ARISTOTLE

AND THE EARLIER PERIPATETICS

VOL. I.

ARISTOTLE

AND

THE EARLIER PERIPATETICS

BEING A TRANSLATION FROM

ZELLER'S 'PHILOSOPHY OF THE GREEKS'

BY

B. F. C. COSTELLOE, M.A.

AND

J. H. MUIRHEAD, M.A.

IN TWO VOLUMES—VOL. I.

NEW YORK

RUSSELL & RUSSELL · INC

1962

185
C
Z 57
v. 1

89191

FIRST PUBLISHED IN 1897
REISSUED, 1962, BY RUSSELL & RUSSELL, INC.
L. C. CATALOG CARD NO: 62-10698

PRINTED IN THE UNITED STATES OF AMERICA

TO

THE MASTER OF BALLIOL

TRANSLATORS' NOTE.

THE following translation embraces Part II. Div. II.
of the third edition of Dr. Eduard Zeller's work on
'The Philosophy of the Greeks in its Historical Development.' It is made with Dr. Zeller's sanction, and
completes the series of volumes issued from time to
time by Messrs. Longmans as translations of the
various sections of that exhaustive work. Mr. Costelloe
is chiefly responsible for the translation of text and
notes up to the middle of Chapter VII., and for
Chapter XIX. to the end; Mr. Muirhead for the middle
portion. In most instances, however, both translators
have revised the sheets. In calling attention to the table
of *Corrigenda,* which is longer than might reasonably
be expected in a work of this kind, the editors desire
to explain that, owing to an accident for which the
translator was not responsible, the sheets of that portion
of the text in which the greater part of them occur

were passed through the press before he had seen them in proof. In dealing with some parts of Zeller's notes a certain liberty has been taken with the German text with a view to condensing the material where this could be done without impairing its value. The treatise is believed to be the only work accessible to English readers which is a complete and accurate exposition of the Aristotelian doctrine. The student will find ample guidance as to Dr. Zeller's plan in the Table of Contents, which is in fact an index of subject matters; and the arrangement adopted by Dr. Zeller is so logical and clear that it has not been considered necessary to burden the translation with an exhaustive verbal index.

CONTENTS

OF

THE FIRST VOLUME

———◇———

CHAPTER IV

STANDPOINT, METHOD, AND DIVISIONS OF THE PHILOSOPHY OF ARISTOTLE

CHAPTER V

LOGIC

CHAPTER VI

INTRODUCTORY INQUIRIES TOUCHING ARISTOTLE'S METAPHYSICS

Addenda and Corrigenda.

Page 74, n. 2. Zeller adds in a later note that Diog. No. 78 gives the *Rhetoric* only 2 books, but this is not decisive.

,, 129, l. 22. Zeller adds in a later note, that many of these may be in great part explained by the supposition that Aristotle did not always *write*, but *dictated* his books.

,, 178, n. 2, *for* Braniss *read* Brandis

,, 188; n. 1, col. 1, l. 12, *for* representation *read* opinion

,, 203, n. 2, l. 4, *insert* 199, n. 2

,, 210, n. 2, col. 1, l. 18, *delete* of

,, 224, n. col 1, ll. 11, 12, *for* a *and* an *read* the same

,, 232, 233, *for* individual [judgments] *read* singular

,, 235, n. col. 2, l. 30, *for* apodeictic *read* assertorial

,, 249, n. 3, col. 2, l. 5, *for* there *read* these

,, 257, n. 1, add a further reference to *De Cœlo*, i. 10 *init.*

,, 288, n. 1, col. 2, ll. 18, 21, *for* equality *read* identity

,, 302, n. 3, col. 2, l. 3, *for* corresponds with *read* assimilates to itself

,, 335, n. 1, l. 4, *for* general *read* universal

,, 346, n. col. 2, l. 15 from bottom, *after* possibility *insert comma*

,, 361, n. col. 1, l. 16, *omit semicolon*

,, 364, l. 8.   Zeller in a later note refers to the criticism of TORSTRIK (*Hermes*, ix. 1875, p. 425), and suggests that the word 'disturbance' might be replaced by 'modification.'

,, 390, n. 3, col. 1, l. 17, *for* Fr. 13 *read* Fr. 12

,, 395, n. col. 1, l. 9, *after* (the ἀΐδιον) *add* that it should be capable of ceasing to be

,, 400, n. 1, col. 2, l. 11, *omit* not

,, ,, ,, l. 33, *after* word *read* is

,, 404, l. 23, *for* object of thought *read* intelligible

,, 405, n. 3, col. 1, l. 12, *for* do *read* are

,, 407, n. 2, col. 2, l. 18, *for* motion *read* moved

,, 412, n. col 1, l. 5, *after* κινοῦν *add* absolutely

,, 415, l. 16, *for* forces *read* Form

,, 417, l. 9, *for* bodies and masses ... related to them *read* not only bodies and magnitudes but everything which possesses them or is related to them

,, 427, n. 3, col. 2, l. 8, *for* masses *read* magnitudes

,, 428, l. 28, *for* after *read* behind

,, 441, n. 2, col. 1, l. 8, *for* forcible *read* forced

,, 454, l. 11, *for* extension *read* extrusion

,, 459, n. 5, col. 1, l. 17, *for* But *read* Again

,, 479, n. 1, col. 1, l. 1, *after* ought *add* in the converse case

,, ,, ,, l. 4, *after* does *add* not

,, 481, n. 1, col. 2, l. 24, *for* oppositions *read* opposites.

,, 497, n. 1, col. 2, l. 3, *for* one who stands ... in front of him *read* in front of the propeller who stands in the line of the axis

,, 504, l. 1, *for* One *read* The

,, 510, l. 2, *for* has raised *read* surrounds

ARISTOTLE

AND THE

EARLIER PERIPATETICS

————

CHAPTER I

THE LIFE OF ARISTOTLE

THE lives and circumstances of the three great philosophers of Athens show a certain analogy to the character and scope of their work. As the Attic philosophy began by searching the inner nature of man and went on from this beginning to extend itself over the whole field of existence, so we find that the life of its great masters was at first confined in narrow limits, and gained, as time went on, a wider range. Socrates is not only a pure Athenian citizen, but a citizen who feels no desire to pass beyond the borders of his city. Plato is also an Athenian, but the love of knowledge takes him to foreign lands and he is connected by many personal interests with other cities. Aristotle owes to Athens his scientific training and his sphere of work; but he belongs by birth and origin to another part of Greece, he spends his youth and a considerable part of his manhood out of Athens, chiefly in the rising Macedonian kingdom; and even when he is in Athens, it is as a stranger, not bound up with the political life of the city, and not hindered by any personal ties from giving to his philosophy that purely theoretic and impartial character which became its distinctive praise.[1]

The birth of Aristotle falls, according to the most probable reckoning, in the first year of the 99th Olympiad,[2]

[1] The old accounts of Aristotle's life now extant are (1) DIOGENES, v. 1–35 (far the most copious) ; (2) DIONYSIUS of Halicarnassus, *Epist. ad Ammæum*, i. 5, p. 727 sq. ; (3) 'Αριστ. βίος καὶ συγγράμματα αὐτοῦ, by the *Anonymus Menagii*; (4) another sketch of his life, known to us in three forms : (*a*) the Βίος first printed in the Aldine ed. of Arist. *Opp.* 1496–98 (which is there ascribed to Philoponus, elsewhere to Ammonius, but belongs to neither), here cited as the *Pseudo-Ammonius* (or *Amm.*); (*b*) the Life published from the Codex Marcianus by Robbe in 1861, cited as *Vita Marciana* (or *V. Marc.*) ; (*c*) the Life cited as the *Latin Ammonius*, preserved in an ancient translation, which approaches more closely to the *Vita Marciana* than to the *Pseudo-Ammonius* itself ; (5) 'Ησυχίου Μιλησίου περὶ τοῦ 'Αριστοτέλους ; (6) SUIDAS, *sub voce* 'Αριστοτέλης. All of these, except (4*b*), are to be found in BUHLE, *Arist. Opp.* i. 1–79. Westermann's appendix to Cobet's *Diogenes*, and his *Vitæ Scriptorum* (at p. 397) also contain (3) and (4*a*) ; Robbe, *op. cit.* gives (4*b*) and (4*c*). ROSE (*Arist. Lib. Ord.* 245), before the publication of (4*b*), ascribed the archetype of (4) to the younger Olympiodorus—a guess which may be called possible but not proven. Of later commentaries, cf. BUHLE, *Arist. Opp.* i. 80–104; STAHR,

Aristotelia i. 1–188 ; BRANDIS, *Gr.-röm. Phil.* ii. b, i. pp. 48–65 ; GROTE'S *Arist.* (1872), i. 1–37, and GRANT'S *Arist.* (1877) pp. 1–29. Stahr discusses (p. 5 sqq.) the lost works of ancient writers which treated of Aristotle's life. We cannot be sure, as to any of the sources mentioned, what their basis or credibility may be. Rose's view that they one and all rest only on spurious texts and fanciful combinations (p. 115) is entirely unproved and improbable. Their value, however, beyond doubt differs widely ; we can only test each statement by its inherent probability.

[2] According to APOLLODORUS *apud* DIOG. 9 ; no doubt on the basis of the statement (*ibid.* 10, DIONYS. and AMMON.) which may be accepted as the safest fixed point as to the date of Aristotle's life, that he died in the archonship of Philocles (Ol. 114, 3), about sixty-three years old (ἐτῶν τριῶν που καὶ ἑξήκοντα, or more exactly, as in Dionys., τρία πρὸς τοῖς ἑξήκοντα βιώσας ἔτη). Dionysius agrees, but erroneously talks of Demosthenes as three years younger than Aristotle, whereas he was born in the same year, or at most in the year before (in the beginning of Ol. 99, 1, or end of Ol. 98, 4); *vide* STAHR i. 30. Gellius' statement (*N. A.* xvii. 21, 25) that Aristotle was born in the seventh year after the freeing of Rome

B.C. 384.[1] Stagira, the city of his birth, was situated in that district of Thrace called Chalcidice,[2] which was at that date a thoroughly Hellenic country, with many flourishing cities, whose people were no doubt in full possession of all Greek culture.[3] His father Nicomachus

from the Gauls also agrees, since that event is referred to the year 364 A.U.C., or 390 B.C. So also the *V. Marc.* p. 3, and the *Ammon. Latin.* p. 12, assert that he was born under Diotrephes (Ol. 99, 1) and died sixty-three years old under Philocles. An otherwise unknown writer, EUMELUS (ap. DIOG. 6), asserts, on the other hand, that Aristotle lived to be seventy; but there is little reason to follow ROSE (p. 116) in preferring this account, since his next words, πιὼν ἀκόνιτον ἐτελεύτησεν, sufficiently show his lack of trustworthiness. In fact, as the manner of Socrates' death is here transferred to Aristotle, so is his age also; possibly by reason of the spurious *Apologia* ascribed to Aristotle (v. p. 35, n. 3, *infra*) and its parallelism with the Platonic *Apologia* of Socrates. But apart from the probability of this explanation, Eumelus is completely displaced by the agreement of all the other testimony, including that of so careful a chronologist as Apollodorus. A reliable tradition as to the age of their founder must have existed in the Peripatetic School. How could all our witnesses, except this one unknown and badly-informed writer, have come to agree upon a false statement of it when the truth could have been easily ascertained?

[1] That he was born in the first half of the Olympiad, or in 384 B.C., follows from the accounts as to his death above, and would also follow from our information as to his residence at Athens, if the figures are to be taken strictly (cf. p. 6, n. 3, *infra*). For if, at seventeen, he came to Athens and was with Plato for twenty years, he must have been thirty-seven years old at Plato's death; so that, if we put his exact age at 36½ and bring down Plato's death to the middle of 347 B.C., his birth would still fall in the latter half of 384 B.C. It is, however, also possible that his stay in Athens did not cover the full twenty years.

[2] So called because most of its cities were colonies of Chalcis in Euboea. Stagira itself was originally colonised from Andros, but perhaps (cf. DIONYS. *ut supra*) received a later contribution of second founders from Chalcis. In 348 B.C., it was, with thirty-one other cities of that district, sacked by Philip, but was afterwards on Aristotle's intercession restored (v. p. 24, *infra*). Vide STAHR, 23, who discusses also the form of the name (Στάγειρος, or Στάγειρα as a neuter plural). We do not know whether Aristotle's family house (mentioned in his will, *ap.* DIOG. 14) was spared in the destruction of the town or was subsequently rebuilt.

[3] Bernays (*Dial. Arist.* ii. 55, 134) calls Aristotle a 'half Greek,' but Grote (i. 3) and

was the body-surgeon and friend of the Macedonian
King Amyntas[1]; and it is natural to suppose that the
father's profession—long hereditary in the family—must
have influenced the mental character and education of the
son, and that this early connection with the Macedonian
Court prepared the way for the employment of Aristotle
in the same Court at a later time.   On neither of these
points, however, have we any positive information.   We
may also assume that Nicomachus took his family with

Grant (p. 2) rightly maintain
against him that a Greek family
in a Greek colony in which only
Greek was spoken, could keep
their nationality perfectly pure.
Aristotle was not an *Athenian*,
and though Athens was his
philosophical home, traces can
yet be found in him of the fact
that his political sense had its
training elsewhere; but he was as
truly a *Hellene* as Pythagoras,
Xenophanes, Parmenides, Anaxagoras, Democritus, or the rest.
The 'un-Greek' element which
Bernays and W. von Hum-
boldt (in his letter to Wolf,
Werke, v. 125) find in Aristotle is
doubtless to be connected not so
much with the place of his birth
as with the characteristics of his
generation and his individual
bent of mind.   The full-born
Athenian Socrates exhibits traits
far more singular and seemingly
un-Greek as compared with his
own people and time than Aristotle, and if the typical writings
of Aristotle appear un-Greek in
comparison with Plato's, still, on
the one hand, this is not true of
his Dialogues, and, on the other
hand, equally great divergencies
are to be found between men
whose surroundings and training
were so closely similar as those of
Schelling and Hegel, or of Baur
and Strauss.

[1] *Vide* DIOG. i. (quoting Hermippus), DIONYS., *Ps. Amm.*, *V.
Marc.*, *Ammon. Latin.*, and SUI-
DAS. The family of Nicomachus,
according to these authorities,
traced its descent, as did so many
medical families, to Asclepius.
TZETZES, *Chil.* x. 727, xii. 638,
gives no ground for doubting
this.   The three recensions of the
Pseudo-Ammonius repeat this
same statement as to the family
of Aristotle's mother, Phaistis, but
erroneously; for Diogenes tells
us she was a Stagirite by birth,
and Dionysius says that she was
a descendant of one of the
colonists from Chalcis.   This
connection might account for the
mention of a country house and
garden at Chalcis in the testa-
ment (DIOG. 14).   The statement in Suidas, *sub voce* Νικόμαχος, that a person of that name
had written six books of Ἰατρικὰ
and one book of Φυσικὰ refers,
according to our text, not to the
father of Aristotle (cf. BUHLE, 83,
STAHR, 34), but to an ancestor
of the same name; though no

him to reside near the king,[1] but we cannot tell how old Aristotle then was, or how long this state of things lasted, or what personal relations resulted from it. Equally little knowledge have we as to the early development of his mind, or the circumstances or method of his education.[2] The sole piece of information we have as to this section of his life is the remark of the Pseudo-Ammonius [3] that after the death of both his parents,[4] one Proxenus of Atarneus [5] took over his education, so that in later life the grateful pupil did the like service for Proxenus' son Nicanor, of whom he took charge while he was a child, and to whom he gave his own daughter in marriage. Notwithstanding the untrustworthy character of our informant,[6] the story seems to be true [7];

doubt the story did refer originally to his father. The Anon. Menagii (with *V. Marc.* 1, and *Ammon. Latin.* 1) mentions a brother and sister of Aristotle.

[1] For Diog. 1, following Hermippus, says expressly: συνεβίω [Νικόμαχος] Ἀμύντᾳ τῷ Μακεδόνων βασιλεῖ ἰατροῦ καὶ φίλου χρείᾳ. He must therefore have taken up his residence in Pella and cannot have left his family in Stagira.

[2] Galen's statement (*Anatom. Administr.* ii. 1, vol. ii. 280 κ) that the Asclepiad families practised their sons ἐκ παίδων in reading, writing, and ἀνατέμνειν, does not help us much, as (apart from the question whether the information is fully credible) we do not know how old Aristotle was at his father's death. It is doubtful whether Galen meant human or animal anatomy; cf. p. 89, n. 1 *fin.*

[3] In all three recensions, p. 43

etc., cf. BUHLE, 1 sq. (lege τροφῆς for φήμης) 10 sq. ROBBE.

[4] In his will (DIOG. 16) Aristotle mentions his mother and orders a monument to be erected to her. Pliny (*H. Nat.* xxxv. 10, 106) mentions a picture of her which Aristotle had painted by Protogenes. There may have been many reasons why his father was not mentioned in the will.

[5] Apparently a relative who had emigrated to Stagira, for his son Nicanor is called Σταγειρίτης and οἰκεῖος Ἀριστοτέλους (SEXT. MATH. i. 258).

[6] What trust is to be placed in a writer who tells us, *inter alia*, that Aristotle was for three years a pupil of Socrates and that he afterwards accompanied Alexander to India? (*Ps. Ammon.* p. 44, 50, 48, *V. Marc.* 2, 5, *Ammon. Lat.* 11, 12, 14).

[7] Aristotle in his will(DIOG.12) directs that Nicanor is to marry

but it throws no further light on that which necessarily interests us most, the history of Aristotle's intellectual growth.[1]

His entrance into the Platonic School [2] gives us our earliest reliable data on the subject. In his eighteenth year Aristotle came to Athens [3] and entered the circle of

his daughter when she is grown up ; he charges him to take care of her and her brothers, ὡς καὶ πατὴρ ὢν καὶ ἀδελφός ; he orders that the portraits of Nicanor, Proxenus, and Nicanor's mother, which he had projected, should be completed, and that if Nicanor completed his journey successfully (*v. infra*), a votive offering he had promised should be set up in Stagira. These arrangements prove that Nicanor was adopted by Aristotle, and that Aristotle owed special gratitude to Nicanor's mother as well as to Proxenus, apparently similar to that he owed his own mother, of whom a similar portrait is ordered. If we assume the truth of the story in the Pseudo-Ammonius it will most naturally explain the whole. Dionysius notes that Nicomachus was dead when Aristotle came to Plato. It might appear that, as Aristotle died at sixty-three, the son of his foster-parents would be too old to marry a daughter not then grown up ; but this does not follow. If Aristotle was a child at his father's death, and Proxenus a young man, the latter might have left a son twenty or twenty-five years younger than Aristotle, and some ten years younger than Theophrastus (then at least forty-seven) whom Pythias was to marry in case of

Nicanor's death (DIOG. 13).—This Nicanor is probably the same Nicanor of Stagira whom Alexander sent from Asia to Greece to announce his consent to the return of the exiles at the Olympian games of 324 B.C.(DINARCH. *Adv. Demosth.* 81, 103, DIODOR. xviii.8; cf. the pseudo-Aristotelian *Rhet. ad Alex.* i, 1421, a, 38, and GROTE, p. 14). And the vow in Aristotle's will probably relates to a journey to Alexander's headquarters where he had given an account of his mission and been detained on service in Asia. It is probably the same Nicanor who was governor of Cappadocia under Antipater (Arrian *apud* PHOT. *Cod.* 92, p. 72, a, 6) and who was made away with, in B.C. 318, by Cassander, for whom he had done good service on sea and land (DIODOR. xviii. 64 sq. 68, 72, 75). The dates agree exactly with what we know of Pythias, as to whom see p. 20, n. 3, *infra*.

[1] We know nothing of the age at which Aristotle came to Proxenus, nor of the manner or place of his education, for it was probably not at Atarneus —see above, p. 5, n. 5.

[2] A silly story in *Ps. Amm.* 44, *V. Marc.* 2, and *Ammon. Latin.* 11 relates that he was sent by the Delphic Oracle.

[3] APOLLODOR. *ap.* DIOG. 9 : παραβαλεῖν δὲ Πλάτωνι, καὶ δια-

Plato's scholars,[1] to which he continued to belong for

τρίψαι παρ' αὐτῷ εἴκοσιν ἔτη, ἑπτὰ καὶ δέκα ἐτῶν συστάντα. This testimony seems to be the basis of the statements of Dionysius (p. 728) that he came to Athens in his eighteenth year, of Diogenes 6, that he came ἑπτακαιδεκέτης, and of the three recensions of the Ammonius Life that he came ἑπτακαίδεκα ἐτῶν γενόμενος. We have also the chronology of Dionysius, who places his arrival in the archonship of Polyzelos (366–7 B.C. Ol. 103, 2), while the statement (*V. Marc.* 3, Ammon. *Latin.* 12) that he came in the archonship of Nausigenes (Ol. 103, 1) takes us to the middle of his seventeenth year instead of the completion of it. Eusebius in his *Chronicle* knows that he arrived at seventeen, but places the event erroneously in Ol. 104, 1.—The statement of Eumelus (*apud* DIOG. 6) that he was thirty years old when he met Plato is combined by Grote (p. 3 sq.) with the accounts of Epicurus and Timæus as to his dissolute youth (cf. *infra*), but without deciding between the two accounts. We have already seen how little credit attaches to Eumelus' account of Aristotle's age and manner of death (p. 2, n. 2) ; but the two statements are connected and fall together, for, as Aristotle composed an elegy and the Dialogue named *Eudemus* in memory of a fellow-student, Eudemus of Cyprus (p. 11, n. 4, *infra*), who went to Sicily with Dion in 357 B.C. and was killed there, it follows that Aristotle, if he were thirty when he came to Athens, would have been born several years before 384.—We do

not know, moreover, when Eumelus lived, or from whom he got his information. If, as is possible, he be Eumelus the Peripatetic, whose Περὶ τῆς ἀρχαίας κωμῳδίας is quoted by a scholiast to Æschines' *Timarch.* (ed. Bekker, *Abh. d. Berl. Akad.* 1836, *Hist.-phil. Kl.* 230, § 39; cf. ROSE, *Arist. Libr. Ord.* 113), he would belong to the Alexandrine, or possibly even the post-Alexandrine period. In no case, as above shown, can he merit our confidence. As to Epicurus and Timæus *vide* p. 9, n. 1, *infra*.—The *Vita Marciana* finds it necessary to refute the story that Aristotle came to Plato in his fortieth year. The *Latin Ammonius* reproduces this in a still more absurd form, to which he adapts other parts of his story ; for he says that it was thought by many that Aristotle remained forty years with Plato. His translation ' xl annis immoratus est sub Platone ' probably means that the text of the archetype was μ' ἔτη γεγονὼς ἦν ὑπὸ Πλάτωνι, or μ' ἐτῶν ὢν ἐνδιέτριβεν, &c. If the latter be supposed, the mistake might well have arisen by the dropping out of ὢν in the translator's MS.

[1] Plato himself was probably at the moment absent on his second Sicilian journey (*vide* ZELLER, *Plato*, p. 32). Stahr (p. 43) suggests that the abovementioned statement that he was three years with Socrates and after his death followed Plato (*Ps. Amm.* 44, 50, *V. Marc.* 2, Ammon. *Lat.* 11, 12, OLYMPIOD. *in Gorg.* 42) arose from a misunderstanding of this circumstance. The archetype may have contained the

twenty years until the master died.[1] It would have
been of the greatest value if we could have known
in detail something of this long period of preparation,
in which the foundations of his extraordinary learning
and of his distinctive philosophical system must have
been laid. Unhappily our informants pass over all the
important questions as to the movement and history of
his mental development in absolute silence, and enter-
tain us instead with all manner of evil tales as to his
life and character. One of these writers had heard that
he first earned his bread as a quack-doctor.[2] Another
alleges that he first squandered his patrimony, then in
his distress went into military service, afterwards, being
unsuccessful, took to selling medicines, and finally took
refuge in Plato's school.[3] This gossip, however, was

statement that Aristotle spent
three years in Athens without
hearing Plato, in attending other
Socratic teachers, for whom the
transcriber erroneously inserted
the name of Socrates himself.
On a similar supposition, we
might guess that the archetype
said that in Plato's absence,
Aristotle was with *Xenocrates*:
or with *Isocrates*, whose name is
often confused with Socrates.
It seems more probable, however, that the origin of the error
lay in the remark in a letter to
Philip (whether genuine or spurious) mentioned in the *Vita
Marciana* and the *Latin Ammonius*, to the effect that Aristotle
made Plato's acquaintance in his
twentieth year—perhaps because
Plato then returned from Sicily,
perhaps because Aristotle had till
then been of the school of
Isocrates.

[1] Cf. p. 6, n. 3, and Dionysius,
ut supra: συσταθεὶς Πλάτωνι
χρόνον εἰκοσαετῆ διέτριψε σὺν αὐτῷ.
or as in *Amm.*, τούτῳ σύνεστιν
ἔτη εἴκοσι.

[2] ARISTOCL. *ap.* EUS. *Præp.
Ev.* xv. 2, 1: πῶς ἄν τις ἀποδέξαιτο
Τιμαίου τοῦ Ταυρομενίτου λέγοντος
ἐν ταῖς ἱστορίαις, ἀδόξου θύρας
αὐτὸν ἰατρείου καὶ τὰς τυχούσας
(hiatus) ὀψὲ τῆς ἡλικίας κλεῖσαι.
The same is more fully cited from
Timæus by POLYB. xii. 7, and
SUIDAS, sub v. Ἀριστοτέλης.

[3] Aristocl. *ut supra*: πῶς γὰρ
οἷόν τε, καθάπερ φησὶν Ἐπίκουρος ἐν
τῇ περὶ τῶν ἐπιτηδευμάτων ἐπι-
στολῇ, νέον μὲν ὄντα καταφαγεῖν
αὐτὸν τὴν πατρῴαν οὐσίαν, ἔπειτα
δὲ ἐπὶ τὸ στρατεύεσθαι συνεῶσθαι,
κακῶς δὲ πράττοντα ἐν τούτοις ἐπὶ
τὸ φαρμακοπωλεῖν ἐλθεῖν, ἔπειτα
ἀναπεπταμένου τοῦ Πλάτωνος περιπάτου πᾶσι, παραλαβεῖν αὐτὸν (lege,
according to Athen. παραβαλεῖν

rightly rejected even by Aristocles.[1] Greater weight attaches to the story of the breach between Plato and his scholar which is said to have occurred some time before the former died. So early a writer as Eubulides the

αὐτὸν, scil. εἰς τὸν περίπατον): cf. the same passage quoted in similar words, *apud* ATHEN. viii. 354, *apud* DIOG. x. 8, and less closely *apud* ÆLIAN. *V. H.* v. 9.

[1] In the first place, it is without any reliable authority. Even in antiquity no other testimony than Epicurus and Timæus is known, and except these two, none, as Athenæus expressly remarks, even of Aristotle's bitterest opponents mentioned these stories. Timæus's reckless slanderousness, however, is well known, and he was embittered against Aristotle by his statements (historically correct as they were) as to the low origin of the Locrians (cf. POLYB. xii. 7, 10; PLUT. *Dio.* 36, *Nic.* 1; DIODOR. v. 1). So also of Epicurus we know that there was hardly one of his philosophic predecessors or contemporaries (not excepting Democritus and Nausiphanes, to whom he was under large obligations) whom he did not attack with calumnies and depreciatory criticism (cf. DIOG. x. 8, 13; SEXT. MATH. i. 3 sq.; CIC. *N. D.* 1, 33, 93, 26, 73; ZELLER, *Ph. d. Gr.* I. p. 946, n). Statements by such men, betraying as they do a tone of hatred, must be taken with great distrust; and their agreement is no guarantee, for it is possible that Timæus copied Epicurus, or (as we may better think) that Epicurus copied him. Not only, however, have we against them the consensus of many far more credible writers who say that Aristotle devoted himself from his eighteenth year to his studies at Athens, but the other story is in itself most improbable. If Aristotle were no more than the σοφιστὴς θρασὺς εὐχερὴς προπετὴς that Timæus calls him, he might perhaps have been ὀψιμαθὴς also. But when we know that apart from philosophical greatness, he was the foremost man of learning of his time, and was also famous as a writer for his graces of style, we must think it unparalleled and incredible that his thirst for learning should have first arisen at thirty after a wasted youth, and that he could then have achieved attainments hardly credible as the work of a long lifetime. All we know of Aristotle from his writings or otherwise impresses us with a sense of personal superiority incompatible with these tales of his youth; not to speak of the argument that if he had squandered his property he could hardly have found means to live at Athens. Grote (cf. p. 6, n. 3, *supra*) does too much honour to Epicurus and Timæus when he treats their testimony as balancing the other. They are probably naked and baseless lies, and therefore we ought not even to infer from them with Stahr (p. 38 sq.) and Bernays (*Abh. d. Bresl. Hist.-phil. Gesellschaft*, i. 193), that Aristotle probably practised medicine in Athens while he was studying natural philosophy.

dialectician accused Aristotle of ingratitude to his master.[1] Others accuse him of annoying Plato by his showy dress, his overbearing manner, and his jeering.[2] Others relate that even in Plato's lifetime he attacked his doctrines and set up a school of his own in opposition to the Platonic,[3] and even that on one occasion he took advantage of the absence of Xenocrates to drive the aged master from his accustomed place of resort in the Academia.[4] Many, even among the ancients, re-

Neither Aristocles nor any of the trustworthy witnesses mention medical practice, and the two who do, refer to it in such a way as only to raise suspicion; while Aristotle apparently reckons himself among the 'laymen,' μὴ τεχνῖται, in medicine (*Divin.* 1, 463, *a.* 6).

[1] ARISTOCL. *ap.* EUS. *Pr. Ev.* xv. 2, 3 : καὶ Εὐβουλίδης δὲ προδήλως ἐν τῷ κατ᾽ αὐτοῦ βιβλίῳ ψεύδεται . . . φάσκων . . . τελευτῶντι Πλάτωνι μὴ παραγενέσθαι τά τε βιβλία αὐτοῦ διαφθεῖραι. Neither of the charges is important. His absence at the time of Plato's death, if that is true, may have had an easy explanation ; Plato, indeed, is said to have died quite unexpectedly (cf. ZELLER, *Plato,* p. 35). The injury to Plato's books, if it means a falsification of the text, is an obvious and absurd calumny. If, as is possible, it refers to Aristotle's criticism of Plato, this, as we shall see, though it is keen and not always just, is no indication of any personal misunderstanding, since to Aristotle it meant only natural and impersonal polemics. Besides Aristocles, Diogenes (ii. 109) also rejects Eubulides' charges as a calumny.

[2] ÆLIAN, *V. H.* iii. 19, describing Aristotle's style of dress in detail.

[3] DIOG. 2 : ἀπέστη δὲ Πλάτωνος ἔτι περιόντος· ὥστε φησὶν ἐ᾽εῖνον εἰπεῖν· Ἀριστοτέλης ἡμᾶς ἀπελάκτισε καθαπερεὶ τὰ πωλάρια γεννηθέντα τὴν μητέρα—and so ÆLIAN, *V. H.* iv. 9, and HELLADIUS *ap.* PHOT. *Cod.* 279, p. 533, b. Similarly THEODORET, *Cur. Gr. Aff.* v. 46, p. 77, says Aristotle often attacked Plato while he was yet alive : PHILOP. *Anal. Post.* 54 a, *Schol. in Arist.* 228, p. 16, that he had especially opposed his master's Ideal Theory ; and AUGUSTINE, *Civ. Dei.* viii. 12, that he had established even then a numerous school.

[4] This occurrence is related by our sole authority (ÆLIAN, *V. H.* iii. 19, cf. iv. 9) in this way : that when Plato was over eighty, and his memory was failing, Aristotle on one occasion, Xenocrates being absent and Speusippus ill, had gone with a band of his own pupils and started a debate with Plato, in which he drove the old man into a corner with such rude pertinacity that Plato withdrew himself from the halls of the Academy into his own garden, and it was

ferred to Aristotle the statement of Aristoxenus that during Plato's Sicilian journey a school was erected in opposition to his own 'by strangers.'[1] All these data, however, are very doubtful, and most of the actual statements deserve no credence.[2] If the assertion of Aristoxenus were to be understood of Aristotle it could not possibly be true, for chronological reasons in the first place,[3] but also because we possess undoubted proofs that Aristotle belonged to Plato's school long after the second Sicilian journey, and held his master in the highest honour.[4] Probably, however,

only when Xenocrates returned, three months afterwards, that he reproached Speusippus for his cowardice and forced Aristotle to restore to Plato the disputed territory.

[1] ARISTOCL. *apud* EUS. *Pr. Ev.* xv. 2, 2 ; τίς δ' ἂν πεισθείη τοῖς ὑπ' Ἀριστοξένου τοῦ μουσικοῦ λεγομένοις ἐν τῷ βίῳ τοῦ Πλάτωνος ; ἐν γὰρ τῇ πλάνῃ καὶ τῇ ἀποδημίᾳ φησὶν ἐπανίστασθαι καὶ ἀντοικοδομεῖν αὐτῷ τινὰς περίπατον ξένους ὄντας. οἴονται οὖν ἔνιοι ταῦτα περὶ Ἀριστοτέλους λέγειν αὐτὸν, Ἀριστοξένου διὰ παντὸς εὐφημοῦντος Ἀριστοτέλην. Among the ἔνιοι was Aelian (iv. 9), who in reference no doubt to the words of Aristoxenus, says of Aristotle : ἀντῳκοδόμησεν αὐτῷ [Plato] διατριβήν. So also the *Vita Marciana*, 3 ; οὐκ ἄρα ἀντῳκοδόμησεν Ἀρ. σχολὴν . . . ὡς Ἀριστόξενος πρῶτος ἐσυκοφάντησε καὶ Ἀριστείδης ὕστερον ἠκολούθησεν ; referring to ARISTIDES, *De quatuorv.* ii. 324 sq. (Dind.), who, however, does not refer to Aristotle by name any more than Aristoxenus, whose account he re-

peats and extends. For Aristides the Latin Ammonius (11) substitutes Aristocles; but the Greek Pseudo-Ammonius (p. 44 sq.) limits itself to the remark : οὐ γὰρ ἔτι ζῶντος τοῦ Πλάτωνος ἀντῳκοδόμησεν αὐτῷ τὸ Λύκειον ὁ Ἀρ., ὥς τινες ὑπολαμβάνουσι.

[2] Cf. STAHR, i. 46 sqq., not refuted by HERMANN, *Plat. Phil.* p. 81, 125.

[3] When Plato returned from his last journey Aristotle was under 24 (cf. p. 2, n. 2, *supra*, and ZELLER, *Plato*, p. 30 sq.) ; is it (apart from other questions) likely that he could so early head a school against a master who was then at the height of his fame ?

[4] The proofs of this are :—(*a*) Aristotle published several Platonic essays (cf. *infra* and ZELLER, *Plato*, p. 26). For many reasons (especially perhaps because of their notable departure from the method of teaching laid down by Plato, cf. ZELL. *Plato*, p. 517 sq.) it is unlikely that these fall between the second and third of Plato's Sicilian

that statement did not refer to Aristotle at all.[1]
Ælian's story as to driving Plato out of the Academy
stands in contradiction with other and older [2] accounts
which show that Plato at that time had long removed
his school from the open spaces of the Gymnasium of the
Academia to his own gardens. But besides, it ascribes
to Aristotle a kind of behaviour which we could not believe of a man of otherwise noble character except on the
most conclusive proofs: whereas here we have nothing
but the testimony of a gossip-grubber, who is known to
repeat without discrimination things that are palpably
untrue. Against the suggestion that Aristotle had by

journeys. (*b*) The *Eudemus* of
Aristotle (cf. *infra*) was written
on the lines of Plato's *Phædo*,
and Aristotle was probably still
in the Platonic School when he
wrote it, which was long after
the third journey, since it is in
memory of a friend who died
352 B.C. (*c*) Olympiodorus (*in
Gorg*. 166, in JAHN'S *Jahrb.
Supplementb*. xiv. 395, and
BERGK, *Lyr. Gr*., p. 504) has
preserved some verses of Aristotle's Elegy on Eudemus, which
thus describe his relation to Plato :

ἐλθὼν δ' εἰς κλεινὸν Κεκροπίης
δάπεδον

εὐσεβέως σεμνῆς φιλίης ἱδρύσατο
βωμόν

ἀνδρὸς, ὃν οὐδ' αἰνεῖν τοῖσι κακοῖσι
θέμις· [Plato]

ὃς μόνος ἢ πρῶτος θνητῶν κατέδειξεν
ἐναργῶς

οἰκείῳ τε βίῳ καὶ μεθόδοισι λόγων,

ὡς ἀγαθός τε καὶ εὐδαίμων ἅμα
γίνεται ἀνήρ.

οὐ νῦν δ' ἔστι λαβεῖν οὐδενὶ ταῦτα
ποτέ.

Buhle (*Arist. Opp*. i. 55) doubts

their genuineness on grounds
that are solved by our view of
their application to the *Cyprian*
Eudemus and *Plato*, instead of
to the *Rhodian* Eudemus and
Aristotle himself. In the corrupt last line, Bernays (*Rh. Mus.
N. F*. xxxiii. 232) reads μουνάξ.
He refers ἀνδρὸς, &c., to Socrates;
but this seems unlikely.

[1] Aristocles (*ut supra*) says
expressly that Aristoxenus always
spoke well of Aristotle, against
which testimony, founded on a
knowledge of his book, the hint
to the contrary in Suidas Ἀριστοξ.
is of no weight. The word περίπατος was used of other schools
besides Aristotle's ; cf. Epicurus,
cited p. 8, n. 3, *supra*, and the
Index Herculanensis, 6, 5, where
it is used of Speusippus, and 7, 9,
of Heraclides. The τινὰς of
Aristoxenus may have referred
to Heraclides himself; cf. ZEL-
LER, *Plato*, p. 30, n. As to the
Index Hercul. see *ibid*. p. 553.

[2] In DIOG. iii. 5, 41; cf.
ZELLER, *Plato*, p. 25, n.

his general behaviour incurred Plato's disapproval and had so been kept at a distance by him,[1] we could bring many statements which imply that the relation between the two philosophers was of an entirely different kind.[2] We may allow no weight, therefore, to these accounts, which in any case are insufficiently attested, and we need take no notice of sundry other stories, whose inaccuracy is apparent.[3] But we have beyond this decisive reasons which negative, not only Ælian's story and the other similar tales, but the whole theory that there was before

[1] Buhle, p. 87, sees a proof of this in the fact that Plato does not mention Aristotle, to which circumstance even Stahr, p. 58, attached some weight. But how could he name Aristotle in *Socratic* dialogues ? And probably all Plato's works, except the *Laws*, were written before Aristotle came to Athens at all.

[2] PHILOPONUS, *Aetern. Mundi* vi. 27 : ['Aρ.] ὑπὸ Πλάτωνος τοσοῦτον τῆς ἀγχινοίας ἠγάσθη, ὡς νοῦς τῆς διατριβῆς ὑπ' αὐτοῦ προσαγορεύεσθαι : and *Ps. Ammon.* 44, says Plato called Aristotle's house οἶκος ἀναγνώστου: cf. also ZELLER, *Plato*, p. 559. To the same tradition belong the very doubtful story cited in ZELLER, *Plato*, p. 26, n., and the account of the altar dedicated with a laudatory inscription by Aristotle to Plato on his death (*Amm.* 46, PHILOPON. *i.q.v.*, *Schol. in Arist.* 11, b, 29), which arose, no doubt, out of a mistranslation of the Elegy to Eudemus, p. 11, n. 4, *supra*.

[3] Such is the idea mentioned by Philoponus (*ut supra*, 11, b, 23 sqq., where in l. 25, *lege* 'Aριστοτέ-λους) and by David (*ibid.* 20, b, 16), that Aristotle was ashamed to mount the teacher's chair while Plato lived, and that this was the origin of the name ' Peripatetic.' There is another theory (PHILOPON. *ut supra*, 35, b, 2, DAVID. *ibid.* 24, a, 6, AMMON. *ibid.* 25, b, and the *Pseudo-Ammon.* p. 47, *V. Marc.* 5, *Ammon. Latin.* 14) that the name of Peripatetics belonged originally to the Platonic school; that when Aristotle and Xenocrates took over that school after Plato's death, or rather that of Speusippus, Aristotle's followers were called Peripatetics of the Lyceum and the others Peripatetics of the Academy ; and that, in the end, the one school were called Peripatetics only, and the other Academics. The origin of this theory is doubtless Antiochus, in whose name Varro in CIC. *Acad.* i. 4, 17 tells an exactly similar story : which indicates that the whole is only an invention of that Eclecticism, developed by Antiochus, which denied that there was any essential difference between Plato and Aristotle.

Plato's death any breach between him and his scholar.
Authorities which are beyond any comparison with
Ælian and the rest in their antiquity and credibility,
assert that Aristotle remained with Plato twenty years,[1]
which plainly could not be true if, although he lived for
that time in Athens, he had separated himself from
Plato before the end. Dionysius, indeed, expressly adds
that in all this time he founded no school of his own.[2]
So even in later years and in passages where he
is contesting the principles of the Platonic School,
Aristotle constantly reckons himself as belonging to it;[3]
and he uses language as to the founder of that school
and his own personal relation to him such as plainly
shows how little the sentiment of respect and affection
for his great master had failed in his mind,[4] even where
their philosophic opposition was accentuated in the
sharpest way. So also we find that he was treated as a
Platonist by contemporary opponents;[5] for Cephisodorus

---

[1] *Vide* p. 6, n. 3, and p. 8,
n. 1, *supra*.

[2] *Ep. ad Amm.* i. 7, p. 733:
συνῆν Πλάτωνι καὶ διέτριψεν ἕως
ἐτῶν ἑπτὰ καὶ τριάκοντα, οὔτε
σχολῆς ἡγούμενος οὐτ' ἰδίαν πε-
ποιηκὼς αἵρεσιν.

[3] Aristotle often brackets himself and the Platonists together:
cf. καθ' οὓς τρόπους δείκνυμεν ὅτι
ἔστι τὰ εἴδη κατὰ τὴν ὑπόληψιν
καθ' ἣν εἶναί φαμεν τὰς ἰδέας, and
the like, *Metaph.* i. 9, 990, b, 8,
11, 16, 23, 992, a, 11, 25, c. 8, 989,
b, 18; iii. 2, 997, b, 3, c. 6, 1002,
b, 14; cf. Alex. and Asclep. on
990, b, 8; and Alex. on 990, b,
16, 991, b, 3, 992, a, 10.

[4] In a well-known passage
of the Ethics which itself

seems to point to charges which
his logical polemic against Plato
had drawn down upon him,
Eth. N. i. 4, *init.*: τὸ δὲ καθόλου βέλτιον ἴσως ἐπισκέψασθαι καὶ
διαπορῆσαι πῶς λέγεται, καίπερ
προσάντους τῆς τοιαύτης ζητήσεως
γινομένης διὰ τὸ φίλους ἄνδρας
εἰσαγαγεῖν τὰ εἴδη. δόξειε δ' ἂν
ἴσως βέλτιον εἶναι καὶ δεῖν ἐπὶ
σωτηρίᾳ γε τῆς ἀληθείας καὶ τὰ
οἰκεῖα ἀναιρεῖν, ἄλλως τε καὶ φιλο-
σόφους ὄντας· ἀμφοῖν γὰρ ὄντοιν
φίλοιν ὅσιον προτιμᾶν τὴν ἀλήθειαν.
Cf. ZELLER, *Plato*, p. 512; cf.
also ZELLER, *Ph. d. Gr.* i. p. 971,
as to Aristotle's own view of his
duty to a teacher.

[5] NUMEN. *apud* EUS. *Pr. Ev.*
xiv. 6, 8.

the Isocratean, in a book directed against Aristotle, attacked the Platonic doctrine and particularly the ' Ideas,' and Theocritus of Chios accused Aristotle of exchanging the Academy for Macedonia.[1] Again, it is established that he stayed in Athens until Plato's death, and immediately thereafter left the city for several years, presumably for no other reason than that then for the first time the tie that bound him to the city was dissolved, because his relation to Plato was then for the first time broken. Finally, we are told [2] that Xenocrates journeyed with him to Atarneus; and it is probable from the language in which Aristotle speaks of that Academic's opinions [3] that they continued to be friends in later times. But in view of the known loyalty of Xenocrates and his unbounded reverence for Plato, it is not to be supposed that he would maintain his relations with Aristotle and keep him company on the visit to Atarneus, if the latter had separated from his master in a disrespectful way, or had, by any such rude conduct as Ælian ascribes to him, insulted the aged teacher not long before his death.

It is of course altogether probable that so independent a mind as Aristotle's would not give up its own judgment even in face of a Plato; that as time

[1] In the epigram noticed at p. 20, n. 3, *infra*: εἵλετο ναίειν ἀντ' Ἀκαδημείας Βορβόρου ἐν προχοαῖς, B. being a river near Pella.

[2] By STRABO (xiii. 1, 57, p. 610), whom we have no reason to disbelieve.

[3] Others have remarked that Aristotle almost never mentions Xenocrates, and that he avoids his name as if on purpose where he is obviously alluding to him (cf. the cases cited, ZELLER, *Plato*, p. 364, n.; and notes on p. 585, and later passages), whereas Speusippus is named in parallel cases. This probably indicates not ill-feeling, but rather a desire to avoid the appearance of personal conflict with one who was teaching beside him at Athens.

went on he began to doubt the unconditional validity of the Platonic system and to lay the foundations of his own : and that he perhaps even in these days laid bare many of the weak points of his teacher with the same uncompromising criticism which we find him using later on.[1]   If a certain difference between the two men had developed out of such relations, or if Plato had not been more ready than many others since, to recognise in his scholar the man who was destined to carry forward and to correct his own work, it would be nothing wonderful. Yet that any such difference actually arose cannot be proved, and cannot even be shown to be very probable [2]: while we have patent facts to disprove the idea that Aristotle brought on any open breach by ingratitude or intentional offence.   The same facts make it very improbable that Aristotle opened any philosophic school of his own during his first residence in Athens.   If he had done so, his friendly relations with Plato and the Platonic circle could hardly have gone on, and it would be unintelligible that he should leave Athens exactly at the moment when the death of his great rival left the field free for himself.[3]

[1] Even in the books ' On Philosophy' (*Arist. Fragm.* 10, 11. p. 1475), apparently written before Plato's death, he had openly combated the Ideal Theory, and in the same treatise (*Fragm.* 17, 18) had maintained the eternity of the world.

[2] We have no right to ascribe to Plato and his circle of friends the later ideas of school-orthodoxy, in any such sense as to suppose that the master could not tolerate the independence of such a scholar as Aristotle. Besides, not to mention Heraclides and Eudoxus, Speusippus himself dropped the Ideal Theory.

[3] The remark of the Pseudo-Ammonius that Chabrias and Timotheus prevented Aristotle from setting up a new school against Plato is absurd. Who could hinder him, if he chose ? Chabrias, moreover, died in 358 B.C.; and Timotheus was banished from Athens for life in the following year, being then a very old man.

If, then, Aristotle was connected with Plato, as one of his school, from his eighteenth to his thirty-seventh year, it follows that we cannot well over-estimate the influence of such a relation upon his course of thought. The effect of that education on Aristotle's philosophic system discloses itself at every point. The grateful scholar has himself[1] commemorated the moral greatness and lofty principles of the man ' whom the base have not even the right to praise.' But the reverence for the master would obviously not prevent Aristotle from turning his attention at the same time to all other sources which might carrry him onward and help to satisfy his insatiable thirst for knowledge. We may safely assume that he did in fact employ his long years of preparation at Athens in busy acquirement of his marvellous learning, and also that he took a keen interest in researches in natural philosophy, though Plato always treated it as of secondary importance. It is also possible that even while he was still a member of Plato's circle he may himself have lectured,[2] without thereby breaking off his relations with Plato or setting himself up against him as the leader of a competing school. We hear, for instance, that Aristotle taught Rhetoric in opposition to Isocrates ;[3] but we know that the great

---

[1] See the lines on p.12 *supra*.

[2] STRABO (xiii. 1, 57, p. 610) says of Hermias that he heard at Athens both Plato and Aristotle.

[3] CIC. *De Orat.* iii. 35, 141 : *Aristoteles, cum florere Isocratem nobilitate discipulorum videret, . . . mutavit repente totam formam prope disciplinæ suæ* [which sounds as if Aristotle had even then a school of his own, though Cicero seems to be without exact information] *versumque quendam Philoctetæ paullo secus dixit. Ille enim turpe sibi ait esse tacere, cum barbaros: hic autem, cum Isocratem pateretur dicere. Ita ornavit et illustravit doctrinam illam omnem, rerumque cognitionem cum orationis exercitatione conjunxit. Neque vero hoc fugit sapientissimum regem Phil-*

orator's relations with Plato were no longer good and that he attacked the philosophers.[1] We have distinct indications also which lead us to assign to this same period the commencement of Aristotle's activity as a writer; and the fact that in the writings of this time he imitated his master, both in matter and form,[2] shows clearly how completely he took on the impress of Plato's spirit and made the Platonic methods his own. In time, of course, and no doubt even before he left Athens, Aristotle acquired as a writer a more independent position; and it is manifest that he had in reality outgrown the position of one of Plato's pupils, long before that relation came visibly to an end by the death of the master.

lippum, qui hunc Alexandro filio doctorem accierit. Again, *ibid.* 19, 62, *Arist. Isocratem ipsum lacessivit,* and *ibid.* 51, 172, *quis . . . acrior Arist. fuit? quis porro Isocrati est adversatus impensius?* In *Tusc.* i. 4, 7, Cicero assumes that Aristotle attacked Isocrates in his lifetime, which would be possible only in his first residence at Athens, for when he returned in 335–4 B.C. Isocrates was many years dead. Cf. QUINTIL. iii. 1, 14 : *Eoque* [*Isocrate*] *jam seniore . . . pomeridianis scholis Arist. præcipere artem oratoriam cœpit, noto quidem illo, ut traditur, versu ex Philocteta frequenter usus :* αἰσχρὸν σιωπᾶν Ἰσοκράτην [δ'] ἐᾶν λέγειν. Diog. (3) with less probability, reads Ξενοκράτην, so misplacing the story as of the time of the founding of the Lyceum. Cicero (*Offic.* i. 1, 4) speaks clearly of contests between Aristotle and Isocrates in his life (*de Arist. et Isocrate . . . quorum uterque suo studio delectatus contemsit alterum*), and Isocrates himself, *Ep.* v. *ad Alex.* 3,

makes a covert attack on Aristotle, which confirms the story : *Panath.* 17 can hardly refer to Aristotle, because of the dates ; cf. SPENGEL, *Abh. d. Bayer. Akad.* vi. 470 sq. Cephisodorus, a pupil of Isocrates, wrote a defence of his master against Aristotle, full of bitter abuse ; *v.* DIONYS. *De Isocr.* c. 18, p. 577 ; ATHEN. ii. 60, d, cf. iii. 122, b ; ARISTOCL. *ap.* EUS. *Pr. Ev.* xv. 24, NUMEN. *ibid.* xiv. 6, 8, THEMIST. *Or.* xxiii. 285, c. This friction did not prevent Aristotle from doing justice to his opponents : in the Rhetoric he quotes examples from no one so readily as Isocrates, and twice quotes Cephisodorus (*Rhet.* iii. 10, 1411, a, 5, 23). Cf. as to the whole subject STAHR, i. 68 sq., ii. 285 sq.

[1] SPENGEL, 'Isokr. und Platon,' *Abh. d. Münch. Akad.* vii. 731, and ZELLER, *Ph. d. Gr.* i. 416, ii. 459, n.

[2] See for proof *infra.* Of the Aristotelian writings known to us the greater part of the Dialogues and some of the rhetorical

That event opens a new chapter of Aristotle's life. So long as Plato led the Academy, Aristotle would not leave it. When Speusippus took his place,[1] Aristotle had nothing to keep him in Athens; since he does not seem to have at first contemplated the foundation of a philosophical school of his own, for which Athens would naturally have been the fittest place. Therefore he accepted, with Xenocrates, an invitation from Hermias, the lord of Atarneus and Assos,[2] who had himself at one time belonged to Plato's school.[3] The prince was the intimate friend of both,[4] and they remained three years with him.[5] Thereafter Aristotle went to Mytilene.[6] This, Strabo says, was for his own safety, because Hermias had fallen into the power of the Persians by treachery; it is probable, however, that Aristotle had left before that event.[7] After the death

texts — perhaps the Συναγωγὴ Τεχνῶν — seem to belong to the first Athenian period.

[1] This choice has caused surprise, but wrongly. It is possible that Plato had a greater personal liking for Speusippus than for Aristotle, or expected from him a more orthodox continuation of his teaching. Speusippus was a much older man, was Plato's nephew, had been brought up by him, had followed him faithfully for a long period of years, and was also the legal heir of Plato's garden near the Academy. Besides, we do not know whether Plato did himself bequeath the succession or not.

[2] BOECKH, ' Hermias,' *Abh. d. Berl. Akad.* 1853, *Hist. Phil. Kl.* p. 133 sq.

[3] STRABO, xiii. 1, 57, p. 610, APOLLODOR. *ap.* DIOG. 9, and DIONYS. *Ep. ad Amm.* i. 5, who agree that Aristotle went to Hermias after Plato's death. The opposite would not follow from the charge cited from Eubulides on p. 10, n. 1, *supra*, even if that were true. Strabo names Assos as the place where Aristotle lived during this period.

[4] Cf. p. 17, n. 2, *supra*. Aristotle's enemies (*apud* DIOG. 3, ANON. MENAG., and SUIDAS, 'Ap.), suggest that this friendship was an immoral one, but this is impossible; BOECKH, *'ibid.* 137.

[5] Apollodorus, Strabo, Dionysius, etc., *ut supra*.

[6] Ol. 108. 4 = 345-4 B.C., in the archonship of Eubulus: see Apollod. and Dionys. *ibid.*

[7] Boeckh, *ibid.* 142, refuting Strabo, has shown this to be probable, though not certain.

of Hermias the philosopher married [1] Pythias, who was either the sister or niece of his friend ; [2] and of his lasting affection for them both he left more than one memorial.[3]

[1] According to ARISTOCLES (*see next note*) citing a Letter to Antipater : τεθνεῶτος γὰρ Ἑρμείου διὰ τὴν πρὸς ἐκεῖνον εὔνοιαν ἔγημεν αὐτὴν, ἄλλως μὲν σώφρονα καὶ ἀγαθὴν οὖσαν, ἀτυχοῦσαν μέντοι διὰ τὰς καταλαβούσας συμφορὰς τὸν ἀδελφὸν αὐτῆς. Strabo (*ut supra*) says Hermias married her to Aristotle in his lifetime, which is negatived by the Letter, if genuine. Aristocl. (*ibid*. 4, 8) says that Aristotle was accused in his lifetime of having flattered her brother to win Pythias, and also that Lyco, the Pythagorean, told a foolish story of Aristotle sacrificing to her after her death as Demeter. Diog. (v. 4) caps this by placing the sacrifice immediately after his marriage. Lucian (*Eun. c.* 9) talks of sacrificing to Hermias ; cf. a like hint in ATHEN. xv. 697 a.

[2] The Anon. Menag., Suidas, s. v. Ἀρ. Ἑρμίας, and Hesych. call her his daughter, the untrustworthy Aristippus (apud DIOG. 3) his concubine. Both are disproved by the fact that Hermias was a eunuch (for the statements of Suid. Hesych. and Anon. Menag. as to this are irreconcilable with DEMETR. *De Eloc.* 293). ARISTOCLES *ap.* EUS. xv. 2, 8 sq. cites a letter of Aristotle to Antipater, and a book by Apellicon of Teos relating to Hermias and Aristotle, and says that Pythias was the sister and adopted daughter of Hermias. Strabo (xiii. 610) calls her niece,

Demetr. of Magnesia (*apud* DIOG. v. 3) daughter or niece. Cf. BOECKH, *ibid.* 140. HARPOCRATION, SUID. s. v. Ἑρμίας, *Etym. M.*, and PHOT. *Lex.*, call her an adopted daughter.

[3] Diog. (6) says he had a monument (whose inscription he cites) erected to Hermias at Delphi. A contemporary lampoon on this by Theocritus of Chios (a witty rhetorician of the Isocratean school and local leader of anti-Macedonian politics) is noticed by DIOG. 11, ARISTOCL. *ut supra*, and PLUT. *De Exil.* 10, p. 603 ; cf. MÜLLER, *Hist. Gr.* ii. 86, and *supra*, p. 15, n. 1. Aristotle also dedicated to Hermias the poem preserved in DIOG. 7, and ATHEN. xv. 695. As to Pythias, the will directs that, as she wished, her remains should be laid beside his own ; as no other burial-place is named, she was probably first buried at Athens, and died, therefore, after Ol. 111, 2, but not very long before Aristotle's death, since the Pythias who was then not marriageable was her daughter (cf. ARISTOCL., SUIDAS and the ANON. MENAG.). After her death Aristotle 'married' (ἔγημε) a certain Herpyllis of Stagira, who bore him a son Nicomachus (ARISTOCL. cf. DIOG. 14) ; and though their union was apparently irregular (*v.* Timæus ap. Schol. in HES. Ἔ. κ. Ἡ. v. 375 ; DIOG. v. 1. *ap.* MÜLLER, *Fragm. Hist. Gr.* i. 211 ; ATHEN. xiii. 589 c, citing Hermippus and call-

In the year 343 or 342 B.C. (Olymp. 109, 2),[1] Aristotle accepted a call to the Macedonian Court [2] to take charge of the education of the young Alexander, then thirteen years old,[3] which before that had not been in the best hands.[4] The invitation probably found him in Mytilene.[5] We have no reliable testimony as to the special reasons which led Philip to think of Aristotle.[6] Most unfortunately, we are almost entirely

ing her a ἑταίρα; SUIDAS and the ANON. MENAG.), yet he must have treated her as his wife, and his will speaks of her with honour, provides for her, and begs his friends ἐπιμελεῖσθαι . . . μνησθέντας ἐμοῦ, καὶ Ἑρπυλλίδος, ὅτι σπουδαία περὶ ἐμὲ ἐγένετο, τῶν τε ἄλλων καὶ ἐὰν βούληται ἄνδρα λαμβάνειν, ὅπως μὴ ἀναξίῳ ἡμῶν δοθῇ (DIOG. 13).—As to Aristotle's daughter we know from Sext. Math. (i. 258), the Anon. Menag. and Suidas *s. v.* 'Αρ., that after Nicanor she had two husbands, Procles of Sparta, and Metrodorus the physician; by the former she had two sons who were scholars under Theophrastus, by the latter a son, Aristoteles, who was commended (being then probably young) by Theophrastus to his friends in his will. Nicomachus was brought up by Theophrastus, but died in youth (μειρακίσκος) in battle (Aristocl. *ap.* EUS. xv. 2, 10; DIOG. v. 29; SUIDAS *s. v.* Θεόφρ. and Νικόμ., confirmed by the terms of Theophrastus' will, *apud* DIOG. v. 51). The six books of *Ethics* and the work on his father's *Physics*, ascribed to him by Suidas, are therefore very doubtful.

[1] This date is given by APOLLOD. ap. DIOG. 10, and DIONYS.

ut supra. The Schol. in Arist. 23 b, 47, says Aristotle was at Alexander's Court at Plato's death, but this is obviously wrong.

[2] Cf. GEIER, *Alexander und Arist.* (Halle, 1856).

[3] Diog. says fifteen, which must be an oversight, for Apollodorus cannot be wrong in such a date (cf. STAHR, p. 85).

[4] PLUT. *Alex.* c. v.; QUINTIL. i. 1, 9.

[5] Stahr (p. 84, 105, A. 2) is not averse to the view that Aristotle first went back from Mytilene to Athens, but none of our biographers know anything of it. On the contrary, DIONYS., *ut supra*, expressly says he went from Mytilene to Philip. Aristotle in a fragment of a letter ap. DEMETR. *De Eloc.* 29, 154, says: ἐγὼ ἐκ μὲν Ἀθηνῶν εἰς Στάγειρα ἦλθον διὰ τὸν βασιλέα τὸν μέγαν ἐκ δὲ Σταγείρων εἰς Ἀθήνας διὰ τὸν χειμῶνα τὸν μέγαν, but this jocular expression, even if the letter is genuine, proves nothing, as it is clearly meant, not as an exact historical statement, but as a rhetorical antithesis between the *termini* of his journeys, leaving out the intermediate points.

[6] According to a well-known story, Philip had told Aristotle,

without information as to the kind of education he gave
the young and ambitious prince, and the influence he
had upon him.[1]   But we should be forced to assume that

before Alexander's birth, that he
hoped he would make a great
man of him (*v.* the letter *ap.* GELL.
ix. 3), but the letter is certainly
spurious, for Philip could not
have written in these extrava-
gant terms to a young man of
27, who had had no chance
to distinguish himself; and,
again, if he had destined him
to be his son's instructor from
birth, he would have brought
him to Macedonia before Ol.
109, 2.   But the prince, who
was deeply interested in science
and art, and no doubt well informed of what was going on in
Athens, may have taken notice
of Aristotle after he had become
one of the most distinguished of
Plato's school, though little
weight attaches to Cicero's statement to that effect (*De Orat.*
iii. 35, 141). It is also possible
that through his father, Aristotle
had relations with the Macedonian court, and he may himself, as Stahr (p. 33) suggests,
have been acquainted in his
youth with Philip, who was the
youngest son of Amyntas and
about his own age.

[1] There was a work, or perhaps a section of a larger work,
' On the Education of Alexander,'
by the Macedonian historian
Marsyas (SUID. s. v. Μαρσ.; cf.
MÜLLER, *Script. Alex. M.* 40, and
GEIER, *Alex. Hist. Script.* 320
sq.). Onesicritus had treated of
it also in a chapter of his *Me-
morabilia* (GEIER, *ibid.* 77; DIOG.
vi. 84). Yet the accounts we have
of it are very scanty, and it is

not certain that any are trustworthy.   Plutarch (*Alex.* c. 7
sq.) praises Alexander's thirst
for knowledge, his delight in
books and learned conversation,
and his passion for the poets and
historians of his people.   He assumes that he was instructed by
Aristotle, not only in ethics and
politics, but in the deeper secrets
of his system, basing this on the
well-known letter (*q. v. ap.* GELL.
xx. 5, quoting Andronicus, and *ap.*
SIMPL. *Phys.* 2 b), in which
Alexander chides Aristotle for
publishing his acroamatic doctrines, and Aristotle replies that
those who had not *heard* them
would not understand them.
Plutarch also connects Alexander's
fancy for medicine, which he
sometimes tried personally on
his friends, with Aristotle's
teaching.   These are, however,
more or less probable guesses,
and what appears most important is least trustworthy, for the
letters turn on the theory of an
acroamatic and esoteric teaching
confined to a few, as to the in-
correctness of which *v.* p. 112, *inf.*
We hear of two books which
Aristotle addressed to his pupil,
Περὶ βασιλείας, and Ὑπὲρ Ἀποίκων,
d.q.v. p. 60, n. 1 *inf.* Plut. (*Alex.* 8)
says Aristotle revised the text of
the *Iliad* for Alexander. As fellow-
pupils of Alexander are named
Marsyas (SUID. Μαρσ.), Callisthenes (JUSTIN. xii. 6; cf. PLUT.
Alex. 55; DIOG. v. 4; ARRIAN.
iv. 10; but *vide* GEIER, *Alex.
Script.* 192 sq.), and perhaps
Cassander (PLUT. *Alex.* 74). At

that influence was important and beneficial, even if we
had less distinct testimony as to the respect of the great
pupil for his teacher, and as to the love of learning
which the philosopher imparted to the king.[1] Alexander
was not only the invincible conqueror, but also a far-
seeing ruler, ripe beyond his years. He was ambitious
to establish the supremacy, not of Grecian arms only,
but also of the Hellenic culture. He withstood for
years the greatest temptations to overweening pride to
which any man could be exposed. In spite of his later
errors, he still stands far above all other world-con-
querors in nobility of spirit, in purity of morals, in love
of humanity, and in personal culture. And for all this
the world has in no small degree to thank the tutor who
formed his apt intelligence by scientific training and
fortified by sound principles his natural instinct for all
that was great and noble.[2] Aristotle himself appears to
have made a kindly use of the influence which his
position gave him, for we hear that he interceded with
the king for individuals and even for whole cities.[3]

the same time Alexander met
Theodectes (PLUT. *Alex.* 17),
and probably also Theophrastus
(*d. q. vide* ÆLIAN. *V. H.* iv. 19).
DIOG. v. 39, but cf. 52. The
fabulous stories as to Alexander's
youth, preserved by the pseudo-
Callisthenes, may be ignored.

[1] PLUT. *Alex.* 8 : Ἀριστοτέλη
δὲ θαυμάζων ἐν ἀρχῇ καὶ ἀγαπῶν οὐχ
ἧττον, ὡς αὐτὸς ἔλεγε, τοῦ πατρὸς,
ὡς δι' ἐκεῖνον μὲν ζῶν, διὰ τοῦτον δὲ
καλῶς ζῶν, ὕστερον δὲ ὑποπτότερον
ἔσχεν [*v. infra*], οὐχ ὥστε ποιῆσαί
τι κακὸν, ἀλλ' αἱ φιλοφροσύναι τὸ
σφοδρὸν ἐκεῖνο καὶ στερκτικὸν οὐκ
ἔχουσαι πρὸς αὐτὸν ἀλλοτριότητος

ἐγένοντο τεκμήριον. ὁ μέντοι πρὸς
φιλοσοφίαν ἐμπεφυκὼς καὶ συντε-
θραμμένος ἀπ' ἀρχῆς αὐτῷ ζῆλος
καὶ πόθος οὐκ ἐξερρύη τῆς ψυχῆς,
as his relation to Anaxarchus,
Xenocrates, and the Indian philosophers Dandamis and Kalanus
showed (notwithstanding THE-
MIST. *Or.* viii. 106, D.).

[2] That he did not act in practice on Aristotelian principles
(PLUT. *Virt. Alex.* i. 6, p. 329 ;
cf. STAHR, p. 99, 2 ; DROYSEN,
Gesch. d. Hellen. i. b, 12 sq.)
proves nothing to the contrary.

[3] *Ps. Amm.* 46, *V. Marc.* 4,
Amm. lat. 13, ÆLIAN, *V. H.* xii. 54.

Of the latter we are told that Stagira (whose refounda-
tion he procured from Philip [1]), Eresus,[2] and Athens,[3]
had at different times to thank him for his advocacy.

When Alexander, at the age of sixteen, was appointed
Regent by his father,[4] Aristotle's teaching must naturally
have come to an end. It cannot afterwards have been
resumed in any regular way, for in the immediately
following years the precocious prince took a most active

[1] So PLUT. *Alex.* c. 7, cf. *Adv.
Col.* 33, 3, p. 1126, and DIO.
CHRYSOST. *Or.* 2 *fin, Or.* 47, 224 R.
On the other hand, DIOG. 4, *Ps.
Ammon.* 47, *V. Marc.* 4, *Ammon.
Latin.* 13, PLIN. *H. Nat.* vii. 29,
109, ÆLIAN. *V. H.* iii. 17, xii. 54,
VALER. MAX. v. 6, ascribe the restoration of Stagira to Alexander.
Plutarch, however, seems on the
whole better informed, and is
confirmed by the expressions of
Aristotle and Theophrastus themselves; cf. p. 25, n. 2, *infra.* Plut.
(*Adv. Col.* 32, 9) and Diog. (4) say
that Aristotle also framed laws
for the restored city, which is
hardly credible. DION (*Or.* 47) relates that he had to contend with
great difficulties in the restoration,
of which he complains in a letter,
which may or may not be genuine.
His work did not last long, for
Dion (*ibid.*) and Strabo (vii. fr. 35)
describe Stagira as uninhabited:
that it succeeded for the time is
clear from p. 25, n. 2, & p. 37, n. 3 & 4.

[2] A doubtful story in *Ps. Amm.*
p. 47, and in *V. Marc.* and
Ammon. Latin. represents Aristotle as saving Eresus from destruction by Alexander.

[3] *V. Marc.* 4 and *Ammon.
Latin.* (13) refer to the service
that Aristotle did the Athenians
in his letter to Philip, and add

that a monument was erected to
him in consequence on the Acro-
polis. The story may be suspected
of resting on a spurious letter;
yet DIOG. (6) also says: φησὶ δὲ
καὶ Ἕρμιππος ἐν τοῖς βίοις, ὅτι πρεσ-
βεύοντος αὐτοῦ πρὸς Φίλιππον ὑπὲρ
Ἀθηναίων σχολάρχης ἐγένετο τῆς
ἐν Ἀκαδημίᾳ σχολῆς Ξενοκράτης·
ἐλθόντα δὴ αὐτὸν καὶ θεασάμενον
ὑπ' ἄλλῳ τὴν σχολὴν ἑλέσθαι περίπατον τὸν ἐν Λυκείῳ. This cannot
be true as stated, for at Speusippus'
death, 339 B.C., Aristotle had
long been Alexander's tutor, and
at that date there could be no
question of embassies to Macedonia. Stahr's theory (p. 67, 72)
of an embassy in Aristotle's first
residence at Athens is untenable.
The story may relate to the two
years between the battle of Chæ-
ronea and Philip's murder, when
Aristotle, already influential at
the Macedonian Court, might by
his intercession have done some
service to Athens which Hermippus could describe by some such
term as πρεσβεύειν. The favour
Alexander showed to the Athenians may have been partly due to
Aristotle's influence (PLUT. *Alex.*
c. 13, 16, 28, 60).

[4] Ol. 110. 1, = 340 B.C., the year of
Philip's campaign against Byzantium. (DIOD. xvi. 77; PLUT. *Alex.* 9.)

part in his father's decisive campaigns : though that circumstance does not exclude the possibility of some continuance of their intellectual pursuits in the intervals of leisure.[1] Aristotle seems at this time to have withdrawn to the city of his birth.[2] At an earlier period he and his pupil had already left Pella.[3] After Alexander ascended the throne, Aristotle must still have remained some time in the north. But with the beginning of the great war with Persia, the reasons that had bound him to Macedonia came to an end, and there was no longer anything to keep him away from that city, which offered at once the most congenial residence[4] and the best field for his teaching work.[5]

[1] During this period Aristotle might or might not be called Alexander's tutor; which accounts probably for the different stories as to the length of his tutorship, given by Dionys. as eight years (his whole residence in Macedonia), and by Justin (xii. 7) as five years, which is itself too long.

[2] That the last period before his return to Athens was spent in Stagira, where his family house was (cf. p. 3, n. 2), is assumed in the fragment quoted p. 21, n. 5, the genuineness of which is not beyond doubt. He must have treated Stagira as his home, since in his will (DIOG. 16) he orders the votive offering for Nicomachus to be erected there. His second wife was of Stagira (*v.* p. 20, n. 3), and Theophrastus owned land in the city (DIOG. v. 52), with which he shows himself to be well acquainted. Cf. *Hist. Plant.* iii. 11, 1 ; iv. 16, 3.

[3] PLUT. (*Alex.* c. 7) says he and Alexander lived at the Nymph-

æum, near Mieza. Stahr (104) takes this to be near Stagira, but Geier (*Alexander und Aristot.* 33) shows it to be S.W. of Pella, in Emathia.

[4] The fragment quoted p. 21, n. 5, says it was the Thracian winter that drove him from Stagira, but this could scarcely be the chief reason.

[5] The *Ps. Ammon.* 47, says Aristotle was, after Speusippus' death, called to Athens by the Athenians, or, according to *V. Marc.* 5, by the Platonic school, the leadership of which he took over in common with Xenocrates (cf. p. 13, n. 3). The three recensions of this biography, however, contain at this point a chaos of fables. The *Ps. Ammon.* says Aristotle taught after this call in the Lyceum, had afterwards to fly to Chalcis, went thence again to Macedonia, accompanied Alexander on his Indian expedition, collected in his travels his 255 forms of government, returned after Alexander's

He returned to Athens[1] in Olymp. 111. 2 (B.C. 335–4) thirteen years after Plato's death. The time thus left for his work in that city was but twelve years,[2] but what he accomplished in that short interval borders on the incredible. Even if we may assume that he had already in great part completed the preparatory work for his philosophy, and that the researches in natural philosophy and the historical collections which supplied the materials for his theoretic labours had perhaps been brought to some kind of conclusion before his return to Athens, it seems certain that almost all his systematic treatises belong entirely to this last period of his life.

death to his native town, and died there twenty-three years after Plato. The *Latin. Ammon.* (14, 17) and the *Vita Marciana* (5, 8) send him with Alexander to Persia collecting his 255 polities, and returning home after the war, and after all this they make him start teaching in the Lyceum, fly to Chalcis and die there, twenty-three years after Plato. The collection of polities in Alexander's campaigns is noticed also by AMMON. *Categ.* 5, b; DAVID, *Schol. in An.* 24, *a*, 34; Ps.-PORPH. *ibid.* 9, b, 26; Anon. *ad Porph.* apud ROSE, *Ar. pseud.* 393. To seek any grains of truth in this confusion would be lost time.

[1] APOLLOD. *apud* DIOG. 10, and DIONYS. *ut sup.*, both agree in naming Ol. 111, 2, but do not indicate whether Aristotle came in the first or second half of the year, *i.e.* end of 335 or spring of 334. For the latter it may be argued that the hostility of Athens to Alexander was only terminated and the Macedonian influence restored after the destruction of Thebes in the summer of 335, and that Alexander did not start on his march into Asia till the spring of 334. For the other view the calculation of Dionys. (*see next note*) may be quoted, but it is probable that this is merely his own deduction from the years given by Apollod.— Ol. 111, 2, for the arrival in Athens; Ol. 114, 3, for his death; therefore, Ol. 114, 2, for the flight to Chalcis.

[2] DIONYS. *ut supra*: ἐσχόλαζεν ἐν Λυκείῳ χρόνον ἐτῶν δώδεκα· τῷ δὲ τρισκαιδεκάτῳ, μετὰ τὴν Ἀλεξάνδρου τελευτὴν, ἐπὶ Κεφισοδώρου ἄρχοντος, ἀπάρας εἰς Χαλκίδα νόσῳ τελευτᾷ. As Alexander died June 323, and Aristotle in autumn 322 (cf. p. 37), this reckoning will be exact if Aristotle came to Athens in the autumn of 335 and left in the autumn of 323. It would also coincide if Aristotle went to Athens in spring 334 and to Chalcis in summer 322, which, however, is otherwise unlikely, as is shown at p. 36, n. 1, *infra*.

Parallel with this comprehensive and strenuous labour
as a writer went on his work as a teacher, since he now
at last began to compete with his great master on a
footing of equality as the founder of a new school. The
open spaces of the Lyceum were the resort that he chose
for his hearers.[1] He was wont to converse with his
scholars as he walked up and down in that gymnasium
between the rows of trees; and from this custom his
school derived the name of the 'Peripatetics.'[2] For a
more numerous audience, however, he would naturally
have to adopt a different form of teaching.[3] Therefore,

---

[1] It was a gymnasium connected with a temple of Apollo
Lykeios, and lay in one of the
suburbs (cf. SUID. HARPOCRA-
TION, and *Schol. in Aristoph. Pac.*
v. 352.

[2] HERMIPPUS *ap.* DIOG. 2,
etc.; CIC. *Acad.* i. 4, 17; GELL.
N. A. xx. 5, 5; DIOG. i. 17;
GALEN. *H. phil.* c. 3; PHILOP.
in q. v. Schol. in Ar. ii. b, 23 (cf.
in Categ. Schol. 35, a, 41 sq.;
AMMON. *in q. v. Porph.* 25, 6;
DAVID, *in Categ.* 23, b, 42 sq.,
and p.13, n.3 *supra*); with DAVID,
Schol. in Ar. 20, b, 16; SIMPL.
in Categ. 1 *fin.* That this derivation is correct rather than the
opposite view of Suidas (s. v.
'Αρ. and Σωκράτης) and Hesych.,
which derives the name from
the Περίπατος of the Lyceum as
the meeting-place of the school
is proved, first, by the form of
the word, which can be derived
only from the verb, and also by
the fact that the word Περίπατος
in the earliest times was not
confined to the Aristotelians (v.
p. 13, n. 3); though later it was

so limited, and they were called
οἱ ἐκ (or ἀπὸ) τοῦ περιπάτου (or
οἱ ἐκ τῶν περιπάτων, STRABO, xiii.
1, 54), as the other schools were
called οἱ ἀπὸ τῆς 'Ακαδημίας, or
οἱ ἀπὸ τῆς στοᾶς (*v.* SEXT. Pyrrh.
iii. 181; Math. vii. 331, 369;
xi. 45, etc.).

[3] GELL. *ut supra*, says that
Aristotle gave two kinds of instruction: the exoteric and the
acroamatic. The former related
to Rhetoric, and the latter to
'*Philosophia remotior*' (= Metaphysics) with Physics and Dialectic. The acroamatic instruction, which was intended only
for those who were tried and
well prepared, occupied the morning; the exoteric lectures, to
which the public was admitted,
the afternoon (cf. QUINTIL. iii. 1,
14, *pomeridianis scholis Ar.
praecipere artem oratoriam caepit*).
The former was called the ἑω-
θινὸς, the latter the δειλινὸς περίπατος: *utroque enim tempore am-
bulans disserebat.* It is impossible, however, to address a large
audience walking; therefore

as had already happened more or less with Plato, the
Socratic fashion of the dialogue had to give place to that
of a continuous lecture, whenever he was dealing either
with a large number of scholars or with subjects in which
there was something essentially new in form and matter
to be explained or some inquiry to be carried through
with scientific accuracy of detail.[1]   On the other hand,
wherever these difficulties did not arise, he did no doubt
retain the habit of philosophic dialogue with his friends
as an alternative method.[2]   In addition to his philosophical teaching he appears also to have revived his
earlier school of Rhetoric,[3] in connection with which
there were exercises in oratory.[4]   It is this, and not

Diog. (3) is doubtless more correct, ἐπειδὴ δὲ πλείους ἐγένοντο
ἤδη καὶ ἐκάθισεν.

[1] Such lectures must be meant
when ARISTOX. (*Harm. elem.* p.
30) says that Aristotle in his
teaching indicated the objects
and method of his inquiry before
giving the development of individual points. It is, as will be
seen, probable as to many of the
Aristotelian writings that they
were either made up from notes
of lectures, or intended as preparatory notes for lectures; and
at the end of the *Topica* Aristotle
directly addresses his audience
(*Soph. El.* 34 *fin.*).

[2] This appears partly from
the nature of the case, since
Aristotle had among his hearers
ripe and notable men like Theophrastus; partly from the fact
that at least in earlier years he
used the form of dialogue even
in his writings; partly from the
fashion of peripatetic teaching,
which supposes conversation : cf.

DIOG. iv. 10, speaking of Polemo :
ἀλλὰ μὴν οὐδὲ καθίζων ἔλεγε πρὸς
τὰς θέσεις, φασὶ, περιπατῶν δὲ ἐπε-
χείρει.   The continuous lecture
on a definite theme is expressed
by πρὸς θέσιν λέγειν : a more cur-
sory treatment by ἐπιχείρειν (cf.
following notes).

[3] Diog. (3) is not a good
witness, since what he appears
to state of Aristotle's later time
seems to be taken from a source
relating to the earlier period of
contest with Isocrates (cf. p. 17,
n. 3).   It is probable, however, from Aristotle's *Rhetoric*
itself that in the oral philosophic
teaching rhetoric was not forgotten, and GELL., *ut supra*,
speaks expressly of rhetorical
teaching in the Lyceum.

[4] DIOG. 3 : καὶ πρὸς θέσιν συν-
εγύμναζε τοὺς μαθητὰς ἅμα καὶ ῥητο-
ρικῶς ἐπασκῶν, the θέσις being
a general topic, not a particular
question (cf. CIC. *Top.* 21, 79,
Ep. ad Att. ix. 4; QUINTIL. iii.
5   5, x. 5, 11; and FREI, *Quæst.*

any popular lectures addressed to large audiences, that is referred to in the story that he received in the morning a small and select circle only and in the afternoon everyone freely.[1] At the same time we must also think of the Aristotelian school as a society of friends having on many sides a common life. For friendship its founder, bred in the intimacy of Plato, always showed by word and act a tender and beautiful enthusiasm; and we hear accordingly that, following the fashion of the Academy, he was wont to gather his scholars about him at common meals and that he introduced a plan of definite regulations for these meetings and for the whole of their common life.[2]

It is said that the aid and appliances which Aristotle needed for his far-reaching labours were provided for him by the favour of the two Macedonian rulers, and especially by the princely generosity of Alexander.[3]

Prot. 150). CIC. *Orat.* 14, 46 : *In hac Ar. adolescentes, non ad philosophorum morem tenuiter disserendi, sed ad copiam rhetorum in utramque partem, ut ornatius et uberius dici posset, exercuit.* Neither says whether the earlier or the later school of rhetoric is meant: probably both; cf. GELL. *ibid.* ἐξωτερικὰ dicebantur, quæ ad rhetoricas meditationes facultatemque argutiarum civiliumque rerum notitiam conducebant . . . illas vero exotericas auditiones exercitiumque dicendi.

[1] Cf. p. 27, n. 3, and GELL. *ibid.*

[2] ATHEN. (i. 3, v. 186 b, cf. 186 e) says he wrote for their common meals νόμοι συμποτικοί,

which may refer, however, to the work mentioned p. 99, n. 1, *infra*; and Diog. (4) preserves a hint of his arrangement for the internal government of the school by officers changing every ten days. Cf. ZELLER, *Ph. d. Gr.* i. 839, n. 1.

[3] According to ÆLIAN (*V. H.* iv. 19), Philip gave him ample means to pursue his investigations, πλοῦτον ἀνενδεῆ, especially in Natural History ; ATHEN. (ix. 398) speaks of Alexander devoting 800 talents to that work ; and PLIN. (*H. Nat.* viii. 16, 44) says Alex. placed under his orders all the hunters, fishers, and fowlers of the kingdom, and all overseers of the royal forests, ponds, and live stock, numbering many thousands. Pliny's story,

However exaggerated the stories of the ancient writers on this subject may seem to be, and however wealthy we may fairly suppose Aristotle himself to have been by inheritance,[1] it is yet clear that the vast scope of his researches forces us to infer that he possessed advantages which he probably could not have commanded but for such kingly assistance. The deep and wide acquaintance with the writings of his people which his own works[2] disclose to us could hardly be possible without the possession of books; and on this head we are expressly told that he was the first who accumulated a great library.[3] Such works, again, as the *Politeiai* and the collection of foreign laws could not be produced without laborious and no doubt costly investigations. The books on Natural History especially and the kindred treatises presuppose researches such as no one could have brought to completion unless he had at his disposal or could set in action something more than the resources of a private individual. It was therefore a happy circumstance that the man whose grasp of mind and rare powers of ob-

---

however, is disproved (*v.* BRAN-DIS, p. 117 sq., and HUMBOLDT, *Kosm.* ii. 191, 427) by the fact that with a few exceptions, such as elephants, Aristotle shows no knowledge of things which would be discovered in Alexander's expedition.

[1] His will proves nothing as to his earlier years, but apart from the calumnies of his opponents, as to his pride and love of display, all we know of his way of life, his choice of residence, his marriage, and the means necessary for his extensive studies, implies that he was not hampered by poverty. As to the worthlessness of the tales of Epicurus and Timæus, cf. p. 9, n. 1 and 3.

[2] Besides the extant works, we know of others concerning Rhetoric, Poetry, and the History of Philosophy.

[3] STRABO, xiii. 1, 54, p. 608 : πρῶτος ὧν ἴσμεν συναγαγὼν βιβλία καὶ διδάξας τοὺς ἐν Αἰγύπτῳ βασιλέας βιβλιοθήκης σύνταξιν. Cf. ATHEN. i. 3, a. GELL. (iii. 17, 3) says Aristotle paid three Attic talents for the works of Speusippus.

servation marked him as the ablest founder of empirical science and of systematic learning, should have been so favoured by fortune that the needful equipment for his great calling was not denied him.

In the last years of Aristotle's life the good relations between him and his great pupil were disturbed.[1] The philosopher may well have taken offence at many of the things which Alexander did in the intoxication of success, at many measures which he found necessary for the consolidation of his conquests, but which were repugnant to the Hellenic traditions and to the self-respect of independent Greeks, and at the harsh and passionate excess into which the young conqueror was betrayed when he was surrounded by flatterers, embittered by personal opposition and made suspicious by treachery.[2] There would be no lack of tale-bearers to carry gossip true and false to the king, for the learned and philosophic members of his Court were plotting in their personal jealousies[3] to oust each other, and even the courtiers and generals doubtless sought to use the scientific proclivities of the prince as points in the game of their ambitions. As the king's relations with Antipater grew more unfriendly, it seems he was prejudiced against Aristotle[4] also, because of the close relations between the philosopher and the general.[5] But the severest blow to the

[1] Cf. p. 23, n. 1, *supra.* The exchange of letters which is cited as a proof of their friendship is unreliable, because we do not know how much is genuine.

[2] Plutarch (cf. p. 23, n. 2, *supra*) says Aristotle was dissatisfied with Alexander's whole political idea of the fusion of the Greeks and Orientals.

[3] For examples *v.* PLUT. *Alex.* c. 52, 53, ARRIAN, iv 9–11.

[4] Cf. PLUT. *ibid.* 74 (though that is after the death of Callisthenes); as to Antipater, cf. PLUT. *Alex.* 39, 49; ARRIAN, vii. 12; CURT. x. 31; DIODOR. xvii 118.

[5] This friendship is proved from the fact that Antipater's

king's attachment to his tutor came through the action
of Callisthenes.[1] The stiff-necked opposition of that
philosopher to the new Oriental fashions of the Court;
the bitter and reckless tone of his diatribes against
them; the pointed way in which he vaunted his independence and drew upon himself the eyes of all the
malcontents of the army; the importance he assumed to
himself as Alexander's historian, and the arrogant airs
he gave himself accordingly, had long caused the king
to look on him with anger and mistrust. This made it
the easier for his enemies to persuade the king of his
complicity in the conspiracy of the nobles which had
placed Alexander's life in the gravest danger, and
Callisthenes lost his life [2] with the conspirators, though
he was doubtless innocent of their treacherous design.
In the heat of his anger the king's suspicions turned
against Aristotle [3] also, for he had brought up Calli-

son, Cassander, was a pupil of
Aristotle (PLUT. *Alex.* 74), by the
letters of Aristotle to Antipater
(Aristocl. *apud* EUS. *Pr. Ev.* xv.
2, 9; DIOG. 27; DEMETR. *Eloc.*
225; ÆLIAN, *V. H.* xiv. 1), and
especially by the fact that Antipater is named as chief executor
in Aristotle's will, *apud* DIOG. 11.
The false story of his complicity
in Alexander's death is based
on this circumstance (*v. infra*).

[1]. As to Callisthenes, see
PLUT. *Alex.* 53–55; *Sto. rep.* 20,
6. p. 1043, *Qu. conv.* i. 6. p. 623;
ARRIAN, iv. 10–14; CURT. viii.
18 sq.; CHARES *apud* ATHEN. x.
434 d; THEOPHRAST. *ap.* CIC.
Tusc. iii. 10, 21; SENECA, *Nat.*

Qu. vi. 23, 2; and of modern
writers, STAHR, *Arist.* i. 121 sq.;
DROYSEN, *Gesch. Alex.* ii. 88
sq.; GROTE, *Hist. of Greece*, xii.
290 sq., etc.

[2] It is highly improbable he
was an accomplice, though we
cannot say how far he was to
blame for exciting by reckless
talk his younger friends.

[3] Alex. writes to Antipater
(PLUT. *Alex.* 55): οἱ μὲν παῖδες
ὑπὸ τῶν Μακεδόνων κατελεύσθησαν·
τὸν δὲ σοφιστὴν [Callisth.] ἐγὼ
κολάσω καὶ τοὺς ἐκπέμψαντας αὐτὸν
καὶ τοὺς ὑποδεχομένους ταῖς πόλεσι
τοὺς ἐμοὶ ἐπιβουλεύοντας. According to Chares (*ap.* PLUT. *ibid.*),
he had at first intended to try
Callisthenes in Aristotle's pres-

sthenes as a kinsman and had afterwards recommended him to the King,[1] though, no doubt, he also warned the reckless young man against imprudence.[2] The suspicion however led to nothing worse than a notable coolness in his relations with Alexander.[3] A story to the effect that Aristotle was concerned with Antipater in the alleged poisoning of Alexander was connected with the death of Callisthenes,[4] but the completely groundless nature of the charge has long ago been proved.[5] So far indeed was Aristotle from having any cause to desire his princely pupil's death that that event in reality brought serious dangers upon himself.

ence. The statement of Dio. Chrys. (*Or.* 64, p. 338) that Alexander meant to kill Aristotle and Antipater is merely a rhetorical exaggeration.

[1] PLUT. *ibid.*; ARRIAN, iv. 10, 1 ; DIOG. 4 ; SUID. Καλλισθ.

[2] DIOG. *ibid.*; VALER. MAX. vii. 2 ; PLUT. *Alex.* 54.

[3] Plutarch says this expressly (cf. p. 23, n. 1, *supra*), and the story in Diog. 10, that Alexander, to mortify his teacher, took Anaximenes of Lampsacus and Xenocrates into favour, would not prove the contrary even if it were more credible ; but it is unworthy of both Alexander and Aristotle. Plutarch, *ibid.*, on the contrary, sees in the king's kindness to Xenocrates, a consequence of Aristotle's teaching. Philoponus (*apud* ARIST. *Meteorol.* ed. Ideler, i. 142) cites a reputed letter of Alexander to Aristotle from India, which proves nothing.

[4] The earliest witness to this story is a certain Hagnothemis (*apud* PLUT. *Alex.* 77) who is said to have heard it from King Anti-

gonus I. Arrian (vii. 27) and Pliny (*H. Nat.* xxx. 16) mention it, but, like Plutarch, treat it as an invention. Xiphilinus (lxxvii. 7, p. 1293) says the Emperor Caracalla deprived the Peripatetics in Alexandria of their privileges on account of the alleged guilt of Aristotle.

[5] The disproof of the charge (cf. STAHR, *Ar.* i. 136 sq. and DROYSEN, *Gesch. d. Hellen.* i. 705 sq,) rests, apart from its moral impossibility, on these grounds : (*a*) Plut. *ibid.* shows expressly that the suspicion of poisoning first arose six years after Alexander's death, when it afforded the passionate Olympias a welcome pretext to slake her hatred against Antipater's family, and to excite public opinion against Cassander who was said to have administered the poison ; (*b*) equal suspicion attaches to the testimony of Antigonus, which must belong to the time when he was at enmity with Cassander, though we do not know whether he made any charge against

For the unexpected news of the sudden death of the dreaded conqueror called out in Athens a wild excitement against the Macedonian rule, which, as soon as the news was fully confirmed, broke into open war. Athens put herself at the head of all who were willing to fight for the freedom of Greece, and before the Macedonian regent Antipater was fully prepared, he found himself beset by superior forces, which he only succeeded in mastering after a long and risky struggle in the Lamian War.[1] From the first this movement threatened, as was to be expected, the prominent members of the Macedonian party. Aristotle

Aristotle; (c) it is significant that the bitterest opponents of Aristotle, to whom no calumny is amiss, such as Epicurus, Timæus, Demochares, Lyco, etc., know nothing of the charge; (d) almost all who speak of Alexander's poisoning preserve the story (which was clearly connected with the first publication of the rumour and was well fitted to catch the popular fancy) that it was accomplished by water from the Nonacrian spring—*i.e.* the Styx— a proof that we are not dealing with history; (e) the accounts Arrian and Plutarch give us from the court chronicles as to the course of Alexander's illness do not in any way suggest poison; (f) if Aristotle's motive was the fate of Callisthenes, that could hardly have caused in him a hatred that would lead six years later to murder, nor could he, after so long a time, have had any fear as to his own safety; (g) it is probable that Aristotle's own adopted son was in Alex-

ander's service, and intrusted with important missions (cf. p. 5, n. 7, *supra*); (h) finally, the rumour of Alexander's poisoning is refuted by the movement of events afterwards. Alexander's death was the signal for an outbreak in Greece, which in the Lamian war brought Antipater himself to great straits. Anyone acquainted with the politics of the day would clearly foresee such a result. If Antipater were not as much taken by surprise as everyone else was by the king's death, he would have made preparations either to stem or to head the rising. If he had been known as the author of that which the Greeks acclaimed as the beginning of freedom, they would not have begun their revolt by attacking him; and if any part in it had been attributed to Aristotle, he would not have had to fly from Athens.

[1] For details, see DROYSEN, *Gesch. d. Hellen.* i. 59 sq.

may not have played a political *rôle*; [1] but, in any case, his relation as tutor to Alexander and his friendship with Antipater were so well known, his own name was so famous, and his personal enemies, no doubt, so many, that he could not escape attack. The charge brought against him of offences against the established religion —in itself baseless enough—must have been simply a pretext for wreaking political and personal vengeance. [2] But Aristotle found it best to retire before the rising storm. [3] He escaped to Chalcis in Eu-

[1] According to Aristocl. *ap.* EUS. *Pr. Ev.* xv. 2, 3, Demochares (doubtless Demosthenes' nephew, *de quo cf.* CIC. *Brut.* 83, 286: *De Orat.* ii. 23, 95; SENECA, *De Ira,* iii. 23, 2; PLUT. *Demosth.* 30; *Vit. X Orat.* viii. 53, p. 847, and SUIDAS) had alleged that letters of Aristotle's had been found which were hostile to Athens; that he had betrayed Stagira to the Macedonians, and that after the destruction of Olynthus he had betrayed to Philip the richest citizens of that city. As the last two are impossible, the first is probably untrue, as Aristocles himself recognised.

[2] The charge was brought by Demophilus on the instigation of the Hierophant Eurymedon, related to the deification of Hermias, and alleged as proofs the poem noticed (p. 20, n. 3), and the alleged sacrifice (p. 20, n. 1): cf. ATHEN. xv. 696 a, 697 a; DIOG. 5; ANON. MENAG., SUIDAS, and HESYCH. Origen (*c. Cels.* i. 65) suggests, out of his own fancy, τινὰ δόγματα τῆς φιλοσοφίας αὐτοῦ ἃ ἐνόμισαν εἶναι ἀσεβῆ οἱ Ἀθηναῖοι. The weakness of the charge proves that it was only

a blind, although perhaps the Hierophant may have hated the philosopher's liberalism. An honest charge of atheism in the Athens of that day was hardly possible, although the mass of the people could still be moved by it. Grote (18 sq.) shows how in this connection the Athenians would be impressed by the story that Aristotle had given heroic honours to an eunuch who was first a slave and then a tyrant. Grote also notices (p. 14) how mortifying the mission of Aristotle's adopted son was for Hellenic pride (*v.* p. 5, n. 7). The further suggestion of Grote (p. 37. cf. GRANT, p. 24) that the enmity of the school of Isocrates had to do with the prosecution of Aristotle may be true, but the fact that Demophilus was a son of Ephorus, and that the latter, and perhaps both, belonged to that school is not sufficient proof. We have still less ground to accuse the Academic school of having any share in it.

[3] His remarks that 'he would not give the Athenians a second chance of sinning against philosophy,' and that 'Athens was the

bœa,[1] where he had a country house, to which he had
sometimes retired before,[2] and his enemies could only
inflict on him unimportant insults.[3]　To Theophrastus [4]
he gave over his teaching work at the Lyceum, as a
substitute during his absence.　But it was not given

place spoken of by Homer where
ὄγχνη ἐπ' ὄγχνῃ γηράσκει, σῦκον
δ' ἐπὶ σύκῳ, in allusion to the
sycophants, are quoted by DIOG. 9 ;
ÆLIAN, iii. 36 ; ORIGEN, *ut supra* ;
EUSTATH. *in Odyss.* H 120,
p. 1573 ; AMMON. p. 48 ; *V. Marc.*
8 ; *Ammon. Latin.* 17, the last
mentioned placing them in a
letter to Antipater. FAVORINUS,
apud DIOG. 9, says the Homeric
line occurred in a written *Apologia,*
which is known also to the *Anon.*
Menag. and to ATHEN. xv. 697 a,
both of whom doubt its genuineness.　One does not see why
Aristotle, once in safety, should
write a useless defence. It was no
doubt a rhetorical exercise in imitation of the Socratic *Apologia* (cf.
the fragment given by Athenæus
with PLAT. *Apol.* 26 D sq.).

[1] Apollodor. *apud* DIOG. 10 is
made to say that this was in
Ol. 114, 3, *i.e.* in the latter half
of 322 B.C. This is improbable, for Strabo (x. 1, 11) and
Heraclides *ap.* DIOG. x. 1 speak
as if he lived a considerable time
in Chalcis ; and besides it is more
likely that the attack on Aristotle
happened in the first uprising
against the Macedonian party
than that it was begun after
Antipater's decisive victories in
Thessaly, and that Aristotle fled
in good time instead of waiting
through the whole of the Lamian
war. Probably, therefore, he left
Athens late in the summer of
323, and Apollodorus only said

what we find in DIONYS. *Ep.*
ad Amm. i. 5, that Aristotle
died in Ol. 114, 3, having fled to
Chalcis.　It is not possible to
assume (with STAHR, i. 147) an
earlier emigration of Aristotle to
Chalcis, on the authority of the
statement of Heraclides that
Aristotle was living in Chalcis
when Epicurus came to Athens,
τελευτήσαντος δ' Ἀλεξάνδρου . . .
μετελθεῖν ['Επίκουρον] εἰς Κολο-
φῶνα. For Aristotle's flight was
due only to the danger that
threatened him at Athens, which
arose only on Alexander's unexpected death ; and he cannot
therefore have gone to Chalcis
before the news reached Athens,
in the middle of 323. Either
Heraclides or Diogenes must be
inexact. The Pseudo-Ammonius
(cf. p. 25, n. 5 *supra*) and David
(*Schol. in Ar.* 26 b. 26) assign impossible dates.

[2] Cf. STRABO, x. 1, 11, p.
448.

[3] In a fragment of a letter to
Antipater probably of this time
(*ap.* ÆLIAN, *V. H.* xiv. 1, cf. p.
44, n. 4 *infra*) Aristotle makes
mention τῶν ἐν Δελφοῖς ψηφισ-
θέντων μοι καὶ ὧν ἀφῄρημαι νῦν.
What this was—whether a monument, proëdria, or other honorary
privilege—we do not know. If it
was given him by Athens, it may
be connected with the services
noticed p. 24, n. 3, *supra*.

[4] DIOG. v. 36 and following
lines, SUID. *s. v.* Θεόφρ.

to Aristotle to enjoy his retirement long. In the following year, that is, in the summer of 322 B.C.[1], he succumbed to a disease from which he had long suffered.[2] So it chanced that of his two great contemporaries he survived Alexander by less than a year, and predeceased Demosthenes only by a short interval. His body is said to have been taken to Stagira.[3] His last will is preserved to us,[4] and it is a monument of his

[1] Apollod. *ap.* DIOG. 10, *V. Marc.* 3, *Ammon. Latin.* 12, and DION. *Ep. ad Amm.* i. 5, give Ol. 114, 3 as the year. It was about the time of Demosthenes' death (APOLLOD. *ibid.*), but a little earlier (GELL. *N. A.* xvii. 21, 35). As that date is given by PLUT. (*Dem.* 30) as the 16th of Pyanepsion Ol. 114, 3 = Oct. 14, 322, Aristotle must have died between July and Sept. of that year.

[2] That he died by illness is stated by Apollod. and Dionys. *ut supra*; cf. GELL. xiii. 5, 1. Censorin. (*Di. Nat.* 14, 16) adds: *hunc ferunt naturalem stomachi infirmitatem crebrasque morbidi corporis offensiones adeo virtute animi diu sustentasse, ut magis mirum sit ad annos sexaginta tres eum vitam protulisse, quam ultra non pertulisse.* The statement of Eumelus *ap.* DIOG. 6 (*de quo v.* p. 2, n. 2, p. 6, n. 3 *supra*) followed by the Anon. Menag. and Suidas, that he poisoned himself with hemlock, or (as Hesych. has it) that he was condemned to drink hemlock, is probably a confusion with the death of Demosthenes or of Socrates. It cannot be historic, because the best evidence is against it, because it is contrary to Aristotle's own principles (*Eth. N.* ii. 11, 1116 a,

12, v. 15 *init.*, ix. 4, 1166 b, 11), and because it does not fit the circumstances, for in Euboea he was in no danger. The tale (found only in ÆLIAS CRETENSIS, p. 507 D) that he threw himself into the Euripus because he could not discover the causes of his visions, and the variant of the same in JUSTIN. cohort. 36, GREG. NAZ. *Or.* iv. 112, or PROCOP. *De Bello Goth.* iv. 579, that his fruitless meditations on a vision wore him out with worry and fatigue, need no refutation, though Bayle (art. Aristotle, n. Z) thinks the latter a fitting end; cf. STAHR, i. 155.

[3] Related only by *V. Marc.* 4 and *Ammon. Latin.* 13, and with the addition that an altar was built on his grave and the council meetings held there ; and that a festival (Ἀριστοτέλεια) was instituted and a month named after him. The evidence is not good; but as he was not only the most illustrious citizen but also the re-founder of Stagira (cf. DIO. *Or.* 47, 224, who says that Aristotle alone had the fortune to be τῆς πατρίδος οἰκιστής) the story is not wholly improbable.

[4] *Apud* DIOG. 11 sq; probably (cf. v. 64) taken, like the wills of Theophrastus, Strato, and Lyco, from Aristo, a noted

faithful attachment and careful provision for all who
were connected with him, including his slaves. Theo-

Peripatetic *circ.* 200–250 (*lege*
'Αρίστων ὁ Κεῖος), who will be
mentioned in his place. Hermippus (*circ.* 200–220) cited the
same record (*v.* ATHEN. xiii.
589 *c.*), which according to *V.
Marc.* 8, and *Ammon. Latin.* 17
was also quoted by Andronicus
and Ptolemæus for the catalogues
of Aristotle's writings, *de q. infra.*
V. Marc. says Aristotle left a
διαθήκη . . . ἣ φέρεται παρά τε 'Αν-
δρονίκῳ καὶ Πτολεμαίῳ μετὰ [τῶν]
πινάκ[ων] τῶν αὐτοῦ συγγραμμάτων
(*Ammon. Latin.* ' cum volumi-
nibus suorum tractatuum ;' cf.
HEITZ, *Verl. Schr. d. Ar.* 34).
The external evidence for the
will is therefore good ; the more
because it is likely that the wills
of Aristotle and his followers
would be carefully preserved by
the Peripatetic school (for which
those of Theoph., Strato, and
Lyco were a kind of foundation
charter), and because Aristo was
himself the immediate successor
of Lyco. The document has also
all internal signs of genuineness,
and the objections which have
been urged against it (cf. GRANT,
26) prove little. It is objected
that it mentions neither a house
in Athens nor a library, both
of which Aristotle possessed. A
forger, however, would never
have omitted the latter, which
was the thing of chief interest
for the school ; but it is very possible that Aristotle had already
made arrangements about it,
which did not require to be repeated in the extant will, that
being rather a set of directions
to friends than, like the three

others quoted, a regular disposition of his whole property. Grant
thinks it unlikely that Pythias
was not yet marriageable or that
Nicomachus was a lad ; but this
is not so. Why may not Aristotle's wife Pythias, perhaps
after the death of older children,
have borne him a daughter ten
years after their marriage ? or
why might Aristotle not have by
a second wife, for whose remar-
riage he provides, a son who
would be a lad when his father
was sixty-three ? Besides, we
know from other sources that the
education of Nicomachus was
taken over by Theophrastus. The
naming of Antipater arouses
in Grant a suspicion that the
forger inserted him as a historic
name ; but it is clearly natural
that Aristotle might appoint him
in order to place the carrying
out of his directions for the
benefit of those depending on
him under the protection of his
powerful friend. And this is all
that is meant when he is named
first in the honorary position of
ἐπίτροπος πάντων, whereas the
carrying out of the business
provisions of the will is left to
Theophrastús and the other ἐπι-
μεληταί. Objection is taken to
the provisions for four statues of
animals which Aristotle is said
to have vowed to Zeus Soter
and Athene the Preserver, for
Nicanor's safety (DIOG. 16), as
being an imitation of the Socratic
votive offering for Asclepios
(PLAT. *Phæd.* 118, A). This,
however, is far-fetched and the
point is unimportant. Little as

phrastus he named as the chief of his school,[1] and to him he left the best part of his inheritance, his books.[2] We are but poorly informed as to the personal traits of Aristotle's character. Excepting a few details as to his personal appearance,[3] almost the only statements we possess are the attacks of his enemies. Most of these charges have already been shown to be worthless—such as those concerning his relations with Plato, with Hermias, with his two wives, and with Alexander, his alleged misconduct in youth, and the political turpitude of his later years.[4] What remains of the stories told

Aristotle believed in vows or in the mythic personalities of Zeus and Athene, yet it is quite natural that he should erect a monument of his love for his adopted son in their common home, Stagira (to which the statues were to be sent), in a fashion which accorded with Greek custom. He himself in *Ethics* iv. 5 reckons votive monuments and offerings among the forms in which the virtue of μεγαλοπρέπεια shows itself.

[1] The pretty story as to the way in which he expressed his choice is well known (GELL. *N. A.* xiii. 5, where 'Eudemus' must be substituted for 'Menedemus'). It is quite credible, and not unlike Aristotle.

[2] STRABO, xiii. 1, 54, p. 608; PLUT. *Sulla*, c. 26; ATHEN. i. 3, a, with which cf. DIOG. v. 52.

[3] DIOG. 2 calls him ἰσχνοσκελὴς and μικρόμματος, and an abusive epigram in the Anthology (iii. 167, Jac.), which deserves no weight, σμικρὸς, φαλακρὸς, and προγάστωρ. We hear of a lisp in pronouncing R, to which the word τραυλὸς (*ap.* DIOG. 2, ANON.

MENAG., SUID., PLUT. *Aud. Poet.* 8, p. 26, and *Adulat.* 9, p. 53) refers. Pausanias (vi. 4, 5) mentions a statue said to be of Aristotle; as to others, *v.* STAHR, i. 161 sq, and as to those extant, especially the life-size sitting statue in the Palazzo Spada at Rome, *v.* SCHUSTER, *Erhalt. Portr. d. griech. Philos.* Leipz. 1876, p. 16, where they are photographed. The sitting statue has a lean face, earnest and thoughtful, showing the lines of severe mental labour, and with a delicate, clear-cut profile. It impresses us with its life-like truth to nature, and the workmanship is so excellent that it may well be an original work dating from the time of Aristotle or his immediate successor. Directions are given in Theophrastus' will (DIOG. v. 51) that the Μουσεῖον begun by him should be finished : ἔπειτα τὴν Ἀριστοτέλους εἰκόνα τεθῆναι εἰς τὸ ἱερὸν καὶ τὰ λοιπὰ ἀναθήματα ὅσα πρότερον ὑπῆρχεν ἐν τῷ ἱερῷ, which probably is to be understood of a statue already erected.

[4] Cf. p. 8 sq.; 19, n. 4; 20, n. 1, 2; 33, n. 4; 35, n. 1, 5,

by his many enemies[1] has for the most part little probability.[2] Nor do the accounts we have give us any right to lay to Aristotle's charge either a self-seeking sort of shrewdness, or a jealous and little-minded greed for fame.[3] The first of these charges concerns chiefly his relations with the Macedonian rulers. The second refers to the criticisms he allows himself to make in writing of his cotemporaries and his forerunners. But it cannot be proved that he ever sought the favour of Philip and

supra. Another calumny is Tertullian's *Ar. familiarem suum Hermiam turpiter loco excedere fecit* (*Apologet.* 46), which in the context can only mean he betrayed him, a tale so senseless and wicked that it required a Tertullian to invent it. The story of Philo of Byblos *ap.* SUID. Παλαίφ., as to immoral relations with the historian Palæphatus of Abydos is equally baseless.

[1] THEMIST. *Orat.* xxiii. 285 talks of a στρατὸς ὅλος of Aristotle's calumniators. By him, Aristocl. (*ap.* EUS. xv. 2) and Diogenes (11, 16) the following are named: Epicurus, Timæus, Eubulides, Alexinus, Cephisodorus, Lyco, Theocritus of Chios, Demochares, and Dicæarchus, within a generation of Aristotle.

[2] Such as the accusations to be found in ARISTOCL. and DIOG., *ut supra*; SUID. 'Αριστ.; ATHEN. viii. 342, xiii. 566; PLIN. *H. N.* xxxv. 16, 2; ÆLIAN, *V. H.* iii. 19; THEODORET, *Cur. Gr. Aff.* xii 51, p. 173; LUCIAN, *Dial. Mort.* 13, 5, and *Paras.* 36; that Aristotle was a glutton, and for that reason went to the

Macedonian Court and flattered Alexander, and that at his death 75 (or even 300) dishes were found in his house: or that he was immoral in relation to Pythias and Herpyllis, and was also enamoured of Theodectes of Phaselis: and again that he was so effeminate that he bathed in warm oil (doubtless for medical reasons, cf. DIOG. 16 and p. 37, n. 2, *supra*), and so miserly that he sold the oil afterwards: or that in his youth he was too fashionable for a philosopher (which, as he was rich and brought up at Court, is possible): and that he was impudent and sneering. If there were any facts underlying these stories, we may conclude from the character of the narrators that they were in any case trivial; and we can see in the passages of Lucian and Theodoret and his quotation from Atticus how Aristotle's own statements as to wealth and pleasure were twisted to support these suspicions.

[3] Even Stahr (i. 173 sq) pays too much attention to these charges.

Alexander by unworthy means,[1] and it was not to be expected that he should applaud or imitate the follies of a Callisthenes. To impute it to him as an offence, that he attached himself to the Macedonian party, is to apply to him an erroneous and inapplicable standard. By birth and training he was a Greek. But while all his personal ties attached him to the royal house to which he and his father owed so much, no one can say that the consideration of the general position of politics ought necessarily to have turned him against their policy. So satisfied was Plato of the untenable character of the existing political relations, that he had advocated sweeping changes. Plato's follower could the less evade the same conviction, since he had a keener insight into men and things, and had clearly detected the conditions on which the vitality of States and forms of government depends. With his practical acumen he could not put his trust in the Platonic ideal of a State ; he was forced to seek the materials for a political reconstruction from among the political relations as they were and the powers already existing. At that day no

---

[1] Stahr thinks it sounds like flattery when Aristotle writes to Alexander (*Arist. Fragm.* No. 611, *apud* ÆLIAN, *V. H.* xii. 54) ὁ θυμὸς καὶ ἡ ὀργὴ οὐ πρὸς ἴσους (1. ἥσσους with Rutgers, Rose and Heitz) ἀλλὰ πρὸς τοὺς κρείττονας γίνεται, σοὶ δὲ οὐδεὶς ἴσος, but if this is genuine Aristotle said no more than the truth, and he wrote, according to Ælian, in order to appease Alexander's wrath against certain persons, for which purpose he tells him that one cannot be angry with inferiors, and that he stood above all men, which was surely true of the conqueror of the Persian Empire. We cannot tell whether the letter is genuine. Heitz (*Verlor. Schr. d. Arist.* 287) suggests that this fragment does not agree with that in Plut. (*Tranqu. An.* 13, p 472 ; *Arist. Fragm.* 614, 1581, b) in which Aristotle is made to compare himself with Alexander, but the letter is much the more doubtful of the two.

new foundation could be found except in the Macedonian
kingdom, for the Greek States were no longer able at
once to maintain their independence against the foreigner
and to reform their inner life. The whole course of
history so far had proved this so conclusively, that even
a Phocion was forced to say, in the Lamian War, that
unless the moral conditions of Greece were altered
there was nothing to be expected from an armed rising
against Macedon.[1] Doubtless such a conviction would
come far less readily to an Athenian statesman than to
a friend of the Macedonian kings, who was a citizen
of a small city like Stagira, once destroyed by Philip,
and then reorganised as a Macedonian town. Can
we blame him if he accepted that view, and, with a
just appreciation of the political situation, attached
himself to that party which alone had a future, and
from which alone, if from any, Greece could still find
salvation from the dissension and decay within, and the
loss of power to face the enemy without? Can we
condemn him if he felt that the old independence of
the Greek cities must come to an end, when its basis
in the civic virtue of their citizens was gone? Can we
object if he believed that in his pupil Alexander was
fulfilled the condition under which he held that
monarchy was natural and just [2]—where one man stands
out so clearly beyond all others in efficiency as to make
their equality with him impossible? Can we complain
if he preferred to see the hegemony of Hellas rather in
the hands of such a man than in those of the ' great
king' of Persia, for whose favour the Greek cities had

[1] PLUT. *Phoc.* 23.   [2] *Polit.* iii. 13 *fin.*

been bidding against each other ever since the Peloponnesian War, and hoped that he would give the Hellenes the only thing they lacked to become the rulers of the world—a political unity ? [1]

As for the charge of jealousy of others' fame, it is true that his philosophical polemics are often cutting and sometimes unfair. But they never take on any personal colour, and it would be impossible to prove that they ever rest on any other motive than the desire to make his point as sharply, and establish it as completely as possible. If he does sometimes give us the impression of insisting on his own discoveries, we ought to set off against this the conscientiousness with which he seeks out every seed of truth, even the remotest, in the work of his predecessors ; and remembering this, we shall find that all that remains is but a very intelligible and very pardonable self-appreciation.

Still less—to pass over minor matters [2]—need we attach any importance to the allegation that Aristotle hoped soon to see philosophy completed.[3] If he did, it would have been only the same self-deception of which many other thinkers have been guilty, including some who have not been, as he was, the teachers of mankind

[1] *Polit.* vii. 7, 1327 b, 29, reckoning the merits of the Greek race : διόπερ ἐλεύθερόν τε διατελεῖ καὶ βέλτιστα πολιτευόμενον καὶ δυνάμενον ἄρχειν πάντων μιᾶς τυγχάνον πολιτείας.

[2] Like the tale told by Valer. Max. viii. 14, 3, as a proof of Aristotle's *sitis in capessenda laude,* which is plainly an idle invention based on a misunder-standing of the *Rhet. ad Alex.* c. 1 *fin.* (cf. *Rhet.* iii. 9, 1410 b, 2).

[3] Cic. *Tusc.* iii. 28, 69 : *Aristoteles veteres philosophos accusans qui existimavissent philosophiam suis ingeniis esse perfectam, ait eos aut stultissimos aut gloriosissimos fuisse : sed se videre, quod paucis annis magna accessio facta esset, brevi tempore philosophiam plane absolutam fore.*

for tens of centuries. In fact, the remark seems to have occurred in an early work of Aristotle's,[1] and to have related not to his own system but to Plato's, which professed to open out a prospect of an early completion of all science.[2]

So far as Aristotle's philosophical writings, the scanty fragments of his letters, the provisions of his will, and our incomplete accounts of his life afford us any picture of his personality, we cannot but honour him. Nobility of principles, a just moral sense, a keen judgment, a susceptibility to all beauty, a warm and lively feeling for family life and friendship, gratitude towards benefactors, affection for relatives, benevolence to slaves and those in need,[3] a loyal love for his wife, and a lofty conception of marriage far transcending the traditional theories of Greece—such are the traits that we can see. They all carry us back to that faculty of moral tact to which in his Ethics he reduced all virtue, backed as it was in him by a wide knowledge of men and by deep reflection. We are bound to suppose that the principles he asserts in his Ethics were the guides of his own life,[4] the recoil from all manner of one-sidedness and excess, and the orderly

[1] In the dialogue Περὶ φιλο-σοφίας, to which it is rightly referred by Rose (*Ar. Fr.* No. 1) and Heitz (*Ar. Fr.* p. 33).

[2] As Bywater (*Journ. of Philol.* vii. 69) also says. In Aristotle's extant works he often refers to the need of further investigation.

[3] As to the former, cf. his will, which provides *inter alia* that none of those who had

personally served him should be sold, and that several should be freed and even started in life. As to the latter, cf. his saying, *ap.* DIOG. 17, οὐ τὸν τρόπον, ἀλλὰ τὸν ἄνθρωπον ἠλέησα.

[4] Cf. his expressions in the Letter to Antipater, *ap.* ÆLIAN, *V. H.* xiv. 1 and *ap.* DIOG. 18. In the former fragment he says as to the withdrawal of former honours (*de q. v.* p. 36, n. 3,

appreciation of things which despises nothing that has
its roots in human nature, but attributes an absolute
value only to the spiritual and moral factors of life.
And if his character, so far as we know it, and in spite
of any little weaknesses which may have attached to
it, seems to us lofty and honourable, still more are
his powers and intellectual achievements altogether
astounding. Never have so great a wealth of knowledge, so careful powers of observation, and so untiring
a zeal for acquisition, been found in combination with
such keenness and power of scientific thinking, with a
philosophic insight so capable of piercing into the
essence of things, with a width of view so fully capable
of at once seeing the unity and coherence of all knowledge, and embracing and subordinating all its branches.
In poetic swing, in richness of fancy, in the insight of
genius, he cannot compete with Plato. His powers lay
wholly on the side of knowledge, not of art.[1] That
fascinating witchery of speech with which Plato holds
us is hardly ever to be found in the extant works of the
Stagirite, though many of those that are lost are praised,
doubtless with justice, for their literary grace.[2] But
he outstrips his master in all those qualities which
mark the full manhood of science—in width and solidity

---

supra) οὕτως ἔχω, ὡς μήτε μοι
σφόδρα μέλειν ὑπὲρ αὐτῶν μήτε μοι
μηδὲν μέλειν ; in the latter, as to
one who had reviled him behind
his back : ἀπόντα με καὶ μαστιγούτω.

[1] The few poetic attempts we
have show no great gift. On the
other hand his wit was noted
(DEMETR. *De Eloc.* 128), and
the apophthegms (*ap.* DIOG.

17 sq) and the fragments of
letters (*ap.* DEMETR. 29, 233)
give proof of it. That it went
with a tendency to banter and
sauciness of speech (ἄκαιρος στω-
μυλία), as Ælian (*V. H.* iii. 19)
tells us of him in his youth, is
possible, though not proved by
the existing testimony.

[2] *De quo infra.*

of research, in purity of scientific method, in ripeness of judgment, in wary discrimination, in his compact brevity and inimitable keenness of statement, and in the definite use and comprehensive development of a scientific terminology. He cannot inspire us, lay hold of our hearts, weld in one the scientific and the moral energies, at all in the same way as Plato does. His work is drier, more professional, more closely confined to the field of cognition than Plato's had been. But within these lines he has, so far as one man might, achieved success. For thousands of years he showed philosophy her way. For the Greeks he inaugurated the age of learning. In every field of knowledge then open to him he enriched the sciences by original investigations, and advanced them by new conceptions. Even if we put at their highest possible measure the help he derived from his forerunners, and the assistance he obtained from scholars and friends, and perhaps also from trained slaves,[1] the range of his achievements still runs so far beyond the common standard, that we can scarcely understand how one man in a short life could accomplish it all, especially since we know that his restless soul had to wring from a weakly body the needful vitality for this gigantic work.[2] Aristotle has fulfilled his historic vocation and solved the philosophic task it set him, as scarce any other ever did. Of what he was as a man we know unhappily too little, but we

[1] Callisthenes of Babylon is said to have sent him information of astronomical observations there (SIMPL. *De Cœlo*, Schol. 503, a, 26, following Porph.), but the story is suspicious because of the addition that these observations went back 31,000 years.
[2] Cf. p. 37, n. 2, and DIOG. v. 16.

have no reason to believe the attacks of his foes, or to refuse to accord to him that favourable judgment which his own Ethics with many subsidiary indications must demand.

CHAPTER II

ARISTOTLE'S WRITINGS

A.—Consideration of the particular works seriatim

THE literary activity of Aristotle startles us at the outset both by its extent and its manysidedness. The works which we have under his name extend over all branches of philosophy, and they exhibit a vast wealth of wide observation and historical learning. Yet to these extant works the ancient catalogues add a great number of others, of which only the titles or slight fragments now remain. Two of these catalogues we have: the first in two recensions, that by Diogenes (V. 21 sqq.), and that called the 'Anonymus Menagii': the other in certain Arabic texts.[1] The first list contains, in Diogenes, 146 titles, most[2] of which the 'Anonymus'[3] has preserved, leaving out[4] a few[5] and adding seven or eight new ones. An appendix adds forty-seven titles— many of which,[6] however, are only repetitions or variants of those already entered—and ten Pseudepigrapha.

---

[1] See both in the *Arist. Fragm.* of Rose and Heitz (*Ar. Opp.* v. 1463, Berlin ed., iv. b, 1 sq., Paris ed.)

[2] According to the earlier text 111, but as completed by Rose from an Ambrosian MS. 132.

[3] According to Rose's probable conjecture (*Ar. Libr. Ord.*

48) he was Hesychius of Miletus, who lived about 500.

[4] As to the possible grounds of this omission cf. HEITZ, *Verlor. Schr. Arist.* p. 15.

[5] 14 by one text, 27 by the other.

[6] If our count is right there are 9, *i.e.* Nos. 147, 151, 154, 155, 167, 171, 172, 174, 182, repeating

Both the sources agree in putting the total number of books at nearly 400.[1] The author of the first catalogue cannot be (as Rose imagines [2]) identified with Andronicus of Rhodes, the well-known editor and arranger of Aristotle's works,[3] though it is not to be doubted that that Peripatetic did compile a catalogue of Aristotle's writings.[4] For even if we could set aside the fact that Andronicus is said to have given the total number at 1,000 books,[5] and the circumstance that the extant index includes [6] the Περὶ ἑρμηνείας, which he rejected,[7] it remains clear that we should look to find in Andronicus's edition those writings above all that are included in our extant *Corpus Aristotelicum*, which is derived, speaking broadly, from his own. This is far from being true of the extant catalogues, for many important parts of the extant *Corpus* are either altogether absent or at least are not to be traced under

Nos. 106, 7, 111, 91, 98, 16, 18, 39 and 11 of the main list.

[1] DIOG. 34, and the ANON. MENAG. at the beginning of his list. The titles in Diog. (reckoning the Letters as one book for each correspondent named and the Πολιτεῖαι as a single book) give 375 books; those in the Anon. as completed by Rose, 391.

[2] *Arist. Pseudepig.* 8 sq.

[3] Cf. ZELLER, *Ph. d. Gr.* Pt. iii. a, 549, 3 (2nd edition).

[4] This is clear from the above-mentioned passage of Plut. (*Sulla*, 26) from the *V. Marc.* 8 (cf. p. 37, n. 4, *supra*) and David, *Schol. in Ar.* 24, a, 19. It is not credible that Andronicus merely adopted the catalogue of Hermippus (*v.* HEITZ, *Ar. Fr.* 12)

which did not at all correspond with his own work. A similar catalogue of the writings of Theophrastus is ascribed to him by the Scholia at the end of his *Metaphysics* and at the beginning of the seventh book of the *Hist. of Plants*.

[5] DAVID, *Schol. in Ar.* 24, a, 19.

[6] This is the more remarkable because we gather from DIOG. 34 that the catalogue was to include only works recognised as genuine. Bernays (*Dial. d. Ar.* 134) therefore supposes that the book was inserted in the catalogue of Andronicus by a later hand.

[7] ALEX. *in Anal. Pri.* 52.

their later names and in their later form.¹ The converse theory ² that the list in Diogenes was meant to contain only those writings which were left out of Andronicus's collection of the didactic works, is negatived by the fact that the list contains many important sections of the *Corpus*, and that it distinctly claims to be a *complete* review of the philosopher's works.³ For similar reasons it is equally impossible that it can owe its origin to Nicolaus of Damascus,⁴ or any other to

---

¹ Of the books contained in our *Corpus Aristotelicum* Diogenes' list mentions only the following : Nos. 141, The *Categories* ; 142, Π. ἑρμηνείας ; 49, Προτέρων ἀναλυτικῶν ; 50, Ἀναλ. ὑστέρων ; 102, Π. ζώων, 9 books (meaning no doubt the *History of Animals*, the spurious tenth book of which is afterwards, No. 107, called Ὑπὲρ τοῦ μὴ γεννᾶν) ; 123, Μηχανικῶν αʹ ; 75, Πολιτικῆς ἀκροάσεως 8 books ; 23, Οἰκονομικὸς αʹ ; 78, Τέχνης ῥητορικῆς αʹ βʹ ; 119, Ποιητικῶν αʹ : and probably also the *Topics*, under two different names, *cf. infra.* Also Nos. 90, Π. φύσεως αʹ βʹ γʹ, and 45 (115), Π. κινήσεως αʹ (which are probably parts of the *Physics*) ; and No. 39, Π. στοιχείων αʹ βʹ γʹ (meaning probably the two books Π. γενέσεως with our book iii. *De Cœlo*, or book iv. *Meteor.*) ; 70, Θέσεις ἐπιχειρηματικαὶ κεʹ (no doubt a recension of the *Problems*) ; 36, Π. τῶν ποσαχῶς λεγομένων (doubtless the treatise. often cited by Ar. under that name, which is now book v. of the *Metaphysics*) ; and 38, Ἠθικῶν (only 5 books). Even assuming that all the suggested correspondences are correct, the list still

omits important parts of our *Corpus*. The Anon. Menag. adds the *Topics* under that name (his No. 52) and the *Metaphysics*, to which he gives 20 books (if the text is right, *de quo infra*). The *First Analytic* is his 134, with 2 books, and the *Ethics* is 39, Ἠθικῶν κʹ (*lege* αʹ–κʹ). His appendix adds : 148, Φυσικὴ ἀκρόασις, ιηʹ (*lege* ηʹ ; 149, Π. γενέσεως καὶ φθορᾶς ; 150, Π. μετεώρων, δʹ ; 155, Π. ζώων ἱστορίας ιʹ ; 156, Π. ζώων κινήσεως (as 3 books) ; 157, Π. ζώων μορίων (only 3 books) ; 158, Π. ζώων γενέσεως (also 3 books) ; 174, Π. ἠθικῶν Νικομαχείων.

² Of Bernays, *Dial. Ar.* 133, and Rose, *ut supra* : cf on the opposite side, HEITZ, *Verlor. Schr.* p. 19.

³ 'Συνέγραψε δὲ πάμπλειστα βιβλία ἅπερ ἀκόλουθον ἡγησάμην ὑπογράψαι διὰ τὴν περὶ πάντας λόγους τἀνδρὸς ἀρετήν,' are the introductory words in DIOG. v.21, but that does not mean that he would exclude the main philosophical treatises. The same is clear from § 34, where Aristotle's power of work is said to be proved ἐκ τῶν προγεγραμμένων συγγραμμάτων, numbering nearly 400.

⁴ For his works on Aristotle

whom the edition of Andronicus was already known. Its compiler must have been [1] a scholar of the Alexandrine period, most probably Hermippus; [2] and he must either not have had the means or not have taken the trouble to give us more than a list of the manuscripts which were to be found [3] in a library accessible to him, presumably that of Alexandria. Otherwise it would be impossible for him to have omitted important works which can, as we shall see, be clearly proved to have been in use during the two centuries preceding the date of Andronicus.[4] The first catalogue, therefore, only shows us what writings appeared under Aristotle's name in the Library of Alexandria.

Of far later date is the other catalogue of Aristotelian writings, which two Arabic writers of the thirteenth century [5] copied from a certain ' Ptolemy '—probably a Peripatetic of the second century A.D., mentioned also by Greek writers.[6] His list seems to have reached the

cf. ZELLER, *Ph. d. Gr.* Pt. iii. a. 556, 2nd ed., and HEITZ, *Verlor. Schr.* 38.

[1] So HEITZ, 46 sq., followed by GROTE, i. 48, SUSEMIHL, *Ar. ü. d. Dichtk.* 19, *Ar. Pol.* xliii., NIETZSCHE, *Rhein. Mus.* xxiv. 181 sq.

[2] We are not expressly told that this scholar and Peripatetic, who wrote about 200 B.C., catalogued the works of Aristotle ; but it is hardly to be doubted, seeing that he wrote a biography of Aristotle in at least two books which Diogenes used (cf. DIOG. v. 1, 2, and ATHEN. xiii. 589, xv. 696), and that his Ἀναγραφὴ τῶν Θεοφράστου βιβλίων is mentioned in the Scholia cited, p. 49, n. 4, *supra* (cf.

HEITZ, *ibid.* 49, *Ar. Fr.* 11). Through what channel it came to the knowledge of Diogenes, we do not know.

[3] Brandis (*Gr.-röm. Phil.* ii. b, 1, 81) has shown that this is probably true of both the catalogues of Aristotle and Theophrastus given by Diogenes.

[4] Diogenes himself elsewhere cites works of Aristotle which are not in his list (BRANDIS, *ibid.*; HEITZ, 17), but this only proves that these references were taken from other sources than those from which he got the Catalogue.

[5] *De q. v.* ROSE, *Ar. Opp.*, p. 1469.

[6] One of these Arabic writers

Arabic copyists in an incomplete form. For while Ptolemy put the total of Aristotle's works at 1,000 Books, their lists comprise only some 100 treatises, counting about 550 Books.[1] Of the component parts of our extant *Corpus* only a few are wanting, and their absence may be partly accidental.[2] Some others are

(Ibn el Kifti, d. 1248, *ap.* ROSE, *ibid.*) says this Ptolemy was an admirer of Aristotle, who wrote a book, *Historiæ Ar. et Mortis ejus et Scriptorum Ordo,* addressed to Aa°las (or A°tlas): the other (Ibn Abi Oseibia, d. 1269, *ibid.*) also speaks of his *Liber ad Galas de vita Ar. et eximia pietate testamenti ejus et indice scriptorum ejus notorum.* Both copy from him biographical details as well as the Catalogue, but seem to know no more of him than that he lived ' *in provincia Rum* ' (*i.e.* the Roman Empire), and that he was a different person from the author of the *Almagest.* What they say, however, corresponds exactly with what David, *Schol. in Ar.* 22, a, 10 (after Proclus, cf. l. 23), says of a Ptolemy who reckoned the total of Aristotle's books (as did Andronicus, cf. p. 49, n. 5) at 1,000, ἀναγραφὴν αὐτῶν ποιησάμενος καὶ τὸν βίον αὐτοῦ καὶ τὴν διάθεσιν : and with the remark in *V. Marc.* 8, as to the same, that to his list of Aristotle's works he added his will. David takes this Ptolemy to be Ptolemæus Philadelphus, but this merely proves the ignorance of David, or the pupil who recorded his lectures ; though we know that Ptolemæus Philadelphus himself was a collector of Aristotle's works (ATHEN. i. 3, DAVID, and AMMON. *Schol. in Ar.* 28, a, 13, 43), and was a pupil of

Strato (DIOG. v. 58). The fact that the Ptolemy who compiled the Catalogue came after Andronicus is clear from the mention of Andronicus at No. 90, and of Apellicon at No. 86. Of the writers of that name known to us, Rose (*Ar. Libr. Ord.* 45) suggests as the same the Neoplatonist Ptolemæus, named by JAMBL. *ap.* STOB. *Ecl.* i. 904, and by PROCLUS *In Tim.* 7. Another was a contemporary of Longinus, but he is said (by PORPH. *V. Plot.* 20) to have written no scientific works. The most probable identification would be with the Peripatetic Ptolemy, whose attack on a definition of grammar by Dionysius Thrax is quoted by SEXT. MATH. i. 60, and by the Schol. in BEKKER'S *Anecd.* ii. 730, and whose date therefore must lie somewhere between Dionysius and Sextus (70–220 B.C.).

[1] An exact reckoning is not possible without going into the variations of the numbering in the different texts. If the 171 *Polities* were counted separately, they would raise the total to about 720.

[2] The most important omissions are the *Ethics* and the *Œconomics* ; besides which there are the *Rhetoric. ad Alex.,* the book upon Melissus, &c.; and the tracts Π. ἀκουστῶν, Π. ἀναπνοῆς, Π. ἐνυπνίων, Π. μαντικῆς τῆς ἐν τοῖς ὕπνοις, Π. νεότητος καὶ γήρως,

named twice over. The fact that this Arabic catalogue was taken from a Greek original is proved by the Greek titles, often hopelessly miswritten, which are set against most of the items.

It is obvious that catalogues of such a character and origin offer no sufficient security either for the completeness of their reckoning or for the authenticity of the writings they include. Nothing but a full and accurate inquiry into the merits of each case can enable us to decide as to the claims of those texts or fragments which are handed down to us under Aristotle's name. Such an inquiry cannot here be fully carried out ; but it will not be out of place to combine with a complete review of all the writings ascribed to Aristotle a concise appreciation of the points to be considered in passing judgment on their authenticity.[1]

To begin at the point where the old catalogues end, we may distinguish from the philosophical treatises those writings which dealt with personal matters—the letters, poems, and occasional pieces. Their number is relatively small ; and if we exclude those whose genuine-

---

Π. ὕπνου καὶ ἐγρηγόρσεως, and Π. χρωμάτων; the Π. κόσμου, Π. ἀρετῶν καὶ κακιῶν, Π. θαυμασίων ἀκουσμά- των, and the Φυσιογνωμική. But as No. 40 includes the *De Memoria et Somno*, so it may be that others of the small scientific tracts are bracketed in the list under one title and number.

[1] As to the works known only by titles or fragments, cf. the thorough inquiry of Heitz (*Verlor. Schrift. d. Ar.*, 1865), refuting Val. Rose, whose learned essays, *De Ar. Librorum Ordine et*

Auctoritate, 1854, and *Ar. Pseud- epigraphus*, 1863, rejected too summarily all the lost and several of the extant books.—The writings named in the ancient Catalogues will be cited in this chapter by Rose's numbers (p. 48, n. 1); of the Catalogues themselves, that of Diogenes will be cited as D., that of the Anonymus Menagii as AN., and the Ptolemy of the Arabic texts as PT. *Ar. Fr.* will be used for the collection of the fragments by Rose in *Ar. Opp.* v. 1463 sq., Berlin ed.; and *Fr. Hz.*,

ness is doubtful or which are certainly forged, there is very little left. A few poems and poetic fragments,[1] and perhaps some part of the matter said to be cited from his *Letters*,[2] may stand. The so-called *Apologia* of Aristotle,[3] and the *Orations* in praise of Plato and Alexander,[4] must be rhetorical inventions of later date.

for that of Heitz in *Ar. Opp.* iv. b, 1 sq. of the Didot edition.

[1] For these, with the notices relating to them, *v.* BERGHK, *Lyr. Gr.* 504 sq., ROSE, *Ar. Pseud.* 598 sq., *Ar. Fr.* 621 sq., p. 1583, and *Fr. Hz.* 333 sq. The most important are those above cited (p. 12, n. 4, p. 20, n. 3), whose genuineness we have no reason to doubt. D. 145 mentions ἔπη and ἐλεγεῖα, and AN. 138; ἐγκώμια ἢ ὕμνους appear in AN. *App.* 180.

[2] The Letters of Aristotle, praised by DEMETR. *Eloc.* 230, SIMPL. *Categ.* 2 γ, *Schol. in Ar.* 27, a, 43, and others (cf. ROSE, *Ar. Ps.* 587, HEITZ, *Verl. Schr.* 285, and *Ar. Fr.* 604–620, p. 1579, *Fr. Hz.* 321 sq.) as the high-water mark of epistolary style, were collected in eight books by one Artemon, otherwise unknown (*v.* DEMETR. *Eloc.* 223, DAVID, *Schol. in Ar.* 24, a, 26, and PT. No. 87). Andronicus is said to have reckoned twenty books (PT. No. 90, cf. GELL. xx. 5, 10), but perhaps it was only twenty letters, which is the number in AN. 137. D. 144 names letters to Philip, letters to the Selybrians, four letters to Alexander (cf. DEMETR. *Eloc.* 234, *Ps. Amm.* 47), nine to Antipater, and seven to others. The letters of or to Diares (*de quo v.* SIMPL. *Phys.* 120), mentioned by PHILOP. *De An.* K. 2, are not in D. All

extant Fragments seem to come from the editions of Artemon and Andronicus. It is difficult to say if any are genuine, since some are certainly not. Not only Rose (*Ar. Ps.* 585, *Ar. Libr. Ord.* 113) but also Heitz (*Verl. Schr.* 280, *Fr. Hz.* 321) considers all the letters forged. That the six now extant (*ap.* STAHR, *Ar.* ii. 169, and *Fr. Hz.* 329) are so is clear, and Heitz holds that they could not even have been in Artemon's collection.

[3] Cf. p. 35, n. 3, *supra*; *Ar. Fr.* 601, p. 1578; *Fr. Hz.* 320.

[4] An Ἐγκώμιον Πλάτωνος is quoted by Olympiod. *in Gorg.* 166 (v. *Jahrb. f. Philol.*, Suppl., xiv. 395, and *Ar. Fr.* 603, *Fr. Hz.* 319); but it is more than suspicious, since no one used what would have been the best source of Platonic biography. A Panegyric on Alexander *ap.* THEMIST. *Or.* iii. 55 (*Ar. Fr.* 602, *Fr. Hz.* 319) is condemned by the Fr. *ap.* RUTIL. LUPUS, *De Fig. Sent.* i. 18, if that belongs to it, Bernays' theory of another Alexander (*Dial. Ar.* 156) being very improbable. An Ἐγκλησία Ἀλεξάνδρου is named by AN. (No. 193) as spurious. Books Π. Ἀλεξάνδρου are ascribed by Eustath. *ap.* DIONYS. *Per.* v. 1140, and AN. *App.* 176, to Aristotle through some confusion between his name and Arrian's. Cf. HEITZ, *Verl. Schr.*

A second section of the writings may include those which dealt with scientific questions, but were yet essentially distinct in form from all the extant treatises, namely, the *Dialogues.*[1] We have repeated proofs[2] that Aristotle, in one class of his works, did make use of the form of dialogue. It is said that his Dialogues differed from those of Plato in the fact that the individuality of the persons conversing was not carried through,[3] and that the author kept the lead of the conversation in his own hands.[4] Of the known works of this kind, the *Eudemus,*[5] the three books *On Philosophy*[6] and the four books *On Jus-*

291, and MÜLLER, *Script. rer. Alex.* pref. v.

[1] Cf. BERNAYS, *Dialoge d. Ar.* (1863), HEITZ, *Verl. Schr.* 141–221, ROSE, *Ar. Pseud.* 23 sq.

[2] Cf. CIC. *Ad Att.* xiii. 19, 4, BASIL. *Ep.* 135 (167) *ap.* ROSE, *Ar. Ps.* 24, PLUT. *Adv. Col.* 14, 4, DIO CHRYS. *Or.* 53, p. 274, ALEX. *ap.* DAVID, *Schol. in Ar.* 24, b, 33, DAVID, *ibid.* 24, b, 10 sq., 26, b, 35; PHILOP. *ibid.* 35, b, 41, and *De An. E.* 2; PROCL. *ap.* PHILOP. *Ætern. M.* 2, 2 (cf. *Ar. Fr.* 10) and *In Tim.* 338 d; AMMON. *Categ.* 6, b (*ap.* STAHR, *Ar.* ii. 255); SIMPL. *Phys.* 2, b; PRISCIAN, *Solut. Procem.* p. 553 b.

[3] BASIL. *Ep.* 135 (167) *ap.* ROSE, *Ar. Pseud.* 24. *Ar. Fr.* 1474. HEITZ, 146.

[4] CIC. *ut supra. Ad Quint. Fr.* iii. 5 does not refer to Dialogues. ' *Aristotelius mos,*' in CIC. *Ad Fam.* i. 9, 23, has a wider sense; and refers to the ' *in utramque partem disputare,*' cf. *De Orat.* iii. 21, 80 ; but see HEITZ, 149.

[5] This remarkable Dialogue

(*de q. v.* BERNAYS, 21, 143 etc., and *Rhein. Mus.* xvi. 236 sq., ROSE, *Ar. Ps.* 52 sq., *Ar. Fr.* 32–43, p. 1479, *Fr. Hz.* 47) is called Εὔδημος (THEMIST. *De An.* 197, and cf. quotations in *Ar. Fr.* 41), or Περὶ ψυχῆς (D. 13, AN. 13, PLUT. *Dio* 22), or Εὔδημος ἢ π. ψυχῆς (PLUT. *Cons. ad Apol.* 27, p. 115, and Simpl. ap. *Ar. Fr.* 42). We learn from PLUT. *Dio* 22, and CIC. *Divin.* 1, 25, 53, that it was dedicated to Aristotle's friend, Eudemus, who died in Sicily 352 B.C. (cf. p. 11 n. 4 *supra*), and it was probably written soon after (KRISCHE, *Forsch.* i. 16). Of the Fragments ascribed to it by Rose, more probable places will be indicated *infra* for Fr. 36, 38, and 43. Aristotle himself seems, in *De An.* i. 4, *init.* to refer to a discussion in the *Eudemus,* cf. *Ar. Fr.* 41.

[6] D. 3, AN. 3 (who by oversight gives four books), BERNAYS, 47, 95, ROSE, *Ar. Ps.* 27, *Ar. Fr.* 1–21, p. 1474, HEITZ, *Verl. Schr.* 179 sq., *Fr. Hz.* 30 sq., BYWATER, ' Aristotle's Dialogue

tice[1] seem to have been the most important. The first two are of particular interest, because they stand in such close relation, not only by their form but by their subjects, to the work of Plato, that there is much to be said for the conjecture that they were written in the period when Aristotle still belonged to the circle of Plato's scholars, and had not yet fully passed over to his later independent position.[2] There are certain other works

on Philosophy,' *Journ. of Philol.* vii. 64 sq. Priscian tells us the work was a dialogue (*Solut. Proœm.* p. 553), and it is confirmed by the statement (PLUT. *Adv. Col.* 14, 4, Procl. *ap.* PHILOP. *Æt. M.* 2, 2; v. *Ar. Fr.* 10) that Aristotle had in his Dialogues attacked and renounced the Ideal Theory; cf. *Ar. Fr.* 11 from the second book Π. φιλοσ. arguing against the Ideal Numbers. These three books are referred to (besides D.) by PHILODEM. Π. εὐσεβείας, col. 22, and following him, by CIC. *N. D.* i. 13, 33. The apparent reference in ARIST. *Phys.* ii. 2, 194, a, 35 (διχῶς γὰρ τὸ οὗ ἕνεκα· εἴρηται δ' ἐν τοῖς περὶ φιλοσοφίας) is as Heitz says (*Verl. Schr.* 180) very suspicious, since Aristotle nowhere else cites his Dialogues; but on the other hand the reference will not apply either to the Book on the Good (which could not be called Π. φιλοσ., cf. p. 61, n. 1, *infra*), nor to *Metaph.* xii. 7, 1072, b, 2, since as Aristotle left that book unfinished he could not quote it in the *Physics.* Rose's rejection of the Π. φιλοσ. is followed by Susemihl, *Genet. Ent. d. plat. Phil.* ii. 534; but the arguments are insufficient.

[1] D. 1, AN. 1, PT. 3, *Ar. Fr.*

71–77, p. 1487, BERNAYS, 48, ROSE, *Ar. Ps.* 87, HEITZ, *Verl. Schr.* 169, *Fr. Hz.* 19. CIC. *Rep.* iii. 8, 12, mentions this as a 'comprehensive' work in four books. According to PLUT. *Sto. rep.* 15, 6, it was attacked by Chrysippus ('Αρ. περὶ δικαιοσύνης ἀντιγράφων): and the attacks of Carneades mentioned by LACTANT. *Epit.* 55 (*ap.* CIC. *Rep.* iii.) seem to have been also specially directed to this work. DEMETR. *Eloc.* 28 cites a passage from it. We are not told that it was a Dialogue, but that is inferred from its position at the head of D. which begins (Bernays, p. 132) with the Dialogues arranged according to number of books. It is, however, true that in the midst of the Dialogues (as No. 12) the *Protrepticus* comes in, which probably was not a Dialogue. Neither probably were Nos. 17–19. It is a question, therefore, whether the Anon. has not here preserved the original order : so that the Dialogues really include only the first thirteen numbers of AN., together with the *Symposion* which was misplaced in that list by reason of the textual error (*v.* p. 58, n. 1).

[2] This is specially true of the *Eudemus.* All the fragments of

which are supposed to have been dialogues, mainly
by reason of the place assigned them in the catalogues;
but some of them are only distantly connected with

this dialogue prove that it was
built on the lines of the *Phædo*.
They have in common not only
their subject, the Immortality of
the Soul, but also the artistic
and philosophic method in which
it is treated. Like the *Phædo*
(60 E), the *Eudemus* was introduced (*Fr.* 32) by a revelation in
a dream, the direct prototype of
which is to be found in the other
Dial. relating to the last days of
Socrates (*Crito*, 44 A). As Plato
concludes his work (108 D sq.)
with an imaginative myth, so the
Eudemus had also its mythic
ornament (cf. *Fr.* 40, where
the words of Silenus, δαίμονος
ἐπιπόνον, etc., remind us also of
Rep. x. 617 D, and *Fr.* 37, which
must be taken in a mystical
sense). As the *Phædo* (69 C)
refers to the doctrines of the
Mysteries, so *Fr.* 30 of the
Eudemus recognises the validity
of the customary honours to the
dead. But the most remarkable
resemblance between the two
Dialogues is in their philosophical contents. Aristotle in the
Eudemus insisted not only on
Immortality, but also on Pre-
existence and Transmigration,
defending in his own way the
theory that the soul in its
entrance into this life forgot
the Ideas (*Fr.* 34, 35). As the
Phædo based the decisive argument for immortality on the
relation of the soul to the idea
of life (105 C sq.), so the *Eudemus*
also called the soul εἶδός τι
(*Fr.* 42). As Plato worked up to
this argument by a detailed refu-

tation of the theory that the soul
was the harmony of its body,
here also Aristotle followed him
(*Fr.* 41). Exactly on Plato's
lines is likewise *Fr.* 36, where the
misery of the soul tied to the body
is imaged in a striking comparison; and even if Bywater (*Journ.
of Phil.* ii. 60) and Hirzel
(*Hermes*, x. 94) are right in referring this *Fr.* to the *Protrepticus*,
still this also seems to have
been on the same lines as the
Eudemus (cf. p. 60, n. 1, *infra*).
Aristotle took a more independent position against Plato in
the books *On Philosophy*. It is
true that the *Frs.* in which he
defends the belief in the gods,
the unity of God, and the rational
nature of the stars (*Fr.* 14, 13,
16, 19, 20, 21, and the *Fr.* ap.
CIC. *N.D.* ii. 49, 125, *de q. v.*
BRANDIS, ii. b, 1, 84; HEITZ,
228, refuting ROSE, *Ar. Ps.* 285),
read like Plato, and that *Fr.* 15
(*de q. v.* BERNAYS, 110, and *Fr.
Hz.* 37) is evidently modelled on
Rep. ii. 380 D. Nevertheless,
Aristotle decisively declared himself in this work (*Fr.* 10, 11, cf.
p. 55, n. 6) against the theory of
the Ideas and Ideal Numbers,
declared the world to be not only,
as Plato said, unending, but also
beginningless (v. *Frs.* 17, 18,
with which BYWATER, 80, well
compares PLUT. *Tranqu. An.* 20,
p. 477); and gave in Book I. (*v.*
Bywater's reconstruction thereof
from PHILOP. in *Nicom. Isag.*:
CIC. *Tusc.* iii. 28, 69; PROCL. *in*
EUCL. p. 28; cf. *Ar. Fr.* 2-9) a
general theory of the develop-

the philosophic system,[1] and others are of doubtful authenticity.[2]

ment of humanity to culture and philosophy, which, although it connects with Plato by the remark (*ap.* PHILOP.) that the spiritual and divine principle, in spite of its own light, appears to us dark διὰ τὴν ἐπικειμένην τοῦ σώματος ἀχλύν, and by the theory of periodic floods whereby humanity was thrown back into savagery (cf. PLATO, *Tim.* 22 D, *Laws*, iii. 677 A, 681 E), indicates clearly an independent view of history which goes beyond Plato not only in relation to the eternity of the world (*Meteor.* i. 14, 352 b, 16; *Polit.* vii. 9, 1329 b, 25; *Metaph.* xii. 8, 1074 a, 38; cf. BERNAYS, *Theophr. ü. d. Frömmigk.* 42), but to the process of spiritual development (*Metaph.* i. 1, 981 b, 13, and 2, 982 b, 11 sq.). Aristotle's interest in scholarly inquiries appears in the passages of this work on the Magi, on Orpheus, on the Seven Wise Men, and on the development of philosophy from their time to his own; and his critical sense is shown in his discussion of the story of Orpheus in *Fr.* 9. Taking all this into consideration, the books *On Philosophy* show, as compared with the *Eudemus*, a remarkable advance in independence of thought, leading to the suggestion that they were written later, perhaps at the end of Plato's life.— Krische (*Forsch.* i. 265) sought to identify the 3 bks. Π. φιλοσ. with *Metaph.* i., xi., xii.; but this is now untenable (cf. HEITZ, 179, and *infra*, p. 76 sq.). It is more probable that they were used for various passages of *Metaph.* i., xii., and for the bk. Π. οὐρανοῦ

(*v.* BLASS, *Rhein. Mus.* xxx. 1875, p. 481). There must be, however, much variation, and Blass' view that certain passages are taken verbally from the Π. φιλοσ. is improbable.

[1] To this class belong the 3 bks. Π. ποιητῶν (D. 2, AN. 2, PT. 6; BERNAYS, 10 sq., 60, 139; ROSE, *Ar. Ps.* 77; *Ar. Fr.* 59 69, p. 1485; HEITZ, *V.S.* 174 sq. ; *Fr. Hz.* 23). That this work was a Dialogue is doubted by MÜLLER, *Fr. Hist.* ii. 185; but it is proved not only by its place in the Catalogues, but also by an express statement in *V. Marc.* p. 2, and by the form of *Fr.* 61. It was probably used as a genuine work of Aristotle by Eratosthenes and Apollodorus, but we cannot be sure that their references (*Fr.* 60 *ap.* DIOG. viii. 51) may not point to another work, possibly the *Politeiai*. Aristotle, however, himself refers at the end of *Poet.* 15 to a discussion in the ἐκδεδομένοι λόγοι, which it is most natural to apply to the Π. ποιητῶν, as in the *Rhetoric* (which ROSE, *Ar. Ps.* 79, suggests) there is no corresponding passage. The few references we have, which are mostly historical notes, show nothing that throws doubt on the genuineness of the work. *Fr.* 66 contains statements as to Homer, evidently from a tradition current in Ios, which (notwithstanding NITZSCH, *Hist. Hom.* ii. 87, MÜLLER, *ut supra*, and ROSE, *Ar. Ps.* 79) do not prove the spuriousness of the book, since they might well have been introduced in the Dial. without being believed by the author.

With the *Dialogues* may be connected another
set of writings, which did not take that form, but were

For the title Π. ποιητῶν we find also
(*Fr.* 65, 66, 69 ; cf. SPENGEL, *Abh.
d. Münchn. Akad.* ii. 213 ; RITTER,
Ar. Poet. x. ; HEITZ, *V. S.* 175)
that of Π. ποιητικῆς, which, unless
it is a mere confusion, indicates
that the work was not purely
historical, but contained discussions on the Art of Poetry as well
as information about the poets.—
After the Dialogues, which made
several books, there follows in
the lists the Πολιτικὸς, which
consisted, according to D. 4, of
2 books, according to AN. 4, of
one (*Fr.* 70, p. 1487 ; ROSE, *Ar.
Ps.* 80 ; BERNAYS, 153 ; HEITZ,
V.S. 189, *Fr. Hz.* 41) ; and thereafter the following, in one book
each ; Π. ῥητορικῆς ἢ Γρύλλος (D. 5,
AN. 5 ; the addition of γ΄ is
obviously a false reading, though
PT. 2 b, *ap.* IBN ABI OSEIBIA
has ' De Arte Rituri iii.' Cf. *Ar.
Fr.* 57 sq. p. 1485 ; ROSE, *Ar.
Ps.* 76 ; BERNAYS, 62, 157 ; HEITZ,
V.S. 189, *Fr. Hz.* 41) ; the
Νήρινθος (D. 6, AN. 6 ; ROSE, *Ar.
Fr.* 53, p. 1484, *Ar. Ps.* 73 ;
BERNAYS, 84 ; HEITZ, *V.S.* 190,
Fr. Hz. 42), doubtless the same
as the διάλογος Κορίνθιος, of which
THEMIST. *Or.* 33, p. 356 speaks ;
the Σοφιστὴς (D. 7 ; AN. 8 ; PT. 2 ;
Ar. Fr. 54–56, p. 1484 ; *Ar. Ps.*
75 ; *Fr. Hz.* 42), of which nothing
remains except a few remarks on
Empedocles, Zeno, and Prota-
goras ; the Μενέξενος (D. 8, AN.
10), of which there are no frag-
ments ; the Ἐρωτικὸς (D. 9 ; AN.
12 ; *Ar. Fr.* 90–93, p. 1492 ; *Ar.
Ps.* 105 ; HEITZ, *V.S.* 191, *Fr.
Hz.* 43) ; the Συμπόσιον (D. 10 ;
AN. 19, where συλλογισμῶν is a

miswriting ; *Ar. Fr.* 107 sq.
p. 1495 ; *Ar. Ps.* 119 ; *Fr. Hz.*
44 ; cf. HEITZ, *V.S.* 192, who
rightly questions the application
of PLUT. *N. P. Suav. V.* 13, 4 to
this Dialogue) ; the Π. πλούτου
(D. 11 ; AN. 7 ; *Ar. Fr.* 86–89,
p. 1491 ; *Ar. Ps.* 101 ; HEITZ,
V. S. 195, *Fr. Hz.* 45) probably
attacked by the early Epicurean,
Metrodorus, if the proper reading
in PHILODEM. *De Virt. et Vit.* ix.
col. 22, be (as seems probable ;
cf. SPENGEL, *Abh. d. Münchn.
Akad.* v. 449, and HEITZ, *l.c.*) not
Π. πολιτείας, but Π. πλούτου—the
Dial. is nowhere quoted by name,
and of the fragments reckoned
as belonging to it Heitz rightly
rejects *Fr.* 88 ; and the Π. εὐχῆς
(D. 14 ; AN. 9 ; *Ar. Fr.* 44–46,
p. 1483 ; *Ar. Ps.* 67 ; *Fr. Hz.* 55 ;
BERNAYS, 122), to which we possess only one reference that can
be identified with certainty, *i.e.
Fr.* 46, which is too closely related to PLAT. *Rep.* vi. 508 E
to permit its rejection.

² If we could say absolutely
that the Dial. Π. εὐγενείας (D. 15 ;
AN. 11 ; PT. 5 ; *Ar. Fr.* 82–85,
p. 1490 ; *Ar. Ps.* 96 ; BERNAYS,
140 ; HEITZ, *V. S.* 202 ; *Fr. Hz.*
55), which was already questioned by PLUT. *Arist.* 27, is not
genuine, it would follow (as Heitz
suggests) that the story that
Socrates was accused of bigamy
in it rests upon some misunderstanding. This, however,
seems hardly probable, because
the story in question appears so
frequently and so early in the
Aristotelian School. As to the
genuineness of the Dialogues

yet distinguished, as it seems, from the strictly scientific treatises by their popular style of treatment. These are (at least in part) ascribable to the same period of Aristotle's work.[1] To that period must also belong

named in the previous note, there are very few as to which we can form an approximate judgment; but there do not seem to be decisive grounds for rejecting any of them.

[1] To the same period with the *Eudemus* belongs also the *Protrepticus* (D. 12; AN. 14; PT. 1 —where it is probably transposed with the Π. φιλοσ. and is therefore said to have three books.— *Ar. Fr.* 47–50, p. 1483; *Fr. Hz.* 46). According to TELES, *circa* 250 B.C., it was addressed to the Cyprian prince Themiso, and was known to Zeno and to his teacher Crates (*v.* STOB. *Floril.* 95, 21). ROSE, *Ar. Ps.* 68 (with a *fortasse*), BYWATER, *Journ. of Phil.* ii. 55, and USENER, *Rhein. Mus.* xxviii. 372, suppose it to have been a Dial., and BERNAYS, 116, gives no opinion; but HEITZ, *V. S.* 196, and HIRZEL, *Hermes*, x. 61, seem to be right in saying that it was a continuous essay. The reasons are (1) that Teles says 'Αρ. προτρεπτικὸν ὃν ἔγραψε πρὸς Θεμίσωνα: and although a Dial. like a drama may be *dedicated* to a man, τινὶ προσγράφειν, yet it cannot be *written to* anyone, πρός τινα γράφειν: (2) that all other προτρεπτικοὶ that we know were essays and not dialogues; even the pseudo-Platonic *Clitophon*, which got an unsuitable second title of Προτρεπτικὸς (Thrasyll. *ap.* DIOG. iii. 60), is no exception to this, for it is not a dialogue, but a speech introduced only by

a couple of conversational remarks, which may therefore as properly be called προτρεπτικὸς as *Menexenus* with its longer conversational preface could be called ἐπιτάφιος (Thras. *ibid.*; AR. *Rhet.* iii. 14, p. 1415, b, 30). If Cicero used it as a model for his *Hortensius* (*Script. Hist. Aug. V. Sal. Gallieni*, c. 2), it may still be questioned whether the dialogue form was part of the imitation. As Usener, *ut supra*, shows, Cicero also used it for the *Somnium Scipionis*, Rep. vi., and, mediately or immediately, Censorinus, *D. Nat.* 18, 11. Bywater, *ut supra*, has also shown (but cf. Hirzel) that Jamblicus used it for his own *Protrepticus.* —Of a kindred nature apparently was the Π. παιδείας (D. 19; AN. 10; PT. 4; *Ar. Fr.* 51, p. 1484; *Ar. Ps.* 72; HEITZ, *V. S.* 307, *Fr. Hz.* 61). As no fragments are preserved, we cannot tell whether the Π. ἡδονῆς (D. 16, cf. 66; AN. 15; PT. 16; HEITZ, *V. S.* 203; *Fr. Hz.* 59) was a dialogue or not. The book Π. βασιλείας (D. 18; AN. 16; PT. 7; *Ar. Fr.* 78, 79, probably also 81, p. 1489; *Fr. Hz.* 59), which was addressed to Alexander, and apparently referred to by Eratosthenes (*ap.* STRABO, i. 4, 9, p. 66), was more probably an essay (*v.* HEITZ, *V. S.* 204) than a dial. (ROSE, *Ar. Ps.* 93,[r] and BERNAYS, 56). On the other hand, the title 'Αλέξανδρος ἢ ὑπὲρ (περὶ) ἀποίκων [-κιῶν], if the text

the treatise *On the Good*.[1] It was an account of the substance of Plato's lectures,[2] and what little is recorded from or of it gives no reason to doubt its genuineness.[3]

be correct, rather suggests a dial. (D. 17; *Ar. Fr.* 80; BERNAYS, 56; *Fr. Hz.* 61. HEITZ, *V. S.* 204, 207, suggests πρὸς 'Αλέξ. ὑπὲρ ἀποίκων καὶ π. βασιλείας. A preferable conjecture would be, ὑπ. ἀποίκων α΄. π. βασιλείας α΄). Other fragments which Rose places among the Dials. will be referred to *infra*.

[1] The Π. τἀγαθοῦ consisted, according to D. 20, of three books; AN. 20, one book; PT. 8, five books: ALEX. *ad Metaph.* iv. 2, 1003 b, 36, 1004 b, 34, 1005 a, 2 repeatedly quotes Book II., and the regular form of citation is ἐν τοῖς π. τἀγ. Apart from the Catalogues, we never hear of this work except in the Aristotelian Commentators, whose notices are collected and discussed by BRANDIS, 'Perd. Ar. Libr. de Ideis et de Bono,' *Gr.-röm. Phil.* ii. b, 1, 84; KRISCHE, *Forsch.* i. 263; ROSE, *Ar. Ps.* 46, *Ar. Fr.* 22–26, p. 1477, and HEITZ, *V. S.* 209, *Fr. Hz.* 79. Brandis (*ibid.*) has shown that none of them except Alexander possessed the work itself. Heitz, p. 203, doubts this even as to Alex., because he in one place (p. 206, 19) distinguishes the ἐκλογὴ τῶν ἐναντίων noticed Ar. *Metaph.* iv. 2, 1004 a, 2 (*de q. infra*) from the second book Π. τἀγαθοῦ, and in another place (p. 218, 10, 14) identifies them. These passages seem, however, only to show that Alexander knew of no ἐκλ. τ. ἐν. as a separate book, but saw in the second book Π. τἀγ. a discussion to which, as far as the sense went, Aristotle might be referring, so

that he was not sure whether Aristotle's reference referred to the Π. τἀγ. or to a special work. If so, this makes rather for than against Alexander's knowledge of the Π. τἀγάθου. SIMPL. *De An.* 6, b, PHILOP. *De An.* C. 2 (cf. *Ar. Fr.* p. 1477 b, 35), SUID. 'Αγαθ. p. 35, b, believe that the words ἐν τοῖς περὶ φιλοσοφίας λεγομένοις in AR. *De An.* i. 2, 404, b, 18, refer to this work, whereas they really refer to Platonic writings (cf. Zeller, II. a. 636, 4). But this proves only that these writers knew the Π. τἀγαθοῦ at second hand. Rose's view that this work was a Dial. is refuted by HEITZ, *V. S.* 217. We cannot tell whether Aristotle published in his lifetime his notes upon the lectures of Plato, or whether they became public after his death. If the ἐκλογὴ τ. ἐναντ., cited by himself, formed part of them, the former would of course be true. It is clear that the book was in use before the end of the third century B.C., and certainly before the time of Andronicus, because of the mention of it in Diog.'s list; cf. p. 48 sq. *supra*.

[2] Referred to by Aristoxenus and others, cf. Zeller, Plato, 26. SIMPL. (*Phys.* 32, b, 104, b, Schol. 334, b, 25, 362, a, 8) mentions, besides Aristotle, Speusippus, Xenocrates, Heraclides and Hestiæus as having published Platonic lectures.

[3] This is proved, against SUSEMIHL, *Genet. Entw. d. plat. Phil.* 2, 533, in Zeller's Plato, *ad loc.*

There is more doubt about the date of the work *On the Ideas*,[1] which Aristotle apparently refers to in the *Metaphysics*,[2] and which Alexander possessed.[3] The *Extracts* from some of Plato's writings [4] and the monographs on earlier and cotemporary philosophers [5]—

[1] This work is named in D. 54, and AN. 45 (which give it one book only) Π. τῆς ἰδέας or Π. ἰδέας. We have references, however, by ALEX. in *Metaph.* 564, b, 15 to the 1st book Π. ἰδεῶν, in 573, a, 12 to the 2nd, and in 566, b, 16 to the 4th (but in the last case we may well read Δ for Δ, with ROSE, *Ar. Ps.* 191, *Ar. Fr.* 1509, b, 36). SYRIAN, *In Metaph.* 901, a, 19, 942, b, 21 speaks of a work Π. τῶν εἰδῶν in two books. The same is meant in PT. 14 by the three books *De imaginibus, utrum existant an non*; but the Arabic title '*fari aiduln*' indicates that their Greek text read not Π. εἰδῶν, but Π. εἰδώλων; cf. ROSE, *Ar. Ps.* 185; *Ar. Fr.* 180–184 p. 1508; *Fr. Hz.* 86 sq.

[2] I. 990 b, 8 sq.; we have not only Alexander's statement that this passage refers to the work on Ideas, but it seems to be the natural inference from Aristotle's text itself that he is referring to some more detailed discussion of the Ideal Theory which is already known to his readers.

[3] Rose (*Ar. Ps.* 186) doubts this, but Alexander's own statements (cited in *Ar. Fr.* 183 *fin.*, 184 *fin.*) indicate as much.

[4] Τὰ ἐκ τῶν νόμων Πλάτωνος (D. 21, as 3 Bks., AN. 23 as 2).—Τὰ ἐκ τῆς πολιτείας α' β' (D. 22. PROCL. in *Remp.* 350 ; *Ar. Fr.* 176, p. 1507).—Τὰ ἐκ τοῦ Τιμαίου καὶ τῶν Ἀρχυτείων (*alias* : καὶ Ἀρχύ-

του; D. 94; AN. 85; SIMPL. *De Cœlo*, Schol. 491, b, 37 : σύνοψιν ἢ ἐπιτομὴν τοῦ Τιμαίου γράφειν οὐκ ἀπηξίωσε); cf. *Fr. Hz.* 79.

[5] Π. τῶν Πυθαγορείων, D. 101 AN. 88 : no doubt the same as is named Συναγωγὴ τῶν Πυθαγορείοις ἀρεσκόντων by SIMPL. *De Cœlo*, Schol. 492, a, 26 and b, 41 sq.; Πυθαγορικὰ (*ibid.* 505, a, 24, 35); Πυθαγορικὸς[-ον ?] (THEO. *Arithm.* 5); Π. τῆς Πυθαγορικῶν δόξης (ALEX. *Metaph.* 560, b, 25), and Π. τῆς Πυθαγορικῆς φιλοσοφίας (JAMBL. *V. Pyth.* 31). Probably the separate title Πρὸς τοὺς Πυθαγορείους, D. 97, is only a part of the same work, as D. gives each of them one book only, while Alexander and Simpl. quote from book 2. The reference in DIOG. viii. 34, cf. 19, probably belongs to this treatise (whether we there read ἐν τῷ περὶ κυάμων, or π. κυάμων only, cf. Cobet). Other notices of the work are collected by ROSE, *Ar. Ps.* 193, *Ar. Fr.* 185–200, p. 1510 ; *Fr. Hz.* 68.—We find also three books Π. τῆς Ἀρχυτείου [-του ?] φιλοσοφίας in D. 92, AN. 83, PT. 9 ; cf. *Ar. Ps.* 211, and *Fr. Hz.* 77, and cf. last note. Also Πρὸς τὰ Ἀλκμαίωνος, D. 96, AN. 87 ; Προβλήματα ἐκ τῶν Δημοκρίτου, 7 (? 2) books, D. 124, AN. 116 (cf. *Ar. Ps.* 213, *Ar. Fr.* 202 p. 1514, *Fr. Hz.* 77 ;) Πρὸς τὰ Μελίσσου, D. 95, AN. 86 ; Πρ. τὰ Γοργίου, D. 98, AN. 89 ; Πρ. τὰ Ξενοφάνους, [-κράτους in MSS.] D. 99 ; Πρ. τὰ

so far as these were genuine [1]—must, however, have been mostly compiled during Aristotle's first residence in Athens, or at least before his return from Macedonia. A collection of Platonic *Divisions* ascribed to him was no doubt a forgery.[2]

Far above all these in historic importance stand the works which set out the peculiar system of the Master in strict philosophical form. Speaking broadly, it is these alone which have survived the first century A.D., and have

---

Ζήνωνος, D. 100 : our treatise *De Melisso*, &c., to which, besides the lost section as to Zeno, another cited at second hand by PHILOP. *Phys*. B. 9 as Πρ. τὴν Παρμενίδου δόξαν seems to have belonged. We know that this work was used by Simplicius (cf. Zeller, i. 474 sq.). There was also the Περὶ τῆς Σπευσίππου καὶ Ξενοκράτους [φιλοσοφίας], D. 93, AN. 84.

[1] We cannot judge as to the genuineness of several, of which we have the titles only. It is not impossible that Aristotle may have left, among his papers, extracts and criticisms on various philosophic systems written down in the course of his studies, and that recensions of these were published. It is also possible that similar collections may have passed themselves off under his name. That the latter was the case with the tracts in our *Corpus* on the Eleatic School is proved in ZELLER, *Ph. d. Gr*. i. 465 sq. It is more difficult to decide as to the authenticity of the work on the Pythagoreans. If all the fables (see ZELLER, *Ph. d. Gr*. i. 285) which appear in *Fr*. 186, were related as historic fact, the book could not be Aristotle's, but in

view of the character of our informants it is very possible that *they* presented as history what *he* had only stated as a Pythagorean tradition. Similarly the meanings of the Pythagorean symbols (*Fr*. 190 sq.) and the contents of *Fr*. 188, which Isidor. *ap*. CLEMENT. *Strom*. vi. 641 falsely attributes to Aristotle himself, are merely references to Pythagorean theories. The rest of the passages cited from this book as to the Pythagorean system give no reason to reject it. The apparent contradiction between *Fr*. 200 (*ap*. SIMPL. *De Cœlo*, Schol. 492, b, 39 sq.) and AR. *De Cœlo* ii. 2, 285, b, 25 is quite reconcileable, without following Alexander in assuming a *falsa lectio*, for which, however, *Fr*. 195, *ap*. SIMPL. *ibid*. 492, a, 18, gives some ground.

[2] This is named in the existing lists only by PT. 53, as '*Divisio Platonis*' (formerly mistranslated '*jusjurandum*' or '*testamentum Pl.*'). It was, perhaps, the same as the Aristotelian διαιρέσεις (*v*. p. 75, n. 2, *infra*) elsewhere mentioned. A similar work, obviously a later recension of the Pseudo-Aristotelian text

thereby transmitted to mediæval and modern times a first-hand knowledge of the Aristotelian philosophy. Their preservation itself is no doubt primarily due to the fact that it was in them that that philosophy was first expounded in the systematic maturity in which he set it forth during the years of his teaching at Athens.

If we take what is now extant or otherwise known to us of this class of works, that which first meets us is the important set of treatises which laid the foundation for all later logic : the *Categories*,[1] the book on

used for the account given of Plato by DIOG. iii. 80, is printed by ROSE, *Ar. Ps.* 677–695 (and after him by *Fr. Hz.* 91), under the title, Διαιρέσεις Ἀριστοτέλους, *de q. v.* ZELL., *Ph. d. Gr.* ii. a. 382.

[1] The title of this work by the common (and probably correct) account is Κατηγορίαι ; but we find it also named as : Π. τῶν Κατηγοριῶν, Κατηγορίαι δέκα, Π. τῶν δέκα κατηγοριῶν, Π. τῶν δέκα γενῶν, Π. τῶν γενῶν τοῦ ὄντος, Κατηγορίαι ἤτοι π. τῶν δέκα γενικωτάτων γενῶν, Π. τῶν καθόλου λόγων, Πρὸ τῶν τοπικῶν (or τόπων) ; cf. WAITZ, *Arist. Org.* i. 81, SIMPL. *in Cat.* 4, β, and DAVID, *Schol. in Ar.* 30, a, 3. The title Τὰ πρὸ τῶν τόπων was known to Andronicus according to Simpl. *ibid.* 95 ζ, Schol. 81, a, 27, and to Boëthius, *In Præd.* iv. p. 191 (who obviously got his knowledge from the same source as Simpl., *i.e.* Porphyry). Herminus, *circa* 160 A.D., preferred it to the ordinary name.   David, however, (*Schol.* 81, b, 25), D. 59, and AN. 57 name a book called Τὰ πρὸ τῶν τόπων, besides the Κατηγορίαι, which is D. 141, AN. 132, PT. 25 b ; and do not appear to

think them the same.   Andronicus was probably right (*ap.* SIMPL. *ut supra*, Schol. 81, a, 27) in identifying the title of Τὰ πρὸ τ. τόπων with the spurious appendix of the so-called ' Postprædicamenta' ; and it may have been invented either, as he supposes, by the writer of that tract, or by some later editor who found the original name, Κατηγορίαι, too limited for the treatise as enlarged by the spurious addition.   Aristotle himself refers to his theory of the Categories (*De An.* i. 1, 5, 402 a, 23, 410 a, 14, *Anal. Pri.* i. 37, cf. the quotations, *infra*, p. 189, n. 2, *q. v.*) as known to his readers, and he assumes this in other places also, which seems to indicate that he had dealt with it in a published work.   There is a more definite reference in *Eth. N.* ii. 1 *init.* to *Categ.* c. 8 (cf. TRENDELENB. *Hist. Beitr.* i. 174). That in *Eth. Eud.* i. 8, 1217, b 27, may possibly refer not to the *Categ.* but to some work of Eudemus, and those in *Top.* ix., (*Soph. El.*) 4. 22. 166, b, 14. 178, a, 5, no doubt refer to the passage as to categories in *Top.* i. 9, *init.*,

which, however, is itself so brief
and undeveloped that it presupposes an early and better account.
Simpl. (*Categ.* 4 ζ, *Schol.* 30, b,
36) and David (*Schol.* 30, a, 24)
say that Aristotle had also referred to this work in another
place—not now extant—under
the title of Κατηγορίαι or Δέκα
Κατ. We are told also that, following Aristotle's example, Eudemus, Theophrastus, and Pha-
nias, wrote not only 'Analytica,'
and works 'Π. ἑρμηνείας,' but
also Κατηγορίαι (AMMON. *Schol.*
28, a, 40, and *in q. v.* Porph. 15 m,
DAVID, *Schol.* 19, a, 34, 30, a, 5,
ANON. *ibid.* 32, b, 32, 94, b, 14 ;
but Brandis in the *Rhein. Mus.* i.
1827, p. 270, rightly denies this as
to Theophrastus, and doubts it as
to Eudemus). The references in
SIMPL. *Cat.* 106, a, 107, a, sq.,
Schol. 89, a, 37, 90, a, 12 do not
prove that Strato referred to Aristotle's *Categories.* On the other
hand, the ancient critics never
doubted the genuineness of the
extant book, although they rejected a second recension (*v.*
SIMPL. *Categ.* 4 ζ, *Schol.* 39, a,
36 ; ANON. *ibid.* 33, b, 30 ; PHILOP.
ibid. 39, a, 19, 142, b, 38 ; AMMON.
Cat. 13, 17, and BOETH. *In
Præd.* 113, all following Adrastus, a noted critic *circa* 100
A. D.; cf. *Fr. Hz.* 114). The only
doubts suggested are by *Schol.*
33, a, 28 sq., and these apparently were not derived from
Andronicus. The internal characteristics of the book, however, are in many ways open
to criticisms, which Spengel
(*Münchn. Gel. Anz.* 1845, 41 sq.),
Rose (*Ar. Libr. Ord.* 232 sq.),
and Prantl (*Gesch. d. Logik,* i.
90, 5, 204 sq. 243) have used to
combat its genuineness, the latter

saying that its compiler might
be found 'in any master of a
peripatetic school of the age
following Chrysippus' (p. 207).
Their critical positions, however,
are not all tenable. Prantl
(*ibid.*) takes exception to the
number 10 ; but in the *Top.* i.
9, the same ten Categories are
given, and we know from Dexipp.
(*In Categ.* 40, *Schol.* 48, a, 46)
and Simpl. (*ibid.* 47, b, 40) that
Aristotle named these ten in
other works also. It is true that
Aristotle generally uses a less
number ; but that may only mean
either that he here adduces all
the ten because his object was
logical completeness, or that he
counted more Categories at an
earlier time than he did later.
He never assumed, as will be
shown later, a fixed number of
them. Again, it is objected that
the Κατηγ. speaks of δεύτεραι
οὐσίαι ; but we find as parallels to
this not only πρῶται οὐσίαι (e.g.
Metaph. vii. 7, 13, 1032, b, 2,
1038, b, 10), but also τρίται οὐσίαι
(*ibid.* vii. 2, 1028, b, 20, 1043,
a, 18, 28). The words of Κατηγ.
c. 5, 2, b, 29 : εἰκότως . . .
μόνα . . . τὰ εἴδη καὶ τὰ γένη
δεύτεραι οὐσίαι λέγονται, are not
to be translated 'the term δεύτ.
οὐσ. is used for genera and species
and rightly so,' since it was not
commonly so used before Aristotle, but rather, 'there is reason
to treat as a second class of substances only genera and species.'
Again, when it is remarked in
Κατηγ. c. 7, 8, a, 31, 39, that,
strictly speaking, πρός τι includes those things only which
not merely stand in a definite
relation to some other thing, but
have their essence in such a relation—οἶς τὸ εἶναι ταὐτόν ἐστι

the parts and kinds of propositions,[1] those on

τῷ πρός τί πως ἔχειν—there is no
need to suspect here any trace
of Stoic influence, since the
πρός τί πως ἔχειν appears also
in AR. *Top*. vi. c. 4, 142, a, 29,
c. 8, 164, b, 4; *Phys*. vii. 3, 247,
a, 2, b, 3, and *Eth. N*. i. 12, 1101,
b, 13. It is true, however, that
all the objections cannot easily
be set aside. Nevertheless, the
treatise bears in general a decisively Aristotelian impress; it is
closely related to the *Topics* in
tone and contents, and the external evidence is heavily in its
favour.—The best conclusion
seems to be, not that the whole
is spurious, but that the seemingly un-Aristotelian elements are
to be explained by the assumption that the genuine body of
the work extends to c. 9, 11, b,
7 only, but that what followed
has dropped out of the recension
we possess, and is replaced only
by the short note, c. 9, 11, b,
8–14. The so-called 'Postpræ-
dicamenta' (c. 10–15) were suspected as early as Andronicus
(SIMPL. *ut supra*, Schol. 81, a,
27; AMMON. *ibid*. 81, b, 37),
and Brandis has now proved they
are added by another hand ('Ü.
d. Reihenfolge d. Bücher d. Ar.
Org.,' *Abh. d. Berl. Akad. Hist.
phil. Kl.* 1833, 267, and *Gr.-röm.
Phil.* ii. b, 406). It is another
question whether it was compiled
from Aristotelian fragments, as he
suggests. The concluding para-
graph, at c. 9, 11, b, 8–14, reads
exactly as if it came in the place
of further discussions which the
editor cut out, justifying himself
by the remark that there was
nothing in them which did not
appear in the earlier part. In
the body of the work it is probable also that passages have
been left out and others added
in this recension; but much of
the inconsequence of exposition
and language may as easily be
due simply to the fact that the
Categ. were the earliest of the
logical writings, and were written
probably many years earlier than
the *Analytics*.

[1] This book, Π. ἑρμηνείας, was
in ancient times rejected as not
genuine by Andronicus (so ALEX.
Anal. pri. 52 a, and *Schol. in Ar.*
161 b, 40; AMMON. *De Interpr.*
6 a, and *Schol.* 97 b, 13; BOETH.
ibid. 97 a, 28; ANON. *ibid.* 94 a,
21; PHILOP. *De An.* A 13, B 4),
followed recently by Gumposch
(*Log. Schr. d. Ar.*, Leipz. 1839)
and Rose (*Ar. Ps.* 232). Brandis
(*Abh. d. Berl. Akad.* 263 sq., cf.
DAVID, *Schol. in Ar.* 24 b, 5)
takes it to be an incomplete
sketch of the work, to which c.
14 (rejected as early as Ammonius
and passed over by Porphyry; cf.
AMMON. *De Interpr.* 201 b;
Schol. 135 b) has probably been
added by a later hand. The external evidence for the work is
good enough. Not only do all
three lists agree in naming it (D.
152, AN. 133, PT. 2), but we are
told that Theophrastus referred
to it in his essay Π. καταφάσεως
καὶ ἀποφάσεως (DIOG. v. 44; ALEX.
Anal. pri. 124, *Schol.* 183 b, 1;
more explicitly, after Alexander,
BOETH. *ibid.* 97, a, 38; ANON.
Schol. in Ar. 94, b, 13; cf. the
Schol. *ap.* WAITZ, *Ar. Org.* i. 40,
who, on *De Interpr.* 17, b, 16,
remarks: πρὸς τοῦτό φησιν ὁ Θεόφραστος, etc.; cf. AMMON. *De
Interpr.* 73, a, 122, b). It seems

conclusions and scientific method in general,[1] on the

also that Eudemus Π. λέξεως (ALEX. *Anal. pri.* 6, b, *Top.* 38, *Metaph.* 63, 15; ANON. *Schol. in Ar.* 146, a, 24) may have been an imitation of this book (not, as *Schol.* 84, b, 15, wrongly suggests, of the Categories; cf. the quotation from Ammon. in preceding note). This last suggestion, however, is uncertain, and the notices as to Theophrastus are not absolutely clear, for the texts show that he did not *name* the Π. ἑρμην. at all. Alexander thought he saw, from the way in which Theophrastus dealt with the subject (*thema*) in his own book, reason to infer that he had Aristotle in mind; but whether he was right in that inference or not, we cannot judge. The Schol. *ap.* Waitz has nothing to show that the reference there quoted from Theophrastus referred to a passage in *this* book, and was not rather a general reference to the frequently recurring Aristotelian law of the excluded middle.— On the other hand, it is singular that while the Π. ἑρμην. is never cited or referred to in any of Aristotle's books (cf. BONITZ, *Ind. Ar.* 102, a, 27), it cites not only the *First Analytic* (c. 10, 19, b, 31 : *Anal.* 46, 51, 6, 36) and the *Topics* (c. 11, 20, 6, 26 : *Top.* ix. 17, 175, b, 39), but also the Π. ψυχῆς (c. 1, 16, a, 8), and that for a proposition which neither the ancient opponents of Andronicus nor modern scholars have been able to find in it (cf. BONITZ, *Ind. Ar.* 97, b, 49, whose suggestion, however, is not satisfactory). Its remarks on Rhetoric and Poetry (c. 4, 17, a, 5) have

no relation to the corresponding treatises of Aristotle. It should be added that the work accords throughout with Aristotle's line of thought, but frequently enlarges in a didactic way on the most elementary points in a fashion which one would suppose Aristotle would not have found necessary at the date at which it must have been written, if by him. The question, therefore, is not only whether it is by Aristotle or by another, but whether it may not, as Grant suggests (*Ar.* 57), have been written out by one of his scholars from oral lectures in which the difficulties of beginners would naturally be kept in view.

[1] Syllogisms are dealt with by the Ἀναλυτικὰ πρότερα in two books, and scientific method by the Ἀναλ. ὕστερα, also in two. The fact that D. 49 and An. 46 give nine books to the Ἀναλ. πρότ. (though An. 134 repeats the title with two only) points probably only to a different division; but it is also possible that other tracts are included, for the ANON. *Schol. in Ar.* 33, b, 32 (cf. DAVID, *ibid.* 30, b, 4, PHILOP. *ibid.* 39, a, 19, 142, b, 38, and SIMPL. *Categ.* 4 ζ) says that Adrastus knew of forty books of Analytics, of which only the four which are extant were counted genuine. — That these are genuine is proved beyond doubt, both by internal evidence, by Aristotle's own references, and by the fact that his earliest pupils wrote works modelled on them (cf. p. 65, *supra,* and BRANDIS, *Rhein. Mus.* NIEBUHR and BR. i. 267). Thus we know

proof by probability,[1] and on fallacies and their dis-

of an Analytic by Eudemus
(ALEX. *Top.* 70), and we have
references to book i. of the
Πρότερα ἀναλ. of Theophrastus
(ALEX. *Anal. pri.* 39, b, 51, a,
131, b, *Schol.* 158, b, 8, 161, b, 9,
184, b, 36; SIMPL. *De Cœlo,* Schol.
509, a, 6). Alexander, in his
commentary, quotes from both on
numerous points in which they
developed or improved Aristotle's
Ἀναλ. πρότ. (cf. *Theophr. Fr.*
[ed. Wimmer], p. 177 sq. 229;
Eudem. Fr. [ed. Spengel], p.
144 sq.). For the *Second Analytic* the references are less
copious; but we know of passages
of Theophrastus through Alexander (ANON. *Schol. in Ar.* 240, b,
2, and *ap.* EUSTRAT. *ibid.* 242,
a, 17), through THEMIST. *ibid.*
199, b, 46, and through PHILOP.
ibid. 205, a, 46, and through an
Anon. Schol. *ibid.* 248, a, 24, of
a remark of Eudemus, all of
which seem to refer to the *Second
Analytic.* We know as to Theophrastus, not only from the form
of the title of the 'Ἀναλ. πρότερα,
but also from express testimony
(*v.* DIOG. v. 42; GALEN, *Hippocr.
et Pl.* ii. 2, vol. v. 213, and
ALEX. *Qu. Nat.* i. 26) that he did
write a *Second Analytic,* and it
is probable that in that, as in
the text, he followed Aristotle.
Aristotle himself cites both
Analytics under that name : *Top.*
viii. 11, 13, 162, a, 11, b, 32 ;
Soph. El. 2, 165, b, 8 ; *Rhet.* i.
2, 1356, b, 9, 1357, a, 29, b, 24,
ii. 25, 1403, a, 5, 12 ; *Metaph.* vii.
12 *init.* ; *Eth. N.* vi. 3, 1139, b,
26, 32; also *De Interpr.* 10, 19, b,
31 ; *M. Mor.* ii. 6, 1201, b, 25 ;
Eth. Eud. i. 6, 1217, a, 17, ii. 6,
1222, b, 38, c. 10, 1227, a, 10 ;

(cf. other references *ap.* BONITZ,
Ind. Arist. 102, a, 30 sq). It is
therefore the original title, and
has always remained in common
use, notwithstanding that Aristotle cites certain passages of
the *First Analytic* with the word
ἐν τοῖς περὶ συλλογισμοῦ (*Anal.
post.* i. 3, 11, 73, a, 14, 77, a, 33),
or that Alexander (*Metaph.* 437,
12, 488, 11, 718, 4) and Pt. 28
call the *Second Analytic* ἀπο-
δεικτική, or that Galen (*De Puls.*
iv. *fin.*, vol. viii. 765 ; *De Libr.
Propr.* vol. xix. 41) chooses to
substitute, as he says, for the
common titles, the names Π.
συλλογισμοῦ and Π. ἀποδείξεως ;
nor have we any right to name
them on internal grounds (with
GUMPOSCH, *Log. Ar.* 115) Π.
συλλογισμοῦ and Μεθοδικά. Brandis justly remarks (*Ue. d. Ar.
Org.* 261 sq.; *Gr.-röm. Phil.* ii.
b, 1, 224, 275) that the *First
Analytic* is far more carefully
and evenly worked out than the
Second (which Aristotle can
hardly have considered as complete), and that the two books of
the *First Analytic* do not appear
to have been written together,
but with an interval.

[1] Aristotle dealt with this
subject in several books, no
doubt in connection with his
rhetorical teaching. We still
have the *Topica* in eight books,
of which, however, the last, and
perhaps the third and seventh
also, seem to have been worked
out long after the others (*v.*
BRANDIS, *Ue. d. Ar. Org.* 255 ;
Gr.-röm. Phil. ii. b, 330). The
genuineness of the work and of
its name is established by citations in Aristotle himself (*De*

proof.[1] Besides these, which are the component parts of our *Organon*, we have also the names of a great

Interpr. 11, 20, b, 26 ; *Anal. pr.* i. 11, 24, b. 12 ; ii. 15, 17, 64, a, 37, 65, b, 16 ; *Rhet.* i. 1, 1355, a, 28, c. 2, 1356, b, 11, 1358, a, 29 ; ii. 22, 1396, b, 4, c. 23, 1398, a, 28, 1399, a, 6, c. 25, 1402, a, 36, c. 26, 1403, a, 32 ; iii. 18, 1419, a, 24). For the art of proof by probabilities Aristotle uses the term ' Dialectic' (*Top.* init., *Rhet.* init., etc.), and he refers to the *Topics* in a similar way as πραγματεία π. τὴν διαλεκτικὴν (*Anal. pri.* i. 30, 46, a, 30). It is probable, therefore, that by μεθοδικὰ (*Rhet.* i. 2, 1356, b, 19) he meant the *Topics*, which in the opening words announce as their object, μέθοδον εὑρεῖν, etc., and in which (i. 12, 105, a, 16 ; viii. 2 *init.*) the relative passage is to be found, rather than, as Heitz (p. 81 sq., *Fr. Hz.* 117) suggests, a lost work; cf. ROSE, *Ar. Libr. Ord.* 120 ; VAHLEN, *Wien. Akad.* xxxviii. 99 ; BONITZ, *Ztschr. Oesterr. Gymn.* 1866, 11, 774. It seems, also, that in several MSS. the *Topics* were headed with the title Μεθοδικὰ, so that an idea arose that they were distinct works. This idea has been attributed to Dionys. (*Ep. I. ad Amm.* 6, p. 729, on *Rhet.* i. 2), but he speaks only of ἀναλυτικὴ καὶ μεθοδικὴ πραγματεία, and does not specially include the *Topics* in the latter. But D. 52 inserts Μεθοδικὰ in eight books, and AN. 49, the like title including seven books, although both know the *Topics* as well. So Diog. (v. 29) distinguishes τά τε τοπικὰ καὶ μεθοδικά ; and Simpl. (*Cat.* 16 a, *Schol.* 47, b, 40), after

Porphyry, appears to regard the latter as belonging, and the former as not belonging, to the ' Hypomnematic' writings. In D. 81 we even find a second entry of Μεθοδικὸν α'.—The theory of Spengel (*Abh. d. Münchn. Akad.* vi. 497) that our text of the *Topics* contains grave *lacunæ* does not seem to be proved by the passages he quotes (*Rhet.* i. 2, 1356, b, 10 ; ii. 25, 1402, a, 34). As to the former, which refers to the *Topics* only for the difference between συλλογισμὸς and ἐπαγωγὴ (cf. BRANDIS, ' Ue. d. Rhet. Ar.' ap. *Philologus*, iv. 13), it is satisfied by *Top.* i. 1, 12. As to the second, which does not apply to *Top.* viii. 10, 161, a, 9 sq., the words καθάπερ καὶ ἐν τοῖς τοπικοῖς, etc., need not be taken as referring to a particular passage, but may be taken as meaning ' of objections there are in Rhetoric, as in Topics, many kinds,' *i.e.* in oratorical use as opposed to disputation,—a remark that might well be made even if these distinctions were not taken in the earlier book. For similar uses of ὥσπερ ἐν τοῖς τοπικοῖς, etc., cf. BONITZ, *Ind. Ar.* 101 b, 44 sq., 52 sq., and VAHLEN, *ut supra*, 140 (where the phrase in *Rhet.* ii. 25 is explained as meaning ' Instances are here used in the same way as in *Topics*, and those of four kinds,' etc.).

[1] The Π. σοφιστικῶν ἐλέγχων, or (as ALEX. *Schol.* 296, a, 12, 21, 29, and Boeth. in his translation have it) Σοφιστ. ἔλεγχοι. Waitz (*Ar. Org.* ii. 528), followed by Bonitz (*Ind. Ar.* 102, a, 49),

number of kindred writings: treatises on Knowledge
and Opinion,[1] on Definition,[2] on Classification by
Genera and Species,[3] on Opposition and Difference,[4]
on Particular Kinds of Conceptions,[5] on Expression
in Speech,[6] on Affirmation and Negation,[7] on Syllog-

shows that Aristotle in the *De
Interpr.* c. 11, 20, b, 26, and
Anal. pri. ii. 17, 65, b, 16, refers
to passages of this work (*i.e.*
c. 17, 175, b, 39, c. 30, and c. 5,
167, b, 21), under the name ἐν
τοῖς Τοπικοῖς; that he reckons
knowledge of fallacies as part of
' Dialectic' (*Soph. El.* c. 9 *fin.*,
ch. 11 *fin.* ; cf. *Top.* i. 1, 100, b,
23); and that c. 34 is the epi-
logue not only for these but for
the whole science of ' Topics.'
Again, however, Aristotle seems
(in c. 2, 165 b, 8; cf. *Rhet.* i. 3,
1359, b, 11; cf. BRANDIS, *Gr.-
röm. Phil.* ii. b, 148) to distinguish the two, in a way, however,
which proves, not that the two
were not meant to form a whole,
but that the treatise on fallacies
was composed later than the
rest of the *Topics.* The lists of
D. and An. do not name the
Σοφ. ἔλ. (for that reading in AN.
125 is, as Rose shows, wrong),
and yet give the Μεθοδικὰ only
eight books, whereas PT. 29,
separates them from the *Topics*
(26 b); possibly, however, in
D. 27, Π. ἐριστικῶν two books,
and AN. 27, Π. ἐριστικῶν λόγων
two books, are the same as our
Σοφ. ἔλ.
[1] Π. ἐπιστήμης, D. 40 ; Π. ἐπιστημῶν, D. 26, AN. 25 ; Π. δόξης,
AN. *App.* 162. The genuineness
of the work is doubtful, because
it is nowhere else referred to.
[2] To this subject refer several

titles in PT.: *i.e.* No. 60, 'Οριστικὰ,
four books (cf. DIOG. v. 50, for the
same title in the list of Theophrastus' works); 63, on the objects of
Definition, two books; 63 b, *De
Contradictione Definitionum*; 63 c,
De Arte Definiendi ; 64, Πρὸς τοὺς
ὁρισμοὺς, two books (cf. the same
from Theophr., DIOG. v. 45),
translated *De Tabula Definiendi.*
As to the collections of definitions and divisions, cf. *infra.*
[3] Π. εἰδῶν καὶ γενῶν, D. 31 ; Π.
εἰδῶν, AN. 28, otherwise unknown.
[4] As to the opposition of
concepts there was a book Π.
τῶν ἀντικειμένων, doubtless the
same as Π. ἐναντίων (D. 30, AN.
32). Simplicius, in his commentary on the *Categ.* (v. *Ar. Fr.* 115–
121, p. 1497, sq. ; *Fr. Hz.* 119),
gives us some further information as to this book and its
casuistical discussions. Rose (*Ar.
Ps.* 130) refers to the age
of Theophrastus. PT. 12 has Π.
διαφορᾶς, four books.
[5] *De Relato* (Π. τοῦ πρός τι),
six books (PT. 84).
[6] *De Significatione*, PT. 78 ;
its Greek title is given as ' *Garam-
kun*,' i.e. Γραμματικὸν or -ῶν. As
to another related title, Π.
λέξεως, cf. *infra.* PT. 54, *Partitio
Conditionum quæ statuuntur in
voce et ponuntur*, four books, may
also have been a grammatical
treatise.
[7] ALEX. *Metaph.* 286, 23, 680,
a, 26, cites this simply as ἐν

isms,[1] and on subjects belonging to the sphere of Topics and Eristics.[2] Probably, however, the most

τῷ π. καταφάσεως; probably, however, it should be (like the corresponding, or possibly identical, work of Theophrastus, named by DIOG. v. 44) Π. καταφάσεως καὶ ἀποφάσεως.

[1] Συλλογισμῶν α' β' (D. 56, AN. 54); Συλλογιστικὸν καὶ ὅροι (D. 57 ; AN. 55 : -κῶν ὅρων) ; Συλλογισμοὶ α' (D. 48).

[2] To this category belong in the first place the treatises placed next to the Μεθοδικὰ in the lists: Τὰ πρὸ τῶν τόπων (D. 59, AN. 57); Ὅροι πρὸ τῶν τοπικῶν, 7 books (D. 55); Τοπικῶν πρὸς τοὺς ὅρους α' β' (D. 60, AN. 59, PT. 62 as three books named *Tabula definitionum quae adhibentur in Topica*, i.e. Πρὸς ὅρους τοπικῶν); *De Definiendo Topico* (i.e. ' On Definition in Topics,' PT. 61) ; Π. ἰδίων (D. 32) ; Π. ἐρωτήσεως καὶ ἀποκρίσεως (D. 44, AN. 44). Brandis, however, believes (*ut supra*) that these names indicate only particular parts of our *Topica*. He takes Τὰ πρὸ τῶν τόπων (elsewhere used for the *Categ.* ; cf. p. 64, n. 1) to be the first book, which in fact we know to have been so called by some (ANON. *Schol. in Ar.* 252, a, 46) ; the Ὅρος τῶν τόπων [as Br. reads it] to be books 2–8; Τοπ. πρὸς τοὺς ὅρους, books 6–7; Π. ἰδίων, book 5 ; and Π. ἐρωτ. κ. ἀποκρ. book 8, as to which we learn from ALEX. *Schol.* 292, a, 14, that many named it so, and others again, with a reference to its first words, Π. τάξεως κ. ἀποκρίσεως. These suggestions seem to commend themselves : except that it is easier to suppose as to the seven

books of Ὅροι πρὸ τῶν τόπων that the text of D. is wrong. The AN. gives instead two titles : 51, Ὅρων βιβλίον α' ; 52, Τοπικῶν ζ'. Here it is natural to refer the Ὅροι to book 1, the first half of which (c. 1-11) consists in definitions and their explanation, and the seven *Topica* to books 2-8. We conjecture, therefore, in view of the fact that both lists have the number seven, that in D. also the Ὅροι was originally distinct from the *Topica*, and that his text read : Ὅροι πρὸ τῶν τοπικῶν α' : Τοπικῶν α'-ζ'. D. 65 and AN. 62 name also Ἐπιχειρημάτων α' β' (PT. 55, 39, B, 83, 1, B) ; D. 33 ; AN. 33, Ὑπομνήματα ἐπιχειρηματικὰ, 3 B ; D. 70, AN. 65, Θέσεις ἐπιχειρηματικαὶ κε'; cf. also THEON, *Progymn.* p. 165 W. (*Rhet.* ed. Sp. II, 69), who ascribes to Aristotle and Theophrastus πολλὰ βιβλία θέσεων ἐπιγραφόμενα, described by ALEX. *Top.* 16, *Schol.* 254, b, 10, as containing τὴν εἰς τὰ ἀντικείμενα δι' ἐνδόξων ἐπιχείρησιν. (Πρὸς θέσιν ἐπιχειρεῖν means ' to develop the *pro* and *con* of a given proposition,' v. *Ind. Ar.* 282, b, 57, 283, a, 6: θέσεις ἐπιχειρηματικαὶ are therefore themes for dialectic development or dialectical exercises with an introduction to the way of working them out.)—The Ἐπιχειρήματα are no doubt identical with the Λογικὰ ἐπιχειρ. the second book of which is quoted by PHILOP. *Schol.* 227, a, 46, and the Ὑπομνήμ. ἐπιχειρ. with that which is cited simply as Ὑπομνήματα by DEXIPP. *Cat.* 40, *Schol.* 48, a, 4, and SIMPL. *Schol.* 47, b, 39 following Por-

ancient of these tracts were in reality productions of the Peripatetic school at dates subsequent to Aristotle's death.

Next to the *Topics* in order of subjects come the Rhetorical Works.[1] Some of these were written before the *Topics* in order of time; others only afterwards and at a long interval. Of the many books of Aristotelian or alleged Aristotelian origin which dealt with the theory of skilled speaking,[2] or treated

phyry. PT. gives three entries of 'amusmata' or 'ifumsmata' (= ὑπομνήματα), *i.e.* No. 69, 2 books; 82, 16 books; and 82, b, 1 book. The references in ATHEN. iv. 173, and xiv. 654 to 'Aρ. ἡ Θεόφραστος ἐν τοῖς ὑπομνήμασι are not to a defined book so named, but are vague and not to be identified. What relation the Προτάσεις named in PT. (No. 79 = 33[? 23] books, and No. 80 = 31 [? 7] books) bear to the Θέσεις ἐπιχ. we cannot say, but we also find two entries in D. (46 and 47), and one in AN. (38) of Προτάσεις α΄. The Ἐπιχειρηματικοὶ λόγοι, cited by Aristotle in the opening of c. 2. Π. μνημ. is not a separate work (cf. THEM. 97, a, p. 241), but the first chapter of the work itself (449, b, 13 sq., 450, a, 30 sq., 450, b, 11 sq.; cf. BONITZ, *Ind. Ar.* 99, a, 38). Under the head of *Topics* fall also the Ἐνστάσεις, D. 35, AN. 36, PT. 55, b; the Προτάσεις ἐριστικαὶ δ΄, D. 47, AN. 44; Λύσεις ἐριστικαὶ δ΄, D. 28, AN. 29; and Διαιρέσεις σοφιστικαί, δ΄, D. 29, AN. 31.—As to the Ἐριστικοὶ λόγοι, cf. p. 68, n. 1 *fin.* A tract Παρὰ τὴν λέξιν, named by SIMPL. *Schol.* 47, b, 40, was doubted, as he says, even by the

ancients (cf. *Ar. Fr.* 113, p. 1496; ROSE, *Ar. Ps.* 128; *Fr. Hz.* 116). It dealt probably (cf. *Soph. El.* 4) with the fallacies παρὰ τὴν λέξιν. AN. 196 names among the Pseudepigrapha a work Περὶ μεθόδου.
[1] Cf. *Rhet.* i, 1 *init.* c. 2, 1356, a, 21; *Soph. El.* 34, 184, a, 8.
[2] Besides the two extant works, this class includes primarily the Theodectean Rhetoric: *i.e.* D. 82 and AN. 74, Τέχνης τῆς Θεοδέκτου συναγωγὴ [? εἰσαγωγὴ] in one or three books. The extant *Rhetoric* alludes (iii. 9 *fin.*) to an enumeration ἐν τοῖς Θεοδεκτείοις, which must mean a work of Aristotle, and proves, even if *Rhet.* iii. be spurious, the existence of this book in early times. The compiler of the *Rhet. ad Alex.* 1. 1421, b, 1 makes Aristotle speak of ταῖς ὑπ' ἐμοῦ τέχναις Θεοδέκτῃ γραφείσαις; and this reference also must be at least anterior to Andronicus. The words leave it doubtful whether the writer meant a *Rhetoric* dedicated to Theodectes, or one written by Aristotle but published by Theodectes in his own name. Later classical writers several times attribute to the name 'Rhetoric of Theodectes' the

of the history of rhetoric,[1] or set out rhetorical

atter meaning, in itself most improbable (cf. Θεοδεκτικαὶ τέχναι, ANON. in *Ar. Fr.* 125, p. 1499, *Fr. Hz.* 125; QUINTILIAN, ii. 15, 10, gives this explanation with an '*ut creditum est*': VALER. MAX. viii. 14, 3 gives it more distinctly); or else they name Theodectes directly as the author (CIC. *Orat.* 51, 172, 57, 194; QUINTIL. iv. 2, 63 : and later writers *ap.* ROSE, *Ar. Ps.* 141, *Ar. Fr.* 123; *Fr. Hz.* 124 sq.; compare the similar treatment of the title *Nicomachean Ethics* by Cicero and others, *de quo* p. 97 *inf.*; or else they ascribe to Aristotle *and* Theodectes the opinions they find in this book (DIONYS. *Comp. Verb.* 2, p. 8, *De Vi Demos.* 48, p. 1101; QUINTIL. i. 4. 18; *Ar. Fr.* 126). If it is genuine, which the *Fr.* at least give no reason to doubt, we should consider it certainly not as a work written *by* Theodectes and published by Aristotle after his death, but as a work of Aristotle dedicated *to* Theodectes, in which view, since that orator did not survive the date of Alexander's Eastern expedition, and had become known to Alexander through Aristotle (PLUT. *Alex.* 17 *fin.*), it would have been composed during the years of Aristotle's residence in Macedonia. The name Τέχναι (in the *Rhet. ad Alex.*; cf. ROSE, *Ar. Ps.* 139) seems to indicate that it had more than one book, though the plural Θεοδέκτεια (*Rhet.* iii. 9) would not necessarily do so. For further details *v.* ROSE, *Ar. Ps.* 135 sq., and HEITZ, 85 sq.— As to the remaining titles in our lists which relate to Rhetoric,

the Τέχνη[s] α' of D. 79, AN. 73 probably meant the extant *Rhet. ad Alex.* In D. 80 the MSS. vary between ἄλλη τέχνη and ἄλλη τεχνῶν συναγωγή. If the former is right it would mean a second recension of our *Rhetoric*: if the latter, a recension of the Τεχνῶν συναγωγή : in neither case would it imply separate works.— Of the special tracts, the Γρύλλος has been mentioned p. 58, n. 1, *supra*: probably AN. *App.* 153, Π. ῥητορικῆς is merely a duplicate of it. In the title, Π. λέξεως α' β' (D. 87, AN. 79, Π. λέξ. καθαρᾶς : cf. on a similar book by Eudemus, p. 698, n. 3) Brandis in the *Gr.-röm. Phil.* ii. b, 1. 79 detects book 3 of our *Rhetoric*, whose first twelve chapters deal with that subject. This is the more probable that D. 78 gives the *Rhetoric* only two books, although AN. 72 has three books. The others, *i.e.* D. 85, AN. 77, Π. μεγέθους α' (*de quo* cf. *Rhet.* i. 3, 1359, a, 16, ii. 18 sq. 1391, b, 31, 1393, a, δ); D. 88, AN. 80, Π. συμβουλίας [-ῆς] α' (v. *Ar. Fr.* 136, p. 1501, *Ar. Ps.* 148, *Fr. Hz.* 126): AN. *App.* 177, Π. ῥήτορος ἢ πολιτικοῦ : AN. *App.* 178, Τέχνη ἐγκωμιαστική, were doubtless all spurious, as was also the Μνημονικὸν (D. 117, AN. 109) which would be dealt with as an aid to Rhetoric. PT. 68, Παραγγέλματα seems to be the same as the Παραγγ. ῥητορικῆς attributed to Theophrastus by DIOG. v. 47, but was in any case not by Aristotle.

[1] An exposition of all the rhetorical theories (τέχναι) down to Aristotle's own time was given in the Τεχνῶν συναγωγὴ (D. 77, as two books : AN. 71, and PT.

examples,[1] we have only one preserved to us,[2] in which, however, we possess without doubt the most mature statement of his rhetorical doctrine. The *Rhetoric* addressed to Alexander is now universally admitted to be spurious.[3]

24, as one book), D. 89, Συναγωγῆς α' β', and D. 80, Ἄλλη τεχνῶν συναγωγὴ· (if that is the right reading) seem to be duplicates only. We hear of it in Cic. *De Invent.* ii. 2, 6, *De Orat.* ii. 38, 160, *Brut.* 12, 48, etc. : v. *Ar. Fr.* 130–135, p. 1500; *Ar. Ps.* 145 ; *Fr. Hz.* 122. The same work or an abstract of it seems to be meant by Demetr. Magn. (*ap.* Diog. ii. 104) by the title Ἐπιτομὴ ῥητόρων.

[1] Ἐνθυμήματα ῥητορικὰ α', D. 84, An. 76 ; and Ἐνθυμημάτων διαιρέσεις α' (D. 84 ; An. 88, miswritten Ἐνθ. καὶ αἱρέσεων). To the same class belonged An. 127, Προοιμίων α' ; but *l.* Παροιμιῶν, as in D. 138. With these should be reckoned the Χρεῖαι—a collection of striking remarks, like Plutarch's Apophthegms, quoted by Stob. *Floril.* 5, 83, 7, 30, 31, 29, 70, 90, 43, 140, 57, 12, 93, 38, 116, 47, 118, 29. But as a saying of Zeno the Stoic is quoted from it (57, 12), and as we can hardly credit Aristotle with such a collection of anecdotes, it must either be a forgery or else the work of a later writer of the same name, like the grammarian mentioned *ap.* Diog. v. 35. Rose believes (*Ar. Ps.* 611) that Ἀριστοτέλους is a misreading for Ἀρίστωνος. The same book seems to be what is meant in Stob. (38, 37, 45, 21) by the citation : ἐκ τῶν κοινῶν Ἀριστοτέλους διατριβῶν. See its *Fr. ap.* Rose, *Ar. Ps.* 611, and *Fr. Hz.* 335.—The two orations,

Ἐγκώμιον λόγου and Ἐγκώμιον πλούτου, are counted as pseudepigrapha in An. 190, 194. The various proverbs and apophthegms quoted from Aristotle (Rose, *Ar. Ps.* 606 sq.; *Fr. Hz.* 337 sq.) are collected from different sources.

[2] *I.e.* the three books of the *Rhetoric.* The date of its composition must be the last residence of Aristotle at Athens ; cf. Brandis in ' Ar. Rhet.' *Philol.* iv. 8. That it has suffered interpolations and transpositions (*e.g.* in book ii. c. 18–26 ought to precede c. 1–17) was proved by Spengel, *Abh. d. Münchn. Akad.* vi. 483, followed by Vahlen, ' Z. Krit. Ar. Schr.' *Wien. Akad.* xxxviii. 92, 121. The genuineness of book iii. has been questioned by Sauppe, *Dionys. u. Ar.*, Gött. 1863, p. 32 ; Rose, *Ar. Ps.* 137 n. ; Heitz, p. 85, 89 ; Schaarschmidt, *Samml. Plat. Schr.* 108, whose view has been followed in Zeller, *Plato*, p. 55.

[3] This work was known to the author of our earliest list (*v.* D. 79, but its authenticity is not to be thought of. Spengel (Συναγ. τεχν. 182, Anaxim. *Ars Rhet.* Proleg. ix. sq., cf. 99 sq.) attributes it, excepting the first and last chapters, to Aristotle's contemporary Anaximenes of Lampsacus. This suggestion, however, is very questionable ; cf. Rose, *Ar. Lib. Ord.* 100 ; Kampe, in the *Philol.* ix. 106 sq. 279 sq. For, apart

Of the writings devoted to the development of his philosophic system, the first place is given to collections of Definitions [1] and Divisions [2]—regarded as aids to

from the arbitrariness of the separation of the part attributed to Anaximenes from the rest, the influence of the school of Aristotle betrays itself throughout, not only in the persistence of a method of didactic definitions and divisions, but also in the tenor of particular passages. Cf., *e.g.*, c. 2 *init.* (with *Rhet.* l. 3); c. 3, 1424, a, 12–19 (*Polit.* vi. 4, 1318, b, 27–38); c. 5, 1427, a, 30 (*Eth. N.* v. 10, 1135, b, 11 sqq., *Rhet.* i. 13, 1374, b, 6); c. 8, 1428, a, 19 sqq. (*Rhet.* ii. 25, 1402, b, 12 sqq.); c. 8, 1428, a, 25 (*Anal. pr.* ii. 27 *init.*); c. 9 *init.* (*Rhet.* i. 2, 1357, b, 28); c. 12 *init.* (*Rhet.* ii. 21, 1394, a, 22); and the distinction of ἐνθύμημα and γνώμη in c. 11 sq., though differently put, is of Aristotelian origin (cf. *Rhet.* ii. 21, 1394, a, 26); c. 17 (*Rhet.* i. 15, 1376, b, 31 sq.); c. 28 *init.* 29 *init.* (*Rhet.* iii. 9, 1410, a, 23).

[1] D. 64, AN. 61, Ὁρισμοὶ, 13 books: PT. 59: Ὅροι, 16 books, was certainly a later work of the School, analogous to the Platonic *Definitiones.* As to the other title, AN. 51, Ὅρων βιβλίον αʹ, cf. p. 71, n. 2, *supra.*

[2] Besides the 'Platonic Divisions' mentioned p. 63, n. 2, the lists name the following of this class: D. 42, Διαιρέσεις ιζʹ [AN. 41, Π. διαιρέσεων]; D. 43, AN. 42, Διαιρετικῶν αʹ [Rose *leg.* -κὸν, as in the duplicate title D. 62]; PT. 52 gives the Διαιρέσεις (which might extend to any length according to the subjects chosen), 26 books. Whether the work was different from or identical (as

seems more probable) with the Platonic Διαιρέσεις, it cannot be genuine. The quotation in ALEX. *Top.* 126, *Schol.* 274, a, 42, from Aristotle, ἐν τῇ τῶν ἀγαθῶν διαιρέσει (*Ar. Fr.* 110, p. 1496; *Fr. Hz.* 119), is satisfied by *M. Mor.* i. 2, 1183, b, 20 sq., cf. *Eth. N.* i. 12, 1101, b, 11, but may have found its way from that source into the Διαιρέσεις also.—Aristotle himself names an Ἐκλογὴ τῶν ἐναντίων, in *Metaph.* iv. 2, 1004, a, 1, where, after the remark that all oppositions finally go back to that of the ἓν or ὂν and its opposite, he adds: τεθεωρήσθω δ' ἡμῖν ταῦτα ἐν τῇ ἐκλογῇ τῶν ἐναντίων: in the parallel passage, xi. 3, 1061. a, 15, it is only ἔστωσαν γὰρ αὗται τεθεωρημέναι: cf. 1004, b, 33, πάντα δὲ καὶ τἆλλα ἀναγόμενα φαίνεται εἰς τὸ ἓν καὶ τὸ πλῆθος· εἰλήφθω γὰρ ἡ ἀναγωγὴ ἡμῖν. To the same refers also x. 3, 1054, a, 29: ἔστι δὲ τοῦ μὲν ἑνὸς, ὥσπερ καὶ ἐν τῇ διαιρέσει τῶν ἐναντίων διεγράψαμεν, τὸ ταὐτὸ καὶ ὅμοιον καὶ ἴσον, etc.; and the ταὐτὸν and ὅμοιον were themselves given in *Metaph.* iv. 2, 1003, b, 35, as examples of the εἴδη τοῦ ἑνὸς treated of in the Ἐκλογὴ τ. ἐν.: cf. also x. c. 4 *ad fin.* But in *Met.* xii, 7, 1072, b, 2 the words ἡ διαίρεσις δηλοῖ refer, not to a treatise, but to the division of two kinds of οὗ ἕνεκα given just before. Whether the reference to the Ἐκλογὴ τ. ἐν. indicates a separate treatise or a section of the work 'On the Good,' even Alexander did not know (cf. p. 61, n. 1); but since the subject

correct appreciation of the subject—but none of these appear to have been genuine. Most important, therefore, is the treatise *On the First Philosophy* [1]—a torso which is now arbitrarily bound up [2] with a number of other fragments, some genuine, some spurious, to form our *Metaphysics*. [3] Probably, however, the genuine

on which Aristotle cites the Ἐκλογὴ seems to have been dealt with in the second book Π. τἀγαθοῦ, it is probable that Aristotle had only that book in view.

[1] This is the name by which the work was originally cited; v. *De Motu Anim.* 6, 700, b, 8. That Aristotle himself so named it, is probable from *Metaph.* vi. 1, 1026, a, 15, 24, 30, xi. 4, 1061, b, 19; *Phys.* i. 9, 192. a, 35, ii. 2 *fin.*; *De Cœlo*, i. 8, 277, b, 10; *Gen. et Corr.* i. 3, 318, a, 6; *De An.* i. 1, 403, b, 16; for πρώτη φιλοσοφία we also find φιλοσοφία alone (*Metaph.* xi. 3, 4, 1061, b, 5, 25), θεολογικὴ (*Metaph.* vi. 1, 1026, a, 19, xi. 7, 1064, b, 3), ἡ περὶ τὰ θεῖα φιλοσοφία (*Part. An.* i. 5, 645, a, 4), σοφία (*Metaph.* i. 1, 2), and μέθοδος περὶ τῆς ἀρχῆς τῆς πρώτης (*Phys.* viii. 1, 251, a, 7), as Aristotle's expression for the subject of the book; and accordingly the book itself is also spoken of as σοφία, φιλοσοφία, θεολογία (ASCLEP. *Schol. in Ar.* 519, b, 19, 31). Cf. BONITZ, v. 5, *Arist. Metaph.* ii. 3 sq.

[2] We first find the name μετὰ τὰ φυσικὰ in Nicolaus of Damascus, who (acc. to the Schol. to THEOPH. *Metaph.* p. 323, Brand.) wrote a Θεωρία τῶν Ἀρ. μετὰ τὰ φυσικά : afterwards in PLUT. *Alex.* 7, and since then constantly. As this Nicolaus was

a younger contemporary of Andronicus, the title (which never appears before, and is permanent after that date) may safely be referred to Andronicus himself, whose collection of Aristotle's writings alone explains it; for it means, not as SIMPL. *Phys.* 1, and the Neoplatonist HERENNIUS (*ap.* BONITZ, *Ar. Metaph.* ii. 5) supposed, the Supernatural, but that which in the order of doctrinal development, and of the works as collected, followed after the books on the Natural Sciences (cf. ALEX. *Metaph.* 127, 21; ASCLEP. *Schol.* 519, b, 19). It is named in the lists by AN. 111, AN. *App.* 154, and PT. 49. The latter has the usual Greek reckoning of thirteen books; the former has at 111 κ′, at 154 ι′ ; which leaves it uncertain whether the editions referred to were incomplete, the one having only A–K, and the other A–I, or whether K and I are corruptions of N, *i.e.* A–N.

[3] The question of the arrangement of our *Metaphysics* has been so far established by Brandis in ' Ar. Met.', *Abh. d. Berl. Akad.* 1834, Hist. Phil. Kl. p. 63–87, *Gr.-röm. Phil.* ii. b. 1, 541 sq., and by Bonitz (*Ar. Met.* ii. 3–35), that it is sufficient to refer the reader for earlier theories to the comprehensive account given by Bonitz at p. 30.

portions were brought into this connection immediately

The main body of the work, begun but not finished by Aristotle, is made up of books i., iii. (B), iv., vi.–ix. In these, after the critical and historical introduction in book i., one and the same inquiry, that as to Being as such, is methodically carried on, although it is neither brought to a conclusion, nor in parts submitted to final revision. Book x. seems to have been intended for a somewhat further advanced section of the same inquiry (cf. x. 2 *init*. with iii. 4, 1001, a, 4 sq., and x. 2, 1053, b, 16 with vii. 13), but as it is not brought by Aristotle into any express connection with book ix., it has almost the appearance of a separate treatise. Between these connected books there is inserted, in book v., an inquiry into the different meanings of thirty philosophical conceptions and terms, which stands in no connection with either the preceding or the following book. The Aristotelian authorship of this section is beyond doubt. Aristotle himself quotes it (in *Metaph*. vii. 1 *init*., x. 1; cf. *Gen. et Corr*. ii. 10, 336, b, 29, *Phys*. i. 8, 191, b 29), with the words ἐν τοῖς περὶ τοῦ ποσαχῶς or π. τοῦ ποσ. λέγεται ἕκαστον. The view of Susemihl (*Genet. Entw. d. Plat. Phil*. ii. 536) that these citations are not satisfied by our book v., and that it is an un-Aristotelian tract which has taken the place of a genuine book with similar contents, is as decisively disproved as that of Rose (*Ar. Libr. Ord*. 154) that the book is entirely unworthy of Aristotle. The book is alluded to in other

passages of the *Metaph*. (*e.g.* x. 4, 1055, a, 23, with which cf. v. 10, 1018, a, 25, and x. 6, 1054, b. 34, cf. v. 15, 1021, a. 25); and a discussion reserved in v. 7 *ad fin*. for another place is to be found in ix. c. 7. The tract Π. τοῦ ποσαχῶς, however, cannot have originally formed part of the work 'On the First Philosophy.' It must have been written much earlier—as is shown by the citations in the *Phys*. and in the *Gen. et Corr*.—and as an aid to the exact use and understanding of philosophic terms; and as such it appears in D. 36, and in AN. 37 with the special addition Π. τ. ποσ. λέγ. ἢ τῶν κατὰ πρόσθεσιν. Nevertheless, Ar. *Met*. vi. 2 *init*., alludes unmistakably to v. 7, 1017, a, 7, 22 sq., 31, in the words : ἀλλ' ἐπεὶ τὸ ὂν ἁπλῶς λεγόμενον λέγεται πολλαχῶς, ὧν ἐν μὲν ἦν τὸ κατὰ συμβεβηκὸς, etc., in a way which indicates, by the word ἦν, that the discussion had already come under the reader's notice. It appears, therefore, that Aristotle actually intended to incorporate our book v. or the contents of it in this part of his work, but never was able to finish the literary connection. As to book xi., the second half (c. 8, 1065, a, 26 sq.), is a compilation from the *Physics*, obviously not genuine. The first half exactly corresponds in content with books iii., iv., and vi.; and is therefore either an early sketch of the argument afterwards expanded in them, or else, as Rose (*Ar. Libr. Ord*. 156) supposes, a later abstract of them. A point in favour of the latter view is the objectionable recurrence, seven times, of the particle γὲ μὴν, which is otherwise unknown in Aristotle's writing (EUCKEN, *De Ar. Dic. Rat.* i. 10; *Ind. Ar.* 147, a, 44 sq.) In view, however, of the arguments from the contents of the book themselves adduced in support of the other view by Bonitz (*Ar. Met.* ii. 15, 451), this peculiarity is not decisive, especially as the general style of the book has Aristotle's characteristics, and as similar phenomena as to particles are found elsewhere. [Thus τὲ . . τὲ occurs in Aristotle almost exclusively in the *Ethics* and *Politics* (EUCKEN, 16); δέ γε almost exclusively in the *Physics* (*ibid.* 33), in which also μέντοι, καίτοι, and τοίνυν are much commoner than in the other works (*ibid.* 35, 51): ἄρα recurs oftener in the later books of the *Metaph.* than in the earlier (*ibid.* 50): and among the ten books of the *Ethics*, there are many variants as between the three last and the sections i.–iv. or v.–vii., which again vary from one another in diction (*ibid.* 75 sq.). In this first half of book xi. five of the seven cases of γὲ μὴν occur in c. 2. Besides, γὲ is so often inserted by the copyists that it is always possible some early scribe is partly responsible.] Book xii. appears as an independent treatise, which refers to none of the preceding books, but seems to allude to the *Phys.* viii. 10 (esp. 267, b, 17 sq.) in c. 7, 1073, a, 5, and in c. 8, 1073, a, 32, to *Phys.* viii. 8 sq., and also to the *De Cœlo* ii. 3 sq. It is remarkable that while c. 6–10 develop in some detail the views of Aristotle as to the Godhead and other eternal Essences, c. 1–5 on the contrary give us

the doctrine of changeable substances and their causes only in narrow compass, and in a style condensed often to the point of obscurity. This, with the fact that in these chapters the formula μετὰ ταῦτα [*sc.* λεκτέον] ὅτι occurs twice (*i.e.* 3 *init.*, and 1070, a. 4) indicates that it was not a book published by Aristotle, but a set of notes intended as a basis for lectures, in which many points were only hinted at in the the briefest way, with the knowledge that they would be made plain by oral development. The main theme of the lectures consisted of the points which in the second half of book xi. are treated with special care; while the more general metaphysical inquiries which were to serve as an introduction or basis for them were only lightly sketched. The matter the lectures dealt with was no doubt intended to be included in the work on the First Philosophy; and c. 6-10 are, as far as matter is concerned, exactly fitted to be the conclusion of it. C. 1-5, on the other hand, include nothing which is not contained in the earlier books. The polemic of Rose (*Ar. Libr. Ord.* 160) against this book—which, as will be seen in the next note, is specially well fortified with external evidence —has no value as against its Aristotelian authorship, but only as to its connection with our *Metaph.* The relation of the remaining two books to the rest is not clear; but there is no reason to hold with Rose (p. 157) that only xiv. is genuine. Aristotle must have originally meant to include them in the same book, for xiii. 2, 1076, a, 39, refers

after Aristotle's death.[1]   Of the other writings mentioned which would have stood in close relation with

to iii. 2, 998, a, 7 sq., xiii. 2, 1076,
b, 39, to iii. 2, 997, b, 12 sq.,
xiii. 10, 1086, b, 14 to iii. 6.
1003, a, 6 sq., and in viii. i. 1062,
a, 22 he contemplates a treatment of Mathematics and the
Ideas, which, as appears by xiii.
init., was intended to serve as an
introduction to Theology (cf.
BRANDIS, 542, 413 a).   On the
other hand, in xiv. 1, the obvious
reference to x. 1 is not noticed,
and vii. and viii. are not referred
to at all in xiii. and xiv. (BONITZ,
p. 26).   It is inconceivable that
Aristotle would have repeated a
considerable section almost word
for word, as is the case with the
present text of i. 6, 9, and xiii.
4, 5.   But book i., as a whole,
must, as well as book iii., which
cites it (iii. 2, 996, b, 8, cf. i. 2,
982, a, 16, b, 4, and 997, b, 3,
cf. i. 6 sq.) be older than book
xiii.   It seems to me, therefore,
the most probable conjecture
that the argument in i. 9, which
is apparently more mature than
that in book xiii., was inserted
on a second revision of book i.,
after Aristotle had decided to
exclude books xiii. and xiv. from
the scope of his main work on
Metaphysics.   Book ii. (*a*), a
collection of three small essays,
written as an introduction to Physics rather than to Metaphysics
(v. c. 3 *Schol.*), is certainly not by
Aristotle.   The majority of the
ancient commentators (οἱ πλείους)
attributed it to a nephew of
Eudemus, Pasicles of Rhodes
(Schol. ap. *Ar. Opp.* 993, a, 29 ;
Schol. in Ar. 589, a. 41 ; the so-
called Philoponus [BEKKER'S

Anon. Urbin.] in the Introd. to
a, where the name is Pasicrates ;
and Asclep. *Schol.* 520 a, 6, except that he has erroneously
transferred the story from *a* to
A).   That it was inserted after
the other books were collected is
clear, not only from its designation, but from the way in which
it breaks the connection of the
closely consecutive books A and
B, for which reason many of the
ancients wished to make it a
preface to the *Physics*, or at least
to book i. of the *Metaph.* (*Schol.*
589, b, 1 sq.)   SYRIAN (*ap.*
SCHOL. 849, a, 3) mentions that
some critics proposed to reject A.
These, like Asclepius, probably
confused it with *a* : if not, Syrian
was right in thinking their suggestion laughable.

[1] This seems probable (cf.
ZELLER, *Abh. d. Berl. Akad.*
1877, Hist. Phil. Kl. 145) because
of the circumstance that most of
the genuine books of our *Metaphysics* were in use at the date
of the oldest peripatetic books or
fragments which we possess, and
that they seem to have been
gathered together in the same
series of books with the rest at a
very early date.   Book i., as
above stated, was not only the
model for Theophrastus in book
i. of his *History of Physics*, but
has also left clear traces in what
we know of Eudemus, and is the
source of the point of view taken
by the author of the treatise on
Melissus, &c.   Books iii. (B) and
iv. are referred to by Eudemus,
the fourth by Theophrastus also ;
book vi. by Theophrastus ; book

the *Metaphysics*, only a few can be considered to be

vii. by Eudemus; book ix. by
Theophrastus; book xii. by Theophrastus, Eudemus, the writer of
the *Magna Moralia*, and the
writer of the Π. ζῴων κινήσεως;
book xiii. by Eudemus; book xiv.
apparently by Theophrastus; and
the fifth, the tract Π. τοῦ
ποσαχῶς λεγόμενον, by Strato; cf.
the following: (1) *Metaph.* 1,
981, a, 12 sq., EUDEM. *Fr.* 2,
Speng.; (2) i. 3, 983, b, 20,
THEOPHR. *Fr.* 40; (3) *ibid.* l.
30, EUD. *Fr.* 117; (4) i. 5, 986,
b, 18; *De Melisso*, Xenoph.
etc., see vol. i. 468, 484; (5) *ibid.*
l. 21 sq., THEOPHR. *Fr.* 45; (6)
ibid. l. 27, THEOPHR. *Fr.* 43,
44, EUD. *Fr.* 11, S. 21, 7; (7) i, 6,
THEOPHR. *Fr.* 48; (8) i. 6, 987,
b, 32, EUD. *Fr.* 11, S. 22, 7, Sp.;
(9) i. 8, 989, a, 30, THEOPHR.
Fr. 46; (10) iii. 2, 996, b, 26, iv.
3, 1005, a, 19, EUD. *Fr.* 4; (11)
iii. 3, 999, a, 6, *Eth. Eud.* i. 8,
1218, a, 1; (12) iv. 2, 1009, b, 12,
21, THEOPHR. *Fr.* 42; (13) iv.
6, 1011, a, 12, c. 7, 1012, a, 20,
THEOPHR. *Fr.* 12, 26; (14) v. 11,
Strato *apud* SIMPL. *Categ. Schol.
in Arist.* 90, a, 12–46; (15) vi. 1,
1026, a, 13–16, THEOPHR. *Fr.* 12,
1; (16) vii. 1, 1028, a, 10, 20,
EUD. *Fr.* 5; (17) ix. 9, 1051, b,
24, THEOPHR. *Fr.* 12, 25; (18)
xii. 7 *init.*, cf. c. 8, 1073, a, 22,
De Motu An. 6, 700, b, 7; (19)
xii. 7, 1072, a, 20, THEOPHR. *Fr.*
12, 5; (20) xii. 7, 1072, b, 24, c.
9, 1074, b, 21, 33, *Eth. Eud.* vii.
12, 1245, b, 16, *M. Mor.* ii. 15,
1213, a, 1; (21) xii. 10, 1075, b,
34, THEOPHR. *Fr.* 12, 2; (22)
xiii. 1, 1076, a, 28, *Eth. Eud.* i. 8,
1217, b, 22; (23) xiv. 3, 1090,
b, 13, THEOPHR. *Fr.* 12, 2. Since,
therefore, the parts of our

Metaph., like book xii., which
did not in fact belong to the
main treatise, are in use as commonly and at as early a date as
those parts which did, it must be
conjectured that the whole was
put together in the period immediately following Aristotle's
death. This theory receives remarkable confirmation from the
fact that already in the Π. ζῴων
κινήσεως (c. 6, 700, b. 8), which
belongs undoubtedly to the third
century B.C., book xii. itself is
quoted by the title reserved by
Aristotle for his main treatise on
Metaph.: i.e. ἐν τοῖς περὶ τῆς
πρώτης φιλοσοφίας (cf. BONITZ,
Ind. Ar. 100, a, 47 sq.; the suspicion thrown on the passage by
KRISCHE, *Forsch.* 267, 3. and
HEITZ, *V. S.* 182, is groundless).
We may assume, then, with some
probability that immediately after
Aristotle's death the finished
sections of the work on First
Philosophy (*i.e.* books i., iii., iv.,
vi.–x.) were bound up with the
other sketches and notes of a
like character left by him (*i.e.*
xi. first part, xii., xiii., and xiv.),
and that at the same time book v.
was inserted between iv. and vi.;
but that book α, and the second
half of xi., were first attached by
Andronicus to this work, with
which they were not connected
either by origin or contents.
Naturally, we cannot with certainty affirm by whom the first
redaction was undertaken. But
the statement of ALEX. (ap.
Metaph. 760, b, 11 sq.), that it
was Eudemus, deserves all consideration; while the different
story told by ASCLEP. (*Schol. in
Ar.* 519, b, 38 sq.) is open to the

genuine, and these must have belonged to Aristotle's earlier period.[1]

The works on Natural Philosophy form the largest bulk of all Aristotle's productions. We have first a series of important investigations which Aristotle himself connected together. They deal with the general basis and conditions of the material universe, of the earth and the heavenly bodies, of the elements with their properties and relations, and of meteorological phenomena. These are the *Physics*,[2] the two con-

gravest doubts. Cf. further, p. 155 sqq.

[1] Besides the Books on Philosophy (p. 55, n. 5, and 57), on the Good, and on the Ideas (p. 61, n. 1, 62, n. 1), the Περὶ εὐχῆς was probably genuine (*v.* p. 58, n. 1, fin.). The three books Π. τύχης (AN. *App.* 152) and the Μαγικὸς were not. The latter is named by Diog. (i. 1. 8, ii. 45), and was also evidently used by Plin. (*H. N.* xxx. 1, 2) as Aristotle's, but it is reckoned by AN. (191) among the Pseudepigrapha, and we know from Suidas ('Αντισθ.) that it was attributed sometimes to the Socratic Antisthenes, sometimes to the Antisthenes who was a Peripatetic of Rhodes *circa* 180 B.C. (*lege*, by Bernhardy's happy conjecture, 'Ροδίῳ for 'Ρόδωνι). On this book, vide *Ar. Fr.* 27–30, p. 1479; *Fr. Hz.* 66; HEITZ, *V. S.* 294,8; ROSE, *Ar. Ps.* 50, who considers it to be a Dialogue.— Of the Θεολογούμενα, which was ascribed to Aristotle by Macrob. (*Sat.* i. 18), the 'Theogony' mentioned by Schol. Eur. Rhes. (28), and the τελεταί spoken of by Schol. Laur. in APOLL. RHOD. iv. 973 (*v.* these and other quotations

ap. ROSE, *Ar. Ps.* 615; *Fr. Hz.* 347) seem to have formed part. It is referred by Rose to the hand of Aristocles of Rhodes, a contemporary of Strato ; but this seems unlikely : cf. Heitz, *V. S.* 294. It cannot, however, have been a genuine work of Aristotle, and it seems to have contained, not philosophical inquiries as to the Godhead, but collections and probably explanations of myths and religious usages.—The Π. ἀρχῆς, from its position in the list of D. 41, seems rather to have been a metaphysical or physical tract than a political one, but we know nothing of it.—As to a 'Theology of Aristotle,' which originated in the Neoplatonic School and is preserved to us in an Arabic translation, *v.* DIETERCI, *Abh. d. D. morgenl. Gesellsch.* 1877, 1, 117.

[2] Φυσικὴ ἀκρόασις in 8 books (in AN. 148, *leg.* η' for ιη'), as its own MSS., and those of SIMPL. *Phys.* init., AN. 148, PT. 34, &c., name the treatise. Aristotle himself commonly calls only the first books φυσικὰ or τὰ περὶ φύσεως (*Phys.* viii. 1, 251, a, 8, cf. iii. 1,

nected works *On the Heavens* and *On Growth and*

viii. 3, 253, b, 7, cf. ii. 1, 192, b, 20, viii. 10, 267, b, 20, cf. iii. 4 ; *Metaph.* i. 3, 983, a, 33, c, 4, 985, a, 12, c, 7, 988, a, 22, c, 10, xi. 1, 1059, a, 34, cf. *Phys.* ii. 3, 7 ; *Metaph.* i. 5, 986, b, 30, cf. *Phys.* i. 2 ; xiii. 1, c, 9, 1086, a, 23, cf. *Phys.* i.). The later books he usually calls τὰ περὶ κινήσεως (*Metaph.* ix. 8, 1049, b, 36, cf. *Phys.* viii., vi. 6 ; *De Cælo* i. 5, 7, 272, a, 30, 275, b, 21, cf. *Phys.* vi. 7, 238, a, 20, c, 2. 233, a, 31, viii. 10 ; *De Cælo* iii. 1, 299, a, 10, cf. *Phys.* vi. 2, 233, b, 15 ; *Gen. et Corr.* i. 3, 318, a, 3, cf. *Phys.* viii. ; *De Sensu* c, 6, 445, b, 19, cf. *Phys.* vi. 1 ; *Anal. post.* ii. 12, 95, b, 10). But in *Phys.* viii. 5, 257, a, 34 ἐν τοῖς καθόλου περὶ φύσεως refers to B. vi. 1, 4, *Metaph.* viii. 1, and φυσικὰ to B. v. 1 ; in *Metaph.* i. 8, 989, a, 24, xii. 8, 1073, 32, the phrase τὰ π. φύσεως refers not merely to the whole of the *Physica,* but also to other works on Natural Science (cf. BONITZ and SCHWEGLER *ad loc.*). For more general references see B, iii. 4, *De Cælo* i. 6, 274, a, 21, ἐν τοῖς περὶ τὰς ἀρχὰς, B. iv. 12, vi. 1, *De Cælo* iii. 4, 303, a, 23, περὶ χρόνου καὶ κινήσεως, and see IND. ARIST. 102, b, 18 sqq.— D. 90, 45 (115) names a Π. φύσεως and a Π. κινήσεως, but the former with three books only, and the latter with one (cf. p. 50, n. 1). SIMPL. (*Phys.* 190, a, 216, a, 258, b, and 320, a) says that Aristotle and his ἑταῖροι (*i.e.* Theophrastus and Eudemus) spoke of the first 5 books as Φυσικὰ or Π. ἀρχῶν φυσικῶν and of books vii. and viii. as Π. κινήσεως. No doubt Porphyry, however, was right (*ap.* SIMPL. 190, a) when he in-

cluded book v. with book vi., with which it is so closely connected, under the name Π. κινήσεως. For though in the time of Adrastus (*ap.* SIMPL. 16, 2, a) many may have named i.–v. Π. ἀρχῶν [φυσικῶν], as others named the whole, while vi.–viii. bore the title Π. κινήσεως under which Andronicus (SIMPL. 216, a) also cited them, yet it cannot be shown that this was so in the earliest period. When Theophr. cited book v. as ἐκ τῶν φυσικῶν he may easily have meant not only this whole treatise but others also (*ut supra* : and cf. SIMPL. 216, a). When Damasus the biographer and follower of Eudemus (*ap.* SIMPL. 216, a, where it is impossible to read *Damascius* the Neoplatonist) speaks of ἐκ τῆς περὶ φύσεως πραγματείας τῆς Ἀρ. τῶν περὶ κινήσεως τρία, it does not follow that he means vi., vii., viii., and not rather v., vi., viii. (cf. ROSE, *Ar. Libr. Ord.* 198 ; BRANDIS, ii. b, 782). Indeed book vii. gave even ancient critics the impression of a section not properly fitted into the general connection, and SIMPL. (*Phys.* 242, a) tells us that Eudemus passed it over in his revision of the whole work. It need not on that account be classed as spurious (with ROSE, 199), but rather (with BRANDIS, ii. b, 893 sq.) as a collection of preliminary notes which do not belong to the Treatise on Physics. The text has taken on many interpolations and alterations from a paraphrase, known even in the time of Alexander and Simplicius (*v.* SIMPL. 245, a, b, 253, b, and cf. SPENGEL, *Abh. d. Münchn.*

Decay [1] and the *Meteorology*.[2] Connected with these leading works (so far as they are not to be classed as sections of them under special names, or as spurious),

Akad. iii. 313 sq.),. but the original text is to be found in the smaller edition of Bekker and in that of Prantl. The Aristotelian origin of B. vi. c, 9, 10 is rightly maintained by Brandis (ii. b, 889) against Weisse.

[1] The Π. οὐρανοῦ in 4, and the Π. γενέσεως καὶ φθορᾶς in two books. The current division of these books, however, can hardly be derived from Aristotle, for books iii. and iv. of the Π. οὐρανοῦ are more nearly connected with the other treatise than are the earlier books. Aristotle recognises both by a short reference to their contents in the beginning of the *Meteorol.*, and by citing *De Cœlo* ii. 7 in *Meteorol.* i. 3 . . . περὶ τὸν ἄνω τόπον . . . ἐν τοῖς περὶ τοῦ ποιεῖν καὶ πάσχειν διωρισμένοις; to the *Gen. et Corr.* i. 10 (not *Meteor.* iv.) *De Sensu* c, 3, 440, b, 3, 12 (ἐν τοῖς περὶ μίξεως); to the *Gen. et Corr.* ii. 2, *De An.* ii. 11, 423, b, 29, *De Sensu*, c, 4, 441, b, 12 (ἐν τοῖς περὶ στοιχείων). A work Π. οὐρανοῦ is ascribed by SIMP.(*De Cœlo*, Schol. in Ar. 468, a, 11, 498, b, 9, 42, 502, a, 43) also to Theophrastus, who is said to have followed the lines of Aristotle's book. With this exception the earliest witnesses to the existence of the work are Xenarchus and Nicolaus of Damascus (*v.* BRANDIS, *Gr.-röm. Phil.* ii. b, 952), but there is no doubt of the authenticity either of these books or of the Π. γενέσεως. From STOB. *Ecl.* i. 486, 536 we cannot, with IDELER

Ar. Meteorol. i. 415, ii. 199 (nor from CIC. *N. D.* ii. 15, and PLUT. *Plac.* v. 20) infer that the Π. οὐρανοῦ was originally more complete or existed in a recension different from ours.

[2] AN. *App.* 150, Μετεωρολογικά; PT. 37, Π. μετεώρων δ' ἢ μετεωροσκοπιά; PT. 76 do. with two books only. This work, as above observed, places itself, in its opening chapter, in immediate connection with the works last discussed; and its genuineness is beyond doubt. Aristotle himself does not name it (for *De Plant.* ii. 2, 822, b, 32 is a spurious book), but he frequently recalls its doctrines; cf. BONITZ, *Ind. Ar.* 102, b, 49. According to ALEX. *Meteor.* 91 and Olympiod. *ap.* IDELER, *Ar. Meteor.* i. 137, 222, 286, Theophrastus in his μεταρσιολογικὰ (DIOG. v. 44) seems to have imitated it. Ideler (*ibid.* i. vii. sq.) shows that it was known to Aratus, Philochorus, Agathemerus, Polybius, and Posidonius. Eratosthenes, however, seems not to have known it; cf. *ibid.* i. 462. Of the four books, the last seems from its contents not to have originally belonged to the same treatise. ALEX. (*Meteor.* 126, a) and AMMON. (*ap.* Olympiod. in IDELER, *Ar. Meteor.* i. 133) prefer to connect it with the Π. γενέσεως; but it is not adapted to that work either. Since it has all the appearance of being Aristotelian, and is cited by Aristotle (*Part. An.* ii. 2, 649, a, 23; cf. *Meteor.*

are a variety of other treatises on natural philosophy.[1]

iv. 10, *Gen. An.* ii. 6, 743, a, 6 ; cf. *Meteor.* iv. 6, 383, b, 9, 384, a, 33), it must be taken to be an isolated section, which was not contemplated, in this form, when the *Meteorology* was begun (v. *Meteor.* i. 1 *ad fin.*), but which in the end took the place of the further matter that remained to be dealt with at the end of book iii., which obviously does not itself bring the treatise to a close. As Bonitz (*Ind. Ar.* 98, b, 53) notices in criticising Heitz, this book (c. 8, 384, b, 33) cites *Meteor.* iii. 677, 378, a, 15 (cf. on this subject IDELER, *ibid.* ii. 347–360 ; SPENGEL, ' Ueb. d. Reihenfolge d. naturwissensch. Schriften d. Arist.,' *Abhandl. d. Münchn. Akad.* v. 150 sq. ; BRANDIS, *Gr.-röm. Phil.* ii. b, 1073, 1076 ; ROSE, *Arist. Libr. Ord.* 197). The doubts alluded to by Olympiod. *ibid.* i. 131, as to book i. are unsupported ; the reasons given by Ideler (i. xii. sq.) for holding that two recensions of the *Meteor.* existed in antiquity are not convincing. The points which he supposed to have been found in another edition of this, are for the most part referable to other works, and where that is not so (SEN. *Qu. Nat.* vii. 28, 1 ; cf. *Meteor.* i. 7, 344, b, 18) our informant may be in error. But it is possible that these points may have come from an edition that had been expanded by a later hand or largely added to ; cf. BRANDIS, p. 1075.

[1] The *Physics* have the following titles : Π. ἀρχῶν ἢ φύσεως α′ (AN. 21), ἐν τοῖς π. τῶν ἀρχῶν τῆς ὅλης φύσεως (THEMIST. *De An.* ii. 71, 76), ἐν τοῖς π. τῶν

ἀρχῶν (*ibid.* 93), Π. κινήσεως (D. 45, 115 ; AN. 102, 1 B ; PT. 17, 8 B ; the same again as *Auscultatio physica*, at No. 34 ; and perhaps also as Π. ἀρχῆς at D. 41). In what relation the same work stands to the titles : Π. φύσεως (D. 90 as three books, AN. 81, as one) ; Φυσικὸν α′ (D. 91) ; or Π. φυσικῶν α′ (AN. 82) is not clear. AN. *App.* 170, PT. 85 : Π. χρόνου might also be only an extract including *Phys.* iv. 10–14, though it is preferable to think of it as a special treatise by some of the Peripatetics. Aristotle himself refers with the words ἐν τοῖς π. στοιχείων in the *De An.* ii. 11, 423, b, 28, and the *De Sensu*, 4, 441, a, 12, to the *Gen. et Corr.* ii. 2 sqq. Whether in D. 39, AN. 35, the title Π. στοιχείων γ′ only refers to this work (possibly in connection with *De Cœlo* iii. and iv., cf. p. 50, n. 1 ; or with *Meteor.* iv., cf. *Fr. Hz.* 156), or whether it means a special collection of several Aristotelian tracts relating to the elements, or whether there was a separate treatise (which could not be considered genuine) must remain an open question.—So, again, as to the book Π. τοῦ πάσχειν ἢ πεπονθέναι (D. 25) : Aristotle in *De An.* ii. 5, 417, a, 1, and in *Gen. Anim.* iv. 3, 768, b, 23 refers by the formula, ἐν τοῖς π. τοῦ ποιεῖν καὶ πάσχειν, to *Gen. et Corr.* i. 7 sq., a reference doubted by Trendelenburg (*De An.* ibid.) and by Heitz (*V. S.* 80), but which it seems impossible, on comparison of the passages, to reject (cf. with *Gen. An.* p. 324, *a*, 30 sq. ; with *De An.* 416, b, 35, and 323, a, 10 sq. ; with *De An.* 417

Another class of writings, less directly akin, are the

a, 1, τοῦτο δὲ πῶς δυνατὸν ἢ ἀδύνατον, εἰρήκαμεν, etc., and 325, b, 25, πῶς δὲ ἐνδέχεται τοῦτο συμβαίνειν, πάλιν λέγωμεν, etc.). It suggests itself, therefore, either to apply the title in DIOG. to this section only or to the whole of book i. If, however, a separate treatise is meant, then it seems more likely that it was analogous to the *Gen. et Corr.* than that (as TREND. *Gesch. d. Kategor.*, 130, supposes) it treated generally of the categories of Action and Passion.— With Physics also was connected the tract *De quæstionibus hylicis*, PT. 50, and perhaps also PT. 75, *De accidentibus universis*, both without doubt spurious. So must be also AN. *App.* 184, Π. κόσμου γενέσεως, which cannot have been written by Aristotle, who so decisively combats the idea of a beginning of the world. The book Π. κόσμου (which is not even known to our three lists) was written at the earliest 50–1 B.C.; cf. ZELLER, *Ph. d. Gr.* iii. a, 558. The so-called quotation from a work Π. μίξεως, given by Minoides Mynas, in his edition of Gennadius against Pletho (*Fr. Hz.* 157), belongs perhaps to the διαιρέσεις spoken of p. 75, n. 2.—Many of the books we hear of as related to the subject of the *Meteor.* seem to have been spurious. A work Π. ἀνέμων (ACHILL. TAT. *in Ar.* c. 33, 158 A; *Fr. Hz.* 350; ROSE, *Ar. Ps.* 622) was ascribed to Aristotle, probably by a confusion between him and Theophrastus (*de q. v.* DIOG. v. 42; ALEX. *Meteor.* 101, b, 106, a, etc.); and so with the Σημεῖα χειμώνων (D. 112, or *ap.* AN. 99,

Σημασία[ι] χειμώνων, or in the title ap. *Ar. Opp.* ii. 973, Π. σημείων), for the *Fr.* of which v. *Ar. Fr.* 237 sq. 1521; *Fr. Hz.* 157; *Ar. Ps.* 243 sq. The Π. ποταμῶν (PS.-PLUT. *De Fluv.* c. 25 *ad fin.*; HEITZ, *V. S.* 297; *Fr. Hz.* 349) seems to have been a late compilation. Of much earlier date (according to Rose, either by Theophrastus or of his time) is AN. *App.* 159; PT. 22, Π. τῆς τοῦ Νείλου ἀναβάσεως, *de q. v.* ROSE, *Ar. Ps.* 239 sq.; *Ar. Fr.* p. 1520; *Fr. Hz.* 211. The treatises *De Humoribus* and *De Siccitate*, ap. PT. 73, 74, cannot be genuine, as they are mentioned nowhere else. As to the Π. χρωμάτων, well founded objections have been raised by Prantl (*Ar. ü. d. Farben*, Münch., 1849, p. 82; cf. 107, 115, 142, etc.).— Alex. in *Meteor.* 98, b, and Olympiod. in *Meteor.* 36, a (*ap.* IDELER, *Ar. Meteor.* i. 287 sq.) allege that Aristotle wrote a book Π. χυμῶν, but neither seems to have known it. So Michael of Ephesus, *De Vita et M.* 175, b, remarks that Aristotle's Π. φυτῶν καὶ χυλῶν was lost, so that it was necessary to rely on Theophrastus. Aristotle himself alludes in *Meteor.* ii. 3, 359, b, 20, to some more extended inquiry into the qualities of things relating to the sense of taste; and since in the late *De Sensu*, c. iv. *ad fin.*, further inquiries on the same subject are projected as part of the work on Plants, it is a question whether we should refer the allusion in *Meteor.* ii. to a separate book Π. χυμῶν, and not consider it rather as a later interpolation referring to *De Sensu*‘

mathematical, mechanical, optical, and astronomical
tracts.[1]

c. 4, and *De An.* ii. 10.—Aristotle
contemplates at the end of *Meteor.* iii. a work on Metals, and
the commen*ators mention a
μονόβιβλος π. μετάλλων. See
SIMPL. *Phys.* 1, a; *De Cælo,*
Schol. in Ar. 468, b, 25 ; DAMASC.
De Cælo, ibid. 454, a, 22; PHILOP.
Phys. a, 1, m. (who, however, on
the *Meteorologia,* i. 135 id., speaks
as if he did not know such a
tract); OLYMPIOD. *in Meteor.* i.
133 id. Some, with more reason,
attribute the book to Theophrastus (POLLUX, *Onomast.* vii. 99,
x. 149; cf. DIOG. v. 44; THEOPHR.
De Lapid. init.; ALEX. *Meteor.*
126, a, ii. 161 Id.; and see
ROSE, *Arist. Ps.* 254 sq., 261
sq.; *Ar. Fr.* 242 sq. S. 1523;
Fr. Hz. 161). Against the idea
that *Meteor.* iii. 7, 378, b, 5 ; iv.
8, 384, b, 34, refers to the Π. μετ.
(on which see HEITZ, p. 68), see
BONITZ, *Ind. Ar.* 98, b, 53. We
know nothing of the *De metalli
fodinis* (Hadschi Khalfa, *ap.*
WENRICH, *De Auct. Gr. Ve·s.
Arab.* 160). The tract on the
Magnet (Π. τῆς λίθου, D. 125;
AN. 117; ROSE, *Ar. Ps.* 242;
Fr. H. 215) was probably spurious. That *De lapidibus,* which
was much used by the Arabs
(HADSCHI KH. *loc. cit.* 159; see
MEYER, *Nicol. Damasc. De plantis,* praef. p. xi.; ROSE, *Ar. Libr.
Ord.* 181 sq., *Ar. Ps.* 255 sq.),
was certainly so.

[1] Μαθηματικὸν α' (D. 63; AN.
53), Π. τῆς ἐν τοῖς μαθήμασιν
οὐσίας (AN. *App.* 160), Π. μονάδος
(D. 111; AN. 100), Π. μεγέθους
(D. 85; AN. 77, unless this was
a Rhetorical tract; see p. 72, 2

ad fin.). The Π. ἀτόμων Γραμμῶν
(*Ar. Opp.* ii. 968 sq.), which in
our lists is only named by PT.
10, and never cited by Aristotle
himself, was also ascribed with
much likelihood to Theophrastus
by SIMPL. *De Cælo,* Schol. in
Ar. 510, b, 10, and PHILOP. *Gen. et
Corr.* 8 b, whereas PHILOP. ad
Gen. et Corr. 37, a, and ad *Phys.*
m. 8, treats it simply as by Aristotle. Its genuineness is doubted
also by Rose (*Ar. Libr. Ord.* 193).
The reference in EUTOC. ad *Ar-
chim. de Circ. Dimens. proœm.*
does not mean that Aristotle
wrote a book on squaring the
circle ; the allusion is merely to
Soph. El. 11, 174, b, 14 or *Phys.* i.
2, 185, a, 16. Without further
explanation Simpl. (*Categ.* 1 ζ)
names Aristotle's γεωμετρικά τε καὶ
μηχανικὰ βιβλία ; but the extant
Μηχανικὰ (in D. 123; AN. 114,
called μηχανικὸν [-ῶν], but more
correctly *ap.* PT. 18, Μηχ. *προβλήματα*) are certainly not from
the hand of Aristotle; cf. ROSE,
Ar. Libr. Ord. 192.—D. 114,
'Οπτικὸν α' [-ῶν, *sc.* προβλημάτων];
AN. 103, 'Οπτικὰ βιβλία ; cf.
DAVID *in Categ* Schol. 25, a, 36 ;
ANON. *Proleg. in Metaph.* ap.
ROSE, *Ar. Ps.* 377, and *Fr. Hz.* 215:
'Οπτικὰ προβλήμ., *V. Marc.* p. 2 and
p. 8. It is clear from a reference
in a Latin translation of Hero's
κατοπτρικὰ (*circ.* 230 B.C.) *ap.*
ROSE, *Ar. Ps.* 378; *Ar. Fr.* 1534 ;
Fr. Hz. 216, and from the Pseud.
Ar. *Problems,* xvi. 1 *ad fin.,* that
such a book had currency under
Aristotle's name at an early date,
Its genuineness is not, however,
assured, though it is very pro-

Next to the *Physics* and the related treatises come the numerous and important works dealing with life. Some of these are descriptive, others are inquiries. To the former class belong the *History of Animals* [1] and the

bable that among Aristotle's genuine *Problems* there were some in Optics The *De Speculo*, attributed by Arabic and Christian Middle-Age writers to Aristotle, appears to be only Euclid's Κατοπτρικὰ (ROSE, *Ar. Ps.* 376).—D. 113; AN. 101, report an Ἀστρονομικὸν; and Aristotle himself refers to such a work in *Meteor.* i. 3, 339, b, 7 (ἤδη γὰρ ὦπται διὰ τῶν ἀστρολογικῶν θεωρημάτων ἡμῖν), *ibid.* c. 8, 345, b, 1 (καθάπερ δείκνυται ἐν τοῖς περὶ ἀστρολογίαν θεωρήμασιν), and *De Cælo*, ii. 10, 291, a, 29 (περὶ δὲ τῆς τάξεως αὐτῶν etc. ἐκ τῶν περὶ ἀστρολογίαν θεωρείσθω· λέγεται γὰρ ἱκανῶς); SIMPL. on the *De Cælo*, Schol. 497, a, 8, appears to have the same in his mind. The existence of the book is accepted, of modern scholars, by Bonitz (*Ind. Ar.* 104, a, 17 sq.) and Prantl (*ad* Π. οὐρ. p. 303); while Heitz (*S. V.* p. 117) thinks it probable, though in *Fr. Hz.* 160 he refuses to decide. Blass (*Rhein. Mus.* xxx. 504) applies the references to writings by other hands. Ideler (*Ar. Metaph.* i. 415) assumes a varying recension of the *De Cælo*, which has no probability. It does not seem probable that this Astronomical—or as Aristotle would have called it (*v.* HEITZ, *ibid.*) Astrological—work took the form of Problems, since Aristotle repeatedly speaks of θεωρήματα. Not to it, but to late interpolated tracts, are the

titles to be referred which are mentioned by Hadschi Khalfa (p. 159–161): *De siderum arcanis, De sideribus eorumque arcanis, De stellis labentibus,* and *Mille verba de astrologia judiciaria.* As to the accuracy of the other mathematical and related writings, we can decide nothing. The attempt of Rose (*Ar. Libr. Ord.* 192) to prove that *none* of them can be Aristotle's does not succeed.

[1] Π. τὰ ζῷα ἱστορία (Π. ζῴων ἱστορίας ι', AN. *App.* 155; the same is meant by D. 102 and AN. 91, Π. ζῴων, nine books, and by PT. 42). The Arabic writers count ten, fifteen, or nineteen books, and had no doubt expanded the extant text by various added tracts; cf. WENRICH, *De Auct. Græc. Vers.* 148. Aristotle quotes it by various names: ἱστορίαι [-ία] π. τὰ ζῷα (*Part. Anim.* iii. 14, 674, b, 16; iv. 5, 680, a, 1; iv. 8 *ad fin.*; iv. 10, 689, a, 18; iv. 13, 696, b, 14; *Gen. An.* i. 4, 717, a, 33; i. 20, 728, b, 13; *Respir.* c. 16, *init.*); ἱστορίαι π. τῶν ζῴων (*Part. Anim.* ii. 1, *init.* c. 17, 660, b, 2; *Gen. Anim.* i. 3, 716, b, 31; *Respir.* c. 12, 477, a, 6), ζωϊκὴ ἱστορία (*Part. Anim.* iii. 5, *fin.*), ἱστορία φυσικὴ (*Part. Anim.* ii. 3, 650, a, 31; *Ingr. An.* c. 1, *fin.*), and simply ἱστορίαι or ἱστορία (*De Respir.* 16, 478, b, 1; *Gen. Anim.* i. 11, 719, a, 10; ii. 4, 740, a, 23; c. 7, 746, a, 14; iii. 1, 750, b, 31; c. 2, 753, b, 17; c. 8 *fin.*; c. 10 *fin.*; c. 11 *fin.*

In its contents, however, it is
rather a Comparative Anatomy
and Physiology than a description of animals. As to the plan
of it, cf. J. B. MEYER, *Ar.
Thierk.* 114 sq. Its genuineness
is beyond question, though as to
the tenth book, it must be taken
to be, not merely with Spengel
(*De Ar. Libro X Hist. Anim.*
Heidelb. 1842), a retranslation of
a Latin translation of a section
written by Aristotle to follow
book vii., but wholly spurious;
with Schneider (iv. 262, i. xiii.),
Rose (*Ar. Libr. Ord.* 171), and
Brandis (*Gr.-röm. Phil.* ii. 6,
1257). Apart from anything else
the un-Aristotelian assumption
of a female semen would prove
this of itself. No doubt this
book is the same as that in
D. 107, AN. 90, ὑπὲρ [περὶ] τοῦ
μὴ γεννᾶν. As to Alexander's reported assistance for the whole
work, cf. p. 29 sq. *supra*; and as
to the sources used by Aristotle,
cf. ROSE, *Ar. Libr. Ord.* 206 sq.—
Besides this History of Animals,
there were known to the ancients
various similar works. Athenæus,
for example, uses one work different (as is clear from his own
words) from our *Hist. An.*, under
the names ἐν τῷ π. Ζῴων, ἐν τοῖς
π. Z. (ROSE, *Ar. Ps.* 277, and
HEITZ, 224, unnecessarily read
Ζωϊκῶν), ἐν τῷ π. Ζῳϊκῶν, ἐν τῷ
ἐπιγραφομένῳ Ζῳϊκῷ, ἐν τῷ π. Ζῴων
ἢ [καὶ] Ἰχθύων, ἐν τῷ π. Ζῳϊκῶν
καὶ Ἰχθύων, ἐν τῷ π. Ἰχθύων; but
at the same time he curiously
cites our *Hist. An.* v., as πέμπτον
π. ζῴων μορίων (see the notes of
Schweighäuser on the passages
in question; e.g. ii. 63, b; iii. 88;
c. vii. 281 sq., 286, b; and the
Index, and see ROSE, *Ar. Ps.*
276 sq.; *Ar. Fr.* Nr. 277 sq.;

HEITZ, 224 sq.; *Fr. Hz.* 172). So
CLEMENS, *Pædag.* ii. 150, C (cf.
ATHEN. vii. 315, e) seems to
refer to the same lost work, and
Apollonius (*Mirabil.* c. 27) mentions it, distinguishing it expressly from the extant *Hist. An.*
(Π. ζῴων). Parts of this lost work
are probably indicated by the
names: Π. θηρίων (ERATOSTH.
Catasterismi, c. 41, and therefrom the Scholion in GERMAN-
ICUS, *Aratea Phænom.* v. 427,
Arat. ed. BUHLE, ii. 88); Ὑπὲρ
τῶν μυθολογουμένων ζῴων (D. 106;
AN. 95); ὑπὲρ τῶν συνθέτων ζῴων
(D. 105; AN. 92); Π. τῶν φωλευόντων (PTOL. 23, '*fari tufu-
lin*'). DIOG. v. 44 attributes a
treatise of that name, doubtless
the same, to Theophrastus, from
which come the *Fragm.* 176–178,
Wimm. *apud* ATHEN. ii. 63;
c. iii. 105 d; vii. 314, b. To it
also refers the notice in PLUT.
Qu. Conv. 8, 9, 3, which ROSE,
Ar. Fr. 38, refers to the
Dialogue ' Eudemus,' and HEITZ,
Fragm. Ar. 217, to the ἰατρικὰ.
The citations from this and similar works, sometimes under the
name of Aristotle, sometimes of
Theophrastus, will be found in
ROSE, *Ar. Ps.* 276–372; *Ar. Fr.*
257–334, p. 1525 sq.; *Fr. Hz.*
171 sq. PLIN. (*H. Nat.* viii. 16,
44) says Aristotle wrote about
fifty, and ANTIGONUS (*Mirab.* c.
60 [66]) says about seventy books
on Animals. Of all these it is
clear that none but the first nine
of our *Hist. An.* were genuine.
The work which Athen. used
(which is not Aristotle's style, to
judge by the *Fr.*) seems to have
been a compilation from them
and other sources, belonging, in
view of the passage quoted from
Antigonus, to the third century B.C.

Anatomical Descriptions.[1] The latter class begin with the three books *On the Soul,*[2] on which several other anthropological tracts follow.[3] The further investi-

[1] The 'Ανατομαὶ (seven books, in D. 103, AN. 93) are very often cited by Aristotle (cf. BONITZ, *Ind. Ar.* 104, a, 4, and *Fr. Hz.* 160), and it is not possible with Rose (*Ar. Libr. Ord.* 188) to explain these references away. We know from *H. An.* i. 17, 497, a, 31, iv. 1, 525, a, 8, vi. 11, 566, a, 15 ; *Gen. An.* ii. 7, 746, a, 14 ; *Part. An.* iv. 5, 680, a, 1 ; and *De Respir.* 16, 478, a, 35, that the 'Ανατομαὶ were furnished with drawings, which were perhaps the principal point of the work. The Schol. on *Ingr. An.* 178, b (after Simpl. *De Anima*), can hardly have cited the work from his own knowledge. Apuleius (*De Mag.* c. 36, 40) talks of a work of Aristotle, Π. ζῴων ἀνατομῆς, as universally known ; but it is seldom mentioned elsewhere, and Apuleius himself possibly meant the Π. ζῴων μορίων. The extract from the work—ἐκλογὴ ἀνατομῶν, D. 104, AN. 94, APOLLON. *Mirab.* c. 39—was certainly not by Aristotle. Heitz (*Fr.* 171) rightly rejects Rose's opinion (*Ar. Ps.* 276) that the ἀνατομαὶ were one work with the ζῴϊκα. AN. 187 gives an ἀνατομὴ ἀνθρώπου among the *Pseudepigr.* Aristotle did no human anatomy (cf. *H. An.* iii. 3, 513, a, 12, i. 16 *init.* and see LEWES, *Aristotle*).

[2] The Π. ψυχῆς is often cited by Aristotle in the lesser treatises presently to be mentioned (BONITZ, *Ind. Ar.* 102, b, 60 sq.), and in the *Gen. An.* ii. 3, v. 1, 7, 736, a, 37, 779, b, 23, 786, b, 25, 288, b, 1, *Part. An.* iii. 10, 673,

a, 30, *De Interpr.* i. 16, a, 8, *De Motu An.* c. 6 *init.* and c. 11 *ad fin.*, and must therefore be earlier than these books. Ideler (*Ar. Meteor.* ii. 360) is not correct in saying that the reverse follows from the end of *Meteor.* i. 1. The words in the *Ingr. An.* c. 19 *ad fin.* which name this book as only projected and the Π. ζῴων μορίων as in existence, are (with Brandis ii. 6, 1078) to be considered as a gloss only. Of its three books the first two seem in a more complete state than the third. Torstrik, in the preface to his edition of 1862, has shown that there are preserved traces of a second recension of book ii., and that confusing repetitions have crept into the present text of book iii., through a combination of two recensions made before the date of Alexander of Aphrodisias ; and the same appears to be true of book i. also. Singularly enough D. and AN. do not mention the work ; but PT. 38 has it ; whereas D. 73 and AN. 68 give Θέσεις π. ψυχῆς α'. The *Eudemus* ought also to be reckoned with Aristotle's psychology : see the accounts of it at pp. 55, n. 4, 56, n. 2, *supra*.

[3] To this class belong the following extant treatises, which all relate to the κοινὰ σώματος καὶ ψυχῆς ἔργα (*De An.* iii. 10, 433, 20) :— (1) Π. αἰσθήσεως καὶ αἰσθητῶν. Its proper name probably was Π. αἰσθήσεως only (cf. IDELER, *Ar. Meteor.* i. 650, ii. 358) ; and it is cited by Aristotle in the Π. ζ. μορίων and the Π. ζ.

γενέσεως (BONITZ, *Ind. Ar.* 103, a, 8 sq.), *De Memor.* c. 1, *init.*, *De Somno* 2, 456, a, 2 (*De Motu Anim.* c. 11 *fin.*), and announced as coming in the *Meteor* i. 3, 341, a, 14.—TRENDELENBURG, *De An.* 118 (106) sq. (*contra* ROSE, *Ar. Libr. Ord.*. 219, 226 ; BRANDIS, *Gr.-röm. Phil.* ii. b, 2, 1191, 284 ; BONITZ, *Ind. Ar.* 99, b, 54, 100, b, 30, 40) believes that the Π. αἰσθ. is mutilated, and that it is a separated section of it which is preserved as the ἐκ τοῦ περὶ ἀκουστῶν, *Ar. Opp.* ii. 800 sq. It is certain that some of the references in later writings cannot be satisfactorily verified in our present text. According to the *Gen. An.* v. 2, 781, a, 20, and *Part. An.* ii. 10, 656, a, 27, it was explained ἐν τοῖς περὶ αἰσθήσεως that the canals of the organs of sense started from the heart ; but, on the contrary, in the only applicable passage of the extant treatise (c. 2, 438, b, 25) we are told that the organs of smell and sight are seated near the brain, out of which they are formed, but those of taste and touch in the heart. It is not until the *De Vita et M.* c. 3, 469, a, 10 that he adds that the heart is the seat of perception for the other senses also (only not φανερῶς as for these) ; and here l. 22 sq. refers to the passage of the Π. αἰσθ. just cited (for it is only there, and not in the *Part. An.* ii. 10, as cited *Ind. Ar.* 99, b, 5, that the different positions are assigned to the organs of sense). From these facts it does not follow that a section dealing with this point is omitted in our text, but rather that the words ἐν τοῖς π. αἰσθ. in *Gen. An.* v. 2 and *Part. An.* ii. 10 are to be taken in a wide sense, as including all the anthropological treatises which are introduced by Π. αἰσθ. 1 *init.*, as by a common preface.—The same explanation will account for the statement in *Part. An.* ii. 7, 653, a, 19 that Aristotle would speak ἐν τε τοῖς π. αἰσθήσεως καὶ π. ὕπνου διωρισμένοις of the causes and effects of sleep. The subject is to be found only *De Somno*, 2, 3, 458, a, 13 sq, and no fitting place for its introduction can be found in our Π. αἰσθ. Probably it did not occur in the original text either ; and we are to understand the reference as indicating by Π. αἰσθ. the general, and by Π. ὕπνου the particular description of one and the same treatise (in which view τε should perhaps be dropped).—So finally in *Gen. An.* v. 7, 786, b, 23, 788, a, 34 there are allusions to investigations as to the voice ἐν τοῖς π. ψυχῆς and π. αἰσθήσεως. These are to be referred chiefly to *De An.* ii. 8, and secondarily to c. 1, 437, a, 3 sq., 446, b, 2 sq., and 12 sq., whereas the beginning of c. 4 of the *De An.* itself tells us that it was beyond the plan of that treatise to give any detailed account of voice and tone, such as we find in the extant fragment Π. ἀκουστῶν. The last-named work is never cited by Aristotle, and contains no express references to any of his books. In fact its own broad and sketchy methods of exposition show it to be the work not of the founder, but of a later scholar of the Peripatetic school, probably however of one of its earliest generations. (2) Π. μνήμης καὶ ἀναμνήσεως, PT. 40, is quoted in the *De Motu An.* c. 11, *ad fin.* and by the Commentators. The book of Mnemonics noticed

p. 72, n. 2 *fin. supra*, has nothing to do with it. (3) Π. ὕπνου καὶ ἐγρηγόρσεως cited *De Longit. V., Part. An., Gen. An., Motu An.*, and announced as in contemplation (*Ind. Ar.* 103, a, 16 sq) by *De An.* iii. 9, 432, b, 11, *De Sensu*, c. 1, 436, a, 12 sq. It is frequently connected with (2) (but clearly for external reasons only) as if they were one treatise, Π. μνήμης καὶ ὕπνου (GELL. vi. 6, ALEX. *Top.* 279, Schol 296, b, 1, copied SUID. μνήμη, Alex. *De Sensu*, 125, b, MICHAEL, *in Arist De Mem.* 127, a, *Ptol.* 4). It is, however, clear from Arist. *Divin. in Somn.* c. 2, *fin.*, that it was in fact bracketed with (4) Π. Ἐνυπνίων and (5) Π. τῆς καθ' Ὕπνον μαντικῆς. (4) is also in the *De Somno*, 2, 456, a, 27, announced as in preparation. (6) Π. μακροβιότητος καὶ βραχυβιότητος, cited, not by name, *Part. An* iii. 10, 673, a, 30, and by name ATHEN. viii. 353, a, PT. 46, and perhaps also AN. *App.* 141. (7) Π. ζωῆς καὶ θανάτου : to which (8) Π. ἀναπνοῆς, is in Aristotle's view so closely related that they form one whole (*De Vita et M.* c. 1, *init.* 467, b, 11, *De Respir.* c. 21, 486, b, 21). There was a third tract, Π. νεότητος καὶ γήρως, spoken of by Aristotle (467, b, 6, 10), to which our editors ascribe the first two chapters of the Π. ζωῆς καὶ θανάτου, but clearly without reason, for it seems more probable either that Aristotle never wrote the tract or that it was lost at a very early date (cf. BRANDIS, 1191, BONITZ, *Ind. Ar.* 103, a, 26 sq, HEITZ, p. 58).—Inasmuch as the *De Vita et Morte*, c. 3, 468, b, 31 (cf. *De Respir.* c. 7, 473, a, 27) mentions the Essay on the Parts of Animals as already exist-

ing (cf. ROSE, *Ar. Libr. Ord.*, who wrongly refers to *Hist. An.* iii. 3, 513, a, 21), and as the Essay on Life and Death is spoken of in the *De Longit. V.* c. 6, 467, b, 6 as the conclusion of the inquiries concerning animals, Brandis (1192 sq.) suggests that only the first half of the so-called ' Parva Naturalia' (Nos. 1-5) was composed immediately after the *De Anima* ; and that the rest of these (which in Ptolemy's catalogue stand at No. 46 sq. divided from the books on Sense, Sleep, and Memory by the books on Zoology) were not written until after the works on the Parts, the Movement, and the Generation of Animals, though projected earlier. And it is true that in the *De Generat. Anim.* iv. 10, 777, b, 8, we hear that inquiries into the reason of the varying duration of life are projected, and these are not further dealt with in that work. But on the other hand the *Part. An.* iii. 6, 669. a, 4 refers to *De Respir.* c. 10, 16, and the same iv. 13, 696, b, 1, and 697, a, 22, to *De Respir.* c. 10, 13 ; and *Gen. An.* v. 2, 781, a, 20, as already observed, to *De Vita et Morte*, 3, 469, a, 10, sq. (cf. *Ind. Ar.* 103, a, 23, 34, sq., where the other references are more problematical). If Brandis is right, these references must have been added, as does sometimes happen, to works previously completed. As to the genuineness of the writings already named, it is guaranteed not only by internal evidence, but by the references referred to.—Another projected tract, Π. νόσου καὶ ὑγιείας (*De Sensu* c. 1, 436, a, 17, *Long. Vit.* c. 1, 464, b, 32, *Respir.* c. 21, 480, b, 22, *Part. An.* ii. 7,

gations *On the Parts of Animals,*[1] with the connected essays on the Generation[2] and the Movement of

653, a, 8), was' probably never written (though Heitz, p. 58 and *Fr. Ar.* 169, thinks otherwise). It is unknown to ALEXANDER, *De Sensu,* 94, and therefore it is likely that the *De Sanitate et Morbo* known by the Arabic writers (Hadschi Khalfa *apud* WENRICH, 160) was a forgery. Two books Π. ὄψεως (AN. *App.* 173) and one Π. φωνῆς (*ibid.* 164) could hardly be genuine (cf. p. 86, n. 1).—A book Π. τροφῆς seems to be referred to as existing in the *De Somno,* c. 3, 456, b, 5 (the reference in *Meteor.* iv. 3, 381, b, 13 being too uncertain), and it is spoken of as a project in *De An.* ii. 4 *fin., Gen. An.* v. 4, 784, b, 2, *Part. An.* ii. 3, 650, b, 10, and c. 7, 653, b, 14, and c. 14, 674 a, 20, and iv. 4, 678, a, 19. The reference in *De Motu An.* 10, 703, a, 10 (cf. MICHAEL EPHES. *ad loc.* p. 156, a) is not to a Π. τροφῆς, but to the Π. πνεύματος: for the words τίς μὲν οὖν ἡ σωτηρία τοῦ συμφύτου πνεύματος εἴρηται ἐν ἄλλοις clearly relate to the words τίς ἡ τοῦ ἐμφύτου πνεύματος διαμονή; (Π. πνευ. *init.*). (So BONITZ, *Ind. Ar.* 100, a, 52; but ROSE, *Ar. Libr. Ord.* 167 makes them refer to the Π. ζῷ. κινήσ. itself, and HEITZ, *Fr. Ar.* 168 to the Π. τροφῆς.) The work is named in PT. No. 20, where it is wrongly given three books. It dealt with food and other matters in an aphoristic style; and that it is later than Aristotle is clear from the fact that it recognised the distinction of veins and arteries, which was unknown to him (cf. *Ind. Ar.* 109, b, 22, sq.). In any case it is

Peripatetic ; cf. further *ap.* ROSE, *Ar. Libr. Ord.* 167, sq., and Brandis, p. 1203, who both with Bonitz reject the book.

[1] Π. ζῴων μορίων four books— (in AN. *App.* 157, three books) : cited in the *De Gen. An., Ingr. An., Motu An.* (cf. *Ind. Ar.* 103, a, 55 sq), and the *De Vita et M.* and *De Respir.* (*de q. v.* p. 91, *supra*)—but the *De Somno,* 3, 457, b, 28 might be referred to *De Sensu,* 2, 438, b, 28, though *De Somno,* c. 2, 455, b, 34 may be better paralleled by *Part. An.* iii. 3, 665, a, 10 sq., than by *De Sensu,* 2, 438, b, 25 sq. It is spoken of as projected in *Meteor.* i. 1, 339, a, 7, and *Hist. An.* ii. 17, 507, a, 25. The first book is a kind of introduction to the zoological works, including the treatises on the Soul, and the activities and conditions of life, and it cannot well have been originally meant for this place (cf. SPENGEL, ' On the order of Aristotle's books on Natural Philosophy,' *Abh. d. Münch. Akad.* iv. 159, and the others there cited).

[2] Π. ζῴων γενέσεως, five books (in AN. *App.* 158, three books, PT. No. 44, five books, *ibid.* No. 77, the same work in two books ; the errors are of no significance). It is often referred to by Aristotle, but only in the future (cf. *Ind. Ar.* 103, b, 8 sq.). DIOG. omits it ; but its genuineness is beyond doubt. Book v., however, seems not to belong to it, but to be an appendix to the works on the Parts and Generation of Animals, just as the

Animals,[1] complete his zoological system. Later in date, but earlier in their place in his teaching, were the lost books *On Plants*.[2] Other treatises touching this

' Parva Naturalia ' are to the *De Anima*. For summaries of the contents of the *Part. An.* and the *Generat. Anim.* see MEYER, *Arist. Thierk.* 128 sq., and LEWES, *Ar.* c. 16 sq. The tract *De Coitu* (Hadschi Khalfa, *ap.* Wenrich, p. 159) was spurious: for it cannot be referred, as Wenrich refers it, to the title Π. μίξεως in *De Sensu*, c. 3 (cf. p. 83, n. 1, *supra*). As to the book Π. τοῦ μὴ γεννᾶν, *v.* p. 88, *supra*.

[1] Π. ζῴων πορείας, cited by that name in *Part. An.* iv. 11, 690, b, 15 and 692, a, 17, as the Π. πορείας καὶ κινήσεως τῶν ζῴων in *Part. An.* iv. 13, 696, a, 12, and as Π. τῶν ζῴων κινήσεως in the *De Cœlo*, ii. 2, 284, b, 13, cf. *Ingr. An.* c. 4, 5, c. 2, 704, b, 18; yet it itself cites (c. 5, 706, b, 2) the *Part. An.* iv. 9, 684, a, 14, 34, as an earlier work. According to its concluding words in c. 19 (which, as already suggested at p. 89, n. 2, may be spurious) it is later than the Π. ζῴων μορίων, to which also its introductory words seem to refer back; and yet it is frequently cited in that work, and at its close (*Part. An.* 697, b, 29) there is no hint of an essay on Movement as still to come. Probably it was, in fact, composed while the larger work was in progress.—The tract Π. ζῴων κινήσεως can hardly be authentic; among other reasons, because it cites the Π. πνεύματος (cf. p. 89, n. 3 *fin.*). Rose (*Ar. Libr. Ord.* 163 sq.) and Brandis (ii. b, 1, p. 1271, 482) declare it spurious : Barthélemy St. Hilaire

(*Psych. d'Arist*. 237) accepts it as genuine. Of the Indices, AN. *App.* No. 156, and PT. No. 41, have the Π. ζῴων κινήσεως, and PT. No. 45, Π. ζῴων πορείας.

[2] Π. φυτῶν β' (D. 108, AN. 96, PT. 48). Promised by Aristotle in *Meteor*. i. 1, 339, a, 7, *De Sensu* c. 4, 442, b, 25, *Long. Vitæ*, 6, 467, b, 4, *De Vita* 2, 468, a, 31, *Part. An.* ii. 10, 656, a, 3, *Gen. An.* i. 1, 716, a, 1, v. 3, 783, b, 20, and cited in *H. An.* v. 1, 539, a, 20, *Gen. An.* i. 23, 731, a, 29 (in the last, it is wrong to change the perfect tense into the future in the words of citation). Though both these references must have been inserted after the books were complete, it is possible that Aristotle may have inserted them. ALEX. p. 183, on *De Sensu*, *l.c.*, remarks that a book on Plants by Theophrastus was extant, but none by Aristotle. So MICHAEL EPHES. on *De Vita et M.* 175 b, SIMPLICIUS PHILOP. &c. (*apud* ROSE, *Ar. Ps.* 261, HEITZ, *Fr. Ar.* 163) say the contrary, but we need not suppose they spoke from personal knowledge of the Π. φυτῶν. Quintil. (xii. 11, 22) proves nothing for, and Cic. (*Fin.* v. 4, 10) nothing against, their genuineness. What ATHEN. (xiv. 652 a, 653 d, &c.) cites from them (*Ar. Fr.* 250-4) may as probably be taken from a false as from a genuine book. The two Aristotelian references mentioned make it, however, overwhelmingly probable that Aristotle did write two books on Plants, which were

still extant in the time of Hermippus, though they were afterwards displaced by the more elaborate work of Theophrastus (so HEITZ, *Ar. Fr.* 250, and *Verl. Schrift.* 61, though ROSE, *Ar. Ps.* 261, thinks the books by Theophrastus were ascribed to Aristotle). According to ANTIGONUS (*Mirabil.* c. 169, cf. 129, *ap. Ar. Fr.* 253, *Fr. Hz.* 223) Callimachus as well as Theophrastus seems to have borrowed from these two books. So did the compiler of the Φυτικὰ, as to which POLLUX, x. 170 (*ap. Ar. Fr.* 252, *Fr. Hz.* 224) could not say whether they belonged to Theophrastus or to Aristotle, but which no doubt, like the ζωϊκὰ mentioned at p. 88, *supra*, were compiled by a later disciple for lexicographical purposes. In like manner, Athenæus and other similar collectors also used these books (cf. ROSE and HEITZ, *ibid.*); and they sometimes distinguish between the phrases used by Aristotle and by Theophrastus (*Ar. Fr.* 254, *Fr. Hz.* 225). — The two extant books Π. φυτῶν are emphatically un-Aristotelian. In the older Latin text they have passed already through the hands of two or three translators. Meyer (Pref. to NICOL. DAM. *De Plantis*, ii. ed. 1841) ascribes them in their original form to Nicolaus of Damascus, though possibly they are only an extract from his book, worked over by a later hand. Jessen's suggestion (*Rhein. Mus.* 1859, vol. xiv. 88) that Aristotle's genuine work is contained in the work of Theophrastus is in no way supported by the fact that the latter closely agrees with

what Aristotle elsewhere says, or promises to discuss in his Π. φυτῶν : for we know how constantly the earlier Peripatetics adopted the teaching and the very words of Aristotle. On the other hand, the only passage cited verbally from Aristotle's books (ATHEN. xiv. 652 a, *ap. Ar. Fr.* 250) is not in those of Theophrastus, so far as we have them ; and the latter contain no direct reference to any of the Aristotelian writings—a circumstance which would be incredible in a work so extensive which touched at so many points the earlier Aristotelian treatises. The very passage (*Caus. Pl.* vi. 4, 1) in which Jessen finds one main proof of his theory points to several later modifications of an Aristotelian doctrine which had arisen in the School after his death. Theophrastus, in contrast with Aristotle's view, speaks of male and female plants (cf. *Caus. Pl.* i. 22, 1, *Hist.* iii. 9, 2, &c.). But a decisive argument is to be found in the fact that not only does the text of Theophrastus speak of Alexander and his Indian expedition in a way (*Hist.* iv. 4, 1, 5, 9, *Caus.* viii. 4, 5) which would be hardly possible in Aristotle's lifetime, but it also refers to what happened in the time of King Antigonus (*Hist.* iv. 8, 4) and the Archons Archippus, B.C. 321 or 318 (*Hist.* iv. 14, 11) and Nicodorus, B.C. 314 (*Caus.* i. 19, 5). It would likewise be clear on a full comparison that the diction and manner of statement in the Theophrastic books makes it impossible to attribute them to Aristotle.

field of work, such as the Anthropology,[1] the Physiogno-
mics,[2] the works on Medicine,[3] Agriculture,[4] and Hunt-

[1] Π. Ἀνθρώπου φύσεως, only
named in AN. *App.* 183. There
are a few items which seem to
have belonged to this tract, *apud*
ROSE, *Ar. Ps.* 379, *Ar. Fr.* 257–
264, p. 1525, *Fr. Hz.* 189 sq.

[2] Φυσιογνωμονικὰ (Bekker, 805),
[-κὸν α´ in D. 109, but -κα β´ in
AN. 97]. An extended recension of this work is indicated by
the numerous references to
physiognomic theories not to be
found in our text, which occur in
a treatise on Physiognomy written probably by Apuleius (*apud*
ROSE, *Anecd. Gr.* 61 sq.; cf. *Fr.
Hz.* 191, and ROSE, *Ar. Ps.* 696 sq.).

[3] D. mentions two books of
Ἰατρικά : the ANON. two books Π.
ἰατρικῆς : *ibid.* APP. 167, seven
books Π ἰατρικῆς : PT. 70 five
books of Προβλήματα ἰατρικὰ (from
which it appears that the ἰατρικὰ
in the list of Diog. were also
problems, book i. of our extant
Problems being made up of such
medical questions and answers):
Vita Marc. p. 2 R, Προβλήματα
ἰατρικὰ : PT. 71 Π. διαίτης : *ibid.*
74 b, *De Pulsu* : *ibid.* 92, one
book ἰατρικὸς : Hadschi Khalfa
ap. WENRICH, p. 159, *De San-
guinis Profusione* : COEL. AUREL.
Celer. Pass. ii. 13, one book *De
Adjutoriis* (perhaps a mistake
in the name). Galen in HIPPOCR.
De Nat. Hom. i. 1, vol. xv. 25 K,
knows of an Ἰατρικὴ συναγωγὴ in
several books, bearing Aristotle's
name, which was nevertheless
recognised as being the work of
his pupil, Meno; and this is possibly identical with the Συναγωγὴ
in two books named by Diog. 89
(as WENRICH, p. 158, suggests).

For the little that remains of it,
see ROSE, *Ar. Ps.* 384 sq., *Ar. Fr.*
335–341, p. 1534; *Fr. Hz.* 216,
but on *Fr.* 362 cf. p. 88, *supra.*
The genuineness of these writings, or at least of some of them,
cannot be maintained. That Aristotle held that medical subjects
should be treated in a technical
way, and not from the point of
view of natural science, is evident from his own declaration
which he makes, p. 9, 1 *fin.* (cf.
De Sensu, i. 1, 436, a, 17; *Longit.
V.* 464, b, 32; *De Respir.* c. 21,
fin.; *Part. An.* ii. 7, 653, a, 8),
and such an indefinite statement
as that of Ælian (*V. H.* ix. 22)
cannot prove the contrary. As
to the composition Π. νόσου καὶ
ὑγιείας ʼsee p. 91 *fin.*—Galen (as
Heitz *ibid.* justly remarks) can
have known of no composition of
Aristotle on medical science,
since he never mentions any
such, although he quotes the
philosopher more than six hundred times.

[4] AN. 189 mentions the Γεωργικὰ
amongst the Pseudepigrapha.
PT. 72, on the other hand, gives 15
(or 10) books *De Agricultura* as
genuine, and the statement in
GEOPON. iii. 3, 4 (*Ar. Fr.* 255
sq. p. 1525) on the manuring
of almond-trees seems to have
been taken from this, and not
from the treatise on plants
Rose (*Ar. Ps.* 268 sq.; *Hz. Fr.*
165 sq.) mentions other things
which may perhaps have come
from this source. That Aristotle
did not write about agriculture
or similar subjects is clear
from *Polit.* i. 11, 1258, a, 33, 39.

ing,[1] are,without exception, spurious. The *Problems* [2]
are no doubt based on Aristotelian materials; [3] but our
extant collection under that name can only be described
as a set of gradually gathered and unequally developed
productions of the Peripatetic school, which must
have existed in many other forms parallel to our own.[4]

[1] In the Index of Ptolemy, No. 23, Hadschi Khalfa gives (Π. τῶν φωλευόντων): *De Animalium Captura, nec non de Locis, quibus deversantur atque delitescunt,* i.

[2] With regard to this treatise see the exhaustive article by Prantl 'Ueb. d. Probl. d. Arist.' among the *Abh. d. Münch. Akad.* vi. 341–377; ROSE, *Arist. Libr. Ord.* 199 sqq.; *Ar. Ps.* 215 sqq.; HEITZ, *Verl. Schr.* 103 sqq., *Fr. Ar.* 194 sqq.

[3] Aristotle refers in seven places to the Προβλήματα or Προβληματικὰ (PRANTL, *ibid.* 364 sq.; *Ind. Ar.* 103, b, 17 sqq.), but only one of these quotations suits to a certain extent the extant 'Problems; ' and the same is true (PR. *ibid.* 367 sqq.) of the majority of the later references.

[4] PRANTL, *ibid.* has abundantly proved this, and he has also shown (*Münch. Gel. Anz.* 1858, No. 25) that among the 262 further problems which are given by Bussemaker in vol. iv. of the Didot edition of Aristotle, and some of which were at one time erroneously ascribed to Alexander of Aphrodisias (cf. USENER, *Alex. Aphr. Probl.,* Lib. iii., iv., Berl. 1859, p. ix. sqq.), there is probably nothing written by Aristotle. The same is true of those which Rose (*Ar. Ps.* 666 sqq.) takes from a Latin MS.

of the 10th century. The character ascribed in the text to the collection of ' Problems ' may also explain the many varying statements as to its title and the number of books it included. In the MSS. they are sometimes called Προβλήματα, sometimes Φυσικὰ προβλήματα, and sometimes with the addition κατ' εἶδος συναγωγῆς ('arranged in accordance with the matter'). Gellius generally says, *Problemata* (xix. 4), *Prob. physica* (xx. 4, quoting *Probl.* xxx. 10): Προβλήματα ἐγκύκλια ; Apul. (*De Magia,* c. 51) has *Problemata* ; Athenæus and Apollonius (*vid.* Indices and Prantl, 390 sq.) always Προβλήματα φυσικά; Macrob. (*Sat.* vii. 12) *Physicæ quæstiones.* To collections of problems are also referable the titles : Φυσικῶν λη' κατὰ στοιχεῖον (D. 120, AN. 110 ; as to the words κ. στοιχ., the explanation of which in Rose, *Ar. Ps.* 215, is not clear, they are to be understood of the arrangement of the different books in the alphabetical order of their headings); Προβλήματα (68 or 28 B, PT. 65); Ἐπιτεθεαμένων προβλημάτων β' (D. 121, AN. 112); Ἐγκυκλίων β' (D. 122, AN. 113, Προβλήματα ἐγκύκλ. 4 bks., PT. 67); *Physica Problemata, Adspectiva Probl.* (AMMON. LATIN. p. 58); Ἄτακτα ιβ' (D. 127, [ἀ]διατάκτων ιβ' AN. 119). *Præ-*

Turning to Ethics and Politics, we have on the former subject three comprehensive works,[1] of which,

missa Quæstionibus (PT. 66, says the Greek title is '*brbimatu bruagrawa*,' *i.e.* Προβλημάτων προγραφὴ, or Προαναγραφή); Συμμίκτων ζητημάτων οβ' (AN. 66 with the additional clause: ὥς φησιν Εὔκαιρος ὁ ἀκουστὴς αὐτοῦ); David (*Schol. in Ar.* 24, b, 8) also speaks of 70 books Π. συμμίκτων ζητημάτων, and the *Vita Marc.* p. 2, R of Φυσικὰ προβλήματα in 70 books; Ἐξηγημένα (or Ἐξητασμένα) κατὰ γένος ιδ' (D. 128, AN. 121). With regard to the Προβλήματα μηχανικὰ, ὀπτικὰ, ἰατρικὰ, cf. p. 86, n. 1, and 95, n. 3. The spurious composition Π. προβλημάτων, to which besides D. 51 (and also AN. 48, although the περὶ is here wanting) Alex. *Top.* 34, *Schol. in Ar.* 258, a, 16, also refers, seems to have contained a theory as to setting and answering problems. See ROSE, *Ar. Ps.* 126, *Fragm.* 109, p. 1496, *Fr. Hz.* 115. On the other hand, book xxx. of our Problems cannot well be meant (as Heitz, 122, believes) by the ἐγκύκλια, *Eth. N.* 1, 3, 1096, a, 3. Aristotle seems rather to indicate what he calls in other places ἐξωτερικοὶ λόγοι, and *De Cælo*, i. 9, 279, a, 30 Τὰ ἐγκύκλια φιλοσοφήματα. Cf. BERNAYS, *Dial. of Arist.* 85, 93 sqq. 171; BONITZ, *Ind. Ar.* 105, a, 27 sqq. More on this *infra.*

[1] Ἠθικὰ Νικομάχεια 10 B., Ἠθικὰ Εὐδήμια 7 B., Ἠθικὰ μεγάλα 2 B. Of our catalogues D. 38 only names Ἠθικῶν ε' *al.* δ'; (although DIOG. elsewhere (*Vita*, 21) cites the seventh book of the Ethics in connection with *Eth. Eud.* vii. 12, 1245, b, 20); AN. 39 has Ἠθικῶν κ (*e.g.* the *Eth. Nic.*, the last book of which is κ),

and then again in the Appendix 174: Π. ἠθῶν (-ικῶν) Νικομαχείων ὑποθήκας (which seems to be an extract from the same work); PT. 30 sq. the Great Ethics in two books, the Eudemian Ethics in eight. Aristotle himself quotes (*Metaph.* i. 1, 981, b, 25, and in six passages of the *Politics*) the ἠθικά, meaning doubtless the Nicomachean Ethics (cf. BENDIXEN in *Philologus* x. 203, 290 sq.; *Ind. Ar.* 103, b. 46 sqq., and 101, b, 19 sqq.). Cic. (*Fin.* v. 5, 12) believes that the *Libri de Moribus* of Nicomachus are ascribed to Aristotle, inasmuch as the son would write very much like his father. Diogenes also (viii. 88) quotes *Eth. N.* x. 2 with the words: φησὶ δὲ Νικόμαχος ὁ Ἀριστοτέλους. On the other hand Atticus (*apud* EUS. *Pr. Ev.* xv. 4, 6) gives all three Ethics with their present names as Aristotelian; likewise Simpl. *in Cat.* 1, ζ, 43, ε and Schol. Porphyr. *Schol. in Ar.* 9, b, 22, who says the Eudemian Ethics were addressed to Eudemus, the Μεγάλα Νικομάχια (*M. Mor.*) to Nicomachus the father, and the Μικρὰ Νικομάχια (*Eth. N.*) to Nicomachus, the son of Aristotle. The same story is told by DAVID, *Schol. in Ar.* 25, a, 40. EUSTRAT. (*in Eth. N.* 141, a; cf. Arist. *Eth. Eud.* vii. 4 *init.* c. 10, 1242, b, 2) speaks of the Eudemian Ethics as the work of Eudemus, that is to say, he repeats this statement after one of the earlier writers whom he used (cf. p. 72, b), and who was, it would seem, not altogether unlearned: on the other hand, on his own supposition, or

however, only one—the *Nicomachean Ethics*—is of
directly Aristotelian authorship.[1]　A mass of smaller

following an equally worthless
authority (1, b, m), he represents
Eth. N. as dedicated to a certain
Nicomachus, and *Eth. Eud.* to a
certain Eudemus. A Scholion also
which is attributed to ASPASIUS
(*vid.* Spengel ' On the Ethical Writings
under the name of Aristotle,'
in the *Abh. d. Münch. Akad.* iii.
439–551, p. 520, cf. ' Schol. in Ar.
Eth.' *Class. Journal*, vol. xxix.
117) must suppose Eudemus to
be the author of the Eudemian
Ethics, since on this supposition
alone can he attribute the treatise
on Pleasure to him, *Eth. N.*
vii. 12 sqq. The Commentaries
known to us (by Aspasius, Alexander,
Porphyry, Eustratius) are
concerned only with the Nicomachean
Ethics. For further
materials, cf. SPENGEL, *ibid.* 445
sqq.
[1] Schleiermacher (' On the
Ethical Works of Aristotle,' for
1817, *W. W. Z. Philos.* iii. 306
sqq.) gave it as his opinion that,
of the three ethical works, the
so-called Great Ethics is the
oldest, and the Nicomachean
Ethics the latest, but the treatise
of Spengel already cited makes
the opposite view clear, viz. that
the genuine work of Aristotle
is the Nicomachean Ethics, that
the Eudemian Ethics is a supplementary
work by Eudemus, and
that the Great Ethics is an extract
taken directly from the Eudemian.
But the position of
the three books which are
common to the Nicomachean and
Eudemian Ethics (*Nic.* v.–vii.,
Eud. iv.–vi.) is still a moot
point. Spengel (480 sqq.) believes
that they belong originally
to the Nicomachean Eth., but
that, after the corresponding sections
of the Eudemian Eth. were
lost at an early period, they were
employed to fill up the blanks in
the Eudemian Eth.; he is inclined
to look upon the treatise
on pleasure, *Nic.* vii. 12 sqq.,
which Aspasius also attributes to
Eudemus (see preceding note,
fin.), as a fragment of the Eudemian
Ethics (p. 518 sqq.), but
without wishing to exclude the
possibility of its being a sketch
intended by Aristotle for the
Nicomachean Eth., and later on
replaced by x.1 sqq. In his *Arist.
Stud.* i. 20 (against which Walter
argues in *Die Lehre v. d. prakt.
Vernunft*, 88 sqq.) *Nic.* vi. 13 is
also attributed to Eudemus.　On
the other hand Fischer (*De Ethicis
Eudem. et Nicom.* Bonn, 1847),
and with him also Fritzsche
(*Arist. Eth. Eud.* 1851, Prolegg.
xxxiv.) refer only *Nic.* v. 1–14 to
the Nicomachean, and *Nic.* v. 15,
vi., vii., to the Eudemian Ethics.
Grant (*Ethics of Aristot.* i. 49
sqq.) refers the whole of these
three books to the Eudemian;
whilst Bendixen (*Philologus*, x.199
sqq., 263 sqq.) on the contrary, for
reasons worthy of note, defends
the Aristotelian origin of the
whole, including vii. 12–15.
Brandis (*Gr.-röm. Phil.*ii. b, 1555
sq.), Prantl (*D. dianoët. Tugenden
d. Ar.* Münch. 1852, p. 5 sqq.),
and in the main also Ueberweg
(*Gesch. d. Phil.* i. 177 sq. 5th ed.),
and Rassow (*Forsch. üb. d. nikom.
Ethik*, 26 sqq. cf. 15 sqq.) agree
with the conclusions of Spengel;
the last-named with this modification,
which has much to
support it, that *Nic.* v.–vii.,
though essentially Aristotelian,

tracts is also named,[1] but probably few of them were
genuine. Of the sociological writings only one—the

has been submitted to the after-
work of another pen, and has
perhaps, in consequence of a
mutilation, been supplied from
the Eudemian Ethics.

[1] Such are (besides the Dialogues mentioned on p. 56, n. 1,
59 sq., Π. δικαιοσύνης, 'Ερωτικὸs,
Π. πλούτου, Π. εὐγενείαs and Π.
ἡδονῆs), the following : the small
composition, still extant, Π.
ἀρετῶν καὶ κακιῶν (*Arist. Opp.*
1249-1251), which is the work of
a half-Academic, half-Peripatetic
Eclectic, hardly earlier than the
first century before Christ ; Προτάσεις π. ἀρετῆs (D. 34, AN. 342) ;
Π. ἀρετῆs (AN. *App.* 163); Π. δικαίων
β' (D. 76, AN. 64—PT. 11, 4 B.) ;
Π. τοῦ βελτίονοs α' (D. 53, AN.
50) ; Π. ἐκουσίου (-ίων) α' (D. 68,
AN. 58) ; Π. τοῦ αἱρετοῦ καὶ τοῦ
συμβεβηκότος α' (D. 58 ; Π. αἱρετοῦ
καὶ συμβαίνοντος, AN. 56). It is
not probable that Aristotle composed a treatise Π. ἐπιθυμίαs :
In the beginning of the *De Sensu*,
he proposes future researches into
the faculty of desire, but we do
not hear that they were carried
out ; what we find in Seneca (*De
Ira*, i. 3. 9, 2, 17, 1, iii. 3, 1) may
more probably have been contained in the writing Π. παθῶν
(or -ουs) ὀργῆs (D. 37, AN. 30),
the supposed remnants of which
Rose (*Ar. Ps.* 109 sqq., *Ar. Fr.*
94-97, No. 1492) and Heitz
(*Fr.* 151 sq.) have put together.
Whether it was a dialogue (Rose)
or a treatise (Heitz) cannot with
certainty be determined ; the
latter seems the more probable
opinion. Its genuineness is, to
say the least, undemonstrable,

and the title does not sound
Aristotelian. D. 61, AN. 60 have
also Πάθη α'. Further (besides
the 'Ερωτικὸs mentioned on p. 59),
'Ερωτικὰ (AN. *App.* 181 ; PT. 13, 3
B.) and 4 B. of Θέσεις ἐρωτικαὶ
(D. 71, AN. 66 ; PT. 56, 1 B.) are
mentioned, both of them doubtless equally spurious. AN. 162
reckons Π. σωφροσύνης among the
Pseudepigrapha. Π. φιλίας α'
(D. 24, AN. 24, PT. 25) is supposed not to be a copy from *Eth.
N.* viii. ix., but a special treatise,
which can hardly be genuine.
Still less can Aristotle have
been the author of Θέσεις φιλικαὶ
β' (D. 72, AN. 67). Of the
two writings Π. συμβιώσεως ἀνδρὸs
καὶ γυναικὸs (AN. *App.* 165)
and Νόμους (-οι) ἀνδρὸs καὶ γαμε-
τῆs (*ibid.* 166), the former is mentioned by other writers several
times (*e.g.* by Clemens, Olympio-
dor., and David in the passages
given by ROSE, *Ar. Ps.* 180 sq.,
Ar. Fr. 178 sq., p. 1507). Rose (*De
Ar. Libr. Ord.* 60 sqq.) has pointed
out two Latin translations of these
Νόμοι (or the writing Π. συμβιώσ.,
if both are not merely different
titles of the same book) which
profess to be the second book
of the *Economics* : see *Ar. Pseud.*
644 sqq. ; *Fr. Hz.* 153 sqq. PLU-
TARCH, ATHENÆUS, and others
quote from a writing Π. μέθης,
perhaps a dialogue ; cf. ROSE,
Ar. Ps. 116 sqq., *Ar. Fr.* 98-106,
p. 1493 sq.; *Fr. Hz.* 64 sq. It was
certainly not genuine ; it may
have been identical with the
writing of the same name by
Theophrastus (HEITZ, *ibid.*), only
in that case Athenæus, who,

eight books of the *Politics* [1]—is preserved; but though it contains some of his most mature and admirable work it is unhappily left, like the *Metaphysics*, unfinished.[2] The *Œconomics* cannot be considered genuine.[3] Of all the rest we have lost everything

in addition to these two, quotes a third by Chamæleon, must have been indebted for his quotations to various writers, to whom it was known by different names —a not very probable supposition. What is quoted from it is concerned, partly with historical, partly with physiological discussions; whether drunkenness was regarded also from a moral point of view we do not know. Nor do we know any more as to the contents of the Νόμοι συσσιτικοὶ (in the MSS., of D. 139, Νόμος συστατικὸς, of AN. 130 Νόμων συστατικῶν α΄, for the circumstance of the Platonic republic being mentioned in it (PROCL. *in Remp.* 350, *Ar. Fr.* 177, p. 1507) gives us no indication; hence we cannot determine whether Rose (*Ar. Ps.* 179) is right in supposing that there was a discussion in it on the arrangement of, and good behaviour at symposia, or Heitz (*Ar. Fr.* 307), in believing that it contained a collection of the customs relating to them. Π. συσσιτίων ἢ συμποσίων (AN. *App.* 161) is identical with it; not so, however, the three books Συσσιτικῶν προβλημάτων (AN. 136), the title of which makes us think not so much of questions with regard to meals, as of questions such as are proposed at a meal, like Plutarch's Συμποσιακὰ προβλήματα. For the Παραγγέλματα cf. p. 72, n. 2 *fin.*

[1] Aristotle puts this work in the closest connection with the Ethics, by treating the latter as auxiliary to politics (*Eth. N.* i. 1, 1094 a, 26 sqq., 1095, a, 2, c. 2 *init.* c. 13, 1102, a, 5, vii. 12 *init.*; *Rhet.* i. 2, 1356, a, 26). He expects from politics the realisation of the principles laid down by Ethics (*ibid.* x. 10). But he does not mean both to be merely two parts of one composition (cf. *Polit.* vii. 1, 1323, b, 39, c. 13, 1332, a, 7, 21, ii. 1, 1261, a, 30, iii. 9, 1280, a, 18. c. 12, 1282, b, 19). Even apart from the citation *Rhet.* i. 8 *fin.*, and the mention of it in the catalogue (D. 75, AN. 70), its genuineness cannot be doubted, however seldom it is named by ancient writers (see the remarks of SPENGEL, 'Ueb. d. Politik d. Arist.,' *Abh. d. Münchn. Akad.* v. 44 *infra*).

[2] For further information, see the section on the political philosophy of Aristotle, ch. xiii., *infra*.

[3] Of the second book (as to the beginning of which see ROSE, *Arist. Libr. Ord.* 59 sq.) this has long been admitted, but Göttling (*Arist. Œcon.* p. vii. xvii.) considers the first to be a section of a genuine Aristotelian writing; it seems more probable that it is the work of a later writer based on *Polit.* i. (See end of ch. xxi., *infra.*) D. 23, AN. 17 name Οἰκονομικὸς (or -ον) α΄. Cf. p. 99 *supra* on another pretended second book.

except a few fragments.[1] Among them the loss of

[1] The political writings named, besides those quoted, are the following: (1) Πολιτεῖαι, a collection of facts with regard to 158 states (D. 145, AN. 135, the text of which BERNAYS, *Rh. Mus.* vii. 289, with the approval of ROSE, *Ar. Ps.* 394, has evidently improved), which, according to the fragments and the statements of CIC. *Fin.* v. 4, 11, and PLUT. *N. P. Su. V.* 10, 4 (who names the work κτίσεις καὶ πολιτεῖαι) not only treated of the constitution, but also of the usages, customs, situation of the towns, the history of their foundation, their local traditions, &c. PT. 81 gives the number of cities as 171 (or 191, according to the view of HERBELOT, *Bibl. Or.* 971, a): AMMON. *V. Ar.* 48 gives 255: *Ammon. Lat.* p. 56, Ps.-Porphyr. *Schol. in Ar.* 9, b, 26, and David, *ibid.* 24, a, 34, say 250, and Philop. *ibid.* 35, b, 19, about 250, but the increase does not seem to be founded on any later extension of the collection, but merely on clerical mistakes (cf. ROSE, *Ar. Ps.* 394). Simpl. (*Categ.* 2, γ. *Schol.* 27, a, 43) seems by the words ἐν ταῖς γνησίαις αὐτοῦ πολιτείαις to point to the existence of spurious Polities; ρνη' (158) instead of γνησίαις may be the true reading (HEITZ, *Ar. Fr.* 219), though IDELER, *Ar. Meteor.* i., xii. 40 can hardly be right in substituting ἐπιστολαῖς for πολιτείαις). The numerous fragments of the large collection are found in MÜLLER, *Fragm. Hist.* ii. 102 sqq. (cf. BOURNOT, in *Philolog.* iv. 266 sqq.); ROSE, *Ar. Ps.* 402 sqq.; *Ar. Fr.* 343–560, p. 1535 sqq.; *Fr. Hz.* 218 sqq. The genuineness of the work, which ROSE (*Ar. Libr. Ord.* 56 sq., *Ar. Ps.* 395 sq.) disputes, has no weighty arguments against it (as HEITZ, p. 246 sqq. shows); and even if the external evidence, of which that of TIMÆUS (*apud* POLYB. xii. 5, 11) is the oldest producible, did not utterly exclude Rose's supposition that the work was published and circulated in his name soon after Aristotle's death, nevertheless the internal improbability of that theory would be much strengthened by it. The declarations of DAVID, *ibid.*, and the Schol. to Porphyry's *Isagoge* (*vid.* ROSE, *Ar. Ps.* 399, *Ar. Fr.* 1535) favour the supposition that the different states in the Polities are taken in alphabetical order; and this explains why the Athenians (according to *Fr.* 378, where, however, the reading is uncertain) are treated in the 1st book, and the Ithacans in the 42nd (*Fr.* 466). The circumstance that the numerous fragments all contain merely isolated notes, without reference to a uniform complete treatise, will not (as ROSE, *Ar. Ps.* 395 holds) serve as a proof of the spuriousness of the work; but, in conjunction with the fact that the Aristotelian writings nowhere refer to the work in question (for even *Eth. N.* x. 10, 1181, b, 17, refers to the Politics; cf. HEITZ, 231 sq.), it supports the view (HEITZ, 233 sq.) that the Polities was not a literary completed whole, but a collection by Aristotle, for his own use, of facts which he had gathered partly by personal observation and inquiries, and partly from

Aristotle's collection of forms of government in various cities, is simply irreparable.[1]

Our *Poetics* [2] is only a fragment; but not even so

writings. If this be so, copies would only be circulated after his death. A chapter out of the Πολιτεία Ἀθηναίων may have given rise to the title Π. τῶν Σόλωνος ἀξόνων (AN. *App.* 140 : cf. MÜLLER, *ibid.*, 109, 12).—A similar collection was (2) the Νόμιμα βαρβαρικὰ, which are quoted under this title by APPOLLON. *Mirabil.* 11 ; VARRO, i. 1, vii. 70 ; AN. *App.* 186 (νομίμων βαρβ. συναγωγὴ); from this title also the designations Νόμοι α' β' γ' δ' (D. 140), νομίμων δ' (AN. 131), seem to have been wrongly transcribed. To them the νόμιμα 'Ρωμαίων (AN. *App.* 185) and the νόμιμα Τυρρηνῶν (ATHEN. i. 23, d) probably belonged. Among the few fragments (*apud* MÜLLER, *ibid.* 178 sqq., ROSE, *Ar. Ps.* 537 sqq., *Ar. Fr.* 561-568, p. 1570, *Fr. Hz.* 297 sq.), Nos. 562, 563 and 564 can only be attributed to Aristotle under the supposition that he did not give their contents in his own name, but as traditions somewhere current. — (3) The Δικαιώματα τῶν πόλεων (AMMON. *Differ. Vocab.*, Νῆες) or Δικ. Ἑλληνίδων πόλεων (*V. Marc.* p. 2, R) seem to have dealt with quarrels between the Hellenic states and their settlement; they are also named more briefly Δικαιώματα (D. 129, AN. 120, HARPOCRAT. Δρυμός).—(4) The Θέσεις πολιτικαί β' (AN. 69 ; the same is the right reading in D. 74) were in any case spurious. The ANON. 5 applies the name Π. πολιτικῆς to the Gryllos, but that must be a mistake (see above, p. 59). — On the

Πολιτικὸς cf. p. 57; on Π. βασιλείας and Ὑπὲρ ἀποίκων, p. 60, *sub fin.* ; on Π. ῥήτορος ἢ πολιτικοῦ, p. 72, n. 2, towards the end ; on Π. ἀρχῆς, p. 81, n. 1, *fin.*; on a bungling forgery of the Middle Ages, *Secretum secretorum* (or, *Aristotelis ad Alexandrum regem de moribus rege dignis*), cf. GEIER, *Arist. und Alex.* 234 sq; ROSE, *Arist. Libr. Ord.* 183 sq, *Ar. Ps.* 583 sq.

[1] Since this was written the Athenian Πολιτεία has been recovered.

[2] This writing, in our editions, is entitled : Π. ποιητικῆς. Aristot. himself mentions it in the *Politics* (viii. 7, 1341, b, 38), as a future work ; in the *Rhetoric* (i. 11 *fin.*, iii. 1, 1404, a, 38, c. 2, 1404, b, 7, 28, 1405, a, 5, c. 18, 1419, b, 5, with which cf. p. 74, n. 1), as already existing, with these words : ἐν τοῖς περὶ ποιητικῆς, or (1404, b, 28) ἐν τ. π. ποιήσεως. The Indices name: Πραγματείας τέχνης ποιητικῆς β' (D. 83), τέχνης ποιητ. β' (AN. 75), *De arte poëtica secundum disciplinam Pythagoræ*, PT. *Fr.* (this addition is caused by the combination of two different titles : cf. ROSE, *Ar. Ps.* 194). PS.-ALEX. *Soph. El.* Schol. in Ar. 299, b, 44, has ἐν τῷ π. ποιητ.; likewise HERM. *in Phædr.* 111, and AST, ἐν τῷ π. π.; SIMPL. *Cat. Schol.* 43, a, 13, 27 : ἐν τῷ π. π. ; DAVID, *ibid.* 25, b, 19, τὸ π. π.; on the other hand AMMON. *De interpr.* Schol. 99, a, 12, ἐν τοῖς π. ποι.; BOETH. *De interpr.* 290, *in libris quos de arte poëtica scripsit.* The more ancient authorities are acquainted with two

much as this remains of Aristotle's other contributions to the theory and history of Art or of his dissertations on the poets.[1] Nor is there much left of the other

books on Poetry (a third is mentioned only in the quotations given on p. 58, n. 1, with regard to the writing Π. ποιητῶν), the more modern only with one; except in so far as they copy more ancient writers, as we must suppose was the case with Ammonius and Boëthius. From this alone we might suppose that the writing in question originally had a greater extension than it now has, but this becomes certain from the references to such parts of it as are missing in our recension, as for instance the discussion on the Catharsis promised in *Polit.* viii. 7, 1341, b, 38, which would naturally have come in the section on Tragedy, and, as we learn from sure traces, actually did occur there (cf. BERNAYS, 'Grundz. d. Abh. d. Arist. üb. d. Wirkung d. Trag.' *Abh. d. hist.-phil. Ges. in Breslau*, 160 sqq., 197 sq.; SUSEMIHL, p. 12; VAHLEN, p. 81 sq. of his edition, and others); the examination of Comedy, promised *Poet.* c. 6 *init.*, and quoted *Rhet.* i. 11 *fin.*, of which Bernays (*Rh. Mus.* viii. 561 sqq.) has pointed out valuable remnants in Cramer's *Anecd. Paris.*, vol. i. app. (now in Susemihl, p. 208 sq., Vahlen, 76 sq.); and the discussion on Synonyms, which Simpl. mentions, *Categ.* Schol. 43, a, 13, 27. In other places also our text shows many greater or smaller gaps, as also interpolations (as c. 12 and many smaller ones), and inversions (the most considerable that of chap. 15, which ought to

come after chap. 18), which sufficiently prove that we only possess Aristotle's work in a mutilated and hopelessly corrupt condition. We cannot here inquire how its present condition may be explained (SUSEMIHL, *ibid.*, p. 3 sq., gives an enumeration of the different, and in part widely diverging attempts at explanation). It may be true, as SUSEMIHL concludes, that the carelessness of the writing, the caprice of the copyists, and the freaks of accident account for most of the mischief; but we cannot make these factors responsible for the interpolations, except in so far as they may have rendered possible the introduction of some marginal notes into the text.

[1] Of the Dialogue Π. ποιητῶν γ′ we have already spoken on p. 58. Besides this AN. 115 gives Κύκλον π. ποιητῶν, likewise in three books. This title may have arisen, by duplication and corruption, from that of the Dialogue, or it may (according to HEITZ; 178) designate a work distinct from it: but the 'κύκλον' may also have sprung from the 'ἐγκύκλιον' (or -ίων) which is found in No. 113.—Allied to it, it would seem, are Π. τραγῳδιῶν α′ (D. 136, AN. 128) and Κωμικοὶ (EROTIAN, *Exp. Voc. Hippocr.* s. v. 'Ηρακλ. νόσον). Müller (*Hist. Gr.* ii. 82), though not rightly, takes the Διδασκαλίαι (D. 137; AN. 129; ROSE, *Ar. Ps.* 550 sq., *Ar. Fr.* 575–587, p. 1572 sq.; HEITZ, 255, *Fr. Hz.* 302 sq.), —seemingly a chronological cata-

books named to us, which dealt with subjects outside
the main lines of the Aristotelian system ; [1] and among

logue based on the existing in-
scriptions of the tragedies performed in Athens—as a part of
the book on tragedies. — Further, a series of writings relating
to poets is named, which took
the form of problems: 'Απορημάτων ποιητικῶν α' (AN. *App.* 145) ;
Αἰτίαι ποιητικαί (*ibid.*
146, where
αἰτίαι seems to indicate the form
of treatment which is proper to
the ἀπορήματα or προβλήματα, viz.
that the διὰ τί is sought, and the
reply consists in giving the διότι
or the αἰτία); 'Απορημάτων 'Ομη-
ρικῶν ζ' (D. 118 ; AN. 106 ζ';
HEITZ, 258 sq., *Fr. Hz.* 129;
ROSE, *Ar. Ps.* 148 sq., *Ar. Fr.*
137–175, p. 1501 sq.) or, as the
Vita Marc. p. 2. names it, 'Ομ.
ζητήματα ; Προβλημάτων 'Ομηρι-
κῶν ι' (AN. *App.* 147; PTOL.
91 ; AMMON. *V. Ar.* 44; AMM.
LAT. 54, probably a duplication
of the ἀπορήματα); 'Απορήματα
'Ησιόδου α' (AN. *App.* 143);
'Απορ. 'Αρχιλόχου, Εὐριπίδους,
Χοιρίλου γ' (*ibid.* 144). To these
the 'Απορήματα θεῖα (AN. 107)
seem also to belong. The treatise: Εἰ δέ ποτε "Ομηρος ἐποίησεν
τὰς 'Ηλίου βοῦς ; (AN. *App.* 142),
is no doubt only one of the Homeric problems.—Of these writings
the ones which are more likely
to have an Aristotelian origin
are the Queries on Homer; but
even these may have had later
additions made to them. On the
other hand the genuineness of
the Πέπλος (AN. 105; AN. *App.*
169 ; ROSE, *Ar. Ps.* 563 sqq., *Ar.
Fr.* 594–600, p. 1574 sq.; *Fr.
Hz.* 309 sqq.; cf. BERGK, *Lyr.
Gr.* 505 sqq.; MÜLLER, *Fragm.*

Hist. ii. 188 sqq.) cannot be
maintained. More ancient seems
to be the book Π. μουσικῆς, which
both DIOG. (116, 132) and AN.
(104, 124) give us in two places,
and which is identical with the
musical problems noticed by
LABBEUS, *Bibl. nova*, 116 (see
BRANDIS, ii. b, 94) ; but it is no
more genuine than the Π.
καλοῦ (D. 69, AN. 63, Π. κάλ-
λους).

[1] To these belong certain minor,
mostly historical works, 'Ολυμπιο-
νῖκαι α' (D. 130, AN. 122); Πυ-
θιονικῶν ἔλεγχοι α' (D. 134 and
probably also AN. 125); Πυθιονῖκαι
α' (D. 131, AN. 123, with the
strange title, Πυθιονίκας βιβλίον
ἐν ᾧ Μέναιχμον ἐνίκησεν) ; Πυθικὸς
α' (D. 133), possibly only a different title for the same writing ;
Νῖκαι Διονυσιακαὶ α' (D. 135, AN.
126, Νικῶν Διον. ἀστικῶν καὶ λη-
ναίων α'). About these writings
cf. ROSE, *Ar. Ps.* 545 sqq., *Ar.
Fr.* 572–574, p. 187; HEITZ, 254
sq., *Fr. Hz.* 300 sq.; MÜLLER,
Hist. Gr. ii. 182 sq.—Further
Π. εὑρημάτων (CLEMENS, *Strom.*
i. 308, A, where, however, an Aristotelian work with this title
which could not be genuine
seems to be designated: notes
which may have come from the
work are given by MÜLLER, *ibid.*
181 sq.).—Π. θαυμασίων ἀκουσμάτων
quoted by ATHEN. (xii. 541; cf.
Θαυμ. ἀκ. c. 96) and, with the title
ἐν θαυμασίοις, perhaps also by AN-
TIGON. *Mirabil.* c. 25 (cf. Θαυμ.
ἀκουσμ. c. 30), a 'collection of
strange phenomena,' the genuineness of which cannot be admitted.
For further information on this

these also there is no doubt that many spurious titles have crept in.

B.—*General Questions touching the Aristotelian Writings.*

ON a general survey of the works which are preserved or known to us as Aristotelian, it is evident that they— apart from the letters and poems—were of two different kinds. The component parts of our *Corpus Aristotelicum* are without exception didactic treatises in scientific form.[1] And almost all of these which can be called genuine are, as will be seen, connected together by express references in a way that is only to be explained by the theory that they were addressed to one circle of readers as the connected and mutually explanatory parts of one whole. It is quite different in the case of the writings which were afterwards styled 'hypomnematic'—notes, that is to say, made by

work see WESTERMANN, Παρα-δοξόγραφοι, p. xxv. sqq., and especially ROSE, *Ar. Libr. Ord.* 54 sq., *Ar. Pseud.* 279 sq., who refers the main body of the work, consisting of chaps. 1–114, 130–137, 115–129, 138–181, to the middle of the third century. An enlarged treatment of this, or a more extensive specimen of the same sort of work, is perhaps the Παράδοξα, from the second book of which Plut. (*Parall. Gr. et Rom.* c. 29, p. 312) quotes something which is not found in our Θαυμ. ἀκ.—Παροιμίαι α′ (D. 138; cf. AN. 127), a collection of proverbs, the existence of which seems to be proved, *inter alia*, by ATHEN. ii. 60 d, although Heitz (*Verl.* *Schr.* 163 sq.; *Fragm.* 219) is doubtful whether there was an Aristotelian work on this subject. We cannot prove whether the references in Eustath. *in Od.* N 408 and SYNES. *Enc. Calvit.* c. 22 (*Ar. Fr.* No. 454, No. 2) belong to this or to other works. In addition to these there are two titles which are so indefinite that they furnish no safe clue to the contents of the writings to which they correspond: Παραβολαί(D.126); Ἄτακτα (to which προβλήματα or ὑπομνήματα may be supplied) ιβ′ (D. 127; cf. p. 96, foot).

[1] The 'wonderful stories' are perhaps the only exceptions, but they are not Aristotelian.

Aristotle merely for his own use, and therefore not thrown by him into any such literary form and unity as the works designed for publication.[1] None of the extant works which are genuine is of this class,[2] but several of those which are lost seem to have belonged to it.[3] From these two classes of works, however, there is to be distinguished a third. Cicero, Quintilian, and Dionysius of Halicarnassus praise Aristotle not only for scientific greatness, but equally for the grace and richness of his exposition—'the golden stream of his speech.'[4] This must have referred to works designed

---

[1] Simpl. (*in Categ.* Schol. in Ar. 24, a, 42): ὑπομνηματικὰ ὅσα πρὸς ὑπόμνησιν οἰκείαν καὶ πλείονα βάσανον συνέταξεν ὁ φιλόσοφος : these writings cannot, however, be taken as πάντη σπουδῆς ἄξια, and hence we may not draw from them any proofs for the Aristotelian doctrine: ὁ μέντοι Ἀλέξανδρος τὰ ὑπομνηματικὰ συμπεφυρμένα φησὶν εἶναι καὶ μὴ πρὸς ἕνα σκοπὸν ἀναφέρεσθαι, and for this very reason the others are distinguished from them as συνταγματικά. David (*Schol.* 24, a, 38): ὑπομνηματικὰ μὲν λέγονται ἐν οἷς μόνα τὰ κεφάλαια ἀπεγράφησαν δίχα προοιμίων καὶ ἐπιλόγων καὶ τῆς πρεπούσης ἐκδόσεσιν ἀπαγγελίας. Cf. HEITZ, *Verl. Schr.* 24 sq.

[2] The Problems, which might occur as an instance, cannot have been written down for his own use alone, since Aristotle often quotes them (see above, p. 96), thereby implying that they are known to his readers. Other instances, such as the Melissus, etc., cannot be supposed genuine. Even if it be true that particular portions of

our *Corpus* were intended to serve as the basis for lectures, or were compiled from them, they would not on that account be merely 'hypomnematical writings.'

[3] *E.g.*, those mentioned on p. 62, n. 4, 5, and perhaps also the *Polities* (p. 101); whether the Περὶ τἀγαθοῦ is also one (as already noted on p. 61, n. 2 *fin.*), seems doubtful.

[4] CIC. *Top.* 1, 3: the works of Aristotle are not only recommended by their contents, *sed dicendi quoque incredibili quadam cum copia tum etiam suaritate. De Invent.* ii. 2, 6 (on the Συναγωγὴ τεχνῶν): Aristotle has left the old orators *suavitate et brevitate dicendi* far behind. *De Orat.* i. 11, 49 : *si item Aristoteles, si Theophrastus, si Carneades . . . eloquentes et in dicendo suaves atque ornati fuere. De Fin.* i. 5, 14 (on Epicurus): *quod ista Platonis Aristotelis Theophrasti orationis ornamenta neglexerit. Acad.* ii. 38, 119 : *reniet flumen orationis aureum fundens Aristoteles.* QUINTIL. *Inst.* xi. 83 : *quid Aristotelem ? Quem dubito*

by him for publication. It is not applicable to any of
those which are now extant; and of these, indeed, the
two Latin writers probably knew but a small part.[1]
We are driven to suppose, therefore, that it was to other
works, lost to us, that they ascribed this kind of excel-
lence. The critic who judges of literary form by purely
scientific criteria will find, it is true, much to praise in
our extant Aristotle. He will acknowledge the apt discrimination of all his ideas, the inimitable precision
and compactness of his diction, and his masterly
handling of an established terminology. But of the
qualities which Cicero emphasises, or any graceful movement of a rich and rolling eloquence, he will find even
in the most popular of the extant books but little trace;
while in other parts the dry methods of treatment, the
rough brevity of statement, the involved construction
of long sentences, often broken by anacolutha and
parentheses, stand in plain contradiction to Cicero's
description. We can, however, gather for ourselves,
even from the scanty fragments of the lost books, that
some of these were written in a style far more rich and

*scientia rerum an scriptorum
copia an eloquendi suavitate . . .
clariorem putem.* DIONYS. *De
Verb. Cop.* 24: of the philosophers, Democritus, Plato, and
Aristotle are the best as to style.
De Cens. Vet. Script. 4: παρα-
ληπτέον· δὲ καὶ 'Αριστοτέλη εἰς
μίμησιν τῆς τε περὶ τὴν ἑρμηνείαν
δεινότητος καὶ τῆς σαφηνείας καὶ
τοῦ ἡδέος καὶ πολυμαθοῦς.
[1] Except the *Topics* and *Rhetoric*, we have no reason for supposing that any of them knew
by personal reading the extant

books. Of the others, however,
Cicero used several of the writings mentioned on p. 55 sqq., the
books on Philosophy, the *Eudemus*, the *Protrepticus*, perhaps
also the Πολιτικὸς, Π. βασιλείας
and Π. πλούτου; cf. *Fin.* ii. 13,
40; *Acad.* ii. 38, 119; *N. D.* ii.
15, 42, 16, 44, 37, 95, 49, 125;
Divin. i. 25, 53; *Fragm. Hort.
apud* Augustine *c. Jul.* iv. 78;
Fin. v. 4, 11; *Ad Quint. Fr.* iii.
5; *Ad Att.* xii. 40, 2, xiii. 28, 2;
Off. ii. 16, 56: and above, p. 60,
n. 1.

ornate, and approached far more closely to the literary graces of the Platonic Dialogues, than any of the scientific treatises now contained in our *Corpus*.[1] This difference is to be explained, not merely by the earlier date of the writings in question, but also by the fact that they were not intended to serve the same purpose as the others, nor designed for the same audiences.[2]

Aristotle himself occasionally refers to certain statements of his doctrine, published by him, or then in common use, in terms which seem to imply that a portion of his writings (including these writings in which the references in question occur) were not in the same sense, given to the public.[3] And from his

---

[1] On this point see what is preserved in Nos. 12–14, 17 sq., 32, 36, 40, 48, 49, 71, 72 of the Fragments (Academy edition) from the *Eudemus*, *Protrepticus*, Π. φιλοσοφίας, Π. δικαιοσύνης, and above, p. 56, n. 2.

[2] We shall discuss this immediately.

[3] *Poet.* 15, 1454, b, 17: εἴρηται δὲ περὶ αὐτῶν ἐν τοῖς ἐκδεδομένοις λόγοις ἱκανῶς. *De An.* i. 4 *init.*: καὶ ἄλλη δέ τις δόξα παραδέδοται περὶ ψυχῆς, πιθανὴ μὲν πολλοῖς ... λόγους ὥσπερ δ' εὐθύνας (for which Bernays, *Dial. d. Ar.* 15 sqq, erasing λόγους, reads: ὥσπερ εὐθύνας δὲ) δεδωκυῖα καὶ τοῖς ἐν κοινῷ γιγνομένοις λόγοις· ἁρμονίαν γάρ τινα αὐτὴν λέγουσι, &c. In the first of these places, Bernays says (*ibid.* 13) that 'published' here means the same as 'already published' (the same explanation of the words is given by Rose, *Ar. Ps.* 79), yet one

may well doubt whether this gloss is allowable. The predicate ἐκδεδομένοι would certainly not be there without a purpose, but is meant to distinguish the λόγοι ἐκδεδομένοι from certain other λόγοι. Neither can we translate ἐκδεδομένοι in such a way as to make 'the writings published by me' a mere periphrasis for 'my writings;' partly because such a turn of phrase is not found in Aristotle. When he refers, without indicating a particular work, to something that has gone before, he is accustomed to say merely, ἐν ἄλλοις, ἐν ἑτέροις or πρότερον. Again the fact that he does not say ὑπ' ἐμοῦ ἐκδεδομένοι shows that the emphasis falls on ἐκδεδομένοι, as such, and that the λόγοι ἐκδεδομένοι are meant as an antithesis to μὴ ἐκδεδομένοι. Only we have no right to assume that things μὴ ἐκδεδομένοι mean things published later. The anti-

commentators we further learn that one of the points

thesis to 'published' is not 'later published,' but 'not published;' and from the perfect ἐκδεδομένοι to read 'such as had already been published at the time of the writing of the *Poetics*, and so were earlier than that work,' is shown to be impossible by the reflection of UEBERWEG on this passage (*Arist. üb. d. Dichtk.*, p. 75) that every author puts himself, in regard to the reader, in the time at which his work will be in the reader's hands. Hence, if the *Poetics* were to be laid before the whole reading world, *i.e.* published, just like the λόγοι to which they referred, they would not be designated in contradistinction to the latter, by the predicate ἐκδεδομένοι, since each of them would be, in relation to their reader, equally a λόγος ἐκδεδομένος. Rose wished to refer the λόγοι ἐκδεδ., first to former passages in the *Poetics* (*Ar. Libr. Ord.* 130), and later (*Ar. Pseud.* 79) to the *Rhetoric*, but he was subsequently (*Ar. Ps.* 714) right in withdrawing both, since the discussion for which the *Poetics* refer to the λόγοι ἐκδεδ. is found neither in the *Rhetoric* nor in the *Poetics* (cf. BERNAYS, *ibid.* 138): and, even apart from this, the latter could never have been so indicated. Nor can we on the other hand (as ROSE, *Ar. Ps.* 717, maintains) refer the expression to writings on Poetry by the Platonic school, for we clearly must confine it to Aristotelian writings: and in the second passage, *De An.* i. 4, the λόγοι ἐν κοινῷ γιγνόμενοι cannot be understood (as TORSTRIK, *Arist. de An.* 123 supposes, he being perhaps preceded by the

authors of the variant λεγομένοις instead of γιγνομ.) of conversations, such as would occur in educated circles, or (as Rose, *Ar. Ps.* 717, thinks) of expressions of opinion coming from the Platonic school ; for the εὐθύνας δεδωκυῖα refers to some criticism, known to the reader, of the supposition that the soul is the harmony of its body, and cannot mean vague conversations of third persons (cf. also BERNAYS, *ibid.*, 18 sq.). Neither can one refer them to oral statements made by Aristotle to his pupils (PHILOP. : see following note), partly because Aristotle never elsewhere refers to such statements, and in a treatise which, though perhaps primarily intended as a textbook for his school, yet gives no indication anywhere of being meant only for his personal pupils, he could not well appeal to them ; partly because the Philosopher had really inserted the criticism referred to in one of his own writings (cf. following note). The latter fact indicates that it is wrong (as SIMPL. does ; see following note) to refer the λόγοι ἐν κοινῷ γιγν. to the Platonic *Phædo*, for which this expression would not be a sufficient indication, nor would it correspond (cf. BERNAYS, p. 20) with the manner in which it is in other places mentioned (cf. *Meteorol.* ii. 2, 355, b, 32). Finally, though Ueberweg (*Gesch. d. Phil.* i. 173, 5th ed.) understands by the λόγοι ἐν κ. γιγν. (extending the explanation of Philoponus) discussions which occurred in actual conversations, or in writings arranged in the

to which he so refers was to be found in the *Eudemus*.[1]
We find other and more frequent references of his to
the ' Exoteric Discourses ' as the place where he had
dealt with such and such a subject.[2] Opinions, however, differ as to the meaning of that name and the

form of dialogues, it seems clear
that the latter could not be so
named, and that there was here
no reason for mentioning the
dialogue form of such discussions.
From the point of view of grammar, owing to the present tense of
γιγνομένοις (to which BONITZ, *Ind.
Arist.* 105, a, 46, rightly calls
attention), they cannot be explained as: 'the speeches submitted (*i.e.* which have been
submitted) to publication,' for in
that case it would have been
γενομένοις. It can only mean, as
Bernays translates in his
Dial. d. Arist. 29, 'the discourses existing in a state of
publication, available for the use
of all,' taking the ἐν κοινῷ here in
the same sense as in the expressions : ἐν κοινῷ κατατίθεσθαι, ἐν
κοινῷ ἀφιέναι (*in medio relin-
quere*, *Metaph.* i. 6, 987, b, 14).
A similar meaning to that of the
λόγοι ἐν κοινῷ γιγνόμενοι seems to
be attached to ἐγκύκλια or ἐγκύκλια φιλοσοφήματα, of which
mention is made in *Eth.* i. 3, 1096,
a, 2 (καὶ περὶ μὲν τούτων ἅλις·
ἱκανῶς γὰρ καὶ ἐν τοῖς ἐγκυκλίοις
εἴρηται περὶ αὐτῶν) and *De Cœlo*, i.
9, 279, a, 30 (καὶ γὰρ καθάπερ ἐν
τοῖς ἐγκυκλίοις φιλοσοφήμασι περὶ
τὰ θεῖα πολλάκις προφαίνεται τοῖς
λόγοις ὅτι τὸ θεῖον ἀμετάβλητον
ἀναγκαῖον εἶναι, &c.). Ἐγκύκλιος
can, just as well as ἐν κοινῷ
γιγνόμενος, mean *in medio positus*
—Bernays' rendering, *Dial. d.*

Ar. 124, ' writings in the common
strain,' is not so appropriate. The
phrase is so explained by Simplicius (in *De Cœlo*, Schol. 487, a, 3 :
where he says that Aristotle uses
ἐγκύκλ. φιλ. to signify τὰ κατὰ
τὴν τάξιν ἐξ ἀρχῆς τοῖς πολλοῖς
προτιθέμενα, *i.e.* the ἐξωτερικὰ).
We also see from *Ar. Fr.* 77, 1488,
b, 36 sqq., and *Fr.* 15, 1476, b, 21,
that the matter for which Aristotle refers to the ἐγκύκλια, was
actually treated in two of his
Dialogues. Cf. BERNAYS, *ibid.*
84 sqq., 93 sq., 110 sqq.

[1] It is shown by the passages
quoted in Rose, *Ar. Fr.* 41, p.
1481 sq., and Heitz, *Ar. Fr.* 73,
p. 51, from Philoponus, Simplicius, Themistius, and Olympiodorus (the common source for
whom may have been Alexander),
that Arist. in the *Eudemus*, after
following the *Phædo*, devoted
a searching examination to the
theory that the soul is the harmony of its body, the principal
heads of which examination are
given by them. Hence the passages in question must refer to
this dialogue, although Philoponus (*De An.* E, 2) leaves us the
choice between it and the ἄγρα-
φοι συνουσίαι πρὸς τοὺς ἑταίρους,
and Simplicius (*De An.* 14,
a) connects it with the
Phædo.

[2] All the passages are quoted
below.

relation of these ' Exoteric Discourses' to our extant *Corpus*. The ancients who mentioned them always referred to them as a separate class of Aristotle's works, distinguished from the technical scientific treatises by a less strict method of treatment.[1] But they differ among themselves as to details. Cicero [2] and Strabo [3] speak of the exoteric works in general terms as popular statements.[4] The former, however, is unmistakeably thinking only of the Dialogues,[5] which we also find described as ' exoteric ' in Plutarch.[6] According to Gellius, the treatises which dealt with

[1] The only exceptions are two late Byzantine and altogether untrustworthy interpreters of the *Ethics*, Eustratius (90, a) and the Pseudo-Andronicus (Heliodorus, *circ*. 1367, cf. p. 69, n. 1), the former of whom understands by ἐξωτερικοὶ λόγοι the common opinion, the latter, oral instruction.

[2] *Fin*. v. 5, 12 : about the highest good, Aristotle and Theophrastus have written *duo genera librorum, unum populariter scriptum, quod* ἐξωτερικὸν *appellabant, alterum limatius* [ἀκριβεστέρως, in a more severe style], *quod in commentariis reliquerunt,*' but in essentials they both agree.

[3] XIII. 1, 54, p. 609 : because the Peripatetics, after Theophrastus, had not his works and those of Aristotle, πλὴν ὀλίγων καὶ μάλιστα τῶν ἐξωτερικῶν, they happened μηδὲν ἔχειν φιλοσοφεῖν πραγματικῶς [going deeply into the subject, scientific] ἀλλὰ θέσεις ληκυθίζειν.

[4] Likewise SIMPL. *Phys*. 2, b:

the Aristotelian writings are divided into acroamatic and exoteric, οἷα τὰ ἱστορικὰ καὶ τὰ διαλογικὰ καὶ ὅλως τὰ μὴ ἄκρας ἀκριβείας φροντίζοντα. —PHILOP. *De An*. E, 2 (*ap*. STAHR, *Arist*. ii. 261) : τὰ ἐξωτερικὰ συγγράμματα, ὧν εἰσι καὶ οἱ διάλογοι . . . ἅπερ διὰ τοῦτο ἐξωτερικὰ κέκληται ὅτι οὐ πρὸς τοὺς γνησίους ἀκροατὰς γεγραμμένα.

[5] Cf. *Ad Att*. iv. 16, 2 : *quoniam in singulis libris* [of the discourse on the State] *utor prooemiis, ut Aristoteles in iis quæ* ἐξωτερικοὺς *vocat*. In contradistinction to the Dialogues, the strictly scientific works are called (see preceding note) *commentarii*, continuous expositions, corresponding to the αὐτοπρόσωπα or ἀκροατικὰ of the Greek interpreters (see p. 112, n. 1, and 113, n. 2).

[6] *Adv. Col*. 14, 4, p. 1115 : Aristotle everywhere attacks the Ideas: ἐν τοῖς ἠθικοῖς ὑπομνήμασιν (synonymous with Cicero's *commentarii* ; see preceding note), ἐν τοῖς φυσικοῖς, διὰ τῶν ἐξωτερικῶν διαλόγων.

Rhetoric, Topics, and Politics were named 'exoteric,' and those which related to Metaphysics, Physics, and Dialectics ' acroatic,' [1] the reason being that the former, as Galen explained, were meant for everyone ; the latter only for the philosopher's scholars.[2] Alexander, in a letter which appears in Andronicus,[3] is supposed to complain to his master of the publication of the ' acroatic ' writings ; but inasmuch as Aristotle is expressly stated to have published them, the notion that *he* objected to their publication cannot have been in the mind of the writer of that fragment. At a later time we do find this assumption also,[4] and we find connected with it the further theory that Aristotle purposely adopted in his ' acroatic '

[1] *N. A.* xx. 5 : Aristotle's lectures and writings were divided into two classes, the ἐξω-τερικὰ and the ἀκροατικά. Ἐξωτερικὰ *dicebantur quæ ad rhetoricas meditationes facultatemque argutiarum civiliumque rerum notitiam conducebant,* ἀκροατικὰ *autem vocabantur in quibus philosophia remotior subtiliorque agitabatur quæque ad naturæ contemplationes disceptationesque dialecticas pertinebant.* In the Lyceum the morning was devoted to the latter, the evening to the former (cf. p. 27, n. 3). *Libros quoque suos, earum omnium rerum commentarios, seorsum divisit, ut alii exoterici dicerentur, partim acroatici.*

[2] *De Subst. Fac. Nat.* vol. iv. 758 K : Ἀριστοτέλους ἢ Θεοφράστου τὰ μὲν τοῖς πολλοῖς γεγραφότων, τὰς δὲ ἀκροάσεις τοῖς ἑταίροις.

[3] Cf. GELL. *ibid.* ; PLUT. *Alex.* 7 ; *vide supra,* p. 22, n. 1. The wording : οὐκ ὀρθῶς ἐποίησας ἐκδοὺς τοὺς ἀκροατικοὺς τῶν λόγων,

shows that the distinction between the λόγοι ἀκροατικοὶ and ἐξωτερικοὶ must have been known to the author of the letter.

[4] Thus PLUT. *Alex.* c. 7 : ἔοικε δ' Ἀλέξανδρος οὐ μόνον τὸν ἠθικὸν καὶ πολιτικὸν παραλαβεῖν λόγον, ἀλλὰ καὶ τῶν ἀπορρήτων καὶ βαρυτέρων [βαθυτ.] διδασκαλιῶν, ἃς οἱ ἄνδρες ἰδίως ἀκροαματικὰς καὶ ἐποπτικὰς [as in mysteries] προσαγορεύοντες οὐκ ἐξέφερον εἰς πολλοὺς, μετασχεῖν. CLEMENS, *Strom.* v. 575, A : not only the Pythagoreans and the Platonists, but all schools have secret doctrines and secret writings : λέγουσι δὲ καὶ οἱ Ἀριστοτέλους τὰ μὲν ἐσωτερικὰ εἶναι τῶν συγγραμμάτων αὐτῶν [-οῦ] τὰ δὲ κοινά τε καὶ ἐξωτερικα On the same theory, in the *Rhet. ad Alex.* c. 1, 1421, a, 26 sq., Aristotle is requested by Alexander to observe the strictest secrecy with regard to this work, while Aristotle, on his part, lays a reciprocal duty of silence on Alexander.

works a form of exposition which must make them unintelligible to any but his scholars;[1] while at the same time it is said that it was here only that he disclosed his views in their full logical connection.[2] On this theory the 'exoteric' writings were broadly distinguished from the 'acroatic,' just by the fact that they were intended for a wider public, and that they were therefore put in a more popular form, did not cover the more difficult classes of inquiry, and substituted for a severe and scientific method of proof one more accommodated to general comprehension.[3]

[1] This idea is expressed in the answer of Aristotle to Alexander (see GELL. *ibid.*), when he replies to the reproach of the latter with regard to the ἀκροατικοὶ λόγοι: Ἴσθι οὖν αὐτοὺς καὶ ἐκδεδομένους καὶ μὴ ἐκδεδομένους· ξυνετοὶ γάρ εἰσι μόνοις τοῖς ἡμῶν ἀκούσασιν. See also THEMIST. *Or.* xxvi. 319, A sq., where it is said that Aristotle did not find the same discourses suitable for the masses as for the philosophers, and therefore withdrew the highest secrets of his teaching (the τέλεα ἱερὰ, the μυστικὸν) from the former by using obscure language. SIMPL. *Phys.* 2, b, referring to the letters just mentioned, says: ἐν τοῖς ἀκροαματικοῖς ἀσάφειαν ἐπετήδευσε, &c. For the same view see *Categ.* Schol. 27, a, 38, DAVID, *Categ.* Schol. 22, a, 20; 27, a, 18 sq. In the same sense LUCIAN, *V. Auct.* c. 26, calls Aristotle διπλοῦς, ἄλλος μὲν ὁ ἔκτοσθεν φαινόμενος ἄλλος δὲ ὁ ἔντοσθεν, exoteric and esoteric.

[2] Alexander remarks, *Top.* 52, that Aristotle speaks at one time λογικῶς in order to unfold the truth as such, at another διαλεκ-

τικῶς πρὸς δόξαν. He instances the *Topics*, the ῥητορικὰ and the ἐξωτερικά. 'καὶ γὰρ ἐν ἐκείνοις πλεῖστα καὶ περὶ τῶν ἠθικῶν καὶ περὶ τῶν φυσικῶν ἐνδόξως λέγεται.' But the example of the *Topics* and the *Rhetoric* shows that this only refers to the basis of the opinions laid down in these writings, the argument from the universally acknowledged (the ἔνδοξον), and not to the teaching as such. The later writers, as a rule, express themselves in the same sense; thus SIMPL. *Phys.* 164, a: ἐξωτερικὰ δέ ἐστι τὰ κοινὰ καὶ δι' ἐνδόξων περαινόμενα ἀλλὰ μὴ ἀποδεικτικὰ μηδὲ ἀκροαματικά. As to AMMON. and DAVID, see following note; and cf. PHILOP. *Phys.* p. 4. On the other hand DAVID, *Schol. in Ar.* 24, b, 33, changes the statement of Alexander (which he quotes in order to refute it) into: ὅτι ἐν μὲν τοῖς ἀκροαματικοῖς τὰ δοκοῦντα αὐτῷ λέγει καὶ τὰ ἀληθῆ, ἐν δὲ τοῖς διαλογικοῖς τὰ ἄλλοις δοκοῦντα, τὰ ψευδῆ.

[3] Besides the testimony already adduced, the statements found in the Neoplatonic com-

The theory just mentioned can be traced as far back as Andronicus, perhaps even farther;[1] but this does not put its correctness beyond question. It is, however, confirmed in the main, even if it requires correction in one point or another, by the utterances of Aristotle himself as to the ' Exoteric Discourses.' It is true that in a general sense he may describe as ' exoteric ' any topic which does not belong to the inquiry immediately

mentators go to establish this point. Thus the so-called Ammon. in *Categ.* 6, b sqq. (see also STAHR, *Aristotelia,* ii. 255 sqq.), who, after some other divisions of the the Aristotelian writings, among ' syntagmatic ' ones distinguishes αὐτοπρόσωπα καὶ ἀκροαματικὰ and διαλογικὰ καὶ ἐξωτερικὰ. The former are written πρὸς γνησίους ἀκροατὰς, the latter πρὸς τὴν τῶν πολλῶν ὠφέλειαν; in the former Aristotle expresses his own opinion with a strictly scientific argument, in the latter τὰ δοκοῦντα αὐτῷ, ἀλλ' οὐ δι' ἀποδεικτικῶν ἐπιχειρημάτων, καὶ οἷς οἷοί τέ εἰσιν οἱ πολλοὶ ἐπακολουθεῖν. Similarly, only at greater length, DAVID, *Schol.* 24, a, 20 sqq., who likewise divides the συνταγματικὰ into αὐτοπρόσωπα or ἀκροαματικὰ and διαλογικὰ ἃ καὶ ἐξωτερικὰ λέγονται and considers the former to have been written πρὸς τοὺς ἐπιτηδείους τῇ φιλοσοφίᾳ, the latter πρὸς ἀνεπιτηδείους πρὸς φιλοσοφίαν, and hence the former δι' ἀναγκαστικῶν λόγων, the latter διὰ πιθανῶν. Cf. p. 111, n. 4.

[1] In proof of this statement we cannot attach so much importance to the passage just given from David as Heitz does (*Verl. Schr.* 25 sq.). The fact that David (24, b, 5) expressly appeals to Ammonius (Π. ἑρμηνείας) and to the commentary on the *Categories* passing under Ammonius' name (which, although in its present form it does not come from Ammonius, yet seems to have originated in one written by him), indicates that Ammonius was David's proximate authority; and though he (Ammonius) certainly made use of earlier writers (and principally Alexander, whom David at 24, b, 33 attacks, and from whom his quotation of the Aristotelian *Eudemus* is probably taken, like that in PHILOP. *De An.* E, 2 sq.; *Ar. Fr.* p. 1481, No. 41), still we do not know how much has been added to their testimony. On the other hand we must trace the statements in Cicero, Strabo, and Gellius (*vide supra*, p. 111, n. 2–6, 112, n. 1), to Tyrannio and Andronicus, and the letters mentioned on p. 112, n. 3 etc., prove that the latter was aware of the distinction between exoteric and acroatic writings, and of the suggestion that the last mentioned were only intended to be understood by the pupils of the philosopher.

in hand,[1] or any discussion which does not go very deeply into the subject.[2] It is also true that the title does not always and necessarily denote a distinct class of *writings*.[3] Nevertheless there are passages where we have every reason to refer it to such a class ;[4] and that

[1] *Polit.* i. 5, 1254, a, 33 ; ἀλλὰ ταῦτα μὲν ἴσως ἐξωτερικωτέρας ἐστὶ σκέψεως. Similarly, *ibid.* ii. 6, 1264, b, 39 ; 'in the *Republic* Plato has only imperfectly treated of legislation, τὰ δ' ἄλλα τοῖς ἔξωθεν λόγοις πεπλήρωκε τὸν λόγον.' The term ' ἔξωθεν λόγοι ' covers in this case writings of the most speculative character. In like manner Eudemus *Fr.* 6 (SIMPL. *Phys.* 18, b), where instead of the ἔχει δ' ἀπορίαν . . . . ἴσως δὲ οὐ πρὸς τὸν λόγον of Aristotle (*Phys.* i. 2, 185, b, 11) we read : ἔχει δὲ αὐτὸ τοῦτο ἀπορίαν ἐξωτερικήν.

[2] *Phys.* iv. 10, *init.*: πρῶτον δὲ καλῶς ἔχει διαπορῆσαι περὶ αὐτοῦ [τοῦ χρόνου] καὶ διὰ τῶν ἐξωτερικῶν λόγων. The ἐξωτ. λόγοι here mean the discussion which follows immediately, and which is called exoteric (in the same way as Aristotle, in other places, puts the logical in opposition to the physical, *vid. infra*, p. 174, n. 2), because it does not aim at a strict and adequate notion of time (the τί ἐστιν ὁ χρόνος, 218, a, 31), but only takes into consideration certain preliminary properties of it. The question is not here of exoteric *writings* ; but Prantl is none the less wrong (*Arist. Physik*, 501, 32) in maintaining that by the exoteric discourses we are to understand, not only in the present instance, but everywhere, only those conversations on interesting subjects which

at that time were everywhere in vogue even at social gatherings. That this does not fit other passages will be shown immediately ; as for the passage in question, such a rendering is forbidden by the strictly dialectical and genuinely Aristotelian style of the discussions from p. 217, b, 32 to p. 218, a, 30.

[3] Thus, besides the passage given in the preceding note from the *Physics*, the Eudemian *Eth.* ii. 1, 1218, b, 33, introduces the division of possessions into the external and the spiritual with the remark : καθάπερ διαιρούμεθα καὶ ἐν τοῖς ἐξωτερικοῖς λόγοις. In the parallel passage, *Eth. N.* i. 8, 1098, b, 10, Aristotle says : he wishes to speak about happiness καὶ ἐκ τῶν λεγομένων περὶ αὐτῆς, by which, according to the context, only the prevailing views concerning happiness can be meant. It is to these, therefore, that the ἐξωτ. λόγοι of Eudemus must also refer.

[4] This is true especially of *Polit.* vii. i. 1323, a, 21 : νομίσαντας οὖν ἱκανῶς πολλὰ λέγεσθαι καὶ τῶν ἐν τοῖς ἐξωτερικοῖς λόγοις περὶ τῆς ἀρίστης ζωῆς καὶ νῦν χρηστέον αὐτοῖς. That by this he does not mean mere oral expressions of opinion in the conversations of daily life is clearly shown by what immediately follows. For Aristotle continues : ὡς ἀληθῶς γὰρ πρός γε μίαν διαίρεσιν

the writings referred to were of a more popular type
than our extant Aristotelian texts is made probable

οὐδεὶς ἀμφισβητήσειεν, etc. His
point may be stated thus : 'from
the arguments in the ἐξωτερικοὶ
λόγοι, it will be univeısally recognised that the conditions of
happiness include not only external and bodily good things but also
and pre-eminently spiritual good
things : although it is true that in
common life we are wont to content
ourselves with far too small a proportion of such spiritual good.'
This line of reasoning necessarily
implies that the ἐξωτερικοὶ λόγοι
in question, with which the current
opinion of society is said to be in
partial agreement, are not the
same as any form of expression
of that current opinion (cf. BER-
NAYS, *Dial. d. Arist.* 40). Then,
again, the words : πρός γε μίαν διαίρεσιν οὐδεὶς ἀμφισβητήσειεν point
to definite explanations, set down
in writing, not merely existing
in the intangible medium of oral
conversation. It would be easier
to connect them with oral discourses of Aristotle himself (as
ONCKEN does in *Staatsl. d. Arist.*
i. 44–59). We cannot, however,
base this view on the present
λέγομεν (together with the διοριζόμεθα, *Pol.* iii. 6, 1278, b, 32),
since Aristotle not only quotes
the writings of others very frequently in this way, but not unfrequently even his own; cf.
Pol. vii. 13, 1332, a, 8 : φαμὲν δὲ
καὶ ἐν τοῖς ἠθικοῖς; *Phys.* viii. 1,
251, a, 9 ; φαμὲν δή, etc. (*Phys.*
iii. 1); *De Cælo*, i. 7, 275, b, 21 ;
λόγος δ' ἐν τοῖς περὶ κινήσεως
(ἐστίν) ; *Metaph.* v. 30 *fin.*; λόγος
δὲ τούτου ἐν ἑτέροις ; *Eth.* vi. 3,
1139, b, 26 ; ὥσπερ καὶ ἐν τοῖς

ἀναλυτικοῖς λέγομεν ; *ibid.* 32 :
ὅσα ἄλλα προσδιοριζόμεθα ἐν τοῖς
ἀναλυτικοῖς. And, on the other
hand, the νῦν χρηστέον αὐτοῖς is
adverse to this explanation. That
is meant to designate what follows as something extracted from
the exoteric discourses ; but Aristotle would be far more likely to
use such a formula if he was quoting something from a former work
than if he was merely repeating
in writing what he had already
orally delivered. This latter, from
the nature of the case, he must
have had occasion to do as often
as a modern university teacher
does it. The fact, then, that he
expressly mentions that he is
'making an extract from the ἐξωτερικοὶ λόγοι,' points, as in the
De Cælo, ii. 13, 295, a, 2, and
Meteor. iii. 2, 372, b, 10 (where
some of the writings which we
possess are quoted with the same
χρηστέον) to an existing written
work. And an *Aristotelian* writing must be meant, since that
which follows out of the ἐξωτερικοί λόγοι sounds perfectly Aristotelian, and forms a whole with
what Aristotle gives in his own
name (ἡμεῖς δὲ ἐροῦμεν, l. 38).
Lastly, although something similar to that which is here quoted
from the ἐξωτ. λόγοι is found in
some passages of the *Ethics* (i.
6 sqq. x. 6 sqq.), which Zeller,
in his second edition, brought
into connection with this quotation, yet he now concedes
to Bernays *ibid.* 71 sq. ; cf.
ONCKEN, *ibid.* 43, 5 ; VAHLEN,
Arist. Aufs. ii. 6) that Aristotle
would not by the designation

both by the express distinction that is drawn between

ἐξωτερικοὶ λόγοι have mentioned the *Ethics*, which in the *Politics* he repeatedly quotes as ἠθικὰ, and puts in the closest connection with them (*vid.* p. 127, n. 2, cf Zeller's 2nd ed.). Bernays' theory (73 sqq.), that the first chapter of the seventh book of the *Politics* strikingly diverges from the usual style of his scientific works, and bears distinct traces of having been extracted from a dialogue can scarcely be supposed after Vahlen's forcible objections (*Arist. Aufs.* ii.) to be established; Zeller, however, feels bound to agree with Bernays that by the 'exoteric discourses' in this passage is meant a written work of the philosopher's which is lost to us, and which Aristotle here seems to follow pretty closely, for which very reason he refers to it, and not to the *Ethics*, though the parallel passages in the latter were closely connected with it in meaning. — Less convincing with regard to this, in spite of what Bernays says to the contrary (*ibid.* 38, 51 sqq.), appears to be *Polit.* iii. 6, 1278, b, 30: ἀλλὰ μὴν καὶ τῆς ἀρχῆς τοὺς λεγομένους τρόπους [the δεσποτεία, the οἰκονομικὴ, and the πολιτικὴ ἀρχὴ] ῥᾴδιον διελεῖν · καὶ γὰρ ἐν τοῖς ἐξωτερικοῖς λόγοις διοριζόμεθα περὶ αὐτῶν πολλάκις. These words, looked at in themselves, might refer not only (as ONCKEN, *ibid.*, suggests) to oral disquisitions, but also (by taking the διοριζόμεθα as the collective 'we') to conversations not connected with the School or even with scientific philosophy. That Aristotle here 'refers to the ἐξωτ. λόγοι, not for the existence' (more correctly

'distinction') ' of different kinds of dominion, but for the *exact limitation* of their difference' (as Bernays, p. 38 asserts), cannot be inferred from the διοριζόμεθα, since this expression designates not only the *exact* distinction, the 'carefully-weighed logical antithesis,' but *any* kind of distinction whatever. If we compare with it the perfectly analogous use of λέγομεν, διοριζόμεθα, &c., in the passages given above (p. 115), we shall be prepared to give the same meaning to the διοριζόμεθα here, and when we have persuaded ourselves, from other passages, that Aristotle names certain writings λόγοι ἐξωτερικοί, the passage appears to fit this interpretation. (And there are certainly some among the lost Aristotelian writings in which the distinction here touched upon may have been given; particularly the πολιτικὸς and Π. βασιλείας : *v. supra*, p. 58, n. 1, and 60, n. 1).—The like is true of *Eth.* vi. 4 *init.*: ἕτερον δ' ἐστὶ ποίησις καὶ πρᾶξις · πιστεύομεν δὲ περὶ αὐτῶν καὶ τοῖς ἐξωτερικοῖς λόγοις. The connection here unquestionably *allows* us to suppose that the words refer to discussions in Aristotelian writings of a character different from that of the scientific works which we possess, as for instance the Dialogue on the Poets or *Gryllos*; but that it *forbids* any other supposition Bernays (p. 39, 57 sqq.) has not made out. If anybody wished to give to the passage, instead of the narrow meaning assumed by Bernays, the broader one, 'this has already been proved in my other writings,' neither the meaning of ἐξωτερικὸς nor the context would stand in his way, since the rendering of the former would be analogous to the examples quoted on p. 115, n. 1, and as regards the latter the question whether Aristotle here refers to scientific or popular writings, is indifferent. If, on the other hand, we wished to understand the ἐξωτ. λόγοι of the λεγόμενα—'what is said by others'—we could parallel the expression by an appeal to Eudemus (see preceding note). Bernays, referring to this, finds it impossible to believe that we are to draw the explanation of such a corner-stone of the Peripatetic system as the connection of ποίησις and πρᾶξις, from the common conversation of well educated persons : but if so, he ought to find it no less absurd to draw from the very same source an explanation of the centre of gravity of all Ethics, the notion of Εὐδαιμονία. And yet we find in *Eth.* i. 8, *init.* incontestably : σκεπτέον δὴ περὶ αὐτῆς . . . καὶ ἐκ τῶν λεγομένων περὶ αὐτῆς. This may not mean that we are to seek *the scientific definition* of happiness ' in the conversation of the educated ; ' but neither would this be affirmed in *Eth.* vi. 4 *init.* about that of ποίησις and πρᾶξις, if we were to understand the ἐξωτ. λόγοι in this passage of the λεγόμενα. The appeal to universal conviction would be to establish a *general* distinction of ποίησις from πρᾶξις ; and this is Aristotle's way : τῷ γὰρ ἀληθεῖ πάντα συνᾴδει τὰ ὑπάρχοντα (*Eth.* i. 8).—Much more definitely may we discern in *Eth.* i. 13, 1102, a, 26 an intention of appealing to some Aristotelian writings in the

words : λέγεται δὲ περὶ αὐτῆς [sc. τῆς ψυχῆς] καὶ ἐν τοῖς ἐξωτερικοῖς λόγοις ἀρκούντως ἔνια καὶ χρηστέον αὐτοῖς. οἷον τὸ μὲν ἄλογον αὐτῆς εἶναι τὸ δὲ λόγον ἔχον. For though it is by no means so incredible as Bernays, p. 36, believes, that the distinction between the rational and the irrational in the soul may have made its way from the Platonic school into wider circles (Epicharmus, at a much later period, comes very near to it with his νοῦς ὁρᾷ, &c.), and though it could scarcely be said to be an actual impossibility to interpret the words ἐξωτ. λόγοι as referring to opinions current outside the school, yet the introductory words here too much resemble those given above from *Polit.* vii. 1, and the λέγεται ἀρκούντως ἔνια καὶ νῦν χρηστέον αὐτοῖς here points too obviously to written discussions, for us to be able to refer this quotation to mere λεγόμενα. If it refers to an Aristotelian work, this must be one of the lost writings—most probably the *Eudemus* ; for the quotation does not agree with Π. ψυχῆς iii. 9, 432, a, 22 sqq., and this work would not be cited by such a reference, but, as always in other places, by ' ἐν τοῖς περὶ ψυχῆς.' — Neither in *Metaph.* xiii. 1, 1076, a, 28 (on the Ideas as such he will only speak ἁπλῶς καὶ ὅσον νόμου χάριν — τεθρύλληται γὰρ τὰ πολλὰ καὶ ὑπὸ τῶν ἐξωτερικῶν λόγων) can we understand by the ἐξωτ. λόγοι oral discussions of others. It must mean the work of Aristotle himself, since this alone could dispense him from a fuller criticism of the doctrine of Ideas ; and that we are to look for such work neither in the philo-

the exoteric and the scientific treatises,[1] and by the terms
that are used in describing the former.[2] It is not to be

sopher's doctrinal discussions nor
in his strictly scientific writings
is suggested not only by the designation ἔξωτ. λόγοι, but also
by the καὶ (καὶ ὑπὸ τ. ἐξ. λ.),
by which the ἔξωτ. λόγοι are distinguished from other not exoteric λόγοι. Still more clearly
does this appear from Eudemus,
when the latter, probably remembering this passage, in *Eth.* i. 8,
1217, b, 22 says likewise of the
Ideas : ἐπέσκεπται δὲ πολλοῖς περὶ
αὐτοῦ τρόποις καὶ ἐν τοῖς ἐξωτερικοῖς
λόγοις καὶ ἐν τοῖς κατὰ φιλοσοφίαν.
Cf. following note.

[1] This is indicated by the express statement in the passages
quoted in the preceding note,
especially from *Polit.* vii. 1, *Eth.*
i. 13, *Metaph.* xiii. 1, that certain
points have been sufficiently explained ' even in the exoteric discourses : ' that is, inasmuch as we
should less expect such discussions in them. Eudemus puts it
more definitely, by putting the
ἐξωτερικοὶ λόγοι (see preceding
note, *fin.*) in opposition to the
λόγοι κατὰ φιλοσοφίαν. Since the
latter are scientific inquiries,
the former can only be popular
discourses ; and, since (as we have
seen) writings are meant by
them, they can only be popular writings. Now it might indeed appear that the criticism
of the doctrine of Ideas, to which
Eth. Eud. i. 8, and *Metaph.* xiii.
1, *loc. cit.* refer, would of all
things have been least suited for
popular writings ; but we have
already seen on p. 76, n. 3, 56,
n. 2 *med.* that he opposed this
doctrine, with the greatest re-

solution, in the Dialogue on Philosophy.

[2] Ἐξωτερικὸς in Aristotle means
(1) that which *exists* outside,
the external ; and (2) that
which *goes* out, refers to the
external. The word has the
former meaning when for instance a foreign province is called
an ἐξωτερικὴ ἀρχὴ (*Polit.* ii. 10,
1272, b, 19), or when hand and
foot are styled ἐξωτερικὰ μέρη
(*Gen. An.* v. 6, 786, a, 26) ; to
these uses cf. the ἐξωτερικὰ ἀγαθὰ,
Pol. vii. 1, 1323, a, 25. In the
second meaning the expression
is used in the combination :
ἐξωτερικαὶ πράξεις (*Pol.* vii. 3,
1325, b, 22, 29). If now, in the
phrase ἔξωτ. λόγοι, we propose to
give it the *first* meaning, we cannot, by exoteric discourses, in
those passages where Aristotelian
writings of a particular class or
the inquiries contained in them
are meant, understand such discourses as lie outside the discussion in which they are referred
to as ' other discourses' (like the
ἐξωτερικωτέρα σκέψις and the ἔξωθεν λόγοι, p. 115, n. 1 and 3) ; nor
yet (as Bernays thinks in *Dial. d.
Ar.* 92 sq.) such as do not enter
into the essence of a thing, but
are external to it (as p. 115, n. 2).
The latter meaning would not
suit, partly because this would
be a strange way of speaking of
' popular treatises,' partly because
it would not fit those cases in
which Aristotle again takes up in
later works, as being suitable and
adequate, what he had said in
the ἐξωτερικοὶ λόγοι (as in the
passages of the *Politics, Ethics,*

inferred either from the words ἐξωτερικοὶ λόγοι themselves, or from the surrounding facts, that Aristotle's Dialogues alone were meant. There may have been, and in fact there appear to have been, other works also which were adapted to the understanding of the general public.[1]

As to the later theories, the idea that the Master did not intend his strictly scientific work for publication at all is refuted by the contemporary record of the complaints that were made because he published them : [2] and the idea that he designedly chose for them a style obscure and unintelligible to the lay mind is disproved by the visible characteristics of the texts themselves. The truth is that, except in cases where we ought to consider them as mere sets of notes for his own use, he takes all manner of trouble to aid the reader, by the use of a strictly devised scientific terminology, by clear definitions, by explanations and illustrations, by methodical processes of thought, and by warnings against possible obscurities, ambiguities or misconceptions. If it be true nevertheless that there occur many particular points of

and *Metaphysics* given on p. 115, n. 4). Such writings could only be called exoteric, in this use of the word, in the sense that they were known and in use even outside the Aristotelian school. But it comes to very much the same thing also if we start (as Zeller prefers to do), with the *second* meaning of ἐξωτερικὸς, and understand the ἐξωτ. λόγοι to signify such works as were intended for outsiders or for the general public, the same, in fact, as are included in the terms λόγοι ἐκδεδομένοι or ἐν κοινῷ γιγνόμενοι. That such writings were of a more

popular character was implied in the designation, but not directly expressed in the adjective ἐξωτερικὸς as such. When Eudemus puts the λόγοι ἐξωτ. in opposition to those κατὰ φιλοσοφίαν (see preceding note), we might understand the latter to mean ' such as were intended to serve for scientific instruction '; but at the same time there is nothing against the translation ' both in those intended for the general public and in the scientific treatises.'

[1] Cf. p. 60, n. 1.
[2] Cf. p. 22, n. 1, 112, n. 3.

difficulty, the reasons are to be found anywhere rather than in the writer's intention. Besides, it is obvious that any such theory attributes to the philosopher a very childish sort of mystification, wholly destitute of any reasonable motive.

It does seem, however, to be true that it was only a portion of his writings which Aristotle *published,* in the sense of making express provision for their dissemination to a wide circle of general readers. Others which were more closely connected with his oral teaching seem to have been designed primarily for the use of his scholars as classbooks.[1] It was in the case of the former only that he took pains to cultivate that eloquence and artistic completeness and that popular style of exposition for which his ' exoteric ' works were famous. The sole aim of the second set of texts was scientific investigation for its own sake, and they were therefore distinguished by a stricter logic and a less artistic dress. It seems that of the former class by far the greater part, if not the whole, consisted of those writings which Aristotle wrote before the opening of the Peripatetic School at Athens, and chiefly while he was still one of the Platonic circle : of all of which nothing remains but a few fragments.[2] On

[1] But without our having to suppose that they were forbidden to communicate them to others.

[2] 'In this sense', says Prof. Zeller, 'I had already expressed myself in the second edition, p. 98, as to the probable state of facts with regard to the distinction between exoteric and esoteric writings. On the other hand, I then believed that, in the Aristotelian passages which mention the ἐξωτερικοὶ λόγοι, I could everywhere translate that phrase as meaning such discussions as do not belong to the sphere of the inquiry actually under investigation. (Thus also SCHWEG-LER, *Gesch. d. griech. Phil.* 194.) I have now rejected this opinion, and think that the general meaning of ἐξωτερικὸς, to designate something external, or relating to the external, is more

such a theory there may have been a great difference in form between the 'exoteric' and the 'acroatic' texts,

appropriate. It follows that even in the combination ἐξωτερικοὶ λόγοι this expression will apply not only to such discussions as lie outside a specified subject (as p. 115, n. 1), or are concerned only with what is external to it (p. 115, n. 2), but also to such as are current outside a particular circle (p. 115, n. 3), or such as are intended for outsiders (p. 115, n. 4). According as we begin from this or that passage in Aristotle, and extend the meaning of the expression in that particular passage to all the other cases, we get this or that rendering of the ἐξωτ. λόγοι. This is the explanation of the fact that even now there are the most diverse opinions on the matter. Of these, the farthest removed from the explanation which has prevailed since the time of Andronicus, which understands by this expression a particular class of Aristotelian writings, is the supposition of MADVIG (Exc. vii. on CIC. *De Fin.*), PRANTL (*Arist. Physik*, p. 501, 32), SPENGEL (' Arist. Studien,' *Abh. d. bayr. Akad.* x. 181 sq.), FORCHHAMMER (*Arist. und die exoter. Reden*, cf. particularly pp. 15, 64), and SUSEMIHL (*Philol. Anz.* v. 674 sq.), that only the conversations of non-philosophical circles are designated by the ἐξωτ. λόγοι. Rather nearer to it are RAVAISSON (*Métaph. d'Arist.* i. 209 sq.) and THUROT (*Etudes sur Aristote*, 209 sq.), who understand by them such dialectic discussions (in contradistinction to the strictly scientific), as proceed by arguments πρὸς δόξαν, occurring either in

Aristotelian writings, or in the oral disputations of the school. These, in their view, may be called exoteric, either because they always have to deal with something foreign to the matter (cf. the ἔξω and ἔσω λόγος, *Anal.* i. 10, 76, b, 24), or because they always treat the subject externally. GROTE (*Aristotle*, 63 sqq.) agrees with them, except that, besides the Aristotelian Dialogues and some extracts from the acroamatic works, he thinks conversations outside the school are referred to. In like manner (though with the exclusion of conversations outside the school) UEBERWEG (*Gesch. d. Phil.* i. 143, 5th ed.). ONCKEN (*Staatsl. d. Arist.* i. 43 sq.) refers the term to oral discussions, allied to the scientific lectures in which the ἐξωτ. λόγοι are mentioned, but of a different class from them. On the other hand RITTER (*Gesch. d. Phil.* iii. 21 sqq.) holds more closely to the statements of the ancient writers about the two classes of Aristotelian pupils and writings, in assuming (p. 29) that all the strictly scientific works were only written by Aristotle as a help to his lectures and were only published, at a later period, by himself or his pupils, and perhaps at first only for the latter ; whereas the remaining writings (which are lost to us), were designed for the use of cultured persons and might, together with any corresponding lectures, be called exoteric. A like position is held, in the main, by BERNAYS (*Dial. d. Arist.*), who by the exoteric discourses under-

and it may be very true that the matter of the former was less advanced than the systematic doctrine of the Master, as we have it from his riper years; but it is entirely beside the mark to suggest that he sought in either the one case or the other to conceal his opinions or to withdraw them from the reader's eye.

It is not only, however, the distinction noted between these ' published ' or ' exoteric' books and the others, which points to the conclusion that the extant, closely reasoned writings of Aristotle were written primarily for his scholars, as classbooks only. In the texts themselves there are many indications which it is hard to reconcile with the idea that they were really *published*, in the full sense of the word, during Aristotle's lifetime.

In the first place there is the remarkable circumstance[1] that a book which is cited in another nevertheless

stands such lectures chiefly. HEITZ (*Verl. Schr. d. Ar.* 122 sqq.), though agreeing with him in substance, prefers to give the expression (with reference to *Phys.* iv. 10 *init.*) the broader meaning, and to make it imply a point of view farther removed from true science. BONITZ (*Ind. Arist.* 104, b, 44 sqq.; *Zeitschriften für östr. Gymn.* 1866, 776 sq.) takes a similar view. STAHR (*Aristotelia,* ii. 239 sqq., cf. especially 275 sq.), and BRANDIS (*Gr.-röm. Phil.* ii. b, 101 sqq.) express themselves less decidedly —the former believing that by the exoteric writings are meant partly those in which something was treated merely in passing, partly and principally those which did not essentially belong to the systematic connection of the philosophical writings, such as the Dialogues, partly a special manner of philosophising; the latter broadly identifying the exoteric writings with the popular ones, but abstaining from further definition of them or of the expression " exoteric discourses." THOMAS (*De Arist. ἐξωτ. λόγοις*) stands quite isolated with his strange whim of looking for Aristotle's exoteric discourses in the greater *Ethics.* Space does not permit me a more searching examination of these various suppositions; the principles on which it would be based are contained in what has been said above. STAHR, *ibid.*, gives all the earlier references which bear upon the question.'

[1] RITTER (iii. 29) and BRANDIS (ii. b, 113) have already

cites that other book itself: or that an earlier treatise
speaks of an inquiry as already completed, and yet a
later treatise says it is in contemplation only. These
cases are not rare. The *Topics* is frequently cited in the
Analytics,[1] and yet cites the latter four times.[2] All four
may belong to a later-written portion of the *Topics*, but
at any rate they cannot be later than the *Analytics*, in
which these same books are cited as well as the earlier
ones.[3] When the *Physics* refers us back to discussions
which, as we know them, exist only in the *Metaphysics*,
it might be said that the reference is to a section which
existed as a separate treatise before the *Metaphysics* was
compiled; [4] but it cannot be doubted that the zoological

noted this and explained in a
similar way.

[1] Cf. p. 67, n. 1. BONITZ
(*Ind. Arist.* 102 sq.) gives the
passages on which the following
explanation is based, so far as
they have not been expressly
cited here.

[2] VII. 3, 153, a, 24 : ἐκ τίνων
δὲ δεῖ κατασκευάζειν [sc. συλλογισμὸν ὅρου] διώρισται μὲν ἐν ἑτέροις
ἀκριβέστερον (cf. *Anal. Post.* ii.
13), viii. 11, 162, a, 11 : φανερὸν
δ᾽ ἐκ τῶν ἀναλυτικῶν (*Anal. Pr.* ii.
2), viii. 13, 162, b, 32 : τὸ δ᾽ ἐν
ἀρχῇ . . . πῶς αἰτεῖται ὁ ἐρωτῶν,
κατ᾽ ἀλήθειαν μὲν ἐν τοῖς ἀναλυτικοῖς
[*Anal. Pr.* ii. 16] εἴρηται, κατὰ
δόξαν δὲ νῦν λεκτέον, ix. 2 (*Soph.
El.*), 165, b, 8 : περὶ μὲν οὖν τῶν
ἀποδεικτικῶν [sc. συλλογισμῶν] ἐν
τοῖς ἀναλυτικοῖς εἴρηται.

[3] *Anal. Pr.* ii. 15, 64, a, 36
(ἔστι δὲ δι᾽ ἄλλων ἐρωτημάτων συλλογίσασθαι θάτερον ἢ ὡς ἐν τοῖς
τοπικοῖς ἐλέχθη λαβεῖν) refers to
Top. viii. and *Anal. Pr.* ii. 17, 65,
b, 15 (ὅπερ εἴρηται καὶ ἐν τοῖς

τοπικοῖς) to the passage *Top.* ix.
4, 167, b, 21, with which what
follows is also closely connected.

[4] In *Phys.* i. 8, 191, b, 2
Aristotle remarks, after a discussion on the possibility of coming
into existence : εἷς μὲν δὴ τρόπος
οὗτος, ἄλλος δ᾽ ὅτι ἐνδέχεται ταὐτὰ
λέγειν κατὰ τὴν δύναμιν καὶ τὴν
ἐνέργειαν · τοῦτο δ᾽ ἐν ἄλλοις διώρισται δι᾽ ἀκριβείας μᾶλλον. This
reference is most probably to a
passage in the *Metaphysics* (for
to refer it to one of the lost
writings is forbidden by the fact
that Aristotle is not accustomed
in other places to quote these
latter, as he cites the dogmatic
writings, with the simple ἐν
ἄλλοις ; cf. p. 108, n. 3). In the
Metaph., however, it not only
agrees with ix. 6 sqq., but also
with v. 7, 1017, a, 35 sqq., *i.e.*
the treatise Περὶ τοῦ ποσαχῶς,
cf. p. 76, n. 3. The same is true
of *Gen. et Corr.* ii. 10, 336, b,
29, as compared with *Metaph.*
v. 7.

tract cited in the *De Cœlo* [1] was written later than that work.[2] The *Meteorology* refers to the *De Sensu* : [3] and yet in its own preamble it described itself as the close of the series of investigations as to inorganic nature, *after* which the works on Animals and Plants were to be taken up. The *Natural History* quotes the book on Plants, which is spoken of in texts that are demonstrably later as being still unwritten.[4] The same treatise on Plants is referred to in an early section of the Περὶ ζῴων γενέσεως as already existing, and in a later one as yet to come.[5] The lost book on Food is quoted in the *De Somno* ; [6] in the later works on the Parts and Generation of Animals, it is promised as in the future.[7] There is a similar relation of cross reference between these same tracts and one of the lesser physiological

---

[1] *De Cœlo*, ii. 2, 284, b, 13 : if the world had a right and left side, it would also be obliged to have an above and below, a before and behind ; διώρισται μὲν οὖν περὶ τούτων ἐν τοῖς περὶ τὰς τῶν ζῴων κινήσεις (*Ingr. An.* 2, 704, b, 18, sqq., *ibid.* c, 4 sq.) διὰ τὸ τῆς φύσεως οἰκεῖα τῆς ἐκείνων εἶναι.

[2] This is proved not only from *Meteorol.* i. 1 *fin.* but also because the History of Animals and Π. ζῴων μορίων are quoted ; see *Ind. Arist.* 100, a, 55 sq.

[3] III. 2 *fin.*: ἔστω δὲ περὶ τούτων ἡμῖν τεθεωρημένον ἐν τοῖς περὶ τὰς αἰσθήσεις δεικνυμένοις (*De Sensu*, 3) διὸ τὰ μὲν λέγωμεν, τοῖς δ' ὡς ὑπάρχουσι χρησώμεθα αὐτῶν. Still more clearly must we, in *Meteor.* ii. 3, 359, b, 21, refer the εἴρηται ἐν ἄλλοις to *De Sensu*, 4.

[4] *H. An.* v. 1, 539, a, 20 :

ὥσπερ εἴρηται ἐν τῇ θεωρίᾳ τῇ περὶ φυτῶν. On the other hand this composition, as has been shown on p. 93, n. 1, is first promised in works which on their part quote in many places the History of Animals, *De Vita et M.*, *Part. An.*, and *Gen. An.*

[5] I. 23, 731, a, 29 : ἀλλὰ περὶ μὲν φυτῶν ἐν ἑτέροις ἐπέσκεπται. On the other hand v. 3, 783, b, 23 : ἀλλὰ περὶ μὲν τούτων (the falling of the leaves in winter) ἐν ἄλλοις τὸ αἴτιον λεκτέον (cf. i. 1, 716, a, 1 : περὶ μὲν οὖν φυτῶν, αὐτὰ καθ' αὑτὰ χωρὶς ἐπισκεπτέον, and p. 93, n. 1).

[6] C. 3, 456, b, 5 : εἴρηται δὲ περὶ τούτων ἐν τοῖς περὶ τροφῆς.

[7] Cf. p. 92, and on the chronological relation of the writings Π. ὕπνου, Π. ζῴων μορίων, Π. ζῴων γενέσεως, see BONITZ, *Ind. Arist.* 103, a, 16 sqq., 55 sqq.

texts,[1] making it impossible to say which comes before
the other. The tract on the Parts of Animals is cited
once in that on the Motion of Animals, which it cites
three times itself.[2]

How are we to treat this peculiarity? Are we so to
pervert the formulæ of reference in all these cases as to
read what ostensibly refers to an earlier writing as if it
were only an indication of something intended in a later
one? This would be negatived by the number of cases in
which the phenomenon recurs—itself a notable fact—and
also by the circumstance that in several cases the assumption of the later treatise as a thing already in existence is
too intimately interwoven with the tenor of the passage
to allow the change.[3] The like reasons stand equally
against the theory that these abnormal references crept
into the text after Aristotle's death.[4] But there is a far

---

[1] Π. ζωῆς καὶ θανάτου, together
with the connected Π. ἀναπνοῆς,
cf. p. 91 sq.

[2] *Ingr. An.* 5, 706, a, 33 :
many animals have the front and
hind parts near one another, οἷον
τά τε μαλάκια καὶ τὰ στρομβώδη
τῶν ὀστρακοδέρμων. εἴρηται δὲ περὶ
τούτων πρότερον ἐν ἑτέροις (*Part.
An.* iv. 9, 684, b, 10 sqq., 34, where
the same is said of the μαλάκιά
τε καὶ στρομβώδη τῶν ὀστρακοδέρμων). On the other hand, *Part.
An.* iv. 11, 690, b, 14 : ἡ δ᾽ αἰτία
τῆς ἀποδίας αὐτῶν (of snakes)
εἴρηται ἐν τοῖς περὶ τῆς πορείας τῶν
ζῴων (c. 8, 708, a, 9 sqq.) διωρισμένοις. *Ibid.* 692, a, 16 : περὶ δὲ
τῆς τῶν καμπύλων κάμψεως ἐν τοῖς
περὶ πορείας (c. 7, 707, b, 7, sqq.)
πρότερον ἐπέσκεπται κοινῇ περὶ
πάντων. With reference to the
same passage, iv. 13, 696, a, 11 :

τὸ δ᾽ αἴτιον ἐν τοῖς περὶ πορείας καὶ
κινήσεως τῶν ζῴων εἴρηται. [3] Thus
Top. vii. 3, 153, a,
24, where two lines would have to
be thrown out in order to remove
the reference, and *Meteorol.* iii.
2 *fin.* (p. 125, n. 3), where
the ὡς ὑπάρχουσι, χρησώμεθα
plainly shows that the reference
is not to a future exposition.
Still more violent than the
changes of text here contested is
the resource (*Ar. Libr. Ord.* 118
sq.) of giving to εἴρηται, when
necessary, the meaning of ῥηθή-
σεται, and of denying the
reference to the future in expressions like εἰς ἐκεῖνον τὸν καιρὸν
ἀποκείσθω. [4] Besides the passages given
in the preceding note, this
suggestion seems especially objectionable in *De Cœlo*, ii. 2 (*vid.*

simpler explanation, if it be true that he did not at once publish those books in which we find references to later texts as already written, but used them for a time only among his scholars and in connection with his oral lectures. In such manuscripts addenda would be introduced—and among them references to works written later would come in from time to time. If the author was never able to give to such a work any final revision for the purpose of publication, it might well happen that in one place a reference would stand in its originally correct form, as to a future work, though in another passage of the same or an earlier text a note might have been incorporated which spoke of the same work as already written. The same theory will explain the fact that the *Politics*—which we have every reason to consider as a book never finished by Aristotle, and published in its unfinished form after his death [1]—is cited in the *Rhetoric*, along with the *Poetics*,[2] which is itself spoken of by the *Politics* in the future tense. [3] The fact is that Aristotle had written a part of the *Politics* before he wrote the *Rhetoric* and *Poetics*. Therefore he could call the *Poetics* a future book in the *Politics*, and yet quote a passage of the *Politics* in the *Rhetoric*. If he

---

supra, p. 125, n. 1) since the εἰ δὲ δεῖ καὶ τῷ οὐρανῷ, &c. (line 18) corresponds with the διώρισται μὲν οὖν (line 13). The whole passage from διώρισται to εὔλογον ὑπάρχειν ἐν αὐτῷ (line 20), could be dispensed with, and it would all have to be taken as a post-Aristotelian interpolation.

[1] Cf. *infra*, ch. xiii.

[2] The *Politics* i. 8, 1366, a, 21 (διηκρίβωται γὰρ ἐν τοῖς πολιτι-

κοῖς περὶ τούτων), the *Poetics* frequently, *vid. supra* p. 102, n. 1.

[3] VIII. 7, 1341, b, 39 : on the ' catharsis ' νῦν μὲν ἁπλῶς, πάλιν δ' ἐν τοῖς περὶ ποιητικῆς ἐροῦμεν σαφέστερον, which, as Bernays (*Abh. d. hist. phil. Ges. in Breslau*, p. 139) rightly supposes, probably refers to a lost section of our *Poetics*, and not to one of the *Politics* (HEITZ, *Verl. Schr.* 100 sq.).

had published the *Rhetoric*, he could not in it have referred as he did to the unpublished *Politics*.[1]

The closing words of the *Topics*[2] seem to indicate that Aristotle's treatises were meant primarily for his scholars. Addressing his readers, he bespeaks their indulgence or their thanks for the theory he has unfolded to them,[3] referring specially to those who have heard his lectures. This does not imply that our *Topics* are only the lecture notes of the Master, or the note-book of one of his hearers. Such a view is negatived both by the wording of the passage,[4] and by the fact that in later writings he often refers to the *Topics* himself[5] in words which cannot be explained away as relating either to a lost book of his own or to another author. Such an address would be out of place in a work which was tendered to an unlimited circle of readers by formal publication, but it is entirely natural if the *Topics* was then issued only to Aristotle's scholars

---

[1] It is more difficult to explain the strange fact that *Rhet.* iii. 1, 1404, b, 22 speaks of the actor Theodorus as if he were still living and acting, whilst *Polit.* viii. 17, 1336, b, 27 treats him as one belonging to the past. But here the question arises, whether we possess, in the third book of *Rhetoric*, the work of Aristotle himself, or the work of a later writer, who, in this passage, which seems to be in the genuine style of Aristotle, may have used one of his earlier works. Cf. p. 72, n. 2.

[2] *Soph. El.* 33 *fin.*: Aristotle had no predecessor for his theory of demonstration; εἰ δὲ φαίνεται θεασαμένοις ὑμῖν . . . ἔχειν ἡ μέθοδος

ἱκανῶς παρὰ τὰς ἄλλας πραγματείας τὰς ἐκ παραδόσεως ηὐξημένας, λοιπὸν ἂν εἴη πάντων ὑμῶν ἢ τῶν ἠκροαμένων ἔργον τοῖς μὲν παραλελειμμένοις τῆς μεθόδου συγγνώμην τοῖς δ' εὑρημένοις πολλὴν ἔχειν χάριν.

[3] Some MSS. read, instead of ὑμῖν and ὑμῶν, ἡμῖν and ἡμῶν; but Aristotle could not possibly have included himself among those whom he thanks, and to whom he apologises.

[4] Which distinguishes among the readers the ' ἠκροαμένοι ' from the rest; only by striking out the ἢ before τῶν ἠκροαμένων could we get a simple address to listeners, but the MSS. all have it.

[5] *Ind. Arist.* 102, a, 40 sqq.

as a memorial of the contents of his lectures or as an auxiliary to them.[1] That this was true of some of his books, must be inferred from other passages also. The synopsis of varying meanings of words, which now forms the fifth book of the *Metaphysics*, could never have been published by Aristotle in its present form as a glossary without beginning or end. It can only have been placed in the hands of his scholars simply as an aid to his teaching. Yet he often refers to it, and that even in texts earlier than the *Metaphysics*.[2] The same argument applies to the often-cited anatomical texts,[3] which must have been limited to a narrow circle because of the drawings which were an essential part of them. If it be true, however, that writings which Aristotle cites were published only to his scholars, it follows that the same must be true of those in which these citations occur; for no one could in a published book refer to an unpublished one, or say that a subject not gone into was fully explained in an inaccessible tract.

The same theory by which we explain the group of peculiarities already noticed, will explain others also. The trick of carelessness in style which is so often re-marked, the repetitions which surprise us in an exposition otherwise compact, the insertions which upset a naturally well-ordered movement of thought are all explained most easily if we suppose that the author never put the finishing touches to the writings in question, and that various matters were at the time of the

[1] As Stahr, *ibid.*, has sup-posed.
[2] Cf. pp. 76, n. 3, 124, n. 4.
[3] About which see p. 89, n. 1.

posthumous publication added to the original text either from parallel copies or from the author's notes.[1] This theory becomes extremely probable when, as in the books *On the Soul*,[2] we find throughout considerable sections clear traces of a double recension, without any reason to say that either recension is not Aristotle's.[3] The same kind of argument would apply also to the *Politics* and *Metaphysics*, but as to these we have independent grounds for the belief that they remained unfinished, and were only published after his death.[4] If this be so, a further inference is forced on us ; for we must conclude that if a certain book was a posthumous publication only, all which refer to it in such a way as to show that they follow it in the series cannot have been issued in Aristotle's life. This line of argument, even if we could apply it with high probability to nothing more than the *De Anima*, would take us a long way ; for that work is cited in many of the books on natural philosophy.[5]

The scope and the modifications of this theory as to the way in which the Aristotelian books were produced, can only be settled by a detailed examination of the indi-

[1] A supposition which a number of scholars have been led to adopt, with various particular modifications : thus RITTER, iii. 29 (*vid. supra*, p. 121, n. 2 mid.) ; BRANDIS, ii. b, 113 ; UEBERWEG, *Gesch. d. Phil.* i. 174, eighth ed., SUSEMIHL, *Arist. Poët.* p. 1 sq., BERNAYS, *Arist. Politik*, 212. It is also probable that Aristotle, instead of *writing*, usually *dictated*: which would account for many of the irregularities of style, such as the lengthy and involved anacolutha.

[2] Cf. p. 89, n. 2. It may be otherwise with the repetitions and disarrangements of the connection in the *Ethics*, especially bks. 5–7. Cf. p. 97, n. 1.

[3] As in Bk. vii. of the *Physics*, on which Spengel has written in *Abh. d. Münch. Akad.* iii. 2, 305 sqq. Cf. PRANTL, *Arist. Phys.* 337.

[4] Cf. p. 76, n. 3, and *infra*, Ch. xiii., *init.*

[5] *Vid. supra*, p. 93, n. 2 ; *Ind. Ar.* 102, b, 60 sqq.

vidual texts. But the peculiarities above referred to, the reference to a class of published or ' exoteric ' works, the habit of citing later books in earlier ones, the tricks of repetition and disorder which indicate the absence of the author's final revision—all these extend through almost the whole of the extant *Corpus*. From this and from the fact that, though the *Topics* and the *De Anima* were apparently written only for Aristotle's pupils, yet they are frequently cited by later treatises,[1] it seems very probable that the whole of our *Corpus*, so far as it is genuine, consists of books which were produced in connection with the teaching in the Lyceum, were intended at first for Aristotle's pupils only, and were made generally accessible by formal publication only after the master's death. Of the great majority of them it may also be assumed, not only from their contents, but also from their express internal correlation that Aristotle is in them working up in writing what he had already given his pupils by way of oral lectures,[2] though it is also likely that when they came to be published by third parties explanations were added and whole passages interpolated from Aristotle's papers or his other lectures.[3] A few of the texts may have served him as aids in his teaching, without being themselves matter of lecturing.[4] One of the books of the *Metaphysics*[5]

---

[1] Cf. p. 129 and 130.

[2] Cf. what has been remarked on p. 128 sq. with regard to the closing words of the *Topics*.

[3] As, from what has been said on pp. 76 and 130, seems to have been the case

in the *Metaphysics* and the *De Anima*.

[4] Like the composition Περὶ τοῦ ποσαχῶς (cf. p. 76, n. 3, at p. 77). One is inclined to think the same of the 'Ανατομαί.

[5] The twelfth, cf. same note, at p. 78.

seems to have been a plan for a lecture course, though
not intended, in its present shape, for communication
to his pupils. This, however, cannot well be true of
any great portion of the extant writings. That theory
is excluded in the first place by the all-pervading
system of cross references, which both in number and
in manner go far beyond anything that Aristotle
could have wanted for himself.[1] Again it is negatived
by the fact that, in spite of all the defects already
referred to, these works are from a literary point of
view far more carefully worked up than they would
have been if they were merely sketches for the lecturer's
own use. Then again, the unusual recurrence of formulæ
of introduction, transition and conclusion, shows that
the author is writing, not for himself, but for others.[2]

[1] Bk. xii. of the *Metaphysics*
has in the first half none at all,
and in the second, which is
worked out much more fully
(since the δέδεικται, c. 7, 1073,
a, 5, relates to c. 6, 1071, b, 20), a
single reference (c. 8, 1073, a, 32 :
δέδεικται δ' ἐν τοῖς φυσικοῖς περὶ
τούτων). It is otherwise in most
of the other works. Still more
decisive, however, is the form of
the references. No one uses for
himself expressions like the
φαμὲν mentioned in p. 115, n. 4, or
circumstantial formulas, like ἔκ
τε τῆς ἱστορίας τῆς περὶ τὰ ζῷα
φανερὸν καὶ τῶν ἀνατομῶν καὶ
ὕστερον λεχθήσεται ἐν τοῖς περὶ
γενέσεως (*Part. An.* iv. 10, 689,
a, 18), and the like (the *Ind. Ar.*
97, b, sqq. furnishes examples), or
like those quoted on p. 115.

[2] To this class belongs the
conclusion of the *Topics* (see p.
128, n. 2); the νῦν δὲ λέγωμεν

(*Soph. El.* c. 2, *fin.*; *Metaph.* vii.
12, *init.*, xiii. 10, 1086, b, 16 and
supra), ὥσπερ λέγομεν, ὥσπερ
ἐλέγομεν (*Eth. N.* vi. 3, 1139, b,
26, *Metaph.* iv. 5, 1010, a, 4, *Rhet.*
i. 1, 1055, a, 28 and *supra*),
καθάπερ ἐπήλθομεν (*Metaph.* x. 2,
init., xiii. 2, 1076, b, 39), καθάπερ
διειλόμεθα (*Metaph.* vii. 1, *init.*),
ἃ διωρίσαμεν, ἐν οἷς διωρισάμεθα,
τὰ διωρισμένα ἡμῖν (*Metaph.* i. 4,
985, a, 11, vi. 4, *fin.*, i. 7, 1028, a,
4), δῆλον ἡμῖν (*Rhet.* i. 2, 1356, b,
9, 1357, a, 29), τεθεώρηται ἡμῖν
ἱκανῶς περὶ αὐτῶν (*Metaph.* i. 3,
983, a, 33); cf. also those sentences in which what has been
discussed before is summed up,
and what is going to be treated
is announced (e.g. *Metaph.* xiii. 9,
1086, a, 18 sqq., *Rhet.* i. 2, 1356,
b, 10 sqq.; *Soph. El.* c. 33, 183,
a, 33 sqq.; *Meteorol.* init.).
ONCKEN (*Staatsl. d. Ar.*, i. 58)
cites, from the *Nicom. Ethics* and

Another unlikely theory[1] is that which suggests that the whole or a great part of our *Corpus* consists of transcripts in which Aristotle's pupils had set down the contents of his lectures. We have seen that they are in all probability closely connected with the lecture courses.[2] But whether they are a mere transcript of these, or a free working-up of the same matter, whether they were designed to repeat as correctly as might be the words of the master, or to leave us a spiritual reproduction of his thoughts, whether in fine they were written by his pupils or by himself, is a very different question. The note-theory may rely on the suggestion that it would explain the carelessness of the methods of

the *Politics* alone, thirty-two passages with such formulas. No one will believe that Aristotle would have had to write down all such expressions in his lecture-book, like a man beginning to teach, who is not sure of a single word.

[1] ONCKEN, *ibid.* 48 sqq. following SCALIGER. O. there remarks (62 sq.) that he thinks he has only made this supposition probable with regard to the *Ethics* and *Politics*, but his reasons would hold equally for the majority of our Aristotelian writings.

[2] Oncken, in proof of this, rightly appeals, besides other passages (p. 59 sq.), to those passages of the *Ethics* in which an audience is spoken of: *Eth.* i. 1, 1095, a, 2, 11 : διὸ τῆς πολιτικῆς οὐκ ἔστι οἰκεῖος ἀκροατῆς ὁ νέος . . . περὶ μὲν ἀκροατοῦ . . . πεφροιμιάσθω τοσαῦτα. *Ibid.* c. 2, 1095, b, 4 : διὸ δεῖ τοῖς ἔθεσιν ἦχθαι καλῶς τὸν

περὶ . . . τῶν πολιτικῶν ἀκουσόμενον. (*Eth.* x. 10, 1079, b, 23, 27 ; vii. 5, 1147, b, 9, are not relevant here ; and *Pol.* vii. 1, 1323, b, 39 : ἑτέρας γάρ ἐστιν ἔργον σχολῆς ταῦτα, only means ' this belongs to another inquiry.') Oncken further proves that, in referring on any point to other works, only such expressions are used as are suited to a person who is *speaking*, such as εἴρηται, λεκτέον, ἄλλος λόγος, &c.; but such language was certainly used in referring to *writings* (like the *Problems* and the ἐξωτερικοὶ λόγοι, see above, p. 96, and p. 115, n. 4), and is often so used in our own days. He also refers to the title πολιτικὴ ἀκρόασις (*ap.* DIOG. v. 24) ; φυσικὴ ἀκρόασις is likewise universally used for the *Physics* (*vid. supr.* p. 81, n. 2) ; but since we do not know with whom these titles originate, not much can be inferred from them.

statement.[1] But on closer inquiry, this argument comes to nothing. For it is not here a question of any such defects as commonly arise in the redaction of well-ordered lectures badly reported, through omissions and repetitions and the erroneous piecing together of the broken argument. It is more a question of peculiarities of style not restrained by the writer, which are too characteristic and too constant in their character to allow us to make chance and the errors of third persons answerable for them.[2] Such an origin might be thought possible if they appeared in some books and not in others. But as they in fact extend, though in varying degrees, through the whole, they can only be ascribed to Aristotle himself. The very style and form of the

---

[1] And this is the chief ground on which Oncken bases his opinion. The defects of our texts are most easily explained ' from the natural defects of a peripatetic monologue ' (he says, p. 62), 'hastily copied in and badly edited from the note-books of the audience.'

[2] With these must be reckoned the formation of the sentences (searchingly investigated by BONITZ, *Arist. Stud.* ii. 3 sqq.) especially the explanations, often of considerable length, which are parenthetically introduced, and the anacolutha consequent on this; the frequent use or absence of certain particles (proofs of which are to be found in EUCKEN, *De Arist. Dicendi Ratione*, and in Bonitz's notice of this work in the *Ztschr. f. d. östr. Gymn.* 1866, 804 sqq.), and similar points. The same is the true view as to the questions

occurring so often in all Aristotelian writings, which are put at one time in simple form, at another (as in *De An.* i. 1, 403, b, 7 sqq., *Gen. et Corr.* ii. 11, 337, b, 5, and in the passages explained by BONITZ, *Arist. Stud.* ii. 16 sq., *ibid.* 6, 333, b, 30) in a disjunctive form, but are not answered. That such unanswered questions could not have occurred in a composition (ONCKEN, *ibid.* 61), one cannot allow — how many, for instance, are found, only to mention one modern writer, in Lessing ! Neither can one admit the supposition (*ibid.* 59), that they were answered, in oral discourse, by the audience or the teacher. They seem to be, both in Aristotle and Lessing, a very natural diversion of an acute and lively Dialectic, which would have been more likely to be removed than retained by any reporter.

writings therefore afford a strong indication that not only their contents but their language is Aristotle's own. A like conclusion follows also (as we have seen [1]) from the series of cross references; for in a lecture a man might allude to one or two past courses, but could hardly refer to a whole series of lectures widely distant in date, as to which he could not assume that the details were in the memory of his present audience.[2] It seems moreover that in many cases, as in the Natural Philosophy, the matter of the various treatises goes too closely into detail for the purposes of oral teaching. Such lectures would have taxed the attention and memory of the most zealous hearer, and it is difficult to see how they could have been transcribed so perfectly.[3] Yet these treatises stand on no different footing from the rest.

We learn that Theophrastus and Eudemus in their *Analytics* followed Aristotle, not only in the general plan, but in details,[4] and we can bring proof that these followers adopted word for word several passages of the extant *Metaphysics*.[5] Eudemus adopted the *Ethics* of

---

[1] See pp. 128, 131.

[2] Note, in relation to this point, how one and the same composition is frequently referred to in the most remote places, and how, on the other hand, the most widely differing texts are cited in the same treatise. Thus the *Physics, De Cœlo, Gen. et Corr., Meteor., De Anima, De Sensu, Part. An.,* are quoted in many passages of the *Metaphysics* and in the *Ethics*; the books on *Generation and Corruption* in the *Meteorology, Metaphysics, De Anima, De Sensu, Part. An., Gen. An.*; the *Metaphysics* quote the *Analytics, Physics, De Cœlo, Ethics,* the ἐκλογὴ τῶν ἐναντίων; in the *Rhetoric,* the *Topics, Analytics, Politics, Poetics,* and the Θεοδέκτεια are quoted.

[3] The notion of formal dictation can hardly be suggested, but if it were, it would imply that our Aristotelian writings were the work of Aristotle himself and *not* his pupils' notes.

[4] Cf. p. 67.

[5] Cf. p. 78, n. 1.

Aristotle, and still more the *Physics*,[1] often verbally, into his own corresponding texts. We actually possess letters in which Eudemus consults Theophrastus as to the text of a particular passage and receives his answer.[2] These facts clearly justify Brandis' remark,[3] that the fashion in which Aristotle's followers clung to the master's writings presupposes that they were dealing with his actual words. As to the *Topics* in particular, it has been already proved that it is not a mere transcript by another hand, but that on the contrary it bears to be and must have been the work of Aristotle (see p. 128).

If it be true that the philosophical works of Aristotle had not yet passed at his death beyond the circle of his personal hearers, this circumstance would make it also intelligible that they might for a long time, even after his death, have been withheld from general publicity, or that they might even by an unlucky accident have been lost to the Peripatetic School. And, according to a curious and well-known story, such an accident was said to have occurred, involving, as was supposed, the loss for two centuries of the texts of Aristotle.

[1] See the section dealing with Eudemus, etc., *infra*, Ch. xix., and notes thereon.

[2] These have reference to *Phys.* v. 2, 226, b, 14, and are found in SIMPL. *Phys.* 216 a, *Schol.* 404, b, 10.

[3] *Gr.-röm. Phil.* ii. b, 114.

CHAPTER III

HISTORY AND ORDER OF THE WORKS OF ARISTOTLE

STRABO and Plutarch say that the works of Aristotle and Theophrastus passed, at the death of the latter, to his heir, Neleus of Scepsis, and that they were stowed away in a cellar by the heirs of Neleus, discovered only in the early part of the last century B.C. by Apellico of Teos in a decayed condition, brought by him to Athens and thence by Sulla as spoils of war to Rome, where they were afterwards used and republished by Tyrannio and Andronicus.[1] From this story the writers named argue that to the Peripatetics who followed Theophrastus, not only the master's chief works, but also his true philosophical system was unknown, but they do not tell us whether this allegation is grounded on their own opinion, or on definite evidence,

[1] The date of this edition must have fallen somewhere about the middle of the last century B.C. For as Tyrannio was in B.C. 71 taken prisoner in Amisus and released by Muræna (cf. ZELLER, *Ph. d. Gr.*, pt. iii. a, 550, 1), he could hardly have settled in Rome before Lucullus' return to Rome (66 B.C.). We know that he was even at the time of his capture a scholar of renown, that he was instructing in B.C. 57 the sons of Cicero, and had some intercourse with the latter and Atticus (CIC. *Ad Qu. Fr.* ii. 5, *Ad Att.* iv. 4, 8). His work at Rome could not, therefore, have extended very far beyond the middle of the century, even though he perhaps lived on into the last third of it. (He died according to Suid. *s. v.* γηραιὸς, in the third year of an Olympiad the number of which has unfortunately been miswritten.) About Andronicus cf. ZELLER, *Ph. d. Gr.*, pt. iii. a, 549, 3, and above, p. 49, n. 6.

and if so, what the nature of the evidence might be.[1]
Later critics found in the tale a welcome explanation of
the incompleteness and irregularities of the existing
Corpus.[2] If in truth the case were exactly as Strabo
and Plutarch say, we should not only not wonder at the
existing defects, but we should rather have expected a
far wider and more hopeless corruption than appears in
fact to exist. For if it were true of the most important

[1] Our authorities for the
above narrative are, as we have
remarked, Strabo (xiii. 1, 54, p.
608) and Plutarch (*Sulla*, 26),
for Suid *Σύλλας* only copies Plutarch. The latter, however, undoubtedly gets his information
from Strabo. The only thing
which the latter does not give is
the remark that Andronicus obtained copies of the Aristotelian
works through Tyrannio, published them, and wrote the *τοὺς
νῦν φερομένους πίνακας*. Plut. may
have added this from what he
knew from other sources, or also
(as Stahr supposes in *Arist.*
ii. 23) from Strabo's historical
work (made use of immediately
afterwards for an incident in
Sulla's residence at Athens). We
have no right to suppose (HEITZ,
Verl. Schr. 10) a source for his
information about Apellico's discovery of books, independent of
Strabo. Hence our only stable
witness for this item is Strabo.
But we do not know to whom the
latter was indebted for his information; the supposition that
it was Andronicus is very unsafe.
Strabo, after the statements as
to the purchase of the Aristotelian books by Apellico, and as to
his faulty editing of them, says :
συνέβη δὲ τοῖς ἐκ τῶν περιπάτων,

*τοῖς μὲν πάλαι τοῖς μετὰ Θεόφρασ-
τον οὐκ ἔχουσιν ὅλως τὰ βιβλία
πλὴν ὀλίγων, καὶ μάλιστα τῶν ἐξωτερικῶν, μηδὲν ἔχειν φιλοσοφεῖν
πραγματικῶς ἀλλὰ θέσεις ληκυθίζειν·
τοῖς δ' ὕστερον, ἀφ' οὗ τὰ βιβλία
ταῦτα προῆλθεν, ἄμεινον μὲν ἐκείνων
φιλοσοφεῖν καὶ ἀριστοτελίζειν,
ἀναγκάζεσθαι μέντοι τὰ πολλὰ
εἰκότα λέγειν διὰ τὸ πλῆθος τῶν
ἁμαρτιῶν.* But we can only suppose this to have been taken from
Andronicus, if we limit the
'younger Peripatetics' (*τοῖς
δ' ὕστερον*, &c.) to those predecessors of Andronicus who
were able to use the editions
of Apellico and Tyrannio, and
it is very questionable whether
anyone could attribute to these
men, who are quite unknown to
us, an improvement of the Peripatetic doctrine, and a closer
insight into Aristotle, such as
might with reason be ascribed to
Andronicus. As little can we
assume Tyrannio or Boëthus
(to whom Grote ascribes it, *Aristotle*, i. 54) as Strabo's source of
information, since the former
would have taken a different view
of his own edition, and the latter
of the younger Peripatetics.

[2] Thus BUHLE, *Allg. Encykl.*
Sect. i. vol. v. 278 sq., and lately
HEITZ; see next page, n. 2.

works that the only source of our extant text was to be
found in these MSS., which rotted for a century and
more in the cellar of Scepsis, till Apellico found them
worm-eaten, ruined by damp, and tossed into a disordered heap—if it be true that he, as Strabo says,
supplied unskilfully the missing portions, and that
Tyrannio and Andronicus also had no further manuscripts they could collate—who then could guarantee
that in any number of cases there would not have been
foreign matter, found among Neleus' MSS., adopted
into Aristotle's text, or connected parts of his own
works separated, and other portions blunderingly bound
together, or lacunæ great and small filled up by the
editor's fancy?

Modern criticism has, however, raised doubts about
Strabo's story [1] which even its defenders cannot altogether silence.[2] That Theophrastus bequeathed his
library to Neleus is beyond doubt.[3] That the MSS. of

[1] After the isolated and disregarded voice of a learned
Frenchman, about the beginning
of the eighteenth century, had
raised doubts as to this narration
(see what Stahr gives in *Arist.*
ii. 163 sq. from the *Journal des
Sçavans* of the year 1717, p. 655
sqq., as to the anonymous composition *Les Aménitez de la
Critique*), BRANDIS (' Ueb. die
Schicksale d. arist. Bücher.'
Rhein. Mus. v. Niebuhr and
Brandis, i. 236 sqq , 259 sqq.; cf.
Gr.-röm. Phil. ii. b, 66 sqq.) was
the first to deal with it seriously.
KOPP (*Rhein. Mus.* iii. 93 sqq.)
supplemented his criticism, and
finally STAHR has discussed the
question with exhaustive parti-

cularity (*Aristotelia*, ii. 1–166, cf.
294 sq.). Later scholars have
mostly followed them.

[2] HEITZ, *Verl. Schr. d. Ar.*
9 sqq., 20, 29 sqq.; GROTE, *Aristotle*, i. 50 sqq.; GRANT, *Ethics
of Ar.* i. 5 sqq., *Aristotle*, 3 sqq.
Certain errors in Strabo's and
Plutarch's representation are indeed admitted by these scholars,
but in the main it is said to be
correct. It is impossible here to
examine in detail the reasons
given for this opinion, but the
grounds for its rejection are
fully dealt with in the text.

[3] Theophrastus' will, *apud*
DIOG. v. 52; cf. ATHEN. i. 3,
where it is added that Ptolemy
Philadelphus bought the whole

Aristotle and Theophrastus belonging to that library passed to the heirs of Neleus and were by them hidden in a canal or cellar to escape a royal book-collector and were afterwards found by Apellico in a desperate condition, there is no need to doubt.[1] All the *facts* which Strabo relates as to the matter may therefore be correct enough. And it is also beyond question that Andronicus' edition of the Aristotelian text-books was of epoch-making importance both for the study of the system and for the preservation of the text. If, however, it be maintained that these writings were nowhere to be found outside the Scepsis cellar and were unknown therefore to the Peripatetic School after the death of Theophrastus, there are the strongest arguments against any such theory.

In the first place, it is almost incredible that an event so singularly notable as the discovery of the lost masterpieces of Aristotle should never have been even alluded to by any of those who, since that time, have concerned themselves with Aristotle, as critics or as philosophers. Cicero says not a word, though he had abundant occasion, for he lived at Rome at the very time when Tyrannio was working among the literary booty of Sulla, and was, in fact, in active intercourse with Tyrannio himself. Alexander, ' the Exegete,' says nothing ; nor does any one of the Greek critics who used the very works of Andronicus, either at first or at second

collection of Neleus and had it brought to Alexandria.

[1] For when Athenæus, or the epitomiser of his introduction, *ibid.*, asserts that the *whole library* of Neleus was taken to Alexandria, this may easily be an inexact expression, just as it is inexact, in the opposite way, when, in v 214, he makes Apellico possess not the *works*, but the *library* of Aristotle.

hand. Andronicus himself seems to have ascribed to
Apellico's discovery so little importance that he based
neither the inquiry into the genuineness of a tract nor
the discussion of a various reading upon any reference
to the MSS. of Neleus.[1] Later editors did not in any
way feel themselves bound by his text,[2] though if
Strabo were right, it could be the only authentic one.

On the other hand, the theory that by the loss of
the works of Aristotle, the followers of Theophrastus
strayed from the original teachings of their school and
lost themselves in mere rhetorical developments, is an
obvious contradiction of the facts. It may be true that
the Peripatetics of the third century strayed away as
time went on from the study of natural philosophy and
metaphysics, but this change took place not on the
death of Theophrastus, but at the earliest on the death
of his successor Strato. So far was he from confining
himself to ethics and rhetoric, that he devoted himself,
on the contrary, with a one-sided preference to physics,
though he by no means neglected logic and metaphysics. He frequently contradicted Aristotle ; but
that could not be by ignorance of the Aristotelian system,
because he attacked it expressly.[3] It does not appear

---

[1] With regard to the first,
cf. the account given on p. 66, n. 1.
as to his doubts about the
Π. Ἑρμηνείας : with respect to
the second point, cf. DEXIPP.
In Arist. Categ. p. 25, Speng.
(*Schol. in Ar.* 42, a, 30) : πρῶτον
μὲν οὐκ ἐν ἅπασι τοῖς ἀντι-
γράφοις τὸ " ὃ δὲ λόγος τῆς οὐσίας "
πρόσκειται, ὡς καὶ Βοηθὸς μνημο-
νεύει καὶ 'Ανδρόνικος—it is not
said that he has settled the dis-

pute by means of Sulla's MSS.
(or, if he had not access to the
latter, at least by means of the
copies of Tyrannio, which, according to Plutarch, he used). It
seems, therefore, that these MSS.
were not the only copies nor
even the original ones of the
works in question. Cf. BRANDIS,
Rhein. Mus. i. 241.

[2] Cf. SIMPL. *Phys.* 101, a.

[3] The proofs will be given,

that the scientific activity of the School came at once to an end, even after Strato's death.[1] The theory that the falling away of the later Peripatetics from Aristotle was due to the loss of his writings from Athens is in every way unnatural. It is much more reasonable to correlate it to the parallel movement in the Academy, which nevertheless was at no loss for texts of Plato.

But who can believe that the most important works of the great philosopher were not extant at the date of his successor's death in any other MSS. than those which Neleus inherited? or that not only in Aristotle's lifetime, but also in the nine Olympiads between his death and that of Theophrastus, not one of his many followers had ever been willing and able to possess himself of the most important sources of the Peripatetic teaching? Who can think that Eudemus, the most loyal of the Aristotelian circle, or Strato, the shrewdest of the Peripatetics, would have done without the Master's books—or that Demetrius of Phalerus did not include them in his zeal for collecting learned works—or that Ptolemy Philadelphus bought other books of Aristotle and Theophrastus for his Library of Alexandria, but omitted to obtain copies of their essential texts?

The story also supposes that the possessors of the manuscripts objected to such uses of them : that Aristotle kept his writings closely under lock and key, and that Theophrastus, for no apparent reason, kept up this

in part, in the following pages. They will also be found in the section on Strato, *infra*, Ch. xx., and notes thereon.

[1] See, at end of vol. ii., the section on the Pseudo-Aristotelian texts (*infra*, Ch. xxi.).

secrecy, and laid it as a duty on his heirs.   All this is
too absurd to need serious refutation.

We are not left, however, wholly to conjecture.
The materials are very scanty for the history of a time
whose philosophic literature by an unhappy accident
we have almost wholly lost; but we can still prove, as
to a great part of Aristotle's books, that they were not
unknown to the learned men of the two centuries that
elapsed between Theophrastus' death and the occupation
of Athens by Sulla.   Whether Aristotle did or did not
himself *publish* his strictly scientific treatises, they were
in any case destined to be the text-books of the School,
and to be used by its members.   Even those numerous
passages in which they refer one to the other offer us a
palpable proof that, in the view of the writer, they were
not only to be read by his scholars, but closely studied
and compared, and, by consequence, that copies were to
be kept and multiplied.   That this was done is clear,
not only from the notices which we find of particular
books, but from certain general considerations also:

If it is true that the Peripatetics lost the genuine
Aristotelianism when the library of Theophrastus
disappeared, it must be because the sources of that
teaching were nowhere else to be found.   But we hear
not only of Theophrastus but of Eudemus also, that he
imitated Aristotle [1] not only in the titles but also in the
contents of his books; and how close was the imitation
both in wording and in the line of thought, we can see
for ourselves in the *Ethics* and *Physics* of Eudemus. [2]

[1] For references see pp. 65
and 68.

[2] Cf. p. 148, n. 4, and in the section on Eudemus at Ch. xix., *inf.*

To do this, Eudemus must have possessed Aristotle's texts; especially if, as a reliable story tells us,[1] he used them at a time when he was not living at Athens.[2] Again, it is beyond doubt that the Alexandrian Library included a large number of Aristotle's works.[3] The compilers of the Alexandrine Canon, who place Aristotle among the model writers of philosophy, may have had chiefly in view the more careful style of his exoteric writings;[4] but in the foundation of that great collection it is not possible that the scientific works of Aristotle can have been left out of account. If the Catalogue of Diogenes[5] comes from the Alexandrine Library, it is proof positive that they were there: but even if that conjecture (in itself extremely probable) were erroneous, the Catalogue still proves in any case that the compiler of

---

[1] *Vide supra*, p. 136, n. 3.

[2] HEITZ (*Verl. Schr.* 13) indeed thinks that if the Aristotelian works had been universally known and published, it would be incomprehensible that Eudemus in his *Physics* (and *Ethics*) should have imitated the words of Aristotle so exactly. It seems, however, that if Eudemus had hesitated to do this with regard to published works, a plagiarism on unpublished ones must have seemed much more unlawful to him. It is impossible, however, to regard his conduct in this light at all, and he himself probably never so regarded it. His *Ethics* and *Physics* were never intended to be anything but elaborations of the Aristotelian works universally known in the Peripatetic School, adapted to the needs of his own tuition.

[3] Besides what has been remarked on p. 142, we have the fact that Ptolemy Philadelphus busied himself zealously about Aristotelian books, paid high prices for them, and thus gave occasion to the forgery of such texts (AMMON. *Schol. in Arist.* 28, a, 43; DAVID, *ibid.*, l. 14; SIMPL. *Categ.* 2, ε). And such accounts as those noticed at p. 64, n. 1 and 67, n. 1, about the two books of the *Categories* and the forty of the *Analytics* which Adrastus found in old libraries, must refer especially to the Alexandrian Library. But it is not to be supposed that the latter obtained only substituted works, and did not possess the genuine ones, by reference to which the forgeries were proved.

[4] See STAHR, *ibid.* 65 sq. on this point.

[5] For which see p. 48 sqq.

it, who lived later than Theophrastus and earlier than Andronicus, had before him a great part of our extant *Corpus Aristotelicum*.[1] Its probable author, Hermippus, was acquainted with the works of Theophrastus (which according to Strabo and Plutarch were buried in Scepsis along with those of Aristotle), as is clear from his catalogue of them, preserved, apparently, by Diogenes.[2] That he at all events knew nothing of the disappearance of the Aristotelian writings, may probably be inferred from the silence of Diogenes on that subject.[3] Another strong evidence of the use of the Aristotelian books in the third century B.C. is to be found in the Stoic teaching, which in its most systematic exposition by Chrysippus follows both in logic and in physics more closely on the Aristotelian than could be possible if the Aristotelian text-books were unknown. There is, indeed, some express evidence that Chrysippus had in fact these texts in view.[4]

---

[1] Cf. p. 50, n. 1.

[2] Cf. the scholion at the end of the *Metaphysics* of Theophrastus: τοῦτο τὸ βιβλίον ’Ανδρόνικος μὲν καὶ ῞Ερμιππος ἀγνοοῦσιν · οὐδὲ γὰρ μνείαν αὐτοῦ ὅλως πεποίηται ἐν τῇ ἀναγραφῇ τῶν Θεοφράστου βιβλίων. From the same list evidently is taken the scholion at the beginning of the seventh book of the *History of Plants* (*apud* USENER, *Anal. Theophr.* 23) : Θεοφράστου περὶ φυτῶν ἱστορίας τὸ η΄. ῞Ερμιππος δὲ περὶ φρυγανικῶν καὶ ποιωδῶν, ’Ανδρόνικος δὲ περὶ φυτῶν ἱστορίας. DIOG. (ii. 55) names a book by Hermippus on Theophrastus, of which it probably formed a part. That the lists in Diog. v. 46 sqq., at least in part and indirectly,

originated with Hermippus, is the more probable since that writer is mentioned immediately before in v. 45.

[3] For, on the one hand, it is not to be supposed that Hermippus in his copious work on Aristotle (mentioned on p. 51, n. 2) would not have mentioned this circumstance, if he had been aware of it ; and, on the other hand, it is very improbable that the author to whom Diogenes is indebted for his many quotations from Hermippus would have passed over this information. Diogenes, to whose literary tastes it must have recommended itself, would have seized upon it, if he found it.

[4] For even if we were not

If the works of Aristotle were first unearthed by Apellico and first fully known through Tyrannio and Andronicus, how could it be said of Critolaus that he imitated the old masters of his school—Aristotle, that is, and Theophrastus?[1] or how of Herillus the Stoic that he based himself upon them,[2] or of Panætius that he was always quoting them?[3] How could we have mention of the constant tendency of Posidonius towards Aristotle?[4] How could Cicero's teacher, Antiochus, have explained the Aristotelian teaching as one with the Academic, and attempted their complete and thorough-going amalgamation?[5] or where could opponents such as Stilpo and Hermarchus have found the material for their attacks on Aristotle?[6] So again, since Andronicus gives us the alleged letter in which Alexander complains to Aristotle about the publication of his doctrine,[7] it follows that long before that date writings of Aristotle, including some of those which were afterwards reckoned 'exoteric,' must have in fact been public property.

Scanty as are the sources open to us, we can ourselves demonstrate the public use before Andronicus, not only of many of the lost works, which, being

inclined to attach much importance to the polemic against one of the discourses mentioned on p. 56, n. 1, yet the expression in PLUT. *Sto. Rep.* 24, p. 1045, supposes acquaintance with Aristotle's dialectical writings.

[1] CIC. *Fin.* v. 5, 14.
[2] *Ibid.* v. 25, 73.
[3] *Ibid.* iv. 28, 79 ; cf. ZELL., *Ph. d. Gr.* pt. iii. a, 503, 3, 2nd ed.

[4] *Ibid.* iii. a, 514, 2.
[5] Fuller particulars, *ibid.* 535 sqq.
[6] Stilpo wrote, according to DIOG. ii. 120, an Ἀριστοτέλης, Hermarchus (*ibid.* x. 25) πρὸς Ἀριστοτέλην. From the expression of Colotes *apud* PLUT. *Adv. Col.* 14, 1, p. 1115, we can, however, conclude nothing.
[7] See pp. 22, n. 1, and 112, n. 3.

exoteric or hypomnematic,[1] are not here in point, but also of the majority of the scientific treatises themselves.

In the case of the *Analytics* we show this by the Catalogue of Diogenes and by the notices as to the use made of them by Theophrastus and Eudemus.[2] For the Categories and the Περὶ ἑρμηνείας, we have the Catalogue.[3] As to the former, Andronicus found in his MS. the spurious 'Post-prædicamenta' added to them, and was acquainted with several recensions, having varying titles and different readings.[4] It follows, therefore, that the *Categories* must have been long before his day in the hands of transcribers.[5] The *Topics* are in the Catalogue of Diogenes,[6] and Theophrastus [7] and

---

[1] The letters, *vide supra* p. 54, n. 2.; the four books, Π. δικαιοσύνης (p. 56, n. 1), taken into consideration by Chrysippus, Teles, Demetrius (Π. ἑρμην.), probably also by Carneades ; the *Protrepticus*, which is known even to Crates, Zeno, and Teles (p. 60, n. 1), the *Eudemus* (p. 56, n. 2), which at any rate Cicero used ; the discourses on Philosophy (p. 55, n. 6) and on Wealth (p. 58, n. 1 end), which, before him, Philodemus, and also Metrodorus, pupil of Epicurus, made use of ; the ἑρωτικὸς, which, according to ATHEN. xv. 674, b, Aristo of Ceos knew ; the dialogue Π. ποιητῶν (p. 58, n. 1), which Eratosthenes and Apollodorus seem to have used ; the Ὀλυμπιονῖκαι, which Eratosthenes (*apud* DIOG. viii. 51), quotes ; the *Didascalics*, which Didymus quotes in the Scholiasts to Aristoph. *Av.* 1379 (cf. HEITZ, *Verl. Schr.* 56); the Παροιμίαι, on account of which Aristotle (according to ATHEN.

ii. 60, d) was attacked by Cephisodorus ; in short (as has been shown at p. 48 s3q.), all the compositions given in the Catalogue of Diogenes, not to mention the spurious but much-used composition Π. εὐγενείας (p. 59, n. 2). The writings on ancient philosophers, among which is included our extant tract on Melissus, &c., are found *apud* DIOG. No. 92–101 (see p. 62, n. 2, *supra*).

[2] See p. 67, n. 1.

[3] See pp. 64, n. 1, 66, n. 1.

[4] See pp. 64 and 66; p. 141, n. 1.

[5] The same would follow from the statement (SIMPL. *Categ., Schol.* 79, a, 1), that Andronicus followed pretty closely the *Categories* of Archytas, since the latter at any rate are imitations of the Aristotelian ; Simplicius, however, bases what is here said merely on his false supposition of their genuineness.

[6] Cf. p. 68, n. 1, and 71, n. 2.

[7] Of Theophrastus this is

his follower Strabo [1] had used them. The *Rhetoric* is imitated and referred to in writings which in all likelihood are themselves earlier than Andronicus; [2] and the same is true of the Theodectine *Rhetoric*.[3] The *Physics* were worked over by Theophrastus and Eudemus, and the latter followed the text so closely that he is actually cited in support of the correctness of a various reading.[4]　　One of the scholars of Eude-

clear from Alexander *In Top.* p. 5, m. (cf. 68, 72, 31), *In Metaph.* 342, 30, 373, 2 (705, b, 30, 719, b, 27). See SIMPL. *Categ. Schol. in Ar.* 89, a, 15.

[1] Cf. ALEX. *Top.*, *infra* (*Schol.* 281, b, 2). Among Strabo's writings is found *apud* DIOG. v. 59, a Τόπων προοίμια.

[2] The former in the *Rhetoric ad Alex.* (*vide supra*, p. 74, n. 3), which Diogenes (No. 79) knows (cf. p. 72, n. 2) as well as our *Rhetoric* (about which see p. 72, n. 2, *ad fin.*); the latter *apud* DEMETRIUS, *De Elocutione*; quotations from our *Rhetoric* are found here, c. 38, 41 (*Rhet.* iii. 8, 1409, a, 1); c. 11, 34 (*Rhet.* iii. 9, 1409, a, 35, b, 16); c. 81 (*Rhet.* iii. 11, *init.*); to it *ibid.* c 34 refers, which is earlier than the author Archedemus, who was probably the Stoic of that name, *circa* 140 B.C.

[3] Which (as shown at p. 72, n. 2) is likewise given in Diogenes, and is named by the *Rhetoric ad Alex.*

[4] We get these facts, apart from other proof, from the exceedingly numerous references to the *Physics* in Simplicius; for instance, about Theophrastus, cf. SIMPL. *Phys.* 141, a and b, and 187, a, 201, b, and the

same author *In Categ. Schol.* 92, b, 20 sq., with THEMIST. *Phys.* 54, b, 55, a, b (*Schol.* 409, b, 8, 411, a, 6, b, 28), and BRANDIS, *Rhein. Mus.* i. 282 thereon ; about Eudemus, SIMPL. *Phys.* 18, b (*Arist. Phys.* i. 2, 185, b, 11); also 29, a : ὁ Εὔδημος τῷ Ἀριστοτέλει πάντα κατακολουθῶν; 120, b, where it is remarked on *Phys.* iii. 8, 208, b, 18 : κάλλιον γὰρ, οἶμαι, τὸ " ἔξω τοῦ ἄστεως " οὕτως ἀκούειν, ὡς ὁ Εὔδημος ἐνόησε τὰ τοῦ καθηγεμόνος, &c.; so 121, b: ἔν τισι δὲ [sc. ἀντιγράφοις] ἀντὶ τοῦ " κοινὴ " " πρώτη." καὶ οὕτω γράφει καὶ ὁ Εὔδημος ; 128, b : Εὔδημος δὲ τούτοις παρακολουθῶν, &c.; 178, b : Eudemus writes, in *Phys.* iv. 13, 222, b, 18, not Πάρων but παρών; 201, b : Εὔδ. ἐν τοῖς ἑαυτοῦ φυσικοῖς παραφράζων τὰ τοῦ Ἀριστοτέλους; 216, a : Eudemus immediately connects with what is found in Aristotle at the end of the fifth book, the beginning of the sixth ; 223, a : in Aristotle an ἐπὶ τάδε repeated in a different context (*Phys.* vi. 3, 234, a, 1) gives an ambiguity in expression, and so Eudemus puts " ἐπέκεινα " instead of the second ἐπὶ τάδε; 242, a (beginning of the seventh book) : Εὔδ. μέχρι τοῦδε ὅλης σχεδὸν πραγματείας κεφαλαίοις ἀκολουθήσας,

mus [1] cited from the *Physics* of Aristotle the three books
' on Movement.' It can also be proved that the same work
was known to Strabo,[2] and Posidonius the Stoic showed
no less acquaintance with it.[3] The *De Cœlo* cannot
be shown with certainty to have been known to any
writer older than Andronicus except Theophrastus.[4]
It is, however, very unlikely that this work disappeared after his time when its continuation—the Περὶ
γενέσεως καὶ φθορᾶς—appears in the Catalogue of
Diogenes,[5] and when the *Meteorology*, which is closely
connected with both the one and the other, is known
to have been used by many writers of that period.[6]
Posidonius, for example, appropriated from it the theory
of the elements,[7] and Strabo disputed its account of the
heaviness and lightness of bodies.[8]   The (spurious)
Mechanics, and the *Astronomy*, are named in the list
in Diogenes.[9]   The *Natural History* was adapted not
only by Theophrastus,[10] but also by the Alexandrine
writer Aristophanes of Byzantium.[11]   That it was not

τοῦτο παρελθὼν ὡς περιττὸν ἐπὶ τὰ
ἐν τῷ τελευταίῳ βιβλίῳ κεφάλαια
μετῆλθε; 279, a: καὶ ὅ γε Εὔδ.
παραφράζων σχεδὸν καὶ αὐτὸς τὰ
Ἀριστοτέλους τίθησι καὶ ταῦτα
τὰ τμήματα συντόμως; 294, b:
Aristotle shows that the first
motor must be immovable—to
which Eudemus adds: τὸ πρώτως
κινοῦν καθ' ἑκάστην κίνησιν. For
further details see ch. xix. *infra*,
and p. 136, n 2.

[1] Damasus: *vide supra*, p. 82.
[2] Cf. SIMPL. *Phys.* 153, a
(155, b), 154, b, 168, a, 187, a,
sqq., 189, b (cf. *Phys.* iv. 10),
214, a.
[3] In the fragment *apud*
SIMPL. *Phys.* 64, b: of which

Simplicius remarks that it is
based on Aristotle (*Phys.* ii. 2).
[4] *Vide supra*, p. 83, n. 1.
[5] That is, if No. 39,   Π.
στοιχείων α' β' γ', refers to it;
about which see p. 50, n. 1.
[6] *Vide supra*, p. 83, n. 1.
[7] SIMPL. *De Cœlo, Schol. in
Ar.* 517, a, 31.
[8] SIMPL. *ibid.* 486, a, 5.
[9] The former No. 123, the
latter 113 : *vide supra*, p. 86, n. 1.
[10] DIOG. v. 49 names as his
Ἐπιτομῶν Ἀριστοτέλους Π. Ζῴων ς'.
[11] According to HIEROCL.
Hippiatr. Præf. p. 4, this grammarian had written an Ἐπιτομὴ of
it, which ARTEMIDOR. *Oneiro-
crit.* ii. 14 calls ὑπομνήματα εἰς

unknown during the Alexandrine period is also shown by the Catalogue of Diogenes (No. 102), and by the existence of a popular compilation from it which was much in use.[1] The *De Anima* was used, after Theophrastus,[2] by the author of the book on the 'Movement of Living Creatures,' who used also the spurious treatise Περὶ πνεύματος.[3] As to the *Problems*,[4] it is more than improbable that the working up of that book for the Peripatetic School began later than the time of Andronicus. The *Metaphysics* was used, as we have seen,[5] not only by Theophrastus and Eudemus, but after them by Strabo and other Peripatetics. It was probably published by Eudemus; though some sections of it do seem to have been first introduced by Andronicus into the then extant Aristotelian treatise on the First Philosophy. Of the *Ethics*, it is obvious that it could not have existed only in Theophrastus's MS. so as to be lost with it, for if so it could not have been worked over either by Eudemus or at a later date by the author of *Magna Moralia*. The *Politics*, if we are to judge by the list of Diogenes, was to be found in the Library of Alexandria,[6] along with the first book of our *Economics*,

---

Ἀριστοτέλην (see Schneider in his edition i. xix). Demetrius also, *De Elocut.* 97, 157 (cf. *H. An.* ii. 1, 497, b, 28; ix. 2. 32, 610, a, 27, 619, a, 16), or perhaps the earlier writer used by him, knows this epitome.

[1] About which see p. 87, n. 1, *ad fin.* From this compilation also the many quotations from the Aristotelian *History of Animals* in Antigonus' *Mirabilia* (c. 16, 22, 27-113, 115) are perhaps taken.

For the present purpose it is of no importance whether they are mediate or immediate witnesses for the use of Aristotle's work.

[2] Upon which see THEMISTOCLES in *De An.* 89, b, 91, a; PHILOP. *De An.* C. 4. Cf. p. 89, n. 1, *supra.*

[3] Cf. p. 89, n. 2 *ad fin.*

[4] As to which cf. p. 96.

[5] See p. 79, n. 1.

[6] *Vide supra*, p. 100, n. 1 p. 100, n. 3.

which is also cited by Philodemus.[1] It is obvious that the author of that book [2] had the *Politics* before him; that Dicæarchus knew it also is indicated by the notices of his *Tripoliticus*.[3] The use of it in the *Magna Moralia* is not so well proven,[4] and we cannot tell to what source Cicero owed the parts of it which he used for his own political works:[5] but it is not doubtful that it must have been accessible to learned persons after the death of Theophrastus. The same is true of the Πολιτεῖαι, for the use of which in the Alexandrine period we have abundant proofs.[6] That the *Poetics*

[1] *De Vit.* ix. (*Vol. Herc.* ii.) col. 7, 38, 47, col. 27, 15, where it is ascribed to Theophrastus.

[2] Whom we have rather to seek in Eudemus or one of his Peripatetic contemporaries than in Aristotle: see ch. xxi. *infra*.

[3] On which see *infra*, ch. xix. *ad fin.*

[4] Although happiness is here, i. 4, 1184, b, 33 sqq., defined as ἐνέργεια καὶ χρῆσις τῆς ἀρετῆς, this has certainly a greater resemblance to *Polit.* vii. 13, 1332, a, 7 (a passage to which NICKES, *De Arist. Polit. Libr.* 87 sq. calls attention) than to *Eth. N.* i. 6, x. 6, 7, *Eud.* ii. 1, since happiness is here certainly called ἐνέργεια κατ᾽ ἀρετὴν (or τῆς ἀρετῆς),but the conjunction of the ἐνέργεια and χρῆσις is wanting. Then the χρῆσις is also spoken of in *Eud.* 1219, a, 12 sqq. 23, *Nic.* i. 9. 1098, b, 31, and thus it is quite possible that only these passages were in the mind of the author of the *Great Ethics*.

[5] ZELLER had already proved in his 2nd ed., that in Cicero's political writings many things are taken from the Aristotelian *Politics*, citing CIC. *Leg.* iii. 6., *Rep.* i. 25 (cf. *Polit.* iii. 9, 1280, 6, 29, c, 6, 1278, b, 8, 19, i. 2, 1253, a, 2); *Rep.* i. 26 (*Pol.* iii. 1, 1274, b, 36, c. 6, 1278, b, 8, c. 7, 1279, a, 25 sqq.); *Rep.* i. 27 (*Pol.* iii. 9, 1280, a, 11, c. 10, 11, 1281, a, 28 sqq., b, 28, c. 16, 1287, a, 8 sqq.); *Rep.* i. 29 (*Pol.* iv. 8, 11). Susemihl (*Arist. Pol.* xliv. 81) also agrees with this. But since Cicero does not name Aristotle in the *Republic*, and *Leg.* iii. 6 only refers to him in very indefinite expressions, he seems not to have drawn immediately on Aristotle, and the question arises: where did he get this Aristotelian doctrine from? Susemihl, p. xlv, thinks, from Tyrannio, but we might also presume Dicæarchus, whom Cicero was fond of using.

[6] The oldest witness for this is Timæus, *apud* POLYB. xii. 5–11, and the latter author himself. There is also, besides Diog. (*Hermippus*) No.145,the Scholiast of Aristophanes, who (according to a good Alexandrine authority)

was also known to the Alexandrine grammarians is placed beyond doubt by recent research.[1]

We may sum up the case by saying that of the genuine portions of the extant *Corpus*, there are only the works on the *Parts*, *Genesis*, and *Movement of Animals*, and the minor anthropological tracts, as to which we cannot show either express proof or high probability for the assertion that they were in use after the disappearance of Theophrastus's library from Athens. Even as to these we have no reason to doubt it—only we cannot positively prove it; and that, when we remember the fragmentary character of our knowledge of the philosophic literature of the period in question, is nothing strange. The belief of Strabo and Plutarch that the scientific writings of Aristotle were after the death of Theophrastus all but wholly withdrawn from access is therefore decisively negatived by the facts. A few of these writings may possibly have suffered the fate which they ascribe to the whole. One book or another may have been lost to the School at Athens when they lost the library of Theophrastus, and may have been again published by Andronicus from the damaged MSS. of Sulla's collection. But that this happened to any or all of the important books is for all reasons antecedently improbable. There must have

quoted the Πολιτεῖαι very often; see *Arist. Fr.* ed. Rose, Nos. 352, 355–358, 370, 373, 407, 420 sq., 426 sq., 470, 485, 498 sq., 525, 533.

[1] Their presence in the Alexandrian library is clear from the Catalogue of Diog. (No. 83), and their having been used by Ari-

stophanes of Byzantium and Didymus from the proofs which Susemihl has collected at p. 20 sq., of his edition (following Trendelenburg, *Grammat. Græc. de Arte Trag. Judic. Rel.*) from the Introductions and Scholia to Sophocles and Euripides.

been copies of the important text-books made during the long life of Theophrastus. He who cared so well for his scholars in every other way, by providing for them gardens and houses and a museum and the means of maintaining it, could never have deprived them of his most precious and most indispensable possession— his own and his master's texts—if a sufficient substitute for them were not at hand. Any theory, therefore, as to an individual book of our collection, that its text rests solely on a MS. from Apellico's library, ought to rest entirely on the internal evidence of the book itself; for Strabo's and Plutarch's suggestion of a general disappearance of the texts could give it no support.

It is not, however, to be denied that many of the books show signs leading to the conclusion that in their present form other hauds than the author's have been at work. We find corruptions of the text, lacunæ in the logical movement, displacement of whole sections, additions that could be made only by later hands, other additions which are Aristotelian but were originally designed for some other context, repetitions which we should not expect in so condensed a style, and which yet can hardly be late interpolations.[1] Strabo's story, however, does not serve for the explanation of these phenomena, for the reason, among others, that such peculiarities are to be found equally in those texts

---

[1] Cf. with regard to this, not to mention other points, what has been said before as to the *Categories* (p. 64, n. 1), Π. ἑρμηνείας (p. 66, n. 1), the *Rhetoric* (p. 72, n. 2), the *Metaphysics* (p. 76, n. 3), the seventh book of the *Physics* (p. 81, n. 2 *ad fin.*), the fourth book of the *Meteorology* (p. 83, n. 2), the tenth book of the *History of Animals* (p. 87, n. 1), Π. ψυχῆς (p. 89, n. 2), bk. v. *De Gen. An.* (p. 92, n. 2), the *Ethics* (p. 98, n. 1), and the *Poetics* (p. 102, n. 2); and the remarks in ch. xiii. *infra* upon the state of the *Politics,*

which we can prove to have been current before Apellico. We must explain them really as arising in part from the circumstances under which these treatises were written and issued,[1] in part from the way they were used for teaching purposes,[2] in part from the carelessness of transcribers and the many accidents to which each transcript was exposed.

If we pass to the discussion of the time and sequence in which the writings of Aristotle were produced, we must remember that this is of far less importance than in the case of the writings of Plato. It is clear that Aristotle commenced his career as a writer during his first residence at Athens,[3] and it is probable that he continued his literary activity in Atarneus, Mitylene and Macedonia. The extant writings, however, seem all to belong to the second Athenian period, although much preparation may probably have been made for them before. The proof of this lies partly in certain traces of the dates of their production, which control not only those books in which they occur, but also all that are later:[4] and partly in the common references

[1] Cf. p. 108 sqq.

[2] How easily, by this means, explanations and repetitions may find their way into the text, and greater or smaller sections may come to be repeated, is perfectly plain, and is proved on a large scale by the parallel case of the Eudemian *Physics* and *Ethics*.

[3] See p. 56 sqq. He left Athens in B.C. 345–4 and returned in 335–4.

[4] Thus *Meteor.* i. 7, 345, a, 1, mentions a comet which was visible when Nicomachus (Ol. 109, 4, B.C. 341) was Archon in Athens, its course and position being accurately described as from subsequent personal inquiry. The *Politics* refer to the Holy War as an event in the past (v. 4, 1304, a, 10), and to the expedition of Phalæcus to Crete, which took place at its conclusion about Ol. 108, 3 (DIODORUS, xvi. 62), with a νεωστὶ (ii. 10, *fin.*), but the same book refers to the assassination of Philip (B.C. 336) in v. 10, 1311, b, 1, without the least indication of its having been a very recent event. The *Rhetoric* in ii. 23,

which even the earliest of them contain to Athens and to the place itself where Aristotle taught.[1] If, then, the view already indicated[2] as to the destination of these texts for his scholars, their connection with his teaching, and the character of their cross references be right, it

1397, b, 31, 1399, b, 12, refers without doubt to past events of the years B.C. 338–336 ; in iii. 17, 1418, b, 27 it mentions Iso-crates' Philippus (B.C. 345) ; of the *Rhetoric* also Brandis shows (*Philologus*, iv. 10 sqq.) that the many Attic orators quoted in it and in the *Poetics* who were younger than Demosthenes, could by no means belong to a time prior to Aristotle's first departure from Athens, and the same is true of the numerous works of Theodectes which are used both here and in the *Poetics*. In *Metaph.* i. 9, 991, a, 1, xii. 8, 1073, b, 17, 32, Eudoxus and the still younger Callippus, and in *Eth. N.* vii. 14, 1153, b, 5, x. 2, *init.*, Speusippus and Eudoxus are spoken of as if they were no longer living. Rose (*Arist. Libr. Ord.* 212 sqq.) has shown with regard to the *History of Animals*, from viii. 9, ii. 5. *init.*, and other passages, that it was only written (or at least completed), some time after the battle of Arbela, in which the Macedonians saw elephants for the first time, and probably not before the Indian expedition. The fact that even much earlier events are intro-duced with a νῦν—as in *Meteor.* iii. 1, 371, a, 30, the burning of the temple of Ephesus (Ol. 106, 1, B.C. 356), and in *Polit.* v. 10, 1312, b, 19, Dion's expedition (Ol. 105, 4 sq.)—proves nothing, by rea-

son of the indefiniteness of that particle. Just as little does it follow from *Anal. Pri.* ii. 24, that Thebes was not yet destroyed at that time ; we might rather gather the contrary, with regard to this work, from *Polit.* iii. 5, 1278, a, 25.

[1] Cf. BRANDIS, *Gr.-röm. Phil.* ii. b, 116. We may give here a few further instances, besides those already noted. *Categ.* 4, 2, a, 1, c, 9 *fin.*: ποῦ, οἷον ἐν Λυκείῳ. *Anal. Pri.* ii. 24: Athens and Thebes, as examples of neigh-bours. Likewise in *Phys.* iii. 3, 202, b, 13; *ibid.* iv. 11, 219, b, 20: τὸ ἐν Λυκείῳ εἶναι. *Metaph.* v. 5, 30, 1015, a, 25, 1025, a, 25: τὸ πλεῦσαι εἰς Αἴγιναν, as an example of a commercial journey. *Ibid.* v. 24, *fin.*: the Athenian festivals Dionysia and Thargelia (Ari-stotle also uses the Attic months e.g. *Hist. An.* v. 11, &c. ; but it is not fair to attach any import-ance to this). *Rhet.* ii. 7, 1385, a, 28: ὁ ἐν Λυκείῳ τὸν φορμὸν δούς. *Ibid.* iii. 2, 1404, b, 22, *Polit.* vii. 17, 1336, b, 27: the actor Theo-dorus. Very frequent mention is also made of Athens and the Athenians (*Ind. Ar.* 12, b, 34 sqq.). Again the observation on the corona borealis (*Meteor.* ii. 5, 362, b, 9) suits the latitude of Athens, as Ideler (i. 567), on this passage, shows.

[2] P. 108 sqq. : especially p. 123 sq. and p. 128 sq.

follows that all of them *must* have been composed during his final sojourn in Athens. Equally decisive, on this head, is the observation that throughout the whole of so comprehensive a collection, there is hardly to be found a single notable alteration of teaching or terminology. All is ripe and ready. All is in exact correspondence. All the important writings are woven closely together, not only by express cross reference, but also by their whole character. There are no scattered products of the different periods of a life. We can only look upon them as the ordered execution of a work planned when the author, having come to a full understanding with himself, had gathered together the philosophic fruit of a lifetime. Even the earlier works which he proposed to connect with his later writing, he revised on a comprehensive plan. Therefore, for our use of these texts, it is no great matter whether a particular book was written sooner or later than any other. The problem, however, must be dealt with nevertheless.

A certain difficulty is caused by the use of cross references already noticed.[1] As such cases are, after all, only exceptions in the general run of the citations, the value of these as an indication of sequence is not so slight as has been supposed. There are, in fact, but few instances in which our judgment as to the order of the writings is placed in doubt by the occurrence of references both ways.

Of the extant books, so far as they are open to this classification,[2] the logical treatises, excepting the tract on

[1] Cf. p. 124 sqq.

[2] This, however, is always the case except with writings the genuineness of which can be opposed on other grounds. Not only are none of these quoted in the genuine works, and only a single one in a spurious compo-

Propositions,[1] may be considered to come first. It is in itself natural and accords with Aristotle's methodical plan of exposition, that he should preface the material development of his system by the formal inquiries which were designed to establish the rules and conditions of all scientific thinking. But it is also made evident by his own citations that the Logic did precede the Natural Philosophy, the *Metaphysics*, the *Ethics* and *Rhetoric*.[2] Of the logical tracts themselves, the *Categories* seems to be the first. The *Topics*, including the book on Fallacies, came next, and then the two *Analytics*: the treatise

sition, but only very few of them refer to other writings. On the other hand, there is not one among the works which we consider as genuine, which does not quote the others, or is not quoted by them, or, at least, implied, whilst in most of them examples of all three connections occur. To explain more fully: I. Of the decidedly *spurious* works : (a) the following are neither quoted nor do they quote others : Π. κόσμου, Π. χρωμάτων, Π. ἀκουστῶν, Φυσιογνωμονικά, Π. φυτῶν (see p. 93), Π. θαυμασίων ἀκουσμάτων, Μηχανικά, Π. ἀτόμων γραμμῶν, Ἀνέμων θέσεις, Π. Ξενοφάνους &c., Ἠθικὰ μεγάλα, Π. ἀρετῶν καὶ κακιῶν, Οἰκονομικά, Ῥητορικὴ πρὸς Ἀλέξανδρον. (b) Π. πνεύματος quotes no other, but is quoted in the spurious treatise Π. ζῴων κινήσεως. (c) On the contrary, the latter itself is never quoted. But it names some other writings ; as does also the *Eudemian Ethics*, supposing that its quotations refer to Aristotelian works. II. Among the remaining

writings, the *Categories* is the only work which quotes no other, and neither is it directly quoted (but cf. p.64). The Π. ἑρμηνείας. Π. τ. καθ' ὕπνον μαντικῆς and the *Rhetoric* quote others, but are not quoted ; Π. ζῴων γενέσεως has many quotations, but is only once cited, as a book planned for the future ; of the *Metaphysics* only bk. v. is quoted or used (cf. pp. 76, n.3, and 79, n.1) in genuine works, bks. i., xii., and xiii. in spurious ones : and the *Metaph.* itself quotes the *Analytics*, the *Physics*, *De Cœlo*, and the *Ethics*.

[1] On which see p. 66, n. 1.

[2] Besides the arguments given on p. 67, n. 1, p. 68, n. 1, we have the decisive passage in *Anal. Post.* ii. 12, 95, b, 10 : μᾶλλον δὲ φανερῶς ἐν τοῖς καθόλου περὶ κινήσεως δεῖ λεχθῆναι περὶ αὐτῶν. The *Physics*, however, is the earliest of the works on Natural Science. A negative line of proof also is found in the fact that in the *Categories*, the *Analytics*, and the *Topics*, none of the other writings are quoted.

on Propositions was added afterwards.[1]　Later than the *Analytics* but earlier than the *Physics* may be placed the treatise which now forms the fifth book of the *Metaphysics*.[2]　The Natural Philosophy came next.　In that section the *Physics* comes first.　It is projected in the *Analytics* and is referred to in the fifth book of the *Metaphysics*; but the latter is cited or presupposed not only in the metaphysical and ethical works but also in the majority of the other tracts concerning Natural Philosophy, while it on the other hand neither cites nor presupposes any one of them.[3]　That the *De Cœlo*,[4] the treatise on *Growth and Decay*, and the *Meteorology*, follow the *Physics* in the order given, is very expressly stated in the *Meteorology* itself.[5] Whether the *Natural History* or the *De Anima* came next is not settled.　It is very possible that the former work, extensive as it is, was begun before the other but completed after it.[6]　With the *De Anima* we must connect those lesser tracts which point back to it some-

[1] See pp. 64, n. 1, p. 67, n. 1, p. 68 sq., and the treatise of Brandis quoted in the first-cited note, which (p. 256 sqq.), by a comparison of the *Analytics* with the *Topics*, establishes the earlier date of the latter.

[2] For, on the one hand, it is mentioned in the *Physics* and *De Gen. et Corr.* (*vide supra*, p. 76, n. 1, p. 124, n. 4); and, on the other, it seems in c. 30 *fin.* to refer to *Anal. Post.* i. 6, 75, a, 18 sqq., 28 sqq.; though the latter point is not certain.

[3] *Vide supra*, p. 81 sqq., *Ind. Arist.* 102, a, 53 sqq., 98, a, 27 sqq.

[4] Which we cannot, like Blass (*Rhein. Mus.* xxx. 498, 505), consider a 'hypomnematical' writing, not merely because of the references made to it, but on other grounds also.

[5] *Meteor.* i. 1, whereon cf. further p. 83, n. 1, *Ind. Arist.* 98, a, 44 sqq., and the quotation of the tract Π. ζῴων πορείας in the *De Cœlo*, ii. 2, given p. 125.

[6] That the completion of the *History of Animals* should not be put too early is clear from what has been said on p. 154, n. 4.

times expressly[1] and always by the nature of their contents. Some of these were no doubt composed after or with the writings on the *Parts*, the *Movement*, and the *Genesis of Animals*.[2] That group of tracts is undoubtedly later than the *Natural History*, the *De Anima*, and the treatises which followed upon it.[3] On the other hand, it is probably earlier than the *Ethics* and *Politics*, inasmuch as it can hardly be supposed that Aristotle would have broken in upon his studies in Natural Philosophy by undertaking extended works lying in a wholly different direction.[4] It would be less difficult to suppose that the ethical writings as a whole came before the physical.[5] This view is not excluded by any express internal references, excepting the reference to the *Physics* in the *Ethics*.[6] We must, nevertheless, decide in favour of the earlier construction of the Natural Philosophy texts, for a thinker who was so clearly convinced as Aristotle was that the student of ethics must have a knowledge of the human soul,[7] must be supposed to have put his inquiry into the soul before his researches into the moral activities and relations. There are, indeed, in the *Ethics* very unmistakable traces of his theory of the soul and of the treatise thereon.[8] Immediately after the *Ethics*

---

[1] Thus Π. αἰσθήσεως, Π. ὕπνου, Π. ἐνυπνίων, Π. ἀναπνοῆς (*Ind. Ar.* 102, b, 60 sqq.).

[2] *Vide supra*, p. 89 sqq.

[3] See pp. 89, n. 2, 89, n. 3, 87, n. 1 : *Ind. Arist.* 99, b, 30 sqq.

[4] The further question of the relative order of the three writings named has been already discussed on p. 91 sq.

[5] Thus ROSE, *Arist. Libr. Ord.* 122 sqq.

[6] *Eth.* x. 3, 1174, b, 2. Cf. *Phys.* vi.–viii.

[7] *Eth.* i. 13, 1102, a, 23.

[8] Though Aristotle in *Eth.* i. 13, 1102, a, 26 sqq. refers, not to *De An.* iii. 9, 432, a, 22 sqq. ii. 3, but to the ἐξωτερικοὶ λόγοι, yet ii. 2 *init.* seems to presuppose

comes the *Politics*.[1] Judging by the internal references, the *Rhetoric* should be later than both, and the *Poetics* should be later than the *Politics* but before the *Rhetoric*. This, however, is probably true only of a part of the *Politics*—or rather only of those parts which Aristotle himself published, for his death seems to have intervened before he had completed that text as a whole.[2] So, again, in our so-called *Metaphysics*, we have in all probability a work which Aristotle left incomplete, and with which several other fragments, some genuine, some spurious, have been amalgamated since.[3]

the bulk of the theoretical writings. But that there are not many more of such traces may perhaps be explained by the fact that Aristotle did not wish to interfere with the practical aim of an ethical work (*Eth.* i. 1, 1095, a, 4, ii. 2, *init.*) by any discussions which were not indispensable to its purpose; cf. i. 13, 1102, a, 23.

[1] See p. 100, n. 1.

[2] See p. 127 *supra*, and *infra*, ch. xiii. And if this supposition is correct, it would also go to make it improbable that the *Ethics*, so closely allied with the *Politics*, should have been written before the works on natural science.

[3] Cf. p. 76 sqq., and with regard to citations of the *Metaphysics*, see p. 156, n. 2. Rose's supposition (*Arist. Libr. Ord.* 135 sqq. 186 sq.) that the *Metaphysics* preceded all the writings on natural science, or at any rate the zoological ones, makes the actual condition of that work an inexplicable puzzle. But there is also the fact that the *Physics*, as well as the *De Cœlo*, are quoted in numerous passages of the *Metaphysics* (*Ind. Ar.* 101, a, 7 sqq.) as already existing, while the *Metaphysics* are referred to in *Phys.* i. 9, 192, a, 35, as merely in the future.

CHAPTER IV

THE STANDPOINT, METHOD, AND DIVISIONS OF THE
PHILOSOPHY OF ARISTOTLE

As Plato connects directly with Socrates, so Aristotle
with Plato. Yet he made a comprehensive use of the
earlier philosophies as well. He was better versed
than any of the earlier teachers in the theories and
writings of his forerunners, and it is with him a
favourite method to preface his own inquiries with a
retrospect of earlier opinions. He is wont to let them
designate the problems to be dealt with. He is eager
to refute their errors, to resolve their doubts, to bring
out the truth which underlay their views. But the
influence of the pre-Socratic systems upon Aristotle is
far less apparent in the general structure of his system
than it is in the treatment of special points. In principle, Plato had refuted them all. Aristotle is not
under the same necessity to distinguish his position
accurately from theirs.[1] He does not, at least in any
of the extant writings, devote any space to such propaideutic efforts as those by which Plato established
the claims of philosophy and the true meaning of know-

[1] Even in *Metaph.* i. 8 their
principles are merely criticised
briefly from an Aristotelian point
of view, and the Eleatics and
Heraclitus, about whom Plato
busied himself so much, are
passed over altogether.

ledge, as against ' the ordinary consciousness ' on the one hand, and the Sophists on the other. Aristotle presupposes throughout that general point of view which characterised the Socratico-Platonic Philosophy of Ideas. His task is to work out, on these general lines, a more perfect system of knowledge, by a more exact definition of the leading principles, by a stricter accuracy of method, and by an extension and improvement of all the scientific data? It is true that in his own writings the rare expressions of agreement with his teacher are almost lost sight of by comparison with his keen and constant polemic against Platonic views.[1] Yet in reality and in the whole his agreement with Plato is far greater than his divergence,[2] and his whole system cannot truly be understood until we treat it as a development and evolution of that of Plato and as the completion of that very Philosophy of Ideas which Socrates founded and Plato carried on.

In the first place, he agrees for the most part with Plato in his general views as to the meaning and office of Philosophy itself. To him, as to Plato, the *object* of

[1] We shall deal later on with this polemic, especially as it was directed against the doctrine of Ideas in *Metaph.* i. 9, xiii., xiv. &c. Only a few passages are found in which Aristotle expressly declares his agreement with Plato. Besides the passages noted on p. 12, and p. 14, n. 4, see *Eth. N.* i. 2, 1095, a, 32 ; ii. 2, 1104, b, 11 ; *De An.* iii. 4, 429, a, 27 ; *Polit.* ii. 6, 1265, a, 10.

[2] Cf. also the valuable remarks of STRÜMPELL, *Gesch. d. theor. Phil. d. Gr.* 177. Ari-

stotle, as we have shown on p. 14, n. 3, not unfrequently includes himself in the first person along with the rest of the Platonic school. But his way of treating such a relation is the opposite to that of Plato. Whilst Plato puts his own view, even where it contradicts the original one of Socrates, into the mouth of his teacher, Aristotle not unfrequently attacks his teacher even where they agree in the main point, and only differ in opinion as to secondary matters.

Philosophy can be only Being as such,[1] *i.e.* Essence, or, to speak more accurately, the universal Essence of that which is actual.[2] Philosophy treats solely of the causes and basis of things,[3] and in fact of their highest and most universal basis, or, in the last resort, of that which presupposes nothing.[4] For the like reasons he ascribes to the philosopher in a certain sense a knowledge of everything, thinking, of course, of the point of unity where all knowledge converges.[5] As Plato had distinguished. ' knowledge,' as the cognition of that which is Eternal and Necessary,

---

[1] *Anal. Post.* ii. 19, 100, a, 6 : ἐκ δ' ἐμπειρίας . . . τέχνης ἀρχὴ καὶ ἐπιστήμης, ἐὰν μὲν περὶ γένεσιν, τέχνης, ἐὰν δὲ περὶ τὸ ὂν, ἐπιστήμης. *Metaph.* iv. 2, 1004, b, 15 : τῷ ὄντι ᾗ ὄν ἐστι τινὰ ἴδια, καὶ ταῦτ' ἐστὶ περὶ ὧν τοῦ φιλοσόφου ἐπισκέψασθαι τἀληθές. *Ibid.* 1005, a, 2, c. 3, 1005, b, 10.

[2] *Metaph.* iii. 2, 996, b, 14 sqq. : τὸ εἰδέναι ἕκαστον . . . τότ' οἰόμεθα ὑπάρχειν, ὅταν εἰδῶμεν τί ἐστιν, &c. ; vii. 1, 1028, a, 36 : εἰδέναι τότ' οἰόμεθα ἕκαστον μάλιστα, ὅταν τί ἐστιν ὁ ἄνθρωπος γνῶμεν ἢ τὸ πῦρ, μᾶλλον ἢ τὸ ποιὸν ἢ τὸ ποσὸν ἢ τὸ ποῦ, &c. ; c. 6, 1031, b, 20 : τὸ ἐπίστασθαι ἕκαστον τοῦτό ἐστι τὸ τί ἦν εἶναι ἐπίστασθαι, and cf. l. 6 ; *ibid.* xiii. 9, 1086, b, 5 : the determination of the notion of the thing is indispensable, ἄνευ μὲν γὰρ τοῦ καθόλου οὐκ ἔστιν ἐπιστήμην λαβεῖν; c. 10, 1086, b, 33 : ἡ ἐπιστήμη τῶν καθόλου; iii. 6 *fin.*: καθόλου αἱ ἐπιστῆμαι πάντων; iii. 4, 999, b, 26: τὸ ἐπίστασθαι πῶς ἔσται, εἰ μή τι ἔσται ἐν ἐπὶ πάντων; *ibid.* a, 28, b, 1; xi. 1, 1059, b, 25. *Anal. Post.* i. 11

[init]., ii. 19, 100, a, 6, i. 24, 85, b, 13 ; and *Eth. N.* vi. 6 *init.*, x. 10, 1180, b, 15. More *infra*, in chapter v.

[3] *Anal. Post.* i. 2 *init.*: ἐπίστασθαι δὲ οἰόμεθ' ἕκαστον . . . ὅταν τήν τ' αἰτίαν οἰώμεθα γιγνώσκειν δι' ἣν τὸ πρᾶγμά ἐστιν . . . καὶ μὴ ἐνδέχεσθαι τοῦτ' ἄλλως ἔχειν. *Ibid.* c. 14, 79, a, 23, ii. 11 *init. Eth. N.* vi. 7, 1141, a, 17. *Metaph.* i. 1, 981, a, 28, 982, a, 1, c. 2, 982, a, 12, 982, b, 2 sqq., vi. 1, *init.* Cf. SCHWEGLER, *Arist. Metaph.* iii. 9.

[4] *Phys.* i. 1, 184, a, 12 : τότε γὰρ οἰόμεθα γινώσκειν ·ἕκαστον, ὅταν τὰ αἴτια γνωρίσωμεν τὰ πρῶτα καὶ τὰς ἀρχὰς τὰς πρώτας καὶ μέχρι τῶν στοιχείων. *Ibid.* ii. 3 *init. Metaph.* i. 2, 982, b, 9 : δεῖ γὰρ ταύτην [that science which is to deserve the name σοφία] τῶν πρώτων ἀρχῶν καὶ αἰτιῶν εἶναι θεωρητικήν; c. 3 *init.*: τότε γὰρ εἰδέναι φαμὲν ἕκαστον, ὅταν τὴν πρώτην αἰτίαν οἰώμεθα γνωρίζειν ; iii. 2, 996, b, 13, iv. 2, 1003, b, 16, iv. 3, 1005, b, 5 sqq.

[5] *Metaph.* i. 2, 982, a, 8, 21, iv. 2, 1004, a, 35.

from Fancy or 'Opinion,' whose sphere is the contingent, so also Aristotle. To him, as to Plato, knowledge arises out of wonder, out of the bewilderment of the common consciousness with itself.[1] To him, its object is exclusively that which is universal and necessary; for the contingent cannot be *known*, but only *opined*. It is an opinion, when we believe that a thing might be otherwise; it is knowledge, when we recognise the impossibility of its being otherwise. So far from 'Opinion' and 'Knowledge' being all the same, it is rather true, as Aristotle holds, that it is utterly impossible to know and to opine about the same subject at the same time.[2] So, again, 'Knowledge' cannot consist in Perception, for that tells us only of individual things, not of the universal, only of facts, not of causes.[3] In like manner Aristotle distinguishes 'Knowledge' from mere 'Experience' by the test that the latter gives us in any matter only a ' *That*,' while the former gives us a ' *Why* ' also : [4] which is the very mark that Plato used to distinguish 'Knowledge' from 'True Opinion.'

---

[1] *Metaph.* i. 2, 982, b, 12 : διὰ γὰρ τὸ θαυμάζειν οἱ ἄνθρωποι καὶ νῦν καὶ τὸ πρῶτον ἤρξαντο φιλοσοφεῖν, &c. *Ibid.* 983, a, 12. Cf. ZELLER, *Ph. d. Gr.*, pt. ii. div. 1, p. 511, 4.

[2] *Anal. Post.* i. 33; cf. *ibid.* c. 6 *fin.* c. 8, *init.* c. 30 sqq.   *Metaph.* vii. 15, vi. 2, 1026, b, 2 sqq.   *Eth. N.* vi. 3, 1139, b, 18, c. 6 *init.* To this line of thought belongs the refutation of the principle, that for everyone that is true which seems true to him, which is dealt with in *Metaph.* iv. 5, 6, much as it is treated in Plato's *Theætetus.*

[3] *Anal. Post.* i. 31 : οὐδὲ δι'

αἰσθήσεως ἔστιν ἐπίστασθαι. For perception has always to do with individuals (more on this subject *infra*). τὸ δὲ καθόλου καὶ ἐπὶ πᾶσιν ἀδύνατον αἰσθάνεσθαι, &c. Even though we could *see* that the angles of a triangle are equal to two right angles, or that in an eclipse of the moon the earth stands between the sun and the moon, yet this would be no knowledge, so long as the universal reasons of these phenomena remained unknown to us.

[4] *Metaph.* i. 1, 981, a, 28.

Finally, Aristotle is at one with Plato also in this, that both of them proclaim Philosophy to be the mistress of all other sciences, and Science in general to be the highest and best that man can reach, and the most essential element of his happiness.[1]

Nevertheless, it is also true that the Aristotelian notion of Philosophy does not completely coincide with the Platonic. To Plato, Philosophy, regarded as to its content, is a term which includes all spiritual and moral perfection, and it comprehends therefore the *practical* as well as the *theoretic* side; and yet, when regarded as to its essence, he distinguishes it very sharply from every other form of human activity. Aristotle, on the contrary, marks it off more strictly from the practical side of life; while, on the other

---

[1] See *Metaph.* i. 2, 982, b, 4 : ἀρχικωτάτη δὲ τῶν ἐπιστημῶν, καὶ μᾶλλον ἀρχικὴ τῆς ὑπηρετούσης, ἡ γνωρίζουσα τίνος ἕνεκέν ἐστι πρακτέον ἕκαστον· τοῦτο δ' ἐστὶ τἀγαθὸν ἐν ἑκάστοις. But that science is one which investigates the highest reasons and causes, since 'the good' and 'the highest end' are included among these. *Ibid.* 1. 24 : δῆλον οὖν, ὡς δι' οὐδεμίαν αὐτὴν ζητοῦμεν χρείαν ἑτέραν, ἀλλ' ὥσπερ ἄνθρωπός. φαμεν ἐλεύθερος ὁ αὑτοῦ ἕνεκα καὶ μὴ ἄλλου ὤν, οὕτω καὶ αὕτη μόνη ἐλευθέρα οὖσα τῶν ἐπιστημῶν· μόνη γὰρ αὐτὴ αὑτῆς ἕνεκέν ἐστιν· διὸ καὶ δικαίως ἂν οὐκ ἀνθρωπίνη νομίζοιτο αὐτῆς ἡ κτῆσις ... ἀλλ' οὔτε τὸ θεῖον φθονερὸν ἐνδέχεται εἶναι, ... οὔτε τῆς τοιαύτης ἄλλην χρὴ νομίζειν τιμιωτέραν· ἡ γὰρ θειοτάτη καὶ τιμιωτάτη ... ἀναγκαιότεραι μὲν οὖν πᾶσαι ταύτης, ἀμείνων δ' οὐδεμία; xii. 7, 1072, b, 24 : ἡ θεωρία τὸ ἥδιστον καὶ ἄριστον. In *Eth. N.* x. 7 : 'theoria' is the most essential ingredient of perfect happiness ; cf. *e.g.* 1117, b, 30 : εἰ δὴ θεῖον ὁ νοῦς πρὸς τὸν ἄνθρωπον, καὶ ὁ κατὰ τοῦτον βίος θεῖος πρὸς τὸν ἀνθρώπινον βίον· οὐ χρὴ δὲ κατὰ τοὺς παραινοῦντας ἀνθρώπινα φρονεῖν ἄνθρωπον ὄντα οὐδὲ θνητὰ τὸν θνητὸν, ἀλλ' ἐφ' ὅσον ἐνδέχεται ἀθανατίζειν καὶ πάντα ποιεῖν πρὸς τὸ ζῆν κατὰ τὸ κράτιστον τῶν ἐν αὑτῷ ... τὸ οἰκεῖον ἑκάστῳ τῇ φύσει κράτιστον καὶ ἥδιστόν ἐστιν ἑκάστῳ· καὶ τῷ ἀνθρώπῳ δὴ ὁ κατὰ τὸν νοῦν βίος, εἴπερ τοῦτο μάλιστα ἄνθρωπος· οὗτος ἄρα καὶ εὐδαιμονέστατος ; c. 8, 1178, b, 28 : ἐφ' ὅσον δὴ διατείνει ἡ θεωρία, καὶ ἡ εὐδαιμονία. Cf. c. 9, 1179, a, 22, *Eth. Eud.* vii. 15 *fin.* See further in chapter xii., *infra*.

hand, he brings it into a closer relation with the experimental sciences. His view is that Philosophy is exclusively an affair of the theoretic faculty. He distinguishes from it very sharply the practical activities (πρᾶξις), which have their end in that which they produce (not, like Philosophy, in the activity itself), and which belong not purely to thought but also to opinion and the 'unreasoning part of the soul.' He distinguishes also the artistic creative effort (ποίησις) which is likewise directed to something outside itself.[1] With Experience, on the other hand, he connects Philosophy more closely. Plato had banished all dealings with the sphere of change and becoming out of the realm of 'Knowledge' into that of 'Opinion.' Even as to the passage from the former to the latter, he had only the negative doctrine that the contradictions of opinion and fancy ought to lead us to go further and to pass to the pure treatment of Ideas. Aristotle, as we shall presently see, allows to Experience a more positive relation to Thought. The latter, with him, proceeds out of the former by an affirmative movement—that, namely, in which the data given in Experience are brought together into a unity.

Furthermore, we find that Plato was but little interested in the descent from the treatment of the Idea to the individual things of the world of appearance—the phenomena. To him, the pure Ideas are the one

---

[1] Besides the passage just given, see *Eth. N.* vi. 2, c. 5, 1140, a, 28, b, 25; x. 8, 1178, b, 20; vi. 1, 1025, b, 18 sqq.; xi. 7; *De An.* iii. 10, 433, a, 14; and *De Cœlo*, iii. 7, 306, a, 16. The same is repeated by Eudemus *Eth.* i 5 *fin.*, and by the author of *Metaph.* ii. 1, 993, b, 20.

essential object of philosophic knowledge. Aristotle concedes that scientific knowledge has to do only with the universal essence of things; yet he does not stop at that point, for he regards it as the peculiar task of Philosophy to deduce the Individual from the Universal (as in ἀπόδειξις, *vide infra*). Science has to begin with the Universal, the Indeterminate; but it must pass on to the Determinate.[1] It has to explain the data, the phenomena.[2] It must not, therefore, think little of anything, however insignificant, for even there inexhaustible treasures of possible knowledge must lie.[3] It is for a like reason that Aristotle makes for scientific thought itself rules less strict than Plato's. He takes

[1] *Metaph.* xiii. 10, 1087, a, 10 : τὸ δὲ τὴν ἐπιστήμην εἶναι καθόλου πᾶσαν . . . ἔχει μὲν μάλιστ' ἀπορίαν τῶν λεχθέντων, οὐ μὴν ἀλλ' ἔστι μὲν ὡς ἀληθὲς τὸ λεγόμενον, ἔστι δ' ὡς οὐκ ἀληθές· ἡ γὰρ ἐπιστήμη, ὥσπερ καὶ τὸ ἐπίστασθαι, διττὸν, ὧν τὸ μὲν δυνάμει τὸ δὲ ἐνεργείᾳ· ἡ μὲν οὖν δύναμις ὡς ὕλη [τοῦ] καθόλου οὖσα καὶ ἀόριστος τοῦ καθόλου καὶ ἀορίστου ἐστὶν, ἡ δ' ἐνέργεια ὡρισμένη καὶ ὡρισμένου τόδε τι οὖσα τοῦδέ τινος.

[2] *Metaph.* i. 9, 992, a, 24 (attacking the doctrine of Ideas): ὅλως δὲ ζητούσης τῆς σοφίας περὶ τῶν φανερῶν τὸ αἴτιον, τοῦτο μὲν εἰάκαμεν (οὐθὲν γὰρ λέγομεν περὶ τῆς αἰτίας ὅθεν ἡ ἀρχὴ τῆς μεταβολῆς) &c. *De Cœlo*, iii. 7, 306, a, 16 : τέλος δὲ τῆς μὲν ποιητικῆς ἐπιστήμης τὸ ἔργον, τῆς δὲ φυσικῆς τὸ φαινόμενον ἀεὶ κυρίως κατὰ τὴν αἴσθησιν. *De An.* i. 1, 402, a, 16 : ἔοικε δ' οὐ μόνον τό τί ἐστι γνῶναι χρήσιμον εἶναι πρὸς τὸ θεωρῆσαι τὰς αἰτίας τῶν συμβεβηκότων ταῖς οὐσίαις . . . ἀλλὰ καὶ ἀνάπαλιν τὰ

συμβεβηκότα συμβάλλεται μέγα μέρος πρὸς τὸ εἰδέναι τὸ τί ἐστιν· ἐπειδὰν γὰρ ἔχωμεν ἀποδιδόναι κατὰ τὴν φαντασίαν περὶ τῶν συμβεβηκότων ἢ πάντων ἢ τῶν πλείστων, τότε καὶ περὶ τῆς οὐσίας ἕξομεν λέγειν κάλλιστα· πάσης γὰρ ἀποδείξεως ἀρχὴ τὸ τί ἐστιν, ὥστε καθ' ὅσους τῶν ὁρισμῶν μὴ συμβαίνει τὰ συμβεβηκότα γνωρίζειν . . . δῆλον ὅτι διαλεκτικῶς εἴρηνται καὶ κενῶς ἅπαντες Cf. c. 5, 409, b, 11 sq.

[3] *Part. An.* i. 5, 645, a, 5 : λοιπὸν περὶ τῆς ζωϊκῆς φύσεως εἰπεῖν, μηδὲν παραλιπόντας εἰς δύναμιν μήτε ἀτιμότερον μήτε τιμιώτερον· καὶ γὰρ ἐν τοῖς μὴ κεχαρισμένοις αὐτῶν πρὸς τὴν αἴσθησιν κατὰ τὴν θεωρίαν ὅμως ἡ δημιουργήσασα φύσις ἀμηχάνους ἡδονὰς παρέχει τοῖς δυναμένοις τὰς αἰτίας γνωρίζειν καὶ φύσει φιλοσόφοις . . . διὸ δεῖ μὴ δυσχεραίνειν παιδικῶς τὴν περὶ τῶν ἀτιμοτέρων ζῴων ἐπισκέψιν· ἐν πᾶσι γὰρ τοῖς φυσικοῖς ἔνεστί τι θαυμαστόν, &c. *De Cœlo*, ii. 12, 291, b, 25.

the content of 'Knowledge,' and of scientific proof, to include not only the Necessary, but also the Usual (τὸ ὡς ἐπὶ τὸ πολύ).[1] He deems it a sign of philosophic crudity that a man should demand the same logical strictness of all kinds of investigation,[2] when in fact it depends on the nature of the subject matter what amount of exactitude can be attained in each of the sciences.[3] Where coercive proof fails him, he is content

[1] *Anal. Post.* i. 30, iii. 12 *fin. Part. An.* iii. 2, 663, b, 27. *Metaph.* vi. 2, 1027, a, 20, xi. 8, 1064, b, sqq. *Eth. N.* i. 1, 1094, b, 19.

[2] *Eth. N.* i. 1, 1094, b, 11–27, c. 7, 1098, a, 26, ii. 2, 1104, a, 1, vii. 1 *fin.* ix. 1, 1165, a, 12 (*Polit.* vii. 7 *fin.* is not in point here). It is chiefly as regards the ethical discussions that Aristotle here denies the claim they have to a thorough accuracy, because the nature of the subject does not allow of any such result ; for in judging of men and the issues of human action, much rests on estimates which are correct only ' in the main ' and ' as a rule.'

[3] According to *Anal. Post.* i. 27, that science is more exact (ἀκριβεστέρα), which besides the ὅτι settles the διότι ; that which has to deal with purely scientific questions, not with their application to some given case (ἡ μὴ καθ' ὑποκειμένου [ἀκριβεστέρα] τῆς καθ' ὑποκειμένου, οἷον ἀριθμητικὴ ἁρμονικῆς), and lastly that which deduces its results from a smaller number of assumptions (*e.g.* Arithmetic as compared with Geometry), or in other words the more abstract (ἡ ἐξ ἐλαττόνων τῆς ἐκ προσθέσεως, as is also said in *Metaph.* i. 2, 982, a, 26, the same

example being adduced). The latter is thus expressed (*Metaph.* xiii. 3, 1078, a, 9) : ὅσῳ δὴ ἂν περὶ προτέρων τῷ λόγῳ (that which, according to its notion or nature, is earlier, or stands nearer to the first principles ; cf. p. 330 sqq.) καὶ ἀπλουστέρων τοσούτῳ μᾶλλον ἔχει τἀκριβές. From this it naturally follows, that the first philosophy, according to Aristotle, is capable of the greatest accuracy (cf. *Metaph.* i. 2, 982, a, 25 : ἀκριβέσταται δὲ τῶν ἐπιστημῶν αἱ μάλιστα τῶν πρώτων εἰσί), and that every other science is capable of so much the less according as it descends more and more to the world of sensible things (cf. *ibid.* 1078, a, 11 sq.); for in the latter πολλὴ ἡ τοῦ ἀορίστου φύσις ἐνυπάρχει (*Metaph.* iv. 5, 1010, a, 3; further *infra*, in ch. vii. sec. 2). Therefore the natural sciences are necessarily less accurate than those which are concerned with what is constant, like the first Philosophy, pure Mathematics, and the doctrine of souls (of which *De An.* i. 1 *init.* extols the ἀκρίβεια); and those which have the transient as their object are less exact than Astronomy (*Metaph.* 1078, a, 11 sqq.). KAMPE (*Erkenntnisstheorie d. Ar.* 254) says, that in the scale of ἀκρίβεια

to put up with arguments possible and probable, and
to postpone a more definite decision until a further
analysis can be had.[1] It is not, however, the essential
problems of philosophy which Aristotle so treats, but
always special questions of ethics or natural philosophy,
for which Plato himself had relaxed the strictness of
his dialectical procedure, and put probability in the
place of scientific proof. The real difference between
them is only this, that Aristotle includes this kindred
branch of knowledge *in* Philosophy; whereas Plato
insists on treating everything except the pure Science
of Ideas as merely matter of intellectual discourse, or
as a condescension of the philosopher to the pressure of
practical needs.[2] Why, asks Aristotle rightly, should
the man who thirsts after knowledge not seek to learn
at least a little, even where he cannot establish all?[3]

Aristotle cannot be justly accused of having com-
promised the unity of all spiritual effort by dividing

---

the science of nature takes the
lowest place: but this would
rather, as has been said in the
preceding note, be true of Ethics
and Politics.

[1] *De Cælo*, ii. 5, 287, b, 28
sqq. c. 12 *init. Gen. An.* iii. 10,
760, b, 27, where to a discussion
on the reproduction of bees he
adds the remark : οὐ μὴν εἴληπταί
γε τὰ συμβαίνοντα ἱκανῶς, ἀλλ' ἐάν
ποτε ληφθῇ, τότε τῇ αἰσθήσει
μᾶλλον τῶν λόγων πιστευτέον, καὶ
τοῖς λόγοις, ἐὰν ὁμολογούμενα
δεικνύωσι τοῖς φαινομένοις. *H. An.*
ix. 37 *fin.* c. 42, 629, a, 22, 27.
Metaph. xii. 8, 1073, b, 10 sqq.
1074, a, 15. *Meteor.* i. 79, *init.* :
περὶ τῶν ἀφανῶν τῇ αἰσθήσει
νομίζομεν ἱκανῶς ἀποδεδεῖχθαι κατὰ

τὸν λόγον, ἐὰν εἰς τὸ δυνατὸν
ἀναγάγωμεν. Cf. EUCKEN, *Meth.
d. Arist. Forsch.* 125 sq. See
further on this subject in the
next chapter.

[2] *Rep.* vi. 511, B, sq. vii. 519,
C, sqq.; *Pl.* 173, E ; *Tim.* 29, B, sq.
and *alib.* Cf. ZELLER, *Ph. d. Gr.*,
Pt. i pp. 490, 516, 536 sq.

[3] *De Cælo*, ii. 12 *init.* : πειρατέον
λέγειν τὸ φαινόμενον, αἰδοῦς ἀξίαν
εἶναι νομίζοντας τὴν προθυμίαν
μᾶλλον ἢ θράσους (it does not occur
to him that he himself might be
accused rather of an unphilosophi-
cal modesty), εἴ τις διὰ τὸ φιλοσοφίας
διψῆν καὶ μικρὰς εὐπορίας ἀγαπᾷ
περὶ ὧν τὰς μεγίστας ἔχομεν ἀπορίας.
Cf. *ibid.* 292, a, 14, c. 5, 287, b, 31
Part. An. i. 5, 644, b, 31.

off the theoretic from the practical activities.[1] That distinction is undeniably justified to the full; but the note of unity is expressly preserved in Aristotle's treatment by the fact that while he presents Θεωρία as the completion of the true human life, he also represents the practical activity as an indispensable element therein, as a moral upbringing is an indispensable condition precedent of ethical knowledge.[2] If it be true that this shutting back of ' Theory ' upon itself, this exclusion from the notion of Philosophy of all practical need and effort (as it becomes apparent, for example, in the Aristotelian sketch of the Divine Life) did in fact prepare the way for the later withdrawal of the Wise Man from practical usefulness, nevertheless we should not overlook the fact that even here Aristotle only followed in the direction indicated before by Plato; for Plato's ' Philosopher' would also, if left to himself, live for ' theory' alone, and only take part in the life of the Republic on compulsion. Least of all can one agree with those who criticise Aristotle because he conceived the office of Philosophy, not from the point of view of an ideal humanly unattainable, but in a way that could be carried out in the actual world,[3] or with those who attack him by praising Plato for distinguishing between the ideal of knowledge and the scientific attainment of men.[4] If such a view of the relation of the ideal to actuality were in itself and in Aristotle's view well founded, it would only follow that he had sought, as

[1] RITTER, *Ges. d. Ph.* iii. 50 sqq.
[2] Besides the passages to be cited *infra*, on the inquiry into the ' highest good,' cf. *Eth. N.* x. 10, 1179, b, 20 sqq. i. 1, 1094, b, 27 sqq.
[3] RITTER, *ibid.* and p. 56 sq.
[4] *Ibid.* ii. 222 sqq.

every philosopher should, not *abstract* ideals, but the actual *essence* of things. Even this, however, is less than the truth. To Aristotle the Idea does in truth reach out beyond the phenomena—it is not entirely realised in any individual phenomenal thing, although it is not an *unactual* ideal even so. Aristotle recognised both sides with equal clearness. He sees that the goal of knowledge is set very high—that it cannot be reached by everyone—that even by the best it can only be imperfectly attained.[1] Yet he is never content to call it wholly unattainable or to limit the demands he makes upon Philosophy (as such) by the weakness of humanity. Indeed, the whole course of this account must have already shown how complete is his real agreement with Plato on just this very point.

In his philosophic method Aristotle likewise follows out in all essentials the lines which Socrates and Plato opened out. His method is the dialectic method, which indeed he himself carried to its highest perfection. With it he combines the observational method of the student of nature ; and even though it be true that he does not succeed in getting a true equilibrium between the two, yet the mere fact that he combined them was one of the highest services rendered to philosophy among the Greeks. By that advance he made good the one-sidedness of the Philosophy of Ideas, so far as that was possible without a complete restatement of its principles. As Socrates and Plato always began by asking for the

---

[1] *Metaph.* i. 2, 982, b, 28, xii. 7, 1072, b, 24 ; *Eth. N.* vi. 7, 1141, b, 2 sqq., x. 7, 1177, b, 30, c. 8, 1178, b, 25 ; cf. *ibid.* vii. 1.

'idea' of each thing they dealt with, and set this kind
of cognition as the basis of all other knowledge, so also
does Aristotle delight to begin with an inquiry into
the 'idea' of whatever his subject for the time being
may be.[1] As Socrates and Plato commonly set out on
such inquiries with the simplest questions—examples
taken from everyday life, commonly accepted beliefs,
arguments from uses of words and ways of speech—so
too is Aristotle wont to find his starting-point for the
definition of such ideas in prevalent opinions, in the
views of earlier philosophers, and particularly in the
expressions and names which are in common use on the
subject and in the meaning of words.[2] Socrates sought
to correct the uncertainty of such beginnings by means
of a dialectical comparison of various opinions and
experiences gathered from all sides. But in Aristotle
this process is far more complete and is directed with
more explicit consciousness to the scientific ends in
view. As a rule, he commences every important inquiry
with an accurate investigation as to the various points
of view from which the matter in hand can be treated,
as to the difficulties and contradictions which arise
from the different views that might be taken, and as to
the reasons which make for or against each view; and
the task which he sets before the philosopher is simply
that of finding, by a more accurate definition of the

---

[1] Thus, for instance, in *Phys.*
ii. 1, iii. 1, iv. 1 sqq. iv. 10 sq.
the notions of Nature, Motion,
Space and Time are investigated;
in *De An.* i. 1 sqq., ii. 1 sq. the
notion of the Soul; in *Eth. N.* ii.
4 sq. the notion of Virtue; in

Polit. iii. 1 sqq. the notion of
the State, and so on.

[2] It will be shown later what
significance universal opinion and
the probable arguments deduced
from it, had with Aristotle as a
foundation for induction.

ideas involved, the solution of the difficulties disclosed.[1] Aristotle is thus working in truth wholly on the ground and along the lines of the Socratico-Platonic method of dialectic. He developed the Socratic Induction into a conscious technical device, and he completed it by the theory of the syllogism which he invented and by all the related logical inquiries. In his own writings he has left us a most perfect example of a dialectical investigation carried through with keen and strict fidelity from all sides of the subject. If we did not know it before, we should recognise at once in Aristotle's philosophic method the work of a scholar of Plato.

With this dialectical process he combines at the same time a mastery in all that concerns the observation of facts, and a passion for the physical explanation of them, which are not to be found in Socrates nor in Plato either. To Aristotle the most perfect definition of an idea is that which exhibits the causes of the thing,[2] for

---

[1] On this also more definite information will be given later.

[2] *De An.* ii. 2 *init.*: οὐ γὰρ μόνον τὸ ὅτι δεῖ τὸν ὁριστικὸν λόγον δηλοῦν . . .' ἀλλὰ καὶ τὴν αἰτίαν ἐνυπάρχειν καὶ ἐμφαίνεσθαι. νῦν δ' ὥσπερ συμπεράσμαθ' οἱ λόγοι τῶν ὅρων εἰσ.'ν· οἷον τί ἐστι τετραγωνισμός; τὸ ἴσον ἑτερομήκει ὀρθογώνιον εἶναι ἰσόπλευρον· ὁ δὲ τοιοῦτος ὅρος λόγος τοῦ συμπεράσματος· ὁ δὲ λέγων ὅτι ἐστὶν ὁ τετραγωνισμὸς μέσης εὕρεσις, τοῦ πράγματος λέγει τὸ αἴτιον. *Anal. Post.* ii. 1. sq.: every inquiry deals with four points, the ὅτι, the διότι, the εἰ ἔστι, the τί ἐστιν. These may, however, be reduced to the two questions : εἰ ἔστι μέσον and τί ἐστι τὸ μέσον· τὸ μὲν γὰρ αἴτιον τὸ μέσον, ἐν ἅπασι δὲ τοῦτο ζητεῖται. And after quoting some examples : ἐν ἅπασι γὰρ τούτοις φανερόν ἐστιν ὅτι τὸ αὐτό ἐστι τὸ τί ἐστι καὶ διὰ τί ἐστιν, &c. *Ibid.* c. 3 *init.* c. 8 *init.*; *ibid.* i. 31, 88, a, 5 : τὸ δὲ καθόλου τίμιον ὅτι δηλοῖ τὸ αἴτιον. *Metaph.* vi. 1, 1025, b, 17: διὰ τὸ τῆς αὐτῆς εἶναι διανοίας τό τε τί ἐστι δῆλον ποιεῖν καὶ εἰ ἔστιν. *Ibid.* vii. 17, 1041, a, 27 : φανερὸν τοίνυν ὅτι ζητεῖ τὸ αἴτιον· τοῦτο δ' ἐστὶ τὸ τί ἦν εἶναι, ὡς εἰπεῖν λογικῶς . ὃ ἐπ' ἐνίων μέν ἐστι τίνος ἕνεκα, . . . ἐπ' ἐνίων δὲ τί ἐκίνησε πρῶτον. Cf. *Anal. Post.* ii. 11 *init.*: ἐπεὶ δὲ ἐπίστασθαι οἰόμεθα ὅταν εἰδῶμεν τὴν αἰτίαν, αἰτίαι δὲ τέτταρες . . . πᾶσαι αὗται διὰ τοῦ μέσου δείκνυνται.

philosophy ought to explain the phenomena.[1] Therefore, in his view (as we shall see presently), it ought to
take account not only of the idea and the final cause of
a thing, but of the efficient and the material causes
also. Holding as decisively as we shall see he does
that a thing is to be explained by its own causes, he
could not well be content with a method which should
look only to the Universal which the 'Idea' gives, and
neglect the immediate definiteness of the things themselves.[2] This is the reason of that careful regard for

[1] *Vid. supr.* p. 167.

[2] In this sense Aristotle not
unfrequently contrasts the *logical*
consideration of a subject (*i.e.*
that which is only concerned with
what is universal in its concept), either with the *analytical*,
which enters more deeply into
the peculiarity of the given case,
(and which he also calls ἐκ τῶν
κειμένων), or with the *physical*
research which draws its result
not from the concept of a phenomenon merely, but from its
concrete conditions. The former,
for instance, *Anal. Post.* i. 21 *fin.*,
c 23, 84, a, 7, cf. c. 24, 86, a, 22, c,
32, 88, a, 19, 30; *Metaph.* vii. 4,
1029, b, 12, 1030, a, 25, c. 17,
1041, a, 28. The latter, *Phys.* iii.
5, 204, b, 4, 10 (cf. a, 34, *Metaph.*
xi. 10, 1066, b, 21), c. 3, 202, a,
21; *De Cælo*, i. 7, 275, b, 12;
Metaph. xii. 1, 1069, a, 27, xiv. 1,
1087, b, 20 (similarly φυσικῶς and
καθόλου, *De Cælo*, i. 10 *fin.* c. 12,
283, b, 17). But here he takes
the logical to be so much the
more imperfect, the further removed it. is from the concrete
definiteness of the object. Cf.
Phys. viii. 8, 264, a, 7: οἷς μὲν οὖν

ἄν τις ὡς οἰκείοις πιστεύσειε λόγοις,
οὗτοι καὶ τοιοῦτοί τινές εἰσιν·
λογικῶς δ' ἐπισκοποῦσι κᾶν ἐκ τῶνδε
δόξειέ τῳ ταὐτὸ τοῦτο συμβαίνειν.
Gen. An. ii. 8, 747, b, 28 : λέγω δὲ
λογικὴν [ἀπόδειξιν] διὰ τοῦτο ὅτι
ὅσῳ καθόλου μᾶλλον πορρωτέρω τῶν
οἰκείων ἐστὶν ἀρχῶν. And after a
proof such as this has been brought
forward, he adds (748, a, 7): οὗτος
μὲν οὖν ὁ λόγος καθόλου λίαν καὶ
κενός. οἱ γὰρ μὴ ἐκ τῶν οἰκείων
ἀρχῶν λόγοι κενοί, &c. (similarly
De An. i. 1, 403, a, 2 : διαλεκτικῶς
καὶ κενῶς ; *Eth. Eud.* i. 8, 1217, b,
21 : λογικῶς καὶ κενῶς). Hence in
such cases he 'much prefers the
physical treatment to the logical
(e.g. *Gen. et Corr.* i. 2, 316, a, 10 :
ἴδοι δ' ἄν τις καὶ ἐκ τούτων, ὅσον
διαφέρουσιν οἱ φυσικῶς καὶ λογικῶς
σκοποῦντες, &c., see ZELLER, *Ph.*
d. Gr., pt. i. p. 869, 1), whereas in
metaphysical researches on Ideas
(*Metaph.* xiii. 5 *fin.*) he thinks the
λογικώτεροι λόγοι are the ἀκριβέ-
στεροι. See further, WAITZ, *Arist.*
Org. ii. 353 sq. ; BONITZ, *Arist.*
Metaph. ii. 187; *Ind. Arist.* 432, b,
5 seq. ; RASSOW, *Arist. de not. def.*
doctr. 19 sq.

facts which has drawn down on him often enough the reproach of an unphilosophic empiricism.[1] He was not only one of the highest speculative thinkers—he was also one of the most accurate and untiring observers, and one of the most erudite men of learning that the world knows. As in his general theory he conceived of experience as the condition precedent of thought, and of perception as the matter out of which thoughts come forth, so in practice he did not fail to provide for his own system a broad substructure of experiential knowledge, and to base his philosophic dicta upon an all-round appreciation of the data of fact. Especially in regard to any theory of nature he insists that we should first know the phenomena and then look about for their causes.[2] We could not, of course, expect to find in him the sureness and accuracy of method which empirical science has in modern times attained. In Aristotle's day it was only in its infancy, and it suffered from the complete lack of the proper aids to observation and of the support of a developed mathematics. We

[1] Thus SCHLEIERMACHER, *Gesch. d. Phil.* p. 120, says of Aristotle: 'We cannot deny that there is a great want of speculative genius,' &c., and on p. 110 he contrasts the older Academics with him, as being 'more speculative'; but he sets out with a principle, according to which Aristotle must certainly come off badly: 'Never has one who first went through a great mass of empirical work become a true philosopher.' Thus also STRÜMPELL, *Theoret. Phil. d. Gr.* 156, who delivers the judgment—which, however, can scarcely be reconciled with his own observations on pp. 184 sqq.,

and appears to be in every way untenable—that Aristotle's general bent made him 'more suited for the collective comprehension of empirical and historical data, than for the solving of metaphysical difficulties.'

[2] Thus *Part. An.* i. 1, 639, b, 7 sqq., 640, a, 14.; *Hist. An.* i. 7, 491, a, 9 sq.; *Meteor.* iii. 2, 371, b, 21; *Anal. Pr.* i. 30, 46, a, 17 sqq. Aristotle appeals here (as in *Part. An.* 639, b, 7) especially to the progress of astronomy about which see *infra*, ch. ix. (middle). Cf. EUCKEN, *Methode d. Arist. Forsch.* 122 sq.

also notice that in Aristotle the empirical effort is still too often crossed by the speculative and dialectic methods which he took over directly from Platonism. Indeed, so far as natural science goes, it would be more just to charge him with too little empiricism than too much.[1] But it would be far truer to say simply that he carried both methods as far as could be expected of his day. The science of the Greeks began with speculation. The empirical sciences only attained to any sort of development at a late date, and largely by the efforts of Aristotle himself. Therefore it was natural that the dialectical method of Socrates and Plato, with its logical dissections and connections of ideas, guided by current opinions and the indications of language, should take precedence of any strict empirical rules. Aristotle stood in a close relation to the dialectical movement, and brought it in theory and practice, as we have just said, to completion. It was not to be expected that the art of empirical investigation should find in him an equally complete exponent, and therefore an accurate discrimination between the two methods was as yet far off. That could only come after the fuller development of the empirical sciences and the direct investigation of the theory of knowledge, which the modern centuries have brought to pass. All the greater is the credit due to Aristotle that his wide and direct scientific instinct led him even so soon to turn to the methods of

---

[1] This charge has been made by Bacon, and, since the above was first written, by Lewes (*Aristotle*, § 91, 97) ; and, through a one-sidedness not uncommon with him, by LANGE, *Gesch. d. Mater.* i. 61 sqq.

observation and to connect them as well as he then could with the dialectical treatment of ideas.[1]

That Aristotle's dialectic had to do with a far more extensive range of empirical data than Plato had to deal with is the reason why Aristotle's methods of exposition are distinguishable at a glance from Plato's by that air of formal logic which they wear. Aristotle does not limit himself to that unfolding of pure ideas which Plato expected of the philosopher,[2] though his own attempts at it were in truth but rare and partial. The ideal processes are for ever interrupted, in Aristotle, by references to experience, by examinations of ambiguous terms, by criticism of other views. The more extensive is the matter which he has to bring under the yoke of science, the more eager is he to see that every step in his far-reaching investigations should be assured on the one hand by a copious induction, and on the other by a careful observance of the rules of logic. His manner of presenting his work seems often dry and tedious as compared with Plato's; for the texts we now possess yield us but rare examples of that richness and charm for which his writings were praised no less than his master's. We miss wholly the dramatic life, the artistic finish, the fine mythical presentment which make us love the Dialogues.[3] But the *Corpus Aristotelicum* exhibits the peculiar qualities of a *philosophic* style in so high a degree that we ought not only

---

[1] For fuller information on the methodological principles of Aristotle and their application, see the next chapter; and EUCKEN, *Die Methode d. Arist. Forschung* (1872); cf. especially pp. 29 sqq. 122 sqq. 152 sqq.

[2] See Zeller's Plato, *passim.*

[3] Cf. p. 106 sq.

not to call him a 'bad writer,'[1] but ought rather to set
him in this respect far above his great forerunner. He
is accused of 'formalism,' though where the discussion
grows more concrete, as in his physics or ethics, this
falls away; but it will not be regarded as a blemish by
those who remember how needful even in Plato's view
this strict logical effort was—how much bewilderment
among ideas must have been cured by keen distinctions
in the meanings of words—how many fallacies will have
been avoided by the exact analysis of the syllogism.
Rather has Aristotle done the world immortal service
in that he established a fixed basis for all scientific
procedure, and won for thought thereby a security
whose value to us we only overlook because we have
grown too used to it to remember that it is great.

If, again, we endeavour to appreciate, so far as at
this point we can, the standpoint and general view of
the universe which we can call Aristotelian, we shall
find two things. On the one hand, no one can overlook
the basis he inherited from Socrates and Plato. Yet,
on the other hand, there is an element of originality
so notable and so sustained as to make us stigmatise
the notion that Aristotle was a kind of dependent
follower of Plato who did nothing but formally work
up and complete his master's thought, as an error
utterly unjust.[2]

Aristotle adheres not only to the Socratic proposition that Science has to do with the idea of things, but
also to the further consequence which takes us into the
heart of Plato's system, that that which is truly actual

[1] RITTER, iii. 28.
[2] BRANISS, *Gesch. d. Phil.*; see KANT, i. 179 sqq. 207 sq.

in a thing is only its essence as thought in the idea of
it, and that all else is 'actual' only in so far as it
partakes of that ideal essentiality. Yet, whereas to
Plato this 'Essential Being' was a thing existing by
itself, which he relegated to a separate ideal world
beyond the world of experience, his follower recognises
the truth that the Idea, as the essence of things, could
not stand separate from the things themselves. Therefore he seeks to present the Idea, not as a Universal
existing for itself apart, but as a common essence of
things indwelling in the particular things themselves.
In lieu of the negative relation to which the sundering
of ideas and phenomena had led with Plato, he posits
rather the positive relation of each to the other and
their mutual dependence. Therefore he calls the sensible element the Matter, and the insensible essence the
Form. He puts it that it is one and the same Being,
here developed into actuality, there undeveloped and
lying as a mere basis. So it comes that, for him,
Matter must, by an inner necessity, strive upward to
Form, and Form equally must present itself in Matter.
In this transformation of Plato's metaphysic, it is easy
to recognise the realism of the natural philosopher
whose aim is the explanation of the actual. Just this
is his strongest and ever recurrent charge against the
Ideal Theory, that it leaves the world of phenomena,
the things of Becoming and Change, unexplained. For
his own part, he finds the very root-definitions of his
metaphysic in his treatment of those processes wherein
is the secret of all genesis and all change, whether by
nature or by art.

Yet Aristotle, too, is barred from completing his
philosophy in these directions by just that dualism of
the philosophy of Ideas which he inherited from Plato.
Hard as he tries to bring Form and Matter together,
still to the last they always remain *two* principles, of
which he can neither deduce one from the other, nor
both from a third. Fully as they are worked out
through the range of finite things, still the highest
entity of all is nothing but the pure Spirit, left outside
the world, thinking in itself—as the highest in man is
that Reason which enters into him from without, and
which never comes into any true unity with the individual side of his being. In this way, Aristotle is at
once the perfection and the ending of the Idealism of
Socrates and Plato : its perfection, because it is the
most thorough effort to carry it throughout the whole
realm of actuality and to explain the world of phenomenal things from the standpoint of the ' Idea '; but
also its ending, since in it there comes to light the impossibility of ever holding together the Idea and the
Phenomenon in any real unity, after we have once
posited, in our definition of the ultimate basis of the
world, an original opposition between them.

If we follow out the development of these principles
in the Aristotelian system, and seek for that purpose to
take a general view of the divisions he adopted, we are
met at once with the unfortunate difficulty that, neither
in his own writings nor in any trustworthy account of
his method, is any satisfactory information on that point
to be found.[1] If we should trust the later Peripatetics

[1] Cf. for what follows : RITTER, iii. 57 sqq.; BRANDIS, ii. b, 130

and the Neo-Platonic commentators, Aristotle had divided all philosophy into *Theoretic* and *Practical*, assigning to the former the office of perfecting the cognitive part of the soul, and to the latter that of perfecting the appetitive. In Theoretic Philosophy, they say, he again distinguished three parts : Physics, Mathematics, and Theology, also called First Philosophy or Metaphysics. Practical Philosophy likewise fell, it is said, into three : Ethics, Economics, and Politics.[1] There are not wanting indications in the Aristotelian writings which serve to support this statement. Aristotle often opposes to each other the theoretical and the practical reason.[2] He distinguishes between inquiries which are directed to Cognition, and those which are directed to Action.[3] Accordingly we find,

---

sqq. ; TEICHMÜLLER, *Arist. Forsch.* ii. 9 sqq. ; WALTER, *Die Lehre v. d. prakt. Vern.* 537 sqq.

[1] Thus AMMON. *in Qu. voc. Porph.* 7, a, sqq. (who adds the fourfold division of Mathematics into Geometry, Astronomy, Music, and Arithmetic), and after him DAVID, *Schol.* 25, a, 1 ; SIMPL. *Phys. init. Categ.* i. ε ; PHILOP. *Schol. in Ar.* 36, a, 6, *Phys. init.* ; ANATOL. *in Fabric. Bibl.* iii. 462 H. ; EUSTRAT. in *Eth. N. init.* ; ANON. *Schol. in Arist.* 9, a, 31. The division into theoretical and practical philosophy had already been given by ALEX. *in Anal. Pri. init.* and DIOG. v. 28. Further, the latter, in part diverging from the others, divides theoretical philosophy into Physics and Logic (which, however, he does not consider so much a

real part as an instrument of Philosophy), practical philosophy into Ethics and Politics, and Politics into the science of the State and the science of the household. ALEX. *Top.* 17, gives as philosophical sciences, Physics, Ethics, Logic and Metaphysics ; but as to Logic cf. below p. 187, n. 2.

[2] *De An.* iii. 9, 432, b, 26, c. 10, 433, a, 14 ; *Eth.* vi. 2, 1139, a, 6, cf. i. 13 *vers. fin.* ; *Polit.* vii. 14, 1333, a, 24. For further information see chap. xi.

[3] *Eth.* i. 1, 1095, a, 5 : ἐπειδὴ τὸ τέλος [τῆς πολιτικῆς] ἐστὶν οὐ γνῶσις ἀλλὰ πρᾶξις. Likewise, *ibid.* x. 10, 1179, a, 35, ii. 2, *init.* : ἐπεὶ οὖν ἡ παροῦσα πραγματεία οὐ θεωρίας ἕνεκά ἐστιν ὥσπερ αἱ ἄλλαι (οὐ γὰρ ἵν' εἰδῶμεν τί ἐστιν ἡ ἀρετὴ σκεπτόμεθα, ἀλλ' ἵν' ἀγαθοὶ γενώμεθα, ἐπεὶ οὐδὲν ἂν ἦν ὄφελος αὐτῆς), &c.

at an early date in his School, a division of Science
into theoretic and practical.¹ He himself, however, is
accustomed to add a third—the ' poietic science '²—
because he distinguishes ποίησις or production from
πρᾶξις or action, both by its source and by its end,
saying that the former originates in the artistic faculty,
the latter in the will,³ and that production has its
end outside itself in the work to be brought into
being, but action has its end in the activity of the

¹ *Metaph.* ii. (*a*), 1, 993, b,
19 : ὀρθῶς δ' ἔχει καὶ τὸ καλεῖσθαι
τὴν φιλοσοφίαν ἐπιστήμην τῆς ἀληθείας. θεωρητικῆς μὲν γὰρ (wherein,
however, the whole of philosophy
is here included) τέλος ἀλήθεια,
πρακτικῆς δ' ἔργον. *Eth. Eud.* i.
1, 1214, a, 8 : πολλῶν δ' ὄντων
θεωρημάτων . . . τὰ μὲν αὐτῶν συν-
τείνει πρὸς τὸ γνῶναι μόνον, τὰ δὲ
καὶ περὶ τὰς κτήσεις καὶ περὶ τὰς
πράξεις τοῦ πράγματος. ὅσα μὲν οὖν
ἔχει φιλοσοφίαν μόνον θεωρητικήν,
&c.

² *Metaph.* vi. 1, 1025, b,
18 sq. : ἡ φυσικὴ ἐπιστήμη . . .
δῆλον ὅτι οὔτε πρακτική ἐστιν οὔτε
ποιητική . . . . ὥστε εἰ πᾶσα διάνοια
ἢ πρακτικὴ ἢ ποιητικὴ ἢ θεωρητική, ἡ
φυσικὴ θεωρητική τις ἂν εἴη ; c. 2,
1026, b, 4 (xi. 7) : οὐδεμιᾷ γὰρ
ἐπιστήμῃ ἐπιμελὲς περὶ αὐτοῦ [sc.
τοῦ συμβεβηκότος] οὔτε πρακτικῇ
οὔτε ποιητικῇ οὔτε θεωρητικῇ. The
same division of ἐπιστήμη in
Top. vi. 6, 145, a, 15 ; viii. 1, 157,
a, 10. Further cf. *Eth. N.* vi.
3–5, c. 2, 1139, a, 27, x. 8, 1718,
b, 20, and on the difference
between poietic and theoretic
science in *De Cœlo,* iii. 7, 306, a,
16 ; *Metaph.* xii. 9, 1075, a, 1, cf.
ix. 2, 1046, b, 2, and Bonitz on this
passage. Though Aristotle here

speaks merely of an ἐπιστήμη (not
of a φιλοσοφία) πρακτικὴ and ποιητικὴ, these passages would justify
our using the latter expression,
since φιλοσοφία is synonymous
with ἐπιστήμη when the latter
signifies not merely knowledge in
general, but science in the special
sense of the term. And since in
Metaph. vi. 1 (*vid. inf.* 183, n. 3)
he gives three φιλοσοφίαι θεωρητι-
καί, this undoubtedly supposes
that there is a non-theoretical, *i.e.*
a practical or poietic philosophy.
But one cannot believe that by
the latter is meant, not that
science which treats of πρᾶξις and
ποίησις (Ethics, Politics, and the
science of Art), but the faculty of
the πρᾶξις and ποίησις itself, namely
φρόνησις and τέχνη (WALTER,
Lehre v. d. prakt. Vern. 540 sq.).
Φιλοσοφία never has this meaning,
and even ἐπιστήμη cannot have it
in this context. So again since certain branches are distinguished
as practical and poietic from
Physics, Mathematics and Metaphysics, which are the theoretic
sciences, the former must likewise be really sciences. And
what other place would be left
for Ethics, &c. ?

³ *Metaph.* vi. 1, 1025, b, 22 :

actor.¹ The two coincide, however, as opposed to the *theoretic* activity in this, that they have to do with the determination of that which *can* be either one way or another, whereas Knowledge has to do with the determination of that which *cannot* be any otherwise than as it is.² Aristotle does also speak of three theoretic Sciences, the first concerning things which are *movable* and *corporeal*, the second referring to things *unmoved though corporeal*, the third dealing with that which is *incorporeal* and *unmoved* : these being Physics, Mathematics, and the First Philosophy,³ which

τῶν μὲν γὰρ ποιητικῶν ἐν τῷ ποιοῦντι ἡ ἀρχὴ ἢ νοῦς ἢ τέχνη ἢ δύναμίς
τις, τῶν δὲ πρακτικῶν ἐν τῷ πράτ-
τοντι ἡ προαίρεσις Hence *Eth.* vi.
5, 1140, b, 22 : in the province of
art it is better to err voluntarily ;
in that of morals involuntarily.

¹ *Eth.* vi. 4 *init.* : ἕτερον δ'
ἐστὶ ποίησις καὶ πρᾶξις ; c. 5, 1140,
b, 3 : ἄλλο τὸ γένος πράξεως καὶ
ποιήσεως . . . . τῆς μὲν γὰρ ποιήσεως
ἕτερον τὸ τέλος, τῆς δὲ πράξεως οὐκ
ἂν εἴη· ἔστι γὰρ αὐτὴ ἡ εὐπραξία
τέλος. *Ibid.* i. 1 *init.*

² *Eth.* vi. 3, 1139, b, 18:
ἐπιστήμη μὲν οὖν τί ἐστιν ἐντεῦθεν
φανερόν . . . . πάντες γὰρ ὑπολαμ-
βάνομεν, ὃ ἐπιστάμεθα μὴ ἐνδέχεσθαι
ἄλλως ἔχειν; c. 4 *init.*: τοῦ δ' ἐνδεχομένου ἄλλως ἔχειν ἔστι τι καὶ
ποιητὸν καὶ πρακτόν, &c. Cf. c. 2,
1139, a, 2 sqq. *De Cœlo*, iii. 7, 306,
a : *vid.supr.* p 167, n. 2 ; *Part. An.*
i. 1, 640, a, 3 : ἡ γὰρ ἀρχὴ τοῖς μὲν
[the theorists] τὸ ὂν, τοῖς δὲ [the
technicists] τὸ ἐσόμενον.

³ *Metaph.* vi. 1 (xi. 7) where
among other things 1026, a, 13 :
ἡ μὲν γὰρ φυσικὴ περὶ ἀχώριστα μὲν
ἀλλ' οὐκ ἀκίνητα, τῆς δὲ μαθηματικῆς ἔνια περὶ ἀκίνητα μὲν οὐ

χωριστὰ δ' ἴσως, ἀλλ' ὡς ἐν ὕλῃ. ἡ
δὲ πρώτη [sc. φιλοσοφία] καὶ περὶ
χωριστὰ καὶ ἀκίνητα . . . ὥστε τρεῖς
ἂν εἶεν φιλοσοφ'αι θεωρητικαὶ, μαθηματικὴ, φυσικὴ, θεολογικὴ. Similarly xii. 1, 1096, a, 30, c, 6 *init.* ;
De An. i. 1, 403, b, 7 sqq. About
the name of the first philosophy,
cf. also p. 76, *supra*. As to Mathematics as the science of numbers
and quantity, and the abstraction
peculiar to it, whereby it does not
consider a body according to its
physical properties, but only from
the point of view of magnitude in
space, and, in determining number and quantity, disregards the
intrinsic condition of that in
which they occur, see *Phys.* ii. 2,
193, b, 31 sqq. ; *Anal. Post.* i. 10,
76, b, 3, c. 13, 79 a, 7 ; *Anal.
Pri.* i. 41, 49, b, 35 ; *Metaph.* xi.
4, c. 3, 1061, a, 28, vii. 10, 1036,
a, 9, xiii. 2, 1077, a, 9 to c. 3 *fin.*,
iii. 2, 997, b, 20, *ibid.* 996, a, 29 ;
De An. iii. 7 *fin.* Detached statements on Mathematics are found
in many places, e.g. *Metaph.* i. 2,
982, a, 26 ; *De Cœlo*, iii. 1, 299, a,
15, c. 7, 306, a, 26 ; *De An.* i. 1,
402, b, 16. Cf. BRANDIS, p. 135

he names also Theology, and treats as the pinnacle of
all knowledge.[1]

If, however, we attempt to apply the suggested
division to the contents of the Aristotelian books,[2] we

sqq. The contradiction which
RITTER, iii. 73 sq., finds in Aristotle, viz. that a sensible sub-
tratum is first denied and afterwards attributed to Mathematics,
and that its object is now designated as removed, now as not
removed, from what is sensible, is
partly solved by the distinction
of the purely mathematical from
the applied sciences, and partly
and chiefly by the remark that
Aristotle nowhere says that the
object of Mathematics *is* a χωριστὸν, but only that it is *considered*
as such, *i.e.* by abstracting from its
sensible nature ; in *Metaph.* xii. 8,
1073, b, 3, moreover, Astronomy
according to the common reading
is not called ' the truest philosophy,' but the οἰκειοτάτη, the
most important of the mathematical sciences for the discussion in hand ; still Bonitz is right
in reading : τῆς οἰκειοτάτης φιλοσοφίᾳ τῶν μαθηματικῶν ἐπιστημῶν.
  [1] *Metaph.* vi. 1, 1026, a, 21
(and almost the same in xi. 7,
1064, b, 1), after what is given in
the preceding note : τὴν τιμιωτάτην [ἐπιστήμην] δεῖ περὶ τὸ τιμιώτατον γένος εἶναι. (For, as is said
in 1064, b, 5 : βελτίων καὶ χείρων
ἑκάστη λέγεται κατὰ τὸ οἰκεῖον ἐπι-
στητόν.) αἱ μὲν οὖν θεωρητικαὶ τῶν
ἄλλων ἐπιστημῶν αἱρετώτεραι, αὕτη
δὲ τῶν θεωρητικῶν. He discusses
at length in *Metaph.* i. 2, why the
first philosophy especially deserves the name σοφία : because,
as perceiving the most universal,
it gives the most comprehensive

knowledge ; because it investigates what is most difficult to be
known ; because the science of
the last reasons is the most accurate (ἀκριβεστάτη) and gives the
most perfect instruction as to
causes ; because, more than any
other, it pursues knowledge for
its own sake ; and because, as the
science of principles, and hence
also of final ends, it must govern
all others. In *Top.* viii. 1, 157, a,
9, the following is given as an
example of a division : ὅτι ἐπιστήμη ἐπιστήμης βελτίων ἢ τῷ ἀκριβεστέρα εἶναι ἢ τῷ βελτιόνων.
Aristotle in *Metaph.* xii. 9, 1074,
b, 29 sq. also supposes that the
value of knowledge is proportioned to that of its object. The
universal pre-eminence of the
theoretical over the practical
and poietic sciences does not,
however, rest on this, nor on their
greater exactness, for some of
them (the zoological and psychological sciences) have no superiority over Ethics in either
respect ; but primarily on the fact
that knowledge is here an end in
itself ; cf. *Metaph.* i. 1, 981, b,
17 sqq. 982, a, 1.
  [2] Thus Ravaisson (*Essai sur
la Métaphysique d'Aristote*, i.
244 sqq.). who wishes to sub-
divide theoretical philosophy
into Theology, Mathematics and
Physics, practical philosophy into
Ethics, Economics and Politics,
and poietic philosophy into
Poetics, Rhetoric and Dialectics.

run at once into manifold troubles. Of all that Aristotle wrote, the only thing which would fall under 'poietic science' is the *Poetics*; for he himself relegates the *Rhetoric* to another section by indicating that it is a side-branch of Dialectics and Politics,[1] and Dialectics cannot be disconnected from Analytics or Logic.[2]

If we were to conclude from this difficulty that the division into *two* groups—theoretic and practical—was preferable to the division into *three*, we should thereby be cutting ourselves loose from the statements of Aristotle himself. It further appears that in the presentation of his system he took no account of the existence of Mathematics. The one mathematical work to which he gives a reference, and which can with certainty be taken to be genuine—the tract on Astronomy—belongs, according to the classification above indicated, to

[1] *Rhet.* i. 2, 1356, a, 25 : ὥστε συμβαίνει τὴν ῥητορικὴν οἷον παραφυές τι τῆς διαλεκτικῆς εἶναι καὶ τῆς περὶ τὰ ἤθη πραγματείας, ἣν δίκαιόν ἐστι προσαγορεύειν πολιτικήν. c. 3, 1359, b, 8 : ὅπερ γὰρ καὶ πρότερον εἰρηκότες τυγχάνομεν ἀληθὲς ἐστιν, ὅτι ἡ ῥητορικὴ σύγκειται μὲν ἔκ τε τῆς ἀναλυτικῆς ἐπιστήμης καὶ τῆς περὶ τὰ ἤθη πολιτικῆς, ὁμοία δ' ἐστὶ τὰ μὲν τῇ διαλεκτικῇ τὰ δὲ τοῖς σοφιστικοῖς λόγοις. *Eth.* i. 1, 1094, b, 2 : ὁρῶμεν δὲ καὶ τὰς ἐντιμοτάτας τῶν δυνάμεων ὑπὸ ταύτην [τὴν πολιτικὴν] οὔσας, οἷον στρατηγικήν, οἰκονομικήν, ῥητορικήν· χρωμένης δὲ ταύτης ταῖς λοιπαῖς τῶν πρακτικῶν ἐπιστημῶν, &c. These expressions seem to have a direct reference to the passage cited from the *Rhetoric*. Aristotle sees in it an application of Dialectics for the

purposes of Politics; and since the character of a science depends on its purpose, he includes it in the practical section. Hence, although in itself an artistic science, and designated as such by Aristotle (e.g. *Rhet.* i. 1354, a, 11 sq. b, 21, 1355, a, 4, 33, b, 11, c. 2, 1356, b, 26 sqq. ; rhetorical theories are also called τέχναι, cf. *supra*, p. 72, 2, 73, 1), still he does not seem to give Rhetoric an independent place in the system, as Brandis does (ii. b, 147), and still more decidedly Döring (*Kunstl. d. Arist.* 78).

[2] So in *Top.* i. 1 *init.* c. 2, it is plainly designated as an auxiliary science to philosophy in general, and especially to the theoretical investigations.

Physics. Of the others, they are either of doubtful authenticity or, in any case, the absence of any references leaves us to suspect that these were not considered an essential part of the connected exposition of his system.[1] The *Physics*, again, is spoken of as the ' second,'[2] not the third, philosophy—as if there were no thought of Mathematics standing between it and the ' First Philosophy : ' and Aristotle himself refers the *Mathematical Axioms* to the ' First Philosophy.'[3]

As regards Practical Philosophy, Aristotle does not divide it into Ethics, Economics and Politics[4]—like the later commentators[5] who were misled in that matter by the spurious Economics. He distinguishes in the first place[6] the main Ethical Science—which he desires to call ' Politics '[7]—from the auxiliary sciences of Economics, Military Tactics, and Rhetoric[8] : and then in ' Politics ' he distinguishes that section which treats of

[1] About these writings cf. p. 86, n. 1, *supra*.

[2] *Metaph.* vii. 11, 1037, a, 14 : τῆς φυσικῆς καὶ δευτέρας φιλοσοφίας.

[3] *Metaph.* iv. 3 *init.* (xi. 4).

[4] Aristotle in *Eth.* vi. 9, 1142, a, 9, besides φρόνησις which relates to individual action, certainly names οἰκονομία and πολιτεία also : but in 1141, b, 31 he has divided Politics (*i.e.* the science of the life in society with the exclusion of Ethics) into οἰκονομία, νομοθεσία, πολιτικὴ, so that, according to .this, Economics forms a part of Politics. Still more definitely Eudemus in *Eth. Eud.* i. 8, 1218, b. 13, combines the πολιτικὴ καὶ οἰκονομικὴ καὶ φρόνησις

as the three parts of practical science ; this division must consequently belong to the oldest Peripatetics.

[5] With whom, besides Ravaisson, RITTER, iii. 302, also agrees.

[6] *Eth.* i. 1, 1094, a, 18 sqq., vi. 9, 1141, b, 23 sqq.

[7] *Eth.* i. 1, *ibid.*, and 1095, a, 2, i. 2 *init.* and *fin.*, ii. 2, 1105, a, 12, vii. 12 *init.*, cf. i. 13, 1102, a, 23. *Rhet.* i. 2, 3, *vid. supr.* p. 185, n. 1.

[8] *Eth.* i. 1, 1094, b, 2 ; *Rhet.* i. 2, 1356, a, 25. Also in the first book of the *Politics*, Economics, as far as Aristotle has treated the subject, is taken to belong to the science of the State.

the moral action of the individual from that which treats of the State.[1]

It is also important to remember that in the above division, whether we take it to be twofold or threefold, there is no place for Logic. The later Peripatetics get over this difficulty by the theory—which is a point of controversy between them and the Stoics—that Logic is not a part of Philosophy, but only an instrument for it.[2] Aristotle himself never hints at this distinction,[3] although he does, of course, treat Logic as a Methodology.[4] Nor will the suggestion help us much ; for since Aristotle *had* worked out his Logic with such scientific care, it must have had *some* definite place in his system.[5] The only conclusion is that the scheme of subdivision, which we deduce from the above-quoted remarks of Aristotle, seems to be in part too wide and in part too narrow for the matter which his books contain.

A different subdivision of the system might be built

---

[1] *Eth.* i. 1, 1094, b, 7. So also in the lengthy discussion, x. 10.

[2] DIOG. v. 28 ; ALEX. in *Pri. Anal.* init., *Schol.* 141, a, 19, b, 25, in *Top.* 41, m, AMMON. *apud* WAITZ, *Arist. Org.* i. 44 *med.* ; SIMPL. *Categ.* 1, ζ, *Schol.* 39, b, and PHILOP. in *Categ. Schol.* in *Ar.* 36, a, 6, 12, 37, b, 46. The same in *Anal. Pri. ibid.* 143, a, 3. ANON. *ibid.* 140, a, 45 sqq. DAVID, in *Categ. Schol.* 25, a, 1, where there are also further fragmentary subdivisions of Logic and the logical writings.

[3] That in *Top.* i. 18 *fin.*, and viii. 14, 163, b, 9, he speaks of logical readiness as an organ of philosophy, is of course beside the point.

[4] *Supra*, p. 91 sq.

[5] No more trustworthy is Ravaisson's statement (*loc. cit.* 252, 264 sq.), that Analytics is no special science, but the form of all science. It is much rather the *knowledge* of this form, which constitutes a particular branch just as much as Metaphysics, which is the knowledge of the universal grounds of all Being. MARBACH, *Gesch. d. Phil.* i. 247, even thinks that ' there can be no doubt that the " Mathematics " which forms a part of philosophy is what is now called Logic.'

188   *ARISTOTLE*

on the other remark, that all propositions and problems
are either ethical, physical, or logical.[1] Under the
logical head, however, Aristotle here comprehends both
formal Logic and the First Philosophy or Metaphysics,[2]
and this alone would prove that he could not here have
meant to indicate a scheme for the presentation of his
system, in which these two departments are kept so
obviously distinct.

If, then, we are forced to give up the attempt to
find in his own isolated remarks any key to the plan of
his work which corresponds with the construction
itself, nothing remains but to gather from the actual
work as we have it, the method of the work he designed.
Abstracting from those of his writings which are intended only as preliminary essays, or devoted to historical materials or collections concerning natural history,
or taken up with philosophic criticism, we distinguish
among Aristotle's writings four main masses. These
are his investigations of Logic, of Metaphysics, of
Natural History, and of Ethics. A fifth would be the

---

[1] *Top.* i. 14, 104, b, 19 : ἔστι δ'
ὡς τύπῳ περιλαβεῖν τῶν προτάσεων
καὶ τῶν προβλημάτων μέρη τρία. αἱ
μὲν γὰρ ἠθικαὶ προτάσεις εἰσὶν, αἱ δὲ
λογικαί . . . . ὁμοίως δὲ καὶ τὰ πο-
βλήματα . . . . πρὸς μὲν οὖν φιλοσοφίαν κατ' ἀλήθειαν περὶ αὐτῶν
πραγματευτέον, διαλεκτικῶς δὲ πρὸς
δόξαν. It is of no importance as
against this, that, in dealing with
the difference between knowledge and representation, Aristotle remarks in *Anal.Post.* i. 33
fin. : τὰ δὲ λοιπὰ πῶς δεῖ διανεῖμαι
ἐπί τε διανοίας καὶ νοῦ καὶ ἐπιστήμης
καὶ τέχνης καὶ φρονήσεως καὶ σοφίας

τὰ μὲν φυσικῆς τὰ δὲ ἠθικῆς θεωρίας
μᾶλλον ἐστίν.

[2] As an instance of logical
propositions *Top. ubi sup.* mentions the principle, which belongs
equally to Methodology or Analytics and to Metaphysics (cf.
Metaph. iv. 2, 1004, a, 9 sqq.,
1005, a, 2), that opposites fall
under the same science. Again,
in the instances given on p. 174,
n. 2, *supra*, λογικὸς at one time
stands for logical, at another for
metaphysical inquiries ; for the
latter also in *Eth. Eud.* i. 8, 1217,
b, 16.

Philosophy of Art, except that Aristotle did not work out any part of it except the *Poetics*. He seems to have forgotten to deduce these various branches of work from the idea and problem of philosophy as a whole, or to reduce them to any simpler plan of division. Of these five, the section of Logic and Methodology ought to come first, not only in the time order of the important texts,[1] but also in the order of exposition—for Aristotle himself describes it as a propaideutic for all other inquiries.[2] After the investigation of scientific method, the 'First Philosophy' must come. For, although the connected exposition of it belongs in time to the close of Aristotle's work,[3] nevertheless it contains the key to the philosophical understanding of the *Physics* and the *Ethics*, and it is from it we must obtain all the definitions, without which we could take not a step in either of these sciences—such as the definitions of the Four Causes, of Form and Matter, of the different senses of Being, of Substance and Accident, of the Mover and the Moved, &c. The very

---

[1] See *supra*, p. 156 seq.

[2] *Metaph.* iv. 3, 1005, b, 2: ὅσα δ᾽ ἐγχειροῦσι τῶν λεγόντων τινὲς περὶ τῆς ἀληθείας, ὃν τρόπον δεῖ ἀποδέχεσθαι, δι᾽ ἀπαιδευσίαν τῶν ἀναλυτικῶν τοῦτο δρῶσιν· δεῖ γὰρ περὶ τούτων ἥκειν προεπισταμένους, ἀλλὰ μὴ ἀκούοντας ζητεῖν. It is much the same for the question in hand, whether the τούτων is referred to ἀναλυτικῶν, or more correctly to the investigations indicated in the words περὶ τῆς ἀληθείας &c., since from the nature of the thing it comes to the same, whether he says, 'One must be acquainted with Ana-lytics,' or 'One must be acquainted with what Analytics has to discuss.' Inadmissible, on the other hand, is Prantl's explanation (*Gesch. d. Log.* i. 137), which refers the τούτων, not to the words with which it is immediately connected, but to the ἀξιώματα, about which Aristotle has spoken above. As a consequence of this translation, Prantl thinks it monstrous that this passage should be used as a proof of the precedence of the Analytics.

[3] *Vid. supr.* p. 76 sqq., and p. 160, n.

name of the ' First Philosophy' expresses the fact that
in the logical order it precedes all other material
investigations, as being concerned with the discussion
of the most universal of all presuppositions.[1] The
Physics follow on after the 'First Philosophy,' and the
Ethics follow the *Physics*, because the latter is presupposed in the former.[2] The *Rhetoric* must be taken
as belonging to Ethics.[3] The philosophy of Art, on the
other hand, forms a section by itself, which is not
brought into any definite connection with the rest.
We can only treat it, therefore, as an appendix. To a
like position we must relegate also Aristotle's occasional
utterances as to Religion—for a Philosophy of Religion,
in the true sense, was not within his view.

[1] Still more plainly than by
the superlative πρώτη φιλοσοφία is
this shown by the comparative :
φιλοσοφία προτέρα (φυσικῆς, μαθηματικῆς), *Metaph.* vi. 1, 1026, a, 13,
30, *Gen. et Corr.* i. 318, a, 5.
[2] *Vid. supra*, p. 159.
[3] See *supra*, p. 185, n. 1.

CHAPTER V

LOGIC

FROM of old, Aristotle has been renowned as the founder of Logic, and he has deserved his fame. We must not, however, overlook the fact that he treated Logic, not as an independent science, but only from the point of view of Methodology, as the 'technique' of his philosophic investigations. In dealing with it, therefore, he does not contemplate by any means a full and uniform account of the powers of thought as a whole, but rather a simple inquiry into the forms and laws of scientific proof. Of the first half of his Logic—the *Topics*—he admits this himself.[1] Of the other and more important section—the *Analytics*—it follows partly from single references which assign to it the place of a Propaideutic of Science,[2] partly from the analogy of the *Topics* aforesaid, but more especially from the whole treatment of the subject. Of the two *Analytics*, the logical masterpieces of Aristotle, the first is concerned with Syllogisms, the second with the laws of Proof.[3] Only in connection with these investigations, and only in so

---

[1] *Top.* i. 1 *init.* : ἡ μὲν πρόθεσις τῆς πραγματείας μέθοδον εὑρεῖν, ἀφ' ἧς δυνησόμεθα συλλογίζεσθαι περὶ παντὸς τοῦ προτεθέντος προβλήματος ἐξ ἐνδόξων καὶ αὐτοὶ λόγον ὑπέχοντες μηθὲν ἐροῦμεν ὑπεναντίον. Cf. c. 2. c. 3 : ἕξομεν δὲ τελέως τὴν μέθοδον,

ὅταν ὁμοίως ἔχωμεν ὥσπερ ἐπὶ ῥητορικῆς καὶ ἰατρικῆς καὶ τῶν τοιούτων δυνάμεων· τοῦτο δ' ἐστὶ τὸ ἐκ τῶν ἐνδεχομένων ποιεῖν ἃ προαιρούμεθα.

[2] *Vid. supra*, p. 189, n. 2.

[3] The common theme of both

far as may be necessary thereto, did he stay to consider the theory of Propositions.[1] It was not until a later period,[2] (if at all) that he extended these hints into a separate treatise in the Περὶ ἑρμηνείας. In the same way, it is from the consideration of the Syllogism that he is led to the logical treatment of Notions. He touches òn Definition in the *Analytics*,[3] merely as a matter connected with Proof; and, in fact, the logical properties of Notions as a whole are only taken up as incidental to the Syllogism.[4] The theory of the Categories, on the other hand, belongs more to Metaphysics than to Logic, because it is not deduced from the *logical* form of the Notion as such, or from the process of thóught involved in its construction, but is derived rather from the natural division of those *real* relations, to which the Categories, according to their content, are referred.[5] The very name of ' Analytica '[6] indicates that in the

is thus designated in *Anal. Pri.* init. : πρῶτον μὲν εἰπεῖν περὶ τί καὶ τίνος ἐστὶν ἡ σκέψις, ὅτι περὶ ἀπό-δειξιν καὶ ἐπιστήμης ἀποδεικτικῆς. Likewise at end of *Anal. Post.* ii. 19 *init.* : περὶ μὲν οὖν συλλογισμοῦ καὶ ἀποδείξεως, τί τε ἑκάτερόν ἐστι καὶ πῶς γίνεται, φανερὸν, ἅμα δὲ καὶ περὶ ἐπιστήμης ἀποδεικτικῆς · ταὐτὸν γάρ ἐστιν.
[1] *Anal. Pri.* i. 1–3. *Anal. Post.* i. 2, 72, b, 7.
[2] *Vid. supr.* p. 66, n. 1.
[3] *Anal. Post.* ii. 3 sqq. and cf. especially c. 10.
[4] The little that has to be mentioned with regard to this will be adduced later. The definition of the ὅρος in *Anal. Pri.* i. 1, 24, b, 16 alone shows (ὅρον δὲ καλῶ εἰς ὃν διαλύεται ἡ πρότασις)

that Aristotle is going by an analytical method, and just as he proceeds from syllogisms to propositions, so in like manner he passes from propositions to notions. Both are merely considered as factors in the syllogism.
[5] Some other writings on Concepts, which were mentioned on p. 70, *supra*, seem to have had a purely logical character; but probably not one of them was the work of Aristotle.
[6] Aristotle not only calls both the principal logical writings Ἀναλυτικά (see p. 67, n. 1), but (*vid. supr.* p. 189, n. 2, and p. 185, n. 1) he uses the same designation for the science of which they treat.

investigations which we should class under ' Formal
Logic,' Aristotle was chiefly concerned to determine
the conditions of scientific procedure, and especially of
scientific processes of proof.[1]

Socrates had revealed the method of forming Conceptions ; Plato had added that of Division ; Aristotle
was the discoverer of the theory of Proof. This is to
him so clearly the one important point, that he resolves into it the whole science of Methodology. It
follows, then, that when the later Peripatetics described
Logic[2] as an ' instrument ' of philosophy,[3] and when
accordingly the logical writings of Aristotle were in
the end published together under the name of the
' Organon,'[4] this was in no way contrary to the

[1] Ἀναλύειν means to reduce a
given thing to the parts of which
it is composed, or to investigate
the conditions through which it
is brought about. In this sense
Aristotle uses ἀνάλυσις and
ἀναλύειν regularly for the reduction of syllogisms to the three
figures, e.g. *Anal. Pri.* i. 32 *init.*:
εἰ . . . τοὺς γεγενημένους [συλλογισ-
μοὺς] ἀναλύοιμεν εἰς τὰ προειρημένα
σχήματα, for which was written
immediately before : πῶς δ' ἀνά-
ξομεν τοὺς συλλογισμοὺς εἰς τὰ προειρημένα σχήματα. Cf. BONITZ,
Ind. Arist. 48, b, 16. And since
every investigation consists in
tracing out the component parts
and conditions of that with
which it is concerned, ἀναλύειν
together with ζητεῖν stands for
' investigate.' Thus *Eth. N.* iii.
5, 1112, b, 15 : (βουλεύεται . . . .
οὐδεὶς περὶ τοῦ τέλους·) ἀλλὰ
θέμενοι τέλος τι, πῶς καὶ διὰ τίνων
ἔσται σκοποῦσι. . . . ἕως ἂν ἔλθωσιν

ἐπὶ τὸ πρῶτον αἴτιον, ὃ ἐν τῇ
εὑρέσει ἔσχατόν ἐστιν · ὁ γὰρ βου-
λευόμενος ἔοικε ζητεῖν καὶ ἀναλύειν
τὸν εἰρημένον τρόπον ὥσπερ διά-
γραμμα. φα'νεται δ' ἡ μὲν ζήτησις οὐ
πᾶσα εἶναι βούλευσις, οἷον αἱ μαθημα-
τικαί, ἡ δὲ βούλευσις πᾶσα ζήτησις,
καὶ τὸ ἔσχατον ἐν τῇ ἀναλύσει
πρῶτον εἶναι ἐν τῇ γενέσει. (Cf.
TRENDELENBURG, *Elem. Log.
Arist.* p. 47 sq.) The ἀναλυτικὴ ἐπιστήμη (*Rhet.* i.4, 1359,b, 10) designates accordingly the art of scientific inquiry, or the introduction
to it, which is scientific methodology ; and similarly τὰ ἀναλυτικὰ
means ' that which deals with
scientific inquiry,' *i.e.* the theory
of it : as in *Metaph.* iv. 3, 1005, b, 2.

[2] On this designation, proved
to have existed since the the time
of Cicero, cf. PRANTL, *Gesch. d. Log.*
i. 514, 27, 535.

[3] *Vid. supr.* p. 187, n. 2.

[4] This name is not used by
any of the Greek commentators

Master's own view.[1]　The further theory that Logic, as being the ' Organon ' of philosophy, could not be also a *part* of philosophy,[2] he would hardly have approved.

In order rightly to comprehend this Science of Method, it will first be necessary for us to go more closely into Aristotle's views concerning the nature and origin of Knowledge.　For it is the conception of Knowledge which determines the aim and the direction of the procedure of Science ; and the natural development of Knowledge in the mind of man must point the way for its systematic development in Science also.

All Knowledge relates to the *Essence of Things*— to the *Universal* properties which remain identical with themselves in all individual things, and to the *Causes* of all that is actual.[3]　Conversely, however, it is true that the Universal is only to be known through

---

till the sixth century, as applied to the *writings* ; it only came to this use later (cf. WAITZ, *Arist. Org.* ii. 293 sq.).　On the other hand, the texts are, before that time, called by them ὀργανικὰ, because they refer to the ὄργανον (or ὀργανικὸν μέρος) φιλοσοφίας ; cf. SIMPL. *in Categ.* 1, ε ; PHILOP. *in Cat.* Schol. 36, a, 7, 15 ; DAVID, *ibid.* 25, a, 3.

[1] PRANTL, *Gesch. d. Log.* i. 136, is in this respect unreasonable, when he denounces ' the schoolmasters of later antiquity,' who, ' infected with the folly of the Stoic philosophy,' wished at any price to represent Logic as the tool of knowledge.　This is really the position and meaning which Aristotle gives it.　The theory that in the same sense as Physics

and Ethics it has its own end in itself and its own object, or that it is meant to be a philosophically established presentment of the activity of human thought and nothing else (*ibid.* p. 138 sq.), is a supposition which can neither be proved from any definite statements of Aristotle, nor from the construction of his logical writings.　The ' real-metaphysical side of the Aristotelian logic,' however, need not on this account be disregarded.　Even if it is regarded as the Science of Method, it may have its foundations in Metaphysics ; and even though it precede the latter, yet it may become necessary, in the end, to reduce it to metaphysical principles.

[2] *Vid. supr.* p. 187, n. 2.

[3] *Vid. supr.* pp. 163 sq., 173 sq.

the Individuals, the Essence only through Appearances, the Causes only through their Effects. This follows in part from Aristotle's metaphysical propositions about the relation of the individual to the universal, which will meet us hereafter; for if it is individual existence alone which can be called originally actual—if the Universals exist, not independently as ' Ideas ' but only in attachment to individual things as ' properties '—it follows that the experiential knowledge of Individuals must necessarily precede the scientific knowledge of Universals.[1] Quite as directly, to Aristotle, will the same conclusion follow from the nature of man's powers of knowledge. For while he unhesitatingly admits that the soul must bear within itself the ground-principle of its knowledge, he is equally positive that it is not possible to attain any real knowledge except by means of experience. All learning presupposes, of course, some present knowledge, to which it joins on.[2] Out of this axiom there arises the doubt, which had given the earlier thinkers so much trouble,[3] about the possibility of learning at all. For either, as it seems, we

---

[1] Aristotle himself points out this connection of his doctrine of perception with his metaphysics in *De An.* iii. 8, 432, a, 2 : ἐπεὶ δὲ οὐδὲ πρᾶγμα οὐθέν ἐστι παρὰ τὰ μεγέθη, ὡς δοκεῖ, τὰ αἰσθητὰ κεχωρισμένον, ἐν τοῖς εἴδεσι τοῖς αἰσθητοῖς τὰ νοητά ἐστι (cf. c. 4, 430, a, 6 : ἐν δὲ τοῖς ἔχουσιν ὕλην δυνάμει ἕκαστόν ἐστι τῶν νοητῶν) τά τε ἐν ἀφαιρέσει λεγόμενα [abstract notions] καὶ ὅσα τῶν αἰσθητῶν ἕξεις καὶ πάθη. καὶ διὰ τοῦτο οὔτε μὴ αἰσθανόμενος μηθὲν οὐθὲν ἂν μάθοι οὐδὲ ξυνείη· ὅταν τε θεωρῇ, ἀνάγκη

ἅμα φάντασμά τι θεωρεῖν· τὰ γὰρ φαντάσματα ὥσπερ αἰσθήματά ἐστι, πλὴν ἄνευ ὕλης.

[2] *Anal. Post.* i. *init*: πᾶσα διδασκαλία καὶ πᾶσα μάθησις διανοητικὴ ἐκ προϋπαρχούσης γίνεται γνώσεως—which he immediately proceeds to prove as to the different sciences, both as regards syllogistic and inductive proof. The like in *Metaph.* i. 9, 992, b, 30; *Eth.* vi. 3, 1139, b, 26.

[3] See Zell., *Ph. d. Gr.* pt. i. 996, and pt. ii. a, 696.

must already be possessed of that knowledge from which
all the rest is to be deduced—which is not in fact true—
or else we have still to acquire it, in which case the said
axiom does not hold for that which is the highest knowledge of all.[1] It was this difficulty that Plato sought to
avoid by his doctrine of ' Anamnesis '—the latent recollection of a prior knowledge. But apart from all the
other objections which he finds to lie against the pre-
existence of the soul,[2] Aristotle is unable to reconcile
himself with this theory, because it seems to him unthinkable that we should *have in us a knowledge without
knowing it* ;[3] not to speak of all the various absurdities
to which a closer analysis of the notion of the existence
of the Ideas in the soul would obviously lead.[4] His
solution lies rather in that conception by means of
which he has answered so many of the questions of
metaphysics and natural philosophy—in the notion of
' Development '—in the distinction between the groundwork of potentiality and the completed actuality.   The
soul, he says, must certainly bear within itself in *some*
sense its knowledge.   For if even our Sense Perception

---

[1] *Anal. Post.* ii. 19, 99, b, 20 :
Every knowledge by argument
supposes acquaintance with the
highest principles (the ἀρχαὶ
ἄμεσοι, *vid. inf.*): τῶν δ' ἀμέσων τὴν
γνῶσιν . . . διαπορήσειεν ἄν τις . . . .
καὶ πότερον οὐκ ἐνοῦσαι αἱ ἕξεις [the
γνῶσις of the ἀρχαὶ] ἐγγίνονται ἢ
ἐνοῦσαι λελήθασιν. εἰ μὲν δὴ ἔχομεν
αὐτὰς, ἄτοπον · συμβαίνει γὰρ ἀκρι-
βεστέρας ἔχοντας γνώσεις ἀποδείξεως
λανθάνειν. εἰ δὲ λαμβάνομεν μὴ
ἔχοντες πρότερον, πῶς ἂν γνωρίζοιμεν
καὶ μανθάνοιμεν ἐκ μὴ προϋπαρχούσης
γνώσεως · ἀδύνατον γὰρ . . . φανερὸν

τοίνυν. ὅτι οὔτ' ἔχειν οἷόν τε, οὔτ'
ἀγνοοῦσι καὶ μηδεμίαν ἔχουσιν ἕξιν
ἐγγίνεσθαι.
[2] Cf. the section as to the relation of soul and body, *infra*, ch. x.
init.
[3] *Anal. Post. loc. cit.*, and
Metaph. i. 9, 992, b, 33.
[4] *Top.* ii. 7, 113, a, 25 : if ideas
were in us they would have also
to move with us, &c. Still Aristotle himself would scarcely
have laid much stress on this
merely dialectical line of attack.

is to be regarded, not as a passive reception of things
given, but rather as an activity for which such reception is the occasion,[1] then the same must *à fortiori* be
true of Thought,[2] which has no outward object at all.
Because our pure thought is not different from the
things thought,[3] therefore there lies in its nature as such
the possibility of knowing with an immediate knowledge
those highest principles, which are presupposed by all
derivative and mediate knowledge as its condition and
starting-point.[4] So far, then, the soul may be de-

[1] *De An.* ii. 5, 417, b, 2 sqq.
Aristotle here says that neither
consciousness nor thought ought
to be called a πάσχειν and an
ἀλλοίωσις, unless we distinguish
two kinds of suffering and
change : τήν τε ἐπὶ τὰς στερητικὰς
διαθέσεις μεταβολὴν καὶ τὴν ἐπὶ τὰς
ἕξεις καὶ τὴν φύσιν. Similarly in iii.
5, 429, b, 22 sqq., iii. 7, 431, a, 5.
[2] *De An.* ii. 417, b, 18 : καὶ τὸ
κατ' ἐνέργειαν [αἰσθάνεσθαι] δὲ
ὁμοίως λέγεται τῷ θεωρεῖν· διαφέρει
δὲ, ὅτι τοῦ μὲν τὰ ποιητικὰ τῆς
ἐνεργείας ἔξωθεν, τὸ ὁρατόν etc.
αἴτιον δ' ὅτι τῶν καθ' ἕκαστον ἡ κατ'
ἐνέργειαν αἴσθησις, ἡ δ' ἐπιστήμη
τῶν καθόλου· ταῦτα δ' ἐν αὐτῇ πώς
ἐστι τῇ ψυχῇ. διὸ νοῆσαι μὲν ἐπ'
αὐτῷ ὅταν βούληται, αἰσθάνεσθαι δ'
οὐκ ἐπ' αὐτῷ· ἀναγκαῖον γὰρ ὑπάρχειν τὸ αἰσθητόν.
[3] *De An.* iii. at 430, a, 2 (following the passage to be cited
presently on p. 199, n. 2), he says :
192, 3 : καὶ αὐτὸς δὲ [ὁ νοῦς] νοητός
ἐστιν ὥσπερ τὰ νοητά. ἐπὶ μὲν γὰρ
τῶν ἄνευ ὕλης τὸ αὐτό ἐστι τὸ νοοῦν
καὶ τὸ νοούμενον · ἡ γὰρ ἐπιστήμη ἡ
θεωρητικὴ καὶ τὸ οὕτως ἐπιστητὸν τὸ
αὐτό ἐστιν. *Ibid.* iii. 7 *init.* : τὸ δ'
αὐτό ἐστιν ἡ κατ' ἐνέργειαν ἐπιστήμη
τῷ πράγματι. *Metaph.* xii. 7, 1074,

b, 38 : ἢ ἐπ' ἐνίων ἡ ἐπιστήμη τὸ
πρᾶγμα; ἐπὶ μὲν τῶν ποιητικῶν ἄνευ
ὕλης ἡ οὐσία καὶ τὸ τί ἦν εἶναι,
ἐπὶ δὲ τῶν θεωρητικῶν ὁ λόγος τὸ
πρᾶγμα καὶ ἡ νόησις.
[4] *Anal. Post.* ii. 19, 100, b, 8 :
ἐπεὶ δὲ . . . . οὐδὲν ἐπιστήμης ἀκριβέστερον ἄλλο γένος ἢ νοῦς, αἱ δ'
ἀρχαὶ τῶν ἀποδείξεων γνωριμώτεραι,
ἐπιστήμη δ' ἅπασα μετὰ λόγου ἐστὶ,
τῶν ἀρχῶν ἐπιστήμη μὲν οὐκ ἂν εἴη,
ἐπεὶ δ' οὐδὲν ἀληθέστερον ἐνδέχεται
εἶναι ἐπιστήμης ἢ νοῦν, νοῦς ἂν εἴη
τῶν ἀρχῶν . . . εἰ οὖν μηδὲν ἄλλο
παρ' ἐπιστήμην γένος ἔχομεν
ἀληθές, νοῦς ἂν εἴη ἐπιστήμης ἀρχή.
Eth. vi. 6 : τῆς ἀρχῆς τοῦ ἐπιστητοῦ
οὔτ' ἂν ἐπιστήμη εἴη οὔτε τέχνη
οὔτε φρόνησις . . . . λείπεται νοῦν
εἶναι τῶν ἀρχῶν. c. 7, 1141, a, 17,
b, 2, c. 9, 1142, a, 25 : ὁ μὲν γὰρ
νοῦς τῶν ὅρων, ὧν οὐκ ἔστι λόγος.
c. 12, 1143, a, 35 (with which cf.
TRENDELENBURG, *Histor. Beitr.*
ii. 375 sqq. ; WALTER, *Die Lehre
v. d. prakt. Vernunft*, etc., 38
sqq.) : ὁ νοῦς τῶν ἐσχάτων ἐπ'
ἀμφότερα· καὶ γὰρ τῶν πρώτων ὅρων
καὶ τῶν ἐσχάτων νοῦς ἐστι καὶ οὐ
λόγος, καὶ ὁ μὲν κατὰ τὰς ἀποδείξεις
τῶν ἀκινήτων ὅρων καὶ πρώτων, ὁ δ'
ἐν ταῖς πρακτικαῖς τοῦ ἐσχάτου καὶ
ἐνδεχομένου etc. (More will be

scribed as the ' place of the Ideas,' [1] and it may be said
of the faculty of Thought that it *is* in itself all that is

said as to the latter, in ch. xi.
and xii. *infra*.) This recognition of principles is an immediate knowledge (ἄμεσον), for the
root principles of all argument
cannot, in their turn, be proved :
(cf. *Anal. Post.* i. 2, 3, 72, a, 7, b,
18 sqq. c, 22, 84, a, 30; ii. 9
init. c. 10, 94, a, 9 ; and *Metaph.* iv.
4, 1006, a, 6, 1011, a, 13 ; more
fully later).   But on this very
account it is always true.   For
error only consists in a false conjunction of perceptions, and hence
arises only in the Proposition by
reason of the conjunction of the
Predicate with a Subject (*Categ.*
4 *fin.* ; *De Interpr.* i. 16, a, 12 ;
De An. iii. 8, 432, a, 11) ; immediate knowledge, on the other
hand, is concerned with pure
conceptions relating to no subject
distinct from themselves, which
we can only know or not know,
but as to which we cannot be
deceived ;   *De An.* iii. 6 *init.* :
ἡ μὲν οὖν τῶν ἀδιαιρέτων νόησις ἐν
τούτοις περὶ ἃ οὐκ ἔστι τὸ ψεῦδος·
ἐν οἶς δὲ καὶ τὸ ψεῦδος καὶ τὸ
ἀληθὲς, σύνθεσίς τις ἤδη νοημάτων
ὡς ἓν ὄντων ; and *ibid.* at the end :
ἔστι δ' ἡ μὲν φάσις τὶ κατά τινος,
ὥσπερ ἡ κατάφασις, καὶ ἀληθὴς ἢ
ψευδὴς πᾶσα· ὁ δὲ νοῦς οὐ πᾶς, ἀλλ'
ὁ τοῦ τί ἐστι κατὰ τὸ τί ἦν εἶναι
ἀληθὴς, καὶ οὐ τὶ κατά τινος·   ἀλλ'
ὥσπερ τὸ ὁρᾶν τοῦ ἰδίου ἀληθὲς, εἰ
ὁ ἄνθρωπος τὸ λευκὸν ἢ μὴ, οὐκ
ἀληθὲς ἀεὶ, οὕτως ἔχει ὅσα ἄνευ
ὕλης. *Metaph.* ix. 10 : ἐπεὶ δὲ . . .
τὸ . . . ἀληθὲς ἢ ψεῦδος . . . ἐπὶ τῶν
πραγμάτων ἐστὶ τῷ συγκεῖσθαι ἢ
διῃρῆσθαι . . . πότ' ἐστὶν ἢ οὐκ ἔστι
τὸ ἀληθὲς λεγόμενον ἢ ψεῦδος . . . .
περὶ δὲ δὴ τὰ ἀσύνθετα τί τὸ εἶναι ἢ

μὴ εἶναι καὶ τὸ ἀληθὲς καὶ τὸ
ψεῦδος ; . . . ἢ ὥσπερ οὐδὲ τὸ
ἀληθὲς ἐπὶ τούτων τὸ αὐτὸ, οὕτως
οὐδὲ τὸ εἶναι, ἀλλ' ἔστι τὸ μὲν
ἀληθὲς τὸ δὲ ψεῦδος, τὸ μὲν θιγεῖν
καὶ φάναι ἀληθὲς . . . τὸ δ' ἀγνοεῖν
μὴ θιγγάνειν·   ἀπατηθῆναι γὰρ περὶ
τὸ τί ἐστιν οὐκ ἔστιν ἀλλ' ἢ κατὰ
συλβεβηκός . . . ὅσα δή ἐστιν ὅπερ
εἶναί τι καὶ ἐνεργείᾳ, περὶ ταῦτα οὐκ
ἔστιν ἀπατηθῆναι ἀλλ' ἢ νοεῖν ἢ μή
. . . τὸ δὲ ἀληθὲς τὸ νοεῖν αὐτά· τὸ
δὲ ψεῦδος οὐκ ἔστιν, οὐδ' ἀπάτη,
ἀλλ' ἄγνοια.   According to these
passages we should understand
by the προτάσεις ἄμεσοι, which express the ultimate principles (*An.
Post.* i. 2, 23, 33, 72, a, 7, 84, b, 39,
88, b, 36), only those propositions
in which the predicate is already
contained in the subject, not
those in which it attaches to a
subject different from itself : or
in other words, only analytical
a priori judgments.   In like
manner the ὁρισμὸς τῶν ἀμέσων
(*ibid.* ii. 10, 94, a, 9) is a θέσις
τοῦ τί ἐστιν ἀναπόδεικτος, in which
nothing is affirmed as to the
existence or non-existence of a
conception, nor of its connection
with a stated subject.   Lastly,
when the principle of contradiction (in *Metaph.* iv. 3 sq. 1005,
b, 11, 1006, a, 3) is designated
as the βεβαιοτάτη ἀρχὴ πασῶν περὶ
ἣν διαψευσθῆναι ἀδύνατον, here also
only the fundamental principle
of all analytical judgments is
in question—the formal identity
of every conception with itself.

[1] *De An.* iii. 4, 429, a, 27 : καὶ
εὖ δὴ οἱ λέγοντες τὴν ψυχὴν εἶναι
τόπον εἰδῶν (see on this ZELLER'S
Plato), πλὴν ὅτι οὔτε ὅλη ἀλλ'

thinkable.[1] This contained knowledge, however, can only become actual knowledge in the active exercise of cognition. It follows, therefore, that, prior to experience, it cannot be in the soul except in the way of a possibility and a basis; and so, according to him, it is, in virtue of the fact that the soul has the faculty of forming its notions out of itself by its own inherent activity.[2]

ἡ νοητική, οὔτε ἐντελεχείᾳ ἀλλὰ δυνάμει τὰ εἴδη.

[1] *De An.* iii. 8 *init.*: νῦν δὲ περὶ ψυχῆς τὰ λεχθέντα συγκεφαλαιώσαντες εἴπωμεν πάλιν ὅτι ἡ ψυχὴ τὰ ὄντα πώς ἐστι πάντα. ἢ γὰρ αἰσθητὰ τὰ ὄντα ἢ νοητά, ἔστι δ' ἡ ἐπιστήμη μὲν τὰ ἐπιστητά πως, ἡ δ' αἴσθησις τὰ αἰσθητά. (Cf. ii. 5 *fin.* iii. 7 *init.*)

[2] *De An.* iii. 4, 429, a, 15 : ἀπαθὲς ἄρα δεῖ εἶναι [before the Nous experiences the effect of the νοητὸν, it must be without πάθος; cf. BONITZ, *Ind. Ar.* 72, a, 36 sqq.], δεκτικὸν δὲ τοῦ εἴδους καὶ δυνάμει τοιοῦτον [sc. οἷον τὸ εἶδος] ἀλλὰ μὴ τοῦτο, καὶ ὁμοίως ἔχειν, ὥσπερ τὸ αἰσθητικὸν πρὸς τὰ αἰσθητὰ, οὕτω τὸν νοῦν πρὸς τὰ νοητά. . . ὁ ἄρα καλούμενος τῆς ψυχῆς νοῦς. . . οὐθέν ἐστιν ἐνεργείᾳ τῶν ὄντων πρὶν νοεῖν . . . καὶ εὖ δὴ etc. (*vid. supr.* p. 198, n. 1). *Ibid.* b, 30 : δυνάμει πώς ἐστι τὰ νοητὰ ὁ νοῦς, ἀλλ' ἐντελεχείᾳ οὐδὲν, πρὶν ἂν νοῇ. δεῖ δ' οὕτως ὥσπερ ἐν γραμματείῳ ᾧ μηθὲν ὑπάρχει ἐντελεχείᾳ γεγραμμένον. ὅπερ συμβαίνει ἐπὶ τοῦ νοῦ. Here (b, 5) and in ii. 5, 417, a, 21 sqq. a still more accurate distinction is made between two meanings of the δυνάμει : we can call a man δυνάμει ἐπιστήμων not only when he has as

yet learned nothing, but possesses the capacity for learning something, but also when he knows something, but has not at a given moment this knowledge actually present to his mind. It was in the latter sense that Plato conceived of innate knowledge, whereas Aristotle conceived of it under the former analogy. This is the meaning of his comparison of the soul with the book that is not yet written on : and it was a misapprehension when this comparison was understood in the sense of the later Sensation-theory of knowledge. (Cf. HEGEL, *Gesch. d. Phil.* ii. 342 sq.; TRENDELENBURG, on this passage, p. 485 sq.) Aristotle only wants to illustrate by it the difference between the δυνάμει and ἐνεργείᾳ. He does not here go on to inform us in what way potential knowledge becomes actual. But, according to what has gone before (429, a, 15), it is not the αἰσθητὰ but the νοητὰ by whose action the tablet of the νοῦς, blank in itself, is written upon, so that we have to deal in fact with a theory far removed from the Sensation-philosophy.

Throughout his whole treatment of this question, there runs a certain obscurity, the grounds of which we can of course indicate, but which we cannot altogether remove without doing violence to the statements of the Master himself. On the one hand, Aristotle contests the possibility of *any* innate knowledge, and insists that all our notions arise out of perception.[1] On the other hand, he speaks of an immediate knowledge of those truths on which all others depend,[2] and allows that all the knowledge which in the course of our lives we gain lay in our soul from the beginning in germ.[3] Of course, this last view is not to be taken to imply that the soul, prior to all experience, carried in itself the said knowledge in so far as the content thereof is concerned, or that the function of such experience was merely to cause it to be brought out into consciousness.[4]

[1] Cf. pp. 195 sq., 205 sq.
[2] P. 197, n. 4.
[3] Cf. pp. 196, n. 1, 197, n. 2, 198, n. 1, and 199, n. 1.
[4] There is no necessity to interpret in that sense the passages given above. On the contrary, when he says in *De An.* iii. 8 (*supra*, p. 199, n. 1) that 'the soul is in a certain sense everything,' he immediately explains this phrase by adding (431, b, 28) : ἀνάγκη δ᾽ ἢ αὐτὰ ἢ τὰ εἴδη εἶναι. αὐτὰ μὲν γὰρ δὴ οὔ · οὐ γὰρ ὁ λίθος ἐν τῇ ψυχῇ, ἀλλὰ τὸ εἶδος · ὥστε ἡ ψυχὴ ὥσπερ ἡ χείρ ἐστιν · καὶ γὰρ ἡ χεὶρ ὄργανόν ἐστιν ὀργάνων, καὶ ὁ νοῦς εἶδος εἰδῶν καὶ ἡ αἴσθησις εἶδος αἰσθητῶν. Since the hand indeed forms and uses the tools, but still can only form them from some given material, this comparison does not carry us further

than the thought that the soul is everything inasmuch as it is capable of having the forms (or images) of all things within itself. That it produces them out of itself is not stated. On the contrary, as the power of perception is called εἶδος αἰσθητῶν, because it *receives* into itself the forms of the αἰσθητά, so the νοῦς may, in the same sense, be called εἶδος εἰδῶν, inasmuch as it is the faculty to *receive* the insensible forms ; and τόπος εἰδῶν (p. 198, n. 1) may be taken in the same sense. The statement that 'universals are in the soul itself' (in *De An.* ii. 5, cited at p. 197, n. 2), occurs in a passage which has no reference to the growth of knowledge in itself, but where Aristotle is endeavouring to illustrate the progress from the power of perception to

For this would take us back again to the theory of innate ideas which Aristotle so decidedly rejects.[1] It would be equally wrong, however, to make him a pure Empiricist, and attribute to him the view that the Universal, 'without any limitation, comes to the soul from the external world.'[2] If this were his view, he could not possibly have derived the highest concepts of all—the *principia* of all knowledge—from that faculty of immediate cognition by which the *Nous* is, according to him, distinguished from all other forms of thinking activity.[3] For it is plain that concepts which we can only come at by an ascent from individuals to universals, cannot be the data of any immediate kind of knowledge, but must be data of that kind of knowledge which is the most entirely mediate of all. Our cognitive faculties, he asserts, do, in fact, take this way to arrive at these *principia*; but he cannot have regarded the thoughts in which these *principia* come for us into consciousness as the mere precipitate of a progressively refined experience, or the act by which we present them to ourselves as only the last of these successive gene-

---

actual perception by the relation of ἐπιστήμη to the θεωρεῖν (p. 417, b, 5 : θεωροῦν γὰρ γίγνεται τὸ ἔχον τὴν ἐπιστήμην). Finally, in *Anal. Post.* ii. 19 (cited at p. 197, n. 4, *supra*) Aristotle says it is impossible to believe that we should come to the knowledge of the highest principles, without possessing previous knowledge; but he looks for that previous knowledge not in any ideas innate in the soul prior to all experience, but simply in the inductive process. Cf. *infra*, ch. v. *ad fin.*

[1] As KAMPE (*Erkenntnisstheorie d. Arist.* p. 192) objects, not without reason, though his citation of *Metaph.* i. 9, 993, a, 7 sqq. is not in point.

[2] So KAMPE, *ibid.* ; but it is hard to reconcile with this exposition his attempt in the next following pages to reduce that true perception which is, for Aristotle, the basis of all knowledge to some kind of Intuitive Thought, essentially differing both from Knowledge and Opinion.

[3] On this see p. 197, n. 4, *supra*.

ralisations upon a matter given in experience. Each of these generalisations consists in an induction,[1] the result of which can only be expressed as a judgment and a conclusion, and which therefore is, like all judgments, either false or true. But, on the other hand, the activity of the *Nous* in knowledge is by him distinguished from all mediate cognition, and what we attain by it is not judgments but ideas—not that which may be either false or true, but that which is always true—that which we may either have or not have, but as to which, if we have it, we cannot be deceived.[2] So, again, as all induction starts from perception, which has relation to that which is compounded of Form and Matter and is sensible, and as the quality of contingency, the possibility of being and not-being, is inseparable from all that is Matter,[3] therefore by induction alone we can never attain to anything which is unconditionally necessary. For those ideas which rest entirely on experience can have no higher certainty than that on which they rest. But of the knowledge of the *principia*, Aristotle holds that it is of all knowledge the most certain,[4] and he will allow nothing to rank among the *principia* except what is necessarily true.[5] It follows, then, that the immediate knowledge referred to can only be an intuition—and that it can only be a spiritual intuition, as contrasted with all sensible perception. But the spirit of man has not these ideas innate in itself. Therefore, the intuition by

---

[1] About which see ch. v. *infra*.
[2] Cf. p. 197, n. 4.
[3] Cf. *infra* in the second part of ch. vii., and the notes there on these points.

[4] *Anal. Post.* i. 2, 71, b, 19, 72, a, 25 sqq.; ii. 19, 100, b, 9.
[5] *Anal. Post.* i. 6 *init*.

which it finds them cannot consist in any self-intuition
or act of introspection, making us conscious of the
principia as of a truth already within us.[1] It must be
something whereby certain thoughts and ideas arise
through an action of that which is thought upon the
spirit thinking it, in some way analogous to that in
which perception arises through an action of that which
is perceived upon the percipient. And Aristotle does,
in fact, base himself on this very analogy when he says
that the *Nous* is related to the thinkable as sense is to
the perceivable ;[2] or that it knows the thinkable because
it ' touches' it ;[3] or that as perception in itself must be
always true, so must thought be, in so far as it relates
to ideas as such.[4]

In this way we get a theory which is for the
moment intelligible and consistent. But the further
questions remain wholly unanswered—What *is* this,
by the intuition of which we get the *principia* of all
mediate knowledge and the most universal of all ideas
and axioms? What kind of being belongs to it? In
what way does it act upon our spirit? Of what sort
are these *principia* which we so attain? Do all of

[1] This was Zeller's view in
his second edition.
[2] *De An.* iii. 4, 429, a, 15 ;
see p. *13. a. 2.*
[3] *Metaph.* ix. 10, 1051, b, 24
(*vid. supr.* p. 197, n. 4): in perception of the ἀσύνθετα is τὸ μὲν
θιγεῖν καὶ φάναι ἀληθές ... τὸ δ'
ἀγνοεῖν μὴ θιγγάνειν ; xii. 7, 1072,
b, 20 : αὐτὸν δὲ νοεῖ δ νοῦς [the
divine νοῦς] κατὰ μετάληψιν τοῦ
νοητοῦ [by taking itself as a
νοητόν]· νοητὸς γὰρ γίγνεται
θιγγάνων καὶ νοῶν. Remembering,

doubtless, the first of these
passages, Theophrastus also says
in *Fr.* 12 (*Metaph.*) 25 : 'If we
begin with observation we can,
up to a certain point, explain
things from their causes : ὅταν δὲ
ἐπ' αὐτὰ τὰ ἄκρα μεταβαίνωμεν οὐκέτι δυνάμεθα, either because these
have no causes, or because our
eye cannot see in a full light, τάχα
δ' ἐκεῖνο ἀληθέστερον ὡς αὐτῷ τῷ νῷ
ἡ θεωρία θιγόντι καὶ οἷον ἀψαμένῳ.'
[4] *De An.* iii. 6 *fin.* ; cited
supr. p. 197, n. 4.

them merely express the formal laws of thought (as does the law of contradiction), or are there also metaphysical ideas which are so given, such as the ideas of Being, of Cause, of God? This might prove to be a natural conclusion from the theory of Aristotle; but it would take us very near to the Platonic teaching as to the intuition of the Ideas, except that, since for Aristotle the 'Forms' of things could not belong to another world, the intuition of them would necessarily be transferred also from the future to the present.

The final explanation of Aristotle's want of clearness on this subject is, however, to be found in the fact that he *had* only half emancipated himself, as we shall see, from Plato's tendency to hypostatise ideas. The 'Forms' had for him, as the 'Ideas' had for Plato, a metaphysical existence of their own, as conditioning all individual things. And keenly as he followed the growth of ideas out of experience, it is none the less true that these ideas, especially at the point where they are farthest removed from experience and immediate perception, are metamorphosed in the end from a logical product of human thought into an immediate presentment of a supersensible world, and the object, in that sense, of an intellectual intuition.

Plato conceived that the picture of the Ideas which slumbers within us could only awake to any sensible intuition by an actual recollection, and that the spiritual eye could only accustom itself to receive the light of the Ideas by a long course of preparation. So with Aristotle is it self-evident that at the beginning of our spiritual development we are at the

farthest possible distance from that knowledge which is
its goal; and that consequently our ascent to knowledge can only come by a gradual approximation to
that goal, through a progressive deepening of our
comprehension, advancing from particulars to universals,
from phenomena to the essence, from effects to causes.
Knowledge, which we neither possess as a perfect gift
of nature nor derive as a consequence from something
higher than itself, must issue out of that which is
lower : that is, out of Perception.[1] The development in
time of our ideas is therefore exactly the inverse of
their logical order. That which is absolutely first is
relatively to us last; and whereas by virtue of its
nature the universal has greater certainty than the
particular, and the principle than the deductions which
depend upon it, yet individuals and things of sense have
more of certainty for us.[2] And in like manner we find

---

[1] *Anal. Post.* ii. 19, 100, a,
10 : οὔτε δὴ ἐνυπάρχουσιν ἀφωρισ-
μέναι αἱ ἕξεις (*vid. supr.* 196, n. 1),
οὔτ' ἀπ' ἄλλων ἕξεων γίνονται
γνωστικωτέρων, ἀλλ' ἀπὸ αἰσθήσεως.

[2] *Anal. Post.* i. 2, 71, b, 33 : πρότερα δ' ἐστὶ καὶ γνωριμώτερα διχῶς ·
οὐ γὰρ ταὐτὸν πρότερον τῇ φύσει
καὶ πρὸς ἡμᾶς πρότερον οὐδὲ γνωριμώτερον καὶ ἡμῖν γνωριμώτερον ·
λέγω δὲ πρὸς ἡμᾶς μὲν πρότερα καὶ
γνωριμώτερα τὰ ἐγγύτερον τῆς
αἰσθήσεως, ἁπλῶς δὲ πρότερα καὶ
γνωριμώτερα τὰ πορρώτερον · ἔστι
δὲ πορρωτάτω μὲν τὰ καθόλου μάλιστα, ἐγγυτάτω δὲ τὰ καθ' ἕκαστα.
Phys. i. 1, 184, a, 16 : πέφυκε δὲ
ἐκ τῶν γνωριμωτέρων ἡμῖν ἡ ὁδός
καὶ σαφεστέρων ἐπὶ τὰ σαφέστερα
τῇ φύσει καὶ γνωριμώτερα · οὐ γὰρ
ταὐτὰ ἡμῖν τε γνώριμα καὶ ἁπλῶς ;

i. 5 *fin.* Cf. *Metaph.* i. 2, 982,
a, 23 ; v. 11, 1018, b, 29 sqq.;
vii. 4, 1029, b, 4 sqq. ; ix. 8,
1050, a, 4 ; *Top.* vi. 4, 141, b, 3,
22 ; *De An.* ii. 2 *init.*, iii. 7,
init. ; *Eth.* i. 2, 1095, b, 2. (Still
more forcibly, referring rather,
however, to PLATO, *Rep.* vii.
init. than to Aristotle, is it expressed in *Metaph.* ii. 1, 993, b,
9.) The apparent contradiction
in *Phys.* i. 1 : ἔστι δ' ἡμῖν πρῶτον δῆλα καὶ σαφῆ τὰ συγκεχυμένα
μᾶλλον · ὕστερον δ' ἐκ τούτων γίνεται γνώριμα τὰ στοιχεῖα καὶ αἱ
ἀρχαὶ διαιροῦσι ταῦτα. διὸ ἐκ τῶν
καθόλου ἐπὶ τὰ καθ' ἕκαστα δεῖ
προϊέναι. τὸ γὰρ ὅλον κατὰ τὴν
αἴσθησιν γνωριμώτερον, τὸ δὲ καθόλου ὅλον τί ἐστιν · πολλὰ γὰρ
περιλαμβάνει ὡς μέρη τὸ καθόλου, is
only a verbal ambiguity. For (as

that the kind of proof which proceeds from the particular
is to us more clear than a deduction from the general.[1]

The way in which actual knowledge is evolved from
the rudimentary possibilities of knowledge is this. The
first stage is always, as we have remarked, sensible
perception. Without this we can have no actual thought.[2]
The man who is deprived of one of the organs of sense
must of necessity also lack all the corresponding knowledge, for the general axioms of every kind of science
can only be discovered by induction, and induction
rests upon perception.[3] Now particular things are the
proper objects of perception;[4] but inasmuch as a
universal, although it may be as yet undistinguished,
is contained in every particular, therefore perception
is also conversant mediately with universals.[5] Or, to
speak more accurately, what the senses perceive is, not
the individual substance of the particular as such, but
rather certain of its properties. These again are related to the particular substance after the manner of a
universal, for they are not a 'this' (τόδε) but a 'such'

TRENDELENBURG on *Arist. De
An.* p. 338, and RITTER, iii. 105,
etc. remark) it is not the *logical,*
but the *sensible* universal which is
here dealt with—the as yet indefinite presentation of an object,
as when, for instance, we represent to ourselves a body as such,
before we clearly distinguish its
constituent parts. In themselves, however, the simple elements are always prior to that
which is made up of them; *De
Cœlo,* ii. 3, 286, b, 16; *Metaph.*
xiii. 2, 1076, b, 18, c. 3, 1078, a, 9.

[1] *Anal. Pr.* ii. 23 *fin.*: φύσει

μὲν οὖν πρότερος καὶ γνωριμώτερος
ὁ διὰ τοῦ μέσου συλλογισμὸς, ἡμῖν
δ' ἐναργέστερος ὁ διὰ τῆς ἐπαγωγῆς.

[2] *De An.* iii. 8, 432, a, 4 (*vid.
supr.* p. 195, n. 1). *De Sensu,* c. 6,
445, b, 16: οὐδὲ νοεῖ ὁ νοῦς τὰ ἐκτὸς
μὴ μετ' αἰσθήσεως ὄντα.

[3] *An. Post.* i. 18.

[4] *An. Post.* i. 18, 81, b, 6 : τῶν
καθ' ἕκαστον ἡ αἴσθησις. The same
idea recurs frequently, *e.g. An.
Post.* i. 2 (*vid. supr.* p. 205, n. 2),
c. 31 (*vide* p. 207, n. 1), *Phys.* i. 5
fin., De An. iii. 5, 417, b, 22, 27,
Metaph. i. 1, 981, a, 15.

[5] *De An.* iii. 8, as at p. 195, n. 1.

(τοιόνδε); and although in perception they never come
under our intuition in the form of a universal, but
always as belonging to this or that thing, and in a
definite individual instance, yet still they are virtually
universals, and out of our perception of them the
thought of the universal can be developed.[1] Now the
way in which it is developed is this. In sensible perception itself the several sensible properties, and therefore also the relative universals, which inhere in the individual substance, are discriminated.[2] Out of such perception is next developed by the help of memory a general

---

[1] *An. Post.* i. 31, *init.* : οὐδὲ δι'
αἰσθήσεως ἔστιν ἐπίστασθαι. εἰ γὰρ
καὶ ἔστιν ἡ αἴσθησις τοῦ τοιοῦδε
καὶ μὴ τοῦδέ τινος [only the τόδε,
however, is an individual substance : οὐδὲν σημαίνει τῶν κοινῇ
κατηγορουμένων τόδε τι ἀλλὰ τοιόνδε; *Metaph.* vii. 13, 1039, a, 1 : of
which more *infra*], ἀλλ' αἰσθάν-
εσθαί γε ἀναγκαῖον τόδε τι καὶ ποῦ
καὶ νῦν. τὸ δὲ καθόλου καὶ ἐπὶ πᾶσιν
ἀδύνατον αἰσθάνεσθαι. οὐ γὰρ τόδε
οὐδὲ νῦν. οὐ γὰρ ἂν ἦν καθόλου
. . . ἐπεὶ οὖν αἱ μὲν ἀποδείξεις
καθόλου, ταῦτα δ' οὐκ ἔστιν αἰσθάνεσθαι, φανερὸν ὅτι οὐδ' ἐπίστασθαι
δι' αἰσθήσεως ἔστιν. So in ii. 19,
100, a, 17 : αἰσθάνεται μὲν τὸ
καθ' ἕκαστον, ἡ δ' αἴσθησις τοῦ
καθόλου ἐστίν, οἷον ἀνθρώπου, ἀλλ'
οὐ Καλλία ἀνθρώπου: *i. e.* Perception, has, it is true, a definite
individual Kallias for its immediate object ; but what it gives
us is the image of a man with
these definite properties, and the
circumstance of this man's being
Kallias has no influence upon the
content of our perception. Cf.
further *De An.* ii. 12, 424, a, 21
sqq.; and *Phys.* i. 5, 189, a, 5. What

is said in the text will establish
the agreement of these passages
with the general doctrine of
Aristotle, about which HEIDER
(*Vergl. d. Aristotel. und Hegel'schen Dialektik*, i. 160, sqq.)
makes too much difficulty. Nor
does *Metaph.* xiii. 10, 1087, a, 15
sqq. contradict it, as KAMPE
believes (*Erkenntnissth. d. Ar.*
85). It is there said that knowledge as δύναμις is τοῦ καθόλου
καὶ ἀορίστου, ἡ δ' ἐνέργεια ὡρισμένη
καὶ ὡρισμένου τόδε τι οὖσα, τοῦδέ
τινος. All that this states is that
the capability of knowing extends
to everything that is knowable,
but that every actual perception
is the perception of a definite
object; and whether this object
is an individual or a universal
conception does not enter into the
question. Καθόλου here signifies
'the indefinite,' as to which cf.
xii. 4, 1070, a, 32; *Gen. An.* ii. 8,
748, a, 7 ; *Eth.* ii. 7, 1107, a, 29.

[2] *De An.* iii. 2, 426, b, 8 sqq.
Hence the αἴσθησις in *An. Post.*
ii. 19, 99, b, 35, cf. *De An.* iii. 3,
428, a, 4, c. 9 *init.*, is called a
δύναμις σύμφυτος κριτική.

representation, for that which has steadily recurred in
several perceptions is fixed and retained by the mind.
Thus arise in the first place experience, and next, when
several experiences have condensed into general principles, art and science [1] also, until at last we reach the most
universal principles of all ; and of these in like manner
a scientific comprehension is only to be gained by a
further methodical repetition of the same process—in
other words, by induction. The result may be put
thus. Plato sought to get at the Idea by turning
the mental eye *away from* the phenomenal world, on
which, in his view, the most that was to be seen
was a reflection of the idea and not the idea itself. Aristotle's theory of the ascent to knowledge rests
it, on the contrary, rather upon a striving after the
universal element *in* appearances as such. In other
words, while both demand abstraction from the immediate data and reflection on the underlying universal,
still the relation between the two elements is quite
different. To Plato the abstraction from the given

[1] *Anal. Post.* ii. 19, 100, a, 2 :
ἐκ μὲν οὖν αἰσθήσεως γίνεται μνήμη,
ὥσπερ λέγομεν, ἐκ δὲ μνήμης πολλάκις τοῦ αὐτοῦ γινομένης ἐμπειρία.
αἱ γὰρ πολλαὶ μνῆμαι τῷ ἀριθμῷ
ἐμπειρία μία ἐστίν. ἐκ δ' ἐμπειρίας ἢ
ἐκ παντὸς ἠρεμήσαντος τοῦ καθόλου
ἐν τῇ ψυχῇ, τοῦ ἑνὸς παρὰ τὰ πολλά,
ὃ ἂν ἐν ἅπασιν ἓν ἐνῇ ἐκείνοις τὸ
αὐτό, τέχνης ἀρχὴ καὶ ἐπιστήμης,
ἐὰν μὲν περὶ γένεσιν, τέχνης, ἐὰν
δὲ περὶ τὸ ὄν, ἐπιστήμης. *Metaph.*
i. 1, 980, b, 28 : γίγνεται δ' ἐκ τῆς
μνήμης ἐμπειρία τοῖς ἀνθρώποις· αἱ
γὰρ πολλαὶ μνῆμαι τοῦ αὐτοῦ πράγματος μιᾶς ἐμπειρίας δύναμιν ἀπο-
τελοῦσιν . . . . ἀποβαίνει δ' ἐπιστήμη
καὶ τέχνη διὰ τῆς ἐμπειρίας τοῖς
ἀνθρώποις . . . . γίνεται δὲ τέχνη,
ὅταν ἐκ πολλῶν τῆς ἐμπειρίας ἐννοη-
μάτων μία καθόλου γένηται περὶ τῶν
ὁμοίων ὑπόληψις. τὸ μὲν γὰρ ἔχειν
ὑπόληψιν ὅτι Καλλίᾳ κάμνοντι τηνδὶ
τὴν νόσον τοδὶ συνήνεγκε καὶ
Σωκράτει καὶ καθέκαστον οὕτω
πολλοῖς, ἐμπειρίας ἐστίν· τὸ δ' ὅτι
πᾶσι τοῖς τοιοῖσδε κατ' εἶδος ἓν
ἀφορισθεῖσι, κάμνουσι τηνδὶ τὴν
νόσον, συνήνεγκεν, . . . τέχνης. In
the same passages is also found
more to the like purpose. In
Phys. vii. 3, 247, b, we have, ἐκ
γὰρ τῆς κατὰ μέρος ἐμπειρίας τὴν
καθόλου λαμβάνουεν ἐπιστήμην.

is the first thing, and only on the presupposition of such abstraction will he recognise the possibility of coming to any knowledge of universal essence at all.

To Aristotle the *direction* of the mind *upon* the common essence of the empirical data is the main point, and it is only as an inevitable consequence of this that abstraction from the particulars of sense comes in. For a like reason, Aristotle also defends the truth of the knowledge derived by sensation against the objectors; for he shows that, notwithstanding the contradictions and deceptions of the senses, a true perception is still possible, and that the actuality of what we perceive is beyond doubt, although its value is relative : in a word, that the doubts attaching to sensible perception [1] are due solely to want of caution in the use we make of it.[2] He even maintains that perception of itself never leads us astray, and that it is in our imaginations and our judgments that we are first exposed to error.[3]

---

[1] Cf. *Metaph.* iv. 5, 6, 1010, b, sqq., where, among other things (1010, b, 30 sqq.), it is stated that although we might say in a certain sense that without a perceiving being there would be no αἰσθητὰ as such, still it is impossible to say that without the αἴσθησις the ὑποκείμενα ἃ ποιεῖ τὴν αἴσθησιν could not exist—οὐ γὰρ δὴ ἤ γ' αἴσθησις αὐτὴ ἑαυτῆς ἐστιν, ἀλλ' ἔστι τι καὶ ἕτερον παρὰ τὴν αἴσθησιν, ὃ ἀνάγκη πρότερον εἶναι τῆς αἰσθήσεως· τὸ γὰρ κινοῦν τοῦ κινουμένου πρότερόν ἐστι. Likewise *Cat.* c. 7, 7, b, 36 : τὸ γὰρ αἰσθητὸν πρότερον τῆς αἰσθήσεως δοκεῖ εἶναι. τὸ μὲν γὰρ αἰσθητὸν ἀναιρεθὲν συναναιρεῖ τὴν αἴσθησιν, ἡ δὲ αἴσθησις τὸ αἰσθητὸν οὐ συναναιρεῖ . . . ζῴου

VOL. I.

γὰρ ἀναιρεθέντος αἴσθησις μὲν ἀναιρεῖται, αἰσθητὸν δὲ ἔσται, οἷον σῶμα, θερμὸν, γλυκὺ, πικρὸν καὶ τἄλλα ὅσα ἐστὶν αἰσθητά.

[2] To this refer *Metaph.* iv. 5, 1010, b, 3 sqq., 14 sqq. ; xi. 6, 1062, b, 13 sqq.

[3] *De An.* iii. 3. 427, b, 11 : ἡ μὲν γὰρ αἴσθησις τῶν ἰδίων ἀεὶ ἀληθὴς καὶ πᾶσιν ὑπάρχει τοῖς ζῴοις, διανοεῖσθαι δ' ἐνδέχεται καὶ ψευδῶς καὶ οὐδενὶ ὑπάρχει ᾧ μὴ καὶ λόγος. *Ibid.* 428, a, 11 : αἱ μὲν [the αἰσθήσεις] ἀληθεῖς ἀεί, αἱ δὲ φαντασίαι γίνονται αἱ πλείους ψευδεῖς. Similarly ii. 6, 418, a, 11 sqq. ; and in *Metaph.* iv. 5, 1010, b, 2 : οὐδ' ἡ αἴσθησις ψευδὴς τοῦ ἰδίου ἐστὶν, ἀλλ' ἡ φαντασία οὐ ταὐτὸν τῇ αἰσθήσει.

He shows in fact that simple-minded confidence in the truth of sensible perceptions which is natural to every uncritical consciousness. This is in his case the more easy to understand because he has as little notion as the other Greeks of making any close inquiry into the part which a subjective activity plays in the construction of our experience, and refers it simply to an operation of the objects upon us whereby they impress their images upon the soul ;[1] while, on the other hand, the philosopher who attributed so high a value to observation, and the naturalist who required so wide a basis of empirical facts, could hardly be expected to take sufficient account of the attacks which some of his predecessors had made upon the trustworthiness of the senses.[2] Of course he does not seek to deny the delu-

[1] See the account of Aristotle's theory of sensation, *infra*, ch. x. *ad fin.*

[2] It has been shown at p. 209, n. 1, how Aristotle, in *Cat.* 7, treats as given objectively even those sensible properties which Democritus had already shown to be merely subjective (ZELL. *Ph. d. Gr.* i. 772, l. 783, 2). Similarly in *Phys.* viii. 3, in combating the opinion (of Parmenides), πάντα ἠρεμεῖν, he follows up the striking remark (254, a, 30) that such a view could not explain δόξα and φαντασία as movements of the soul (it would have been more exact to say ' of the changing series of mental images ') with the sweeping observation that to investigate such a view is ζητεῖν λόγον ὧν βέλτιον ἔχομεν ἢ λόγου δεῖσθαι, and κακῶς κρίνειν τὸ πιστὸν καὶ τὸ μὴ πιστὸν καὶ ἀρχὴν καὶ μὴ ἀρχήν. The same objection holds, in his opinion against the theories

that everything is always being moved, or that one thing is always moved and another never. πρὸς ἅπαντα γὰρ ταῦτα ἱκανὴ μία πίστις· ὁρῶμεν γὰρ ἔνια ὁτὲ μὲν κινούμενα ὁτὲ δ' ἠρεμοῦντα. *Ibid.* 253, a, 33, in opposing the doctrine πάντ' ἠρεμεῖν, he says, τούτου ζητεῖν λόγον ἀφέντας τὴν αἴσθησιν, ἀρρωστία τίς ἐστι διανοίας, and such speculations seem to him abnormal and non-natural. All such questions as how we know whether we are awake or asleep, whether we are in our sound senses, &c., Aristotle considers altogether misleading : πάντων γὰρ λόγον ἀξιοῦσιν οὗτοι εἶναι . . . λόγον γὰρ ζητοῦσιν ὧν οὐκ ἔστι λόγος· ἀποδείξεως γὰρ ἀρχὴ οὐκ ἀπόδειξίς ἐστι. (*Metaph.* iv. 6, 1011, a, 8 sqq. cf. below, p. 247, n. 2). He thinks it a self-evident proposition that we can only decide upon the sensible properties of things—as upon the good and the evil, the beautiful and the

sions of sense, but he believes that our sensations, as such, are not to blame. He holds that each sense represents to us always, or almost always, with truth the special colour, sound, etc., which it perceives, but that illusion first arises in the referring of these properties to definite objects, and in the discriminating of that which is immediately given in perception from that which is only got by abstraction therefrom.[1]

To these views, then, as to the nature or origin of knowledge, the arrangement of Aristotle's theory of scientific knowledge—his Analytics—corresponds. It is the function of Science to explain the phenomena by their principles, which must be sought for in the Universal Causes and Laws. The deduction, therefore, of the

ugly—in a normal state of the senses and the mind.

[1] In this sense Aristotle himself illustrates his principle in *De An.* iii. 3, 428, b, 18 : ἡ αἴσθησις τῶν μὲν ἰδίων ἀληθής ἐστιν ἢ ὅτι ὀλίγιστον ἔχουσα τὸ ψεῦδος. δεύτερον δὲ τοῦ συμβεβηκέναι ταῦτα· καὶ ἐνταῦθα ἤδη ἐνδέχεται διαψεύδεσθαι· ὅτι μὲν γὰρ λευκὸν, οὐ ψεύδεται, εἰ δε τοῦτο τὸ λευκὸν, ἢ ἄλλο τι [whether the white thing is, *e.g.*, a cloth or a wall], ψεύδεται. (So also at the end of c. 6.) τρίτον δὲ τῶν κοινῶν καὶ ἑπομένων τοῖς συμβεβηκόσιν, οἷς ὑπάρχει τὰ ἴδια· λέγω δ' οἷον κίνησις καὶ μέγεθος, ἃ συμβέβηκε τοῖς αἰσθητοῖς περὶ ἃ μάλιστα ἤδη ἔστιν ἀπατηθῆναι κατὰ τὴν αἴσθησιν. (About these κοινὰ see also *De Sensu*, c. i. 437, a, 8.) *De Sensu*, iv. 442, b, 8 : περὶ μὲν τούτων [the κοινὰ just mentioned] ἀπατῶνται, περὶ δὲ τῶν ἰδίων οὐκ ἀπατῶνται, οἷον ὄψις περὶ χρώματος καὶ ἀκοὴ περὶ ψόφων. *Metaph.* iv.

5, 1010, b, 14. We can only trust the deliverance of each sense with regard to its own particular objects, those of sight with regard to colour, &c.: ὧν [αἰσθήσεων] ἑκάστη ἐν τῷ αὐτῷ χρόνῳ περὶ τὸ αὐτὸ οὐδέποτέ φησιν ἅμα οὕτω καὶ οὐχ οὕτως ἔχειν. ἀλλ' οὐδ' ἐν ἑτέρῳ χρόνῳ περὶ τὸ πάθος ἡμφισβήτησεν, ἀλλὰ περὶ τὸ ᾧ συμβέβηκε τὸ πάθος. The same wine may taste to us at one time sweet, at another not: ἀλλ' οὐ τό γε γλυκὺ οἷόν ἐστιν ὅταν ᾖ, οὐδεπώποτε μετέβαλεν, ἀλλ' ἀεὶ ἀληθεύει περὶ αὐτοῦ καὶ ἔστιν ἐξ ἀνάγκης τὸ ἐσόμενον γλυκὺ τοιοῦτον. Perception shows us primarily (as has been already said on pp. 206-7) only certain sets of qualities. The subjects to which these qualities belong are not immediately and exclusively determined by perception ; nor are those other properties which are only inferred from what we perceive.

particular from the universal and of effects from causes, or in one word *Demonstration*, forms the task of Science : for in such deduction, according to Aristotle, consists all Proof. The premises, however, from which these deductive proofs must start cannot be themselves deduced by the same method. Nor are they immediately given in any innate kind of knowledge. It is only by working upwards from phenomena that we can reach the principles that underlie them : only from particulars that we can rise to universals. To do this scientifically is the business of *Induction*. Demonstration and Induction are accordingly the two component parts of the scientific process, and the essential subjects of Methodology. Both, however, presuppose the general elements of Thought, and cannot be explained without a knowledge of them. Aristotle, therefore, prefaces his theory of Proof with an examination of the Syllogism ; and in connection with this he finds himself compelled to go more closely into the nature of the Judgment and the Proposition, as being the component parts of the Syllogism. It was not till a later period of his work (as we have already explained) that he went on to treat them separately, and even then this part of his Logic remained distinctly undeveloped. The same remark applies still more strongly to his doctrine of Concepts.[1] Nevertheless, it is with these last that we must begin, in order to proceed thereafter to the theory of judgments, and lastly to the Syllogism—inasmuch as certain definite views as to concepts are always presupposed by Aristotle in his discussion of Syllogistic Logic.

[1] Cf. pp. 192 sqq.

It was the search for general concepts which gave
to philosophy under Socrates that new direction which
not only Plato but also Aristotle followed in all
essentials. As a natural result of this, we find that
Aristotle, generally speaking, takes for granted the
Socratico-Platonic theory of the nature of concepts and
the problem of abstract thought.[1] But as we shall find
him in his metaphysics contradicting Plato's doctrine
of the independent reality of the Universal which we
think in the Concept, so also in the matter of the
logical handling of concepts he feels it necessary in
connection with this criticism to obtain more accurate
and definite conclusions on many points.[2] Plato had
required that in conceptual definition attention should
be restricted to the essential as opposed to the accidental
properties of things;[3] and yet at the same time he had
exalted all general notions to an absolute independence
as Ideas, without any further distinction between conceptions of property and substance.[4] This distinction
Aristotle introduces, for to him, as we shall see, the individual thing alone is Substance. But he does not merely
separate the accidental from the essential.[5] He goes on

[1] Cf. pp. 162 sq. and 172 sq.
[2] For the following, besides
PRANTL (*Gesch. d. Log.* i. 210
sqq.), and the other general
works, cf. KUHN, *De Notionis
Definitione qual. Arist. constitu-
erit*, Halle, 1844; RASSOW, *Arist.
de Notionis Definitione Doctrina*,
Berl. 1843.
[3] See ZELL. *Ph. d. Gr.* pt. i.
p. 518 sq.
[4] *Ibid.* 584 sqq.
[5] As to the distinction of the
συμβεβηκὸς from the καθ' αὐτὸ

cf. *Anal. Post.* i. 4, 73, a, 34 sqq.;
Top. i. 5, 102, b, 4; *Metaph.* v.
7, c. 9 *init.*, c. 18, 1002, a, 24
sqq., c. 30, 1025, a, 14, 28, c. 6
init.; WAITZ, in *Categ.* 5, b, 16;
Anal. Post. 71, b, 10. According
to these passages everything belongs to any object ' καθ' αὐτὸ '
which is, mediately or immediately, contained in the concept
of that object; and all is ' κατὰ
συμβεβηκὸς ' which does not follow
from the concept. To be a biped
belongs to any man καθ' αὐτὸ,

to make a further subdivision of the latter head by distinguishing the Universal from the Genus, and both from the Concept or conceptual Essence of things.[1] A *Universal* is everything that appertains to several objects in common, not merely by accident, but by virtue of their nature.[2] If this common element is a qualification of the essence derived from some other more general, then the Universal is a property-concept, and indicates an essential property.[3] If it is of the essence of the things in question, then the Universal becomes a *Genus*.[4] If to the common distinguishing

for every man, as such, is a biped. To be educated is to him κατὰ συμβεβηκός. A συμβεβηκὸς is (*Top.* ibid.) ὃ ἐνδέχεται ὑπάρχειν ὁτῳοῦν ἑνὶ καὶ τῷ αὐτῷ καὶ μὴ ὑπάρχειν. Hence, what is said of a thing καθ' αὑτὸ is true of all things which fall under the same concept; but what is said κ. συμβεβηκὸς is only true in particular cases; and therefore all universal determinations are καθ' αὑτό. *Metaph.* v. 9, 1017, b, 35: τὰ γὰρ καθόλου καθ' αὑτὰ ὑπάρχει, τὰ δὲ συμβεβηκότα οὐ καθ' αὑτὰ ἀλλ' ἐπὶ τῶν καθ' ἕκαστα ἁπλῶς λέγεται. Cf. note 2, below. For more about the συμβεβηκὸς, see the second part of ch. vii., *infra*.

[1] Thus *Metaph*. vii. 3 *init.*: οὐσία in common usage means many different things: τὸ τί ἦν εἶναι καὶ τὸ καθόλου καὶ τὸ γένος . . . καὶ τέταρτον τούτων τὸ ὑποκείμενον.

[2] *Anal. Post.* i. 4, 73, b, 26: καθόλου δὲ λέγω ὃ ἂν κατὰ παντός τε ὑπάρχῃ καὶ καθ' αὑτὸ καὶ ᾗ αὑτό. φανερὸν ἄρα ὅτι ὅσα καθόλου ἐξ ἀνάγκης ὑπάρχει τοῖς πράγμασιν; *Part. An.* i. 4, 644, a, 24: τὰ δὲ καθόλου κοινά· τὰ γὰρ πλείοσιν ὑπάρχοντα καθόλου λέγομεν. (Like-

wise *Metaph*. vii. 13, 1038, b, 11.) Cf. last note but one.

[3] Such an essential quality Aristotle calls a καθ' αὑτὸ ὑπάρχον, a πάθος καθ' αὑτὸ, or a συμβεβηκὸς καθ' αὑτὸ, understanding in the last case by συμβεβηκὸς (the term being used in a sense different from that discussed above) broadly that ὃ συμβαίνει τινὶ, *i.e.* a quality; cf. *Metaph*. v. 30 *fin.* c. 7, 1017, a, 12, iii. 1, 995, b, 18, 25, c. 2, 997, a, 25 sqq. iv. 1, iv. 2, 1004, b, 5, vi. 1, 1025, b, 12, vii. 4, 1029, b, 13; *Anal. Post.* i. 22, 83, b, 11, 19, c. 4, 73, b, 5, c. 6, 75, a, 18, c. 7, 75, a, 42; *Phys.* i. 3, 186, b, 18, ii. 2, 193, b, 26, c. 3, 195, b, 13, iii. 4, 203, b, 33; *De An.* i. 1, 402, b, 16; *Rhet.* i. 2, 1355, b, 30; WAITZ, on *Anal. Post.* 71, b, 10; TRENDELENBURG, *De An.* 189 sq.; BONITZ, on *Metaph*. 1025, a,

[4] *Top.* i. 5, 102, a, 31: γένος δ' ἐστὶ τὸ κατὰ πλειόνων καὶ διαφερόντων τῷ εἴδει ἐν τῷ τί ἐστι κατηγορούμενον. ἐν τῷ τί ἐστι δὲ κατηγορεῖσθαι τὰ τοιαῦτα λεγέσθω, ὅσα ἁρμόττει ἀποδοῦναι ἐρωτηθέντα τί ἐστι τὸ προκείμενον (*e.g.* in a man: τί ἐστι; ζῷον). *Metaph*. v. 28,

qualities included in the notion of the Genus are added other marks which are again essential with reference to a certain part of the whole class, and by which such part is distinguished from the rest of the same Genus, then we arrive at the *Species*, which, accordingly, is made up of the Genus and the *specific differences*.[1] If,

1024, a, 36 sqq., where, among different meanings of γένος, the following are given : τὸ ὑποκείμενον ταῖς διαφοραῖς, τὸ πρῶτον ἐνυπάρχον ὃ λέγεται ἐν τῷ τί ἐστι ... οὗ διαφοραὶ λέγονται αἱ ποιότητες (that these two descriptions apply to the same meaning of γένος is shown by Bonitz on this passage). *Ibid.* x. 3, 1054, b, 30 : λέγεται δὲ γένος ὃ ἄμφω ταὐτὸ λέγονται κατὰ τὴν οὐσίαν τὰ διάφορα ; x. 8, 1057, b, 37 : τὸ γὰρ τοιοῦτον γένος καλῶ, ᾧ ἄμφω ἓν ταὐτὸ λέγεται, μὴ κατὰ συμβεβηκὸς ἔχον διαφοράν. *Top.* vii. 2, 153, a, 17 : κατηγορεῖται δ' ἐν τῷ τί ἐστι τὰ γένη καὶ αἱ διαφοραί. Every γένος is consequently a καθόλου, but not every καθόλου a γένος ; cf. *Metaph.* iii. 3, 998, b, 17, 999, a, 21, xii. 1, 1069, a, 27, &c., with i. 9, 992, b, 12, vii. 13, 1038, b, 16, 25 sq. ; and BONITZ on *Metaph.* 299 sqq. To the distinction between genus and property is also partly referable the statement in *Categ.* c. 2, 1, a, 20 sqq. c. 5, that everything either (1) καθ' ὑποκειμένου τινὸς λέγεται, ἐν ὑποκειμένῳ δὲ οὐδενί ἐστιν, or (2) ἐν ὑποκειμένῳ μέν ἐστι καθ' ὑποκειμένου δὲ οὐδενὸς λέγεται, or (3) καθ' ὑποκειμένου τε λέγεται καὶ ἐν ὑποκειμένῳ ἐστίν, or (4) οὔτ' ἐν ὑποκειμένῳ ἐστὶν οὔτε καθ' ὑποκειμένου λέγεται. Of these divisions, the fourth comprises particular things : the first refers to genera and (c. 5,

3, a, 21) specific differences : the second to properties, activities and conditions—in fact, the συμβεβηκότα. To the first belongs the term ' man,' to the second the term ' grammar,' and to the fourth the term ' Socrates.' But the uncertainty of the whole division immediately appears in the description of the third class, for if there are notions which are predicated both καθ' ὑποκειμένου and ἐν ὑποκειμένῳ—*i.e.* which are at once genera and properties (the example Aristotle gives is the concept of ' science,' which is in the soul as its ὑποκείμενον, and is also predicated of each of the particular sciences)—then the genera and properties cannot be distinct and co-ordinate classes of universals. How undefined was the boundary between a ' genus' and a ' property' will be seen also in his treatment of Substance (on which see the first part of ch. vii., *infra*).

[1] *Metaph.* x. 7, 1057, b, 7 : ἐκ γὰρ τοῦ γένους καὶ τῶν διαφορῶν τὰ εἴδη (for instance, the specific concepts ' black ' and ' white ' are made up of the generic notion χρῶμα and the distinguishing qualities διακριτικὸς and συγκριτικός : white is the χρῶμα διακριτικὸν, black is the χρῶμα συγκριτικόν). *Top.* vi. 3, 140, a, 28 : δεῖ γὰρ τὸ μὲν γένος ἀπὸ τῶν ἄλλων χωρίζειν [the generic concept distinguishes

finally, an object is in this way, by the aggregate of its distinctive marks, so defined that the definition as a whole is applicable to no other object, then we have its *Concept*.[1] The object of the Concept is therefore the

what belongs to a genus from every other], τὴν δὲ διαφορὰν ἀπό τινος ἐν τῷ αὐτῷ γένει. *Ibid.* vi. 6, 143, b, 8, 19. (Further instances of the manner of using διαφορὰ are given by WAITZ, *Arist. Org.* i. 279; BONITZ, *Ind. Ar.* 192, a, 23.)—These distinguishing marks of species, Aristotle calls διαφορὰ εἰδοποιὸς (*Top.* vi. 6, 143, b, 7; *Eth.* x. 3, 1174, b, 5). From other properties he distinguishes them by their being able to be predicated of a subject (καθ᾽ ὑποκειμένου λέγονται), but not being in a subject (ἐν ὑποκειμένῳ οὐκ εἰσί)—*i.e.* they do not subsist in a subject which would exist before themselves, or which might be conceived independently of them, but in one which *by* them alone *is* this definite subject (*Cat.* 5, 3, a, 21 sq.; cf. c. 2, 1, a, 24 sq.); they are not accidental but essential determinations (*Metaph.* vii. 4, 1029, b, 14, 1030, a, 14; *Top.* vi. 6, 144, a, 24 : οὐδεμία γὰρ διαφορὰ τῶν κατὰ συμβεβηκὸς ὑπαρχόντων ἐστί, καθάπερ οὐδὲ τὸ γένος · οὐ γὰρ ἐνδέχεται τὴν διαφορὰν ὑπάρχειν τινὶ καὶ μὴ ὑπάρχειν); they belong to the concept of the subject of which they are affirmed, and hence everything that is implied in them is also true of the species and of the individuals to which they belong (*Cat.* c. 5, 3, a, 21 sqq. b, 5). It can hence be said of them, that they (together with the genus) ' form the substance ' (*Metaph.* vii. 12, 1038, b, 19 : cf. following note)

and that they ' express something substantial ' (*Top.* vii. 2, *vid. supr.* p. 214, n. 4 ; and yet, looked at in themselves, they are not substances but qualities, for they express not a τί, but a ποιόν τι (*Top.* iv. 2, 122, b, 16,. c. 6, 128, a, 26, vi. 6, 144, a, 18, 21 ; *Phys.* v. 2, 226, a, 27 ; *Metaph.* v. 14 *init.*). The apparent contradiction between Aristotle's different statements on the subject (brought out by TRENDELENBURG, *Hist. Beitr. z. Phil.* i. 56 sqq., and BONITZ, on *Metaph.* v. 14) may be solved in the manner indicated; cf. WAITZ, *ut supra.*

[1] *Anal. Post.* ii. 13, 96, a, 24. Many properties of things are also accidental to other things which fall under the same genus. Τὰ δὴ τοιαῦτα ληπτέον [in the determination of concepts] μέχρι τούτου, ἕως τοσαῦτα ληφθῇ πρῶτον, ὧν ἕκαστον μὲν ἐπὶ πλεῖον ὑπάρξει [is accidental also to other things], ἅπαντα δὲ μὴ ἐπὶ πλέον. ταύτην γὰρ ἀνάγκη οὐσίαν εἶναι τοῦ πράγματος—which will be further illustrated below. *Ibid.* 97, a, 18: we get the concept (λόγος τῆς οὐσίας) of a given object by dividing the genus into its species, and then the species to which our object belongs into its sub-species, and thus proceeding till we arrive at a group ὧν μηκέτι ἐστὶ διαφορά, *i.e.* that which is indivisible into any farther sets of opposed species, to one or other of which the object in question would belong (but about the actual tenableness of this

Substance, or more accurately the determinate Substance or peculiar Essence of the things in question ;[1] and the theory, cf. BONITZ, *Arist. Metaph.* ii. 346, 1). So also *Metaph.* vii. 12, 1037, b, 29 : οὐθὲν γὰρ ἕτερόν ἐστιν ἐν τῷ ὁρισμῷ, πλὴν τό τε πρῶτον λεγόμενον γένος καὶ αἱ διαφοραί (or as it stands 1038, a, 8 : ὁ ὁρισμός ἐστιν ὁ ἐκ τῶν διαφορῶν λόγος). The genus is divided into its species, the latter into their sub-species, and this is continued ἕως ἂν ἔλθη εἰς τὰ ἀδιάφορα (*ibid.* l. 15); and since in this series every subsequent *differentia* includes the preceding one (*e.g.* the δίπουν includes the ὑπόπουν), therefore the intermediate terms which fall between the genus and the lowest specific difference do not need to be repeated in the definition (cf. also *Part. An.* i. 2 *init.*). So it follows (*Met.* ibid. 1038, a, 28) : ὅτι ἡ τελευταία διαφορὰ ἡ οὐσία τοῦ πράγματος ἔσται 'καὶ ὁ ὁρισμός : in which, however, we have to understand by the τελευταία διαφορά, not only the last specific difference as such, but the specific concept as determined by it, which embraces the higher species and the genus.

[1] For the designation of that which is thought of in the concept, Aristotle makes use of various expressions. Besides οὐσία and εἶδος (of which we shall have more to say in dealing with the Metaphysics), we have to notice in this connection his way of marking out the idea which a word expresses by placing a ὅπερ before it, as : ὅπερ ὄν, or ὅπερ ἕν (*Phys.* 3, 186, a, 32 sqq.), for 'Being, as such,' or 'One, as such' (cf. BONITZ, *Ind. Arist.* 533, b, 36 sqq.); and also his

special use of εἶναι with a dative annexed (for instance, τὸ ἀνθρώπῳ εἶναι, &c., τὸ ἑνὶ εἶναι τὸ ἀδιαιρέτῳ ἐστὶν εἶναι, *Metaph.* x. 1, 1052, b, 16 : οὐ γάρ ἐστι τὸ σοὶ εἶναι τὸ μουσικῷ εἶναι, *ibid.* vii. 4, 1029, b, 14, cf. *Ind. Ar.* 221, a, 34); and the phrase τὸ τί ἦν εἶναι.—In the second of these expressions the dative must (according to TRENDELENBURG, *Rh. Mus.* 1828, 481; SCHWEGLER, *Ar. Metaph.* iv. 371) be taken possessively, so that ἀνθρώπῳ εἶναι is equivalent to εἶναι τοῦτο ὅ ἐστιν ἀνθρώπῳ = 'to be that which belongs to man'; and so τὸ ἀνθρώπῳ εἶναι designates the manner of being that is peculiar to man = 'Man's Being'; whereas ἄνθρωπον εἶναι only signifies the condition of one who is a man, or the actual participation in human nature. For the proof of this explanation such passages as the following will serve : τὸ εἶναι αὐτῷ ἕτερον, τὸ ζῆν τοῖς ζῶσι τὸ εἶναί ἐστιν (BONITZ, *Ind. Ar.* 221, a, 42, 54 sq., *Arist. Stud.* iv. 377). The fact that the article is never put before the dative (for Aristotle does not say τὸ τῷ ἀνθρώπῳ εἶναι) does not stand in the way; for the τῷ in this case after τὸ would be very awkward as a matter of diction; and moreover this very omission of the article makes it clearer that in the ἀνθρώπῳ εἶναι we are dealing with that 'being' which belongs to man *as such.*—The τί ἦν εἶναι is also, as a rule, construed with the dative of the object (τὸ τί ἦν εἶναι ἑκάστῳ, &c.; cf. *Ind. Ar.* 764, a, 60 sq.); for it is (as ALEX. says, in *Schol.* 256, b, 14 on *Top.* 24 m.)

Concept itself is nothing else but *the thought of this*

equivalent to ὁ τί ἐστι τὸ εἶναι αὐτῷ δηλῶν λόγος. But to this account must be added the explanation of the force of the peculiar imperfect, which is meant to designate that in things which does not belong to the moment, but which throughout the whole course of their existence has represented their proper *esse*, *i.e.* the essential as distinguished from the contingent and transitory. (Cf. PLATO, *Theæt.* 156, A : the Heracliteans maintain ὡς τὸ πᾶν κίνησις ἦν καὶ ἄλλο οὐδέν, and other examples *apud* SCHWEGLER, *ut supra*, 373 sq.). Hence τὸ τί ἦν εἶναι ἀνθρώπῳ properly means, ' that which in a man was his proper *esse*,' the true ' being ' of man, that belonging to him which is also called the πρώτη οὐσία ἴδιος ἑκάστῳ (*Metaph.* vii. 13, 1038, b, 10; vii. 7, *vid. inf.*; vii. 5 *fin.*) But this is simply his Ideal Being, that of which we think, when we abstract from what is contingent to the phenomenal man before us, and from the material element on which that contingency rests; cf. *Metaph.* vii. 4, 1029, b, 19 : ἐν ᾧ ἄρα μὴ ἐνέσται λόγῳ αὐτὸ, λέγοντι αὐτὸ, οὗτος ὁ λόγος τοῦ τί ἦν εἶναι ἑκάστῳ. So ch. 7, 1032, b, 14 : λέγω δ' οὐσίαν ἄνευ ὕλης τὸ τί ἦν εἶναι. *Ibid.* xii. 9, 1075, a, 1 : ἐπὶ μὲν τῶν ποιητικῶν ἄνευ ὕλης ἡ οὐσία καὶ τὸ τί ἦν εἶναι [sc. τὸ πρᾶγμά ἐστι]. And ch. 8, 1074, a, 35 : τὸ δὲ τί ἦν εἶναι οὐκ ἔχει ὕλην τὸ πρῶτον· ἐντελέχεια γὰρ. The τί ἦν εἶναι, therefore, goes with the εἶδος. *Metaph.* vii. 7, 1032, b, 1 : εἶδος δὲ λέγω τὸ τί ἦν εἶναι ἑκάστου καὶ τὴν πρώτην οὐσίαν. *Ibid.* ch. 10, 1035, b, 32 : εἶδος δὲ λέγω τὸ τί

ἦν εἶναι. *Phys.* ii. 2, 194, a, 20 : τοῦ εἴδους καὶ τοῦ τί ἦν εἶναι. In *Phys.* ii. 3, 194, b, 26 : one of the four causes is τὸ εἶδος καὶ τὸ παράδειγμα· τοῦτο δ' ἐστὶν ὁ λόγος ὁ τοῦ τί ἦν εἶναι καὶ τὰ τούτου γένη— this being what Aristotle, in *Metaph.* i. 3, 983, a, 27, calls τὴν οὐσίαν καὶ τὸ τί ἦν εἶναι, but immediately afterwards τὸν λόγον also. In fact, all these expressions are constantly interchanged by him. Compare, for example, the *De An.* ii. 1, 412, b, 10, where οὐσία ἡ κατὰ τὸν λόγον is explained by τὸ τί ἦν εἶναι; *Metaph.* vi. 1, 1025, b, 28 : τὸ τί ἦν εἶναι καὶ τὸν λόγον; vii. 5, 1030, b, 26 : τὸ τί ἦν εἶναι καὶ ὁ ὁρισμός (similarly *Part. An.* i. 1, 642, a, 25, cf. *Phys.* ii. 2, *ut supra*); *Eth.* ii. 6, 1107, a, 6 : κατὰ μὲν τὴν οὐσίαν καὶ τὸν λόγον τὸν τί ἦν εἶναι λέγοντα.—The τί ἦν εἶναι stands to the simple τί ἐστι as the particular and definite to the universal and indefinite. Whilst ' τί ἦν εἶναι ' only designates the form or peculiar being of a thing, the question, ' τί ἐστιν;' may be answered by giving either the matter only or that which includes both matter and form, or even by giving merely a property; and even when it is answered by giving the ideal form, the answer need not embrace the whole concept of the thing, but may be confined to the genus, or the specific difference (the proof of this is given by SCHWEGLER, *Arist. Metaph.* iv. 375 sqq.). The τί ἦν εἶναι is, consequently, a definite species of the τί ἐστι (hence *De An.* iii. 6, 430, b, 28 : τοῦ τί ἐστι κατὰ τὸ τί ἦν εἶναι = ' Being on its essential side ') ; and thus, as very com-

Essence.[1] And this is arrived at by the process of making the Universal of the Genus determinate by means of the aggregate of distinguishing marks.[2] But

monly happens in Aristotle, the latter may be used in the narrower meaning of the τί ἦν εἶναι, whereas the other phrase never has the looser sense of the τί ἐστι, so as to designate merely the matter of the thing or a mere property, or a generic universal without the specific differences. — The like relation exists between εἶναι with the dative and εἶναι with the accusative : τὸ λευκῷ εἶναι designates the idea of what is white : τὸ λευκὸν εἶναι, the property of being white. Cf. SCHWEGLER, *loc. cit.* p. 370; *Phys.* iii. 5, 204, a, 23, *et alibi.*—Aristotle undoubtedly introduced the formula τὸ τί ἦν εἶναι. Even if Stilpo really used it (see ZELLER, *Ph. d. Gr.* pt. i. 223, 3), he probably took it from Aristotle. Again, Antisthenes could hardly have used the mere τί ἦν to designate the concept : at least, this does not follow from the references in ZELL. *ibid.* p. 252, n. 1.—The following writers treat at length of the τί ἦν εἶναι and the allied phrases : TRENDELEN-BURG (who was the first to examine this subject thoroughly), *Rhein. Mus. v. Niebuhr und Brandis,* ii. (1828), 457 sqq.; *De Anima,* 192 sqq., 471 sqq.; *Hist. Beitr.* i. 34 sqq.; SCHWEGLER, *ut supra,* 369 sqq. (who cites other authors); HERTLING, *Mat. u. Form. b. Arist.* 47 sq.

[1] *Anal. Post.* ii. 3, 90, b, 30, 91, a, 1 : ὁρισμὸς μὲν γὰρ τοῦ τί ἐστι καὶ οὐσίας . . . ὁ μὲν οὖν ὁρισμὸς τί ἐστι δηλοῖ. *Ibid.* ii. 10 *init.* : ὁρισμὸς . . . λέγεται εἶναι λόγος τοῦ τί ἐστι. (The same *ibid.*

94, a, 11.) *Top.* vii. 5, 154, a, 31 : ὁρισμός ἐστι λόγος ὁ τὸ τί ἦν εἶναι σημαίνων. *Metaph.* v. 8, 1017, b, 21 : τὸ τί ἦν εἶναι οὗ ὁ λόγος ὁρισμὸς, καὶ τοῦτο οὐσία λέγεται ἑκάστου. So also vii. 4, 1030, a, 6, cf. a, 16, b, 4, and ch. 5, 1030, b, 26; also *Part. An.* i. 1, 642, a, 25. Hence Aristotle also designates the concept (in .the subjective meaning) by the expressions : ὁ λόγος ὁ ὁρίζων τὴν οὐσίαν (*Part. An.* iv. 5, 678, a, 34), ὁ λόγος ὁ τί ἐστι λέγων (*Metaph.* v. 13, 1020, a, 18) and similar phrases. (Λόγος or λόγος τῆς οὐσίας, in relation to the objective meaning of λόγος, stands for the form or the Being of things : *e.g. Gen. An.* i. 1, 715, a, 5, 8; *De An.* i. 1, 403, b, 2; ii. 2, 414, a, 9, &c.; and cf. preceding note.)—By the nature of the case ὅρος is synonymous with ὁρισμὸς, *e.g.* in *Top.* i. 5 *init.* : ἔστι δ' ὅρος μὲν λόγος ὁ τὸ τί ἦν εἶναι σημαίνων. So ch. 4, 101 b, 21, and ch. 7, 103, a, 25; *Anal. Post.* i. 3, 72, b, 23 ; ii. 10, 97, b, 26; *Metaph.* vii. 5, 1031, a, 8; ch. 13, 1039, a, 19 ; viii. 3, 1043, b, 28; ch. 6, 1045, a, 26; *Poet.* ch. 6, 1449, b, 23. But the same word, in a further sense, signifies either of the two terms of a proposition (subject and predicate), and is therefore the standing expression for the three terms of the syllogism ; *Anal. Pri.* i. 1, 24, b, 16 : ὅρον δὲ καλῶ εἰς ὃν διαλύεται ἡ πρότασις, etc., ch. 4, 25, b, 32, ch. 10, 30, b, 31, ch. 34, 48, a, 2 ; *Anal. Post.* i. 10, 76, b, 35 *et supra.*

[2] Cf. pp. 215, n. 1, 216, n. 1. Aristotle expresses the relation

the essence of things, according to Aristotle, consists
only in their form.[1] It is therefore only with the
form that the Concept is concerned, and no concept of
sensible objects *as such* can be presented to the mind.[2]
For although a definite relation of Form to Matter does
belong to the peculiar Essence and therefore also to

between these two elements, by
designating the genus as the
matter and the specific difference
as the form of the concept ; and
by this he explains how in the
concept the two are one. The
genus is that, in other words,
which, in itself indefinite, first
becomes definite in the specific
concept—the substratum (ὑποκείμενον), whose properties are the
matter, and whose form is made
up of the distinguishing marks.
But the substratum never actually
exists without properties, nor the
matter without form, and therefore neither does the genus exist
outside the species, but only in
them ; looked at in itself, it only
contains the universal presupposition, the possibility of that
which exists in reality in the
lowest species ; *Metaph.* viii. 6,
cf. ch. 2, 1043, a, 19 : v. 6, 1016, a,
25 : ch. 28, 1024, b, 3 : vii. 12, 1038,
a, 25 : x. 8, 1058, a, 23 : cf. ch. 3,
1054, b, 27; *Phys.* ii. 9 *fin.*; *Gen. et
Corr.* i. 7, 324, b, 6 (*Part. An.* i. 3,
643, a, 24, does not come in here).

[1] Cf. p. 217, n. 1. More fully
treated in the account of Aristotle's Metaphysics, *infra*, ch. vii.

[2] See p. 219, n. 1, and *Metaph.* vii. 11, 1036, b, 28 : τοῦ γὰρ
καθόλου καὶ τοῦ εἴδους ὁ ὁρισμός. So
ch. 15 *init.* : by Substance is meant
sometimes the λόγος alone, sometimes the λόγος σὺν τῇ ὕλῃ συνει-
λημμένος (the σύνολον). ὅσαι μὲν

οὖν (sc. οὐσίαι) οὕτω [in the sense
of the σύνολον] λέγονται, τούτων
μὲν ἔστι φθορά · καὶ γὰρ γένεσις ·
τοῦ δὲ λόγου οὐκ ἔστιν οὕτως ὥστε
φθείρεσθαι · οὐδὲ γὰρ γένεσις (οὐ
γὰρ γίγνεται τὸ οἰκίᾳ εἶναι ἀλλὰ τὸ
τῇδε τῇ οἰκίᾳ) . . . διὰ τοῦτο δὲ καὶ
τῶν οὐσιῶν τῶν αἰσθητῶν τῶν καθ'
ἕκαστα οὔθ' ὁρισμὸς οὔτ' ἀπόδειξίς
ἐστιν, ὅτι ἔχουσιν ὕλην ἧς ἡ φύσις
τοιαύτη ὥστ' ἐνδέχεσθαι καὶ εἶναι
καὶ μή · διὸ φθαρτὰ πάντα τὰ καθ'
ἕκαστα αὐτῶν. εἰ οὖν ἥ τ' ἀπόδειξις
τῶν ἀναγκαίων καὶ ὁ ὁρισμὸς ἐπι-
στημονικὸς, καὶ οὐκ ἐνδέχεται,
ὥσπερ οὐδ' ἐπιστήμην ὁτὲ μὲν ἐπιστήμην ὁτὲ δ' ἄγνοιαν εἶναι, ἀλλὰ
δόξα τὸ τοιοῦτόν ἐστιν (*vid. supra*
p. 163), οὕτως οὐδ' ἀπόδειξιν οὐδ'
ὁρισμὸν, ἀλλὰ δόξα ἐστὶ τοῦ ἐνδεχομένου ἄλλως ἔχειν, δῆλον ὅτι οὐκ
ἂν εἴη αὐτῶν οὔτε ἀπόδειξις. As soon
as we perceive it no longer, we
do not know whether it is now
the same as we think it to be. (Cf.
Top. v. 3, 131, b, 21 ; *Anal. Pri.*
ii. 21, 67, a, 39.) And in ch. 10,
1035, b, 34 : τοῦ λόγου μέρη τὰ τοῦ
εἴδους μόνον ἐστὶν, ὁ δὲ λόγος ἐστὶ
τοῦ καθόλου · τὸ γὰρ κύκλῳ εἶναι
καὶ κύκλος καὶ ψυχῇ εἶναι καὶ ψυχὴ
ταὐτά · τοῦ δὲ συνόλου ἤδη, οἷον
κύκλου τουδὶ, τῶν καθέκαστά τινος
ἢ αἰσθητοῦ ἢ νοητοῦ (λέγω δὲ νοη-
τοὺς μὲν οἷον τοὺς μαθηματικοὺς,
αἰσθητοὺς δὲ οἷον τοὺς χαλκοῦς καὶ
τοὺς ξυλίνους—but even the
former have a ὕλη, only it is a ὕλη
νοητή, 1036, a, 9 sqq.), τούτων δὲ

the Concept of any object,[1] yet it is not *this object* of sense itself, but only *this determinate mode* of sensible existence, only the universal form of the object, which can be defined.[2] It follows as a consequence of this that the conception does not relate to individual objects of sense[3] as such; but this applies also to all Individuals in general. Knowledge, in fact, aims always at a Universal,[4] and the words of which a definition is made up are themselves general terms.[5] Each concept

οὐκ ἔστιν ὁρισμὸς ἀλλὰ μετὰ νοήσεως ἢ αἰσθήσεως γνωρίζονται, ἀπελθόντας [-τα] δ᾿ ἐκ τῆς ἐντελεχείας οὐ δῆλον πότερόν ποτε εἰσὶν ἢ οὐκ εἰσίν, ἀλλ᾿ ἀεὶ λέγονται καὶ γνωρίζονται τῷ καθόλου λόγῳ · ἡ δ᾿ ὕλη ἄγνωστος καθ᾿ αὑτήν.

[1] As in the concept of the house (*Metaph*. vii. 15, see preceding note), the soul, the axe (*De An*. i. 403, b, 2 : ii. 1, 412, b, 11), of the σιμὸν (*Metaph*. vii. 5, &c.), in fact in all concepts of material and natural things. Cf. *Phys*. ii. 9 *fin*.: although the material causes are subservient to the ideal or final causes, still in explaining natural phenomena we must give both; ἴσως δὲ καὶ ἐν τῷ λόγῳ ἐστὶ τὸ ἀναγκαῖον [*i.e.* because the physical or material causes belong to the concepts of things]. ὁρισαμένῳ γὰρ τὸ ἔργον τοῦ πρίειν, ὅτι διαίρεσις τοιαδί · αὕτη δ᾿ οὐκ ἔσται, εἰ μὴ ἕξει ὀδόντας τοιουσδί · οὗτοι δ᾿ οὔ, εἰ μὴ σιδηροῦς. ἔστι γὰρ καὶ ἐν τῷ λόγῳ ἔνια μόρια ὡς ὕλη τοῦ λόγου. Cf. *Metaph*. vii. 10, 1035, a, 1, b, 14, and ch. 11, 1037, a, 29.

[2] If on the one hand we deny that matter belongs to the concept of a thing, and on the other are obliged to admit that

numberless things cannot be defined without giving their matter, this seems, at first sight, a contradiction. In the passage referred to (*Metaph*. vii. 10) Aristotle seeks to escape this contradiction by saying that in such cases, not this individual object, formed by the combination of a specific concept with this definite matter, is defined, but only its form; it is not *this* circle, but *the* circle, or the κύκλῳ εἶναι, not *this* soul, but *the* soul, the ψυχῇ εἶναι. But the difficulty is, indeed, by no means removed in this way. If, for instance, the soul is the 'Entelechy' of an organic body (*De An*. ii. 1), the τί ἦν εἶναι τῷ τοιῷδε σώματι (*Metaph. ibid.*.1035, b, 16), then a matter constituted in a stated way belongs to the concept of the soul.

[3] *Metaph*. vii. 15, 1039, b, 27, as at p. 220, n. 2, *supra*.

[4] *Vid. supra*, p. 163, n. 2.

[5] *Metaph. ibid*. 1040, a, 8: not only are sensible things incapable of definition, but also ideas: τῶν γὰρ καθ᾿ ἕκαστον ἡ ἰδέα, ὥς φασι, καὶ χωριστή. ἀναγκαῖον δ᾿ ἐξ ὀνομάτων εἶναι τὸν λόγον· ὄνομα δ᾿ οὐ ποιήσει ὁ ὁριζόμενος, ἄγνωστον

embraces several individuals, or at least can embrace
several ;[1] and even if we descend to the lowest species
we are still always met by universal determinations
only. Within these, the individual entities are distinguished no longer by anything relating to species,
but only by accidental marks of difference.[2]   Between

γὰρ ἔσται. τὰ δὲ κείμενα κοινὰ
πᾶσιν. ἀνάγκη ἄρα ὑπάρχειν καὶ
ἄλλῳ ταῦτα· οἷον εἴ τις σὲ ὁρί-
σαιτο, ζῷον ἐρεῖ ἰσχνὸν ἢ λευκὸν ἢ
ἕτερόν τι ὃ καὶ ἄλλῳ ὑπάρξει.
    [1] *Loc. cit.* l. 14, Aristotle pro-
poses the objection : μηθὲν κωλύειν
χωρὶς μὲν πάντα πολλοῖς, ἅμα δὲ μόνῳ
τούτῳ ὑπάρχειν (which is really
the case in the determination of
concepts, *vid. supra*, p. 216, n. 1),
and he gives among other answers
this (cf. BONITZ, on this passage)
at l. 27 : 'even though an object
be the only one in its species, like
the sun and the moon, still its
concept could only contain such
things ὅσα ἐπ' ἄλλου ἐνδέχεται,
οἷον ἐὰν ἕτερος γένηται τοιοῦτος,
δῆλον ὅτι ἥλιος ἔσται· κοινὸς ἄρα ὁ
λόγος, &c.' Similarly, in *De
Cælo*, i. 9, 278, a, 8 : supposing
there were only one circle, οὐθὲν
ἧττον ἄλλο ἔσται τὸ κύκλῳ εἶναι καὶ
τῷδε τῷ κύκλῳ, καὶ τὸ μὲν εἶδος, τὸ
δ' εἶδος ἐν τῇ ὕλῃ καὶ τῶν καθ'
ἕκαστον. *Ibid.* b, 5 : there is only
one world, but still the οὐρανῷ
εἶναι and the τῷδε τῷ οὐρανῷ εἶναι
are two different things.
    [2] *Metaph.* vii. 10 (*vid. supr.* p.
220, n. 2) : ὁ λόγος ἐστὶ τοῦ καθόλου.
Anal. Post. ii. 13, 97, b, 26 : αἰεὶ
δ' ἐστὶ πᾶς ὅρος καθόλου.   The
determination of concepts may
be continued till all specific
differences are exhausted, and
the τελευταία διαφορὰ is reached ;

but below this there only remain
individuals which are no longer
specifically distinguished (see
Metaph. x. 9, 1058, a, 34 sqq.
and *supra*, p. 216, n. 1), and are in
a sense ὅμοια (*Anal. Post.* ii. 13,
97, a, 37, b, 7) ; these, however,
continue to form a multiplicity,
and, in fact, an indefinite multiplicity, and for this reason cannot
be the object of science and of
the concept ; *Metaph.* iii. 4, *init.* :
εἴτε γὰρ μὴ ἔστι τι παρὰ τὰ καθέκαστα, τὰ δὲ καθέκαστα ἄπειρα, τῶν
δ' ἀπείρων πῶς ἐνδέχεται λαβεῖν
ἐπιστήμην ; cf. ii. 2, 994, b, 20
sqq. ; *Top.* ii. 2, 109, b, 14 ;
Anal. Post. i. 24, 86, a, 3 sqq.
and *ibid.* c. 19–21, the proof that
argument cannot be continued to
infinity either upwards or downwards.   In this Aristotle exactly
follows Plato : see ZELL. *Ph. d. Gr.*
pt. i. p. 524, 3, 587, 1.—Aristotle designates singulars by the phrases :
τὰ καθ' ἕκαστα (or κ. ἕκαστον), τὸ
ἀριθμῷ ἕν (*Metaph.* iii. 4, 999, b, 34 ;
Categ. c. 2, 1, b, 6, *et supra* ; see
WAITZ on this passage), τὰ τινὰ,
ὁ τὶς ἄνθρωπος, &c. (*Categ. ibid.*
1, 4, b ; *Anal. Post.* i. 24, 85, a,
34 ; *Metaph.* vii. 13, 1038, b, 33),
τόδε τι (*Categ.* c. 5, 3, b, 10 ;
Metaph. ix. 7, 1049, a, 27 *et supra* ;
see WAITZ on this passage of the
Categories), also τὰ ἄτομα (e.g.
Categ. c. 2, 1, b, 6, c. 5, 3, a, 35 ;
Metaph. iii. 1, 995, b, 29. It is true

this accidental difference and the specific differences lie
those attributes which belong exclusively to the members of a certain species, without, however, being directly
included in their Concept ; and Aristotle calls these *Properties* (ἴδια).[1] But in a wider sense this name is also
used by him to include specific differences on the one
side and accidental qualities on the other.[2]

What falls under one Concept must be, so far as
this is the case, identical.[3] What does not fall under

that the lowest species, which
do not divide into sub-species
—the ἀδιάφορα, *vid. supra*, p. 216,
n. 1—are given the same name :
but in that case, whenever this
meaning does not appear from
the context itself, he uses, not
merely τὰ ἄτομα, but ἄτομα εἴδη
and similar expressions (cf.
Metaph. iii. 3, 999, a, 12, v. 10,
1018, b, 6, vii. 8 *fin.*, x. 8, 9,
1058, a, 17, b, 10, xi. 1, 1059, b,
35) or τὰ ἔσχατα, because in de-
scending from the most universal
they come last (*Metaph.* xi. 1,
1059, b, 26 ; *Eth. N.* vi. 12, 1143,
a, 29, 33 ; *De An.* iii. 10, 433, a,
16 ; *De Mem.* c. 2, 451, a, 26).

[1] In *Top.* i. 4, 101, b, 17, he
distinguishes γένος, ἴδιον, and
συμβεβηκός ; and as soon as he
has divided the ἴδιον again into
ὅρος and ἴδιον in the narrower
sense, he defines the latter, c. 5,
102, a, 17 : ἴδιον δ' ἐστὶν ὃ μὴ
δηλοῖ μὲν τὸ τί ἦν εἶναι, μόνῳ δ'
ὑπάρχει καὶ ἀντικατηγορεῖται τοῦ
πράγματος [is related to it as
an interchangeable concept], οἷον
ἴδιον ἀνθρώπου τὸ γραμματικῆς εἶναι
δεκτικόν, &c.

[2] Already (*loc. cit.*) he distinguishes the ποτὲ ἢ πρός τι ἴδιον
from the ἁπλῶς ἴδιον, and in the

5th book, which deals with the
topical treatment of the ἴδια
(c. 1) he distinguishes the ἴδιον
καθ' αὑτὸ from the ἴδιον πρὸς
ἕτερον, the ἀεὶ ἴδιον from the ποτὲ
ἴδιον. He himself, however, remarks (129, a, 32) of the ἴδιον
πρὸς ἕτερον, and it is true in any
case of the ποτὲ ἴδιον, that it belongs to the συμβεβηκότα. On the
other hand, he gives as examples
of the ἴδ. καθ' αὑτὸ and ἀεὶ essential marks such as ζῷον ἀθάνατον,
ζῷον θνητὸν, τὸ ἐκ ψυχῆς καὶ σώματος συγκείμενον (128, b, 19, 35,
129, a, 2). Cf. preceding note.

[3] Aristotle does not say so in
these words, but it is shown by
his discussions on the various
meanings of ταὐτὸν. In *Top.* i. 7
(cf. viii. 1, 151, b, 29 ; 152, b, 31)
three of these are distinguished :
γένει ταὐτὸν is what belongs to one
genus, εἴδει ταὐτὸν what belongs
to one species (cf. *Metaph.* x. 8,
1058, a, 18), and ἀριθμῷ ταὐτὸν, ὧν
ὀνόματα πλείω τὸ δὲ πρᾶγμα ἕν.
This last kind of identity may
be expressed in various ways :
κυριώτατα μὲν καὶ πρώτως ὅταν
ὀνόματι ἢ ὅρῳ τὸ ταὐτὸν ἀποδοθῇ,
καθάπερ ἱμάτιον λωπίῳ καὶ ζῷον
πεζὸν δίπουν ἀνθρώπῳ, δεύτερον δ'
ὅταν τῷ ἰδίῳ, καθάπερ τὸ ἐπιστήμης

one concept is different.¹ Complete Identity, however, implies unity of matter also, for individuals between which there is no difference of a species are yet different numerically, because in each of them the same concept presents itself in a different matter.² Conceptual distinction in the highest degree gives us *Contrary Opposition*; whereas simple difference produces *Contradictory Opposition*. For *Contraries* (ἐναντία) are such as, within the same Genus, lie as far as possible asunder.³ Contrary opposition, in fact, is

δεκτικὸν ἀνθρώπῳ, . . . τρίτον δ᾽ ὅταν ἀπὸ τοῦ συμβεβηκότος, οἷον τὸ καθήμενον ἢ τὸ μουσικὸν Σωκράτει. There is a somewhat different division in *Metaph*. v. 9. Aristotle there distinguishes, first, the ταὐτὰ κατὰ συμβεβηκὸs and ταὐτὰ καθ᾽ αὑτὰ; then the ταὐτὸν εἴδει and ἀριθμῷ, both of which are affirmed partly of that which has a Matter, partly of that which has an Essence (fuller at x. 3,1054, a, 32 : that is identical in number which both in Matter and in Form is one). As a general explanation he gives us a formula which is easily reducible ¬to the one cited above : ἡ ταὐτότης ἑνότης τίς ἐστιν ἢ πλειόνων τοῦ εἶναι ἢ ὅταν χρῆται ὡς πλείοσιν (as in αὐτὸ αὑτῷ ταὐτόν). Since, however (according to ch. 10, 1018, a, 35), Unity and Being can be used in different senses, the meaning of the ταὐτὸν, ἕτερον, &c. must vary accordingly.

¹ *Metaph*. v. 9, 1018, a, 9 : ἕτερα δὲ λέγεται ὧν ἢ τὰ εἴδη πλείω ἢ ἡ ὕλη ἢ ὁ λόγος τῆς οὐσίας· καὶ ὅλως ἀντικειμένως τῷ ταὐτῷ λέγεται τὸ ἕτερον. On εἴδει and γένει ἕτερον, cf. *ibid*. x. 8, v.

10, 1018, a, 38 sqq. and ch. 28, 1024, b, 9.
² See preceding note and p. 222, n. 2. That the individual differences of things must be based on Matter will be further shown later on, in the second part of ch. vii. *infra*.
³ Aristotle states this definition, *Categ*. c. 6, 6, a, 17; *Eth. N.* ii. 8, 1108, b, 33, as one already in use (ὁρίζονται) ; but in *Metaph*. x. 4 *init*., he puts it forward in his own name, and he there establishes the proposition that opposites must belong to the same genus, by observing expressly : τὰ μὲν γὰρ γένει διαφέροντα οὐκ ἔχει ὁδὸν εἰς ἄλληλα, ἀλλ᾽ ἀπέχει πλέον καὶ ἀσύμβλητα (*e.g.* a sound and a colour are not *opposed* to one another, because they cannot at all be compared, they are ἀσύμβλητα). Yet, on the other hand, we read in *Metaph*. v. 10, 1018, a, 25 : ἐναντία λέγεται τά τε μὴ δυνατὰ ἅμα τῷ αὐτῷ παρεῖναι τῶν διαφερόντων κατὰ γένος, καὶ τὰ πλεῖστον διαφέροντα τῶν ἐν τῷ αὐτῷ γένει, καὶ τὰ πλεῖστον διαφέροντα τῶν ἐν ταὐτῷ δεκτικῷ (that the ἐναντία are

nothing but specific difference made absolute.[1] _Contradictory_ opposition, on the other hand, is the relation

accidental to one and the same δεκτικὸν is confirmed by _Metaph._ x. 4, 1055, a, 29; _De Somn._ No. 1, 453, b, 27), καὶ τὰ πλεῖστον διαφέ-ροντα τῶν ὑπὸ τὴν αὐτὴν δύναμιν, καὶ ὧν ἡ διαφορὰ μεγίστη ἢ ἁπλῶς ἢ κατὰ γένος ἢ κατ' εἶδος. τὰ δ' ἄλλα ἐναντία λεγεται τὰ μὲν τῷ τὰ τοιαῦτα ἔχειν, τὰ δὲ τῷ δεκτικὰ εἶναι τῶν τοιούτων, &c. (and the like in x. 4, 1055, a, 35), and _Categ._ c. 11 _fin._ also has: ἀνάγκη δὲ πάντα τὰ ἐναντία ἢ ἐν τῷ αὐτῷ γένει εἶναι [like black and white], ἢ ἐν τοῖς ἐναντίοις γένεσιν [like just and unjust], ἢ αὐτὰ γένη εἶναι [like good and evil]. SIMPL. cites something similar (_In Categ. Schol._ 84, a, 6; _Ar. Fr._ 117) from the treatise Π. ἀντικειμέ-νων, about which cf. p. 70, n 4.— The more mature and correct statement is that which is given in _Metaph._ x. (_e.g._ good and evil could not be contraries if they did not fall under the same generic concept, that of moral behaviour); and, in fact, Aristotle himself (at 1055, a, 23 sqq.) resolves the earlier statements by bringing them into line with the idea of the ἐναντ.ον as there defined. It is only in reference to that definition of the ἐναντίον that we can understand Aristotle's important axiom (_Metaph._ iii. 2, 996, a, 20; iv. 2, 1004, a, 9, 1005, a, 3; xi. 3, 1061, a, 18; _An. Pri._ i. 36, 48, b, 5; _De An._ iii. 3, 427, b, 5, _et alibi_; see BONITZ and SCHWEGLER on _Metaph._ iii. 2, _loc. cit._), τῶν ἐναν-τίων μία ἐπιστήμη. That is the _same_ science which deals with the _same_ things; things which

belong to different genera, like sound and colour, belong also to different sciences: cf. _loc. cit._ 1055, a, 31.—Further, from the same definition of the ἐναντίον (_ibid._ 1055, a, 19, cf. _De Cœlo,_ i. 2, 269, a, 10, 14, and _Phys._ i. 6, 189, a, 13) Aristotle deduced the principle that to each thing there can only be one contrary. Between contraries there may lie an indefinite number of inter-mediate grades, which are com-pounded of these contraries (as colours out of light and dark). Such intermediate grades are not found, however, between every pair of contraries, but only be-tween those pairs of which one or other predicate does not necessa-rily belong to the subject con-cerned, and in which there is a gradual transition from one to the other. (_Metaph._ x. 7; _Categ._ c. 10, 11, b, 38 sqq., 12, b, 25 sqq. cf. SIMPL. _Categ. Schol. in Ar._ 84, a, 15 sqq., 28 sqq.) What Aristotle had in his mind in this doctrine of the ἐναντίον is the scale of changes in the natural sciences; for every change is a transition from one condition to the opposite; _Phys._ v. 3, 226, b, 2, 6, i. 4, 187, a, 31, c. 5, 188, a, 31 sqq.; _Gen. et Corr._ i. 7, 323, b, 29.—To the above definition of the εἴδει ἐναντίον corresponds that of the ἐναντίον κατὰ τόπον in _Meteor._ ii. 6, 363, a, 30, and _Phys._ v. 3, 226, b, 32.— The correct way of formulating oppositions was dealt with in the treatise Π. ἀντικειμένων (_vid. supra_ p. 70, n. 4, and SIMPL. _loc. cit._ 83, b, 39 sqq.; _Ar. Fr._ 116).

[1] The διαφορὰ τέλειος of _Me-_

between such concepts as stand to one another in the relation of Yes to No,[1] of affirmation to negation, and between which, therefore, no third or middle term can lie,[2] and of which as applied to every given object one or other must be true.[3] This kind of opposition, to put it differently, arises when everything which is not contained in a certain concept is collected into one negative expression,[4] *i.e.* where the aggregate of all possible determinations is divided between two concepts by the test of identity with or difference from some given determinant. Between contrary and contradictory opposition Aristotle places that of *privation and possession*,[5] though he is not able quite to establish the difference [6] between this and the other two kinds of

taph. x. 4, 1055, a, 10 sqq., 22 sqq. Since this opposition only occurs between abstract concepts and not between concrete things, the tract Π. ἀντικειμένων maintained that only the concepts (*e.g.* φρόνησις and ἀφροσύνη) were to be called ἁπλῶς ἐναντία, not the beings to which these concepts apply (such as the φρόνιμος and the ἄφρων). SIMPL. *loc. cit.* 83, b, 24 sqq., cf. PLATO, *Phædo,* 103 B.

[1] Aristotle's standing formula for this kind of opposition is therefore, ' ὡς κατάφασις καὶ ἀπόφασις ἀντικεῖσθαι.' In a judgment the like opposition is called ἀντίφασις (*vid.* n. 6, &c., *infra*) ; and in *Phys.* v. 3, 227, a, 8 and *Metaph.* iv. 7 *init.*, v. 10 *init.*, the opposition of concepts is included under the same word.

[2] *Metaph.* iv. 7, xi. 6, 1063, b, 19 ; *Phys. loc. cit.*, and cf. what will be said presently about contradictory judgment. The kind of opposition is the same there as

here : see *Categ.* c. 10, 12, b, 10.

[3] *Categ.* c. 10, 11, b, 16 sqq., 13, a, 37 sqq. ; and *Metaph.* x. 1057, a, 33.

[4] An ὄνομα or ῥῆμα ἀόριστον ; *vid. infra,* p. 232, n. 2.

[5] Ἕξις and στέρησις, *e.g.* 'seeing' and 'blind.' For what follows, cf. TRENDELENBURG, *Hist. Beitr.* i. 103 sqq.

[6] In *Metaph.* v. 22 (and, referring to this, x. 4, 1055, b, 3) Aristotle distinguishes three meanings of the στέρησις : (1) ἂν μὴ ἔχῃ τι τῶν πεφυκότων ἔχεσθαι, κἂν μὴ αὐτὸ ἦν πεφυκὸς ἔχειν, οἷον φυτὸν ὀμμάτων ἐστερῆσθαι λέγεται. (2) ἂν πεφυκὸς ἔχειν, ἢ αὐτὸ ἢ τὸ γένος, μὴ ἔχῃ. (3) ἂν πεφυκὸς καὶ ὅτε πέφυκεν ἔχειν μὴ ἔχῃ. Only in the first meaning would ' privation ' be synonymous with ' negation ' (for ' blind ' = ' not-seeing '), and we could affirm of the opposites κατὰ στέρησιν καὶ ἕξιν that which we are told by *Categ.* c. 10, 13, b, 20 sqq. (that is to say, by the

opposition. Notions of *relation* are adduced as the

author of the *Post-prædicamenta*) can *not* be affirmed of them, namely that 'everything is either one or the other' (either 'seeing' or 'blind'); in such a case, therefore, the relation between στέρη- σις and ἕξις would be reduced to that of ἀντίφασις. In the other two senses of στέρησις this is not the case, for in them the στέρησις itself, as is admitted in *Metaph.* iv. 12, 1019, b, 3 sqq., expresses something positive, and is a kind of ἕξις; and thus, if we take 'privation' in this sense, the opposition of the ἕξις comes under the definition of the ἐναν- τίον.—The distinction of the two in the *Post-prædicamenta* (*Categ.* c. 10, 12, b, 26 sqq.) is founded on the following argument: of those ἐναντία, which have no middle term between them (as 'straight' and 'crooked'), one or other must necessarily apply to everything capable of the dis- tinction (*e.g.* 'every *number* must be either *odd* or *even*'); when, on the other hand, there is a middle term between two ἐναντία, such a conclusion never follows (we cannot say, 'Everything which is capable of colour must be either white or black'); but in the case of στέρησις and ἕξις, neither one nor the other of these results will arise; we cannot say that 'to everything capable of the distinction one or other of such opposites must apply,' for there may be some time at which neither of the two will apply to it—τὸ γὰρ μήπω πεφυκὸς ὄψιν ἔχειν οὔτε τυφλὸν οὔτε ὄψιν ἔχον λέγεται; but neither can we reckon this class of opposites with those between which there

is a middle term—ὅταν γὰρ ἤδη πεφυκὸς ᾖ ὄψιν ἔχειν, τότε ἢ τυφλὸν ἢ ὄψιν ἔχον ῥηθ,σε⸱⸱αι. It is, how- ever, to be observed that (1) so long as the thing in question is *not* πεφυκὸς ὄψιν ἔχειν, it is not δεκτικὸν ὄψεως either, and there- fore the instance adduced is not to the point; and (2), on the other hand, there is much that is intermediate between 'posses- sion' and 'privation,' for there are all the degrees of partial possession: there are not only 'seeing' things and 'blind' things, but also things 'half blind.'—A further distinction of the ἐναντία from the opposites κατὰ στέρησιν καὶ ἕξιν is said to lie in the fact (*Categ.* c. 10, 13, a, 18), that in the former the trans- ition from one to the other is mutual (white can become black and black white), but in the latter only one-sided, from pos- session to privation, and not con- versely. But this is likewise in- correct: not only can things which see become blind or the rich poor, but blind things may become seeing and the poor rich; and even if this is not possible in every actual case, the same is just as true of the ἐναντία them- selves; neither can every sick man get well, nor every black thing become white. For the logical relation of concepts, such a distinction would in any case be of no importance.—Lastly, in *Metaph.* x. 4, 1055, b, 3, 7, 14, it is said that the στέρησις is a kind of ἀντίφασις, namely the ἀντίφασις ἐν τῷ δεκτικῷ, and the ἐναντιότης a kind of στέρησις (thus also in xi. 6, 1063, b, 17); so that, according to this, these three

subjects of a fourth sort of opposition.[1] Of all these
kinds of opposition the general proposition holds good,
that ' opposites fall within one and the same science.'[2]

concepts would form a kind of
gradation from the higher to the
lower. But this also can only be
said when the concept of στέρησις
is not accurately determined ; as
soon as this is done, the relation
of στέρησις and ἕξις falls either
under ἀντίφασις or under ἐναντιότης. To the latter result *Anal.
Post.* i. 4, 73, b, 21 points : ἔστι
γὰρ τὸ ἐναντίον ἢ στέρησις ἢ ἀντίφασις ἐν τῷ αὐτῷ γένει, οἶον ἄρτιον
τὸ μὴ περιττὸν ἐν ἀριθμοῖς ; for, to
be an ἐναντίον, the στέρησις must
express a positive concept, and
this not merely indirectly, like
the ἀντίφασις from which it is
here distinguished. The same is
true of passages like *Metaph.*
vii. 7, 1033, a, 7 sqq., where the
sick person—who is elsewhere
the ἐναντίον of the healthy person—is given as his στέρησις ;
ibid. xii. 4, 1070, b, 11 : ὡς μὲν
εἶδος [αἰτία τῶν σωμάτων] τὸ θερμὸν
καὶ ἄλλον τρόπον τὸ ψυχρὸν ἡ στέρησις, for cold forms a contrary
opposition to warm, and if it is
an εἶδος, it cannot be merely a
negation ; and hence, though it
is given as a negation with other
analogous concepts (*e.g. De Cœlo,*
ii. 3, 286, a, 25), yet Aristotle
himself in other passages admits
that, in certain cases, it is a
natural property, and not merely
a defect (*Part. An.* ii. 2, 649, a,
18), and that it has the power of
acting (*Gen. et Corr.* ii. 2, 329, b,
24), which cannot possibly be
true of a *mere* στέρησις. Cf.
TRENDELENBURG, *loc. cit.* 107
sqq., and STRÜMPELL, *Gesch. d.
theor. Phil.* 27 sq.—The tract

Π. ἀντικειμένων also treated of
στέρησις and ἕξις ; SIMPL. *Schol.
in Ar.* 86, b, 41, 87, a, 2 ; *Ar. Fr.*
119. We shall have to discuss
hereafter the metaphysical signification of στέρησις and its relation to the ὕλη.
    [1] *Cat.* c. 10, 11, b, 17, 24 sqq.;
Top. ii. 2, 109, b, 17, c. 8, 113,
b, 15, 114, a, 13, v. 6, 135, b, 17 ;
Metaph. x. 4, 1055, a, 38, c. 3,
1054, a, 23. Instances of such relative concepts are (see *Cat., loc.
cit.*, and c. 7 ; *Metaph.* v. 15) :
double and half—in fact, the manifold and its part, the ὑπερέχον
and ὑπερεχόμενον ; the active and
the passive ; the measurable and
the measure ; the knowable and
knowledge. Though in *Metaph.* v.
10, two further forms of opposition are named, yet BONITZ, on
this passage, and WAITZ, *Arist.
Org.* i. 308, have demonstrated
that these latter come under the
four already given. Conversely,
Phys. v. 3, 227, a, 7 only mentions
two (ἀντίφασις and ἐναντιότης).
    [2] See n. on p. 225, and as to the
extension of the above principle
to all ἀντικείμενα, cf. *Metaph.* iv. 2,
1004, a, 9 ; *Top.* i. 14, 105, b, 33,
ii. 2, 109, b, 17, viii. 1, 155, b,
30, c. 13, 163, a, 2. The foundation of this proposition lies mainly
in the fact that, of opposites,
one cannot be known without
the other. This has different
causes in different cases : in contradictory opposition, it arises
from the negative concept Non-A
immediately presupposing and
containing the positive one A ;
in correlative concepts it arises

But concepts taken by themselves cannot, so far,
produce *Discourse* of any kind; they are neither true
nor false. Definite expression, and therewith truth
and falsehood likewise, are first found in the *Proposition*.[1] The coupling of the Noun or Name-word
with the Verb or Time-word, of the Subject with the
Predicate,[2] presents us with a unit of discourse (or
spoken thought, λόγος) ;[3] and if this discourse takes
the form of Assertion, if anything is affirmed or denied
in it, we get, as distinguished from other modes of
thought expressed in words,[4] the Proposition [5] or Judgment (ἀπόφανσις)[6]—for which Aristotle regards the
simple Categorical Judgment as the type.[7] A judgment is *true*, when the thought whose inner process is

from their mutually presupposing
one another; in contrary opposition, and in στέρησις and ἕξις
(so far as that applies here) it
arises because the knowledge of
the opposed specific differences
presupposes that of the common
genus.

[1] *Vid. supra*, p. 202, &c.; *De
Interpr.* c. 4, c. 5, 17, a, 17;
Metaph. vi. 4; cf. ZELLER, *Ph.
d, Gr.* pt. i., p. 527, 5; p. 528, 1.

[2] As to ὄνομα and ῥῆμα (the
latter of which, however, includes
both copula and predicate), see
De Interpr. c. 1, 16, a, 13, c. 2,
3, c. 10, 19, b, 11; *Poet.* c. 20,
1457, a, 10, 14; *Rhet.* iii. 2, 1404,
b, 26. This is also Platonic; see
ZELL. *Ph. d. Gr.* pt. 1, pp. 557,
n. 5, 532, n. 2.

[3] *De Interpr.* c. 4 ; and *Rhet.*,
ut supra.

[4] Such as wish, request, &c.
In *Anal. Pr.* i. 1, 24, a, 22;
Top. i. 10, 104, a, 8 (cf. WAITZ,

Arist. Org. i. 352). Interrogation
is put under the concept of
πρότασις, but it is distinguished
as πρότασις διαλεκτικὴ from πρ.
ἀποδεικτικὴ, in that the latter is
λῆψις θατέρου μορίου τῆς ἀντιφάσεως, and the former, on the
other hand, ἐρώτησις ἀντιφάσεως.
Similar definitions of πρότασις
will be found in *De Interpr.* ii.
20, b, 23, and *Anal. Post.* i. 2,
72, a, 8 ; cf. *Soph. El.* 6, 169, a,
8, 14.

[5] Πρότασις ; on the expression
cf. BIESE, *Phil. d. Arist.* i. 128,
2 ; WAITZ, *Arist. Org.* i. 368 ;
BONITZ, *Ind. Ar.* 651, a, 33 sqq

[6] *De Interpr.* c. 4, 17, a, 1 ;
Anal. Pr. i. 1, 24, a, 16.

[7] *De Interpr.* c. 5, 17, a, 20 :
ἡ μὲν ἁπλῆ ἐστιν ἀπόφανσις . . .
ἡ δὲ ἐκ τούτων συγκειμένη . . . ἔστι
δὲ ἡ μὲν ἁπλῆ ἀπόφανσις φωνὴ
σημαντικὴ περὶ τοῦ ὑπάρχειν τι ἢ
μὴ ὑπάρχειν, ὡς οἱ χρόνοι διῄρηνται.

signified by the spoken words,[1] regards that as conjoined
or divided which is so conjoined or divided in actuality :
it is *false* in the opposite case.[2] The most fundamental
distinction between judgments is therefore that of
affirmative and negative.[3] Every affirmation stands
opposed to a negation which forms with it an exclusive
(contradictory) opposition (ἀντίφασις), in such wise
that one or the other of them must be true and no
third is possible.[4] On the other hand, certain affirmative propositions are related to certain negatives (as,
for instance, universal affirmatives to the corresponding

[1] On the definition of speech
as σύμβολον τῶν ἐν τῇ ψυχῇ παθημάτων, see *De Interpr.* c. 1, 16,
a, 3, c. 2 *init.* c. 4, 17, a, 1;
Soph. El. c. 1, 165, a, 6; *De
Sensu*, c. 1, 437, a, 14; *Rhet.* iii.
1, 1404, a, 20. The events in the
soul which words express are,
according to these passages, the
same in all men ; their designation in speech, on the other
hand, is (like written signs) a
matter of convention, and thus
differs in different persons.

[2] *Metaph.* vi. 4, ix. 1 *init.*

[3] *De Interpr.* c. 5 *init.* : ἔστι
δὲ εἷς πρῶτος λόγος ἀποφαντικὸς
κατάφασις εἶτα ἀπόφασις · οἱ δ' ἄλλοι
πάντες συνδέσμῳ εἷς. Further,
ibid. c. 5, 6 ; *Anal. Pr.* i. 1, 24,
a, 16 ; *Anal. Post.* i. 25, 86, b, 33.
The πρότασις καταφατική is also
called κατηγορική, the ἀποφατική
also στερητική. *Anal. Pr.* i. 2,
c. 4, 26, a, 18, 31, c. 6, 28, a, 20,
b, 6, 15, c. 13, 32, b, 1.

[4] *De Interpr.* c. 6, c. 7, 17, b,
16 ; *Anal. Post.* i. 2, 72, a, 11 :
ἀπόφανσις δὲ ἀντιφάσεως ὁποτερον-
οῦν μόριον. ἀντίφασις δὲ ἀντίθεσις
ἧς οὐκ ἔστι μεταξὺ καθ' αὑτήν.

μόριον δ' ἀντιφάσεως τὸ μὲν τὶ κατά
τινος κατάφασις, τὸ δὲ τὶ ἀπό τινος
ἀπόφασις. Cf. p. 226, n. 1 and 2.
We shall have more to say later on
about the law of contradiction
and the excluded middle. According to *De Interpr.* c. 9, an
exception to the rule stated above
is found in such disjunctive propositions as refer to a future
result which is contingent or
depends on free will. As is here
remarked, we can assert nothing
at all about them beforehand,
neither that they will happen,
nor that they will not happen ;
of them (*Gen. et Corr.* ii. 11, 337,
b, 3) only ὅτι μέλλει, but not ὅτι
ἔσται, is true; for the latter excludes the possibility of the event
being otherwise. Hence of them
only the disjunctive proposition is
true, that ' they will either happen
or will not happen.' Of the two
categorical propositions, ' they
will happen ' and ' they will not
happen,' *neither* is true of them.
The latter assertion is remarkable, for we should rather say,
that *one* of the two assertions
is true, but we only find out

universal negatives) in the way of contrary opposition,
which does *not* exclude a third possible case.[1]

But in truth we must not expect a perfectly clear
exposition of these relations from Aristotle. As he
was not yet able to distinguish the Copula expressly
from the Predicate,[2] he was naturally unable to discover the true status of the Negative. He nowhere
states that negation concerns the Copula alone, that it

which by the result. But Aristotle only regards as 'true'
those assertions which assert
actuality; and since this, in the
given case, is itself undetermined,
no definite proposition can, with
truth, be then affirmed. When
it is equally possible that something will happen, and that it
will not happen, the assertion
that it will happen is neither
true nor false; it only *becomes*
one or other, according as a corresponding or a contradictory
state of fact arises. Cf. SIMPL.
Categ. 103, β Bas.: according to
the teaching of the Peripatetic
school only the disjunctive proposition is true, ' A will either
be or not be '; but which part of
this disjunction will be true, and
which false, ἄληπτον εἶναι τῇ
φύσει καὶ ἄστατον. Hence all that
class of assertions, ἤδη μὲν οὐκ
ἔστιν ἢ ἀληθῆ ἢ φευδῆ ἔσται δὲ
ἢ τοῖα ἢ τοῖα.—It is from the
Megareans that Aristotle took the
subject-matter of the ' Aporia '
which he discusses in the passage
cited : cf. ZELLER, *Ph. d. Gr.*
pt. i. p. 220, 1.
   [1] *De Interpr.* c. 7, 17, b, 20:
cf. what has been said at pp.
224–5, about the ἐναντιότης. The
particular affirmative and particular negative propositions which,

according to later terminology,
are opposed as *subcontraries*, are,
in *Anal. Pr.* ii. 8, 59, b, 10,
reckoned among the ἐναντίως ἀντι-
κείμεναι. Aristotle, however, remarks (c. 15 *init.*) that this is
only ' according to the words, not
as to the thing itself.'
   [2] *Vid. supr.* p. 229, n. 2. In *De
Interpr.* c. 10, 19, b, 19, a case
is certainly before his mind, ὅταν
τὸ ἔστι τρίτον προσκατηγορῆται, as
in the proposition ἔστι δίκαιος
ἄνθρωπος. This, however, does
not relate to the separation of
the copula from the predicate,
but only to the fact that,
in existential propositions: ἔστιν
ἄνθρωπος, οὐκ ἔστιν ἄ., &c., the
subject can be expanded by
means of an added adjective,
which itself may be put either
affirmatively (δίκαιος ἄ.), or nega-
tively (οὐ δίκαιος ἄ.): ἔστι δίκ. ἄ.
means 'there is a just man,'
which is different from ἄνθρωπος
δίκαιός ἐστι, 'man is just.' Aristotle nowhere says that every
proposition, or even that the
existential proposition logically
considered, consists of *three*
parts; and the treatise Π. ἑρμη-
νείας even shows a preference for
selecting examples from those
existential propositions which fall
into two parts only.

has to do only with the connection of the subject to the predicate, and does not in fact deny the subject or the predicate itself.[1] The omission caused him to treat propositions with a negative subject or predicate as a special class,[2] whereas there is in fact no ground for doing so.[3]

Aristotle proceeds to consider the *Quantity* of Judgments, distinguishing between those which relate to many objects at once and those which relate to one, and then subdividing the former into universals and particulars. He has therefore a general division into judgments universal, particular, and individual.[4] But

[1] In *Anal. Pr.* i. 46 *init.* c. 3, 25, b, 19, he shows that there is a distinction between μὴ εἶναι τοδὶ and εἶναι μὴ τοῦτο, μὴ εἶναι λευκὸν and εἶναι μὴ λευκὸν, inasmuch as propositions of the last kind have the form of affirmative propositions ; but he does not detect the real reason of this either here or in *De Interpr.* c. 12 (to which BRANDIS, p. 165, refers).

[2] *De Interpr.* c. 3, 16, a, 30, b, 12, he says: οὐκ-ἄνθρωπος is no ὄνομα, and οὐχ-ὑγιαίνει no ῥῆμα ; but he wants to call the former ὄνομα ἀόριστον, and the latter ῥῆμα ἀόριστον : and in c. 10, along with the propositions ἔστιν ἄνθρωπος, οὐκ ἔ. ἄ., &c., he introduces also the corresponding ones made up of negative concepts : ἔστιν οὐκ-ἄνθρωπος, οὐκ ἔστιν οὐκ-ἄ., ἔστιν οὐ-δίκαιος οὐκ-ἄνθρ., οὐκ ἔστιν οὐ-δίκ. οὐκ-ἄνθρ., &c. Theophrastus called these propositions : ἐκ μεταθέσεως (AMMON. *De Interpr.* 128, b, 129, a., and PHILOP. *Schol. in Ar.* 121, a), or κατὰ μετάθεσιν (ALEX. *Analyt.* 134, a.).

[3] For that in which consists the *form* of the judgment—the definite conjunction of the subject with the predicate—remains the same, whether the subject and predicate be positive or negative concepts. And Aristotle himself admits (*Anal. Pr.* i. 3, 25, b, 19, cf. c. 13, 32, a, 31), that expressions such as : ἐνδέχεται μηδενὶ ὑπάρχειν, ἔστιν οὐκ ἀγαθὸν, have a σχῆμα καταφατικὸν.

[4] Still, this is only the case in *De Interpr.* c. 7. Universal judgments, which are also called ἐπὶ τῶν καθόλου ἀποφαίνονται καθόλου, and particulars, which are also called ἐν μέρει or κατὰ μέρος (*Anal. Pr.* i. 1, 24, a, 17, c. 2, 25, a, 4, 10, 20, &c.), are also designated as those which ἐπὶ τῶν καθόλου μὲν μὴ καθόλου δὲ ἀποφαίνονται, *i.e.* in both the subject is a καθόλου, ὃ ἐπὶ πλειόνων πέφυκε κατηγορεῖσθαι, but in the one the predicate is affirmed of the subject in its whole extension, in the other not so. The *Analytics*, on the other hand, does not mention individual

he adds what he calls the 'indefinite judgments,' and thus is led to bring in, here as elsewhere, a distinction which really has nothing to do with the logical form of thought-connection at all, but solely with the grammatical form of the expression.[1]

Aristotle also devotes much attention to the *Modality of Judgments*, on account of the importance of this subject in connection with the *Syllogism*. He distinguishes between judgments which assert actuality, necessity, and possibility,[2] but this division does not coincide with that which is now in use—of Assertory,. Apodeictic, and Problematic—for Aristotle in his classification does not regard subjective degrees of certainty, but the objective nature of things. By 'possible' he does not mean what *may perhaps* exist, but only what *may* exist but does not exist *necessarily*, and therefore *may or may not* exist indifferently.[3] The

judgments (see following note); and although it is true that they are without meaning for the main object of that treatise, which is the doctrine of the syllogism, yet we should expect that, if Aristotle at the time he wrote it had already had his attention called to this form of judgment, he would have expressly stated why he passed it over. We may infer, if the composition Π. ἑρμηνείας be really his, that the peculiar notes of individual judgments must have struck him *after* he had written *Analytics*.

[1] In the *De Interpr.* he adds nothing as to indefinite judgments. In *Anal. Pr.* i. 1, 24, a, 16 (cf. c. 2, 25, a, 4, c. 4, 26, b, 3, etc.) he says: πρότασις . . . ἢ καθόλου ἢ ἐν μέρει ἢ ἀδιόριστος; but the

examples which are there given— τῶν ἐναντίων εἶναι τὴν αὐτὴν ἐπιστήμην, τὴν ἡδονὴν μὴ εἶναι ἀγαθόν, —belong, logically considered, to the class of universal propositions; others which might be adduced, such as ἔστιν ἄνθρωπος δίκαιος, are particular. Aristotle himself makes no further use in the *Analytics* of the προτάσεις ἀδιόριστοι. Theophrastus designated under this name the particular negative (ALEX. *Analyt.* 21, b), or perhaps as AMMON. *De Interpr.* 73, a, states, particular propositions in general.

[2] *Anal. Pr.* i. 2 *init.*: πᾶσα πρότασίς ἐστιν ἢ τοῦ ὑπάρχειν ἢ τοῦ ἐξ ἀνάγκης ὑπάρχειν ἢ τοῦ ἐνδέχεσθαι ὑπάρχειν.

[3] *Anal. Pr.* i. 13, 32, a, 18 λέγω δ' ἐνδέχεσθαι καὶ τὸ ἐνδεχόμε-

corollaries which he deduced from his definitions were partly confuted by critics as old as Theophrastus and Eudemus.[1] To what is called the ' Relation of Judg-

νον, οὗ μὴ ὄντος ἀναγκαίου, τεθέντος δ' ὑπάρχειν, οὐδὲν ἔσται διὰ τοῦτ' ἀδύνατον; l. 28: ἔσται ἄρα τὸ ἐνδεχόμενον οὐκ ἀναγκαῖον κα ἱτὸ μὴ ἀναγκαῖον ἐνδεχόμενον. *Metaph.* ix. 3, 1047, a, 24: ἔστι δὲ δυνατὸν τοῦτο, ᾧ ἐὰν ὑπάρξῃ ἡ ἐνέργεια, οὗ λέγεται ἔχειν τὴν δύναμιν, οὐθὲν ἔσται ἀδύνατον. Likewise c. 4, 1047, b, 9, c. 8, 1050, b, 8: πᾶσα δύναμις ἅμα τῆς ἀντιφάσεώς ἐστιν ... τὸ ἄρα δυνατὸν εἶναι ἐνδέχεται κὶ εἶναι καὶ μὴ εἶναι· τὸ αὐτὸ ἄρα δυνατὸν καὶ εἶναι καὶ μὴ εἶναι; ix. 9 *init.*: ὅσα γὰρ κατὰ τὸ δύνασθαι λέγεται, ταὐτόν ἐστι δυνατὸν τἀναντία : *i.e.* what can be healthy can also be ill, what can rest can also move, he who can build can also destroy.

[1] Aristotle says that in a 'possibility,' the possibility of the contrary is also contained (see preceding note, and *De Interpr.* c. 12, 21, b, 12: δοκεῖ δὲ τὸ αὐτὸ δύνασθαι καὶ εἶναι καὶ μὴ εἶναι· πᾶν γὰρ τὸ δυνατὸν τέμνεσθαι ἢ βαδίζειν καὶ μὴ βαδίζειν καὶ μὴ τέμνεσθαι δυνατόν, &c.), determining the concept by taking that meaning of δύναμις according to which it designates a power of doing or suffering (*Metaph.* ix. 1, 1046, a, 9 sqq., v. 12 *init.*); and it matters not that this possibility of the contrary is not always equally great, and that the ἐνδεχόμενον or δυνατὸν (for these two expressions are really synonymous) at one time designates something which happens as a rule, though not without exceptions, at another something

which may equally happen or not happen (*Anal. Pr.* i. 13, 32, b, 4 sqq.). Hence he maintains in *Anal. Pr.* i. 13, 32, a, 29 (cf. *De Cœlo*, i. 12, 282, a, 4), that from the ἐνδέχεσθαι ὑπάρχειν the ἐνδέχεσθαι μὴ ὑπάρχειν also invariably follows, and from the παντὶ ἐνδέχεσθαι the ἐνδέχεσθαι μηδενὶ and μὴ παντὶ (*i.e.* the possibility of the predicate in question occurring to none, or not to all, for PRANTL, *Gesch. d. Log.* i. 267, explains the words wrongly); for since the possible is nothing necessary, the contrary of all that is (merely) possible may happen.—And for the same reason Aristotle refuses (*ibid.* c. 17, 36, b, 35) to allow, in possible propositions, the simple conversion of the universal negative judgment. For, since the negative judgment, ' it is possible that no B is A,' according to him, includes the affirmative, ' it is possible that every B is A,' so the simple conversion of the former would include the simple conversion of a universal affirmative judgment; and universal affirmative judgments cannot be converted simply. Theophrastus and Eudemus denied these assertions, because they understood by 'possible,' everything that can happen, and lost hold of the statement that it must also at the same time be able not to happen; and thus they included some things necessary in the possible (ALEX. *Anal. Pr.* 51, b, m, 64, b, 72, a, b, m, 73, a). Aristotle

ments ' Aristotle pays as little attention as to the Hypothetical and Disjunctive Syllogisms. Only in what he

himself admits (*Anal. Pr.* i. 3, 25, a, 37; *De Interpr.* c. 13, 22, b, 29 ; cf. *Metaph.* ix. 2 *init.* c. 5, 1048, a, 4, c. 8, 1050, b, 30 sqq.) with regard to the forces of nature (δυνάμεις) which only act in one direction, that the necessary also *may be called* a possible (δυνατὸν), and that, allowing this, universal negative possible-propositions can be converted simply, and that we may conclude from necessity to possibility—but he also adds that this is not true as to *his own* concept of the possible.—Two further points of dispute, on which Alexander wrote a work (ALEX. *Anal.* 40, b, 83, a), arose between Aristotle and his pupils upon the question about the mood of conclusions in syllogisms, the premisses of which are in different moods. Aristotle says that where one premiss is a possible- and the other an actual-proposition, a perfect syllogism can only be had in the case where the major proposition is a possible-proposition ; if, however, it is the minor, we get, first of all, an imperfect syllogism, *i.e.* one in which the conclusion is only obtained by a *deductio ad absurdum* and not immediately from the given premisses, and secondly, in the case of a negative syllogism (more correctly : in all cases), the possibility in the conclusion must be taken in the improper sense (*i.e.* not as confined to that which both can and cannot be) (*Anal. Pr.* i. 15). Theophrastus and Eudemus, on the contrary, were of opinion that even in this case

there was a perfect possible-syllogism (ALEX. *loc. cit.* 56, b). Both sides are right, according to their concepts of the possible. If we understand by ' possible ' everything that can be, including also the necessary, the syllogisms are quite correct and simple : ' Every B is A, every C can be B, therefore every C can be. A '; ' No B is A, every C can be B, therefore it is possible that no C is A.' If, on the other hand, we take ' possible ' to mean only that of which the contrary is likewise possible, we cannot make such syllogisms, because in this supposition the minor, ' every C can be B,' includes the negative proposition, ' every C can be not-B.' And also, as Theophrastus and Eudemus merely adhered to the principle that the modality of the conclusion is conformed to the weaker premiss (ALEX. *ibid.*), they asserted, on the same principle, that when one premiss is assertorial and the other apodeictic, the conclusion is apodeictic (ALEX. *ibid.* 40, a, 42, b, and from him PHILOP. *Schol. in Arist.* 158, b, 18, 159, a, 6), whilst, according to Aristotle (*Anal. Pr.* i. 9 sqq.) it is apodeictic when the major is so. In this case also, according to the meaning which we attach to the modality of propositions, both assertions may be made. If the propositions 'B must be A,' ' B cannot be A,' are supposed to express that between B and A there is (or is not) not a contingent, but a necessary connection, it follows that between every-

says of contradictory opposition [1] do we find the kernel of the late doctrine of disjunctive judgments. On the other hand, he is copious in his treatment of the Conversion of Propositions,[2] laying down the well-known rules,[3] but he treats it solely in connection with his theory of the Syllogism.

This theory of the Syllogism was expounded by Aristotle at full length, and it may truly be called his most original discovery.[4] As he was the first to introduce the name of the Syllogism into the scientific vocabulary,[5] so he was also the first to remark that all connections and all advances in our thought depend upon the syllogistic combination of judgments. A 'Syllogism' is a chain of thoughts, in which, from certain matters assumed, and by virtue of these alone, there issues of necessity some further matter different from them.[6]

---

thing contained in B and A, by the same necessity, there is, or is not, a connection (if all living beings, by reason of a necessity of nature, are mortal, the same is also true of every kind of living beings, *e.g.* of men), as Aristotle, *loc. cit.* 30, a, 21 sqq. shows quite clearly. If, on the other hand, these propositions are meant to state that we are obliged to think A connected or not connected with B, the proposition, ' C must (or cannot) be A ' can only be deduced from the proposition ' B must (or cannot) be A,' when we are obliged to consider C implied in B. If, however, we only know as a fact (assertorially) that C is B, then we only know as a fact, likewise, that C is or is not that which we are obliged to

think connected or not connected with B.

[1] *Vid. supr.* p. 230.

[2] *Anal. Pr.* i. 2, 3, cf. c. 13, 32, a, 29 sqq. c. 17, 36, b, 15 sqq. ii. 1, 53, a, 3 sqq.

[3] Simple conversion of universal negative and particular affirmative judgments, particular conversion (later so-called *conversio per accidens*) of universal affirmative, and no conversion at all of particular negative judgments — for the *conversio per contrapositionem* was not as yet known to him.

[4] As he himself says, *Soph. El.* c. 34, 183, b, 34, 184, b, 1.

[5] Cf. PRANTL, *Gesch. d. Log.* i. 264.

[6] *Anal. Pr.* i. 24. b, 18: συλλογισμὸς δὲ ἐστι λόγος ἐν ᾧ τεθέντων τινῶν ἕτερόν τι τῶν κει-

The principle that this process in its simplest form involves no more than two assumptions, or more accurately
two judgments, from which a third is derived, and that
therefore no syllogistic conclusion can have more than
two premisses, is nowhere expressly proved by Aristotle
in the beginning of his treatise, though he refers to it
later.[1] Now the deduction of a third judgment from two
given judgments can only arise out of some bringing
into connection of the concepts, which in these given
judgments were as yet unconnected.[2] This is impossible, except a mediation be effected between them by
another concept connected with both of them.[3] Every
syllogism must therefore necessarily contain three concepts, no more and no less,[4] and of these the intermediate
is connected in the one premiss with the first and in
the other with the third, in such a way as to bring out
the connection between the first and third in the con-

μένων ἐξ ἀνάγκης συμβαίνει τῷ
ταῦτα εἶναι. (Likewise *Top.* i. 1,
100, a, 25, cf. *Soph. El.* c. 1, 165,
a. 1.) λέγω δὲ ʼτῷ ταῦτα εἶναιʼ τὸ
διὰ ταῦτα συμβαίνειν, τὸ δὲ ʻδιὰ
ταῦτα συμβαίνεινʼ τὸ μηδενὸς ἔξωθεν
ὅρου προσδεῖν πρὸς τὸ γενέσθαι τὸ
ἀναγκαῖον.
[1] *Anal. Pr.* i. 25, 42, a, 32.
As regards terminology, the premisses are generally called προτάσεις (*Metaph.* v. 2, 1013, b, 20:
ὑποθέσεις τοῦ συμπεράσματος); the
minor proposition in *Eth. N.* vi.
12, 1143, b, 3, vii. 5, 1147, b, 9 =
ἡ ἐτέρα (or τελευταία) πρότασις;
the conclusion invariably = συμπέρασμα. In *Anal. Pr.* ii. 1, 53,
a, 17 sqq., however, συμπέρασμα
stands for the subject of the conclusion.

[2] A principle which Aristotle
does not state in this form, but
which follows immediately from
his definition of Judgment, if we
apply it to the case before us.
[3] Cf. *Anal. Pr.* i. 23, b, 30
sqq., but especially 41, a, 2.
[4] *Anal. Pr.* i. c.25,*init. Ibid.*
42,b,1 sqq. on the number of concepts in whole series of syllogisms.
Of the three concepts of a syllogism (ὅροι, *vid. supr.* p. 219, n.1),
that which occurs in both premisses is called μέσος ; that which
comprehends the latter is called
the higher or greater (μεῖζον or πρῶτον ἄκρον) ; that which is comprehended by it, the lower or lesser
(ἔλαττον ἄκρον or ἔσχατον), *Anal.
Pr.* i. 4,25,b, 35, 32, 26,a, 21,c.38
init., and *Anal. Pr.* ii. 23, 68, b.

clusion. But this result may come in three ways. As
all judgments consist in the connecting of a subject
with a predicate (for Aristotle leaves hypothetical and
disjunctive judgments out of his reckoning), and as
the connecting of two judgments into a conclusion, or,
in other words, the deduction of the conclusion from the
premises, rests upon the relation of the intermediate
concept or middle term to the other two, it follows
that the mode of the connecting ('the form of the syllogism') will be determined by the way in which the
middle term is related to the others.[1] Now there are
only three ways possible : the middle term may either
be related as subject to the higher and as predicate to
the lower concept, or as predicate to both, or as subject
to both.[2] Aristotle does not take any direct notice of
a fourth possible case, in which it is the subject of the
lower and predicate of the higher ; but we need not
greatly blame him, for this fourth arrangement can

33 sq.; or the major concept is
called briefly ἄκρον, and the minor
τρίτον.

[1] *Anal. Pr.* i. 23, 41, a, 13, at
the end of the section on the
syllogistic figures, Aristotle, after
having treated of ·the necessity
and significance of the Middle
concept as a connecting-link
between Major and Minor, continues : εἰ οὖν ἀνάγκη μέν τι λαβεῖν
πρὸς ἄμφω κοινὸν, τοῦτο δ' ἐνδέχεται
(ἢ γὰρ τὸ Α τοῦ Γ καὶ τὸ Γ τοῦ Β
κατηγορέσαντας, ἢ τὸ Γ κατ' ἀμφοῖν, ἢ ἄμφω κατὰ τοῦ Γ), ταῦτα δ'
ἐστὶ τὰ εἰρημένα σχήματα, φανερὸν
ὅτι πάντα συλλογισμὸν ἀνάγκη γίνεσθαι διὰ τούτων τινὸς τῶν σχη-
μάτων. Cf. c. 32, 47, a, 40 sqq.,
and the searching discussion in

UEBERWEG'S *Logik*, § 103, p. 276
sqq.

[2] The position of the propositions has, as we know, no influence on the form of the syllogism.
The precedence of the major, customary since then, seemed more
natural to Aristotle than to us.
In laying down a syllogism, he
begins not, as we are accustomed
to do, with the subject, but with
the predicate of the major : A
ὑπάρχει παντὶ τῷ Β, Β ὑπάρχει παντὶ
τῷ Γ : so that, even in his form of
expression, there is a constant
descent from the greater to the
middle concept, and from that
to the lesser. Cf. UEBERWEG,
loc. cit. p. 276.

never occur in a single and rigorous chain of reasoning.[1] We obtain, then, three *Figures* (σχήματα)
which together sum up the categorical syllogism. The
so-called fourth figure of later logic[2] is ignored, and
neither the hypothetical nor the disjunctive syllogisms
are treated of as special forms in any way.[3]

If we ask what syllogisms are possible in these three
figures, it is to be observed that every syllogism must
contain a universal, and must also contain an affirmative
proposition ;[4] that the conclusion can only be universal
when both the premisses are so ;[5] and that in every
syllogism at least one of the premisses must resemble

---

[1] The proof of this cannot be
well given here.

[2] Cf. ZELLER, *Ph. d. Gr.*
iii. a, 738, 2nd ed. : and consult
especially PRANTL, *Gesch. d. Log.*
i. 570 sq.

[3] Whether this is a failing
or, as PRANTL (*Gesch. d. Leg.* i.
295) thinks, an advantage of
Aristotelian logic, it is not necessary here to inquire; but when that
learned writer, as well as BIESE
(*Phil. d. Arist.* i. 155), endeavours
to find that Aristotelian account
of hypothetical syllogisms, which
others miss, in the remarks on
supposition-syllogisms (συλλογισμοὶ ἐξ ὑποθέσεως) at *Anal. Pr.* i.
23, 40, b, 25, 41, a, 21 sqq. c. 29,
45, b, 22, c. 44, he confounds two
different things. Aristotle means
by a 'hypothetical syllogism'
that which begins with an unproved supposition (cf. WAITZ,
on *Anal.* 40, b, 25). We understand by it that of which the
major is a hypothetical judgment. And the two classes do
not by any means necessarily

coincide, for an unproved supposition may be expressed in a
categorical proposition, and conversely a hypothetical proposition may be fully demonstrable.
The same statement, can, in fact,
without changing its meaning,
be expressed both categorically
and hypothetically. Our modern
distinction of categorical and
hypothetical propositions regards
exclusively the form of the judgment, not the scientific certainty
of the proposition.

[4] *Anal. Pr.* i. 24 *init.*: ἔτι τε
ἐν ἅπαντι [sc. συλλογισμῷ] δεῖ
κατηγορικόν τινα τῶν ὅρων εἶναι καὶ
τὸ καθόλου ὑπάρχειν. The former
is not further proved, as Aristotle
supposes it to be clear from his
preceding explanation of the
syllogistic figures. By way of
proving the second, he proceeds :
ἄνευ γὰρ τοῦ καθόλου ἢ οὐκ ἔσται
συλλογισμὸς, ἢ οὐ πρὸς τὸ κείμενον,
ἢ τὸ ἐξ ἀρχῆς αἰτήσεται which will
be explained in detail in what
follows *infra*.

[5] *Loc. cit.* 41. b, 23.

the conclusion, both as to its quality and also as to its modality.[1] Yet Aristotle has nowhere deduced these rules on general principles from the nature of the syllogistic method. They are merely generalisations from his observation of the various forms of syllogism themselves. This analysis, however, he carries out with very great care. He is not satisfied with proving the well-known *moods* for the three figures,[2] but he also investigates minutely the influence which the modality of the premisses in pure and in mixed syllogisms must exercise upon the conclusion and upon the whole syllogistic process.[3] He regards the syllogisms of the first figure alone as 'perfect,' because, according to his view, they alone immediately reveal the necessity of the syllogistic sequence. Both the others yield 'imperfect' syllogisms, and require to be completed through the first. Their demonstrative value rests upon and is proved by the fact that they can be reduced to the first figure, either apagogically or by conversion.[4] These syllogistic forms are of course employed in the *reductio ad impossibile*, as well as in 'hypothetical' arguments generally.[5]

---

[1] *Loc. cit.* l. 27.

[2] For the first figure (to use the Scholastic designations) the moods: *Barbara, Darii, Celarent, Ferio* (*Anal. Pr.* i. 4); for the second: *Cesare, Camestres, Festino, Baroco* (*ibid.* c. 5); for the third: *Darapti, Felapton, Disamis, Datisi, Bocardo, Fresison* (c. 6).

[3] *Anal. Pr.* i. c. 8–23; cf. the discussion in n. 1 to p. 234, *supra*.

[4] See the sections cited, especially c. 4 *fin.*, c. 5 *fin.*, c. 6 *fin.*, c.

7, 29, a, 30, b, 1 sqq., c. 23, cf. c. 1, 24, b, 22 : τέλειον μὲν οὖν καλῶ συλλογισμὸν τὸν μηδενὸς ἄλλου προσδεόμενον παρὰ τὰ εἰλημμένα πρὸς τὸ φανῆναι τὸ ἀναγκαῖον, ἀτελῆ δὲ τὸν προσδεόμενον ἢ ἑνὸς ἢ πλειόνων, ἃ ἔστι μὲν ἀναγκαῖα διὰ τῶν ὑποκειμένων ὅρων οὐ μὴν εἴληπται διὰ προτάσεων. It is not necessary here to defend Aristotle's view.

[5] *Ibid.* c. 23, 41, a, 21 sqq. ; cf. *supra*, p. 238, n. 1.

With equal fulness does Aristotle set forth rules for the proper treatment of these forms in scientific use, and the errors to be avoided. He shows in the first instance what kind of propositions are more difficult to prove but more easy to confute, and *vice versa*.[1] Next he provides rules for the discovery of the fitting premisses, having regard to the quality and quantity of the conclusion to be proved,[2] and in doing so he takes occasion to censure[3] in passing the Platonic method of division.[4] On this head he treats minutely of the rules and methods which must be observed in order to reduce the materials of proof so discovered to the exact syllogistic form.[5] Furthermore he discusses the capacity of syllogisms in relation to the comprehension of their contents;[6] the syllogisms giving true conclusions from false premisses;[7] the *circulus in argu-*

[1] *Ibid.* c. 26.

[2] *Ibid.* c. 27–29, here also (c. 29) with express application to apagogic and supposition-syllogisms.

[3] To seek to define concepts by means of continuous divisions, he says (c. 31), is of no use; we have then to suppose the chief point that is to be proved. When it is a question of the concept of man as a ζῷον θνητὸν, then, he says, from the propositions 'All living beings are either mortal or immortal; man is a living being,' it would only follow that man is either mortal or immortal: that he is a ζῷον θνητὸν is a mere postulate. Hence Aristotle says of division, that it is οἷον ἀσθενὴς [not valid] συλλογισμός. Similarly in *Anal. Post.* ii. 5. Also in *Part. An.* i. 2 sq.;

the Platonic method is blamed because (contrary to the rule given at p. 216, n. 1) it multiplies unnecessarily the intermediate divisions, introduces the same thing under different genera, gives negative qualities, divides from all kinds of opposite points of view, &c. Cf. MEYER, *Arist. Thierkunde*, 71 sqq.

[4] See ZELL. *Ph. d. Gr.* pt. i. 523 sqq.

[5] *Loc. cit.* c. 32–46.

[6] *Anal. Pr.* ii. 1.

[7] *Ibid.* c. 2 *init.* (cf. *Top.* viii. 11 sq., 162, a, 9, b, 13): ἐξ ἀληθῶν μὲν οὖν οὐκ ἔστι ψεῦδος συλλογίσασθαι, ἐκ ψευδῶν δ' ἔστιν ἀληθές, πλὴν οὐ διότι ἀλλ' ὅτι· τοῦ γὰρ διότι οὐκ ἔστιν ἐκ ψευδῶν συλλογισμός (because false premisses give the ground itself, the διότι, falsely; cf. *supra*, p. 173, n. 2). Under what

endo;[1] the 'conversion' of the syllogism;[2] the *Reductio ad absurdum*;[3] syllogisms which result from the conversion of premisses into their opposites,[4] together with the various syllogistic fallacies and the means of meeting them.[5] Lastly he inquires into those kinds of proof which do not arise by *demonstration*, in the strict sense of the word,[6] and establishes the method of argument peculiar to each.[7] We cannot at this point

conditions this is possible in the different figures, is discussed in c. 2–4.

[1] Τὸ κύκλῳ καὶ ἐξ ἀλλήλων δείκνυσθαι. This consists in the conclusion of a syllogism (which, however, must of course be shown to be true from other sources) being used in conjunction with the converse of one premiss to prove the other. For the cases where this is possible, see *loc. cit.* c. 5–7. Against 'the vicious circle' in argument, see *Anal. Post.* i. 3, 72, b, 25.

[2] The destruction of one premiss by the other in conjunction with the contradictory or contrary of the conclusion; *loc. cit.* c. 8–10.

[3] The *Reductio ad absurdum*, ὁ διὰ τοῦ ἀδυνάτου συλλογισμός, c. 11–14, cf. *Top.* viii. 2, 157, b, 34, c. 12, 162, b, 5, and *Anal. Post.* i. 26, where it is remarked that direct proof is of greater scientific value.

[4] *Loc. cit.* c. xv.

[5] The *petitio principii* (τὸ ἐν ἀρχῇ αἰτεῖσθαι), c. 16, cf. *Top.* viii. 13; the μὴ παρὰ τοῦτο συμβαίνειν τὸ ψεῦδος, c. 17; the πρῶτον ψεῦδος, c. 18, cf. *Top.* viii. 10; rules for disputation deduced from this, c. 19, sq.; on deception by too hasty suppositions, c. 21; on proving certain suppositions by the transposition of the propositions in a syllogism, c. 22.

[6] Induction, c. 23; example, c. 24 (cf. *Anal. Post.* i. 1, 71, a, 9; *Rhet.* i. 2, 1356, b, 2, 1357, b, 25, ii. 20); ἀπαγωγὴ (reduction of one problem to another more easy to solve), c. 25; objection (ἔνστασις), c. 26; the syllogism from the probable (εἰκὸς) or certain marks (σημεῖα), which Aristotle calls the 'Enthymeme,' c. 27. The most important of these is 'Induction,' which we shall discuss later on. It consists in the major proposition being proved by the minor and the conclusion. *E.g.*, we may prove apodictically 'All animals which have little gall are long-lived; man, the horse &c. have little gall, and are therefore long-lived;' but the inductive proof will go thus: 'Man, the horse &c., are long-lived; man &c. have little gall; therefore animals which have little gall are long-lived.' This, however, only applies when the minor concept ('animals which have little gall') has an equal extension with the middle concept ('man &c.'), and when the minor proposition ('man &c. have little gall') can be simply transposed, so that in its place 'the animals which have little gall are man &c.' can be put (*loc. cit.* c. 23).

[7] See for a fuller discussion of these points, PRANTL, p. 299–

follow him into these researches, although we undoubtedly owe much to them in the application of the
syllogistic method, and though they prove most clearly
the care with which the great logician worked out
its many-sided detail.

The syllogistic system forms the foundation upon
which Aristotle built the theory of Scientific Proof,
which he set out in the second *Analytics*. All proof
is syllogistic, but not every syllogism is proof. It is
only the *Scientific Syllogism* which deserves this name.[1]
Science consists in the cognition of causes, and the
cause of a phenomenon is that from which it of necessity
arises.[2] Proof, therefore, and apprehension by means of
proof are only possible when something is explained
from its original causes.[3] Nothing can be the subject
of proof except that which is necessary. Proof is a
conclusion from necessary premisses.[4] That which is
ordinarily (though not without exception) true can be

321.—In the selection and sequence of the different sections no
strict order is observed, although
related subjects are put together.
On the division of the *Prior Analytics* as a whole, see BRANDIS, p.
204 sq., 219 sq.

[1] *Anal. Post.* i. 2, 71, ·b, 18 :
ἀπόδειξιν δὲ λέγω συλλογισμὸν
ἐπιστημονικόν. And after giving
the requisites for such an argument, he adds : συλλογισμὸς μὲν
γὰρ ἔσται καὶ ἄνευ τούτων, ἀπόδειξις
δ' οὐκ ἔσται· οὐ γὰρ ποιήσει ἐπιστήμην.

[2] *Loc. cit.* c. 2 init.: ἐπίστασθαι δὲ οἰόμεθ' ἕκαστον ἁπλῶς . . .
ὅταν τήν τ' αἰτίαν οἰώμεθα γινώσκειν
δι' ἣν τὸ πρᾶγμά ἐστιν, ὅτι ἐκείνου

αἰτία ἐστί, καὶ μὴ ἐνδέχεσθαι τοῦτ'
ἄλλως ἔχειν. Further references in
support of this, *supra*, p. 163, n. 3.

[3] *Ibid.* 71, b, 19 : εἰ τοίνυν
ἐστὶ τὸ ἐπίστασθαι οἷον ἔθεμεν,
ἀνάγκη καὶ τὴν ἀποδεικτικὴν ἐπιστήμην ἐξ ἀληθῶν τ' εἶναι καὶ πρώτων
καὶ ἀμέσων [about this below] καὶ
γνωριμωτέρων καὶ προτέρων τοῦ
συμπεράσματος· οὕτω γὰρ ἔσονται
καὶ αἱ ἀρχαὶ οἰκεῖαι τοῦ δεικνυμένου.
Ibid. line 29 : αἴτιά τε . . . δεῖ εἶναι
[sc. that from which a proof is
deduced] . . . ὅτι τότε ἐπιστάμεθα
ὅταν τὴν αἰτίαν εἰδῶμεν.

[4] *Ibid.* c. 4 init. : ἐπεὶ δ'
ἀδύνατον ἄλλως ἔχειν οὗ ἐστὶν
ἐπιστήμη ἁπλῶς, ἀναγκαῖον ἂν εἴη
τὸ ἐπιστητὸν τὸ κατὰ τὴν ἀποδεικ-

included under matters of proof only in a limited sense.¹
On the other hand, the contingent cannot be proved—
cannot even be known scientifically.² And since necessary truth is that only which proceeds from the essence
and the idea of the subject, while everything else is
contingent, so it may be said that all proof relates to
and is founded exclusively upon the essential characteristics of things, and that the concept of each thing
is at once its starting-point and goal.³ The purer and
more perfect the information, therefore, which any
form of Proof secures to us concerning the *conceptual
nature* and the causes of an object, the higher is
the kind of knowledge which it warrants; and so, other
things being equal, a universal proof ranks above a
particular, a positive proof above a negative, a direct
above an apagogic, one which enables us to know the
cause above that which merely instructs us in the fact.⁴

τικὴν ἐπιστήμην. ἀποδεικτικὴ δ'
ἐστὶν ἣν ἔχομεν τῷ ἔχειν ἀπόδειξιν·
ἐξ ἀναγκαίων ἄρα συλλογισμός ἐστιν
ἡ ἀπόδειξις. Cf. note 3 *infra.*

¹ *Metaph.* xi. 8, 1065, a, 4 :
ἐπιστήμη μὲν γὰρ πᾶσα τοῦ ἀεὶ
ὄντος ἢ ὡς ἐπὶ τὸ πολύ, τὸ δὲ
συμβεβηκὸς ἐν οὐδετέρῳ τούτων
ἐστίν. *Anal. Post.* i. 30 : πᾶς γὰρ
συλλογισμὸς ἢ δι' ἀναγκαίων ἢ διὰ
τῶν ὡς ἐπὶ τὸ πολὺ προτάσεων·
καὶ εἰ μὲν αἱ προτάσεις ἀναγκαῖαι,
καὶ τὸ συμπέρασμα ἀναγκαῖον, εἰ δ'
ὡς ἐπὶ τὸ πολύ, καὶ τὸ συμπέρασμα
τοιοῦτον. Cf. p 168, n 1.

² *Anal. Post.* i. 6, 5, a, 18,
c. 30 ; cf. c. 8, c. 33, &c.; *vid.
supra,* p. 164, n. 2.

³ *Ibid.* c. 6 *init.* : εἰ οὖν ἐστὶν
ἡ ἀποδεικτικὴ ἐπιστήμη ἐξ ἀναγκαίων ἀρχῶν (ὃ γὰρ ἐπίσταται οὐ
δυνατὸν ἄλλως ἔχειν) τὰ δὲ καθ'
αὑτὰ ὑπάρχοντα ἀναγκαῖα τοῖς

πράγμασιν . . . φανερὸν ὅτι ἐκ
τοιούτων τινῶν ἂν εἴη ὁ ἀποδεικτικὸς
συλλογισμός· ἅπαν γὰρ ἢ οὕτως
ὑπάρχει ἢ κατὰ συμβεβηκός, τὰ δὲ
συμβεβηκότα οὐκ ἀναγκαῖα. *Ibid.*
at the end: ἐπεὶ δ' ἐξ ἀνάγκης
ὑπάρχει περὶ ἕκαστον γένος ὅσα καθ'
αὑτὰ ὑπάρχει καὶ ᾗ ἕκαστον, φανερὸν
ὅτι περὶ τῶν καθ' αὑτὰ ὑπαρχόντων
αἱ ἐπιστημονικαὶ ἀποδείξεις καὶ ἐκ
τῶν τοιούτων εἰσίν. τὰ μὲν γὰρ
συμβεβηκότα οὐκ ἀναγκαῖα, ὥστ'
οὐκ ἀνάγκη τὸ συμπέρασμα εἰδέναι
διότι ὑπάρχει, οὐδ' εἰ ἀεὶ εἴη, μὴ
καθ' αὑτὸ δέ, οἷον οἱ διὰ σημείων
συλλογισμοί. τὸ γὰρ καθ' αὑτὸ οὐ
καθ' αὑτὸ ἐπιστήσεται, οὐδὲ διότι.
τὸ δὲ διότι ἐπίστασθαί ἐστι τὸ διὰ
τοῦ αἰτίου ἐπίστασθαι. δι' αὑτὸ ἄρα
δεῖ καὶ τὸ μέσον τῷ τρίτῳ καὶ τὸ
πρῶτον τῷ μέσῳ ὑπάρχειν. Cf.
p. 213, n. 5 *supra.*

⁴ *Anal. Post.* i. 14, c. 24–27.

If we take demonstration as a whole, and consider the building up of a scientific system, it is an axiom that the knowledge of the universal must precede that of the particular.[1] The same considerations lead up from another point of view to a principle which is deeply rooted in Aristotle's whole way of thinking : that nothing can be demonstrated except from its own peculiar principles, and that it is inadmissible to borrow proofs from without. Demonstration, he thinks, should start from the essential characteristics of the object in question, and any properties which belong to another genus can only accidentally attach to it, seeing that they form no part of its concept.[2] All demonstration, consequently, hinges on the concept of the thing. Its problem consists in determining, not only the properties which attach to any object by virtue of the conception of it, but also the media by which they are attached to it. Its function is to deduce the particular from the universal, phenomena from their causes.

Is this process of 'mediation' unending, or has it a necessary limit ? Aristotle takes the latter alternative, from three points of view.

[1] *Phys.* iii. 1, 200, b, 24 : ὑστέρα γὰρ ἡ περὶ τῶν ἰδίων θεωρία τῆς περὶ τῶν κοινῶν ἐστίν.

[2] *Anal. Post.* i. 7 *init.* : οὐκ ἄρα ἔστιν ἐξ ἄλλου γένους μεταβάντα δεῖξαι, οἷον τὸ γεωμετρικὸν ἀριθμητικῇ. τρία γάρ ἐστι τὰ ἐν ταῖς ἀποδείξεσιν, ἓν μὲν τὸ ἀποδεικνύμενον τὸ συμπέρασμα· τοῦτο δ' ἐστὶ τὸ ὑπάρχον γένει τινὶ καθ' αὑτό. ἓν δὲ τὰ ἀξιώματα· ἀξιώματα δ' ἐστὶν ἐξ ὧν [sc. αἱ ἀποδείξεις εἰσίν]. τρίτον τὸ γένος τὸ ὑποκείμενον, οὗ τὰ πάθη καὶ τὰ καθ' αὑτὸ συμβεβηκότα δηλοῖ ἡ ἀπόδειξις. ἐξ ὧν μὲν οὖν ἡ ἀπό-δειξις, ἐνδέχεται τὰ αὐτὰ εἶναι· ὧν δὲ τὸ γένος ἕτερον, ὥσπερ ἀριθμητικῆς καὶ γεωμετρίας, οὐκ ἔστι τὴν ἀριθμητικὴν ἀπόδειξιν ἐφαρμόσαι ἐπὶ τὰ τοῖς μεγέθεσι συμβεβηκότα . . . ὥστ' ἢ ἁπλῶς ἀνάγκη τὸ αὐτὸ εἶναι γένος ἢ πῇ, εἰ μέλλει ἡ ἀπόδειξις μεταβαίνειν. ἄλλως δ' ὅτι ἀδύνατον, δῆλον· ἐκ γὰρ τοῦ αὐτοῦ γένους ἀνάγκη τὰ ἄκρα καὶ τὰ μέσα εἶναι. εἰ γὰρ μὴ καθ' αὑτὰ, συμβεβηκότα ἔσται. διὰ τοῦτο . . . οὐκ ἔστι δεῖξαι . . . ἄλλῃ ἐπιστήμῃ τὸ ἑτέρας, ἀλλ' ἢ ὅσα οὕτως ἔχει πρὸς ἄλληλα ὥστ' εἶναι θάτερον ὑπὸ θάτερον ; c.

We may rise from the particular to the general—
from the subject, beyond which there is nothing of
which it can be predicated—to continually higher predicates : and we may, on the other hand, descend from
the most universal point—from that predicate which is
the subject of no other predicate—down to the particular. But in any case we must arrive eventually
at a point where this progression ceases, otherwise we
could never reach an effectual demonstration or definition.[1] The argument excludes also the third hypothesis,
that there may exist an infinite number of intermediate
terms between a definite subject and a definite predicate.[2] If the list of middle terms is not infinite, it
follows that there are things of which there cannot be a
demonstration or derived knowledge.[3] For wherever the
middle terms cease, immediate knowledge must necessarily take the place of demonstration. To demonstrate
everything is not possible. If we attempt it we are
either brought round again to that progression *ad
infinitum* already mentioned, which annuls all possibility of knowledge and Proof, or else to ' arguing in
a circle,' which is equally incapable of producing a
solid demonstration.[4] There remains, therefore, but one

9 *init.* : φανερὸν ὅτι ἕκαστον ἀπο-
δεῖξαι οὐκ ἔστιν ἀλλ' ἢ ἐκ τῶν
ἑκάστου ἀρχῶν, &c. We return
to this later on.

[1] For he says at 83, b, 6, 84,
a, 3 : τὰ ἄπειρα οὐκ ἔστι διεξελθεῖν
νοοῦντα. Cf. note 4 *infra.*

[2] *Ibid.* ch. 19–22. The details
of this treatment, in parts not
very clear, cannot well be repeated here. We have already
seen at p. 222, n, 2, that Aristotle

supposes a limit to the number of
concepts above as well as below.

[3] Ch. 22, 84, a, 30; and so *Metaph.* iii. 2, 997, a, 7 : περὶ πάντων
γὰρ ἀδύνατον ἀπόδειξιν εἶναι· ἀνάγκη
γὰρ ἔκ τινων εἶναι καὶ περί τι καὶ
τινῶν τὴν ἀπόδειξιν.

[4] After Aristotle (*Anal. Post.* i.
2) has shown that the proof-power
of syllogisms is conditional on
the scientific knowledge of the
premisses, he continues, in ch. 3 :

conclusion, that in the last resort demonstration must start from propositions which, by reason of their *immediate certainty*, neither admit nor stand in need of proof.[1] These 'principles' of all proof[2] must possess

'Many conclude from this, that no knowledge at all is possible; others, that everything can be proved.' But he confutes both assertions. Of the former he says : οἱ μὲν γὰρ ὑποθέμενοι μὴ εἶναι ὅλως ἐπίστασθαι, οὗτοι εἰς ἄπειρον ἀξιοῦσιν ἀνάγεσθαι ὡς οὐκ ἂν ἐπισταμένους τὰ ὕστερα διὰ τὰ πρότερα, ὧν μή ἐστι πρῶτα, ὀρθῶς λέγοντες, ἀδύνατον γὰρ τὰ ἄπειρα διελθεῖν. εἴ τε ἵστανται καὶ εἰσὶν ἀρχαὶ, ταύτας ἀγνώστους εἶναι ἀποδείξεώς γε μὴ οὔσης αὐτῶν, ὅπερ φασὶν εἶναι τὸ ἐπίστασθαι μόνον· εἰ δὲ μὴ ἔστι τὰ πρῶτα εἰδέναι, οὐδὲ τὰ ἐκ τούτων εἶναι ἐπίστασθαι ἁπλῶς οὐδὲ κυρίως, ἀλλ' ἐξ ὑποθέσεως, εἰ ἐκεῖνά ἐστιν. He admits that what is deduced would not be *known* if the principles (ἀρχαὶ) are not *known*, and that if mediate knowledge, by way of proof, is the only *knowledge*, then there can be no knowledge of ἀρχαὶ. Yet he himself in the same treatise denies this very thing at p. 72, b, 18 ; cf. *Metaph.* iv. 4, 1006, a, 6 : ἔστι γὰρ ἀπαιδευσία τὸ μὴ γιγνώσκειν, τίνων δεῖ ζητεῖν ἀπόδειξιν καὶ τίνων οὐ δεῖ· ὅλως μὲν γὰρ ἁπάντων ἀδύνατον ἀπόδειξιν εἶναι· εἰς ἄπειρον γὰρ ἂν βαδίζοι, ὥστε μηδ' οὕτως εἶναι ἀπόδειξιν. As to the second of the above propositions, Aristotle states it at p. 72, b, 16, in other words— πάντων εἶναι ἀπόδειξιν οὐδὲν κωλύειν· ἐνδέχεσθαι γὰρ κύκλῳ γίνεσθαι τὴν ἀπόδειξιν καὶ ἐξ ἀλλήλων—and then at ll. 25 sqq. of the same page he goes on to

refute it by reference to his earlier exposition on the subject of ' reasoning in a circle ' (*de quo v. supra*, p. 242, n. 1).

[1] *Anal. Post.* c. 2, 71, b, 20 : ἀνάγκη καὶ τὴν ἀποδεικτικὴν ἐπιστήμην ἐξ ἀληθῶν τ' εἶναι καὶ πρώτων καὶ ἀμέσων καὶ γνωριμωτέρων καὶ προτέρων καὶ αἰτίων τοῦ συμπεράσματος. . . . ἐκ πρώτων δ' ἀναποδείκτων, ὅτι οὐκ ἐπιστήσεται μὴ ἔχων ἀπόδειξιν αὐτῶν [because otherwise if they were not ἀναπόδεικτοι we could, likewise, only know them by proof]; τὸ γὰρ ἐπίστασθαι ὧν ἀπόδειξίς ἐστι μὴ κατὰ συμβεβηκὸς, τὸ ἔχειν ἀπόδειξίν ἐστιν. c. 3, 72, b, 18 : ἡμεῖς δέ φαμεν οὔτε πᾶσαν ἐπιστήμην ἀποδεικτικὴν εἶναι, ἀλλὰ τὴν τῶν ἀμέσων ἀναπόδεικτον. . . . καὶ οὐ μόνον ἐπιστήμην ἀλλὰ καὶ ἀρχὴν ἐπιστήμης εἶναί τινά φαμεν, ᾗ τοὺς ὅρους γνωρίζομεν. Cf. *supra*, p. 197, n. 6, and 210, n. 2, 179, n. 4, and 210, n. 2 *fin.* On the other hand, the circumstance that a thing is always so is no reason for rejecting proof by causes, for even the eternal may have its causes on which it is conditional ; see *Gen. An.* ii. 6, 742, b, 17 sqq.

[2] Ἀρχαὶ, ἀρχαὶ ἀποδείξεως, ἀρχαὶ συλλογιστικαί, ἀ. ἄμεσοι, προτάσεις ἄμεσοι, *Anal. Post.* 72, a, 7, 14, c. 10 *init.* (λέγω δ' ἀρχὰς ἐν ἑκάστῳ γένει ταύτας, ὡς ὅτι ἔστι μὴ ἐνδέχεται δεῖξαι) ; ii. 19, 99, b, 21, cf. p. 197, n. 4 ; *Gen. An.* ii. 6, 742, b, 29 sqq.; *Metaph.* v. 1, 1013, a, 14, iii. 1, 2, 995, b, 28, 996, b, 27, iv. 3, and also cf. *Ind,*

even a higher certainty than anything deduced from them.[1] Consequently, the soul must contain a faculty of immediate knowledge higher and more sure than any mediate cognition. And, in fact, Aristotle finds in the *Nous*—the pure reason—just such a faculty; and he maintains that it never deceives itself, that in every case it either *has* its object or has it *not*, but never has it in a *false* or illusive way.[2]

Yet it must be admitted that he has neither proved the possibility nor the infallibility of any such knowledge. This immediate certainty, he says, is of two kinds. There are three elements in every process of demonstration: that which is proved, the principles from which it is proved,[3] and the object of which it is proved. The first of these is not matter of immediate knowledge, for it is deduced from the other two. These, again, are themselves distinguished in this way, that the axioms are common to different fields of knowledge, but the postulates relating to the special

---

Arist. 111, b, 58 sqq. In *Anal. Post.* i. 2, 72, a, 14, Aristotle proposes to call the unproved premiss of a syllogism θέσις, if it refers to a particular fact, ἀξίωμα if it expresses a universal presupposition of all proof. Again, if a θέσις contains an affirmation as to the existence or non-existence of an object, it is a ὑπόθεσις ; if otherwise, a ὁρισμός. Θέσις is used in a broader meaning in *Anal. Pr.* ii. 17, 65, b, 13, 66, a, 2, and *Anal. Post.* i. 3, 73, a, 9 ; in a narrower one in *Top.* i. 11, 104, b, 19, 35. (For further references see *Ind. Ar.* 327, b, 18 sqq.)—For ἀξίωμα, which is

also used in a wider sense, see *Anal. Post.* i. 7, 75, a, 41, c. 10, 76, b, 14, and *Metaph.* iii. 2, 997, a, 5, 12.—Αἴτημα is distinguished from ὑπόθεσις in *Anal. Post.* i. 10, 76, b, 23 sqq.

[1] *Anal. Post.* i. 2, 72, a, 25 sqq. ; cf. p. 247, n. 1.

[2] *Vide supra*, p. 197 sqq., where Aristotle's view of this 'immediate knowledge' is explained.

[3] *Anal. Post.* i. 7 (as cited *supra*, p. 245, n. 3), and *ibid.* ch. 10, 76, b, 10 : πᾶσα γὰρ ἀποδεικτικὴ ἐπιστήμη περὶ τρία ἐστίν, ὅσα τε εἶναι τίθεται (ταῦτά δ᾿ ἐστι τὸ γένος οὗ τῶν καθ᾿ αὐτὰ παθημάτων ἐστὶ θεωρητικὴ), καὶ τὰ λεγόμενα κοινὰ

matter are peculiar to the particular science.¹ It is only upon postulates which are proper to a particular department that he allows a binding demonstration to be founded.² But these postulates are just as little capable as the universal axioms of being deduced from a higher law.³ They must be supplied to us by our knowledge of that particular object to which they relate.⁴ They are therefore matter of observation—of experience.⁵ How such an experience could come to

ἀξιώματα ἐξ ὧν πρώτων ἀποδείκνυσι, καὶ τρίτον τὰ πάθη . . . τρία ταῦτά ἐστι, περὶ ὅ τε δείκνυσι καὶ ἃ δείκνυσι κ^λ ἐξ ὧν. *Metaph.* iii. 2, 997, a, 8 : ἀνάγκη γὰρ ἔκ τινων εἶναι καὶ περί τι καὶ τινῶν τὴν ἀπόδειξιν. In ch. 6 he gives γένος ὑποκείμενον, πάθη, ἀξιώματα in another order.

¹ *Anal. Post.* i. 7, *cit. supr.* p. 245, n. 3, and *ibid.* c. 10, 76, a, 37 : ἔστι δ' ὧν χρῶνται ἐν ταῖς ἀποδεικτικαῖς ἐπιστήμαις τὰ μὲν ἴδια ἑκάστης ἐπιστήμης τὰ δὲ κοινά . . . ἴδια μὲν οἷον γραμμὴν εἶναι τοιανδὶ καὶ τὸ εὐθύ, κοινὰ δὲ οἷον τὸ ἴσα ἀπὸ ἴσων ἂν ἀφέλῃ ὅτι ἴσα τὰ λοιπά. c. 32 *init.*: τὰς δ' αὐτὰς ἀρχὰς ἁπάντων εἶναι τῶν συλλογισμῶν ἀδύνατον, and after this has been proved at length he says at the end : αἱ γὰρ ἀρχαὶ διτταί, ἐξ ὧν τε καὶ περὶ ὅ· αἱ μὲν οὖν ἐξ ὧν κοιναί, αἱ δὲ περὶ ὃ ἴδιαι, οἷον ἀριθμός, μέγεθος. More about the ἀποδεικτικαὶ ἀρχαὶ or the κοιναὶ δόξαι ἐξ ὧν ἅπαντες δεικνύουσιν will be found in the passages cited at p. 247, n. 2.

² *Vid. supr.* p. 245, n. 3 ; *Gen. An.* ii. 8, 748, a, 7 : οὗτος μὲν οὖν ὁ λόγος καθόλου λίαν καὶ κενός. οἱ γὰρ μὴ ἐκ τῶν οἰκείων ἀρχῶν λόγοι κενοί, ἀλλὰ δοκοῦσιν εἶναι τῶν πραγμάτων οὐκ ὄντες. Cf. p. 174, n. 2, *supra.*

³ *Anal. Post.* i. 9, 76, a, 16

(following on the passage cited *supra,* p. 245, n. 3,) : εἰ δὲ φανερὸν τοῦτο, φανερὸν καὶ ὅτι οὐκ ἔστι τὰς ἑκάστου ἰδίας ἀρχὰς ἀποδεῖξαι· ἔσονται γὰρ [for there *would* be] ἐκεῖναι ἁπάντων ἀρχαὶ καὶ ἐπιστήμη ἡ ἐκείνων κυρία πάντων. Cf. ch. 10, cited p. 248, n. 3 *supra.*

⁴ *Anal. Pr.* i. 30, 46, a, 17 : ἴδιαι δὲ καθ' ἑκάστην [ἐπιστήμην] αἱ πλεῖσται [ἀρχαὶ τῶν συλλογισμῶν]. διὸ τὰς μὲν ἀρχὰς τὰς περὶ ἕκαστον ἐμπειρίας ἐστὶ παραδοῦναι. λέγω δ' οἷον τὴν ἀστρολογικὴν μὲν ἐμπειρίαν τῆς ἀστρολογικῆς ἐπιστήμης. ληφθέντων γὰρ ἱκανῶς τῶν φαινομένων οὕτως εὑρέθησαν αἱ ἀστρολογικαὶ ἀποδείξεις. So in *Hist. An.* i. 7 *init.*: we have first to describe the peculiar properties of animals, and then to discuss their causes : οὕτω γὰρ κατὰ φύσιν ἐστὶ ποιεῖσθαι τὴν μέθοδον, ὑπαρχούσης τῆς ἱστορίας τῆς περὶ ἕκαστον· περὶ ὧν τε γὰρ καὶ ἐξ ὧν εἶναι δεῖ τὴν ἀπόδειξιν, ἐκ τούτων γίνεται φανερόν.

⁵ Cf. preceding note, and the remark in *Eth.* vi. 9, 1142, a, 11 sqq., that young people can make advances in the knowledge of Mathematics, but not in Natural History or the wisdom of life, ὅτι τὰ μὲν [Mathematics] δι' ἀφαιρέσεώς ἐστιν [is an abstract

pass, he does not further inquire. Sense-perception he treats as a simple datum, whose elements he does not try to analyse. He even includes cases which are to us merely judgments upon given materials, among what he calls immediate certainties.[1] It is therefore impossible to give a clear and sufficient account of the faculties to which, according to him, we are indebted for the immediate truths in question.[2]

To enumerate the special presuppositions of all the various sciences is also obviously impossible. Even a general view of the universal axioms is not to be found

science], τῶν δ' αἱ ἀρχαὶ ἐξ ἐμπειρίας.

[1] It is said in *Eth.* iii. 5, 1112, b, 33, that practical reflection (βούλευσις) is concerned with τὰ καθ' ἕκαστα, οἷον εἰ ἄρτος τοῦτο ἢ πέπεπται ὡς δεῖ· αἰσθήσεως γὰρ ταῦτα. *Ibid.* vi. 9, 1142, a, 23 sqq., Aristotle explains that, in contradiction to ἐπιστήμη, φρόνησις is, like νοῦς, an immediate knowledge; but whilst the latter is concerned with the ὅροι, ὧν οὐκ ἔστι λόγος (the ' highest principles,' which in this case are practical principles), φρόνησις is a knowledge τοῦ ἐσχάτου, οὗ οὐκ ἔστιν ἐπιστήμη ἀλλ' αἴσθησις, οὐχ ἡ τῶν ἰδίων [the sensible properties of things] ἀλλ' οἵᾳ αἰσθανόμεθα, ὅτι τὸ ἐν τοῖς μαθηματικοῖς ἔσχατον τρίγωνον (*i.e.* the last thing obtained in analysing a figure in a triangle). Here, therefore, the judgment ' This is a triangle ' is explained as a matter of αἴσθησις (and so also in *Anal. Post.* i. 1, 71, a, 20) and the minor premisses of practical syllogisms, such as ' This deed is just,' ' This is useful,' &c., are re-

ferred to an αἴσθησις in like manner. (See also the discussion of φρόνησις in ch. xii. *infra.*) So in *Eth.* iii. 12, 1143, b, 5, referring to the same class of propositions he says: τούτων οὖν ἔχειν δεῖ αἴσθησιν, αὕτη δ' ἐστὶ νοῦς. Now, although (as is indicated in c. 9 *fin.*) αἴσθησις is here to be taken as in *Polit.* i. 2, 1253, a, 17, in the wider signification of ' consciousness,' still it always means an ' immediate knowledge,' as distinguished from an ἐπιστήμη. KAMPE (*Erkenntnissl. d. Ar.* 220 sq.) finds in the above passages, a proof that Book VI. of the *Nicomachean Ethics* originally belonged to the *Eudemian* ; but *Polit.* i. 2, shows how unfounded is this conclusion. As little does it follow from *Eth.* vi. 3, 1139, b, 33—where the εἰ μὲν γάρ πως πιστεύῃ, &c., does not mean ' we have knowledge when we have *any* conviction,' but ' knowledge consists in *a definite kind* of conviction based on known principles.'

[2] For proof of this, see ch. xii. *infra.*

in Aristotle. He merely seeks to determine which of all principles is the most incontestable, obvious, and unconditional,[1] so that it can involve no possible error. This he finds in the Law of Contradiction.[2] No one can seriously doubt this principle, though many may pretend to do so; but just because it is the highest principle of all, it admits of no demonstration—it cannot, that is to say, be deduced from any higher law. It is certainly possible to defend it against objections of every kind, by showing either that they rest upon misunderstandings, or that they themselves presuppose the axiom in question and destroy themselves in attacking it.[3] He has, however, carefully guarded against any

---

[1] *Metaph.* iv. 3, 1005, b, 11 : βεβαιοτάτη δ' ἀρχὴ πασῶν περὶ ἣν διαψευσθῆναι ἀδύνατον · γνωριμωτά- την τε γὰρ ἀναγκαῖον εἶναι τὴν τοιαύτην (περὶ γὰρ ἃ μὴ γνωρίζουσιν ἀπατῶνται πάντες) καὶ ἀνυπόθετον. ἣν γὰρ ἀναγκαῖον ἔχειν τὸν ὁτιοῦν ξυνιέντα τῶν ὄντων, τοῦτο οὐχ ὑπόθεσις.

[2] Line 19 (xi. 5 *init.*): τὸ γὰρ αὐτὸ ἅμα ὑπάρχειν τε καὶ μὴ ὑπάρ- χειν ἀδύνατον τῷ αὐτῷ καὶ κατὰ τὸ αὐτό · καὶ ὅσα ἄλλα προσδιορισαίμεθ' ἄν, ἔστω προσδιωρισμένα πρὸς λογι- κὰς δυσχερείας. αὕτη δὴ πασῶν ἐστι βεβαιοτάτη τῶν ἀρχῶν. The axiom that 'opposites cannot belong to the same thing in the same re- spect, is only a form of this. And the further principle that 'no one can really ascribe such opposites at once to anything' is so closely connected that sometimes the latter is proved from the former, at other times the former from the latter; cf. *Anal. Post.*, *ut supra*, line 26 : εἰ δὲ μὴ ἐνδέχεται ἅμα ὑπάρχειν τῷ αὐτῷ τἀναντία

(προσδιωρίσθω δ' ἡμῖν καὶ ταύτῃ τῇ προτάσει τὰ εἰωθότα), ἐναντία δ' ἐστὶ δόξα δόξῃ ἡ τῆς ἀντιφάσεως, φανερὸν ὅτι ἀδύνατον ἅμα ὑπολαμβά- νειν τὸν αὐτὸν εἶναι καὶ μὴ εἶναι τὸ αὐτό · ἅμα γὰρ ἂν ἔχοι τὰς ἐναντίας δόξας ὁ διεψευσμένος περὶ τούτου. *Ibid.* c. 6, 1011, b, 15 : ἐπεὶ δ' ἀδύνατον τὴν ἀντίφασιν ἀληθεύεσθαι ἅμα κατὰ τοῦ αὐτοῦ [for which at line 20 he substitutes ἅμα καταφά- ναι καὶ ἀποφάναι ἀληθῶς], φανερὸν ὅτι οὐδὲ τἀναντία ἅμα ὑπάρχειν ἐν- δέχεται τῷ αὐτῷ . . . ἀλλ' ἢ πῇ ἄμφω, ἢ θάτερον μὲν πῇ θάτερον δὲ ἁπλῶς.

[3] In this sense Aristotle in *Metaph.* iv. 4 sq. confutes the statement (which, however, he only ascribes to certain of the older schools as being in his view an inference from their tenets ; cf. ZELLER, *Ph. d. Gr.* part i. 600 sq., 910, 4), that ' an object can both be and not be the same thing at the same time,' by proving that in every statement the principle of non-contradic-

sophistical misuse of it to deny the connection of
different properties in one subject, or the possibility of
becoming and of change, by that detailed exposition of it
in which he shows that it is not absolutely impossible
that contradictions should be predicated of the same
subject, but only that they should be so predicated
together and in the same relation.[1]

By similar arguments to these with which he established the Law of Contradiction, he lays down that of
the Excluded Middle[2] as an incontestable Axiom.[3]
But he does not expressly deduce the one from the
other.

Though Aristotle maintains so decidedly that every
kind of knowledge brought about by demonstration is
doubly conditioned by an immediate and undemonstrable conviction of the mind, yet he is far from representing this conviction as itself incapable of scientific
verification. The starting-point of all demonstration is
undemonstrable—it is incapable of being deduced from
any other principle as from its cause. Yet it can be
shown from the given facts to be the condition which
underlies them, and which their existence presup-

tion is presupposed. In c. 5
init., c. 6 (cf. c. 4, 1007, b, 22,
xi. 6 *init.*), he reduces to the
same principle the dictum (*de
quo v.* ZELLER, *Ph. d. Gr.* part i.
982, 1, 988, 2) that 'that is true
for each one which appears so to
him'; and to this, amongst other
arguments — coinciding broadly
with the Platonic *Theœtetus*—he
especially opposes the objection
(1011, a, 17 sqq. b, 4) that since
every φαινόμενον must be a τινὶ

φαινόμενον, the dictum would
make *everything* a πρός τι.

[1] See preceding note.

[2] Οὐδὲ μεταξὺ ἀντιφάσεως ἐνδέχεται εἶναι οὐδέν ; cf. p. 230, *supra*.

[3] *Metaph.* iv. 7 ; in applying
his argument, Aristotle has
adopted here those reasons
which are borrowed from the consideration of Change in Nature,
evidently wishing to prove his
theory not only as a logical, but
also as a metaphysical principle.

poses. So in the place of Demonstration, comes in Induction.[1] There are thus two lines of scientific thinking which require to be distinguished: the one which leads up to principles, the other which leads down from principles [2]—the movement from the universal to the particular, from that which is *in itself* the more certain to that which is so *for us*; and the reverse movement from the individual, as that which is best known to us, to the universal, which is in its own nature the more sure. In the former direction goes syllogism and scientific demonstration: in the latter goes induction.[3] And by one or other of these ways all knowledge comes to be. That which by virtue of its

---

[1] Cf. with what follows the references on p. 242, n. 6 *supra*. The name ' ἐπαγωγή ' refers either to the *adducing* of particular instances, from which a universal proposition or concept is abstracted (TRENDELENBURG, *Elem. Log. Arist.* 84 : HEYDER, *Vergl. d. arist. und hegel. Dialektik*, p. 212 sq.), or to the *introduction* to these instances of the person to be instructed (WAITZ, *Arist. Org.* ii. 300). In favour of the latter explanation there are certain passages, in which ' ἐπάγειν ' has as its object the person knowing; as *Top.* viii. 1, 156, a, 4 : ἐπάγοντα μὲν ἀπὸ τῶν καθέκαστον ἐπὶ τὰ καθόλου, but especially *Anal. Post.* i. 1, 71, a, 19 : ὅτι μὲν γὰρ πᾶν τρίγωνον ἔχει δυσὶν ὀρθαῖς ἴσας, προῄδει, ὅτι δὲ τόδε . . . τρίγωνόν ἐστιν, ἅμα ἐπαγόμενος ἐγνώρισεν . . . πρὶν δ' ἐπαχθῆναι ἢ λαβεῖν συλλογισμὸν, τρόπον μέν τινα ἴσως φατέον ἐπίστασθαι, &c.; c. 18, 81, b, 5 : ἐπαχθῆναι δὲ μὴ

ἔχοντας αἴσθησιν ἀδύνατον. ' Ἐπάγειν,' however, also means ' to prove by induction,' as in ἐπάγειν τὸ καθόλου, *Top.* i. 18, 108, b, 10 ; *Soph. El.* 15, 174, a, 34.

[2] *Eth. N.* i. 2, 1095, a, 30 ; cf. ZELLER, *Ph. d. Gr.* pt. i. 491, 2 ; and see p. 205, n. 2 *supra*.

[3] Besides Induction, HEYDER (*Vergl. d. arist. und hegel. Dial.* 232 sq.) finds in Aristotle (*Phys.* i. 1, 184, a, 21 sqq.) indications of another process, by which we should proceed from the universal of sensible perception to the concept, as the more particular and definite—just as in induction we go from the particular in perception to the universal of the concept. But he himself rightly observes that this is only an induction reversed (though this case is not usually made very prominent by Aristotle). When a universal is brought out as that which is common to many individual cases, it is thereby

nature admits of no demonstration must be established by induction.[1] We have already remarked that this undemonstrable element of thought need not necessarily be abstracted from experience, but that Aristotle rather regards the universal axioms as apprehended by the spontaneous activity of the reason.[2] But as he sees that this activity of reason is only gradually developed in the individual under the guidance of experience, so he believes there are no other means of scientifically verifying its content and deliverance but by a comprehensive induction.[3] Many difficulties are involved in this. For inductive reasoning is founded,

separated from the complex in which it presents itself to perception; and this is all that Aristotle has in his mind in the passage cited; cf. p. 205 sq. *supra.*
[1] *Anal. Pri.* ii. 23, 68, b, 13 : ἅπαντα γὰρ πιστεύομεν ἢ διὰ συλλογισμοῦ ἢ δι' ἐπαγωγῆς. *Ibid.* at line 35 ; *vid. supr.* p. 206, n. 1 ; *Eth.* i. 7, 1098, b, 3 : τῶν ἀρχῶν δ' αἱ μὲν ἐπαγωγῇ θεωροῦνται, αἱ δ' αἰσθήσει, &c. ; vi. 3, 1139, b, 26 : ἐκ προγινωσκομένων δὲ πᾶσα διδασκαλία · . . . ἡ μὲν γὰρ δι' ἐπαγωγῆς, ἡ δὲ συλλογισμῷ. ἡ μὲν δὴ ἐπαγωγὴ ἀρχή ἐστι καὶ τοῦ καθόλου, ὁ δὲ συλλογισμὸς ἐκ τῶν καθόλου. εἰσὶν ἄρα ἀρχαὶ ἐξ ὧν ὁ συλλογισμὸς, ὧν οὐκ ἔστι συλλογισμός · ἐπαγωγὴ ἄρα. (TRENDELENBURG, *Hist. Beitr.* ii. 366 sq., and BRANDIS, ii. b, 2, 1443, would like to cut out the last two words, on the ground that *all* unproved knowledge does not rest on induction ; but the form of statement is not more universal than in the other parts of this passage, and the explana-

tion of the whole will be gathered from what is said in the text.) Similarly *Anal. Post.* i. 1 *init. Anal. Post.* i. 18 : μανθάνομεν ἢ ἐπαγωγῇ ἢ ἀποδείξει. ἔστι δ' ἡ μὲν ἀπόδειξις ἐκ τῶν καθόλου, ἡ δ' ἐπαγωγὴ ἐκ τῶν κατὰ μέρος · ἀδύνατον δὲ τὰ καθόλου θεωρῆσαι μὴ δι' ἐπαγωγῆς. *Ibid.* ii. 19, 100, b, 3 : δῆλον δὴ ὅτι ἡμῖν τὰ πρῶτα ἐπαγωγῇ γνωρίζειν ἀναγκαῖον. *Top.* i. 12 : ἔστι δὲ τὸ μὲν [εἶδος λόγων διαλεκτικῶν] ἐπαγωγὴ, τὸ δὲ συλλογισμός . . . ἐπαγωγὴ δὲ ἡ ἀπὸ τῶν καθέκαστον ἐπὶ τὰ καθόλου ἔφοδος . . . ἔστι δ' ἡ μὲν ἐπαγωγὴ πιθανώτερον καὶ σαφέστερον καὶ κατὰ τὴν αἴσθησιν γνωριμώτερον καὶ τοῖς πολλοῖς κοινὸν, ὁ δὲ συλλογισμὸς βιαστικώτερον καὶ πρὸς τοὺς ἀντιλογικοὺς ἐναργέστερον. *Ibid.* c. 8 *init.* ; *Rhet.* i. 2, 1356, a, 35 ; and cf. *supra*, p. 205 sq.
[2] See p. 197 sqq., and 246 sq. *supra.*
[3] See also the citation *infra* (in note 1 on p. 256) from *Top.* i. 2.

as we have shown,[1] upon such a mutual relation of
concepts as will admit of the conversion of the universal
affirmative minor premiss. It assumes that the minor
and the middle of the syllogism have the same extension. In other words, no cogent induction is possible,
unless a predicate can be shown to be common to all the
individuals of that genus of which it is to be predicated.[2]
Such an exhaustive acquaintance with every individual
case is impossible.[3] It would seem, therefore, that
every induction is imperfect, and that every assumption
which bases itself upon induction must remain uncertain. To meet this difficulty, it was requisite to
introduce an abbreviation of the inductive method, and
to find something which would make up for the impossibility of complete observation of every individual
instance. This Aristotle finds in Dialectic or Probable
Demonstration,[4] the theory of which he lays down in
the *Topics*. The value of dialectic consists, he says,
not only in the fact that it is an intellectual discipline,
nor that it teaches argumentation as a fine art: it is
also of essential service in scientific research, inasmuch
as it teaches us to explore and estimate the different

[1] P. 242, n. 6.
[2] Cf. *Anal. Pr.* ii. 24 *fin.*:
[τὸ παράδειγμα] διαφέρει τῆς ἐπαγωγῆς, ὅτι ἡ μὲν ἐξ ἁπάντων τῶν
ἀτόμων τὸ ἄκρον ἐδείκνυεν ὑπάρχειν
τῷ μέσῳ . . ., τὸ δὲ . . . οὐκ ἐξ
ἁπάντων δείκνυσιν. *Ibid.* c. 23,
68, b, 27: δεῖ δὲ νοεῖν τὸ Γ [the
lowest concept in the inductive
syllogism] τὸ ἐξ ἁπάντων τῶν
καθέκαστον συγκείμενον· ἡ γὰρ
ἐπαγωγὴ διὰ πάντων.
[3] Even if we supposed we

knew *all* the cases which *had*
occurred of a particular kind,
still we could never know that
the future would not bring other
experiences differing from them.
The supposition itself is by the
nature of the case impossible, and
even more clearly unprovable.
[4] On this narrower meaning
of the 'dialectical' in Aristotle,
see WAITZ, *Arist. Org.* ii. 435
sqq.; cf. following note.

aspects under which an object can be contemplated. It is specially useful in establishing the scientific principles; for as these cannot be deduced by demonstration from anything more certain than themselves, there is nothing left for us but to get at them from the side of probability.[1] Such an attempt must start from the prevailing tenets of humanity. What all the world, or at least the experienced and intelligent part of it, believes, is always worthy of consideration, since it carries with it a presumption that it rests upon a real experience.[2]

[1] *Top.* i. 1: Ἡ μὲν πρόθεσις τῆς πραγματείας, μέθοδον εὑρεῖν, ἀφ' ἧς δυνησόμεθα συλλογίζεσθαι περὶ παντὸς τοῦ προτεθέντος προβλήματος ἐξ ἐνδόξων, καὶ αὐτοὶ λόγον ὑπέχοντες μηθὲν ἐροῦμεν ὑπεναντίον. . . . διαλεκτικὸς δὲ συλλογισμὸς ὁ ἐξ ἐνδόξων συλλογιζόμενος . . . ἔνδοξα δὲ τὰ δοκοῦντα πᾶσιν ἢ τοῖς πλείστοις ἢ τοῖς σοφοῖς, καὶ τούτοις ἢ πᾶσιν ἢ τοῖς πλείστοις ἢ τοῖς μάλιστα γνωρίμοις καὶ ἐνδόξοις. *Ibid.* i. 2: ἔστι δὴ πρὸς τρία [χρήσιμος ἡ πραγματεία], πρὸς γυμνασίαν, πρὸς τὰς ἐντεύξεις, πρὸς τὰς κατὰ φιλοσοφίαν ἐπιστήμας . . . πρὸς δὲ τὰς κατὰ φιλοσοφίαν ἐπιστήμας, ὅτι δυνάμενοι πρὸς ἀμφότερα διαπορῆσαι ῥᾷον ἐν ἑκάστοις κατοψόμεθα τἀληθές τε καὶ τὸ ψεῦδος. ἔτι δὲ πρὸς τὰ πρῶτα τῶν περὶ ἑκάστην ἐπιστήμην ἀρχῶν. ἐκ μὲν γὰρ τῶν οἰκείων τῶν κατὰ τὴν προτεθεῖσαν ἐπιστήμην ἀρχῶν ἀδύνατον εἰπεῖν τι περὶ αὐτῶν, ἐπειδὴ πρῶται αἱ ἀρχαὶ ἁπάντων εἰσί, διὰ δὲ τῶν περὶ ἕκαστα ἐνδόξων ἀνάγκη περὶ αὐτῶν διελθεῖν. τοῦτο δ' ἴδιον ἢ μάλιστα οἰκεῖον τῆς διαλεκτικῆς ἐστιν· ἐξεταστικὴ γὰρ οὖσα πρὸς τὰς ἁπασῶν τῶν μεθόδων ἀρχὰς

ὁδὸν ἔχει. Aristotle (*Top.* viii. 11, 162, a, 15) calls the dialectical syllogism ἐπιχείρημα. THUROT, *Études sur Arist.* 201 sqq., compares the different statements of Aristotle on the office and use of Dialectics; but he has laid rather too much stress upon the partial inaccuracy of Aristotle's language. Cf. on the *Topics* also p. 68, n. 1, *supra*.

[2] *Divin. in S.* c. 1 *init.*: περὶ δὲ τῆς μαντικῆς τῆς ἐν τοῖς ὕπνοις γινομένης . . . οὔτε καταφρονῆσαι ῥᾴδιον οὔτε πεισθῆναι. τὸ μὲν γὰρ πάντας ἢ πολλοὺς ὑπολαμβάνειν ἔχειν τι σημειῶδες ἡ ἐνύπνια παρέχεται πίστιν ὡς ἐξ ἐμπειρίας λεγόμενον, &c.; *Eth.* i. 8 *init.* vi. 12, 1143, b, 11; *Rhet.* i. 1, 1355, a, 15 (cf. the beginning of ch. xiv. *infra*). For the same reason, *Eth.* vii. 14, 1153, b, 27 appeals to Hesiod (Ἔ. κ. ἡμ. 763): φήμη δ' οὔ τί γε πάμπαν ἀπόλλυται, ἥν τινα λαοὶ πολλοὶ . . . and SYNES. *Calv. Enc.* c. 22 (*Ar. Fr.* No. 2) quotes as Aristotelian: ὅτι [sc. αἱ παροιμίαι] παλαιᾶς εἰσι φιλοσοφίας ἐν ταῖς μεγίσταις ἀνθρώπων φθοραῖς ἀπολομένης ἐγκαταλείμματα περισωθέντα

Such a foundation may appear unstable ; and the sense of this forced on Aristotle the need (which had likewise driven Socrates to form his dialectic) of supplying its deficiencies by combining the different points of view which cross one another in popular opinion, and by balancing them one with the other. From this he got his habit of prefacing his dogmatic dissertations with 'Απορίαι ; of enumerating the different sides from which the subject may be touched ; of testing conclusions by mutual comparison and by established standards ; and, finally, of raising difficulties by this testing process and obtaining a ground for a scientific exposition from their solution.[1] These dialectical elucidations prepare the way for positive scientific conclusions by clearing up the questions which are in issue, by grouping the inductive results under a certain number of general aspects, and by making them explain each other and so combining them into an aggregate result. From them, our thought is led on into the

---

διὰ συντομίαν καὶ δεξιότητα. Cf. also *Polit.* ii. 5, 1264, a, 1 ; *Eth. Eud.* i. 6 *init.*, and, as to the belief in the αἰθήρ, *De Cælo*, 270, b, 19, *Metaph.* xii. 8, and *Meteor.* 339, b, 27. With this is connected Aristotle's preference for proverbial sayings and ' gnomes,' about which cf. p. 104, n. 1 (on the Παροιμίαι).

[1] *Metaph.* iii. 1 *init.* : ἔστι δὲ τοῖς εὐπορῆσαι βουλομένοις προὔργου τὸ διαπορῆσαι καλῶς· ἡ γὰρ ὕστερον εὐπορία λύσις τῶν πρότερον ἀπορουμένων ἐστί, λύειν δ' οὐκ ἔστιν ἀγνοοῦντας τὸν δεσμόν, &c. *Eth. N.* vii. 1 *fin.* : δεῖ δ', ὥσπερ ἐπὶ τῶν ἄλλων, τιθέντας τὰ φαινόμενα

καὶ πρῶτον διαπορήσαντας οὕτω δεικνύναι μάλιστα μὲν πάντα τὰ ἔνδοξα περὶ ταῦτα τὰ πάθη, εἰ δὲ μὴ, τὰ πλεῖστα καὶ κυριώτατα· ἐὰν γὰρ λύηταί τε τὰ δυσχερῆ καὶ καταλείπηται τὰ ἔνδοξα, δεδειγμένον ἂν εἴη ἱκανῶς. Cf. *De Cælo*, i. 10 *init. Anal. Post.* ii. 3 *init.*, and WAITZ on this passage ; also *Phys.* iv. 10 *init.*, *Meteorol.* i. 13 *init.*, *De An.* i. 2 *init.*, *Longit. Vit.* c. 1, 464, b, 21, &c. In *Top.* viii. 11, 162, a, 17, the ἀπόρημα is defined as συλλογισμὸs διαλεκτικὸs ἀντιφάσεως. These Aristotelian ' Apories ' served the Scholastics as a model for their *disputatio pro et contra*.

explicit problems, the true solution of which brings us to philosophic knowledge.[1]

It is true that neither this theory nor the actual practice of Aristotle can satisfy the stricter requirements of modern science.

Whether we consider his procedure in the working out from the observed facts of the laws and definitions of Science, or in the establishment of natural phenomena themselves, we must admit that it shows serious omissions and defects. Of Induction, for example, he says that it consists in the collection, from *all* the instances of a given class, of a proposition which expresses as a universal law that which was true of all these particular cases.[2] In truth, Induction consists in inferring such a proposition from *all the cases known to us*; and in considering the principle on which the inductive method rests, the main point is to inquire how we are justified in concluding from *all the cases known to us*, a law for *all like cases*. Aristotle can hardly be blamed for not raising exactly this question, since none of his successors succeeded in stating it clearly until Stuart Mill wrote his Logic; and even he could find no answer but an inadequate and self-contradictory theory. But it was an inevitable result of Aristotle's position that his theory of Induction does not help us over the real difficulty, which is to ascertain how the correctness of an inductive proof can be assumed in spite of the fact that the range of experiences on which it rests is not *complete*. The fact is that Aristotle, as we have

---

[1] *Metaph.* iv. 2, 1004, b, 25 :
ἔστι δὲ ἡ διαλεκτικὴ πειραστικὴ περὶ
ὧν ἡ φιλοσοφία γνωστική.

[2] Cf. *supra*, p. 242, n. 6, and p. 255.

already indicated, has tried to fill up the gap by the
invention of the ' proof from probability,' and by the
dialectical treatment of the ἀπορίαι. In the latter his
acuteness and his scientific width of view are conspicuous
throughout. But it cannot make up for a satisfactory
and methodical comparison of observed facts, if only for
the reason that the theories discussed are not themselves
based on pure observation, but on the ἔνδοξον—on
views, that is, in which guesses, inferences and fancies
have, or at least may have, become mixed up with
actual experience. Even where Aristotle is dealing
with actual observation, he falls, in many respects, far
short of the standard which we are accustomed to set
to the scientific observer. As to the conditions of a
trustworthy observation, or the methods to be applied
for establishing the correctness of one's own observations
or controlling the accuracy of information given by
others, we have only here and there a chance remark.
As he is too little conscious of the part which a subjective mental activity plays in all perception,[1] so it
was natural that his method should not adequately
provide for the subjective control of the errors of observation.

In his own work there is, on this side of it, much to
criticise. It is true that he has brought together,
especially in the zoological writings, an extraordinary
volume of statements of fact, the overwhelming majority
of which (so far as they can now be verified [2]) have been

[1] Cf. p. 210 and *infra*, ch. x.
[2] For this is not always possible, partly because it is often
uncertain which animal is meant
by this or that name, partly
because not all the animals mentioned by Aristotle are sufficiently
known to us.

found to be correct. Most of these, of course, are
patent enough to any observer ; but there are also many
cases among them where careful investigation would be
required.[1] The methods of experiment he did not
altogether neglect.[2] His historical studies excite our

[1] Thus we see from *Part.
An.* iii. 4, 665, a, 33 sqq. (cf.
LEWES, *Arist.* § 394), that he had
made experiments on the development of the embryo in the egg,
since he there remarks that we
often find in eggs, even on the
third day, the heart and the
liver as isolated points. So in
Gen. An. ii. 6, he makes remarks
on the order of appearance of the
different parts of the body ; from
which, as even LEWES (§ 475) admits, we see that Aristotle studied
embryonic development. A statement, long considered fabulous,
about the appearance of a placenta
in a kind of shark (*H. An.* vi. 10,
565, b, 1) has been confirmed (by
Joh. MÜLLER, *Abh. d. Berl. Ak.*
1840, *Phys. math. Kl.* 187, cf.
LEWES, *loc. cit.* § 205) ; the same is
the case (cf. LEWES, § 206–208)
with Aristotle's statements about
the embryo of the ink-fish (*Gen.
An.* iii. 8, 758, a, 21) ; about fishes
which build a nest (*H. An.* viii.
30, 607, b, 19) ; about the eyes of
the mole (*De An.* iii. 1, 425, a,
10, *H. An.* i. 9, 491, b, 28 sqq.),
and about a gland which a certain
kind of stag has under the tail
(*H. An.* ii. 15, 506, a, 23, cf. W.
Rapp in *Müller's Archiv. f. Anat.*
1839, 363 sq.). With regard to his
description of the cephalopods,
LEWES remarks (§ 340 sq.) that it
could only spring from a great
familiarity with their forms, and
we see in it the unmistakeable
traces of personal knowledge.

All the more odd is it that Lewes
should complain of Aristotle's
failure to mention the freshness
of the sea breeze, the play of the
waves, &c. This is to blame Aristotle for not having the bad taste
to drop from the realism of a
zoological description into the
style of a *feuilleton*, or the im-
pertinence to explain to people
who had the sea daily before
their eyes the things they had
known all their lives.

[2] EUCKEN, *Meth. d. Arist.
Forsch.*, p. 163 sqq., gives instances from *Meteor.* ii. 3, 359, a,
12, 358, b, 34 (*H. An.* viii. 2,
590, a, 22) ; *H. An.* vi. 2, 560,
a, 30 (*Gen. An.* iii. 1, 752, a, 4) ;
De An. ii. 2, 413, b, 16 ; *De
Respir.* iii. 471, a, 31 ; *H. An.*
vi. 37, 580, b, sqq. (if this was
really an experiment, and not
rather a chance observation).
Then again there are others introduced with a λέγουσιν, *Gen.
An.* iv. 1, 765, a, 21 (which is
later on disputed by himself),
and *Hist. An.* ii. 17, 508, b, 4
(though in *Gen. An.* iv. 6, 774, b,
31 the same is stated in his own
name). Some of these experiments are of such a questionable
kind, that we may well doubt
whether Aristotle himself con-
ducted them ; and, on the whole,
he appeals to experiments so
seldom that we cannot avoid seeing how little he, or Greek
science in general, recognised
their value.

high admiration by their extent and their accuracy.[1]
To received accounts he so far takes a critical attitude
that he is careful to correct many false views,[2] to direct
attention to the untrustworthiness of some of his
authorities,[3] and to attack even universally accepted
myths.[4] Where he lacks adequate means of observation, he is willing to reserve his judgment; [5] where there
might be a tendency to close an inquiry too precipi-
tately, he gives us warning that we should first weigh
all the objections suggested by the matter in hand
before we decide.[6] In a word, he shows himself not
only an untiring inquirer whose thirst [7] for the knowledge of all things great and small was never satisfied,

---

[1] Besides the numberless items
of information from the History
of the Greek States, of Philosophy,
of Poetry, and of Rhetoric, which
the extant works contain, we
may refer here to what is quoted
to us from the *Politics* and other
lost works; *de quo vide* p. 101,
n. 1; 73, n. 1; 62, n. 5; 58, n. 1;
103. n. 1, and 104, n. 1.

[2] Thus in the cases named by
EUCKEN (*loc. cit.* 124), *Gen. An.*
iii. 5, 755, b, 7 sqq., 756, a, 2;
ch. 6, 756, b, 13 sqq., 757, a, 2 sqq.;
iv. 1, 765, a, 16 sqq., 21 sqq.;
H. An. viii. 24, 605, a, 2 sq.

[3] As in *Hist. An.* viii. 28, 606,
a, 8, ii. 1. 501, a, 25, where certain statements of Ctesias are
called in question as untrustworthy; in *Gen. An.* iii. 5, 756,
a, 33, where he says that fisher-
men frequently overlook the occurrence in question: οὐθεὶς γὰρ
αὐτῶν οὐθὲν τηρεῖ τοιοῦτον τοῦ
γνῶναι χάριν. So in *Hist. An.*
ix. 41, 628, b, 8: αὐτόπτῃ δ' οὔπω

ἐντετυχήκαμεν. But, on the other
hand, in c. 29, 37, 618, a, 18,
620, b, 23, he appeals to eye-
witness.

[4] As in doubting the genuineness of the poems of Orpheus,
and the existence of their supposed author; as to which see
ZELLER, *Ph. d. Gr.* vol. i. 50.

[5] Cf. *supra*, p. 169, n. 1.

[6] *De Cælo*, i. 13, 294, b, 6:
ἀλλ' ἐοίκασι μέχρι τινὸς ζητεῖν,
ἀλλ' οὐ μέχρι περ οὗ δυνατὸν τῆς
ἀπορίας· πᾶσι γὰρ ἡμῖν τοῦτο σύν-
ηθες, μὴ πρὸς τὸ πρᾶγμα ποιεῖσθαι
τὴν ζήτησιν ἀλλὰ πρὸς τὸν τἀναντία
λέγοντα· καὶ γὰρ αὐτὸς ἐν αὐτῷ
ζητεῖ μέχρι περ ἂν οὗ μηκέτι ἔχῃ
ἀντιλέγειν αὐτὸς αὑτῷ· διὸ δεῖ τὸν
μέλλοντα καλῶς ζητήσειν ἐνστα-
τικὸν εἶναι διὰ τῶν οἰκείων ἐνστά-
σεων τῷ γένει, τοῦτο δ' ἐστὶν ἐκ
τοῦ πάσας τεθεωρηκέναι τὰς δια-
φοράς.

[7] Τὸ φιλοσοφίας διψῆν: *vide
supra*, p. 169, n. 3.

but also an observer of care and common sense. Nevertheless, we find that glaringly incorrect statements are not rare in Aristotle, and occur sometimes in cases where, even with the simple methods to which he was limited, the correction of the error should have been easy enough.[1] And still more commonly do we find that he draws from insufficient and incomplete data conclusions much too rash and sweeping, or that he forces his facts to conform to some general theory which has itself no adequate experiential basis. In his inductions he is often far too rash, and by basing them on various popular assumptions he leaves them without any sure foundation. He shows himself but little

---

[1] Cf. EUCKEN, *loc. cit.* 155 sqq. Such cases are: that Aristotle gives the male sex more teeth than the female (*Hist. An.* ii. 3, 501, b, 19; on the conjectured cause of this error see LEWES, *Arist.* § 332, A. 19); that the human male has three sutures in the skull, and the female only one running around it (*ibid.* i. 8, 491, b, 2); that man has only eight ribs on each side (*ibid.* i. 15, 493, b, 14)—a supposition, as it would seem, universally held at that time, and explained by supposing that it was founded, not on anatomical observations of human corpses, but on observations of living bodies; cf. p. 89, n. 1; that the lines in the hand indicate longer or shorter span of life (*ibid.* 493, b, 32 sq.); that the hinder part of the skull is empty (*H. An.* i. 8, 491, a, 34; *Part. An.* ii. 10, 656, b, 12; *Gen. An.* v. 4, 784, b, 35). Further examples in LEWES,

§ 149 sqq., 154 sqq., 315, 332, 347, 350, 352, 386 sq., 398, 400, 411, 486. When, however, it is said that Aristotle in the *Part. An.* iii. 6, 669, a, 19, asserted that only man has a pulsation of the heart (so LEWES, § 399, c, where he adds: 'According to this passage one might think that Aristotle never held a bird in his hand;' and EUCKEN, 155, 2), this is an inaccurate accusation. Aristotle distinguishes, in *De Respir.* 20, 479, b, 17, the σφυγμὸς or heart-beat always going on, from the πήδησις τῆς καρδίας = the strong throb of the heart in passion. And even the latter he does not confine to men, for he says in the tract referred to that it sometimes becomes so strong that animals die of it. All that is said in the passage cited is: ἐν ἀνθρώπῳ τε γὰρ συμβαίνει μόνον ὡς εἰπεῖν—*i.e.* the passion-throb occurs *almost* exclusively in Man.

skilled in the art of analysing the phenomena methodically into their real factors, of following out each fact to its causes and the laws of its action, and of unravelling the conditions of the causal nexus. He has not mastered—even in the degree which with the scanty technical skill of Greece was possible to him—the best methods of establishing and analysing facts, of checking observations and theories, or of applying experiment to science. He does not, in a word, come up to the standard to which in our day a student of nature is expected to attain. There is nothing strange in this; rather would it be strange if it were otherwise.

If Aristotle were without the faults we note in his theory and practice, he would not only be far more in advance of his own time than in fact he was—he would have belonged to another and much later period of human thought. Before science could attain to that certitude, correlation and exactness of procedure by which we excel the ancients, it was necessary in all ranges of scientific and historical inquiry that the facts should be collected and all manner of experiments made, that the laws of particular classes of phenomena should be sought out and gradually universalised, that hypotheses should be proposed for the elucidation of various series of facts, and these again continually checked and revised by the facts themselves. To this end no general disquisitions on methodology, but only scientific work itself could assist. Until the experimental sciences had passed far beyond the position at which they stood in Aristotle's time, it was not possible that either the methodology or the methods of experimental knowledge should really advance beyond the form in which he stated them. In the then state of science it was already a great thing that observed facts should be collected in such vast masses and with such care. It was not to be expected that they should also be with the like care tested, or that his personal observations should be exactly discriminated from information otherwise received, and the value of the latter critically appraised. Many of the assertions which we find absurd, were probably taken by Aristotle from others in all good faith, and were not doubted by him, merely because the knowledge of nature which he possessed gave him no reason to think them impossible. When we are surprised by the rashness with which the Greeks often built hypotheses or theories upon facts whose falsity is obvious to us at first sight, we do not stop to think how utterly they were ignorant of all our aids to accurate observation, and how greatly this poverty of tools must have hindered every sort of helpful experiment. To fix time without a watch, to compare degrees of heat without a thermometer, to observe the heavens without a telescope and the weather without a barometer—these and the like were the tasks which the natural philosophers of Greece had to set themselves. Where there is no basis for accuracy as to facts, the difficulties that attend the classification of phenomena, the discovery of natural laws, and the correction of hypothesis by experience are so vastly increased, that we cannot wonder if scientific inquiry rises but slowly and insecurely above the levels of prescientific fancy. The service which Aristotle nevertheless did for the world in the collection of data, and the acuteness with which he strove to explain the facts he knew, cannot but be appreciated if we try to judge him by any standards that conform to the knowledge and the opportunities of his day.

To enter into the details of Aristotle's *Topics*, or to examine his refutation of the Sophistic fallacies, are equally beyond our present scope. No wider view of his scientific principles is to be got from them, but only an application of them to a field beyond the limits of Science properly so called.[1] But this is the proper place to touch upon his researches into Definition, which we find partly in the second *Analytics*, partly in the *Topics*.[2] As the Concept forms the starting point of all scientific research, so we may say conversely that a complete acquaintance with the Concept—which is Definition—is the goal toward which it strives. Knowledge is indeed nothing but insight into the grounds of things, and in the concept this insight is summed up. The 'what' is the same as the 'why.' We apprehend the *concept* of the thing as soon as we apprehend its *causes*.[3] So far, Definition has the same problem as Demonstration. In both we try to discover the means by which the object has been brought to be what it is.[4] Nevertheless, they do not, with Aristotle, entirely coincide. In the first place, it is clear that

---

[1] BRANDIS, pp. 288–345 gives a sketch of both.

[2] Besides the general works on Aristotelian Logic, see KÜHN, *De notionis definitione*, etc., and RASSOW, *Arist. de notionis definitione* (cf. *supra*, p. 212, n. 2);

HEYDER, *Vergl. d. arist. u. hegel. Dialektik*, p. 247 sqq., and KAMPE, *Erkenntnissth. d. Arist.* 195 sqq.

[3] *Vid. supra*, p. 163, n. 2, and p. 173, n. 2.

[4] *Vid. supra*, p. 173, n. 2.

everything which admits of demonstration does not
equally admit of definition ; for negatives, particulars,
and propositions predicating properties, can all be demonstrated, whereas definition is always universal and
affirmative, and is not concerned with mere properties
but with the substantial essence only.[1] The converse
is no less true—not everything that can be defined
admits of demonstration, as may be seen at once
from the fact that demonstrations must start from
undemonstrable definitions.[2]   Indeed, it seems to be
true in general, that the contents of a definition are
undemonstrable by syllogisms : for demonstration *presupposes* a knowledge of the essence of the object, while
this is precisely what definition seeks.   The one points
out that a property belongs as predicate to a certain
subject; the other does not concern itself with individual properties, but with the essence itself.   The one
inquires for a ' *that*,'[3] the other for a ' *what* '; [4] and
in order to specify *what* anything is, we must first know
that it is.[5]   Here, however, we must draw a distinction.
The fact is that a definition cannot be derived through a
single syllogism.   We cannot take that which is asserted
in the definition of an object and use it as the predicate
of a middle term in our major premiss, in order to attach
it again in the conclusion to the object which was to
be defined: for if, in such a process, we are dealing
with not merely one or other of the properties, but
with the whole concept of the object, then it must

[1] *Anal. Post.* ii. 3.
[2] *Ibid.* 90, b, 18 sqq. (cf.
supra, p. 246 sqq.).   Another
kindred reason is there given
also.

[3] ὅτι ἢ ἔστι τόδε κατὰ τοῦδε ἢ
οὐκ ἔστιν.
[4] *Anal. Post.* ibid. 90, b, 28
sqq.; cf. c. 7, 92, b, 12.
[5] *Ibid.* c. 7, 92, b, 4.

follow that both major and minor premisses would be alike definitions —the one of the middle term and the other of the minor. A proper definition, however, cannot be applied to any other object except the one to be defined.[1] Consequently, in every definition, the subject and the predicate must be equal in comprehension and extension, so that the universal affirmative proposition which expresses the definition, must always be simply convertible. Therefore it follows that, by such a process as we have described, we should only be demonstrating the same by the same,[2] and should get, not a real definition, but a verbal explanation.[3]

Plato's method of arriving at the idea by means of division is no better ; for the division presupposes the concept.[4] The same objection also applies to the method[5] of assuming a definition and proving its validity *a posteriori* by reference to individuals ; for how can we feel certain that the hypothesis which we assumed, does really express the idea of the object, and not merely a number of particular marks ?[6] If, lastly, we endeavoured to bring definition within the province

[1] *Vid. supra*, p. 216 sqq.

[2] *Anal. Post.* ii. 4. As an illustration he uses the definition of the soul as 'a self-moving number.' If we wished to establish this by means of the syllogism : 'everything that is itself the cause of life is a self-moving number ; the soul is itself the cause of life, &c,' this would be insufficient, for in this way we could only prove that the soul is a self-moving number, and not that its *whole* essence, its concept, is contained in this definition. In order to show this, we should have to argue : 'the concept of that which is itself the cause of life consists in its being a self-moving number ; the concept of the soul consists in its being itself the cause of life,' &c.

[3] *Anal. Post.* ii. c. 7, 92, b, 5, 26 sqq.; cf. c. 10 *init.* i. 1, 71, a, 11 ; *Top.* i. 5 *init.* ; *Metaph.* vii. 4, 1030, a, 14.

[4] *Vid. supra*, p. 241, n. 3.

[5] Which one of the philosophers of that time (we know not who) had likewise made.

[6] *Anal. Post.* ii. c. 6, and also WAITZ.

of the epagogic process, we should be met with the difficulty that induction never brings us to a ' what,' but always to a ' that.'[1] But although definition can neither be obtained by demonstration nor by induction, so long as they are separately used, yet Aristotle thinks it possible to reach it by a union of the two. When experience in the first instance has taught us that certain characteristics appertain to an object, and we begin to search for their causes, or for the conception which links them to their subject, we are so establishing by demonstration the essence of the thing ;[2] and if we continue this process until the object is defined in all its aspects,[3] we at last obtain the concept of it. Although syllogistic demonstration, therefore, may be insufficient to constitute a perfect definition, yet it helps us to find it,[4] and in this sense definition may be said to be under another form a demonstration of the essence.[5] This process is admissible in every case but that of things the being of which is not dependent on any causes outside themselves ; and the conception of

[1] *Loc. cit.* c. 7, 92, a, 37 : Induction shows that something in general is of such and such a kind, by proving that it is so in all particular instances ; but this is equivalent to proving merely a ὅτι ἔστιν ἢ οὐκ ἔστιν, not the τί ἐστι.

[2] *Ibid.* c. 8, 93, a, 14 sqq.

[3] It is necessary at this point to fill out the too short hints of Aristotle's statement by reference to the argument cited at p. 216, n. 1 *supra*, from *Anal. Post.* ii. 13.

[4] *Anal. Post.* ii. 8 *fin.* : συλλογισμὸς μὲν τοῦ τί ἐστιν οὐ γίνεται οὐδ' ἀπόδειξις, δῆλον μέντοι διὰ συλλογισμοῦ καὶ δι' ἀποδείξεως · ὥστ' οὔτ' ἄνευ ἀποδείξεως ἔστι γνῶναι τὸ τί ἐστιν οὗ ἐστιν αἴτιον ἄλλο, οὔτ' ἔστιν ἀπόδειξις αὐτοῦ.

[5] *Ibid.* c. 10, 94, a, 11 : ἔστιν ἄρα ὁρισμὸς εἷς μὲν λόγος τοῦ τί ἐστιν ἀναπόδεικτος, εἷς δὲ συλλογισμὸς τοῦ τί ἐστι, πτώσει διαφέρων τῆς ἀποδείξεως, τρίτος δὲ τῆς τοῦ τί ἐστιν ἀποδείξεως συμπέρασμα : the fuller explanation of which is given above. That definitions of the latter kind do not suffice, Aristotle tells us in *De An.* ii. 2 ; *vid. supra*, p. 173, n. 2.

these can only be postulated as immediately certain, or elucidated by induction.[1]

From these researches into the nature and conditions of Definition we obtain some important rules as to the method by which in practice it is arrived at. Since the essential nature of an object [2] can only be defined genetically by the indication of its causes, Definition must embrace those distinctive characteristics by which the object is actually made to be what it is. It must, by Aristotle's rule, be got at by means of that which is prior and more known; nor must these principles be such as are prior in our knowledge, but such as are prior and more known in themselves. It is allowable to prefer the former only in the case of scholars who are incompetent to understand the latter; but in such a case they get nothing which really elucidates the essence of the object.[3] This rule, indeed, follows from the axiom that Definition consists of the genus and the specific differences: for the genus is

---

[1] *Anal. Post.* ii. c. 9 : ἔστι δὲ τῶν μὲν ἕτερόν τι αἴτιον, τῶν δ᾽ οὐκ ἔστιν. ὥστε δῆλον ὅτι καὶ τῶν τί ἐστι τὰ μὲν ἄμεσα καὶ ἀρχαί εἰσιν, ἃ καὶ εἶναι καὶ τί ἐστιν ὑποθέσθαι δεῖ ἢ ἄλλον τρόπον φανερὰ ποιῆσαι. Cf. preceding note and *Anal. Post.* ibid. 94, a, 9 : ὁ δὲ τῶν ἀμέσων ὁρισμὸς θέσις ἐστὶ τοῦ τί ἐστιν ἀναπόδεικτος. *Metaph.* ix. 6, 1048, a. 35 : δῆλον δ᾽ ἐπὶ τῶν καθέκαστα τῇ ἐπαγωγῇ ὃ βουλόμεθα λέγειν, καὶ οὐ δεῖ παντὸς ὅρον ζητεῖν, ἀλλὰ καὶ τὸ ἀνάλογον συνορᾷν; and above, p. 253. To Induction also belongs the process which is described in *De An.* i. 1, 402, b, 16 : ἔοικε δ᾽ οὐ μόνον τὸ τί ἐστι γνῶναι χρήσιμον εἶναι πρὸς τὸ θεωρῆσαι τὰς αἰτίας τῶν συμβεβηκότων ταῖς οὐσίαις . . . ἀλλὰ καὶ ἀνάπαλιν τὰ συμβεβηκότα συμβάλλεται μέγα μέρος πρὸς τὸ εἰδέναι τὸ τί ἐστιν : for a definition is only correct when it explains all the συμβεβηκότα (*i.e.* the καθ᾽ αὑτὸ συμβεβηκότα, the essential properties; *vid.* p. 214, n. 3 *supra*) of an object. On immediate knowledge, cf. p. 246 sqq., 197 sqq.

[2] Of course with the exception of the ἄμεσα just mentioned, *i.e.* that which is conditional on no principle other than itself.

[3] *Top.* vi. 4; cf. p. 205, n. 2 *supra*.

prior and more certain than its contents, and the differentiæ are prior to the species which they mark off.[1] Inversely we obtain the same result: for if Definition consists in specifying the aggregate determining characteristics by which the object is conditioned in its essential nature, it must include the genus and the differentiæ, for these are simply the scientific expression of those causes which in their coincidence produce the object.[2] But these, in their turn, are definitely related to one another in an order of superiority and inferiority. The genus is narrowed by the first of the differentiating marks ; then the species so produced is further narrowed by the second, and so on. It is not, therefore, a matter of indifference in what order the separate properties shall follow in any definition.[3] A definition, in fact, implies not a mere enumeration of the essential marks,[4] but also the completeness[5] and the proper sequence of them.[6] Bearing this in mind, it will be found that in the descent from universals to particulars the practice of

---

[1] *Loc. cit.* 141, b, 28 ; cf. *supra,* p. 215, n. 1, 216, n. 1.

[2] This follows from the passages cited *supra,* p. 173, n. 2, compared with pp. 215, n. 1, 244, n. 3. By reason of this connection *Topics* vi. 5 sq., immediately after the remarks on the πρότερα καὶ γνωριμώτερα, gives rules for the correct determination of the definition by γένος and διαφοραί.

[3] *Anal. Post.* ii. 13, 96, b, 30; cf. 97, a, 23 sqq.

[4] Τὰ ἐν τῷ τί ἐστι κατηγορούμενα, αἱ τοῦ γένους διαφοραί. It is obvious that only such things

can occur in the definition; cf. p. 217 sqq., *Anal. Post.* ii. 13, 96, b, 1 sqq., i. 23, 84, a, 13., *Top.* vi. 6 ; and other passages WAITZ on *Categ.* 2, a, 20.

[5] It has been already remarked on p. 246, that the number of intermediate grades must be a limited one. Cf. also *Anal. Post.* ii. 12, 95, b, 13 sqq.

[6] *Anal. Post.* ii. 13, 97, a, 23 : εἰς δὲ τὸ κατασκευάζειν ὅρον διὰ τῶν διαιρέσεων τριῶν δεῖ στοχάζεσθαι, τοῦ λαβεῖν τὰ κατηγορούμενα ἐν τῷ τί ἐστι, καὶ ταῦτα τάξαι τί πρῶτον ἢ δεύτερον, καὶ ὅτι ταῦτα πάντα.

progressive division is our surest method, while a correspondingly gradual building up of concepts is equally proper to the upward process towards the universal.[1] And thus Plato's method, though Aristotle could not accept it as a satisfactory process for deducing definitions, was yet recognised and further worked out by him as a means to their discovery.[2]

Supposing, then, that we have defined and surveyed the whole field of the knowledge of concepts on this method, we shall obtain a system of ideas such as Plato looked for,[3] carrying us in an unbroken line from the Summa Genera through all the intermediate members down to the lowest species. And since scientific deduction must consist in the specification of causes, and since each specific difference in the upward scale implies the introduction of a new cause, and every added cause creates a corresponding differentia, it results that our logical structure must exactly correspond with the actual sequence and concatenation of causes. Plato never undertook actually to set forth that derivation of everything knowable out of unity, which he saw ahead as the end and goal of science. Aristotle

---

[1] Aristotle includes both, without further separating them, in the concept of Division. For this he gives full rules in *Anal. Post.* ii. 13, 96, b, 15–97, b, 25; *Top.* vi. 5, 6; *Part. Anim.* i. 2, 3. Like Plato (ZELLER, *Ph. d. Gr.* pt. i. p. 524 sq.), he also considers that the most important thing is that the division should be continuous, should omit no intermediate grade, and should totally exhaust the object to be divided; and lastly (to which Plato devoted less attention), that it should not proceed by means of deduced or contingent differences, but by the essential ones. Cf. preceding note.

[2] Two further rules, contained especially in the sixth book of the *Topics*—where he enumerates at length the mistakes made in defining—are omitted here.

[3] See ZELL. *ibid.* p. 525, 588.

considers such a demonstration to be quite impracticable. The highest genera, according to him, are no more capable of being derived from any one higher principle than are the special postulates of each science.[1] They are connected, not by any complete community of nature, but only by a kind of analogy,[2] and the reason

[1] *Anal. Post.* i. 32, 88, a, 31 sqq., &c.; *vid. supra* p. 246. sqq. Aristotle says, in *Metaph.* xii. 4, 1070, b, 1 (παρὰ γὰρ τὴν οὐσίαν καὶ τἆλλα τὰ κατηγορούμενα οὐθέν ἐστι κοινόν), that the categories especially can be deduced neither from one another nor from a higher common genus: v. 28, 1024, b, 9 (where the same is said of Form and Matter); xi. 9, 1065, b, 8; *Phys.* iii. 1, 200, b, 34; *De An.* i. 5, 410, a, 13; *Eth. N.* i. 4, 1096, a, 19, 23 sqq.; cf. TRENDE-LENBURG, *Hist. Beitr.* i. 149 sq. The concepts, which one would be most inclined to consider the highest genera, ' Being ' and ' One,' are no γένη: *Metaph.* iii. 3, 998, b, 22; viii. 6, 1045, b, 5; x. 2, 1053, b, 21; xi. 1, 1059, b, 27 sq.; xii. 4, 1070, b. 7; *Eth. N. ibid.*; *Anal. Post.* ii. 7, 92, b, 14; *Top.* iv. 1, 121, a, 16, c. 6, 127, a, 26 sqq. Cf. TRENDELENBURG, *loc. cit.* 67; BONITZ and SCHWEG-LER on *Metaph.* iii. 3 (more on p. 276 *infra*). Therefore the principle ' that eventually every-thing is contained in a single highest concept as in a common genus,' which STRÜMPELL, *Gesch. d. theor. Phil. d. Gr.* p. 193, gives as an assertion of Aristotle, is not really Aristotelian.

[2] In *Metaph.* v. 6, 1016, b, 31, four kinds of Unity are dis-tinguished (somewhat different is the other fourfold enumera-tion in *Metaph.* x. 1, in which the unity of analogy does not occur) : the unity of number, of species, of genus, and of analogy. Each of these unities includes in it the subsequent unities (*i.e.* that which in number is one is also one in species, &c.) ; but not *vice versa.* Hence the unity of Analogy can occur even in those things which belong to no common genus (cf. *Part. An.* i. 5, 645, b, 26: τὰ μὲν γὰρ ἔχιουσι τὸ κοινὸν κατ' ἀναλογίαν, τὰ δὲ κατὰ γένος, τὰ δὲ κατ' εἶδος). It occurs in everything ὅσα ἔχει ὡς ἄλλο πρὸς ἄλλο. It consists in identity of relation (ἰσότης λόγων), and hence supposes at least four members (*Eth. N.* v. 6, 1131, a, 31). Its formula is : ὡς τοῦτο ἐν τούτῳ ἢ πρὸς τοῦτο, τόδ' ἐν τῷδε ἢ πρὸς τόδε (*Metaph.* ix. 6, 1048, b, 7; cf. *Poet.* 21, 1457, b, 16). It is found not only in quantitative identity, such as arithmetical and geometrical (*Eth. N.* v. 7, 1131, b, 12, 1132, a, 1), but also in qualitative identity, such as similarity (*Gen. et Corr.* ii. 6, 333, a, 26 sqq.), or in identity of operation (cf. *Part. An.* i. 5, 645, b, 9 : τὸ ἀνάλογον τὴν αὐτὴν ἔχον δύναμιν; *ibid.* i. 4, 644, b, 11; ii. 6, 652, a, 3), and in fact in all categories (*Metaph.* xiv. 6, 1093, b, 18). Besides those in the passages just mentioned, other instances are given in *De Part.*

why the sciences are not all one, is just because each class of actual existences has its own peculiar sort of knowledge which applies to it.[1] If it be true that among the sciences we find one which is a science of first principles—the ' First Philosophy '—we must not expect it to develop its subject-matter out of any single principle of being. On the contrary, we shall find it necessary, before proceeding to any further researches, that we should inquire into all the most general points of view from which the world of actual existence can be considered, or, in other words, enumerate the highest generic concepts themselves.

This it is with which the doctrine of the Categories is concerned, and these form accordingly the true connecting link, in Aristotle's philosophic system, between Logic and Metaphysics.

Anim., Anal. Pri. i. 46, 51, b, 22, and *Rhet.* iii. 6 *fin.* That which cannot be deduced from any other thing (the highest principles), must be explained by analogy, as, for example, the concepts of Matter, of Form, &c.; cf. *Metaph.* ix. 6 (*vid. sup.* p. 269, n. 1); xii. 4, 1070, b, 16 sqq., and *Phys.* i. 7, 191, a, 7. This is the account given by TRENDELENBURG in his *Hist. Beitr.* i. 151 sqq. ' Analogy ' is of special importance to Aristotle in his study of Natural History; see thereon *infra*, and cf. MEYER, *Arist. Thierkunde*, 334 sqq

[1] *Anal. Post.* i. 28 *init.*: μία δ' ἐπιστήμη ἐστὶν ἡ ἑνὸς γένους . . .

ἑτέρα δ' ἐπιστήμη ἐστὶν ἑτέρας, ὅσων αἱ ἀρχαὶ μήτ' ἐκ τῶν αὐτῶν μήθ' ἕτεραι ἐκ τῶν ἑτέρων. *Metaph.* iii. 2, 997, a, 21: περὶ οὖν τὸ αὐτὸ γένος τὰ συμβεβηκότα καθ' αὐτὰ τῆς αὐτῆς [ἐπιστήμης] ἐστὶ θεωρῆσαι ἐκ τῶν αὐτῶν δοξῶν. *Ibid.* iv. 2, 1003, b, 19: ἅπαντος δὲ γένους καὶ αἴσθησις μία ἑνὸς καὶ ἐπιστήμη. *Ibid.* 1004, a, 3: τοσαῦτα μέρη φιλοσοφίας ἐστὶν ὅσαιπερ αἱ οὐσίαι . . . ὑπάρχει γὰρ εὐθὺς γένη ἔχοντα τὸ ἓν καὶ τὸ ὄν· διὸ καὶ αἱ ἐπιστῆμαι ἀκολουθήσουσι τούτοις. The relation between this and the concept of the First Philosophy will be examined *infra*.

CHAPTER VI

INTRODUCTORY INQUIRIES TOUCHING ARISTOTLE'S METAPHYSICS

1. *The Categories* [1]

ALL the objects of our thought fall, according to Aristotle, under one or other of the following ten concepts : Substance, Quantity, Quality, Relation, Where, When, Situation, Possession, Action, Passion.[2] These highest concepts—the Categories [3]—neither mean to him merely subjective forms of thought, which would be utterly foreign to his Realism, nor are they merely concerned with logical relations. What they ex-

---

[1] TRENDELENBURG, *Gesch. d. Kategorieenlehre* (*Hist. Beitr.* i. 1846), pp. 1–195, 209–217; BONITZ on Aristotle's Categories, *Aristotel. Stud.* vi. H. (first published in the *Sitzungsbericht der Wiener Akad., Hist.-philol. Kl.* 1853, B. x. 591 sqq.); PRANTL, *Gesch. d. Log.* i. 182 sqq., 90 sq.; SCHUPPE, *Die arist. Kategorieen.* (*Gymn. progr. Gleiwitz*, 1866); cf. BRENTANO'S essay *Von der mannigfachen Bedeutung des Seienden nach Ar.*, published in 1862.

[2] *Categ.* c. 2 *init.* : τῶν λεγομένων τὰ μὲν κατὰ συμπλοκὴν λέγεται, τὰ δ' ἄνευ συμπλοκῆς.

C. 4 *init.* : τῶν κατὰ μηδεμίαν συμπλοκὴν λεγομένων ἕκαστον ἤτοι οὐσίαν σημαίνει ἢ ποσὸν ἢ ποιὸν ἢ πρός τι ἢ ποῦ ἢ ποτὲ ἢ κεῖσθαι ἢ ἔχειν ἢ ποιεῖν ἢ πάσχειν. *Top.* i. 9 *init.* : μετὰ τοίνυν ταῦτα δεῖ διορίσασθαι τὰ γένη τῶν κατηγοριῶν, ἐν οἷς ὑπάρχουσιν αἱ ῥηθεῖσαι τέτταρες [ὅρος, γένος, ἴδιον, συμβεβηκός]. ἔστι δὲ ταῦτα τὸν ἀριθμὸν δέκα, τί ἐστι, ποσὸν, ποιὸν, πρός τι, ποῦ, ποτὲ, κεῖσθαι, ἔχειν, ποιεῖν, πάσχειν.

[3] Aristotle uses various expressions to designate them (cf. TRENDELENBURG, *loc. cit.* at p. 6 sqq., and BONITZ, *ut supra*, at p. 23 sqq., and in the *Ind. Arist.*

press is rather the different forms of the Actual.[1] Not all forms of the Actual, however, are categories or divisions of categories ; but only those which represent the different formal points of view under which the Actual may be treated. Therefore he does not reckon among the

378, a, 5 sqq.). He calls them τὰ γένη (*scilicet*, τοῦ ὄντος, cf. *De An.* i. 1, 402, a, 22), τὰ πρῶτα *Metaph.* vii. 9, 1034, b, 7), also διαιρέσεις (*Top.* iv. 1, 120, b, 36, 121, a, 6), and πτώσεις (*Metaph.* xiv. 2, 1089, a, 26, with which cf. *Eth. Eud.* i. 8, 1217, b, 29), τὰ κοινὰ πρῶτα (*Anal. Post.* ii. 13, 96, b, 20, and *Metaph.* vii. 9, 1034, b, 9); but most frequently κατηγορίαι, κατηγορήματα, γένη or σχήματα τῶν κατηγοριῶν (τῆς κατηγορίας).—BONITZ (with whom LUTHE, *Beitr. zur Logik*, ii. 1 sqq. agrees) rightly explains the last expression by simply translating κατηγορία = 'assertion'; and consequently γένη or σχήματα τ. κατ. = ' the chief genera or fundamental forms of assertion,' = ' the various senses in which an object can be spoken of.' The same meaning is conveyed also by the shorter κατηγορίαι = 'the various modes of assertion,' or κατηγορίαι τοῦ ὄντος (*Phys.* iii. 1, 200, b, 28 ; *Metaph.* iv. 28, 1024, b, 13, ix. 1, 1045, b, 28, xiv. 6, 1093, b, 19, &c.); the latter phrase implying that every such assertion is concerned with being.--The meaning of ' predicate,' which κατηγορία often has in other places, and which BRENTANO (*loc. cit.* 105 sq.) and SCHUPPE give it here, does not suit the Aristotelian categories, for the latter designate the different senses of the τὰ κατὰ μηδεμίαν συμπλοκὴν λεγόμενα,

whereas the predicate, as such, can only occur in the proposition. Hence it is needless to ask the question (over which SCHUPPE, *loc. cit.* 21 sq., gives himself unnecessary trouble) in what sense ' Substance,' which is not a predicate-concept (*vide infra*, ch. vii. *init.*), can belong to the scheme of the categories. Any concept becomes a predicate by being asserted of something, and this may occur even with concepts expressing substance (cf. *Metaph.* vii. 3, 1029, a, 23, τὰ μὲν γὰρ ἄλλα τῆς οὐσίας κατηγορεῖται αὕτη δὲ τῆς ὕλης). For instance, in the proposition, 'this man is Socrates,' Socrates is predicate. From this *logical* function, which a substance-concept may take on *in a proposition*, it by no means follows that such an idea, when regarded out of this special relation and with reference solely to the content of the idea itself, is to be regarded as signifying anything dependent, or in the nature of a property or συμβεβηκός. —STRÜMPELL is mistaken in saying (*Gesch. ὰ theor. Phil. b. d. Griechen*, p. 211) that the categories treat of the various ways of predicating or the distinctions to be drawn in the ways of combining concepts, though in other respects he correctly apprehends the merely formal character of the categories.

[1] *Metaph.* v. 7, 1017, a, 22 :

categories either those concepts which are so universal
as to be predicable of things of the most different kinds,
and to have a different meaning according to the relation in which they are used (such as the concepts of
Being and of Unity ¹), or any of those more definite
expressions which concern the concrete condition of

καθ' αὐτὰ δὲ εἶναι λέγεται ὅσαπερ
σημαίνει τὰ σχήματα τῆς κατη-
γορίας· ὁσαχῶς γὰρ λέγεται, τοσαυταχῶς τὸ εἶναι σημαίνει (cf.
Eth. N. i. 4, 1096, a, 23). Hence
the categories are called κατηγορίαι τοῦ ὄντος (see preceding
note). That of which they represent the various meanings is
the ὄν (*Metaph.* vi. 2 *init.* ix. 1,
1045, b, 32 ; *De An.* i. 5, 410, a,
13 : ἔτι δὲ πολλαχῶς λεγομένου τοῦ
ὄντος, σημαίνει γὰρ τὸ μὲν τόδε τι,
&c.) ; cf. *Ind. Arist.* 378, a, 13
sqq.—Logical relations of concepts, on the other hand (such as
ὅρος, γένος, ἴδιον, συμβεβηκὸς), are
not expressed in separate categories, but run indifferently
through them all. In answer to
the question τί ἐστι; for instance,
you may get according to circumstances an οὐσία, a ποσὸν, &c. :
see *Top.* i. 9.—As little are the
categories concerned with the
opposition of true and false,
which has reference, not to the
nature of things, but to our relation to them (*Metaph.* vi. 4, 1027, b,
29). Yet Aristotle sometimes does
make, after all, an ontological
application of the categories, as
when, for example, he deduces
the different kinds of change
from the circumstance that one
kind is concerned with things as
to their substance, another as to
their quality, a third as to quan-

tity, and a fourth as to place ; cf.
following note.
¹ These two concepts (which
κατὰ πάντων μάλιστα λέγεται τῶν
ὄντων, according to *Metaph.* iii.
3, 998, b, 22 sqq. ; x. 2, 1053, b,
16 sqq. ; viii. 16, 1045, b, 6, cf.
supra, p. 272, n. 1), are no γένη,
but predicates which may be
applied to all that is possible.
That they cannot be genera,
Aristotle proves in *Metaph.* iii. 3,
by observing that ' a genus can
never be predicated of the mark
which stands to it as a specific
difference, but that Being and
Unity must be predicable of
every mark which can be added
to the ὄν and the οὐσία.'—Both the
concepts are used in various
meanings. *Metaph.* v. 7, gives
four senses of ' Being,' while ix.
10 (cf. xiv. 2, 1089, a, 26, where
the κατὰ συμβεβηκὸς λεγόμενον ὄν
is omitted) gives three, one of
these being that κατὰ τὰ σχήματα
τῶν κατηγοριῶν, which suggests
that a different kind of Being corresponds to each category, and
therefore implies that ' Being '
cannot as such coincide with any
single category. The same is
true of ' Unity ': τὸ ἓν ἐν παντὶ
γένει ἐστί τις φύσις, καὶ οὐθενὸς
τοῦτό γ' αὐτὸ ἡ φύσις, τὸ ἓν (=
' there is nothing whose essence
consists in Unity as such '). It
likewise occurs in all categories,

any object and its physical or ethical properties.[1]
Equally does he exclude from the number of categories
those general metaphysical conceptions which serve to
explain concrete peculiarities and processes, such as
the conceptions of the Actual and the Possible, of
Form and Matter, and of the four kinds of Cause.[2] The

but adds to the concept of the object, of which it is predicated, no new mark ; and Aristotle concludes from this, ὅτι ταὐτὸ σημαίνει πως τὸ ἓν καὶ τὸ ὂν (*Metaph*. x. 2, 1054, a, 9 sqq.), the τὸ ἓν καὶ τὸ ὂν ταὐτὸν καὶ μία φύσις τῷ ἀκολουθεῖν ἀλλήλοις . . . ἀλλ᾽ οὐχ ὡς ἑνὶ λόγῳ δηλούμενα (*Metaph*. iv. 2, 1003, b, 22), and that both have the same extension (ἀντιστρέφει, xi. 3, 1061, a, 15 sq., cf. vii. 5, 1030, b, 10, c. 16, 1040, b, 16). Upon ' Unity,' cf. also *Metaph*. x. 1 sqq. (where in particular 'unity of measure' is treated of), and the references at p. 272, n. 2 *supra*; and see also HERTLING, *De Arist. notione unius*, Berl. 1864. As to the ὂν, see particularly BRENTANO, *Von der mannigfachen Bedeutung des Seienden*.

[1] For this reason such a concept as Movement (or Change) is not put among the categories ; it is rather, according to Aristotle, a physical concept which, through the different categories, receives its further determination as substantial change, qualitative or quantitative change, or movement in space (*Phys*. v. 1 *fin*., c. 2 *init*., *ibid*. 226, a, 23, iii. 1, 200, b, 32 ; *Gen. et Corr*. i. 4, 319, b, 31 ; *De Cœlo*, iv, 3, 310, a, 23 ; *Metaph*. xii. 2, 1069, b, 9 ; more about this *infra*). He allows that, looked at in itself, it may

be put in the category of Action and Passion (*Top*. iv. 1, 120, b, 26 ; *Phys*. v. 2, 225, b, 13, iii. 1, 201, a, 23 ; *De An*. iii. 2, 426, a, 2 ; TRENDELENBURG, *Hist. Beitr*. i. 135 sqq.), and in this sense it is even used in *Metaph*. viii. 4, 1029, b, 22, to illustrate how the categories other than Substance have a substratum, yet it does not itself *become* a category. Still less would it be a category if we were to accept the belief of the later Peripatetics (which is not established by *Metaph*. v. 13, 1020, a, 26 ; SIMPL. *Categ*. 78, δ, § 29 Bas.) that it belonged to the category of the ποσὸν, or as others preferred (SIMPL. *ibid*. 35, δ, § 38) to the πρός τι.—So also, when Eudemus (*Eth. Eud*. 1217, b, 26) gives Motion (in place of Action and Passion) among the categories, it is not Aristotelian. Other Peripatetics, notably Theophrastus, said more correctly, that it ' runs through many categories' (SIMPL. *ibid*. 35, δ, § 38 ; *Phys*. 94, a).—In the same way ' the Good' is to be found in various categories (*Eth. N*. i. 4, 1096, a, 19, 23).

[2] None of these concepts is reckoned among the categories or comprised under any one of them. On the contrary, when Aristotle is considering the various meanings of ' Being,' he mentions the distinction of δυν-

purpose of ' categories' is not to describe things by their
actual qualities, nor yet to set forth the general conceptions which are needful for this purpose. They are
confined to pointing out the different sides which may
be kept in view in any such description. In Aristotle's
intention, they are meant to give us, not real conceptions, but only the framework into which all real
conceptions are to be set, whether they are confined to
one division of the framework or extend to several.[1]

ἁμει and ἐντελεχείᾳ, with the distinction of truth and falsity, as
matters to be superadded to the
distinctions expressed by the
categories (*Metaph.* v. 7, 1017, a,
7, 22, 31, 35, vi. 2 *init.*, ix. 10
init., c. 1, 1045, b, 32, xiv. 2,
1089, a, 26; *De An.* i. 1, 402, a, 22,
cf. TRENDELENBURG, *Gesch. der
Categorieenlehre, ut supra*, p. 157
sqq. ; BONITZ, *ut supra*, p. 19
sq.), but themselves running
through the various categories
indifferently (*Phys.* iii. 1, 200, b,
26 ; *Metaph.* ix. 10 *init.* : τὸ δὲ
κατὰ δύναμιν καὶ ἐγέργειαν τούτων).
Aristotle does not tell us why
they cannot be reckoned among
the categories ; but the reason
seems to be that indicated above,
viz. that these ideas do not merely
relate, like those of substance,
quality, &c., to the formal character and the formal differences
of that which falls under them,
but designate definite real relations of actual being.

[1] Thus also BRANDIS, ii. b,
394 sqq. On the other hand TREN-
DELENBURG, *ibid.* 162 sq. explains the absence of ' Possibility
and Actuality ' from the categories by saying that the latter
are ' separated predicates,' whilst
the former is ' no real predicate.'
It seems, however, that precisely
the opposite is the case. The
categories are *not themselves* directly taken as predicates, but
only as designating the *place* of
certain predicates in the scale ;
whereas the distinction of Possible and Actual is based on real
and definite facts, the contrast
between the different conditions
of development in individual
things, and the opposition in the
universe as a whole between the
corporeal and the spiritual. The
one kind of distinction is only an
abstract, metaphysical expression
of the other. But it is not possible entirely to agree with BONITZ
when he says on p. 18, 21, that
the categories ' are only meant to
render possible a survey of what
is contained in the empirical
data,' and hence that ' such concepts are excluded as extend
beyond the comprehension of
empirical data, to any kind of
explanation of them.' For the
concept of Motion is given by
experience just as much as that
of Action and Passion, and the
concept of Substance is as valuable for ' explaining the data ' as
that of form and matter, or of

Of the completeness of this framework, Aristotle is convinced,[1] but he nowhere tells us how he came to set

actuality and possibility.—Nor does it seem possible to say with BRENTANO (*loc. cit.* p. 82 sq.), that the categories are 'real concepts,' if by this we are to understand such concepts as designate the common object-matter of a series of experiences, such as are the concepts of weight, extension, thought, &c. For those very categories which are most frequently and universally applied—substance, quantity, quality, relation, action, and passion—designate merely formal relations, and hence are adapted to cover and apply to a content of the most diverse character; and though this is not so absolutely true of others—such as ποῦ, ποτὲ, or κεῖσθαι—that peculiarity only proves that Aristotle was not able strictly to carry out through them all the point of view with which he started his category-scheme as a whole. BRENTANO himself, at p. 131 sq., admits that ' the distinction of the categories is not a real distinction.'

[1] PRANTL, *Gesch. d. Log.* i. 204 sqq., denies that Aristotle adopted any absolutely fixed number of categories; but it is clear, not only from the enumerations given at p. 274, n. 2 and p. 282, n. 3, but also from many other expressions, that he did. Thus we have in *Soph. El.* c. 22, *init.*: ἐπείπερ ἔχομεν τὰ γένη τῶν κατηγοριῶν— namely, the ten enumerated in *Top.* i. 9, to which at c. 4, 166, b, 14, after mentioning τὶ (ταὐτὸ), ποιὸν, ποσὸν, ποιοῦν, πάσχον, διακείμενον (really only a kind of ποιὸν, the διάθεσις : see *Categ.* c.

8, 10, a, 35 sqq. *Metaph.* v. 20), he refers back with the words : καὶ τἆλλα δ' ὡς διῄρηται πρότερον. *De An.* i. 1, 402, a, 24: πότερον τόδε τι καὶ οὐσία ἢ ποιὸν ἢ ποσὸν ἢ καί τις ἄλλη τῶν διαιρεθεισῶν κατηγοριῶν. *Ibid.* c. 5, 410, a, 14: σημαίνει γὰρ τὸ μὲν τόδε τι τὸ δὲ ποσὸν ἢ ποιὸν ἢ καί τινα ἄλλην τῶν διαιρεθεισῶν κατηγοριῶν. *Anal. Pri.* i. 37: τὸ δ' ὑπάρχειν τόδε τῷδε . . . τοσαυταχῶς ληπτέον ὁσαχῶς αἱ κατηγορίαι διῄρηνται. *Metaph.* xii. 1, 1069, a, 20 : πρῶτον ἡ οὐσία, εἶτα τὸ ποιὸν, εἶτα τὸ ποσόν ; vi. 2, 1026, a, 36: τὰ σχήματα τῆς κατηγορίας, οἷον τὸ μὲν τί, τὸ δὲ ποιὸν, τὸ δὲ ποσὸν, τὸ δὲ ποῦ, τὸ δὲ ποτὲ, καὶ εἴ τι ἄλλο σημαίνει τὸν τρόπον τοῦτον ; vii. 4, 1030, a, 18 : καὶ γὰρ τὸ τί ἐστιν ἕνα μὲν τρόπον σημαίνει τὴν οὐσίαν καὶ τὸ τόδε τι, ἄλλον δὲ ἕκαστον τῶν κατηγορουμένων, ποσὸν, ποιὸν καὶ ὅσα ἄλλα τοιαῦτα ; xii. 4, 1070, a, 33 : it is a question of, πότερον ἕτεραι ἢ αἱ αὐταὶ ἀρχαὶ στοιχεῖα τῶν οὐσιῶν καὶ τῶν πρός τι, καὶ καθ' ἑκάστην δὲ τῶν κατηγοριῶν ὁμοίως. Likewise in *Metaph.* vii. 9, 1034, b, 9, xiv. 2, 1089, a, 7; *Phys.* iii. 1, 200, b, 26, after mentioning some of the categories, he refers to the rest with a mere ' αἱ ἄλλαι κατηγορίαι,' as to something well known, and in *Anal. Post.* i. 22, 83, b, 12, a, 21, the impossibility of an infinitely extended argument is proved by the assertion that the number of categories is limited to those there named. The completeness of Aristotle's list of categories is also supposed by the proof referred to at the end of p. 276, n. 2, that

out these categories and no others;[1] and among the
categories themselves there is so little indication of
any fixed principles for their evolution [2] that we are

there are only three kinds of
motion (in the narrower sense),
qualitative, quantitative, and
local (*Phys.* v. 1 sq.), inasmuch
as that theorem is proved by the
process of exclusion. ' Motion,'
Aristotle argues, ' does not occur
in the categories of substance,
&c. : therefore only those three
categories remain.'

[1] Even in the lost writings no
such demonstration seems to
have occurred ; otherwise the
early commentators would have
appealed to it. Whereas, on the
contrary, SIMPL. *Schol. in Ar.*
79, a, 44, says : ὅλως οὐδαμοῦ περὶ
τῆς τάξεως τῶν γενῶν οὐδεμίαν
αἰτίαν ὁ Ἀριστοτέλης ἀπεφήνατο.

[2] To TRENDELENBURG (in his
dissertation *De Arist. Categoriis*
[Berl. 1833] and the *Elementa
Logices Aristotelicæ*, p. 54) belongs the credit of having first
endeavoured to find one. But
even his repeated explanation in
Hist. Beitr. i. 23 sqq., 194 sq. has
not persuaded us that he has
really succeeded in doing so. It
seems rather that the objections
which RITTER, iii. 80, and still
more exhaustively BONITZ, *loc.
cit.* 35 sqq., have brought against
his opinion, are well justified.
TRENDELENBURG (and after him
BIESE, *Phil. d. Arist.* i. 54 sq.)
believes that in setting out these
ten genera Aristotle was proxi-
mately influenced by grammatical distinctions He suggests
that οὐσία corresponds to the
substantive, ποσὸν and ποιὸν to
the adjective ; with πρός τι correspond such forms of expres-

sion as those referred to in
Categ. c. 7 ; ποῦ and ποτὲ are represented by the adverbs of place
and time; the last four categories are to be looked for in the
verb, for ποιεῖν and πάσχειν translate into a general concept the
force of the active and passive
voices, as κεῖσθαι renders one side
of the intransitive, and ἔχειν the
special force of the Greek perfect.—But, in the first place, as
BONITZ, p. 41 sqq., fully proves,
Aristotle himself nowhere gives
any indication of his having
arrived at his categories in this
way. On the contrary, he does
not distinguish the parts of
speech on any such method as
that which Trendelenburg's
theory of the categories would
presuppose, for he nowhere expressly distinguishes the adverbs,
he treats the adjective (as ῥῆμα)
along with the verb, and in fact
the only ' parts of speech ' which
he names (apart from the article
and conjunction) are the ὄνομα
and the ῥῆμα. It is therefore
not probable that grammatical
forms to which, as ' parts of
speech' he paid no attention,
should nevertheless have guided
him in distinguishing the classes
of concepts. And, again, the
two series do not in fact correspond to any such extent as we
should have expected if Trendelenburg's supposition were
correct. For ' quantity' and
' quality ' may just as well be expressed by substantives (*e.g.* λευκότης, θερμότης, &c., *Categ.* c. 8,
9, a, 29) or verbs (λελεύκωται,

reduced to supposing that he obtained them empirically, by putting together the main points of view from which the data of experience can be practically treated. It is true that a certain logical progress is to be found among them. We begin with the Substantial—the Thing. Next in order to this, he deals with Quali-

&c.) as by adjectives; 'action and passion' as well by substantives (πρᾶξις, πάθος, &c.) as by verbs; 'time' not only by adverbs but also by adjectives (χθιζὸς, δευτεραῖος, &c.); very many substantives designate no substance (*Categ.* c. 5, 4, a, 14, 21); and for 'relation' a corresponding grammatical form cannot be found.—BRENTANO, *loc. cit.* p. 148 sqq., also seeks to defend the Aristotelian categories against the charge of having no scientific derivation and suggests another scheme. He believes that in arranging them Aristotle first distinguished 'substance' from 'accidents,' and, among the latter, distinguished the *absolute* from the *relative*; and that he went on to divide the former into (1) *inherences* (material = ποσὸν, and formal = ποιόν); (2) *affections* (ποιεῖν and πάσχειν, to which, at one time, Aristotle added ἔχειν); (3) *external circumstances* (ποῦ and ποτὲ, and, for a time, κεῖσθαι). The question is not, however, whether it is *possible* to bring the ten categories into some logical scheme (for that could be done with any series, unless it were merely put together at haphazard), but whether *Aristotle arrived at them* by means of a logical deduction. And against any such supposition

there are two facts: first, that Aristotle in speaking of the categories, never indicates such a deduction, and next, that none can be found into which they naturally fit. Even in Brentano's ingenious scheme, this is not the case. If the ten categories had come about in the way he suggests, they would have been enumerated by Aristotle in a corresponding order. Instead of that, the πρός τι, which, according to Brentano, should come last, stands in the middle in every enumeration (see p.274, n. 1 and p.282, n.3), and its regular place (the only exception being *Phys.* v. 1) is immediately after the '*inherences*.' After it, again, the '*affections*' do not follow (as they should according to Brentano's order), but the '*external circumstances*.' Nor is the distinction of *inherences* and *affections* itself Aristotelian.—So far as a logical disposition of the categories *ex post facto* is concerned, ZELLER gives on p. 288 *infra*, that which he prefers, although he does not believe that Aristotle arrived at his list of categories by any method in which he had in his mind beforehand either that or any other logical scheme into which they were to fit.

ties: first (in the ποσὸν and ποιὸν), those qualities
which belong to a thing in itself, and then (in the πρός
τι), those which belong to a thing in its relation to
other things. From these he passes to the external
conditions of sensible existence—Space and Time.
And he ends the list with the concepts which express
changes and the conditions thereby produced. This
cannot be called a deduction in the strict sense ; for that,
according to Aristotelian principles, was not possible
in the case of the highest general conceptions at all.[1]
In fact, the order of the categories is not always
the same.[2] It even seems that ten is somewhat arbitrarily fixed as their number. Aristotle himself so
far recognises this, that in his later writings he passes
over the categories of Possession and Situation, in
places where he apparently intends to give a complete
enumeration.[3] It is possible that it may have been the
example of the Pythagoreans,[4] and the predilection

---

[1] Vide supra, pp. 246 and 272.

[2] Examples will be found in
what follows, and also at p. 279,
n. 1. The most striking thing
with regard to this is that in
Cat. c. 7, contrary to the otherwise constant rule, and even to
the order given in c. 4, πρός τι
precedes ποιόν. No satisfactory
reason can be found for this, but
it would be rash to conclude anything from it against the genuineness of the work, since a later
writer would probably be less
likely to permit a divergence
from the order given than would
Aristotle himself, for whom it
was not firmly established.

[3] Anal. Post. i. 22, 83, a, 21 :
ὥστε ἢ ἐν τῷ τί ἐστιν [κατηγορεῖται]

ἢ ὅτι ποιὸν ἢ ποσὸν ἢ πρός τι ἢ ποιοῦν ἢ πάσχον ἢ ποῦ ἢ ποτὲ, ὅταν ἐν
καθ' ἑνὸς κατηγορηθῇ. Ibid. b, 15 :
τὰ γένη τῶν κατηγοριῶν πεπέρανται·
ἢ γὰρ ποιὸν ἢ ποσὸν ἢ πρός τι ἢ
ποιοῦν ἢ πάσχον ἢ ποῦ ἢ ποτέ (the
οὐσία to which the latter are opposed as συμβεβηκότα has been
already mentioned). Phys. v. 1
fin. : εἰ οὖν αἱ κατηγορίαι διῄρηνται
οὐσίᾳ καὶ ποιότητι καὶ τῷ ποῦ καὶ
τῷ ποτὲ καὶ τῷ πρός τι καὶ τῷ ποσῷ
καὶ τῷ ποιεῖν ἢ πάσχειν, ἀνάγκη
τρεῖς εἶναι κινήσεις (cf. p. 279, n. 1
fin.). Metaph. v. 8, 1017, a, 24 :
τῶν κατηγορουμένων τὰ μὲν τί ἐστι
σημαίνει, τὰ δὲ ποιὸν, τὰ δὲ ποσὸν,
τὰ δὲ πρός τι, τὰ δὲ ποῦ τὰ δὲ ποτέ.

[4] See ZELL. Ph. d. Gr. pt. 1,
325.

for a decimal system inherited from them by the Platonists,[1] which made it at first seem to Aristotle natural that he should find a round number of categories. But we cannot well suppose any further connection between his doctrine and the Pythagorean ;[2] nor is the conjecture[3] much more probable, that he borrowed his categories from the school of Plato.[4] It is true that almost all of them appear in Plato's writings ;[5] but we cannot attribute any great weight to this coincidence, for the reason that in Plato they are merely used as occasion arises, without any attempt to arrive at a full enumeration of *all* the categories in one scheme.

Among the categories themselves, much the most

[1] ZELLER, *ibid.* p. 857 sqq.

[2] As PETERSEN supposed in *Philos. Chrysipp. Fundamenta,* p. 12.

[3] ROSE, *Arist. Libr. Ord.* 238 sqq.

[4] In the first place, there is no trace whatever of the ten categories among the Platonists ; and it is not likely that information about so notable a point would neither have been transmitted through their writings nor through Chrysippus and other scholars of the Alexandrian period to the later Peripatetics, and through them to us. And again, the theory of the categories is so closely connected with the other opinions of Aristotle that it is not likely to have sprung up on other ground. Take, for example, merely the fundamental statements as to the οὐσία and its relation to properties, on which the whole division of the categories in Aristotle is based. These are certainly not Platonic ; in fact it is one chief point of dispute between Aristotle and his master that the latter conceded to ideas of quality the position of substances and made the ποιόν an οὐσία. —We might rather suppose (as UEBERWEG does in his *Logik.* § 47, at p. 100) that Aristotle was led to his theory of Categories in his recoil against the theory of Ideas, and, in particular, by the reflection that the Ideas only represented things under the form of substantiality, whereas things in the actual world exhibit many different forms of existence. But as this explanation itself presupposes the distinction of substance from properties, &c., too much importance must not be attached to the theory.

[5] See TRENDELENBURG, *Hist. Beitr.* i. 205 sqq.; BONITZ, *ut supra,* p. 56. PRANTL, *Gesch. d. Log.* i. 73 sqq., and ZELLER, *Ph. d. Gr.* pt. i. p. 589.

important is that of *Substance*, which may here be fitly
treated at once in detail. Substance, in the strict sense,
is individual Substance. That which can be set out in
parts is a Quantum.[1] If these parts are divided, then
the Quantum is a discrete Quantum, a multitude; if
they are interdependent, then it is a constant Quantum,
a *quantity* ;[2] if they are in a definite position (θέσις),
the quantity is extensive ; if they are only in an order
(τάξις) without position, then it is non-extensive.[3]
The undivided, or the unity by means of which quantity
is distinguished, is the measure of it. This is the distinguishing mark of quantity, that it is measurable and
has a measure.[4] As *Quantitas* belongs to a divisible

[1] *Metaph.* v. 13 *init.*: ποσὸν
λέγεται τὸ διαιρετὸν εἰς ἐνυπάρχοντα,
ὧν ἑκάτερον ἢ ἕκαστον ἕν τι καὶ
τόδε τι πέφυκεν εἶναι. The ἐνυπάρχοντα, however, are, the constituent parts as distinguished from
the logical elements of the concept. Thus, *e.g.*, in *Metaph.* iii. 1,
995, b, 27, c, 3 *init.* he inquires
whether the γένη or the ἐνυπάρχοντα are the highest principles ;
ibid. viii. 17 *fin.* the στοιχεῖον
is defined as that εἰς ὃ διαιρεῖται
[sc. τὶ] ἐνυπάρχον [Acc.] ὡς ὕλην.
Similarly in viii. 2, 1043, a, 19, cf.
Gen. An. i. 21, 729, b. 3 : ὡς ἐνυπάρχον καὶ μόριον ὂν εὐθὺς τοῦ γινομένου
σώματος μιγνύμενον τῇ ὕλῃ. *Ibid.*
c. 18, 724, a, 24 : ὅσα ὡς ἐξ ὕλης
γίγνεσθαι τὰ γιγνόμενα λέγομεν, ἔκ
τινος ἐνυπάρχοντος . . . . ἐστίν.
Cat. c. 2, 1, a, 24, c, 5, 3, a, 32,
&c. (*Ind. Arist.* 257, a, 39 sqq.)
The ποσὸν is consequently that
which is made up of parts, like a
body, and not of logical elements,
like a concept. But since num-

ber and time are also ποσὰ, we
must not suppose that these
'parts' are merely material ones
and in *Metaph.* v. 13, the τόδε τι
must be understood not of individual substance, but in a wider
sense, as signifying anything
numerically distinct (ἀριθμῷ ἕν).

[2] *Metaph.* v. 13 (where also
ποσὸν καθ' αὑτὸ and κατὰ συμβεβηκός is spoken of). *Cat.* 6 *init.*
TRENDELENBURG, *ibid.* p. 82.
treats further of discrete and
continuous quantities, with special reference to *Cat.* 6, *Phys.* v.
3, 227, a, 10 sqq. and *Metaph.*
loc. cit.

[3] *Cat.* c. 6 *init.*, *ibid.* 5, a, 15
sqq. Aristotle does not here express the opposition of that
which has and that which has not
extension in any general form,
but merely by means of examples
(of the former—line, surface,
body; of the latter—time, number, word).

[4] *Metaph.* x. 1, 1052, b. 15

and substantial whole, so *Qualitas* expresses the differences whereby the conceptual whole is divided; for under *Qualitas*, in the stricter sense of the word,[1] Aristotle understands nothing else but the distinguishing mark, or further determination wherein a given Universal particularises itself. As the two chief divisions of qualities, he notes those which express an essential distinction, and those which express a movement or activity.[2] Elsewhere he names four determinations of quality as the most important,[3] but these again fall

sqq.; *Cat.* c. 6, 4, b, 32. This follows immediately from the above definition of ποσόν: that which can be divided into parts can also be built up of parts and be measured by them.—Further marks of ποσόν (*Cat.* c. 6, 5, b, 11 sqq.) are that nothing is opposed to it, and that it is what it is and neither more nor less, and that the concept of equality and inequality belongs peculiarly to it.

[1] The generic concepts (δεύτεραι οὐσίαι) are sometimes also called ποιὸν, or more correctly ποιὰ οὐσία (*Cat.* c. 5, 3, b, 13 ; cf. *Metaph.* vii. 1, 1039, a, 1); and sometimes the συμβεβηκότα are comprised under the same term (*Anal. Post.* i. 22, 83, a, 36).

[2] In *Cat.* c. 8 the concept of ποιότης is not explained except by reference partly to forms of speech and partly to examples. In *Metaph.* v. 14, 1020, b, 13, however, there is an enumeration of its different meanings thus: σχεδὸν δὴ κατὰ δύο τρόπους λέγοιτ' ἂν τὸ ποιὸν, καὶ τούτων ἕνα τὸν κυριώτατον · πρώτη μὲν γὰρ ποιότης ἡ τῆς οὐσίας διαφορά . . . τὰ δὲ

πάθη τῶν κινουμένων ἢ κινούμενα καὶ αἱ τῶν κινήσεων διαφοραί. To the first class belong, among other things, the qualitative distinctions of numbers ; to the second, ἀρετὴ and κακία. With regard to the διαφορὰ see *supra*, p. 215, n. 1. Therefore Quality expresses a determination of form, for that is true of the διαφορὰ ; *Metaph.* viii. 2, 1043, a, 19 : ἔοικε γὰρ ὁ μὲν διὰ τῶν διαφορῶν λόγος τοῦ εἴδους καὶ τῆς ἐνεργείας εἶναι, ὁ δ' ἐκ τῶν ἐνυπαρχόντων τῆς ὕλης μᾶλλον.

[3] *Cat.* c. 8. The four εἴδη ποιότητος (besides which, we are told, 10, a, 25, others might occur) are the following : (1) ἕξις and διάθεσις, which are distinguished inasmuch as ἕξις expresses a lasting state, while διάθεσις is used sometimes for every state whatsoever, and sometimes for a transitory one (cf. *Metaph.* v. 19, 20; BONITZ and SCHWEGLER on this passage ; TRENDELENBURG, *Hist. Beitr.* i. 95 sqq. WAITZ, *Arist. Org.* i. 303 sqq.) Instances of ἕξις are ἐπιστῆμαι and ἀρεταί; of mere διάθεσις, health and sickness. (2) Ὅσα

under the same heads.[1] He treats as the peculiar mark of *Qualitas*, the opposition of the like and the unlike.[2] But in dividing off this category from others Aristotle finds himself in difficulties.[3] To the category of *Relativity*[4] belongs that of which the peculiar essence consists in a definite relation to something else;[5] and in this sense Relativity is the category which ' expresses

κατὰ δύναμιν φυσικὴν ἢ ἀδυναμίαν λέγεται (a class which, however, cannot be strictly distinguished from the ἕξεις and διαθέσεις ; see TRENDELENBURG, *ibid.* 98 sqq. More about the δύναμις later). (3) The passive qualities, παθητικαὶ ποιότητες, also called πάθος in the meaning of ποιότης καθ᾽ ἣν ἀλλοιοῦσθαι ἐνδέχεται (*Metaph.* v. 21), and distinguished from the πάθη (which fall under the category of πάσχειν), by their duration. Aristotle, however, understands by them not only the qualities which are produced by a πάθος (such as white and black colour) but also those which produce a πάθος or an ἀλλοίωσις on our senses : cf. *De An.* ii. 5 *init.* (4) Figure (σχῆμα καὶ μορφή).

[1] For the first two and a part of the third express ' activities and movements '; the rest, ' essential properties.'

[2] *Cat.* c. 8, 11, a, 15 ; on the other hand (*ibid.* 10, b, 12, 26), the ἐναντιότης and the μᾶλλον καὶ ἧττον (= ' difference of degree') do not belong to all quantities. The notion of Similarity, cf. *Top.* i. 17 ; *Metaph.* v. 9, 1018, a, 15, x. 3, 1054, a, 3, and *infra*, p. 287, n. 2.

[3] For, on the one hand, the remark in *Cat.* c. 8, 10, a, 16, that the concepts of rarity and denseness, roughness and smoothness, designate no *quality*, but a *situ-*

ation of the bodily parts (*i.e.* a κεῖσθαι), would (as TRENDELENBURG rightly perceives, *Hist. Beitr.* i. 101 sq.) equally apply to many other things which Aristotle includes under Quality; whilst, on the other hand, the impossibility of a constant definition of the categories is seen from the fact that a generic concept (*e.g.* ἐπιστήμη) may belong to the πρός τι, when a corresponding specific concept (γραμματική) belongs to the ποιὸν (*Cat.* c. 8, 11, a, 20 ; *Top.* iv. 124, b, 18 ; whereas in *Metaph.* v. 15, 1021, b, 3, ἰατρική is counted under πρός τι, that it may follow its generic concept, ἐπιστήμη).

[4] That the category of Relativity, in *Cat.* c. 7, precedes that of Quality (*vide supra*) is contrary to the natural relation of both, as is clear, not only in all other enumerations and in the express explanation in *Metaph.* xiv. 1, 1088, a, 22, but indirectly also (in *Cat.* c. 7 itself) from the fact that the ὅμοιον and ἴσον (qualitative and quantitative equality) is in 6, b, 21 counted as πρός τι ; cf. *Top.* i. 17 ; TRENDELENBURG, *ibid.* p. 117.

[5] Thus *Cat.* c. 7, 8, a, 31 : ἔστι τὰ πρός τι οἷς τὸ εἶναι ταὐτόν ἐστι τῷ πρός τί πως ἔχειν : where the earlier verbal explanations are expressly declared (at the

the least reality.'[1] Aristotle distinguishes three kinds of Relativity,[2] which are again reduced to two.[3] In this, however, he is not consistent throughout,[4] nor has he been able to find any sure marks of this category,[5] or to avoid confusing it in many ways with others.[6]

beginning of the chapter) to be insufficient. Cf. *Top.* vi. 4, 142, a, 26, c. 8, 146, b, 3.

[1] *Metaph. ut supra* : τὸ δὲ πρός τι πάντων [for which ALEX. read πασῶν] ἥκιστα φύσις τις ἢ οὐσία τῶν κατηγοριῶν ἐστι, καὶ ὑστέρα τοῦ ποιοῦ καὶ ποσοῦ, &c. ; b, 2 : τὸ δὲ πρός τι οὔτε δυνάμει οὐσία οὔτε ἐνεργείᾳ. *Eth. N.* i. 4 ; 1096, a, 21 : παραφυάδι γὰρ τοῦτ᾽ ἔοικε καὶ συμβεβηκότι τοῦ ὄντος.

[2] *Metaph.* v. 15 : the πρός τι appears in the following forms : (1) καθ᾽ ἀριθμὸν καὶ ἀριθμοῦ πάθη (and in other related forms) ; to this head belong the ἴσον, ὅμοιον, ταὐτὸν in so far as these are concerned with relations to a given unity : ταὐτὰ μὲν γὰρ ὧν μία ἡ οὐσία, ὅμοια δ᾽ ὧν ἡ ποιότης μία, ἴσα δὲ ὧν τὸ ποσὸν ἕν (the latter also in *Gen. et Corr.* ii. 6, 333, a, 29) ; (2) κατὰ δύναμιν ποιητικὴν καὶ παθητικήν, like the θερμαντικὸν and the θερμαντόν ; (3) in the sense which comprises such expressions as μετρητὸν, ἐπιστητὸν, διανοητόν. The first two kinds come also in *Phys.* iii. 1, 200, b, 28.

[3] *Metaph. ibid.* 1021, a, 26 : In the first two of the cases adduced the πρός τι is called τῷ ὅπερ ἐστὶν ἄλλου λέγεσθαι αὐτὸ ὃ ἐστὶν (double is ἡμίσεος διπλάσιον, that which warms θερμαντοῦ θερμαντικὸν). In the third case it is τῷ ἄλλο πρὸς αὐτὸ λέγεσθαι (what can be measured or thought has its proper essence indepen-

dently from the fact that it is measured or thought, and only becomes a relative in so far as that which measures and thinks enters into relation with it). The like also in *Metaph.* x. 6, 1056, b, 34, 1057, a, 7.

[4] Another division is found in *Top.* vi. 4, 125, a, 33 sqq.

[5] The various peculiarities of the Relative which are mentioned in *Cat.* c. 7 are all found, as is there remarked, only in a part of that class : *e.g.* the ἐναντιότης (6, b, 15, cf. *Metaph.* x. 6, 1056, b, 35, c. 7, 1057, a, 37, and also TRENDELENBURG, 123 sqq.), the μᾶλλον καὶ ἧττον, the property of correlatives to be simultaneous (*Cat.* 7, b, 15), which is not found in the relative of the second class (the ἐπιστητὸν, &c., see note 3, *supra*). But it is a universal mark of every relative, to have a corresponding correlative (τὸ πρὸς ἀντιστρέφοντα λέγεσθαι, *Cat.* 6, b, 27 sqq.), which, in the main, tallies with the statement made at first (c. 7 *init.*) and afterwards repeated (8, a, 33), that the πρός τι is ὅσα αὐτὰ ἅπερ ἐστὶν ἑτέρων εἶναι λέγεται ἢ ὁπωσοῦν ἄλλως πρὸς ἕτερον, the latter statement differing merely by being less exact. Individual substances (πρῶται οὐσίαι) cannot be relative ; but generic concepts (δεύτεραι οὐσίαι) may be. *Cat.* 8, a, 13 sqq.

[6] Thus in *Cat.* c. 7, 6, b, 2, the ἕξις, διάθεσις, αἴσθησις, ἐπι-

The remaining categories are dealt with so briefly in the treatise on the *Categories*—and, indeed, wherever Aristotle mentions them—that an extended account of them cannot be given here.[1]

The essential meaning of the theory of the categories lies in the fact that it indicates to us how to distinguish the different meanings of concepts and the different corresponding relations of the actual. Thus, in the first place, the original and unchangeable essence or substance of each thing is distinguished from all that is derivative.[2] Among things which are derivative, a division is again made between the qualities, the activities, and the external circumstances. Of the qualities, one class belong to things in themselves, and in this case they express sometimes a quantitative and sometimes a qualitative determination—that is to say, they have relation either to the substratum or to the form ;[3]

στήμη, θέσις are referred to πρός τι, of which, however, the first four belong also to Quality, the last to Position ; ποιεῖν and πάσχειν, according to *Metaph.* v. 15, 1020, b, 28, 1021, a, 21, are relative concepts ; the parts of a whole (πηδάλιον, κεφαλή, &c.) are also said to be relative (*Cat.* c. 7, 6, b, 36 sqq., cf., however, 8, a, 24 sqq.). Also Matter (*Phys.* ii. 2, 194, b, 8); and if so, why not Form as well ?

[1] In the abrupt ending of the genuine *Categories*, c. 9 (as to which, see the latter part of n. 1 to p. 64, *supra*) it is merely said of the category of ποιεῖν and πάσχειν, that it is susceptible of opposition and of More and Less. As to the other categories, there is nothing but a reference to what

has gone before. *Gen. et Corr.* i. 7, treats Action and Passion more at length, but that passage deals with the physical meaning of these terms, and we shall have to mention it later on. Ἕξις is discussed etymologically in *Metaph.* v. 15, and in *Cat.* c. 15 (in the *Postpræ-dicamenta*).

[2] Cf. note 4 on next page.

[3] As TRENDELENBURG, p. 103, rightly remarks, the Quale is related to the Form, the Quantum to the Matter ; *vide supra*, 284, n. 1 and 4, p. 285, n. 2, cf. p. 219, n. 2. Thus similarity also, which, according to Aristotle, consists in qualitative equality (see p. 286, n. 3, 287, n. 2), is defined, in another place, as equality of Form (*Metaph.* x. 3, 1054, b, 3 : ὅμοια δὲ ἐὰν μὴ ταὐτὰ

another class belong to things only in relation to other things—that is to say, they are relative.[1] With regard to activities, the most far-reaching opposition is that of Action and Passion ; on the other hand, the categories of Possession and Situation, as has been already remarked,[2] have only a precarious rank, and are afterwards dropped by Aristotle himself *sub silentio*. Finally, as regards external circumstances, these are taken on the one hand in terms of Space, and on the other in terms of Time, in the categories of the Where and the When. In strictness, however, both of these ought to have been ranged under the Category of Relation ; and perhaps it was this kinship which led Aristotle to place them as a rule next in order after that category.[3] All the categories, however, lead back to Substance as their base.[4]

ἁπλῶς ὄντα . . . . κατὰ τὸ εἶδος ταῦτα ᾖ), in *Metaph*. iv. 5, 1010, a, 23 sqq. ποσὸν and ποιὸν are transposed with ποσὸν and εἶδος, and in *Metaph*. xi. 6, 1063, a, 27, ποιὸν is taken as φύσις ὡρισμένη, ποσὸν (like Matter, *vide infra*) as ἀόριστος.

[1] All concepts of relation refer to something which is conditioned; substances are not πρός τι : *vide supra*.

[2] *Vide supra*, p. 282.

[3] That this is not without exception is clear from p. 282, n. 3.

[4] *Anal. Post*. i. 22, 83, b, 11 : πάντα γὰρ ταῦτα [ποιὸν, &c.] συμβέβηκε καὶ κατὰ τῶν οὐσιῶν κατηγορεῖται (about συμβεβηκὸς in this meaning see p. 275 sqq.). Similarly l. 19, *ibid*. a, 25, c. 4, 73, b, 5. *Phys*. i. 1, 185, a, 31 : οὐθὲν γὰρ τῶν ἄλλων χωριστόν ἐστι

παρὰ τὴν οὐσίαν· πάντα γὰρ καθ' ὑποκειμένου τῆς οὐσίας λέγεται (but what is asserted καθ' ὑποκειμένου is a συμβεβηκὸς in the further sense: *Anal. Post*. i. 4, 73, b, 8 ; *Metaph*. v. 30 *fin*. &c) ; c. 7, 190, a, 34 : καὶ γὰρ ποσὸν καὶ ποιὸν καὶ πρὸς ἕτερον καὶ ποτὲ καὶ ποῦ γίνεται ὑποκειμένου τινὸς διὰ τὸ μόνην τὴν οὐσίαν μηθενὸς κατ' ἄλλου λέγεσθαι ὑποκειμένου τὰ δ' ἄλλα πάντα κατὰ τῆς οὐσίας ; iii. 4, 203, b, 32. *Metaph*. vii. 1, 1028, a, 13, *ibid*. l. 32 : πάντων ἡ οὐσία πρῶτον καὶ λόγῳ καὶ γνώσει καὶ χρόνῳ (cf. the whole chapter); c. 4, 1029, b, 23, c. 13, 1038, b, 27, ix. 1 *init*. xi. 1, 1059, a, 29, xiv. 1, 1088, b, 4 : ὕστερον γὰρ [τῆς οὐσίας] πᾶσαι αἱ κατηγορίαι. *Gen. et Corr*. i. 3, 317, b, 8. Hence in all the enumerations οὐσία goes first. Cf. also *infra*, ch. vii. *init*.

An inquiry, therefore, into Substance, or Being as such, must be the starting-point in the investigation of the Actual.

2. *The First Philosophy as the Science of Being.*

As Science in general has for its task the investigation of the grounds of things,[1] so the highest Science must be that which refers to the last and most universal of the grounds of things. For this gives us the most comprehensive knowledge, everything else being comprehended under the most universal. It gives us the knowledge which is most difficult to attain, as the most universal principles are the furthest removed from sense experience. It gives us the surest knowledge, since it has to do with the most simple concepts and principles. It gives us the most instructive knowledge, because it points out the highest grounds, and all instruction is a setting forth of the grounds of things. It gives us that knowledge which is most truly an end to itself, in that it is concerned with the highest object of knowledge. It gives us that which dominates all other knowledge, for it establishes that end to which all knowledge serves.[2]   But any knowledge which is to

---

[1] *Vide supra*, p. 163 sqq. For this we may especially cite *Metaph.* i. 1, where, with reference to prevailing views as to wisdom, it is shown (981, b, 30) that ὁ μὲν ἔμπειρος τῶν ὁποιανοῦν ἐχόντων αἴσθησιν εἶναι δοκεῖ σοφώτερος, ὁ δὲ τεχνίτης τῶν ἐμπείρων, χειροτέχνου δὲ ἀρχιτέκτων, αἱ δὲ θεωρητικαὶ τῶν ποιητικῶν μᾶλλον. Hence : ὅτι μὲν οὖν ἡ σοφία περί τινας αἰτίας καὶ ἀρχάς ἐστιν ἐπιστήμη, δῆλον.

[2] *Metaph.* i. 2, where the above is thus summed up (982, b, 7): ἐξ ἁπάντων οὖν τῶν εἰρημένων ἐπὶ τὴν αὐτὴν ἐπιστήμην πίπτει τὸ ζητούμενον ὄνομα [σοφία] · δεῖ γὰρ ταύτην τῶν πρώτων ἀρχῶν καὶ αἰτιῶν εἶναι θεωρητικήν. Cf. iii. 2, 996, b, 8 sqq. *Eth. N.* vi. 7. *Metaph.* vi. 1, 1026, a, 21 : τὴν τιμιωτάτην [ἐπιστήμην] δεῖ περὶ τὸ τιμιώτατον γένος εἶναι. αἱ μὲν οὖν θεωρητικαὶ τῶν ἄλλων ἐπιστημῶν αἱρετώτεραι, αὕτη δὲ τῶν θεωρητικῶν.

set forth the ultimate grounds of things must clearly
include all actuality, for these ultimate grounds are
simply those which explain Being as such.[1] Other
sciences, such as Physics and Mathematics, may limit
themselves to a particular sphere, the conception of
which they take no further. The science of the ultimate
grounds of things must go through the whole world of
things, and must take them back, not to finite principles,
but to their eternal causes, and, in the last resort, to
that which is unmoved and incorporeal, from which
proceeds all movement and formation in the corporeal
world.[2] This science is the First Philosophy, which

[1] *Metaph.* iv. 1: ἔστιν ἐπιστήμη τις ἣ θεωρεῖ τὸ ὂν ᾗ ὂν καὶ τὰ
τούτῳ ὑπάρχοντα κιθ' αὐτό. αὕτη δ'
ἐστὶν οὐδεμιᾷ τῶν ἐν μέρει λεγομένων ἡ αὐτή· οὐδεμία γὰρ τῶν ἄλλων
ἐπισκοπεῖ κιθόλου περὶ τοῦ ὄντος
ᾗ ὄν, ἀλλὰ μέρος αὐτοῦ τι ἀποτεμό-
μεναι περὶ τούτου θεωροῦσι τὸ
συμβεβηκός . . . ἐπεὶ δὲ τὰς ἀρχὰς
καὶ τὰς ἀκροτάτας αἰτίας ζητοῦμεν,
δῆλον ὡς φύσεώς τινος αὐτὰς
ἀναγκαῖον εἶναι καθ' αὑτήν. . . . διὸ
καὶ ἡμῖν τοῦ ὄντος ᾗ ὂν τὰς πρώτας
αἰτίας ληπτέον. Cf. note 2 and
supra, ch. iv. *passim.*
[2] See the previous note, and
see also *Metaph.* vi. 1: αἱ ἀρχαὶ
καὶ τὰ αἴτια ζητεῖται τῶν ὄντων,
δῆλον δὲ ὅτι ᾗ ὄντα. Every science
has to do with certain principles
and causes. ἀλλὰ πᾶσαι αὗται
[ἰατρικὴ, μαθηματικὴ, &c.] περὶ ἔν
τι καὶ γένος τι περιγραψάμεναι περὶ
τούτου πραγματεύονται, ἀλλ' οὐχὶ
περὶ ὄντος ἁπλῶς οὐδὲ ᾗ ὄν, οὐδὲ τοῦ
τί ἐστιν οὐθένα λόγον ποιοῦνται·
ἀλλ' ἐκ τούτου αἱ μὲν αἰσθήσει
ποιήσασαι αὐτο δῆλον, αἱ δ' ὑπόθεσιν
λαβοῦσαι τὸ τί ἐστιν οὕτω τὰ καθ'

αὑτὰ ὑπάρχοντα τῷ γένει περὶ ὅ εἰσιν
ἀποδεικνύουσιν ἣ ἀναγκαιότερον ἣ
μαλακώτερον. . . . ὁμοίως δὲ οὐδ'
εἰ ἔστιν ἣ μὴ ἐστι τὸ γένος περὶ ὅ
πραγματεύονται οὐδὲν λέγουσι διὰ
τὸ τῆς αὐτῆς εἶναι διανοίας τό τε τί
ἐστι δῆλον ποιεῖν καὶ εἰ ἔστιν. So
it is with Physics and Mathematics, the former being concerned with that which is moved
and in which the Form is not
separated from the Matter, the
latter being at the best concerned
with that which is abstracted
from Matter and Movement, but
which does not exist of itself/as
immaterial and unmoved (cf. p.
183, n. 3): εἰ δὲ τί ἐστιν ἀΐδιον καὶ
ἀκίνητον καὶ χωριστὸν, φανερὸν ὅτι
θεωρητικῆς τὸ γνῶναι. οὐ μέντοι
φυσικῆς γε . . . οὐδὲ μαθηματικῆς,
ἀλλὰ πρότερας ἀμφοῖν. The object
of this science is the χωριστὰ καὶ
ἀκίνητα· ἀνάγκη δὲ πάντα μὲν τὰ
αἴτια ἀΐδια εἶναι, μάλιστα δὲ ταῦτα
ταῦτα γὰρ αἴτια τοῖς φανεροῖς τῶν
θείων: In them, if anywhere, τὸ
θεῖον must be sought; with them
stands or falls the possibility of

Aristotle also names Theology,[1] and its task is to investigate all actuality and the ultimate grounds thereof, which, as being ultimate, are necessarily also the most universal, and concern, not any part of the actual, but the whole.

It is true that the possibility of such a science is open to much question. How can one and the same science treat of causes which are of different kinds, and which do not act collectively together? And, on the other hand, if we were to refer the causes of each *genus* to a special science, how could any one of these sciences claim to be that which is described above—since in this case the qualities claimed for it would rather be divided up among the special sciences?[2] Again, it is a question whether the First Philosophy is to draw into its scope the principles of scientific procedure, or whether these belong at all to any definite science, inasmuch as all sciences make use of them and it is impossible to assign any definite object to which they relate.[3] Or, again, is it to be a single science, or more than one, which will deal with all classes of the actual? If there are more than one, the next question is, whether they are all of the same kind or no, and which of them is the First Philosophy. If there be only one, then it would seem that that one must include all

---

a First Philosophy : if there is nothing else besides natural substances, Physics is the first science ; εἰ δ' ἐστί τις οὐσία ἀκ'νητος, αὕτη προτέρα καὶ φιλοσοφία πρώτη καὶ καθόλου οὕτως ὅτι πρώτη· καὶ περὶ τοῦ ὄντος ἡ ὃν ταύτης ἂν εἴη θεωρῆσαι καὶ τί ἐστι καὶ τὰ ὑπάρχ-

οντα ᾗ ὄν.

[1] *Metaph. loc. cit. et alib.* ; *vid. supra.*

[2] *Metaph.* iii. 1, 995, b, 4, c. 2 *init.*

[3] *Ibid.* c. 1, 995, b, 6, c. 2, 996, b, 26 ; cf. *supra*, ch. v. *passim.*

objects of knowledge, and thereby the multiplicity of
the special sciences would disappear.[1] Finally we may
ask whether this single science is to relate only to substances or to their qualities also. The first alternative
seems inadmissible, because it would be then impossible
to say what kind of science had to do with the qualities
of Being. The latter seems untenable, because substances cannot be known by the same method of
demonstration as qualities.[2]

Aristotle answers these questions by remarking
that not only that which falls under the same conception,
but also that which relates to the same object, belongs
to one and the same science.[3] This, he says, is the case
as regards Being. Only that which is itself Substance,
or is somehow related to substance, can be named Being.
All those conceptions which are in question denote
either that which is Substantial, or else qualities, activi
ties and circumstances of Substance, and in the end they
all lead up to certain elementary pairs of opposites, and
opposites fall under the same science.[4] For these
reasons he concludes that it is one and the same science
which has to deal with all Being as such.[5] The difficulty

[1] *Metaph. ibid.* 995, b, 10, c.
2, 997, a, 15.

[2] C. 1, 995, b, 18, c. 2, 997, a,
25. Among the συμβεβηκότα ταῖς
οὐσίαις must be counted also the
concepts of ταὐτὸν, ἕτερον, ὅμοιον,
ἐναντίον, &c. enumerated in 995,
b, 20; cf. iv. 2, 1003, b, 34 sqq.
1004, a, 16 sqq. The further
Apories of the third book, which
are concerned not only with the
concept of the First Philosophy
but also with its contents, will
be mentioned later on.

[3] *Metaph.* iv. 2, 1003, b, 12:
οὐ γὰρ μόνον τῶν καθ' ἓν λεγομένων
ἐπιστήμης ἐστὶ θεωρῆσαι μιᾶς, ἀλλὰ
καὶ τῶν πρὸς μίαν λεγομένων φύσιν.
Ibid. l. 19, 1004, a, 24, cf. note 4;
and as to the difference between
καθ' ἓν and πρὸς ἓν, see *Metaph.*
vii. 4, 1040, a, 34 sqq.

[4] On this point see p. 224,
supra.

[5] *Metaph.* iv. 2: τὸ δὲ ὂν
λέγεται μὲν πολλαχῶς, ἀλλὰ πρὸς
ἓν καὶ μίαν τινὰ φύσιν (for which
later : ἅπαν πρὸς μίαν ἀρχὴν) καὶ

that this science must needs resume in itself the content
of all other sciences, is removed in Aristotle's mind by
the distinction he draws between the different senses of
Being. As Philosophy in general has to do with
Essential Being, so there will be as many sections of
Philosophy as there are kinds of Essential Being.[1] As
Being determinate is distinguished from Being in
general, so is the First Philosophy as the universal
science distinguished from the special sciences. It
deals with the particular also, not in its particularity,
but as a form of Being. It abstracts from the peculiarities whereby a particular thing distinguishes itself from
others, in order to have regard to that only in it which
appertains to all Being.[2] The objection that Substance
itself must needs be treated in other ways than that

οὐχ ὁμωνύμως . . . . τὰ μὲν γὰρ ὅτι
οὐσίαι ὄντα λέγεται, τὰ δ' ὅτι πάθη
οὐσίας, τὰ δ' ὅτι ὁδὸς εἰς οὐσίαν, ἢ
φθοραὶ ἢ στερήσεις ἢ ποιότητες ἢ
ποιητικὰ ἢ γεννητικὰ οὐσίας, ἢ τῶν
πρὸς τὴν οὐσίαν λεγομένων, ἢ τούτων
τινὸς ἀποφάσεις ἢ οὐσίας · διὸ καὶ τὸ
μὴ ὂν εἶναι μὴ ὂν φαμέν. The consideration of One also belongs to
this science, for the ἓν and the ὂν
are (*ibid*. 1003, b, 22.) ταὐτὸν καὶ
μ'α φύσις τῷ ἀκολουθεῖν, ὥσπερ
ἀρχὴ καὶ αἴτιον, ἀλλ' οὐχ ὡς ἑνὶ
λόγῳ δηλούμενα . . . δῆλον 'οὖν
ὅτι καὶ τὰ ὄντα μιᾶς θεωρῆσαι ᾗ
ὄντα. πανταχοῦ δὲ κυρίως τοῦ
πρώτου ἡ ἐπιστήμη καὶ ἐξ οὗ τὰ
ἄλλα ἤρτηται καὶ δι' ὃ λέγονται. εἰ
οὖν τοῦτ' ἐστὶν ἡ οὐσία, τῶν οὐσιῶν
ἂν δέοι τὰς ἀρχὰς καὶ τὰς αἰτίας
ἔχειν τὸν φιλόσοφον. . . . διὸ καὶ τοῦ
ὄντος ὅσα εἴδη θεωρῆσαι μιᾶς ἐστιν
ἐπιστήμης τῷ γένει τά τε εἴδη τῶν
εἰδῶν. Further, 1004, a, 9 sqq.

25, b, 27 sqq.
[1] *Metaph*. iv. 2, 1004, a, 2,
&c.
[2] *Metaph*. iv. 2, 1004, a, 9 sqq.
Since the concepts of the One
and the Many, of Identity and
Distinction, &c., relate to one
and the same object, therefore
one and the same science must
deal with them ; 1004, b, 5 :
ἐπεὶ οὖν τοῦ ἑνὸς ᾗ ἓν καὶ τοῦ ὄντος
ᾗ ὂν ταῦτα καθ' αὐτά ἐστι πάθη,
ἀλλ' οὐχ ᾗ ἀριθμοὶ ἢ γραμμαὶ ἢ πῦρ.
δῆλον ὡς ἐκείνης τῆς ἐπιστή,μης καὶ
τί ἐστι γνωρίσαι καὶ τὰ συμβεβηκότ'
αὐτοῖς. As the mathematical
and physical properties of things
form a special province, οὕτω καὶ
τῷ ὄντι ᾗ ὂν ἔστι τινὰ ἴδια, καὶ
ταῦτ' ἐστι περὶ ὧν τοῦ φιλοσόφυυ
ἐπισκέψασθαι τἀληθές. *Ibid*. 1005,
a, 8. This is further illustrated
in xi. 3, 1061, a, 28 sqq.

which proceeds by deducing its essential attributes would not trouble Aristotle,[1] since the same thing would be true of the fundamental conceptions of any science whatever. To the question whether the First Philosophy would also deal with the general principles of scientific procedure, Aristotle answers in the affirmative, inasmuch as these principles themselves relate to Being in general rather than to any particular class of Being. In fact, he proceeds immediately to a detailed investigation of the law of Contradiction and the Excluded Middle, which by reason of its relation to Methodology has been already discussed at p. 251. By Aristotle, however, these inquiries are in the present connection treated ontologically, as giving knowledge of the actual, for which reason he includes them in his First Philosophy.[2]

3. *The Fundamental Questions of Metaphysics and their Treatment by earlier Philosophers.*

The forerunners of Aristotle had left him a series of problems in the way of metaphysical inquiry for which he found it necessary to obtain a new solution. The most important of these, to the answering of which the fundamental ideas of his system are immediately directed, were the following :

1. First of all, how are we to think of the actual? Is there nothing but corporeal existence, as the pre-Socratic natural philosophy assumed? Or is there, beside and above that, something uncorporeal, as

---

[1] It is nowhere expressly answered in the *Metaphysics.*
[2] *Metaph.* iv. 3.

Anaxagoras, the Megarians and Plato said? Are the ultimate grounds of things of the nature of matter only, or is form to be distinguished from matter as a peculiar and a higher principle?

2. Connected with this is the question of the relation of the Individual to the Universal. What is that which is essential and in the last resort actual? Is it the individual things or the universal ideas, or is there perhaps in truth only one universal Being? The first was the common view which had lately come out, bluntly enough, in the Nominalism of Antisthenes; the second was the theory of Plato; the third that of Parmenides and of Eucleides after him.

3. Seeing that unity of being and manifold existence are both given in experience, how can we hold these two together in thought? Can the One be at the same time a manifold, including in itself a number of parts and qualities? Can the Many come together in an actual unity? These questions also were variously answered. Parmenides and Zeno had denied that the two ideas could be reconciled, and had therefore declared the manifold to be a delusion, while the Sophists used the assumption of the manifold for their theory of argument, as Antisthenes for his theory of knowledge.[1] The Physicists of the Atomic and Empedoclean schools limited the relation between the Many and the One to that of an external and mechanical juxtaposition of parts. The Pythagoreans found in number, and Plato, with keener philosophic insight, in his Ideas, a means of combining a multitude of different

---

[1] See ZELLER, *Ph. d. Gr.* pt. 1, pp. 985 etc.

determinations of being in an inner unity, while the corresponding relation in sensible things explained itself, according to Plato, by impact.

4. Equally different were the views held as to the passing of the one into another—that is, as to the theory of Change and Becoming. How can being become not-being, or not-being being? How can anything come to be or cease to be? How is movement possible, or change? Such were the questions that Parmenides and Zeno had asked in doubt, and the Megarians and the Sophists had repeated their questionings. The like difficulties drove Empedocles and Anaxagoras, Leucippus and Democritus to explain the coming to be and ceasing to be of all things by the combinations and separations of unchangeable matter. Plato himself so far agreed with them that he confined change to the sphere of appearances, and excepted from it all that was truly actual.

Aristotle has all these questions clearly in view. To the first two problems related most [1] of the ἀπορίαι with which he opens his great work on Metaphysics, after the introductory discussions of the first book. Are sensible things the only essential being, or is there besides them some other? Is the ʻotherʼ of one kind, or is it manifold like the Ideas and mathematical entities of Plato? [2] The limitation of Being to sensible things is contradicted by the series of arguments on which Plato had already based his Ideal Theory: such as, that the

[1] With the exception of those just mentioned, which are concerned with the office of the First Philosophy in general.

[2] *Metaph.* iii. 2, 997, a, 34 sqq. (xi. 1, 1059, a, 38, c. 2, 1060, b, 23), iii. 6, viii. 2.

particular things of sense, passing and indistinct as they are, can be no object of knowledge ;[1] and that all the world of sense, as passing, presupposes an eternal—as moved, presupposes an unmoved—as formed, presupposes a forming cause.[2] These Platonic assumptions, however, as we presently find, are beset by all manner of difficulties. The problem returns in the form of the question [3] whether the ultimate grounds of things are to be sought for in their genera, or in their constituent parts—the latter being the basis of their material conditions, the other the basis of their formal determinations.[4] For either view plausible arguments may be adduced. On the one hand there is the analogy of corporeal things, whose constituent parts we name when we have to explain their character. On the other hand there are the conditions of knowledge, which we attain to by a process of determination through concepts in the assignment of genera and species. And as between these again there arises immediately the question, whether the highest genera or the lowest species ought to be treated as the true *principia*. The former would be universal, including all individual existence as an *ultimate* principle should do. The latter would be determinate conceptions, and out of such only could the individual in its peculiarity of character be obtained.[5]

[1] *Metaph.* vii. 15, 1039, b, 27; iv. 5, 1009, a, 36, 1010, a, 3, cf. i. 6, 987, a, 34; xiii. 9, 1086, a, 37, b, 8.

[2] *Ibid.* iii. 4, 999, b, 3 sqq.

[3] *Metaph.* iii. 3 : πότερον δεῖ τὰ γένη στοιχεῖα καὶ ἀρχὰς ὑπολαμβάνειν ἢ μᾶλλον ἐξ ὧν ἐνυπαρχόντων ἐστὶν ἕκαστον πρῶτον (xi. 1, 1059,

b, 21).

[4] *Vide supra*, ch. v.

[5] *Metaph.* iii. 998, b, 14 sqq. (xi. 1, 1059, b, 34). Among the varied and often intricate forms of Aristotle's dialectic, it is only possible to state here the leading line of reasoning.

On the like considerations rests the other difficulty, to which Aristotle rightly gives special prominence [1]—the question whether it is only individual things that are actual, or whether the universal of the genera be actual also.[2] The former theory seems untenable because the sphere of individual existences is unlimited and of that which is unlimited no knowledge is possible, and since all knowledge in any case is of universals. The latter is open to all the objections which lie against the theory of a universal existing independently, or the Ideal Theory of Plato.[3] An application of this question to a particular case is contained in the further inquiry, whether the conceptions of the One and of Being denote anything substantial or are only predicates for some subject of a different nature. Those who accept universals at all (*e.g.* Number) as in any way substantial, must affirm the first proposition ; but the opposite opinion is not only supported by the analogy of the whole world of concrete things, but also by the argument that you cannot treat the One as substance without denying, as did Parmenides, the existence of

---

[1] *Metaph.* iii. 4 *init.* c. 6 *fin.* (cf. vii. 13 sq.), xiii. 6, xi. 2 *init.*, *ibid.* 1060, b, 19. In the first passage this Apory is called the πασῶν χαλεπωτάτη καὶ ἀναγκαιοτάτη θεωρῆσαι; similarly in xiii. 10, 1086, a, 10; and we shall find later on, that its importance and difficulty rest not merely on the opposition of Aristotle to Plato, but also on the intrinsic contradiction involved in the foundations of his own system.

[2] That this Apory coincides with that adduced on p. 298, Aristotle himself asserts in

Metaph. iii. 4, 999, b, 1 : εἰ μὲν οὖν μηθέν ἐστι παρὰ τὰ καθ᾽ ἕκαστα, οὐθὲν ἂν εἴη νοητὸν ἀλλὰ πάντα αἰσθητά, and hence he here again adduces the reasons, which were there mentioned.

[3] *Metaph.* iii. 4, c. 6, 1003, a, 5, cf. p. 161, 4. Only another expression for the above is the question (iii. 4, 999, b, 24, xi. 2 *fin.*), whether the ἀρχαὶ are εἴδει ἓν or ἀριθμῷ ἕν : τὸ γὰρ ἀριθμῷ ἓν ἢ τὸ καθέκαστον λέγειν διαφέρει οὐθὲν (999, b, 33 cf. c. 6, 1002, b, 30).

the Many, as such.[1] To the same head belongs the
question whether Numbers and Figures are Substances
or no, and to this also opposite answers are possible.
For as the qualities of bodies are mere predicates from
which we distinguish the bodies themselves as their
substrata, and as these bodies presuppose, as their
elements, the surface, the line, the point, and unity, it
would seem that surface and unity must be as substantial as body is; while on the other hand these have
not any existence for themselves but only in corporeal
things, and they do not come to be and cease to be, as
Substances do.[2] Yet another difficulty which leads back
to the relation of the individual to the Universal is this.
The *principia* must on the one hand, as it seems, be of
a potential character, since possibility precedes actuality :
on the other hand, they must be actual, since otherwise
Being would be merely accidental.[3] Individual things,
indeed, do actually exist : whereas the universal concept,
except in so far as it has found for itself a place in
individual entities, exists only potentially. And finally,
if there be besides the corporeal, an uncorporeal, and
beside the changing, an eternal, the final question must
be whether both of these have the same *principia*[4] or
not. If we say Yes, it seems impossible to explain the
difference between them. If we say No, then we must

---

[1] *Metaph.* iii. 4, 1001, a, 3
sqq., and, referring to this, x. 2,
xi 1, 1059, b, 27, c. 2, 1060,
a, 36.

[2] *Metaph.* iii. 5 (cf. xi. 2, 1060,
b, 12 sqq., and on p. 1002, b, 32 :
viii. 5 *init.* c. 3, 1043, b, 15). We
shall meet with further objections to this view in the criticism

of the Pythagorean and Platonic
doctrines.

[3] *Ibid.* iii. 6, 1002, b, 32 cf.
BONITZ and SCHWEGLER on this
passage.

[4] As Plato supposed, in full
accordance with Aristotle's view.
Cf. ZELLER, *Ph. d. Gr.* pt. i. p. 628
sq. 805 sq.

decide whether the *principia* of the changeable are
themselves changeable or unchangeable. If they be
changing, then we must go back to deeper *principia,*
with which the same dilemma will recur. If they be
unchangeable, then we have to explain how it can be
that out of the unchanging, in one case the changeable,
in another the unchangeable, arises.[1] The like difficulty, in truth, applies to all the different classes of
Being. How, for example, is it possible that things
which fall under wholly different categories, such as
those of Substance and Relation, can lead back to
principles that are one and the same ?[2]

The other questions stated above—those relating to
the unity of the manifold, and the possibility of change—
were clearly present to Aristotle's mind, and he sought
in the first principles of his Metaphysics to find a solution for them. The combination of the manifold into
unity, concerns him chiefly as leading up to the inquiry
how the genus and the differentia can be one in conception ;[3] though he recognises that the same question
may be raised in all cases where things of a different
nature are combined.[4] Aristotle's answer, in all such

---

[1] *Metaph.* iii. 4, 1000, a, 5
sqq. (xi. 2, 1060, a, 27).

[2] *Ibid.* xii. 4. Aristotle
answers (*ibid.* 1070, b, 17) that
the final grounds of things are
only analogically the same for
all.

[3] This question also occurs in
Anal. Post. ii. 6, 92, a, 29. In
De Interpr. c. 5, 17, a, 13, it is
proposed, discussed more fully
in *Metaph.* vii. 12, again touched
upon in viii. 3, 1043, b, 4 sqq.,

1044, a, 5, and settled in the
manner stated in the text by viii.
6.

[4] Thus with regard to numbers (*Metaph.* viii. 3, 1044, a, 2,
c. 6 *init.*), and to the relation
between soul and body (c. 6,
1045, b, 11 ; *De An.* ii. 1, 412, b,
6 sqq.) ; but also in many other
cases : cf. *Metaph.* viii. 6, 1045,
b, 12 : καίτοι ὁ αὐτὸς λόγος ἐπὶ
πάντων, &c.

cases, as will be seen, is in its essence one and the
same. It is based upon the relation of the possible
and the actual—of Matter and Form.[1] The problems
of Becoming and Change are of still greater importance
for the Aristotelian system. If a thing comes to be,
does it arise out of being or out of not-being? If a
thing ceases to be, does it become something, or nothing?
Does change mean the becoming of opposite out of
opposite, or of the same out of the same? The one
seems to be impossible—because nothing can come out
of nothing, nor can anything return to nothing, nor
take on it the qualities of its opposite (e.g. warmth the
qualities of cold). The other alternative is equally
impossible, because it is absurd that anything should at
a definite time come to be that which it already is.[2] A
similar case is the analogous problem whether those
things which act upon each other are likes or opposites.[3]
In all these questions, difficulties are brought to light
which are soluble only by a careful inquiry into the
first principles of philosophy.

[1] Cf. *Phys.* i. 2 *fin*, where
Lycophron and others are blamed
for running into difficulties by
the inference that one must at
the same time be many : ὥσπερ
οὐκ ἐνδεχόμενον ταὐτὸν ἕν τε καὶ
πολλὰ εἶναι, μὴ τἀντικείμενα δέ·
ἔστι γὰρ τὸ ἓν καὶ δυνάμει καὶ
ἐντελεχείᾳ.

[2] Cf. *Phys.* i. 6, 189, a, 22, c.
7, 190, b, 30, c. 8 *init.* ibid. 191,
b, 10 sqq., *Gen. et Corr.* i. 3 *init.*
ibid. 317, b, 20 sqq. *Metaph.* xii.
1 *fin.*

[3] See *Gen. et Corr.* i. 7; *Phys.*
i. 6, 189, a, 22, c. 7, 190, b, 29,
c. 8 191, a, 34. To Aristotle

this question coincides with the
other, as to Change, since that
which acts corresponds with
that which suffers : ὥστ᾽ ἀνάγκη
τὸ πάσχον εἰς τὸ ποιοῦν μεταβάλλειν
(*Gen. et Corr.* i. 7, 324, a, 9).
Hence it is true that, on the one
hand, things which are not opposed cannot act upon one
another : οὐκ ἐξίστησι γὰρ ἄλληλα
τῆς φύσεως ὅσα μήτ᾽ ἐναντία μήτ᾽
ἐξ ἐναντίων ἐστὶ (*ibid.* p. 323, b,
28) ; but on the other hand,
neither can absolute opposites :
ὑπ᾽ ἀλλήλων γὰρ πάσχειν τἀναντία
ἀδύνατον (*Phys.* i. 7, 190, b, 33).

The contributions which his forerunners had made towards their solution, did not in any way satisfy Aristotle.[1] He takes exception to most of the pre-Socratic philosophies primarily because of their materialism, which made it impossible for them to reach out to the first principles of the incorporeal;[2] and he further objects that they practically took no account of ideal and final causes.[3]

The earlier Ionic school is criticised by him because of the difficulties which beset every one of their presuppositions,[4] because of their tendency to overlook the moving cause,[5] and because of the superficial way in which they erected an arbitrarily chosen element into the universal basis of things, whereas the sensible qualities and changes of bodies are conditioned by the opposition of different elements.[6]

The same criticism holds for Heraclitus, in so far as he agrees with the Ionic school in assigning a material element as the basis.[7] To his peculiar doctrine as to the flux of all things and the meeting of opposites, Aristotle has other objections. He thinks that the doctrine of the flux is on the one hand not accurately thought out, while on the other hand it overlooks the

---

[1] For what follows cf. STRÜM-PELL, *Gesch. d. theor. Phil. d. Gr.* 157–184; BRANDIS, ii. b, 2, p. 589 sqq. Aristotle's criticism of earlier philosophers is here dealt with only in so far as it concerns their fundamental doctrines.

[2] *Metaph.* i. 8 *init.* cf. iv. 5, 1009, a, 36, 1010, a, 1.

[3] *Metaph.* i. 7, 988, a, 34 sqq. b, 28, *Gen. et Corr.* ii. 9, 335, b, 32 sqq., *Gen. An.* v. 1, 778, b, 7.

[4] See *De Cœlo*, iii. 5, *Metaph.* i. 8, 988, b, 29 sqq.

[5] *Metaph.* i. 8, 988, b, 26; *Gen. et Corr.* ii. 9, 335, b, 24

[6] *Gen. et Corr.* ii. 1, 329, a, 8; *De Cœlo*, iii. 5, 304, b, 11, cf. *ibid.* i. 3, 270, a, 14; *Phys.* i. 7, 190, a, 13 sqq. iii. 5, 205, a, 4.

[7] Aristotle, indeed, generally puts him along with Thales, Anaximenes, &c.; see ZELLER, *Ph. d. Gr.* pt. i. 585, 1.

fact that every change presupposes a substratum ; that under alterations of matter, the form maintains itself ; that it is not all kinds of change which could go on *ad infinitum* ; and that from the changeableness of earthly things we ought not to draw any conclusion as to the universe as a whole.[1] The theory of the unity of opposites he dismisses by the argument that Heraclitus is in conflict with the Law of Contradiction.[2]

The objections to Empedocles cover various points of detail regarding his natural philosophy which cannot be gone into here, but they reach also to the fundamentals of his system. His assumptions as to the immutability of the original matter are held to involve the impossibility of qualitative change, of the passage of the elements into one another as seen in experience, and of their combination into unity in the derivative forms of matter, and also of the doctrines, upheld by Empedocles himself, as to the quantitative identity of the elements and their co-existence in 'the Sphere.'[3] Aristotle also objects that the derivation of these elements is not shown, and that they are not carried back to the original divisions of material being,[4] which are only incompletely presented in the definite kinds of matter known to us as fire, water, &c.[5] He remarks that the opposition of heavy and light is not explained

[1] *Metaph.* iv. 5, 1010, a, 15 sqq.; *Phys.* viii. 3, 253, b, 9 sqq.

[2] See ZELLER, *Ph. d. Gr.* i. 600 sq., and 483, 1.

[3] *Metaph.* i. 8, 989, a, 22–30; *Gen. et Corr.* ii. 1, 329, b, 1, c. 7, 334, a, 18, 26, c. 6 *init. ibid.* i. 1, 314, b, 10, 315, a, 3, c. 8, 325, b, 16. In *De Cælo*, iii. 7 *init*, he gives a detailed refutation of the atomistic reduction (by EMPEDOCLES) of ἀλλοίωσις to ἔκκρισις.

[4] The opposites 'warm and cold,' &c., on which Aristotle bases his own theory of the elements.

[5] *Gen. et Corr.* i. 8, 325, b, 19, ii. 3, 330, b, 21.

at all,[1] and that in the theory of the pores and effluxes
an explanation of the mutual influence of bodies is
put forward which would logically lead to absolute
Atomism.[2] The two 'causes of motion' in the Empedoclean system he considers not to be properly deduced
from first principles nor to be sufficiently distinguished,
since Love not only unites but also divides, and Hate not
only divides but also unites ;[3] and he remarks that since
no laws of their working are laid down, an inordinate
scope is left, in the fashioning of the world, to Chance.[4]
He holds the assumption of alternating states of the
world to be arbitrary and untenable,[5] and the theory of the
composition of the soul out of the elements to be beset
with difficulties of all kinds.[6] Finally, Aristotle believes
that the philosophy of Empedocles would lead in the end
to a sensationalism which would make all truth uncertain.[7]

The criticisms on the Atomic theory are of a similar
kind. Aristotle admits that the theory has a very
plausible basis. If we start from the Eleatic presuppositions, and if we desire nevertheless to save the ideas
of the manifold and of movement, then an Atomic
theory is the most convenient way of escape. So if we
think it an impossibility to suppose bodies to be actually
divisible *ad infinitum*, the only alternative seems to lie
in the assumption of indivisible atoms as their ultimate

[1] *De Cœlo*, iv. 2, 309, a, 19.

[2] *Gen. et Corr.* i. 8; cf.
ZELLER, *Ph. d. Gr.* part i. 695,
3.

[3] See ZELLER, *Ph. d. Gr.* pt. i.
698, 2, and *Metaph.* iii. 8, 986,
a, 25.

[4] *Gen. et Corr.* ii. 6, 333, b, 2
sqq. (cf. ZELLER, *ibid.* 703, 1) ;

Part. An. i. 1, 640, a, 19 ; *Phys.*
viii. 1, 252, a, 4.

[5] *Phys.* viii. 1, 251, b, 28 sqq. :
De Cœlo, i. 10, 280, a, 11 ; *Metaph.*
iii. 4, 1000, b, 12.

[6] *De An.* i. 5, 409, b, 23–410,
b, 27 ; *Metaph.* iii. 4, 1000, b, 3.

[7] *Metaph.* iv. 5. 1009, b, 12 ;
cf. ZELLER, *ibid.* 727, 1.

constituents.[1]   Aristotle, however, neither admits these
Eleatic presuppositions, nor does he concede that the
division of bodies can ever reach its limit,[2] or that the
coming of definite things into being could be treated
as a combination of *minima*, or their passing out of
existence as a resolution into atoms.[3]   Rather does he
hold that indivisible bodies are impossible, since every
fixed quantity can be divided into fixed quantities, which
again must be divisible.[4]   He says that atoms which are
neither qualitatively distinguished nor capable of acting
on each other could not explain the different qualities
and the interaction of bodies or the passage of the
elements into one another or the processes of becoming
and change.[5]   The theory that the atoms are infinite in
number and kind is also rejected, because the phenomena can be explained without this hypothesis, since all
differences of quality or of form are reducible to certain fundamental types, and since the situation and
movement of the elements in nature are also limited
by number; and it is Aristotle's view that a limited
number of original entities is always to be preferred to
an infinity of them, because the limited is better than
the limitless.[6]   The assumption of empty space, so far

---

[1] *Gen. et Corr.* i. 8, 324, b, 35
sqq. c. 2, 316, a, 13 sqq.; cf.
ZELLER, *ibid.* 764 sqq.

[2] *Gen. et Corr.* i. 2, 317, a, 1
sqq.   But Aristotle expresses
himself more exactly on this
point, though without explicit
reference to the Atomic theory,
in *Phys.* iii. 6 sq.

[3] *Gen. et Corr.* i. 2, 317, a,
17 sqq.

[4] *Phys.* vi. 1 ; *De Cœlo*, iii. 4,
303, a, 20.

[5] *Gen. et Corr.* i. 8, 325, b, 34
sqq. c. 9, 327, a, 14 ; *De Cœlo*, iii.
4, 303, a, 24 ; *ibid.* c. 7, c. 8, 306,
a, 22 sqq.   We shall have more
to say on this subject later.

[6] *De Cœlo*, iii. 4, 303, a, 17 sqq.
29 sqq. b, 4 ; cf. *Phys.* i. 4 *fin.*
viii. 6, 259, a, 8.

from being necessary [1] to explain phenomena such as those of movement, would rather be inconsistent with the characteristic movement of bodies and the differences of weight, for in a vacuum nothing could have any particular place towards which it would tend, and everything would necessarily move with equal quickness.[2] He finds that movement and its different kinds are, in the Atomic Philosophy, simply presupposed, and not deduced from first principles.[3] He objects that the school completely overlooks the teleology of nature, and that instead of giving us any principles on which phenomena rest, it refers us to an unsolved necessity, or to the assertion that in fact things have always been as they are.[4] There are further polemical passages, which can only here be mentioned in passing: against the theory of an infinite number of co-existent worlds;[5] against Democritus' explanation of sense-perception;[6] against his doctrine concerning the soul,[7] and his acceptance of sensory appearance as truth.[8]

The natural philosophy of Anaxagoras is so closely connected with the physics of the Atomists and Empe-

[1] *Phys.* iv. 7-9, cf. c. 6. More on this later.

[2] *Phys.* iv. 8, 214, b, 28 sqq.; *De Cœlo*, i. 7, 275, b, 29, 277, a, 33 sqq. ii. 13, 294, b. 30, iii. 2, 300, b, 8. With regard to the theory of Weight held by Democritus, see further *De Cœlo*, iv. 2, 6; as to the influence of Aristotle's attack upon the changes which Epicurus made in the atomic theory, see ZELLER, *Ph. d. Gr.* pt. iii. a, 378.

[3] *Metaph.* xii. 6, 1071, b, 31.

[4] See ZELLER, *Ph. d. Gr.* pt. i. 788 sqq., and *Gen. An.* v. 8 *vers. fin.*, where Aristotle's criticism of the mechanical explanation of nature by Democritus, is very similar to Plato's criticism in the *Phædo* of that proposed by Anaxagoras.

[5] *De Cœlo*, i. 8; see ZELLER, *ibid.* 797, 2.

[6] *De Sensu*, c. 4, 442, a, 29.

[7] *De An.* i. 3, 406, b, 15; cf. c. 2, 403, b. 29, 405, a, 8.

[8] ZELLER, *ibid.* 822.

docles that it is open for the most part to the same objections. The infinite number of his primary bodies is not only needless, inasmuch as a small number would do equally well, but it is also mistaken inasmuch as it would make all knowledge of things impossible. Again, since the primary differences of kinds of matter are limited in number, so must be the primary bodies also. Since all bodies have a natural magnitude, their constituent parts (the so-called ὁμοιομερῆ) cannot be of indefinite size ; and since all bodies are limited, there cannot be in each thing, as Anaxagoras was logically obliged to hold, constituents belonging to the infinitely various kinds of matter.[1] Further, if primary matter is to be looked for in the simplest bodies, few of the ὁμοιομερῆ could be considered as primary matter.[2] Anaxagoras recognises the existence of change in things, but the doctrine of the unchangeability of their constituent parts is inconsistent with that admission. The continuity of bodies is negated by the infinite number of their constituents,[3] in spite of Anaxagoras's weak attack upon the theory of empty space.[4] Aristotle finds that Anaxagoras is as little able to account for differences of weight as was Empedocles.[5] The original mingling of all kinds of matter, as Anaxagoras states it, would be unthinkable ; [6]

---

[1] *Phys.* i. 4, 187, b, 7 sqq ; *De Cœlo*, iii. 4. For a further remark as to the infinite in space, see *Phys.* iii. 5, 205, b, 1.

[2] *De Cœlo*, iii. 4, 302, b, 14.

[3] *Gen. et Corr.* i. 1 ; *Phys.* iii. 4, 203, a, 19. Further objections of a similar kind, but not especially directed against Anaxagoras, will be dealt with in

the latter part of ch. viii. *infra.*

[4] *Phys.* iv. 6, 213, a, 22.

[5] *De Cœlo*, iv. 2, 309, a, 19.

[6] Besides the physical objections which are raised against it in *Metaph.* i. 8, *Gen. et Corr.* i. 10, 327, b, 19, Aristotle asserts both of this statement and of the corresponding one (that, at all times, everything is in every-

but if it were more correctly stated it would lead to the substitution of ' matter' (conceived of as one and without qualities) for the infinite variety of primary bodies which Anaxagoras assumed.[1] The theory, common to him and others, of a beginning of movement among matter, after infinitely continued rest, would contradict the regularity of the order of nature.[2] Aristotle freely recognises the advance made when Anaxagoras formulated the doctrine of universal mind, but he considers it to be still unsatisfactory, inasmuch as, on the one hand, it did not bear fruit in the explanation of nature, and, on the other hand, as applied even to man, it misconceived the distinction between the spirit and the soul.[3]

With regard to the Eleatics (among whom he takes little account of Xenophanes and Melissus),[4] Aristotle's first point is that their philosophy contains no basis for any explanation of phenomena.[5] Their primary axioms he takes to be vitiated by grave obscurities; they talk of ' the unity of being' without keeping distinct the different meanings of unity; and thus they attribute to being such qualities as negate in turn its unconditional unity (*e.g.* limit in Parmenides, and limitlessness in Melissus). They do not understand that every proposition involves the duality of subject and predicate, of

thing), that it destroys the principle of contradiction. See ZELLER, *Ph. d. Gr.* pt. i. 911.

[1] *Metaph.* i. 8, 989, a, 30.
[2] *Phys.* viii. 1, 252, a, 10 sqq.
[3] See ZELLER, *ibid.* 887, 4, 893, 2; *De An.* i. 2, 404, b, 1, 405, a, 13.
[4] *Metaph.* i. 5, 986, b, 26;

Phys. i. 2, 185, a, 10, i. 3 *init.*, and *De Cælo*, ii. 13, 294, a, 21; on the other hand Parmenides is always treated with respect.
[5] *Metaph.* i. 5, 986, b, 10 sqq.; *Phys.* i. 2, 184, b, 25; *De Cælo*, iii. 1, 298, b, 14; *Gen. et Corr.* i. 8, 325, a, 17; cf. SEXT. *Math.* x, 46,

thing and quality, so that we cannot even say that 'Being is' without distinguishing between Being as substance and the Being we attribute to it as quality—which latter, if there were only *one Being*, would necessarily be something other than Being, *i.e.* not-being.[1] The Eleatics assert the unity of Being and deny not-being, whereas in fact 'Being' is only a common predicate of all things, and 'Not-being' is perfectly thinkable as the negation of some definite kind of being (*e.g.* not large, &c.).[2] They attack the divisibility of Being, and yet at the same time describe it as extended in space.[3] They deny all 'Becoming,' and therefore the multiplicity of things, on the ground that every process of becoming must start either from Being or from Not-being, and both hypotheses are untenable. They overlook a third possibility, which not only makes Becoming conceivable, but is the sole expression of any actual process of becoming—namely, that anything becomes what it is, not out of absolute Not-being, but out of that which is *relatively* not-being.[4]

Aristotle holds that Zeno's polemic against movement rests upon similar misconceptions, inasmuch as he treated space and time not as fixed but as discrete quantities, and argued on the assumption

[1] This is the essential point of the complicated dialectical discussion in *Phys.* i. 2, 105, a, 20–c. 3 *vers. fin.* On the second half of these discussions (c. 3), cf. PLATO, *Parm.* 142, B sq., *Soph.* 244, B sqq.; and see ZELLER, *ibid.* p. 562 sq.

[2] *Phys.* i. 3, 187, a, 3; cf. ZELLER, *ibid.* 563 sq.

[3] *Metaph.* iii. 4, 1001, b, 7; cf. ZELLER, *ibid.* 541.

[4] *Phys.* i. 8, cf. *Metaph.* xiv. 2, 1009, a, 26 sqq. (The point will be treated more in detail in ch. viii. *infra.*) On the other hand, the Eleatic hypothesis is answered in *Gen. et Corr.* i. 8, 325, a, 13 merely by a reference to the opposed facts of experience.

that they consisted of an infinite number of actual
subdivisions, whereas in fact they merely include *potentially* in themselves all possible subdivisions.[1] Still
less importance does he attach to the arguments used
by Melissus to prove that Being is limitless and motionless.[2] How can it be supposed that 'All is One,'
unless we are prepared to ignore all the differences of
things, and to represent even contradictory opposites
as one and the same?[3] Here also Aristotle finds
unproved assumptions as to the principles of things, and
an absolute failure to solve the weightiest questions of
philosophy.

Neither does he find a solution among the Pythagoreans, who attempted a philosophy of nature, although
their principles made movement and change, which are
the basis of all natural processes, inconceivable.[4] They
proposed to explain the corporeal by referring it to
number. Yet how can that which is extended in space
be derivable from numbers, or how can weight arise out
of that which is neither light nor heavy?[5] How, in
fine, can the qualities of things be so derived at all?[6]
What is the meaning of saying that in the formation of
the world, the One, as corporeal size, was 'the centre
which drew unto itself portions of the limitless'?[7]

[1] *Phys.* vi. 9, c. 2, 233, a, 21;
cf. ZELLER, *ibid.* 545 sqq.

[2] *Phys.* i. 3 *init.*; cf. ZELLER,
ibid. 554, 3.

[3] *Phys.* i. 2, 185, b, 19 sqq.

[4] *Metaph.* i. 8, 989, b, 29 sqq.

[5] *Metaph.* i. 8, 990, a, 12 sqq.
iii. 4, 1001, b, 17, xiii. 8, 1083, b,
8 sqq. xiv. 3, 1090, a, 30; *De
Cœlo*, iii. 1 *fin.*

[6] *Metaph.* xiv. 5, 1092, b, 15.
The passage refers to Platonics
and Pythagoreans together. Other
remarks, which refer immediately
to Plato and his school, but also
apply to the Pythagoreans, need
not be here cited.

[7] *Metaph.* xiii. 6, 1080, b, 16,
xiv. 3, 1091, a, 13; cf. ZELLER,
ibid. 381 sq. 349, 4.

Again, where things different in character are explained by one and the same number, are we to distinguish between different classes of numbers by reason of the differences of the things they signify, or are we to deny the variety of these things by reason of the likeness of the numbers that denote them ?[1] How, again, can universal conceptions such as the One and the Infinite be of the nature of substance ?[2] Finally, if we proceed to inquire as to the way in which the Pythagoreans applied their theory of numbers, we come upon singular superficiality and caprice.[3] The theory of number itself is very incompletely worked out,[4] and there are numerous untenable positions in their theory of physics which Aristotle marks with censure.[5]

Not only the earlier schools of Natural Philosophy, but also the later systems called, in Aristotle's view, for fundamental reconsideration. Only one of the later schools can be specially dealt with here, because in this connection there is no account to be taken of the Sophists. What they taught was to Aristotle's mind only a mock wisdom, which dealt in the contingent, the unessential, and the unreal.[6] His task in regard to them was, not

---

[1] *Metaph.* i. 8, 990, a, 18 (cf. ZELLER, *ibid.* 362, 1), vii. 11. 1036, b, 17 cf. xiv. 6, 1093, a, 1, 10.

[2] With regard to Being and the One, this view is explained (against Plato and the Pythagoreans) in *Metaph.* iii. 4, 1001, a, 9, 27 cf. x. 2; and it is there especially remarked that the assertion of the substantiality of the One would destroy the plurality of things. As to the ἄπειρον cf. *Phys.* iii. 5, and also c. 4, 203, a, 1.

[3] *Metaph.* i. 5, 986, a, 6, 987, a, 19.

[4] See ZELLER, *ibid.* 367, 2.

[5] Such as the 'Antichthon' (ZELLER, *ibid.* 383, 4), the harmony of the spheres (*De Cœlo,* ii. 9), a theory about time (*Phys.* iv. 10, 218, a, 33, cf. ZELLER, *ibid.* 406, 3 sq.), and certain views as to the soul (*De An.* i. 2, 404, a, 16, c. 3 *fin.* cf. *Anal. Post.* ii. 11, 94, b, 32).

[6] See ZELLER, *ibid.* 968.

to establish any metaphysical propositions, but to combat the scepticism which brought all manner of truth into question, and to prove the untenable nature of their sophisms.[1] The services rendered by Socrates to philosophy are by no means minimised by Aristotle, although at the same time he emphasises the limitation of Socrates' achievement to the sphere of ethics, and observes that in this connection Socrates did not establish any metaphysical basis.[2] Of the lesser Socratic schools Aristotle criticised only the Megarians, for their assertions about the relation of the possible and the actual,[3] and the Cynics, in regard to their theory of knowledge and ethics.[4]

The attention which Aristotle pays, however, to Plato and the Platonic school is as thoroughgoing as his treatment of the other Socratics is slight. His own system grew directly out of that of Plato. He was compelled, therefore,[5] to distinguish his views from those of Plato exhaustively, and to set out the arguments which led him to go beyond the Platonic school. Thus it is

---

[1] The former in *Metaph.* iv. 5, cf. c. 4, 1007, b, 20, x. 1, 1053, a, 35, xi. 6 *init.*; the latter in the treatise on the fallacies.

[2] Cf. the passages cited, ZELLER, *ibid.* at pp. 94, 2, and 1143 That even the Ethics of Socrates are one-sided, is shown by Aristotle in *Eth. Nic.* iii. 7, 1113, b, 14 sq. c. 11, 1116, b, 3 sqq. 1117, a, 9, vi. 13, 1114, b, 17 sqq.

[3] *Metaph.* ix. 3 (cf. ZELLER, *ibid.* 220, 1). Aristotle here confutes the Megarian principle, that the merely possible is actual, by proving that it would not only destroy all motion and change, but also all possession of skill or power : one who does not now hear would be deaf ; one who is not actually building would be no architect.

[4] The former are spoken of in *Metaph.* v. 29, 1024, b, 32, viii. 3, 1043, b, 23 (cf. ZELLER, *ibid.* 252 sq.), and in *Eth. Nic.* x. 1, 1172, a, 27 sqq. Aristotle attacks the exaggerations of the moral doctrine of the Cynics.

[5] *Supra*, pp. 14, 56 sq., 162, &c.

in no spirit of jealousy or detraction that Aristotle
comes back again and again to discuss the Platonic
doctrines, and to set out their defects from all points of
view with untiring patience; for such a criticism of his
master was unavoidable if he was to defend his own
philosophic individuality, and his right to found a new
school, against the fame of his predecessor and the
prestige of the flourishing Academy. His main criticism, leaving out of account incidental objections, is
directed against three leading points: first, against the
Ideal Theory, as such; secondly, against the later
' Pythagorising statement of the Theory;' and, thirdly,
against the principles laid down concerning the ultimate basis of things, Matter and the One.[1]

The Ideal Theory of Plato rested upon his conviction that it is only the universal essence of things that
can be an object of knowledge. This conviction was
shared by Aristotle.[2] So likewise did Aristotle accept
without criticism Plato's doctrine as to the mutability of
all sensible things (which for Plato was the second
buttress of the Ideal Theory), and the necessity to
pass beyond these to something stable and essential.[3]
But when Plato draws from this the conclusion that it
is only the Universal, as such, which can be actual, and
that it must exist for itself as something substantial
beyond phenomena, Aristotle parts company with him.
This, therefore, is the central point about which revolves
the whole Aristotelian attack on Plato's Metaphysics.
For Aristotle holds as to this assumption that it is

[1] Cf. ZELLER, *Platon. Studien*,
p. 197 sqq.

[2] *Vide supra*, pp. 163,300, &c.
[3] *Vide supra*, p. 300 sqq.

devoid of all scientific basis in itself; that it leads in its results to difficulties and contradictions absolutely insoluble, and that instead of explaining the world of phenomena, it makes them impossible.

He holds that the hypothesis of the Ideas is not established; of the Platonic arguments for it, there is not one that is not open to decisive objections.[1] The ends that Plato sought thereby to attain are and must be attainable otherwise. The content of each of these Ideas is, indeed, exactly the same as the corresponding thing of which it is said to be ' the Idea; ' for in the conception of the *ideal man*, of man as such, exactly the same marks are included as in the conception of *man* in the ordinary sense, there being no difference between the two beyond the addition of the word ' ideal ' (τὸ αὐτό).[2] In this view, the Ideas appear as nothing more than a needless reduplication of the world of things, and the introduction of the Ideas to explain things is to Aristotle as if a man who could not count in small numbers should attempt to count in large ones.[3] But even apart from the failure of proof, the Ideal Theory is in his view in itself untenable; for Substance cannot

---

[1] Cf. *Metaph.* i. 9, 990, b, 8 sqq. xiii. 4, 1079, a.

[2] *Metaph.* iii. 2, 997, b. 5: πολλαχῇ δ' ἐχόντων δυσκολίαν, οὐθενὸς ἧττον ἄτοπον τὸ φάναι μὲν εἶναί τινας φύσεις παρὰ τὰς ἐν τῷ οὐρανῷ, ταύτας δὲ τὰς αὐτὰς φάναι τοῖς αἰσθητοῖς πλὴν ὅτι τὰ μὲν ἀίδια τὰ δὲ φθαρτά · αὐτὸ γὰρ ἄνθρωπόν φασιν εἶναι καὶ ἵππον καὶ ὑγίειαν, ἄλλο δ' οὐδὲν, παραπλήσιον ποιοῦντες τοῖς θεοὺς μὲν εἶναι φάσκουσιν ἀνθρωποειδεῖς δέ · οὔτε

γὰρ ἐκεῖνοι οὐθὲν ἄλλο ἐπο'ουν, ἢ ἀνθρώπους ἀϊδίους, οὔθ' οὗτοι τὰ εἴδη ἀλλ' ἢ αἰσθητὰ ἀίδια. Similarly *Metaph.* vii. 16, 1040, b, 32: ποιοῦσιν οὖν [τὰς ἰδέας] τὰς αὐτὰς τῷ εἴδει τοῖς φθαρτοῖς, αὐτοάνθρωπον καὶ αὐτόϊππον, προστιθέντες τοῖς αἰσθητοῖς τὸ ῥῆμα τὸ αὐτό. *Ibid.* xiii. 9, 1086, b, 10 cf. *Eth. N.* i. 4, 1096, a, 34, *Eud.* i. 8, 1218, a, 10.

[3] *Metaph.* i. 9 *init.* xiii. 4, 1078, b, 32.

be separate from that whereof it is the Substance, nor Genus from that to which (as forming part of the essence) it belongs.[1] This proposition, in fact, summarises the whole difference between the Platonic and Aristotelian systems. Aristotle holds, however, that even if this were waived, the Platonist would only pass out of one difficulty into another. It would appear, for instance, that in reason there could only be Ideas of that which was substantial; and the Platonic school accordingly ascribed Ideas only to natural things. Yet when once it is admitted that the Universal Essence is divided among individual things, it must follow that Ideas should be ascribed also to privative and relative conceptions and to artificial products of all kinds ;[2] and even among the Ideas themselves, the most of them must have Ideas over them to which they stand in the relation of copies, so that it would be true of them that the same thing would be at the same time type and copy.[3] Thus also for every thing—inasmuch as it must fall under a series of genera, superior and subordinate in form—there must be *several* Ideas ;[4] or again, the various general marks which together make up a concept must be themselves so many Substances, and it would follow that one Idea would be made out of many Ideas, or one Substance out of many real Substances,

---

[1] *Metaph.* i. 9, 991, b, 1 : δόξειεν ἂν ἀδύνατον, εἶναι χωρὶς τὴν οὐσίαν καὶ οὗ ἡ οὐσία; xiii. 9, 1085, a, 23, cf. vii. 6, 1031, a, 31, c. 14, 1039, b, 15.

[2] *Metaph.* i. 9, 990, b, 11 sqq. 22, 991, b, 6, xiii. 4, 1079, a, 19, c. 8, 1084, a, 27 ; *Anal. Post.* i.

24, 85, b, 18 ; cf. ZELLER, *Ph. d. Gr.* pt. i. 587, 2.

[3] *Metaph.* i. 9, 991, a, 29, xiii. 5, 1079, b, 34. In the first of these passages we should read : οἷον τὸ γένος, ὡς γένος, εἰδῶν (sc. παράδειγμα ἔσται).

[4] *Metaph.* i. 9, 991, a, 26.

and these sometimes of opposite kinds.[1] Or again, if
the Idea is to be Substance, it cannot at the same time
be a general concept ;[2] for it is not the unity of many
individual things, but an individual itself among other
individuals.[3] Conversely, the things of which it is
predicated could not be true subjects.[4] Of Ideas of
this kind any definition would be as impossible as it is
of other individuals,[5] and since the Idea, like the
individual, is numerically one, it follows that one or
other of the contradictory predicates by which we sub-
divide the genus must always be predicable of it, in
which case it clearly cannot be itself the genus also.[6]

Aristotle considers the assertion that the Ideas contain the essence of things to be inconsistent with the
view that they are at the same time incorporeal. He
represents Plato as speaking sometimes of a ' matter of
the Ideas ' (that being inconsistent with the notion that
they are not in space [7]), and as holding at other times
that in the case of all natural objects matter and the
process of becoming belongs to the essence and conception of them, in which case the conception of them
cannot exist by itself separately.[8] Similarly, he argues
that the ethical conceptions cannot be separated from

---

[1] *Metaph.* vii. 13, 1039, a, 3,
c. 14 ; cf. c. 8, 1033, b, 19, i. 9,
991, a, 29, xiii. 9, 1085 a, 23.

[2] *Metaph.* xiii. 9, 1086, a, 32,
vii. 16, 1040, a, 26 sqq. cf. iii. 6,
1003, a, 5.

[3] *Metaph.* i. 9, 992, b, 9, xiii.
9, *ut supra.*

[4] *Metaph.* vii. 6, 1031,b,15 ; cf.
BONITZ and SCHWEGLER on this
passage, and the citation at

p. 215, *supra,* from *Categ.* c. 2.

[5] *Metaph.* vii. 15, 1040, a, 8–
27.

[6] *Top.* vi. 6, 143,b, 23. Length
in itself must be either ἁπλατὲς
or πλάτος ἔχον, and then the genus
must be at once a species also.

[7] *Phys.* iv. 1, 209, b, 33 ; cf
ZELL. *ibid.* 556 sq., 628 sq.

[8] *Phys.* ii. 2, 193 b, 35 sqq.

their objects. There can be no 'Idea of the Good' standing by itself, for the conception of the Good appears under all possible categories, and determines itself differently according to the different circumstances; and as there are different sciences that deal with the Good, so there are different kinds of good, among which there is, in fact, an ascending scale—a fact which of itself excludes the possibility of a common Idea existing by itself.[1] A further objection is that the theory of Ideas logically carried out would be a process *ad infinitum* : for if an Idea is always to be posited in every case where more things than one meet in a common definition, the common essence of the Idea and its phenomenon must always come in as a third term different from either of them.[2]

Even if the Ideal Theory were better founded and

[1] *Eth. N.* i. 4 (*Eud.* i. 8); cf. preceding notes. As to the principle that what is πρότερον and ὕστερον cannot be reduced to a common generic concept, see *Polit.* iii. 1, 1275, a, 34 sqq. (ZELL., *ibid*, 571 sq.). On the same principle in *Eth. Nic. loc. cit.* Aristotle remarks in criticising the 'Idea of the Good,' that the upholders of the doctrine of Ideas themselves say that there is no Idea of that which stands in the relation of Before and After; but this is actually the case with the Good, for it is found in all the categories : *e. g.*, a substantial good is the Divinity and Reason, a qualitative good is Virtue, a quantitive good is Measure, a relative good is the Useful, &c. Thus these different Goods stand in a relation of Before and After, and can consequently be included in no common generic concept, and therefore in no idea, but (1096, b, 25 sqq.) only in a relation of analogy. (Vide *supra*, p. 276 sqq.)

[2] *Metaph.* i. 9, 991, a, 2, vii. 13, 1039, a, cf. vii. 6, 2, 1031, b, 28. Aristotle expresses this objection here by saying that the doctrine of Ideas leads to the τρίτος ἄνθρωπος. Cf. ZELL., *Plat. Stud.* p. 257, and *Ph. d. Gr.* pt. i. p. 623, 5. He finds the parallel of the τρ'τος ἄνθρωπος (which, however, is equally true of the ideas themselves, cf. *Soph. El*,. c. 22, 178, b, 36) in the change of the universal into an individual of the same name.

less untenable, Aristotle would still say that it could by
no means fulfil the task of a true Philosophy, which is
to exhibit the basis and principles of the world of
appearances. As the Ideas are not *in* things, they
cannot make up the essence of things, and they cannot
contribute anything to the being of things.[1] Even the
relation of the one to the other cannot be stated clearly,
for Plato's own references to some kind of copying and
participation are always unintelligible metaphors.[2] The
principle of motive power, without which no process of
becoming and no explanation of nature is conceivable,
is wholly wanting.[3] So also is the principle of final
cause.[4] Even in regard to the theory of Knowledge,
the Ideas cannot render us that service which Plato
expected from them, for if they are *outside* of things,
then they are not truly the essence of things, and therefore the knowledge of the Idea leads to no sure conclusion as to the thing itself.[5] And how, on the other
hand, could we arrive, asks Aristotle, at any knowledge of the Ideal, since *innate* Ideas are not to be
assumed?[6] All these difficulties will be vastly increased if we are to follow Plato and his school in
translating the Ideas into Numbers, and so interposing

[1] *Metaph.* i. 9, 991, a, 12 (xiii.
5, *init.*).

[2] *Metaph.* i. 9, 991, a, 20, 992,
a, 28 (xiii. 5, 1079, b. 24), i. 6,
987, b, 13, viii. 6, 1045, b. 7, xii.
10, 1075, b, 34.

[3] *Metaph.* i. 9, 991, a, 8. 19 sqq
b, 3 sqq. (xiii. 5) 992, a, 24 sqq.
b, 7, c. 7, 988, b, 3, vii. 8, 1033,
b, 26, xii. 6, 1071, b, 14, c. 10,
1075, b, 16, 27; *Gen. et Corr.* ii. 9,

335, b, 7 sqq. cf. *Eth. Eud.* i. 8,
1217, b, 23.

[4] *Metaph.* i. 7, 988, b, 6, c. 9,
992, a, 29 (where, instead of δίὸ,
δἰ ὅ should be read).

[5] *Metaph.* i. 9, 991, a, 12 (xiii.
5, 1079, b, 15), vii. 6, 1031, a, 30
sqq. cf. *Anal. Post.* i. 22, 83, a,
32 : τὰ γὰρ εἴδη χαιρέτω · τερετί-
σματά τε γάρ ἐστι, &c.

[6] *Vide supra*, p. 202, &c.

between the Ideas and the things of sense the whole science of Mathematics. The difficulties which would thus arise were set out by Aristotle with a painstaking thoroughness most tiresome to the modern mind, though in his day it may possibly have been needful in order to cut off all ways of escape for the Pythagorising school, led by such men as Xenocrates and Speusippus. He asks how we are to think to ourselves the causality of numbers,[1] or how they can contribute to the existence of things.[2] He shows how capricious and contradictory is the application of these numbers to natural objects.[3] He points out the difference in character between conceptual determinations, which are qualitative, and numerical determinations, which are quantitative, remarking that two numbers make up one number, but two Ideas do not make one Idea, and that among the numbers which make up numbers no qualitative differences can be posited, whereas there must be units qualitatively different if there were Ideal Numbers.[4] With minute and careful thoroughness,[5] he controverts the various suggestions as to the relations of mathematics to the Ideal Numbers which were thrown out by Plato and his school and the devices they resorted to in order to maintain a conceivable difference

---

[1] *Metaph.* i. 9, 991, b, 9, with the answer : if things are likewise numbers, one does not see of what use the ideal numbers are to them; if, on the other hand, things are only arranged according to number, the same would be true of the ideas of them, which would not be numbers, but λόγοι ἐν ἀριθμοῖς τινῶν (ὑποκειμένων).

[2] *Metaph.* xiv. 6 *init.*, *ibid.* 1093, b, 21 cf. c. 2, 1090, a, 7 sqq.

[3] *Loc. cit.* from 1092, b, 29; cf. the commentaries on this passage.

[4] Cf. ZELL. *Ph. d. Gr.* pt. i. p. 568 sq. 854, 867 sq. 884.

[5] *Loc. cit.* i. 9, 991, b, 21 sqq. 992, a, 2.

between the Numbers and the units which compose them.[1] But in this, as in other branches of the argument, his main point is always that there is a fundamental contradiction between the notion of a unit of number and the fact of differences of kind. It is not, of course, necessary here to recapitulate those of his objections to Ideal Numbers which apply also to the Ideal Theory in general.[2] But it is to be noticed that, in Aristotle's view, if once we assumed the existence of Ideas and Ideal Numbers, the ordinary mathematical numbers would lose their status, for they could only have the same component parts and therefore the same nature as the Ideal Numbers themselves.[3] The position of magnitudes would be equally dubious; for *quâ* ideal they must go by ideal numbers, and *quâ* mathematical they must go by mathematical number;[4] and from the way in which the theory of magnitudes is deduced, he considers that the further dilemma arises that either it must be possible for a surface to exist without line, and a solid without surface, or else all three must be one and the same.[5]

Finally, as concerns the ultimate principles of things, in which Plato and the Platonists had sought to find the ultimate basis and constituents of their Numbers and Ideas,[6] Aristotle asserts that it is impossible to know the constituent parts of all being, since that

---

[1] *Metaph.* xiii. 6–8.

[2] As in *Metaph.* xiii. 9, 1085, a, 23, and in xiv. 2, 1090, a, 7 sqq. c. 3, 1090, a, 25-b, 5, they are used against Speusippus.

[3] *Metaph.* i. 9, 991, b, 27; xiv. 3, 1090, b, 32 sqq.

[4] *Metaph.* i. 9, 992, b, 13; xiv. 3, 1090, b, 20.

[5] *Ibid.* i, 9, 992, a, 10; xiii. 9, 1085, a, 7, 31.

[6] Cf. ZELLER, *Ph. d. Gr.* pt. i. 628 sq., 805.

knowledge cannot be derived from any prior knowledge.[1]
He doubts whether all being can have the same constituent parts,[2] or whether out of the combination of the
same elements, at one time a number and at another
time a magnitude could arise.[3] He remarks that such
constituent parts can only be ascribed to substances, and
only to those substances which have some admixture of
materiality.[4] He further demonstrates that such constituent parts could neither be thought as individual
nor as universal : not as individual, because they would
not then be cognisable and could not be the constituents of more things or Ideas than one ; not as
universal, because in that case they would not be of the
nature of substance.[5] In another connection, he takes
exception to the variance of the Platonic suggestions as
to the 'material element,'[6] and rejects altogether the
assumption of Speusippus that there are more than one
original but different *principia*.[7] A closer inquiry into
the two Platonic ultimate principles, 'the One,' and
'the Great and Little,' leads Aristotle to declare that
they are both misconceived. He asks how the One can
be a thing existing by itself, when no universal is a
substance. The notion of unity expresses only a

[1] *Metaph.* i. 9, 992, b, 24 ;
against which, indeed, his own
distinction of demonstrative and
inductive knowledge might be
used.

[2] This is suggested, without
mention of Plato, in *Metaph.* xii. 4,
1070, a, 33 sqq. ; cf. what was adduced on pp. 300–301, *supra*.

[3] *Metaph.* iii. 4, 1001, b, 17 sqq.

[4] *Ibid.* i. 9, 992, b, 18 ; xiv. 2
init.

[5] *Metaph.* xiii. 10, 1086, b, 19,
1087, a. 4.

[6] *Metaph.* xiv. 1, 1087, b, 4,
12, 26, c. 2, 1089, b, 11; cf. ZELLER,
Ph. d. Gr. pt. i. p. 628, 3.

[7] Of it the remark in *Metaph.*
xiv. 3, 1090, b, 13 sqq. is true, that
Nature is not ἐπεισοδιώδης ὥσπερ
μοχθηρὰ τραγῳδία, and in xii. 10 *fin.*
the οὐκ ἀγαθὸν πολυκοιρανίη. Further cf. ZELLER, *ibid.* p. 851 sq.
and the passages there adduced.

quality—or, more exactly, a determination of measure. This, however, presupposes something measured, and even that is not necessarily ·anything substantial, but may also be a magnitude, or a quality, or a relation, or any of the most different kinds of things, and, according as it is one or the other of these, ' the One ' will be variously determined, as predicated of one or other of the similar kinds of subjects.[1] Whoever seeks to deny this will be driven to explain ' the One ' as the only Substance, as did the Eleatics—a position which, apart from other objections, would make Number itself impossible.[2] Again, if with Plato we are to say that the One is the same as the Good, then there will arise other intolerable difficulties,[3] not worse, however, than those which would be raised if, with Speusippus, we attempt to distinguish the One from the Good as a special principle by itself.[4] As for ' the Great and Little,' this conception indicates nothing but bare qualities, or rather, bare relations—and these, indeed, of such a kind as could least of all be taken for anything in the nature of substance, since they manifestly require a substratum. How can substances, he asks again, consist of that which is not substantial, and how can constituent parts be at the same time predicates?[5] Or if we are to take this second principle to be more closely related to the first, as not-being is to being, such a theory would be altogether perverse. Plato believed that he could only escape the monism of Parmenides by assuming a prin-

[1] *Metaph.* x. 2; xiv. 1, 1087, b. 33, and xi. 2, 1060, a, 36; cf. *supra*, p. 312, n. 2, and p. 272, n. 2.
[2] *Metaph.* iii. 4, 1001, a, 29.
[3] *Metaph.* xiv. 4, 1091, a, 29, 36 sqq., b, 13, 20 sqq.
[4] *Metaph.* 1091, b, 16, 22, c. 5 *init.*
[5] *Metaph.* i. 9, 992, b, 1; xiv. 1, 1088, a, 15 sqq.

ciple of not-being. This assumption is not necessary
for the purpose, since Being itself is not of one kind
only ; [1] and it would also fail of the purpose, since the
manifold character of Being cannot be explained by the
simple opposition of Being and not-Being.[2] According
to Aristotle, Plato has not sufficiently defined Being and
not-Being, and in his deduction of 'the manifold' from
them he has been thinking of substance only, and not
either of qualities, magnitudes, &c.,[3] or of movement ;
for if the 'Great and Little' produced movement, then
must the Ideas whose matter it is be likewise moved.[4]

The main defect of the Platonic view lies in the position that opposition as such is the first and original principle of all things. If all does arise out of an opposition,
still it is not out of mere opposition as such, which is
negation, but out of relative opposition out of the substratum to which negation attaches. Everything which
comes to be, presupposes a matter out of which it
comes, and this matter is not simply a kind of Not-
Being, but a kind of Being—which *is not* as yet that
which it *is about to become*. The nature of matter in
this regard was misunderstood by Plato. He had in
view merely the opposition of matter as against the
formative principle, and so he thinks of it as the Bad
and the Not-Being, and overlooks the other side of the
question—namely, that it is the positive substratum of
all formative action and of all becoming.[5] By this

---

[1] *Metaph.* xiv. 2, 1088, b, 35
sqq. cf. p. 223, *supra.*
[2] *Ibid.* 1089, a, 12.
[3] *Ibid.* l. 15, 31 sqq.
[4] *Ibid.* i. 9, 992, b. 7.

[5] *Metaph.* xiv. 1 *init.* c. 4,
1091, b, 30 sqq. ; xii. 10, 1075, a,
32 sqq.; *Phys.* i. 9, cf. ZELLER,
Ph. d. Gr. pt. i. p. 614.

oversight he involves himself in this contradiction, that matter tends to its own annihilation, that the evil tends to the good and must of necessity assume it into itself.[1] Further contradictions arise in the considerations that the Great and Little (as was above remarked of the ' Unlimited ' of the Pythagoreans) must be a thing existing for itself, a substance; whereas at the same time as a determination of number and magnitude it cannot possibly be so, and that the same principle would of necessity have to be given in actuality as unlimited, which is a position in fact unthinkable.[2] If, finally, we ask the Platonists in what way the numbers can be deduced from their ultimate principles, distinct statements are entirely wanting. We ask if they arise by a mixture, or by a composition, or by a generation, and there is no answer.[3] We are not told how out of the One and the Many could be produced those units of which numbers are composed,[4] or whether number be itself limited or unlimited.[5] There is no deduction of the first uneven number or of any of the rest except the first ten.[6] We are not shown from whence those unities arise out of which is made up the indefinite duality which, by its combination with the One, is to generate the remaining units:[7] and we are not shown how the duality of the Great and Little can, with the aid of the One, bring forth any numbers which could

[1] *Phys.* i. 9, 192, a, 19.; *Metaph.* xiv. 4, 1092, a, 1.
[2] *Phys.* iii. 5, 204, a, 8–34, cf. c. 4, 203, a, 1 sqq.
[3] *Metaph.* xiv. 5, 1092, a, 21 sqq.; xiii. 9, 1085, b, 4 sqq.; cf. c. 7, 1082, a, 20.

[4] *Metaph.* xiii. 9, 1085, b, 12 sqq. an argument immediately directed against Speusippus.
[5] *Ibid.* 1085, b, 23, c. 8, 1083, b, 36 sqq.; xii. 8, 1073, a, 18.
[6] ZELLER, *ibid.* p. 591, 3.
[7] *Metaph.* i. 9, 991, b, 31.

not arise by the doubling of the One.[1] There are a multitude of similar objections to be found in Aristotle, but these will be more than sufficient.

These criticisms of the Platonic theory are not all of equal value. Not a few of them, at least in the form in which Aristotle directly states them, rest undeniably upon a misunderstanding of Plato.[2] Nevertheless, it cannot be gainsaid that Aristotle has noted the weak points of Plato's theory with a keen insight, and has conclusively exposed its defects. Not only has he completely exhibited the obscurities and dilemmas of the theory of Ideal Numbers, but he has also refuted once for all the Ideal Theory and the assertions of Plato as to the original basis of things. Among the arguments which he uses in his attack, there are two which stand out as decisive, and to which all the others mediately or immediately return : *first*, that all universal concepts (such as those of the One, of Being, of the Great and Little, of the Unlimited, and in fact all the concepts involved in the Ideas) are in no sense substantial, and that they denote only certain qualities and relations, and at the most only the genera and species of things, and not the things themselves ; *second*, that the Ideas are devoid of motive power, and not only cannot explain, but would actually make impossible the changes of phenomena, the coming to be and ceasing to be of things, change and movement, with all the natural properties of things that rest thereon.[3]   In the direction

---

[1] *Metaph.* xiv. 3, 1091, a, 9.

[2] Cf. ZELLER, *Platon. Stud.* 257 sqq.

[3] Aristotle frequently insists on the importance which he himself attached to this objection ; cf., for example, *Metaph.* i. 9, 991, a, 8 : πάντων δὲ μάλιστα

of Aristotle's polemical energy to these points, we may recognise in him the spirit of the Natural Philosopher reaching out towards clear definitions of the actual world and towards an explanation of facts. His powers of abstraction are not inferior to Plato's, and he is superior to him in dialectic skill. But he is determined to give currency to such conceptions only as verify themselves by experience, in that they either combine into unity a series of phenomena, or take them back to their common cause. To the logical Idealism of Plato there is wedded in Aristotle the Realism of the student of Nature.

So far the attempt has been to state the objections Aristotle urged against his predecessors. It is time to turn to his own answers to those questions the solution of which he failed to find in them.

διαπορήσειεν ἄν τις, τί ποτε συμβάλλεται τὰ εἴδη τοῖς ἀϊδίοις τῶν αἰσθητῶν ἢ τοῖς γιγνομένοις καὶ φθειρομένοις· οὔτε γὰρ κινήσεως οὔτε μεταβολῆς οὐδεμιᾶς ἐστιν αἴτια αὐτοῖς; and at 1. 20 : τὸ δὲ λέγειν παραδείγματα αὐτὰ εἶναι καὶ μετέχειν αὐτῶν τἄλλα κενολογεῖν ἐστι καὶ μεταφορὰς λέγειν ποιητικάς· τί γάρ ἐστι τὸ ἐργαζόμενον πρὸς τὰς ἰδέας ἀποβλέπον; and so *ibid.* 992, a, 24 : ὅλως δὲ ζητούσης τῆς φιλοσοφίας περὶ τῶν φανερῶν τὸ αἴτιον τοῦτο μὲν εἴακαμεν (οὐδὲν γὰρ λέγομεν περὶ τῆς αἰτίας ὅθεν ἡ ἀρχὴ τῆς μεταβολῆς), &c.

CHAPTER VII.

CONTINUATION.

The Main Inquiry of Metaphysics.

THERE are three main questions which now fall to be discussed. In so far as the First Philosophy has to do with Actuality in general, with Being as such, it follows that the question of the original essence of the actual, which is the inquiry into the conception of Substance, must precede all other investigations. To this question Plato in his Ideal Theory had answered that that which in a true and original sense is actual was to be sought for only in the common essence of things or in their classes, which are expressed by general conceptions. Aristotle, as has been seen, was not content with the answer : but for that very reason he attributed the more importance to the relation between the individual and the universal. It was in the inaccurate statement of this relation that he found the fundamental error of Plato's view, and he felt that it was from the true conception of the same relation that any revision of Platonism must start. The first question for Philosophy, therefore, must be an inquiry into the conception of ' substance,' which is an inquiry into the relation of the individual to the universal. But inasmuch as Aristotle defines that relation in such a way as to throw

¹ See p. 290 sqq. *supra.*

essential actuality to the side of the individual, it follows that the Form, or the εἶδος, which Plato had made identical with the universal, becomes detached from the universal in Aristotle and takes on an altered meaning. To him Form is essence determinate and developed into full actuality : undetermined universality, which is the possibility of Being, not yet determined this way or that, is considered as Matter in opposition to Form. The relation of Form and Matter accordingly furnishes the second main object of Metaphysics. Form, in fine, is essentially related to Matter, and Matter to Form ; and this relation consists in the fact that Matter becomes definite through Form. This process is Movement. All movement, however, presupposes a first cause of movement, and in this way movement and the first motor constitute the third pair of concepts with which Metaphysics is concerned. In the following pages Aristotle's theory will be set forth under these three heads.

(1) *The Individual and the Universal.*

Plato had taken as the essential element in things 'the universal as it is thought in conception,' and had ascribed Being, in its fullest and original sense, to that only. It was by a limitation of this Being, by a combination of Being with Not-Being, that individual entities could arise. These, therefore, had, outside and above them, as something other than themselves, the universal essences, which were the Ideas. Aristotle denies this, for he finds the fundamental error of the Ideal Theory in this *separation* of the conceptual essence from

the thing itself.[1] A universal is that which belongs to
many things in common,[2] or, more accurately, that
which belongs to them by reason of their nature, and
therefore, necessarily and always.[3] It follows that all
universal concepts denote only certain of the properties
of things; or, in other words, are predicates and not
subjects. Even when a number of these properties are
combined to make the conception of a genus, we get
thereby something which belongs to all the things
pertaining to the genus in question, but by no means
a universal subsisting beside them as distinct. For
Plato's ἓν παρὰ τὰ πολλὰ is substituted Aristotle's
ἓν κατὰ πολλῶν.[4] If, then, the universal is not anything subsisting by itself, it cannot be Substance. It
is true that the name of Substance[5] is used in various

[1] See p. 316, n. 1, *supra. Metaph.*
xiii. 9, 1086, b, 2 : τοῦτο δ' [the
doctrine of Ideas] . . . ἐκίνησε
μὲν Σωκράτης διὰ τοὺς ὁρισμοὺς, οὐ
μὴν ἐχώρισέ γε τῶν καθ' ἕκαστον ·
καὶ τοῦτο ὀρθῶς ἐνόησεν οὐ χωρίσας
. . . ἄνευ μὲν γὰρ τοῦ καθόλου οὐκ
ἔστιν ἐπιστήμην λαβεῖν, τὸ δὲ χωρίζειν αἴτιον τῶν συμβαινόντων δυσ-
χερῶν περὶ τὰς ἰδέας ἐστιν . Cf. c.
4, 1078, b, 30 sq.
[2] *Metaph.* vii. 13, 1038, b, 11 ;
τὸ δὲ καθόλου κοινόν · τοῦτο γὰρ
λέγεται καθόλου ὃ πλείοσιν ὑπάρχειν
πέφυκεν ; iii. 4, 999, b, 34 : οὕτω
γὰρ λέγομεν τὸ καθέκαστον τὸ
ἀριθμῷ ἕν, καθόλου δὲ τὸ ἐπὶ τούτων.
De Interpr. 7, 17, a, 39 ; *Part.
An.* i. 4, 644, a 27, and *supra.*
[3] *Anal. Post.* i. 4, 73, b, 26 :
καθόλου δὲ λέγω ὃ ἂν κατὰ παντός
τε ὑπάρχῃ καὶ καθ' αὐτὸ καὶ ᾗ αὐτό.
φανερὸν ἄρα ὅτι ὅσα καθόλου ἐξ
ἀνάγκης ὑπάρχει τοῖς πράγμασιν ;
c. 31, 87, b, 32 : τὸ γὰρ ἀεὶ καὶ

πανταχοῦ καθόλου φαμὲν εἶναι.
Metaph. v. 9, 1017, b, 35 : τὰ γὰρ
καθόλου καθ' αὐτὰ ὑπάρχει. See also
BONITZ, *Ind. Arist.* 356, b, 4 sqq.
KAMPE, *Erkenntnissth. d. Arist.*
160 sq.
[4] *Anal. Post.* i. 11 *init.* : εἴδη
μὲν οὖν εἶναι ἢ ἕν τι παρὰ τὰ
πολλὰ οὐκ ἀνάγκη, εἰ ἀπόδειξις
ἔσται · εἶναι μέντοι ἓν κατὰ πολλῶν
ἀληθὲς εἰπεῖν ἀνάγκη. *De An.* iii.
8 (see p. 195, n. 1, *supra*).
[5] Aristotle's οὐσία is of course
here and elsewhere translated
by 'substance.' It is strange
to find this translation attacked
(by STRÜMPELL, *Gesch. d. theor.
Phil. b. d. Gr.* 213 sq.; cf.
ZELLER, *Ph. d. Gr.* pt. i. 555,
1) on the ground that Aristotle
nowhere understands by οὐσία
'the unknown, constant, and real
substratum of variable attributes.'
It cannot, however, be expected
that we should cease to use for

senses,[1] but it applies originally only to that which can
neither be stated as a definition of the essence of anything else, nor can depend upon anything else as a
derivative.[2] In other words, Substance is that which is
only subject and never predicate.[3] Or again, Substance
is Being in its original sense, the source from which
all other being is drawn.[4] These conditions Aristotle
finds fulfilled only in individuals. The universal, as he
proved against Plato, does not subsist for itself. Every
universal, even the genus, has its existence only in the
individuals of which it is predicated. It is always in
something other than itself. It denotes not 'this
thing,' but only a stated condition of things. The
individual alone is that which belongs to itself only,
which is not borne up by some other, which is what it
is by reason of itself, and not upon the basis of some

an Aristotelian term the word
which the custom of 1,500 years
has consecrated to it, simply
because Herbart connects the
same word with another sense.

[1] On the different meanings
of οὐσία, s°e p. 374 sq., *infra.*

[2] *Cat.* c. 5 : οὐσία δέ ἐστιν ἡ
κυριωτατά τε καὶ πρώτως καὶ μάλιστα
λεγομένη, ἣ μήτε καθ' ὑποκειμένου
τινὸς λέγεται μήτ' ἐν ὑποκειμένῳ
τινί ἐστιν, οἷον ὁ τὶς ἄνθρωπος ἢ ὁ
τὶς ἵππος. Cf. further TRENDEL-
ENBURG, *Hist. Beitr.* i. 53 sqq.

[3] Aristotle himself elsewhere
so defines it. *Metaph.* v. 8, 1017,
b, 13 : ἅπαντα δὲ ταῦτα λέγεται
οὐσία ὅτι οὐ καθ' ὑποκειμένου λέγεται,
ἀλλὰ κατὰ τούτων τὰ ἄλλα ; vii. 3,
1028, b, 36 : τὸ δ' ὑποκείμενόν
ἐστι καθ' οὗ τὰ ἄλλα λέγεται,
ἐκεῖνο δὲ αὐτὸ μηκέτι κατ' ἄλλου.
διὸ πρῶτον περὶ τούτου διοριστέον·

μάλιστα γὰρ δοκεῖ εἶναι οὐσία τὸ
ὑποκείμενον πρῶτον . . . νῦν μὲν
οὖν τύπῳ εἴρηται τί ποτ' ἐστὶν ἡ
οὐσία, ὅτι τὸ μὴ καθ' ὑποκειμένου
ἀλλὰ καθ' οὗ τὰ ἄλλα. Cf. *Anal.
Pri.* i. 27, 43, a, 25 ; *Longit. V.* 3,
465, b, 6.

[4] *Metaph.* vii. 1 *init.* : τὸ ὂν
λέγεται πολλαχῶς [in the different
categories] . . . φανερὸν ὅτι τούτων
πρῶτον ὂν τὸ τί ἐστιν, ὅπερ σημαίνει
τὴν οὐσίαν . . . τὰ δ' ἄλλα λέγεται
ὄντα τῷ τοῦ οὕτως ὄντος τὰ μὲν
ποσότητας εἶναι, τὰ δὲ ποιότητας,
&c. . . . ὥστε τὸ πρώτως ὂν καὶ οὐ
τὶ ὂν [what is nothing else than
itself and applies to nothing
else ; cf. *Anal. Post.* i. 4, and
the remarks which follow] ἀλλ'
ὂν ἁπλῶς ἡ οὐσία ἂν εἴη ; c. 7,
1030, a, 22 : τὸ τί ἐστιν ἁπλῶς τῇ
οὐσίᾳ ὑπάρχει. See further on
p. 289.

other being.[1] Only in a derivative sense can the
genera be called substances : in so far, that is to say,
as they set forth the common essence of a certain
number of substances;[2] and they claim a kind of

[1] *Cat.* c. 5, 2, a, 34 : τὰ δ' ἄλλα
πάντα ἤτοι καθ' ὑποκειμένων λέγεται
τῶν πρώτων οὐσιῶν ἢ ἐν ὑποκειμέναις
αὐταῖς ἐστίν . . . μὴ οὐσῶν οὖν
τῶν πρώτων οὐσιῶν ἀδύνατον τῶν
ἄλλων τι εἶναι. *Anal. Post.* i. 4,
73, b, 5, where Aristotle calls καθ'
αὐτὸ that ὃ μὴ καθ' ὑποκειμένου
λέγεται ἄλλου τινὸς, οἷον τὸ βαδίζον
ἕτερόν τι ὂν βαδ ζον ἐστὶ καὶ λευκὸν,
ἡ δ' οὐσ α, καὶ ὅσα τόδε τι, οὐχ
ἕτερόν τι ὄντα ἐστὶν ὅπερ ἐστ ν·
τὰ μὲν δὴ μὴ καθ' ὑποκειμένου
[sc. λεγόμενα] καθ' αὐτὰ λέγω, τὰ
δὲ καθ' ὑποκειμένου συυβεβηκ τα.
Metaph. vii. 1, 1028, a, 27 : that
which supports all qualities is
said to be ἡ οὐσία καὶ τὸ καθ'
ἕκαστον . . . τῶν μὲν γὰρ ἄλλων
κατηγορημάτων οὐθὲν χωριστὸν,
αὕτη δὲ μόνη ; c. 3, 1029, a, 27 :
τὸ χωριστὸν καὶ τὸ τόδε τι ὑπάρχειν
δοκεῖ μάλιστα τῇ οὐσίᾳ ; c. 4, 1030,
a, 19 : τὴν οὐσίαν καὶ τὸ τόδε τι ;
c. 10, 1035, b, 28 : καθόλου δ' οὐκ
ἔστιν οὐσία ; c. 12, 1037, a, 27 :
ἡ οὐσ α ἔν τι καὶ τόδε τι σημαίνει
ὡς φαμέν ; c. 13, 1038, b, 10 :
πρώτη οὐσία ἴδιος ἑκίστῳ ἡ οὐχ
ὑπάρχει ἄλλῳ, τὸ δὲ καθ' ὅλου κοινόν.
Ibid. l. 34 : ἔκ τε δὴ τούτων
θεωροῦσι φανερὸν ὅτι οὐθὲν τῶν
καθόλου ὑπαρχόντων οὐσ α ἐστὶ, καὶ
ὅτι οὐθὲν σημα νει τῶν κοινῇ
κατηγορουμένων τόδε τι, ἀλλὰ
τοιόνδε ; c. 16, 1040, b, 23 : κοινὸν
μηθὲν οὐσ α · οὐδενὶ γὰρ ὑπάρχει ἡ
οὐσία ἀλλ' ἢ αὐτῇ τε καὶ τῷ ἔχοντι
αὐτὴν οὗ ἐστὶν οὐσ α. *Ibid. fin.* :
τῶν καθόλου λεγομένων οὐθὲν οὐσία ;
xii. 5 *init.* : ἐπεὶ δ' ἐστι τὰ μὲν χωριστὰ, τὰ δὲ οὐ χωριστὰ, οὐσίαι ἐκεῖνα.

καὶ διὰ τοῦτο πάντων αἴτια ταῦτα ;
iii. 6, 1003, a, 8 : οὐθὲν γὰρ τῶν
κοινῶν τόδε τι σημαίνει, ἀλλὰ
τοιόνδε, ἡ δ' οὐσία τόδε τι. *Soph.*
El. c. 22, 178, b, 37 (cf. *ibid.* 179,
a, 8) : τὸ γὰρ ἄνθρωπος καὶ ἅπαν τὸ
κοινὸν οὐ τόδε τι, ἀλλὰ τοιήνδε τι
ἢ πρός τι ἢ πῶς ἢ τῶν τοιούτων τι
σημαίνει. (This holds even of
the sensible qualities of things ;
see p. 206, *supra*.) *Gen. An.* iv.
3, 767, b, 33 : τὸ καθέκαστον·
τοῦτο γὰρ ἡ οὐσία. All other
categories indicate mere accidents (συμβεβηκ τα) of substance ; cf. p. 289 *supra*. Aristotle
finds it therefore quite natural
(*Metaph.* vii. 16, 1040, b, 26 sq.)
that the ideas should be made
into a χωριστόν if they are taken
for substances. The error of the
doctrine of ideas consisted only
in regarding the universal as
such a substantial idea. (HERT-
LING, *Mat. und Form*, 44, 1, has
misunderstood this statement.)

[2] *Cat.* c. 5, 2, a, 15 : δεύτεραι
δὲ οὐσίαι λέγονται ἐν οἷς εἴδεσιν αἱ
πρώτως οὐσίαι λεγόμεναι ὑπάρχουσι,
ταῦτά τε καὶ τὰ τῶν εἰδῶν τούτων
γένη . . . οἷον ὅ τε ἄνθρωπος καὶ
τὸ ζῷον. And so further on.
Otherwise the expression δευτέρα
οὐσία does not occur in Aristotle.
As, however, he elsewhere uses
πρώτη οὐσία for ' substance in the
primary sense,' and τρίτη οὐσία
for ' third class of substances,'
no objection can be taken, as we
have already remarked (in n. 1
to p. 64).

substantial character with the more right the nearer they approach to individual substances, so that the species deserves to be called substantial in a higher degree than the genus.[1] According to the strict conception of substance, however, that term cannot be applied to them at all, because they are predicated of individuals,[2] and because it is true of them, as of every universal, that they are not a ' This,' but a ' Such ' — not substantive, but adjective—and that they express, not substance, but a condition of substance.[3]

The further marks of substance which Aristotle gives us, likewise refer, in so far as they are really characteristic of that conception, to individual substances only.[4] The so-called secondary substance of

---

[1] *Cat.* c. 5, 2, b, 7 sq. Aristotle, indeed, seems to say the opposite in *Metaph.* viii. 1, 1042, a, 13 : ἔτι ἄλλως [συμβαίνει] τὸ γένος μᾶλλον τῶν εἰδῶν [οὐσίαν εἶναι] καὶ τὸ καθόλου τῶν καθέκαστα ; but he does not intend to express his own view in these words ; cf. vii. 13 ; BONITZ and SCHWEGLER *in loco.*

[2] *Cat.* c. 5, 2, a, 19 sq., b, 15–21.

[3] See n. 1 on last page. *Cat.* c. 5, 3, b, 10 : πᾶσα δὲ οὐσία δοκεῖ τόδε τι σημαίνειν. Of. πρῶται οὐσίαι this holds unconditionally : ἐπὶ δὲ τῶν δευτέρων οὐσιῶν φαίνεται μὲν ὁμοίως τῷ σχήματι τῆς προσηγορίας τόδε τι σημαίνειν . . . οὐ μὴν ἀληθές γε, ἀλλὰ μᾶλλον ποιόν τι σημαίνει· οὐ γὰρ ἕν ἐστι τὸ ὑποκείμενον ὥσπερ ἡ πρώτη οὐσ.α, ἀλλὰ κατὰ πολλῶν ὁ ἄνθρωπος λέγεται καὶ τὸ ζῷον.

[4] The first characteristic of substance was τὸ μὴ καθ' ὑποκειμένου λέγεσθαι. That this is true

only of individual substance has been shown. A second (*Cat.* 5, 3, a, 6 sq., and p. 331, n. 2, *supra*) is τὸ μὴ ἐν ὑποκειμένῳ εἶναι. But this characteristic belongs also to the class, and not to it alone, but likewise (*Cat.* c. 5, 3, a, 21 &c.) to the specific difference, since this is likewise contained in the conception of the thing to which it applies ; while (according to Aristotle, *ibid.*) only that is ἐν ὑποκειμένῳ which does not belong to the conception of that of which it is predicated, but which is a quality in a substance quite independent of it : *e.g.* in the sentence ' the body is white,' λευκὸν is ἐν ὑποκειμένῳ ; on the other hand, in the sentence ' man is two-legged,' δ.πουν is not ἐν ὑποκειμένῳ. A further peculiarity of substance is (*Cat.* c. 5, 3, b, 24) τὸ μηδὲν αὐταῖς ἐναντ'ον εἶναι. And yet Aristotle himself remarks that the same

Aristotle cannot be treated as exactly identical with
quality, but neither can it properly be considered substance. It denotes substance on the side of its qualities
only. For it is the combination of the essential properties of a definite class of substances.[1] In contrast
with it, it is the individual substances alone which
are of that self-sufficient and independently subsisting
nature to which the name of substance, in its original
sense, belongs.

This view, however, is not without its difficulties.
If all knowledge is concerned with the actual,[2] then it
is only the actual, in the highest and truly original
sense of the word, which can furnish the original and
ultimate object of knowledge. If knowledge is the
recognition of reality,[3] it must relate, in the first place,
to real Being, which is the substance of things.[4] If
this substance is individual substance, it follows that,

is the case with determinations
of quantity and many other conceptions. And the same reply
may be made if (*ibid.* l. 33) it
be said that substance is susceptible of no difference of
degree, no greater or less. For
while, perhaps, we might say
that one is more or less of a
'man' than another, yet we
could in no sense say that he is
more or less 'two-legged.' If,
finally (*ibid.* 4, a, 10, b, 3, 17),
we take as the most distinctive
quality of substance : τὸ ταὐτὸν
καὶ ἐν ἀριθμῷ ὂν τῶν ἐναντίων
εἶναι δεκτικὸν, τὸ κατὰ τὴν ἑαυτῆς
μεταβολὴν δεκτικὴν τῶν ἐναντίων
εἶναι, this holds only of individual substance, since to classes
the conceptions of numerical
unity and change are inapplica-

ble. The statement, moreover,
contains a questionable identification of substance with matter,
to which we shall have again to
refer.

[1] *Cat.* c. 5, 3, b, 18 : (after the
passage quoted in n. 3 on p. 333) :
οὐκ ἁπλῶς δὲ ποιόν τι σημαίνει, ὥσπερ
τὸ λευκόν. οὐδὲν γὰρ ἄλλο σημα'νει
τὸ λευκὸν ἀλλ' ἢ ποιόν. τὸ δὲ εἶδος
καὶ τὸ γένος περὶ οὐσίαν τὸ ποιὸν
ἀφορίζει· ποιὰν γάρ τινα οὐσίαν
σημαίνει. Cf. SIMPL. *Kat.* 26, β
Bas., who explains ποιά τις οὐσία
by ποιότης οὐσιώδης.

[2] See p. 162.

[3] *Ibid.* and p. 219, n. 1.

[4] *Metaph.* vii. 4, 1030, b, 4 :
ἐκεῖνο δὲ φανερὸν ὅτι ὁ πρώτως καὶ
ἁπλῶς ὁρισμὸς καὶ τὸ τί ἦν εἶναι τῶν
οὐσιῶν ἐστιν. See also p. 219,
n. 1.

in the last resort, all knowledge is of the individual,
and that individual things furnish, not only the starting-
point, but the whole essential content and object of
knowledge. This conclusion, however, Aristotle decisively rejects. He is convinced that Science relates,
not to the individual, but to the universal, and even
when it descends furthest to particulars, it addresses
itself all the while, not to the individual things, as such,
but to general conceptions only.[1] This contradiction
in his system cannot be met by the observation[2] that it
is only in the realm of natural being that the individual
is first, whereas in the realm of spirits the universal is
first. Aristotle himself knows nothing of any such
distinction. He says, without any kind of limitation,
that knowledge is directed to the universal only, and,
equally without qualification, that it is individual essence only which is substantial; and he chooses the
examples with which he illustrates both propositions
from the natural and the spiritual world alike.[3] Even
God is individual Substance. The fact that Substance
and Form run together proves nothing: for, as will be
seen, there recurs in the working out of the conception
of Form the same difficulty which now engages us
with regard to Substance.

Aristotle himself recognised the full weight of
the difficulty,[4] and he seems to indicate another way

---

[1] Pp. 162 sqq., and 220 sqq.
supra. Cf. in *Anal. Post.* i. 24, 85,
a, 20 sq., the argument that the
general method proof is better
than the particular; and *ibid.*
c. 14, 79, a, 28: τὸ δὲ τί ἐστι τῶν
καθόλου ἐστίν.

[2] BIESE, *Phil. d. Arist.* i. 56 sq.

[3] Cf. with regard to the first,
Metaph. xiii. 10, 1086, b, 33 sq.,
i. 1, 981, a, 7; *Anal. Post.* i. 31;
in regard to the second, *Cat.* c. 5,
3, b, 14 sq.; *Metaph.* vii. 10,
1035, b, 27, c. 16, 1040, b, 21, xii.
5, 1071, a, 2.

[4] *Metaph.* iii. 4 *init.*: ἔστι δ'

of escape in the remark [1] that Knowledge, considered *in posse*, is indeterminate and is directed to the universal, but that in actual practice, on the contrary, it is always directed to something determinate. This, however, does not take us very far. The knowledge of the particular arises only by the application of universal propositions. The certitude of that knowledge depends on their certitude. Such knowledge, therefore, as Aristotle expressly recognises,[2] has not for its object the individual as such, but, on the contrary, the individual is known by it only in the form of universality.[3] On the other hand, if the individual be that which is original actuality, then it ought to be precisely, *quâ* individual, the proper object of knowledge, and the knowledge of the universal ought to depend upon it for its truth and certainty. In fact, it would be the individual—and not, as Aristotle taught,[4] the universal—which should be in its own nature the better known and the more certain.[5]

ἐχομένη τε τούτων ἀπορία καὶ πασῶν χαλεπωτάτη καὶ ἀναγκαιοτάτη θεωρῆσαι, περὶ ἧς ὁ λόγος ἐφέστηκε νῦν· εἴτε γὰρ μὴ ἔστι τι παρὰ τὰ καθέκαστα, τὰ δὲ καθέκαστα ἄπειρα, τῶν δ' ἀπείρων πῶς ἐνδέχεται λαβεῖν ἐπιστήμην ; c. 6 *fin.*: εἰ μὲν οὖν καθόλου αἱ ἀρχαί, ταῦτα συμβαίνει· [viz. οὐκ ἔσονται οὐσίαι· οὐθὲν γὰρ τῶν κοινῶν τόδε τι σημαίνει, ἀλλὰ τοιόνδε, ἡ δ' οὐσία τόδε τι, as he says before,] εἰ δὲ μὴ καθόλου, ἀλλ' ὡς τὰ καθέκαστα, οὐκ ἔσονται ἐπιστηταί· καθόλου γὰρ αἱ ἐπιστῆμαι πάντων. Cf. *Metaph.* xi. 2, 1060, b, 19, xiii. 10, also vii. 13, 1039, a, 14.

[1] *Metaph.* xiii. 10 ; see p. 167, n. 1 *supra.*

[2] See especially p. 220, &c., *supra.*

[3] Τῷ καθόλου λόγῳ, as Aristotle expresses it, *Metaph.* vii. 10 (see pp. 220 sqq., *supra*).

[4] See p. 205, n. 2, *supra.*

[5] RASSOW'S solution (*Aristot. de Notionis Definitione Doctrina,* p. 57) is equally unsatisfactory. He appeals to *Metaph.* vii. 10, 1035, b, 28 (where, moreover, after the words ὡς καθόλου, which stand in opposition to the following καθ' ἕκαστον, we have simply to supply an εἰπεῖν) and c. 4, 1029, b, 19, and tries to solve the contradiction by remarking that in definition and in science generally the individual is regarded

If, conceding this, we were to say that the genus had in itself more of the essential than the species, but that, on the contrary, *for us* the species had more than the genus,[1] we should thereby place ourselves in opposition to the definite statements of Aristotle, who continually insists that all Substance, in the strict sense of the word, *is* individual Substance not that it appears to *us* as such. There is only one case which would make it possible to escape the difficulty : that is, if there were a principle which, being individual, could be at the same time truly universal, for this could be at the same time, as substantial, a basis of actuality, and, as universal, a basis of truth. Such a principle seems to be found in the keystone of Aristotle's entire system— namely, in his theory of Pure Thought, or of God. To him the Divine, as thinking Essence, is Subject ; as the End, Mover and Form of the world, it is also a true universal. The conception of it has existence in one individual Essence, not merely contingently,[2] but by reason of its own nature ; whereas, in all finite things, the universal presents itself, or at least might present itself, in a number of individuals.[3] From this standpoint it would be possible to seek a solution of the difficulties suggested, by saying that in God, as the

not as individual, but from the universal side of its being. That is just the reason why it would require to be otherwise if the individual were the substantial.

[1] BRANDIS, ii. b, 568, whose answer to this question is not altogether clear.

[2] As perhaps that of the sun or of the moon; see p. 222, n. 2,

supra.

[3] *Metaph.* xii. 10, 1074, a, 33 ; ὅσα ἀριθμῷ πολλὰ [everything of which several examples are contained in the same class] ὕλην ἔχει · εἷς γὰρ λόγος καὶ ὁ αὐτὸς πολλῶν, οἷον ἀνθρώπου, Σωκράτης δὲ εἷς · τὸ δὲ τί ἦν εἶναι οὐκ ἔχει ὕλην τὸ πρῶτον, ἐντελέχεια γάρ.

ultimate principle, absolute certitude for thought coincides with absolute actuality of being, but that, in all derivative forms of being, the greater actuality falls to the share of the individual and the greater cognisability to the share of the universal. That this solution, however, would be in accordance with all Aristotle's premisses is not yet proven. Aristotle himself does not draw the distinction. He says without any qualification that all knowledge consists in the cognition of the universal, and that substantiality pertains to individuals alone. Even if we were to limit the first of these propositions to the world of sense,[1] its incompatibility with the second would not disappear. Aristotle's view is not that knowledge is directed to the universal because *we* are incapable of perfectly knowing the individual as such. It is, on the contrary, that *in spite of* the fact that the individual things of sense are better known to us, the universal must furnish the sole object of knowledge in the strict sense, because it is *in itself* more original and more cognisable because it alone possesses that immutability which anything that is to be the object of knowledge must afford.[2] The further conclusion is inevitable, that, in comparison with the individual things of sense, it must possess a higher degree of actuality also. And we shall also find[3] the individual can only arise through the combination

---

[1] As G. v. HERTLING does, *Mat. u. Form b. Arist.* 43, f., remarking that the form of universality is not in all spheres the indispensable condition of knowledge, but only where we are dealing with the knowledge of the material world. Here it is the only resource we have in face of the partial unknowableness of all material things.

[2] See pp. 205 and 220, *supra*.

[3] *Infra*, p. 368.

of Form with Matter. But one cannot understand how reality can belong in a higher degree and a more primary sense to that which is a combination of Form and Matter, of Actual and Possible, than to that which is pure Form as it is known in universal concepts, *i.e.* to the Actual which is limited by no element of mere Possibility.[1] It only remains, then, to recognise in this point, not merely a lacuna, but a deep contradiction in the philosophy of Aristotle.[2] He has set aside the Platonic attempt to hypostatise the universal concepts, but he leaves standing its two main pillars, the assumptions, namely, that it is only the universal that can be the object of knowledge and that the truth of knowledge keeps pace with the actuality of its object.[3] How was it possible to hold these two positions together in thought without involving contradictions?

We need not expect, threfore, to avoid contradictions in working out the further developments of his theory, by which Aristotle sought a solution of the questions which the Ideal theory and the doctrines connected therewith had left unanswered.

---

[1] Even HERTLING fails to make this intelligible, when he goes on to say in the passage just quoted that that only is object of knowledge which is of permanent worth in things. This in the sphere of sense is never the whole thing, but is entangled with all that is accidental and that has its source in matter. He thus suggests the question how the thing in which the permanent worth is mixed with the accidental can be anything more substantial than the form which presents it pure.

[2] Since RITTER, iii. 130, called attention to this difficulty it has been further discussed by HEYDER; cf. *Arist. und hegel. Dial.* 180, 183 sq., and ZELLER's first edition, p. 405 sq., which was followed by BONITZ, *Arist. Metaph.* ii. 569. SCHWEGLER, *Arist. Metaph.* iii. 133. Cf. also STRÜMPELL, *Gesch d. Phil.* 251 sq.

[3] Cf. ZELLER, *Ph. d. Gr.* pt. i 541 sq.

(2) Form and Matter: the Actual and the Possible.

We must now go back to Plato. In the Ideas he had distinguished the non-sensible essence of things from their sensible appearance. Aristotle refused to think of the former as a universal subsisting for itself outside of things. Yet he does not wish to abandon the distinction, and the grounds on which he bases it are the same as those of Plato—namely, that the non-sensible Form can alone be an object of knowledge, and that it alone is permanent amid the change of appearances. He says, as Plato said, that as perception is different from knowledge, it is equally clear that the object of knowledge must be something other than sensible things. All that is sensible is passing and changeful; it is a 'contingent' which may be one way or may be another. What knowledge requires, on the contrary, is an object as unchangeable and necessary as itself, which can as little change into its opposite as knowledge can into ignorance. Of sensible things we can have neither a concept nor a proof; it is the Form alone with which knowledge has to do.[1] Form, indeed, is also the indispensable condition of all Becoming: since everything that becomes, comes to be something from being something else. Becoming, then, consists in this, that some matter takes on a definite Form. This Form must therefore be posited before each case

---

[1] *Metaph.* vii. 11, 15 (see p. 220, *supra*), with which cf. *ibid.* iii 4, 999, b, 1 : εἰ μὲν οὖν μηθέν ἐστι παρὰ τὰ καθ' ἕκαστα, οὐθὲν ἂν εἴη νοητὸν ἀλλὰ πάντα αἰσθητὰ καὶ ἐπιστήμη οὐθενός, εἰ μή τις εἶναι λέγει τὴν αἴσθησιν ἐπιστήμην. ἔτι δ' οὐδ' ἀΐδιον οὐθὲν οὐδ' ἀκίνητον; iv. 5, 1010, a, 25: κατὰ τὸ εἶδος ἅπαντα γιγνώσκομεν.

of Becoming as the aim and end thereof; and even
supposing that in any particular case the Form could
itself originate in the process of Becoming, yet in any
case such a supposition could not be carried *ad
infinitum*, for if it could, we should never arrive at a
true instance of actual Becoming. The fact of Becoming, in other words, is inexplicable unless it be true
that before anything came to be[1] there was a Form[2]
which itself had not come to be.

For the same reason there must also be Matter as
the correlative of Form. The relation of these two
should not be defined, as Plato defined it, merely as one

[1] Εἶδος, μορφή, λόγος (see p. 219,
n. 1, *supra*), οὐσία (*infra*, p. 275),
τὸ τί ἦν εἶναι (see p. 217, n. 1,
supra).

[2] *Metaph.* iii. 4, 999, b, 5:
ἀλλὰ μὴν εἴ γε ἀΐδιον οὐθέν ἐστιν,
οὐδὲ γένεσιν εἶναι δυνατόν· ἀνάγκη
γὰρ εἶναί τι τὸ γιγνόμενον καὶ ἐξ
οὗ γίγνεται καὶ τούτων τὸ ἔσχατον
ἀγένητον εἴπερ ἵσταταί τε καὶ ἐκ
μὴ ὄντος γενέσθαι ἀδύνατον . . .
ἔτι δ' εἴπερ ἡ ὕλη ἐστὶ διὰ τὸ
ἀγέννητος εἶναι, πολὺ ἔτι μᾶλλον
εὔλογον εἶναι τὴν οὐσίαν ὅ ποτε
ἐκείνη γίγνεται. [οὐσία as that
which ὕλη becomes] εἰ γὰρ μήτε
τοῦτο ἔσται μήτε ἐκείνη, οὐθὲν
ἔσται τὸ παράπαν. εἰ δὲ τοῦτο
ἀδύνατον, ἀνάγκη τι εἶναι παρὰ τὸ
σύνολον τὴν μορφὴν καὶ τὸ εἶδος;
vii. 8 *init.*: ἐπεὶ δὲ ὑπό τινός τε
γίγνεται τὸ γιγνόμενον . . . καὶ ἔκ
τινος [*e.g.* out of brass] . . . καὶ ὃ
γίγνεται [*e.g.* a ball] . . . ὥσπερ
οὐδὲ τὸ ὑποκείμενον ποιεῖ τὸν χαλκὸν,
οὕτως οὐδὲ τὴν σφαῖραν εἰ μὴ κατὰ
συμβεβηκός . . . λέγω δ' ὅτι τὸν
χαλκὸν στρογγύλον ποιεῖν ἐστὶν οὐ
τὸ στρογγύλον ἢ τὴν σφαῖραν
ποιεῖν, ἀλλ' ἕτερόν τι, οἷον τὸ εἶδος

τοῦτο ἐν ἄλλῳ. The form, again,
could only come from another
form, and so on *ad infinitum*,
since all coming to be is the embodiment of form in matter.
φανερὸν ἄρα ὅτι οὐδὲ τὸ εἶδος . . .
οὐ γίγνεται . . . οὐδὲ τὸ τί ἦν εἶναι
. . . ὅτι τὸ μὲν ὡς εἶδος ἢ οὐσία
λεγόμενον οὐ γίγνεται, ἡ δὲ σύνοδος
ἡ κατὰ ταύτην λεγομένη γίγνεται,
καὶ ὅτι ἐν παντὶ τῷ γενομένῳ ὕλη
ἔνεστι, καὶ ἔστι τὸ μὲν τόδε τὸ δε
τόδε; c. 9, 1034, b, 7: οὐ μόνον
δὲ περὶ τῆς οὐσίας ὁ λόγος δηλοῖ τὸ
μὴ γίγνεσθαι τὸ εἶδος, ἀλλὰ περὶ
πάντων ὁμοίως τῶν πρώτων κοινὸς ὁ
λόγος, οἷον ποσοῦ ποιοῦ, &c. It is
not the ball, nor is it the brass,
that comes to be, but the brass
ball, not ποιὸν but ποιὸν ξύλον;
xii. 3 *inst.*: οὐ γίγνεται οὔτε ἡ ὕλη
οὔτε τὸ εἶδος, λέγω δὲ τὰ ἔσχατα,
πᾶν γὰρ μεταβάλλει τὶ καὶ ὑπό τινος
καὶ εἴς τι. ὑφ' οὗ μὲν, τοῦ πρώτου
κινοῦντος· ὃ δὲ, ἡ ὕλη· εἰς ὃ δὲ, τὸ
εἶδος. εἰς ἄπειρον οὖν εἴσιν, εἰ μὴ
μόνον ὁ χαλκὸς γίγνεται στρογγύλος,
ἀλλὰ καὶ τὸ στρογγύλον ἢ ὁ χαλκός·
ἀνάγκη δὲ στῆναι. *Ibid.* 1070, a, 15,
viii. 3, 1043, b, 16, c. 5, 1044, b, 22.

of opposition, in the sense that all true Being would
fall exclusively to the share of Form, and that there
would remain for Matter only the sphere of Not-Being.
Here again arises the old question of the possibility of
Becoming.[1] It might seem that out of Being nothing
could come to be, since it is already : and out of Not-
Being nothing also, for *ex nihilo nihil fit*. Aristotle
finds it possible to avoid this difficulty only by saying
that all which comes to be starts in the process of
Becoming out of that which *is* only in a relative sense
and in a relative sense *is not*. That from which anything
comes to be cannot be absolutely Not-Being, but at the
same time it cannot be that which it is only on its
way to become. There remains, therefore, as the only
possible alternative, that it is that which it is to be in
possibility, but not as yet in actuality. If, for example,
an uneducated man becomes an educated man, he does
so out of the condition of a man not educated, but as
truly out of the condition of a man capable of education.   In fact, it is not the uneducated, as such, that
becomes educated, but it is the uneducated *man*—the
subject, that is, which has a predisposition towards
education, but in actuality is not yet educated.

All Becoming is a passing over of possibility into
actuality. Becoming, in general, therefore, presupposes
a substratum whose essence it is to be pure possibility,
which has not in any relation become actuality.[2]   All

---

[1] Cf. pp. 302, 309 sqq.

[2] This relation is fully developed in *Phys.* i. 6–10, from which
the following are extracts : c. 7 :
φαμὲν γὰρ γίνεσθαι ἐξ ἄλλου ἄλλο
καὶ ἐξ ἑτέρου ἕτερον ἢ τὰ ἁπλᾶ

λέγοντες ἢ συγκείμενα [the former,
if I say ' the man becomes cultured,' or 'the uncultured becomes cultured '; the latter, if I
say ' the uncultured man becomes
a cultured man ']. τῶν δὲ γινομ-

becomes that which it comes to be out of its opposite. What becomes warm must before have been cold. He who becomes a man of knowledge must before have been without knowledge.[1] Opposites as such, however, can-

ένων ὡς τὰ ἁπλᾶ λέγομεν γίνεσθαι, τὸ μὲν ὑπομένον λέγομεν γίνεσθαι, τὸ δ' οὐχ ὑπομένον. ὁ μὲν γὰρ ἄνθρωπος ὑπομένει μουσικὸς γινόμενος ἄνθρωπος. καὶ ἔστι, τὸ δὲ μὴ μουσικὸν καὶ τὸ ἄμουσον οὔτε ἁπλῶς οὔτε συντιθέμενον ὑπομένει. διωρισμένων δὲ τούτων ἐξ ἁπάντων τῶν γιγνομένων τοῦτο ἔστι λαβεῖν ἐάν τις ἐπιβλέψῃ, ὥσπερ λέγομεν, ὅτι δεῖ τι ἀεὶ ὑποκεῖσθαι τὸ γινόμενον, καὶ τοῦτο εἰ καὶ ἀριθμῷ ἐστιν ἕν, ἀλλ' εἴδει γε οὐχ ἕν . . . οὐ γὰρ ταὐτὸν τὸ ἀνθρώπῳ καὶ τὸ ἀμούσῳ εἶναι. καὶ τὸ μὲν ὑπομένει, τὸ δ' οὐχ ὑπομένει· τὸ μὲν μὴ ἀντικείμενον ὑπομένει (ὁ γὰρ ἄνθρωπος ὑπομένει) τὸ μουσικὸν δὲ καὶ τὸ ἄμουσον οὐχ ὑπομένει. *Ibid.* 190, a, 31: in the case of all else that becomes the οὐσία is the substratum of the change; ὅτι δὲ καὶ αἱ οὐσίαι καὶ ὅσα ἄλλα ἁπλῶς ὄντα ἐξ ὑποκειμένου τινὸς γίνεται, ἐπισκοποῦντι γένοιτ' ἂν φανερόν. This he goes on to prove by the examples of plants, animals, products of art and chemical changes(ἀλλοιώσεις), and then proceeds : ὥστε δῆλον ἐκ τῶν εἰρημένων, ὅτι τὸ γινόμενον ἅπαν ἀεὶ συνθετόν ἐστι, καὶ ἔστι μέν τι γινόμενον, ἔστι δέ τι ὃ τοῦτο γίνεται, καὶ τοῦτο διττόν· ἢ γὰρ τὸ ὑποκείμενον ἢ τὸ ἀντικείμενον. λέγω δὲ ἀντικεῖσθαι μὲν τὸ ἄμουσον, ὑποκεῖσθαι δὲ τὸ ἄνθρωπον, καὶ τὴν μὲν ἀσχημοσύνην καὶ τὴν ἀμορφίαν ἢ τὴν ἀταξίαν τὸ ἀντικείμενον, τὸν δὲ χαλκὸν ἢ τὸν λίθον ἢ τὸν χρυσὸν τὸ ὑποκείμενον. φανερὸν οὖν . . . ὅτι γίγνεται πᾶν ἔκ τε τοῦ ὑποκειμέ-

νου καὶ τῆς μορφῆς . . . ἔστι δὲ τὸ ὑποκείμενον ἀριθμῷ μὲν ἕν, εἴδει δὲ δύο, viz. (1) matter as such and (2) the negation of form (στέρησις) as property (συμβεβηκὸς) of matter. It is just this distinction, c. 8 goes on, which solves the difficulty previous philosophers felt in dealing with the possibility of becoming which they ended by totally denying: οὔτε γὰρ τὸ ὂν γίνεσθαι (εἶναι γὰρ ἤδη) ἔκ τε μὴ ὄντος οὐδὲν ἂν γενέσθαι . . . ἡμεῖς δὲ καὶ αὐτοί φαμεν γίγνεσθαι μὲν οὐδὲν ἁπλῶς ἐκ μὴ ὄντος, ὅμως μέντοι γίγνεσθαι ἐκ μὴ ὄντος, οἷον κατὰ συμβεβηκός· ἐκ γὰρ τῆς στερήσεως, ὅ ἐστι καθ' αὐτὸ μὴ ὄν, οὐκ ἐνυπάρχοντος γίγνεταί τι [*i.e.* a thing becomes what it is not from its negative which in and for itself does not exist : man, for example, becomes what he is not—cultured from being uncultured] . . . εἷς μὲν δὴ τρόπος οὗτος, ἄλλος δ' ὅτι ἐνδέχεται ταὐτὰ λέγειν κατὰ τὴν δύναμιν καὶ τὴν ἐνέργειαν. *Gen. et Corr.* i. 3, 317, b, 15 : τρόπον μέν τινα ἐκ μὴ ὄντος ἁπλῶς γίνεται, τρόπον δὲ ἄλλον ἐξ ὄντος ἀεί. τὸ γὰρ δυνάμει ὂν ἐντελεχείᾳ δὲ μὴ ὂν ἀνάγκη προϋπάρχειν λεγόμενον ἀμφοτέρως. Cf. *Metaph.* xii. 2 (an exposition in complete agreement with that of the *Physics*); *ibid.* c. 4, 1070, b, 11, 18, c. 5, 1071, b, 8, iv. 5, 1009, a, 30 and p. 341, n. 2, *supra.*

[1] See *infra,* and *Phys.* ii. 5, 205, a, 6.

not change into their opposites, nor even act upon their opposites. Cold does not become warmth : ignorance does not become knowledge ; but the former cease when the latter begin. Becoming is not the passing over of one property into the opposite property, but the passage out of one condition into the opposite condition, by the interchange of one property with another. Thus it follows that all Becoming presupposes some Being on the basis of which such an interchange takes place, and which underlies as their subject the changing properties and conditions, and maintains itself in them. This substratum certainly is in a sense the opposite of that which it is to become, but it is so not in itself, but derivatively. It has not as yet those properties which it is to receive, and in place of them it has their opposites ; and in so far it stands in a negative relation to that which is to come out of it. This negative relation, however, concerns not its own essence, but only the determinations of quality which attach to it.[1] As

[1] Cf. besides the above nn. and p. 323 sq., *Phys.* i. 6, 189, a, 20 : for the explanation of phenomena it is not enough to assume two principles standing to one another in the relation of opposites, ἀπορήσειε γὰρ ἄν τις πῶς ἢ ἡ πυκνότης τὴν μανότητα ποιεῖν τι πέφυκεν ἢ αὕτη τὴν πυκνότητα. ὁμοίως δὲ καὶ ἄλλη ὁποιαοῦν ἐναντιότης, &c ; c. 7, 190, b, 29 : διὸ ἔστι μὲν ὡς δύο λεκτέον εἶναι τὰς ἀρχὰς, ἔστι δ' ὡς τρεῖς. καὶ ἔστι μὲν ὡς τἀναντία, οἷον εἴ τις λέγοι τὸ μουσικὸν κ‹ὶ τὸ ἄμουσον ἢ τὸ θερμὸν καὶ τὸ ψυχρὸν ἢ τὸ ἡρμοσμένον καὶ τὸ ἀνάρμοστον ἔστι δ' ὡς οὔ · ὑπ' ἀλλήλων γὰρ πάσχειν τἀναντία

ἀδύνατον. We obtain three principles (ἀρχαὶ) (*ibid.* 191, a, 12) if besides ὑποκείμενον and λόγος we take especial account of στέρησις, otherwise only two. A thing's opposite is its principle in so far as its matter is infected with στέρησις or the contrary of the form it is going to receive ; something other than its opposite is its principle in so far as the matter in itself is as capable of the one determination as of the other ; c. 9, 192, a, 16 : Plato errs in identifying the material simply with the non-existent. ὄντος γάρ τινος θείου καὶ ἀγαθοῦ καὶ ἐφετοῦ, τὸ μὲν ἐναντίον αὐτῷ φαμὲν εἶναι,

it is a presupposition of all Becoming, this substratum
cannot ever itself have had a commencement ; and since
everything which perishes resolves itself finally into the
same substratum, it is imperishable also.[1] This beginningless basis of Becoming[2] is Matter ;[3] and so we
have Matter alongside of Form as a second term.[4]

The notion and the relation of these two principles
is more accurately determined in the doctrine that
Form is the Actual and Matter the Possible.[5] Both

τὸ δὲ ὃ πέφυκεν ἐφίεσθαι καὶ ὀρέγεσθαι αὐτοῦ κατὰ τὴν ἑαυτοῦ φύσιν.
τοῖς δὲ συμβαίνει τὸ ἐναιτίον ὀρέγεσθαι τῆς ἑαυτοῦ φθορᾶς. κα'τοι
οὔτε αὐτὸ ἑαυτοῦ οἷόν τε ἐφίεσθαι
τὸ εἶδος διὰ τὸ μὴ εἶναι ἐνδεές,
οὔτε τὸ ἐναντίον. φθαρτικὰ γὰρ
ἀλλήλων τὰ ἐναντία. ἀλλὰ τοῦτ'
ἔστιν ἡ ὕλη, ὥσπερ ἂν εἰ θῆλυ
ἄρρενος καὶ αἰσχρὸν καλοῦ (see
p. 325, n. 1, supra). Phys. iv. 9,
217, a, 22 : ἐστὶν ὕλη μία τῶν ἐναντίων, θερμοῦ καὶ ψυχροῦ καὶ τῶν
ἄλλων τῶν φυσικῶν ἐναντιώσεων,
καὶ ἐκ δυνάμει ὄντος ἐνεργείᾳ ὂν
γίνεται, καὶ οὐ χωριστὴ μὲν [sc.
τῶν ἐναντίωσεων] ἡ ὕλη, τῷ δ' εἶναι
ἑτέρον.

[1] See p. 341, n. 2, supra. Phys.
i. 9, 192, a, 28 : ἄφθαρτον καὶ ἀγέν-
νητον ἀνάγκη αὐτὴν εἶναι. εἴτε γὰρ
ἐγίγνετο, ὑπόκεισθαί τι δεῖ πρῶτον,
τὸ ἐξ οὗ ἐνυπάρχοντος . . . εἴτε
φθείρεται, εἰς τοῦτο ἀφίξεται ἔσχατον.

[2] Τὸ ὑποκείμενον, τὸ δεκτικὸν, p.
342, n. 2, besides following notes
and Gen. et Corr. i. 10, 328, b, 10 :
θάτερον μὲν δεκτικὸν θάτερον δ' εἶδος.
De An. ii. 2, 414, a, 9 : μορφὴ καὶ
εἶδός τι καὶ λόγος καὶ οἷον ἐνέργεια
τοῦ δεκτικοῦ. Ibid. l. 13 : ὥστε
λόγος τις ἂν εἴη [ἡ ψυχὴ] καὶ εἶδος,
ἀλλ' οὐχ ὕλη καὶ τὸ ὑποκείμενον.

[3] Phys. ibid. l. 31 : λέγω γὰρ
ὕλην τὸ πρῶτον ὑποκείμενον ἑκάστῳ,
ἐξ οὗ γίνεταί τι ἐνυπάρχοντος μὴ
κατὰ συμβεβηκός. Gen. et Corr. i.
4 fin. : ἔστι δὲ ὕλη μάλιστα μὲν
καὶ κυρίως τὸ ὑποκείμενον γενέσεως
καὶ φθορᾶς δεκτικὸν, τρόπον δέ τινα
καὶ τὸ ταῖς ἄλλαις μεταβολαῖς.
Metaph. i. 3, 983, a, 29 : ἑτέρον δὲ
[αἰτ'αν φαμὲν εἶναι] τὴν ὕλην καὶ
τὸ ὑποκείμενον. Cf. foregoing nn.

[4] Cf. the foregoing and the
next n. As στέρησις constitutes
of itself no independent principle,
but merely belongs to matter as
such, i.e. to matter as still formless, it is assigned a place beside
form and matter only in a very
few passages and with a certain
reservation ; see Phys. i. 7 (p.
344, n. 1) ; Metaph. xii. 2, 1069,
b, 32, c. 4, 1070, b, 10, 18, c. 5,
1071, a, 6, 16.

[5] De An. ii. 1, 412, a, 6 :
λέγομεν γένος ἕν τι τῶν ὄντων τὴν
οὐσίαν, ταύτης δὲ τὸ μὲν ὡς ὕλην,
ὃ καθ' αὑτὸ μὲν οὐκ ἔστι τόδε τι,
ἑτέρον δὲ μορφὴν καὶ εἶδος, καθ' ἣν
ἤδη λέγεται τόδε τι καὶ τρίτον τὸ
ἐκ τούτων. ἔστι δ' ἡ μὲν ὕλη
δύναμις, τὸ δ' εἶδος ἐντελέχεια. So
c. 2, 414, a, 14 sq. ; Gen. et Corr.
ii. 9, 335, a, 32 : ὡς μὲν οὖν ὕλη
τοῖς γεννητοῖς ἐστιν αἴτιον τὸ δυνα-

conceptions have been obtained entirely out of the consideration of the distinction between the two poles

τὸν εἶναι καὶ μὴ εἶναι. Metaph. vii. 7, 1032, a, 20 : ἅπαντα δὲ τὰ γιγνόμενα ἢ φύσει ἢ τέχνῃ ἔχει ὕλην. δυνατὸν γὰρ καὶ εἶναι καὶ μὴ εἶναι ἕκαστον αὐτῶν, τοῦτο δ᾽ [that which can be or not be] ἐστὶν ἐν ἑκάστῳ ὕλη ; c. 15 (v. supra) ; viii. 1, 1042, a, 27 : ὕλην δὲ λέγω ἣ μὴ τόδε τι οὖσα ἐνεργείᾳ δυνάμει ἐστὶ τόδε τι ; c. 2, 1042, b, 9 : ἐπεὶ δ᾽ ἡ μὲν ὡς ὑποκειμένη καὶ ὡς ὕλη οὐσία ὁμολογεῖται, αὕτη δ᾽ ἐστὶν ἡ δυνάμει. Ibid. 1043, a, 12 : ἡ ἐνέργεια ἄλλη ἄλλης ὕλης καὶ ὁ λόγος ; l. 20 : τοῦ εἴδους καὶ τῆς ἐνεργείας ; l. 27 : ἡ μὲν γὰρ ὡς ὕλη [οὐσία ἐστὶν] ἡ δ᾽ ὡς μορφὴ ὅτι ἐνέργεια ; c. 3 init. : τὴν ἐνέργειαν καὶ τὴν μορφήν . . . τῆς ἐνεργείας καὶ τοῦ εἴδους ; c. 6, 1045, a, 23 : εἰ δ᾽ ἐστὶν . . . τὸ μὲν ὕλη τὸ δὲ μορφή, καὶ τὸ μὲν δυνάμει τὸ δὲ ἐνεργείᾳ ; ix. 8, 1050, a, 15 : ἡ ὕλη ἐστὶ δυνάμει, ὅτι ἔλθοι ἂν εἰς τὸ εἶδος· ὅταν δέ γ᾽ ἐνεργείᾳ ᾖ, τότε ἐν τῷ εἴδει ἐστίν ; b, 2, 27 : ἡ οὐσ᾽α καὶ τὸ εἶδος ἐνέργειά ἐστιν . . . ἡ οὐσία [τῶν φθαρτῶν] ὕλη καὶ δύναμις οὖσα, οὐκ ἐνέργεια ; xii. 5, 1071, a, 8 : ἐνεργείᾳ μὲν γὰρ τὸ εἶδος . . . δυνάμει δὲ ἡ ὕλη ; l. 18 : πάντων δὴ πρῶται ἀρχαὶ τὸ ἐνεργείᾳ πρῶτον, τὸ εἴδει, καὶ ἄλλο ὃ δυνάμει. Such passages could easily be multiplied to prove that τὸ δυνάμει ὂν corresponds precisely to ὕλη, τὸ ἐνεργείᾳ ὂν to εἶδος. Even the statement (BONITZ, Arist. Metaph. ii. 398) that ὕλη refers rather to πρώτη, δυνάμει ὂν rather to ἐσχάτη ὕλη (see p. 348, n. 1, infra), does not seem correct. If to the question πότε δυνάμει ἐστὶν ἕκαστον ; Aristotle (Metaph. ix. 7) replies by means

of the ἐσχάτη ὕλη, he must make the same reply to the question as to the ὕλη ἑκάστου, the matter of these determinate things. If the earth cannot be said to be δυνάμει ἄνθρωπος, neither can it be called according to Metaph. viii. 4, 1044, a, 35, b, 1 sq., 'the matter of man'; and what the same passage calls δυνάμει οἰκία, 1049, b, 8 sq. designates ὕλη. On the other hand, πρώτη ὕλη is simply δυνάμει ὄν. So far, therefore, as there remains any distinction between the two pairs of conceptions, it c ncerns not so much their actual content as the point of view from which we regard it. In the antithesis of form and matter we distinguish between different elements, in that of ἐνεργείᾳ and δυνάμει between different states or conditions of things. The former refers to the relation of substance to attribute ; the latter, to the relation of the earlier to the later condition, of the incomplete to the complete. But since the very essence of matter consists in possibility of form in actuality, we can conceive no case in which more than a grammatical change is necessary in order that we may substitute the latter for the former expressions. And vice versa we may in most cases substitute matter and form for the possible and the actual. The only difficulty that can possibly arise is in the case where we are speaking, not of two things related to one another as the possible to the actual, but of one and the same

between which all Change and Becoming moves.[1] If we abstract in any given case from all that a given object is about for the first time to become, we shall have a definite Matter which is in want of a definite Form, and is consequently as yet only capable of receiving it. If we abstract entirely from anything which is a product of Becoming—that is to say, if we think to ourselves a kind of object which has not as yet become anything, then we shall have pure Matter without any determination by Form. This will be that which is nothing, but can become everything—the Subject, namely, or substratum to which no one of all the thinkable predicates belongs, but which precisely on that account is equally receptive of them all. In other words, it is that which is all in Possibility and nothing in Actuality : it is purely potential Being,[2]

---

thing as it passes from possibility to actuality, cf. *Phys.* ii. 3, 195, b, 3, viii. 4, 255, a, 33; *De An.* ii. 5, 417, a, 21 sq.; *Gen. An.* ii. 1, 735, a, 9; but even here it can always be shown that a thing is δυνάμει only in so far as it has the ὕλη in itself. Although, therefore, δυνάμει and ἐνεργείᾳ have, logically considered, a wider range than ὕλη and εἶδος (since, while the latter express only a relation of two subjects to one another, the former express also a relation of one subject to itself), metaphysically there is no distinction between them.

[1] That Aristotle's conception of matter and with it the distinction between matter and form thus originated in the attempt to explain 'becoming,' which

seemed to presuppose it, is clear also from the statement that nothing to which 'becoming' is inapplicable can be said to have a matter ; *Metaph.* viii. 5, 1044, b, 27 : οὐδὲ παντὸς ὕλη ἐστὶν ἀλλ' ὅσων γένεσίς ἐστι καὶ μεταβολὴ εἰς ἄλληλα. ὅσα δ' ἄνευ τοῦ μεταβάλλειν ἔστιν ἢ μὴ, οὐκ ἔστι τούτων ὕλη. Cf. vii. 7 (previous n.)

[2] Τὸ δυνάμει ὄν. A somewhat different meaning attaches to δύναμις when it indicates power or faculty in the sense of the ἀρχὴ μεταβλητική, whether we speak of a faculty for doing or for suffering, a rational or an irrational power (cf. *Metaph.* ix. 1–6, v. 12); Aristotle, however, again mixes up both significations (cf. BONITZ on *Metaph.* 379 sq., and p. 234, n. 1, *supra*).

without any kind of actual existence.[1] If conversely
we take an object and abstract from it everything
that is merely rudimentary and only on its way
to completion, if we think of the end of its growth
as fully attained, we obtain the pure and complete realisation of its conception, to which nothing
formless, no matter that is still unformed, any longer
attaches. The Form, or intelligible essence of a thing,
corresponds with its perfect realisation, and Form in
general with Actuality.[2] Just as a statue is contained
only potentially in the unwrought material, and comes
into actual existence only through the Form which
the artist communicates to the material, Aristotle under-

From this second meaning of
δύναμις we have Aristotle's application of it to the material in
which a determinate power
resides, as in *Part. An.* ii. 1,
646, a, 14 sq., where moist and
dry, warm and cold substances,
Gen. An. i. 18, 725, b, 14, where
certain liquids, *Meteor.* ii. 3, 359,
b, 12, where salts and alkalis,
De Sensu, 5, 444, a, 1, where
fragrant scents are called δυνάμεις.

[1] This pure matter, which, however (see *infra*), is never present as
such, Aristotle calls πρώτη ὕλη.
Its opposite in this sense is ὕλη
ἐσχάτη (ἴδιος, οἰκεία ἑκάστου), or
the matter which unites itself,
immediately, without requiring
further preparation, with a determinate form. Πρώτη ὕλη is the
material as it precedes all elementary differences; the ἐσχάτη
ὕλη, *e.g*, of the statue is the
stone or brass; the ἐσχάτη ὕλη of

man is τὰ καταμήνια. *Metaph.* v.
4, 1015, a, 7, c. 24 *init.*, viii. 6,
1045, b, 17. c. 4, 1044, a, 15, 34,
b. 1, ix. 7, 1049, a, 24. Some
verbal confusion is caused by
the fact that the expression
πρώτη ὕλη is applied equally to
matter which is absolutely, and
to matter which is only relatively, first (to the ὅλως πρώτη
and to the πρὸς αὐτὸ πρώτη ὕλη);
see *Metaph.* v. 4, viii. 4, 1044,
a, 18, 23; *Phys.* ii. 1, 193, a, 28,
and cf. *Metaph.* v. 4, 1014, b, 26.
Cf. BONITZ, *Ind. Arist.*, 786,
b, 10.

[2] Ἐνέργεια or ἐντελέχεια (in
the concrete τὸ ἐνεργείᾳ ὄν, τὸ
ἐντελεχείᾳ ὄν), expressions which
properly differ as activity or
actualisation differs from completeness or actuality, but which
are commonly used by Aristotle
without distinction. Cf. *infra*,
p. 379 sq.

stands by Potentiality in general Being as mere susceptibility—indeterminate, undeveloped self-existence, capable, indeed, of becoming a definite reality, but not yet made into one. By Actuality, on the other hand, he means the same being considered as a developed totality or Being which has wrought out all that it contains into full existence. When accordingly he identifies Form with actual, Matter with potential, being, he means to say that the former is the totality of the qualities which the latter does not possess but is capable of acquiring.[1] Matter as such, the so-called πρώτη ὕλη,[2] is without form or definite character, being just that which precedes all Becoming and all formation; the centre of indifference to all opposites and definite qualities; the substratum which as yet possesses none of the qualities that make the Form of things.[3]

[1] *Metaph*. ix. 6, 1048, a. 30 : ἔστι δ' ἡ ἐνέργεια τὸ ὑπάρχειν τὸ πρᾶγμα μὴ οὕτως ὥσπερ λέγομεν δυνάμει. λέγομεν δὲ δυνάμει οἷον ἐν τῷ ξύλῳ Ἑρμῆν καὶ ἐν τῇ ὅλῃ τὴν ἡμίσειαν, ὅτι ἀφαιρεθε΄η ἂν, καὶ ἐπιστήμονα καὶ τὸν μὴ θεωροῦντα, ἂν δυνατὸς ᾖ θεωρῆσαι. τὸ δ' ἐνεργείᾳ. δῆλον δ' ἐπὶ τῶν καθέκαστα τῇ ἐπαγωγῇ ὃ βουλόμεθα λέγειν, καὶ ὀ δεῖ παντὸς ὅρον ζητεῖν, ἀλλὰ καὶ τὸ ἀνάλογον συνορᾷν, ὅτι ὡς τὸ οἰκοδομοῦν πρὸς τὸ οἰκοδομικὸν, καὶ τὸ ἐγρηγορὸς πρὸς τὸ καθεῦδ νν, καὶ τὸ ὁρῶν πρὸς τὸ μύον μὲν ὄψιν δὲ ἔχον, καὶ τὸ ἀποκεκριμένον ἐκ τῆς ὕλης πρὸς τὴν ὕλην, καὶ τὸ ἀπειργασμένον πρὸς τὸ ἀνέργαστον. ταύτης δὲ τῆς διαφορᾶς θάτερου μόριον ἔστω ἡ ἐνέργεια ἀφωρισμένη, θατέρῳ δὲ τὸ δυνατόν ; c. 8, 1050, a, 21 ; *Phys.* i. 7, 191, a, 7 : ἡ δ' ὑποκειμένη φύσις ἐπιστητὴ κατ' ἀναλογίαν.

ὡς γὰρ πρὸς ἀνδριάντα χαλκὸς ἢ πρὸς κλίνην ξύλον ἢ πρὸς τῶν ἄλλων τι τῶν ἐχόντων μορφὴν ἡ ὕλη καὶ τὸ ἄμορφον ἔχει πρὶν λαβεῖν τὴν μορφὴν, οὕτως αὕτη πρὸς οὐσίαν ἔχει καὶ τὸ τόδε τι καὶ τὸ ὄν. *Ibid.* iii. 1, 201, a, 29.

[2] See p. 348, n. 1, *supra*

[3] *Metaph* vii 3, 1029, a, 20 : λέγω δ' ὕλην ἣ καθ' αὑτὴν μήτε τὶ μήτε ποσὸν μήτε ἄλλο μηθὲν λέγεται οἷς ὥρισται τὸ ὄν ; c. 11, 1037, a, 27 : μετὰ μὲν γὰρ τῆς ὕλης οὐκ ἔστιν [λόγος], ἀόριστον γάρ ; ix. 7, 1049, a, 24 : εἰ δέ τί ἐστι πρῶτον, ὃ μηκέτι κατ' ἄλλου λέγεται ἐκείνινον [of such and such a nature], τοῦτο πρώτη ὕλη ; viii. 1, see p. 315, n. 5, *supra*, iv. 4, 1007, b, 28 : τὸ γὰρ δυνάμει ὂν καὶ μὴ ἐντελεχείᾳ τὸ ἀόριστόν ἐστι. *Phys.* i. 7 ; see above, n. 1, and iv. 2, 209, b, 9 : passing from this it becomes

Considered in this aspect, it is also unlimited or infinite, not in the spatial sense (for Aristotle, as we shall see, does not admit the existence of infinity in space), but in the wider sense according to which the infinite is that which, as fixed and circumscribed by no determinate Form, has reached no conclusion or completion.[1] And since what is wholly indeterminate cannot be known, Matter, as such, is unknowable. It is only by analogy that we can gain any conception of it, by supposing a substratum for things of sense in general which is related to them in much the same way as a special material is to the things that are made out of it.[2] To Form, on the other hand, we attribute all the qualities of things, all definiteness, limitation, and intelligibility. Form

---

περιεχόμενον ὑπὸ τοῦ εἴδους [the form] καὶ ὡρισμένον . . . ἔστι δὲ τοιοῦτον ἡ ὕλη καὶ τὸ ἀόριστον. *De Cœlo*, iii. 8, 306, b, 17 : ἀειδὲς καὶ ἄμορφον δεῖ τὸ ὑποκείμενον εἶναι μάλιστα γὰρ ἂν οὕτω δύναιτο ρυθμίζεσθαι, καθάπερ ἐν τῷ Τιμα'ῳ γέγραπται, τὸ πανδεχές.

[1] By ἄπειρον Aristotle understands, first of all, the unlimited in space, and in this sense he examines the conception in *Phys.* iii. 4 sq. But finding that in actuality there is no such infinite space, he finally identifies the unlimited with the ἀόριστον or ὕλη. Cf. *ibid.* c. 6, 207, a, 1 : the notion commonly entertained of infinity is wholly false, οὐ γὰρ οὗ μηδὲν ἔξω, ἀλλ' οὗ ἀεἰ τι ἔξω ἐστὶ, τοῦτ' ἄπειρόν ἐστιν . . . ἄπειρον μὲν οὖν ἐστιν οὗ κατὰ ποσὸν λαμβάνουσιν ἀεί τι λαβεῖν ἔστιν ἔξω. οὗ δὲ μηδὲν ἔξω, τοῦτ' ἐστὶ τέλειον καὶ ὅλον (*De Cœlo*, ii. 4, 286, b, 19, repeated)

. . . τέλειον δ' οὐδὲν μὴ ἔχον τέλος · τὸ δὲ τέλος πέρας . . . οὐ γὰρ λίνον λίνῳ συνάπτειν ἐστὶ τῷ ἅπαντι καὶ ὅλῳ τὸ ἄπειρον . . . ἔστι γὰρ τὸ ἄπειρον τῆς τοῦ μεγέθους τελεοτη-τος ὕλη καὶ τὸ δυνάμει ὅλον, ἐντελεχε'ᾳ δ' οὔ . . . καὶ οὐ περιέχει ἀλλὰ περιέχεται, ᾗ ἄπειρον. διὸ καὶ ἄγνωστον ᾗ ἄπειρον · εἶδος γὰρ οὐκ ἔχει ἡ ὕλη . . . ἄτοπον δὲ καὶ ἀδύνατον, τὸ ἄγνωστον καὶ τὸ ἀόριστον περιέχειν καὶ ὁρίζειν; c. 7, 207, b, 35 : φανερὸν ὅτι ὡς ὕλη τὸ ἄπειρόν ἐστιν αἴτιον, καὶ ὅτι τὸ μὲν εἶναι αὐτῷ στέρησις, τὸ δὲ καθ' αὑτὸ ὑποκείμενον τὸ συνεχὲς καὶ αἰσθητόν. iv. 2, see previous note.

[2] *Phys.* iii. 6; see previous note ; *ibid.* i. 7, *Metaph.* ix. 6 ; see p. 349, n. 1, *supra*, *Metaph.* vii. 10, 1036, a, 8 : ἡ δ' ὕλη ἄγνωστος καθ' αὑτήν. Cf. also p. 220, n. 2, *supra*; for parallels from Plato, cf. ZELLER, *Ph. d. Gr.* pt. i. p. 621, 2.

and Matter, therefore, require nothing further to mediate between them in order to produce a whole, but are immediately united: Form is the definiteness of Matter in itself indefinite; Matter receives into itself directly the lacking definiteness of Form. When the Potential passes into the Actual, these elements do not stand opposed to one another as two separate things, but one and the same thing looked at as Matter is the Potentiality of that of which the Actuality is its Form.[1]

But just as we may not regard Form and Matter in their mutual relation as two heterogeneous substances, so neither may we regard either of them in any case as a single substance, so as to imply that one Matter and one Form constitute the fundamental elements which in various combinations produce the aggregate of things. Aristotle recognises, indeed, in the Divine Spirit a being which is pure Form without Matter. Yet he does not treat this as the intelligible idea of all Forms, the universal, spiritual substance of all things, but as an individual being, beside which all other individual beings exist as so many substances. In like manner Aristotle recognises a fundamental matter. which, while in the elements and generally in all particular kinds of matter it assumes different forms and qualities, yet is in itself one and the same in all bodies. Yet this primitive

[1] *Metaph.* viii. 6, 1045, b, 17: to the question how the elements of a conception or of a number can be one, Aristotle answers that they are related to one another as matter and form (see p. 220, n. 2, *supra*): ἔστι δ' ὥσπερ εἴρηται καὶ ἡ ἐσχάτη ὕλη [cf. p. 348, n. 1] καὶ ἡ μορφὴ ταὐτὸ καὶ ἓν τὸ μὲν δυνάμει τὸ δὲ ἐνεργείᾳ. [So BONITZ reads, but BEKKER has: ταὐτὸ καὶ δυνάμει τὸ ἕν.] ἓν γάρ τι ἕκαστον καὶ τὸ δυνάμει καὶ τὸ ἐνεργείᾳ ἕν πώς ἐστιν.

matter is never present except in the definite form of one of the elements.[1] Nor can it be otherwise, since pure, indeterminate Matter is mere Potentiality without any Actuality whatsoever. This original corporeal Matter, moreover, does not exhaust the conception, and Aristotle goes on to speak also of an incorporeal Matter which he finds, for example, in conceptions and in mathematical figures. To this belongs whatever, without being itself corporeal, stands to something else in the same relation as corporeal Matter stands to Form.[2] Hence we see that not only does each of these conceptions denote a single existence or definite class of things, but they are used, though undoubtedly obtained in the first instance by abstraction from corporeal things,[3] wheresoever a relation subsists analogous to that which they originally express.[4] Thus in analysing conceptions into their

---

[1] *Phys.* iii. 5, 204, b, 32 : οὐκ ἔστι τοιοῦτον σῶμα αἰσθητὸν παρὰ τὰ στοιχεῖα καλούμενα, otherwise the four elements must needs resolve themselves into this, which is not the case. *Gen. et Corr.* ii. 1, 329, a, 8. *Ibid.* l. 24 : ἡμεῖς δὲ φαμὲν μὲν εἶναί τινα ὕλην τῶν σωμάτων τῶν αἰσθητῶν, ἀλλὰ ταύτην οὐ χωριστὴν, ἀλλ' ἀεὶ μετ' ἐναντιώσεως. ἐξ ἧς γίνεται τὰ καλούμενα στοιχεῖα. *Ibid.* i. 5, 320, b, 12 sq.

[2] *Metaph.* viii. 6, 1045, a, 33 : ἔστι δὲ τῆς ὕλης ἡ μὲν νοητὴ ἡ δ' αἰσθητή, καὶ ἀεὶ τοῦ λόγου τὸ μὲν ὕλη τὸ δ' ἐνέργειά ἐστιν ; vii. 11, 1036, b, 35 : ἔσται γὰρ ὕλη ἐνίων καὶ μὴ αἰσθητῶν· καὶ παντὸς γὰρ ὕλη τίς ἐστιν ὃ μή ἐστι τί ἦν εἶναι καὶ εἶδος αὐτὸ καθ' αὑτὸ ἀλλὰ τόδε τι . . . ἔστι γὰρ ἡ ὕλη ἡ μὲν αἰσθητὴ ἡ δὲ

[1] νοητή. *Ibid.* c. 10, 1036, a, 9 : ὕλη δ' ἡ μὲν αἰσθητή ἐστιν ἡ δὲ νοητὴ . . . νοητὴ δὲ ἡ ἐν τοῖς αἰσθητοῖς ὑπάρχουσα μὴ ᾗ αἰσθητά, οἷον τὰ μαθηματικά.

[3] This is evident from the examples which Aristotle uses in illustration ; cf. pp. 341, n. 2, 342, n. 2, and 345 n. 5, *sup.* Of matter he remarks also in *Gen. et Corr.* i. 4, 320, a, 2, that we are to understand by it μάλιστα καὶ κυρίως τὸ ὑποκείμενον γενέσεως καὶ φθορᾶς δεκτικόν.

[4] *Metaph.* xii. 4 : τὰ δ' αἴτια καὶ αἱ ἀρχαὶ ἄλλα ἄλλων ἐστιν ὡς, ἔστι δ' ὡς ἂν καθόλου λέγῃ τις καὶ κατ' ἀναλογίαν, ταὐτὰ πάντων . . . οἷον ἴσως τῶν αἰσθητῶν σωμάτων ὡς μὲν εἶδος τὸ θερμὸν καὶ ἄλλον τρόπον τὸ ψυχρὸν ἡ στέρησις, ὕλη δὲ τὸ δυνάμει ταῦτα πρῶτον καθ' αὑτό . . . πάντων δὲ οὕτω μὲν εἰπεῖν

two elements, Aristotle attributes to the genus the
same significance as Matter, while he identifies the
specific difference with the Form.[1] Similarly in the
scheme of the universe, in physiology, in zoology, in
psychology, the upper and the lower spheres and elements,[2] the soul and the body,[3] the male and the female,[4]
the Active and the Passive Reason,[5] stand to one another
in the same relation as the Form and the Matter. The
same is true, it need hardly be remarked, of Potentiality
and Actuality. These also express a definite relation
which may subsist between all possible kinds of objects,
and which can best be explained by analogy.[6] Aristotle
applies them in precisely the same way as Matter and
Form. He uses them, for instance, to elucidate the connection between the genus and the specific differences,
and in general to show the possibility of several properties belonging to one and the same thing.[7] By them he
explains the relation between the passive and the active

οὐκ ἔστιν, τῷ ἀνάλογον δὲ, ὥσπερ
εἴ τις εἴποι ὅτι ἀρχαί εἰσι τρεῖς, τὸ
εἶδος καὶ ἡ στέρησις καὶ ἡ ὕλη. ἀλλ'
ἕκαστον τούτων ἕτερον περὶ ἕκαστον
γένος ἐστίν ; c. 5, 1071, a, 3 : ἔτι
δ' ἄλλον τρόπον τῷ ἀνάλογον ἀρχαὶ
αἱ αὐταί, οἷον ἐνέργεια καὶ δύναμις.
ἀλλὰ καὶ ταῦτα ἄλλα τε ἄλλοις καὶ
ἄλλως. L. 24 : ἄλλα δὲ ἄλλων
αἴτια καὶ στοιχεῖα, ὥσπερ ἐλέχθη,
τῶν μὴ ἐν ταὐτῷ γένει, χρωμάτων,
ψόφων, οὐσιῶν, ποσότητος, πλὴν τῷ
ἀνάλογον· καὶ τῶν ἐν ταὐτῷ γένει
ἕτερα, οὐκ εἴδει, ἀλλ' ὅτι τῶν καθ'
ἕκαστον ἄλλο ἥ τε σὴ ὕλη καὶ τὸ
κινῆσαν καὶ τὸ εἶδος καὶ ἡ ἐμὲ, τῷ
καθόλου δὲ λόγῳ ταὐτά.
  [1] See p. 219, n. 2, *supra*.
  [2] *De Cœlo*, iv. 3, 4, 310, b, 14,

312, a, 12, *Gen. et Corr.* i. 3, 318,
b, 32, ii. 8, 335, a, 18.
  [3] *De An.* ii. 1, 412. b, 9 sq c.
2, 414, a, 13 sq. and often.
  [4] *Gen. An.* i. 2 *init.*, ii. 1, 732,
a, 3, ii. 4, 738, b, 20, and often.
Metaph. i. 6, 988, a, 5, v. 28,
1024, a, 34.
  [5] *De An.* iii. 5.
  [6] *Metaph.* ix. 6 ; see p. 349, n.
1, *supra*. *Ibid.* 1048, b, 6 : λέγεται
δ' ἐνεργείᾳ οὐ πάντα ὁμοίως, ἀλλ' ἢ τὸ
ἀνάλογον, ὡς τοῦτο ἐν τούτῳ ἢ πρὸς
τοῦτο, τὸ δ' ἐν τῷδε ἢ πρὸς τόδε· τὰ
μὲν γὰρ ὡς κίνησις πρὸς δύναμιν, τὰ
δ' ὡς οὐσία πρός τινα ὕλην. Cf. xii.
5, 1071, a, 3, cited p. 352, n. 4.
  [7] *De An.* iii. 5.

understanding.[1] It follows that one and the same thing may be viewed in one aspect as Matter, in another as Form: as Potentiality in the first, as Actuality in the second. The elements, for instance, which contain the material of all other bodies, are Forms of the primitive Matter; the brass which supplies the material for a statue has its own peculiar Form as a specific metal. While the soul in general is viewed as the Form of the body, yet even in its own highest and most immaterial part a distinction is made between two elements which are related to one another as Form and Matter.[2] Indeed, we shall find that everything except the ' eternal immaterial substances ' contains some element of Matter,[3] while on the other hand, as we already know,[4] Matter never actually presents itself to us except as endowed with Form.

We may therefore distinguish several stages[5] in the development of Matter into Form. The first purely formless Matter lies at the foundation of all things : but it is also true that everything has its own peculiar and ultimate Matter. Between these two lie all the material formations through which the original Matter has to pass before it becomes the particular Matter with which the Form of the thing immediately unites itself.[6] The same holds true of the δύναμις.[7] We ascribe potential knowledge

---

[1] *Metaph.* viii. 6, 1045, a, 23, b, 16. *Phys.* i. 2 *fin.*; see p. 219, n. 2, p. 351, n. 1, p. 301, n. 3 and 4, *supra*.

[2] Cf. *Gen. et Corr.* ii. 1, 329, a, 32 ; *Phys.* iii. 1, 201, a, 29; *De An.* p. 375 sq , 440.

[3] Cf. p. 352, n. 2.

[4] See p. 352, n 1, *supra*, and compare p. 348, n. 1.

[5] Cf. the passages quoted

p. 348, n. 1, *e.g. Metaph.*viii. 4, 1044, a, 20 : γίγνονται δὲ πλείους ὕλαι τοῦ αὐτοῦ, ὅταν θατέρου ἡ ἑτέρα ᾖ, οἷον φλέγμα ἐκ λιπαροῦ καὶ γλυκέος, εἰ τὸ λιπαρὸν ἐκ τοῦ γλυκέος, ἐκ δὲ χολῆς τῷ ἀναλύεσθαι εἰς τὴν πρώτην ὕλην τὴν χολήν.

[6] See p. 351, n. 1.

[7] *Phys.* viii. 4, 255, a, 33; *De An.* ii. 5, 417, a, 21 sq.

not only to the man of learning when he is conceived as
not actually engaged in scientific activity, but also to
the learner, and even to man in general.   But the
sense in each case varies, and we have to distinguish
between the degrees of proximity to ἐνέργεια.[1] Nothing
attains the realisation of that which it had at first the
mere capacity to be, except by degrees ; and in the universe at large there are an infinite number of intermediate
stages between mere Potentiality or the first Matter,
and complete Actuality, which is pure Form or God.

Now in the phenomenal world, Form presents itself
under the aspect of a threefold principle of causality,
while Matter contains the ground of all impressibility
and of all incompleteness, of natural necessity and chance.

Aristotle is in the habit of enumerating four kinds
of Cause [2]—the material, the conceptual or formal, the
efficient and the final.[3]   These, however, on closer

---

[1] *Gen. An.* ii. 1, 735, a, 9 :
ἐγγυτέρω δὲ καὶ πορρωτέρω αὐτὸ
αὐτοῦ ἐνδέχεται εἶναι δυνάμει, ὥσπερ
ὁ καθεύδων γεωμέτρης τοῦ ἐγρηγορ-
ότος πορρωτέρω καὶ οὗτος τοῦ θεωρ-
οῦντος.
[2] Ἀρχαί. On the meaning of
this expression see *Metaph.* v. 1,
with the comments of SCHWEG-
LER and BONITZ, and also xi. 1 *fin.*,
Gen. et Corr. i. 7, 324, a, 27, *Phys.*
i. 5, 188, a, 27, viii. 1 *fin.*, *Gen. An.*
v. 7, 788, a, 14 ; also *Poet.* c. 7, 1450,
b, 27 ; WAITZ, *Arist. Org* i. 457 sq.,
the *Ind. Arist.* under ἀρχή, and
p. 247, n, 2, *supra.* Ἀρχή indicates
the first in every series, and in
this sense it is used for all kinds
of causes, but more especially of
first causes, *i.e.* such as are de-
ducible from no higher. Cf.

Metaph. v. 1, 1013, a, 17 : πασῶν
μὲν οὖν κοινὸν τῶν ἀρχῶν τὸ πρῶτον
εἶναι ὅθεν ἢ ἔστιν ἢ γίγνεται ἢ
γιγνώσκεται· τούτων δὲ αἱ μὲν
ἐνυπάρχουσαί εἰσιν αἱ δὲ ἐκτός.
Anal. Post. i. 2, 72, a, 6 ; *Top.* iv.
1, 121, b, 9.
[3] *Phys.* ii. 3, 194, b, 23 : ἕνα
μὲν οὖν τρόπον αἴτιον λέγεται τὸ ἐξ
οὗ γίνεταί τι ἐνυπάρχοντος, οἷον
χαλκὸς τοῦ ἀνδριάντος, &c.   ἄλλον
δὲ τὸ εἶδος καὶ τὸ παράδειγμα· τοῦτο
δ' ἐστὶν ὁ λόγος ὁ τοῦ τί ἦν εἶναι
καὶ τὰ τούτου γένη [*i.e.* the classes
above it] . . . ἔτι ὅθεν ἡ ἀρχὴ τῆς
μεταβολῆς ἢ πρώτη ἢ τῆς ἠρεμήσεως
. . . ἔτι ὡς τὸ τέλος· τοῦτο δ' ἐστὶ
τὸ οὗ ἕνεκα (= *Metaph.* v. 2) ;
195, a, 15 : one class of causes is
ὡς τὸ ἐξ οὗ αἴτια, and of these τὰ
μὲν ὡς τὸ ὑποκείμενον, τὰ δὲ ὡς τὸ

inspection, are found to be resolvable into the two first mentioned. The concept of a thing is not different from its end, since to realise an end is to actualise a concept. But it is likewise possible to identify the concept with the efficient cause, whether it sets the thing in motion from within as its soul, or whether the motion comes from without. Even in the latter case it is the conception of the thing which produces motion, alike in works of nature and of art. Only man can beget man. Only the conception of health can determine the physician to labour in producing health.[1] In like

τί ἦν εἶναι; next we have causes ὅθεν ἡ ἀρχὴ τῆς μεταβολῆς ἢ στάσεως καὶ κινήσεως; lastly τὸ τέλος καὶ τἀγαθόν. *Metaph.* i. 3 *init.*: τὰ δ' αἴτια λέγεται τετραχῶς, ὧν μἰαν μὲν αἰτίαν φαμὲν εἶναι τὴν οὐσίαν καὶ τὸ τί ἦν εἶναι . . . ἑτέραν δὲ τὴν ὕλην καὶ τὸ ὑποκείμενον, τρίτην δὲ ὅθεν ἡ ἀρχὴ τῆς κινήσεως, τετάρτην δὲ ἀντικειμένην αἰτίαν ταύτῃ, τὸ οὗ ἕνεκα καὶ τἀγαθόν. *Ibid.* viii. 4, 1044, a, 32, *Anal. Post.* ii. 11 *init.*, *De Somno*, 2, 455, b, 14, *Gen. An.* i. 1 *init* , v. 1, 778, b, 7, and elsewhere; cf. *Ind. Arist.* 22, b, 29. On the different terms used for the four causes, *ibid.* and WAITZ, *Arist. Org.* ii. 407; on what follows, RITTER, iii. 166 sqq. The further modifications of the doctrine of the four causes in *Phys.* ii. 3, 195, a, 26 sq. (cf. *Metaph.* v. 2, 1013, b, 28), are unimportant, as is also the distinction of the οὗ ἕνεκα into person and thing, on which cf. *De An.* ii. 4, 415, b, 2 : τὸ δ' οὗ ἕνεκα διττόν, τὸ μὲν οὗ τὸ δὲ ᾧ. See also *Phys.* ii. 2, 194, a, 35, and *Metaph.* xii. 7, 1072, b, 2 (where we must read ἔστι γὰρ τινὶ τὸ οὗ ἕνεκα καὶ

τινός—the end is in the one case to heal the *sick*, and in the other to establish *health*).

[1] *Phys.* ii. 7, 198, a, 24 : ἔρχεται δὲ τὰ τρία εἰς τὸ ἓν πολλάκις · τὸ μὲν γὰρ τί ἐστι καὶ τὸ οὗ ἕνεκα ἕν ἐστι [cf. 198, b, 3], τὸ δ' ὅθεν ἡ κίνησις πρῶτον τῷ εἴδει ταὐτὸ τούτοις · ἄνθρωπος γὰρ ἄνθρωπον γεννᾷ. Cf. i. 7, 190, b, 17 sq. *De An.* ii. 4, 415, b, 7 : ἔστι δὲ ἡ ψυχὴ τοῦ ζῶντος σώματος αἰτία καὶ ἀρχή. ταῦτα δὲ πολλαχῶς λέγεται. ὁμοίως δ' ἡ ψυχὴ κατὰ τοὺς διωρισμένους τρόπους τρεῖς αἰτία · καὶ γὰρ ὅθεν ἡ κίνησις αὐτή, καὶ οὗ ἕνεκα, καὶ ὡς ἡ οὐσία τῶν ἐμψύχων σωμάτων ἡ ψυχὴ αἰτία, which he goes on to prove more fully. *Metaph.* xii. 5, 1071, a, 18 : πάντων δὴ πρῶται ἀρχαὶ τὸ ἐνεργείᾳ πρῶτον, τὸ εἴδει, καὶ ἄλλο ὃ δυνάμει. Elsewhere now one and now another of these three causes is identified with the third. So *Metaph.* viii. 4, 1044, b, 1 : ἴσως δὲ ταῦτα (i.e. εἶδος and τέλος) ἄμφω τὸ αὐτό. *Gen. An.* i. 1 *init.*: ὑπόκεινται γὰρ αἰτίαι τέτταρες, τό τε οὗ ἕνεκα ὡς τέλος, καὶ ὁ λόγος τῆς οὐσίας · ταῦτα μὲν

manner we shall in the highest cause, which is God,
find the pure Form, the ultimate end of the world and
the source of its movement united in one. Nor does
Aristotle in his physics distinguish more than two kinds

οὖν ὡς ἕν τι σχεδὸν ὑπολαβεῖν δεῖ,
τρίτον δὲ καὶ τέταρτον ἡ ὕλη καὶ
ὅθεν ἡ ἀρχὴ τῆς κινήσεως. *Ibid.*
ii. 1, 732, a 3, where the female
is called the ὕλη, the male the
αἰτία κινοῦσα πρώτη, ᾗ ὁ λόγος
ὑπάρχει καὶ τὸ εἶδος, and c. 6,
742, a, 28 ; where, as in i. 1, the
formal and the final cause are
identified, and only three principles are enumerated: the τέλος
or οὗ ἕνεκα, the ἀρχὴ κινητικὴ καὶ
γεννητικὴ and the χρήσιμον ᾧ
χρῆται τὸ τέλος. *Part. An.* i. 1,
641, a, 25 : τῆς φύσεως διχῶς
λεγομένης καὶ οὔσης τῆς μὲν ὡς
ὕλης τῆς δ᾽ ὡς οὐσίας [which =
εἶδος]· καὶ ἔστιν αὕτη καὶ ὡς ἡ
κινοῦσα καὶ ὡς τὸ τέλος. *Phys.* ii.
8, 199, a, 30 : καὶ ἐπεὶ ἡ φύσις
διττὴ ἡ μὲν ὡς ὕλη ἡ δ᾽ ὡς μορφή,
τέλος δ᾽ αὕτη . . . αὕτη ἂν εἴη ἡ
αἰτία ἡ οὗ ἕνεκα. *Ibid.* c. 9, 200,
a, 14 : τὸ δ᾽ οὗ ἕνεκα ἐν τῷ λόγῳ.
L. 34 : τὸ τέλος τὸ οὗ ἕνεκα καὶ ἡ
ἀρχὴ ἀπὸ τοῦ ὁρισμοῦ καὶ τοῦ λόγου.
The artist's method is nature's
also : ἐπεὶ ἡ οἰκία τοιήνδε, τάδε
δεῖ γίγνεσθαι . . . οὕτως καὶ εἰ
ἄνθρωπος τοδὶ, ταδί. *Part. An.*
i. 1, 639, b, 14 : φαίνεται δὲ
πρώτη [αἰτία] ἣν λέγομεν ἕνεκά
τινος· λόγος γὰρ οὗτος. *De An.*
i. 1, 403, b, 6: τὸ εἶδος, ἕνεκα
τωνδί. *Gen. et Corr.* ii. 9, 335,
b, 5 : ὡς μὲν ὕλη τοῦτ᾽ ἐστιν αἴτιον
τοῖς γενητοῖς, ὡς δὲ τὸ οὗ ἕνεκεν
ἡ μορφὴ καὶ τὸ εἶδος· τοῦτο δ᾽
ἐστὶν ὁ λόγος ὁ τῆς ἑκάστου οὐσίας,
and previously : εἰσὶν οὖν [αἱ
ἀρχαὶ τῆς γενέσεως] καὶ τὸν
ἀριθμὸν ἴσαι καὶ τῷ γένει αἱ αὐταὶ

αἵπερ ἐν τοῖς ἀϊδίοις τε καὶ πρώτοις·
ἡ μὲν γάρ ἐστιν ὡς ὕλη, ἡ δ᾽ ὡς
μορφή· δεῖ δὲ καὶ τὴν τρίτην ἔτι
προσυπάρχειν. *Metaph.* xii. 3, see
p. 341, n. 1, *fin. Metaph.* vii. 7 *init.*:
πάντα τὰ γιγνόμενα ὑπό τέ τινος
γίγνεται καὶ ἔκ τινος καὶ τί. Of the
ὑφ᾽ οὗ it is said further on : καὶ
ὑφ᾽ οὗ, ἡ κατὰ τὸ εἶδος λεγομένη
φύσις ἡ ὁμοειδής [sc. ᾧ γιγνομένῳ]·
αὕτη δ᾽ ἐν ἄλλῳ. ἄνθρωπος γὰρ ἄνθρωπον γεννᾷ, and further, 1032, b,
11 : ὥστε συμβαίνει τρόπον τινὰ ἐξ
ὑγιείας τὴν ὑγίειαν γίνεσθαι, καὶ
τὴν οἰκίαν ἐξ οἰκίας, τῆς ἄνευ ὕλης
τὴν ἔχουσαν ὕλην· ἡ γὰρ ἰατρική
ἐστι καὶ ἡ οἰκοδομικὴ τὸ εἶδος τῆς
ὑγιείας καὶ τῆς οἰκίας· λέγω δ᾽
οὐσίαν ἄνευ ὕλης τὸ τί ἦν εἶναι.
(Cf. *Gen. An.* ii. 4, 740, b, 28 :
ἡ δὲ τέχνη μορφὴ τῶν γινομένων ἐν
ἄλλῳ. *Part. An.* i. 1, 610, a, 31 :
ἡ δὲ τέχνη λόγος τοῦ ἔργου ὁ ἄνευ
τῆς ὕλης ἐστίν; so in *Gen. et
Corr.* ii. 9, 335, b, 33, 35, μορφή
corresponds to τέχνη; the art,
however, is elsewhere treated as
the true efficient cause, the
artist only as a secondary cause ;
e.g. *Gen. et Corr.* i. 7, 324, a, 34.)
Metaph. xii. 4 *fin.*: ἐπεὶ δὲ τὸ
κινοῦν ἐν μὲν τοῖς φυσικοῖς
ἀνθρώποις (read ἀνθρώπῳ, approved
by SCHWEGLER and BONITZ)
ἄνθρωπος, ἐν δὲ τοῖς ἀπὸ διανοίας
τὸ εἶδος ἢ τὸ ἐναντίον, τρόπον τινὰ
τρία αἴτια ἂν εἴη, ὡδὶ δὲ τέτταρα·
ὑγίεια γάρ πως ἡ ἰατρική, καὶ οἰκίας
εἶδος ἡ οἰκοδομικὴ, καὶ ἄνθρωπος
ἄνθρωπον γεννᾷ; c. 3 *fin.*: ἡ γὰρ
ἰατρικὴ τέχνη ὁ λόγος τῆς ὑγιείας
ἐστίν. Speaking of health again,

of Cause, necessary and final,[1] in the operation of Matter and that of Form or concept.[2] This is the only distinction, therefore, which we must regard as fundamental; that between formal, efficient and final causes is merely a secondary subdivision. For though the three are not always combined in the individual,[3] yet in themselves and in their essence they are one, and it is only in the phenomena of sense that they are found separate.[4] The created universe has several causes; the eternal has only one—the essential concept itself.[5]

Again, as the Form is at once the efficient and the final force, so Matter as formless and indeterminate[6]

it is said in *Gen. et Corr.* i. 7, 324, b, 15, that as the οὗ ἔνεκα it is not ποιητικόν.

[1] For a fuller discussion on this, see pp. 349, &c. *supra*. At this point, it will be enough to refer the reader to *Part. An.* i. 1. Cf. p. 642, a, 1: εἰσὶν ἄρα δύο αἰτίαι αὗται, τό θ' οὗ ἕνεκα καὶ τὸ ἐξ ἀνάγκης. The opposition is indicated in l 17 in the words: ἀρχὴ γὰρ ἡ φύσις μᾶλλον τῆς ὕλης, with which cf. further the passages quoted in the foregoing note from *Phys.* ii. 8, and *Part. An.* i. 1.

[2] For although in *Gen. An.* v. 1, 778, a, 34, the moving cause is classed along with the necessary and efficient, yet as RITTER, appealing to *Phys.* ii. 9, 200, a, 30, rightly remarks, the moving cause is not here considered by itself, but only as united with matter. Cf. also *ibid.* l. 14: ἐν γὰρ τῇ ὕλῃ τὸ ἀναγκαῖον, τὸ δ' οὗ ἕνεκα ἐν τῷ λόγῳ.

[3] So that, as is remarked *Phys.* ii. 3, 195, a, 8, of two things each may be the cause of

the other, but in a different sense: physical exercise, *e.g.*, may be the efficient cause of health, health the final cause of exercise. This is the meaning of πολλάκις in *Phys.* ii. 7 (p. 356, n. 1).

[4] Cf. *Metaph.* ix. 8, 1049, b, 17: τῷ δὲ χρόνῳ πρότερον [sc. ἐνέργεια δυνάμεως] ὧδε· τὸ τῷ εἴδει τὸ αὐτὸ ἐνεργοῦν πρότερον [*i.e.* every potentiality presupposes a similar actuality], ἀριθμῷ δ' οὔ—for, as this is explained, the seed indeed precedes the plant which springs from it, but this seed itself comes from another plant, so that it is still the plant that produces the plant. *Ibid.* vii. 9, 1034, b, 16: ἴδιον τῆς οὐσίας . . . ὅτι ἀνάγκη προϋπάρχειν ἑτέραν οὐσίαν ἐντελεχείᾳ οὖσαν ἣ ποιεῖ, οἷον ζῷον, εἰ γίγνεται ζῷον.

[5] *Gen. An.* ii. 6, 742, b, 33: ἀρχὴ δ' ἐν μὲν τοῖς ἀκινήτοις τὸ τί ἐστιν, ἐν δὲ τοῖς γινομένοις ἤδη πλείους, τρόπον δ' ἄλλον καὶ οὐ πᾶσαι τὸν αὐτόν· ὧν μία τὸν ἀριθμὸν, ὅθεν ἡ κίνησίς ἐστιν.

[6] See p. 318 sq. *supra*.

is at once the passive subject of all impressions and the
cause of all blind operations unregulated by any purpose.
Matter alone can receive impressions, for all πάθος is a
process of determination, and nothing is susceptible of
such a process but that which is not yet determined :
nothing, that is, but the indeterminate and therefore
determinable—in other words, nothing but Matter,
which can exhibit every activity and every quality,
for the simple reason that, taken in itself, it has no
quality or operative force.[1] But though Matter is
wholly devoid of any such active and positive force,
Aristotle nevertheless attributes to it every obstruction
to the plastic energy exercised by Form. To what
other source, indeed, could this be traced? And so,
since Form always works with a purpose, it is in Matter
that we must seek the ground of all phenomena that
are independent of this final purpose and antagonistic to
it, the principle of blind natural necessity and chance.
The first of these obstructive forces is to be explained by
Nature's need of certain materials and the consequent dependence of her creatures upon the same. Though this
material element is in no sense efficient cause, yet it is
an indispensable condition of the realisation of Nature's
ends. Though it is not necessary in itself, it is so con-
ditionally : for if a certain particular being has to be pro-

---

[1] *Gen. et Corr.* i. 7, 324, b, 4 :
ὅσα μὲν οὖν μὴ ἐν ὕλῃ ἔχει τὴν
μορφήν, ταῦτα μὲν ἀπαθῆ τῶν ποιητικῶν, ὅσα δ' ἐν ὕλῃ, παθητικά. τὴν
μὲν γὰρ ὕλην λέγομεν ὁμοίως ὡς
εἰπεῖν τὴν αὐτὴν εἶναι τῶν ἀντικειμένων ὁποτερουοῦν, ὥσπερ γένος ὄν.
ibid. l. 18 : ἡ δ' ὕλη ᾗ ὕλη παθητι-
κόν; ii. 9, 335, b, 29 : τῆς μὲν γὰρ ὕλης
τὸ πάσχειν ἐστὶ καὶ τὸ κινεῖσθαι, τὸ
δὲ κινεῖν καὶ ποιεῖν ἑτέρας δυνάμεως.
Of Matter as moved and Form as
mover we shall have more to say
immediately.   How exclusively
passivity was limited by Aristotle
to Matter, appears especially in
his anthropology.

duced certain particular materials must be ready to
hand.¹ For the same reason, the extent to which Nature

¹ Plato had already sharply
distinguished the αἴτια from the
συναίτια, the efficient causes (δι'
ὧν γίγνεταί τι) from the indispensable conditions (ἄνευ ὧν οὐ
γίγνεται); cf. *Div.* i. 642 sqq.
Aristotle also adopts this distinction. His whole view of
nature turns on the opposition
between design and natural necessity, between what is required
by the conception or form of a
thing and what proceeds from
the nature of its material: the
former is the δι' ὅ, the latter the
οὗ οὐκ ἄνευ; the former is independent and unconditioned, the
latter is for a purpose and con-
ditionally necessary. To these
two there is added a third kind
of necessity, viz. compulsion,
which, however, does not further
concern us here (upon this as
distinguished from the necessity
of the conception, cf. *Phys.* viii. 4,
254, b, 13; *An. Post.* ii. 11, 94, b,
37; *Metaph.* v. 5, 1015, a, 26
sqq., vi. 2, 1026, b, 27, xi. 8, 1064,
b, 33) Cf. *Metaph.* xii. 7, 1072, b,
11 : τὸ γὰρ ἀναγκαῖον τοσαυταχῶς,
τὸ μὲν βίᾳ ὅτι παρὰ τὴν ὁρμὴν, τὸ
δὲ οὗ οὐκ ἄνευ τὸ εὖ, τὸ δὲ μὴ ἐνδεχόμενον ἄλλως ἀλλ' ἁπλῶς. *Part.
An.* i. 1, 639, b, 21: τὸ δ' ἐξ ἀνάγκης οὐ πᾶσιν ὑπάρχει τοῖς κατὰ
φύσιν ὁμοίως . . . . ὑπάρχει δὲ τὸ
μὲν ἁπλῶς τοῖς ἀϊδίοις, τὸ δ' ἐξ
ὑποθέσεως καὶ τοῖς ἐν γενέσει πᾶσιν.
Ibid. 642, a, 1 : εἰσὶν ἄρα δύο αἰτίαι
αὗται, τό θ' οὗ ἕνεκα καὶ τὸ ἐξ
ἀνάγκης· πολλὰ γὰρ γίνεται ὅτι
ἀνάγκη. ἴσως δ' ἄν τις ἀπορήσειε
ποίαν λέγουσιν ἀνάγκην οἱ λέγοντες
ἐξ ἀνάγκης· τῶν μὲν γὰρ δύο τρόπων
οὐδέτερον οἷόν τε ὑπάρχειν, τῶν

διωρισμένων ἐν τοῖς κατὰ φιλοσοφίαν
[the necessity imposed by the
conception and that of compul-
sion]. ἔστι δ' ἔν γε τοῖς ἔχουσι
γένεσιν ἡ τρίτη. λέγομεν γὰρ τὴν
τροφὴν ἀναγκαῖόν τι κατ' οὐδέτερον
τούτων τῶν τρόπων, ἀλλ' ὅτι οὐχ
οἷόν τε ἄνευ ταύτης εἶναι. τοῦτο δ'
ἐστὶν ὥσπερ ἐξ ὑποθέσεως. *Gen.
An.* i. 4, 717, a, 15 : πᾶν ἡ φύσις
ἢ διὰ τὸ ἀναγκαῖον ποιεῖ ἢ διὰ τὸ
βέλτιον ; ii. 6, 743, b, 16 : πάντα
δὲ ταῦτα, καθάπερ εἴπομεν (743, a,
36), λεκτέον γίνεσθαι τῇ μὲν ἐξ
ἀνάγκης, τῇ δ' οὐκ ἐξ ἀνάγκης ἀλλ'
ἕνεκά τινος; iv. 8, 776, b, 32 : δι'
ἀμφοτέρας τὰς αἰτίας, ἕνεκά τε τοῦ
βελτίστου καὶ ἐξ ἀνάγκης. *Phys.*
ii. 2 *init.*: τὸ δ' ἐξ ἀνάγκης πότερον
ἐξ ὑποθέσεως ὑπάρχει ἢ καὶ ἁπλῶς ;
usually we look for the necessity
in the nature of the material
parts; ἀλλ' ὅμως οὐκ ἄνευ μὲν
τούτων γέγονεν, οἱ μέντοι διὰ ταῦτα
πλὴν ὡς δι' ὕλην . . . ὁμοίως δὲ καὶ
ἐν τοῖς ἄλλοις πᾶσιν, ἐν ὅσοις τὸ
ἕνεκά του ἐστιν, οὐκ ἄνευ μὲν τῶν
ἀναγκαίαν ἐχόντων τὴν φύσιν, οὐ
μέντοι γε διὰ ταῦτα ἀλλ' ἢ ὡς ὕλην
. . . ἐξ ὑποθέσεως δὴ τὸ ἀναγκαῖον,
ἀλλ' οὐχ ὡς τέλος· ἐν γὰρ τῇ ὕλῃ
τὸ ἀναγκαῖον, τὸ δ' οὗ ἕνεκα ἐν τῷ
λόγῳ. L. 30: φανερὸν δὴ ὅτι τὸ
ἀναγκαῖον ἐν τοῖς φυσικοῖς τὸ ὡς
ὕλη λεγόμενον καὶ αἱ κινήσεις αἱ
ταύτης. *De An.* ii. 4, 416, a, 9 :
δοκεῖ δέ τισιν ἡ τοῦ πυρὸς φύσις
ἁπλῶς αἰτία τῆς τροφῆς καὶ τῆς
αὐξήσεως εἶναι . . . τὸ δὲ συναίτιον
μέν πως ἐστιν, οὐ μὴν ἁπλῶς γε
αἴτιον, ἀλλὰ μᾶλλον ἡ ψυχή. *Gen.
et Corr.* ii. 9, 335, b, 24 sq. : it is
not the matter which is the producing cause, for it is merely passive and moved; the κυριωτέρα

can realise her end—the mode and the perfection in which the Form manifests itself—are conditioned by the character of these materials : that is, by their capacity for receiving and exhibiting the Form. Just in proportion as this capacity is wanting, will the formations be imperfect and dege'nerate from their true patterns and the proper purposes of nature, or perhaps we shall have productions which serve no end at all, but are developed incidentally as the result of some natural coherence and necessity, in the course of the realisation of Nature's purposes.[1]

αἰτία is τί ἦν εἶναι and the μορφή. The physical is the mere tool of the causative conception ; heat does not any more of itself effect production than the saw saws of itself. *Part. An.* iii. 2, 663, b, 22 : πῶς δὲ τῆς ἀναγκαίας φύσεως ἐχούσης τοῖς ὑπάρχουσιν ἐξ ἀνάγκης ἢ κατὰ τὸν λόγον φύσις ἕνεκά του κατακέχρηται, λέγωμεν. Similarly Aristotle distinguishes (*Anal. Post.* ii. 11, 94, b, 27) ἕνεκά τινος and ἐξ ἀνάγκης and enumerates (*Metaph.* v. 5) the commoner applications of ἀναγκαῖον : to that οὗ ἄνευ οὐκ ἐνδέχεται ζῆν, &c. ; ὡς συναιτίου, to that which is βίαιον and to that which is ἀναγκαῖον in the proper sense τὸ ἁπλοῦν (= ἁπλῶς ἀναγκαῖον) viz. the μὴ ἐνδεχόμενον ἄλλως ἔχειν. Quite in conformity with this is the statement of Eudemus *apud* SIMPL. *Phys.* 63, a, that matter and aim are the two causes of motion. Within the sphere of conditional necessity there is again (*Gen. An.* ii. 6, 742, a, 19 sq. ; where, however, l. 22, we must read, not οὗ ἕνεκα but with Cod. PS. and Wimmer τούτου ἕν.) a twofold distinction made between that which as efficient cause conditions the

production of anything and that which is necessary to it as the instrument of its activity : the former must precede in origin the thing which it aims at producing ; the latter must follow it. Cf. on the whole subject WAITZ, *Arist. Org.* ii. 409 sq.

[1] *Part. An.* iv. 2, 677, a, 15 : καταχρῆται μὲν οὖν ἐνίοτε ἡ φύσις εἰς τὸ ὠφέλιμον τοῖς περιττώμασιν, οὐ μὴν διὰ τοῦτο δεῖ ζητεῖν πάντα ἕνεκα τίνος, ἀλλά τινων ὄντων τοιούτων ἕτερα ἐξ ἀνάγκης συμβαίνει διὰ ταῦτα πολλά. So according to *Gen. An.* v. 1, 778, a, 30, only that has an end to serve which appears universally in all nature's productions or in certain classes of them ; individual varieties on the other hand have none : the eye has an end to serve ; the fact that it is blue has none : *ibid.* c. 8 *fin.*, mention is made of phenomena ὅσα γίνεσθαι συμβαίνει μὴ ἕνεκά του ἀλλ' ἐξ ἀνάγκης καὶ διὰ τὴν αἰτίαν τὴν κινητικήν. According to *Metaph.* viii. 4, 1044, b, 12, the eclipses of the moon appear to serve no end ; ὕει ὁ Ζεὺς οὐχ ὅπως τὸν σῖτον αὐξήσῃ, ἀλλ' ἐξ ἀνάγκης · τὸ γὰρ ἀναχθὲν ψυχθῆναι δεῖ καὶ τὸ ψυχθὲν ὕδωρ

We shall hereafter have occasion to observe how deeply
this view is rooted in Aristotle's whole theory of Nature,
and how many phenomena he accounts for by the resistance of Matter to Form. Again the same property
of Matter is also the source of all contingency in
Nature.¹ By 'the contingent,'² Aristotle, who was the
first carefully to examine this conception,³ understands in general all that can equally well belong or
not belong to a thing: that which is neither contained
in its essence nor supported by the necessity of its
being,⁴ and which accordingly is neither necessary nor
normal.⁵ That we must assume the existence of

γενόμενον κατελθεῖν· τὸ δ' αὐξά-
νεσθαι τούτου γενομένου τὸν σῖτον
συμβαίνει. ὁμοίως δὲ καὶ εἴ τῳ
ἀπόλλυται ὁ σῖτος ἐν τῇ ἅλῳ, οὐ
τούτου ἕνεκα ὕει ὅπως ἀπόληται,
ἀλλὰ τοῦτο συμβέβηκεν (*Phys.* ii.
8, 198, b, 18); individual organs
of animals are without purpose:
the bile is a περίττωμα καὶ οὐχ
ἕνεκά τινος (*Part. An.* ibid. l. 13),
the stag has no use for its antlers
(*ibid.* iii. 2, 663, a, 6, 664, a, 7).
The same is true of all superfluous materials which are un-
employed; such materials are
ἄχρηστον or even τῶν παρὰ φύσιν
τι (*Gen. An.* i. 18, 725, a, 1, 4);
we must therefore decide even in
reference to one and the same
material whether it serves a purpose or not: lymph (ἰχὼρ), *e g*,
which consists partly of half-as-
similated and partly of corrupted
blood, is in the former aspect
αἵματος χάριν, in the latter ἐξ
ἀνάγκης (*Part. An.* ii. 4 *fin.*).
Necessity of this latter kind, as
is indicated in the passage quoted
above from *Phys.* ii. 8, coincides
with contingency.

¹ Whether also of all freedom
of choice in man, from which
alone contingent effects really
spring (to it alone at least these
are referred in *De Interpr.* c. 9,
18, b, 31, 19, a, 7), Aristotle does
not tell us. In *Phys.* i. 5, 196, b, 17,
sq., he expressly excludes free
purpose, as such, from the domain
of τύχη.
² Συμβεβηκὸς in the narrower
sense, τὸ ἀπὸ τύχης.
³ As he says himself, *Phys.* ii. 4.
⁴ *An. Post.* i. 4, 73, a, 34, b,
10 : Aristotle calls καθ' αὐτὰ, ὅσα
ὑπάρχει τε ἐν τῷ τί ἐστιν . . . καὶ
ὅσοις τῶν ἐνυπαρχόντων αὐτοῖς αὐτὰ
ἐν τῷ λόγῳ ἐνυπάρχουσι τῷ τί ἐστι
δηλοῦντι . . . ὅσα δὲ μηδετέρως
ὑπάρχει, συμβεβηκότα ; further, τὸ
μὲν δι' αὐτὸ ὑπάρχον ἑκάστῳ καθ'
αὐτὸ, τὸ δὲ μὴ δι' αὐτὸ συμβεβηκός.
Top. i. 5, 102, b, 4 : συμβεβηκὸς
δέ ἐστιν ... ὃ ἐνδέχεται ὑπάρχειν
ὁτῳοῦν ἑνὶ καὶ τῷ αὐτῷ καὶ μὴ
ὑπάρχειν ; cf. p. 234, n. 1, on ἐνδεχόμενον and δυνατὸν, p. 213, n. 4,
p. 214, n. 3, on συμβεβηκός.
⁵ *Metaph.* v. 30, *init.* : συμβεβηκὸς λέγεται ὃ ὑπάρχει μέν τινι

such a principle, and not ascribe everything to the
operation of necessity, Aristotle proves in the first place
by the witness of universal experience,[1] aud in particular
by the fact of the Freedom of the Will.[2] But he finds
the true rationale of all contingency in the fact that all
finite existence contains the potentiality of being and
not-being, and that Matter as the indeterminate renders
opposite determinations possible.[3] It follows from this
property of Matter that many things happen independently of the final action of efficient causes. The latter
have always a definite object in view, but they frequently
fail of its perfect accomplishment[4] owing to the indeterminate nature of the Matter which they use, while
at other times, owing to the same disturbing cause, they
incidentally produce results which they did not originally design.[5] A contingent or accidental event is

καὶ ἀληθὲς εἰπεῖν οὐ μέντοι οὔτ᾽ ἐξ
ἀνάγκης οὔτ᾽ ἐπὶ τὸ πολύ. The
same definition is given vi. 2,
1026 b, 31 sqq. (xi. 8). *Phys.* ii.
5 *init.*; *De Cœlo*, i. 12, 283, a, 32:
τὸ μὲν γὰρ αὐτόματόν ἐστι καὶ τὸ
ἀπὸ τύχης παρὰ τὸ ἀεὶ καὶ τὸ ὡς
ἐπὶ τὸ πολὺ ἢ ὂν ἢ γινόμενον. *Phys.*
ii. 8, 138, b, 34 : might not the
appearance of design in nature
be explained by supposing that
of her chance productions only
those survive which are fitted
to live ? No : ταῦτα μὲν γὰρ καὶ
πάντα τὰ φύσει ἢ ἀεὶ οὕτω γίνεται
ἢ ὡς ἐπὶ τὸ πολύ, τῶν δ᾽ ἀπὸ τύχης
καὶ τοῦ αὐτομάτου οὐδέν. So *De
Cœlo*, ii. 8, 289, b, 26.

[1] *Phys. ibid.* 196, b, 13.
[2] *De Interpr.* c. 9, 18, b, 31,
19, a, 7.
[3] *De Interpr.* c. 9, 19, a, 9 :
there must be contingency, ὅτι

ὅλως ἔστιν ἐν τοῖς μὴ ἀεὶ ἐνεργοῦσι
τὸ δυνατὸν εἶναι, καὶ μὴ ὁμοίως.
Metaph. vi. 2, 1027, a, 13 : ὥστε
ἡ ὕλη ἔσται αἰτία, ἡ ἐνδεχομένη
παρὰ τὸ ὡς ἐπὶ τὸ πολὺ ἄλλως, τοῦ
συμβεβηκότος ; vii. 7 (see p. 345,
n. 5, *supra*), v. 30, 1025, a, 24: οὐδε
δὴ αἴτιον ὡρισμίνον οὐθὲν τοῦ
συμβεβηκότος, ἀλλὰ τὸ τυχόν,
τοῦτο δ᾽ ἀόριστον. Cf. n. 5 *infra*.
[4] See pp. 360 sqq. *supra*,
Gen. An. iv. 10, 778, a, 4 :
βούλεται μὲν οὖν ἡ φύσις τοῖς
τούτων [τῶν ἄστρων] ἀριθμοῖς ἀριθμεῖν τὰς γενέσεις καὶ τὰς τελευτάς,
οὐκ ἀκριβοῖ δὲ διά τε τὴν τῆς ὕλης
ἀοριστίαν καὶ διὰ τὸ γίνεσθαι πολλὰς
ἀρχάς, αἳ τὰς γενέσεις τὰς κατὰ
φύσιν καὶ τὰς φθορὰς ἐμποδίζουσαι
πολλάκις αἴτιαι τῶν παρὰ φύσιν
συμπιπτόντων εἰσίν. See further
p. 341 sqq.
[5] See n. 3, *supra*. *Phys.* ii.

caused by the diversion of free or compulsory purposeful action to results alien from its purpose through the influence of external circumstances.[1] Now, since these disturbing circumstances are always found in the nature of the material means by which ends are realised, and in the system of nature to which these means belong, Contingency, in Aristotle's sense of the word, may be defined as the disturbance by intermediate causes of an activity directed to a purpose.[2] But activity in obedience to a purpose is that by which the essence or conception of an object is realised.[3] That which does not proceed from it is unessential; and there-

5, 196, b, 17 : τῶν δὲ γινομένων τὰ μὲν ἕνεκά του γίγνεται, τὰ δ' οὔ . . . ἔστι δ' ἕνεκά του ὅσα τε ἀπὸ διανο'ας ἂν πραχθείη καὶ ὅσα ἀπὸ φύσεως. τὰ δὴ τοιαῦτα ὅταν κατὰ συμβεβηκὸς γένηται, ἀπὸ τύχης φαμὲν εἶναι . . . τὸ μὲν οὖν καθ' αὑτὸ αἴτιον ὡρισμένον, τὸ δὲ κατὰ συμβεβηκὸς ἀόριστον· ἄπειρα γὰρ ἂν τῷ ἑνὶ συμβα'η. It is chance, for instance, if one comes to a place for another purpose and is rewarded in a way he had not thought of ; or if he (Metaph. v. 30) digs a hole and finds a treasure ; or if he desires to sail to one place and is carried to another ; or, generally, if from action directed to a definite end something else results, by reason of the intervention of external circumstances, than that which was intended (ὅταν μὴ τοῦ συμβάντος ἕνεκα γένηται, οὗ ἔξω τὸ αἴτιον, Phys. ii. 6, 197, b, 19). If the action is one of voluntary choice (προαιρετὸν) such a chance (according to the passage just quoted from Phys. ii.) must be

called τύχη, otherwise αὐτόματον, so that the latter is the wider conception. Both, however, stand equally opposed to purposed action; ὥστ' ἐπειδὴ ἀόριστα τὰ οὕτως αἴτια, καὶ ἡ τύχη ἀόριστον (Phys. ii. 5, 197, a, 20).

[1] Akin to this, but unimportant for our present investigation, is the coincidence in time of two circumstances between which no causal relation of any kind exists, e.g. a walk and an eclipse of the moon. Such a coincidence (which is the purest and simplest case of contingency) Aristotle calls σύμπτωμα, Divin. p. S. i. 462, b, 26 sqq.

[2] See p. 356 sqq. supra.

[3] Metaph. vi. 2, 1026, b, 13 : ὥσπερ γὰρ ὀνόματι μόνον τὸ συμβεβηκός ἐστι. διὸ Πλάτων τρόπον τινὰ οὐ κακῶς τὴν σοφιστικὴν περὶ τὸ μὴ ὂν ἔταξεν. εἰσὶ γὰρ οἱ τῶν σοφιστῶν λόγοι περὶ τὸ συμβεβηκὸς ὡς εἰπεῖν μάλιστα πάντων. L. 21 : φαίνεται γὰρ τὸ συμβεβηκὸς ἐγγύς τι τοῦ μὴ ὄντος.

fore Aristotle says that the contingent borders on the
non-existent.[1] After what has been already said about
the nature of Knowledge, it scarcely needs, therefore, to
be explicitly stated that such a principle as Contingency
can be no object of Science.

While it is obvious from what has just been said
about the nature of Matter, that it is something far more
primordial than might have been expected from the first
definition given of its concept, this becomes still clearer
from other considerations. From ' Matter ' Aristotle is
not contented with deducing merely what one is apt to
consider as accidental and unessential, but also certain
properties of things which essentially belong to the
conception of them and contribute to determining their
generic character. The distinction, for example, between
male and female is said to be merely one of material;[2]
and yet procreation, which depends upon it,[3] occupies a
most important place in the scheme of the philosopher.[4]

---

[1] *Anal. Post.* i. 6, 75, a, 18, c.
30, 33 *init. Metaph. ibid.* 1026,
b, 2, 1027, a, 19 (xi. 8).

[2] *Metaph.* vii. 5, 1030, b, 21, sex
is reckoned one of the essential
attributes, the καθ' αὑτὰ ὑπάρχοντα;
but x. 9 *init.* it is asked διὰ τί
γυνὴ ἀνδρὸς οὐκ εἴδει διαφέρει . . .
οὐδὲ ζῷον θῆλυ καὶ ἄρρεν ἕτερον τῷ
εἴδει, καίτοι καθ' αὑτὸ τοῦ ζῴου
αὕτη ἡ διαφορὰ καὶ οὐχ ὡς λευκότης
καὶ μελανία, ἀλλ' ᾗ ζῷον, καὶ τὸ
θῆλυ καὶ τὸ ἄρρεν ὑπάρχει; and the
answer is that a distinction in
kind rests on ἐναντιότητες ἐν τῷ
λόγῳ alone, not on those ἐν τῇ
ὕλῃ. τὸ δὲ ἄρρεν καὶ θῆλυ τοῦ ζῴου
οἰκεῖα μὲν πάθη, ἀλλ' οὐ κατὰ τὴν
οὐσίαν, ἀλλ' ἐν τῇ ὕλῃ καὶ τῷ σώματι.

διὸ τὸ αὐτὸ σπέρμα θῆλυ ἢ ἄρρεν
γίγνεται παθόν τι πάθος. Cf. *Gen.
An.* iv. 3, 767, b, 8 sqq., ii. 3,
737, a, 27, and p. 353, n. 4, *supra.*

[3] *De An.* ii. 4, 415, a, 26, and
other passages. That this is incompatible with the statement
in *Metaph.* x. 9, was rightly
remarked by ENGEL, *Ueb. d.
Bedeut. d. ὕλη Arist., Rhein.
Mus.* N.F. vii. 410.

[4] It is even stated, *Gen. An.*
i. 2, 716, a, 17, b, 8, that the
sexual distinction, depending as
it does on difference of function,
is κατὰ τὸν λόγον and is one οὐ
κατὰ τὸ τυχὸν μόριον οὐδὲ κατὰ
τὴν τυχοῦσαν δύναμιν.

Similarly we shall have occasion to observe that the lower animals, which Aristotle always represents as even in their physical nature different in kind from human beings, are yet at the same time to be regarded as imperfect formations which have been prevented (owing, we must suppose, to the properties of Matter) from developing into the form of man. Furthermore, it is to Matter that we must refer the mutability and corruptibility of earthly things;[1] and the same must be

---

[1] This follows from the general consideration that all Change and Becoming presupposes a material (see p. 342, n. 2 sq. *supra*) which, as δυνάμει ὄν contains the possibility alike of being and not-being (*Gen. et Corr.* ii. 9 ; *Metaph.* vii. 7, and other passages. Cf. p. 345, n. 5), as Aristotle himself distinctly says. Cf. *Metaph.* vii. 15 (see p. 220, n. 2, *supra*), ix. 8, 1050, b, 7 : ἔστι δ' οὐδὲν δυνάμει ἀίδιον. [Or as this is expressed *Phys.* iii. 4, 203, b, 30 : ἐνδέχεσθαι γὰρ ἢ εἶναι οὐδὲν διαφέρει ἐν τοῖς ἀιδίοις.] λόγος δὲ ὅδε. πᾶσα δύναμις ἅμα τῆς ἀντιφάσεώς ἐστιν [the possibility of being involves the possibility of not being, &c.] . . . τὸ ἄρα δυνατὸν εἶναι ἐνδέχεται καὶ εἶναι καὶ μὴ εἶναι (cf. p. 234, n. 1), . . . τὸ δ' ἐνδεχόμενον μὴ εἶναι φθαρτόν (similarly, xiv. 2, *init.*). The motion, therefore, of every perishable thing is combined with effort, for only thus is the possibility of the opposite state (the δύναμις τῆς ἀντιφάσεως, ll. 25, 30 sqq.) overcome: ἡ γὰρ οὐσία ὕλη καὶ δύναμις οὖσα, οὐκ ἐνέργεια, αἰτία τούτου; viii. 4, 1044, b, 27 : οὐδὲ παντὸς ὕλη ἐστὶν ἀλλ' ὅσων γένεσίς ἐστι καὶ μεταβολὴ εἰς

ἄλληλα. ὅσα δ' ἄνευ τοῦ μεταβάλλειν ἔστιν ἢ μή, οὐκ ἔστι τούτων ὕλη ; vii. 10, 1035, a, 25 : ὅσα μὲν οὖν συνειλημμένα τὸ εἶδος καὶ ἡ ὕλη ἐστὶν . . . ταῦτα μὲν φθείρεται εἰς ταῦτα . . . ὅσα δὲ μὴ συνείληπται τῇ ὕλῃ, ἀλλ' ἄνευ ὕλης . . . ταῦτα δ' οὐ φθείρεται ἢ ὅλως ἢ οὔτοι οὕτω γε (similarly it is said of immaterial forms, xii. 3, 1070, a, 15 : οὐδ' ἔστι γένεσις καὶ φθορὰ τούτων, ἀλλ' ἄλλον τρόπον εἰσὶ καὶ οὐκ εἰσὶν οἰκία τε ἡ ἄνευ ὕλης καὶ ὑγίεια καὶ πᾶν τὸ κατὰ τέχνην : not the form as such, but only its union with this or that material has a beginning and end) ; xii. 1, 1069, b, 3 : ἡ δ' αἰσθητὴ οὐσία μεταβλητή; 2, 1069, b, 24 : πάντα δ' ὕλην ἔχει ὅσα μεταβάλλει. *Longit.* v. 3, 465, b, 7 : ᾧ μή ἐστιν ἐναντίον καὶ ὅποι μή ἐστιν ἀδύνατον ἂν εἴη φθαρῆναι. But we may not infer from this the indestructibility of any material thing : ἀδύνατον γὰρ τῷ ὕλην ἔχοντι μὴ ὑπάρχειν πως τὸ ἐναντίον. πάντῃ μὲν γὰρ ἐνεῖναι τὸ θερμὸν ἢ τὸ εὐθὺ ἐνδέχεται, πᾶν δ' εἶναι ἀδύνατον ἢ θερμὸν ἢ εὐθὺ ἢ λευκόν· ἔσται γὰρ τὰ πάθη κεχωρισμένα ['for in this case these qualities would be independent exist-

said of all badness and imperfection,[1] although the per-

ences ']. εἰ οὖν, ὅταν ἅμα ᾖ τὸ
ποιητικὸν καὶ τὸ παθητικὸν, ἀεὶ τὸ
μὲν ποιεῖ τὸ δὲ πάσχει, ἀδύνατον
μὴ μεταβάλλειν. *De Cælo,* i. 12,
283, a, 29 : nothing that is without beginning can have an end,
and nothing that is without end
can have had a beginning, since
this could only be if it were its
nature at one time to be, at
another not to be. τῶν δὲ
τοιούτων ἡ αὐτὴ δύναμις τῆς
ἀντιφάσεως καὶ ἡ ὕλη αἰτία τοῦ
εἶναι καὶ μή.
  [1] *Metaph.* ix. 9, 1051, a, 15 ;
Aristotle seems, indeed, to assert
the very opposite of this : ἀνάγκη
δὲ καὶ ἐπὶ τῶν κακῶν τὸ τέλος καὶ
τὴν ἐνέργειαν εἶναι χεῖρον τῆς
δυνάμεως · τὸ γὰρ δυνάμενον ταῦτὸ
ἄμφω τἀναντία. δῆλον ἄρα ὅτι οὐκ
ἔστι τὸ κικὸν παρὰ τὰ πράγματα ·
ὕστερον γὰρ τῇ φύσει τὸ κακὸν τῆς
δυνάμεως. But this only means
that since every δύναμις contains
the possibility of opposite determinations (see p. 234, n. 1, *supra*)
to what is merely δυνάμει ὂν we
cannot attribute one of two
mutually exclusive qualities,
such as good and bad, as the
Platonists had done in explaining matter as evil (cf. *Div.* i.
642, 6, 721, 737). Nevertheless,
the ultimate cause of evil can
only reside in the δυνάμει ὄν, in
other words, in matter, and this
is indicated by Aristotle himself when, in the passage just
quoted, he proceeds : οὐκ ἄρα οὐδ'
ἐν τοῖς ἐξ ἀρχῆς καὶ τοῖς ἀιδίοις
οὐθέν ἐστιν οὔτε κακὸν οὔτε ἁμάρ-
τημα οὔτε διεφθαρμένον · καὶ γὰρ ἡ
διαφθορὰ τῶν κακῶν ἐστίν. There
is no imperfection in the eternal,
since it exists continually ἐνεργείᾳ, and therefore excludes the

possibility of opposites, since its
conception has for ever been
realised in it and will always
continue to be realised. Evil
and imperfection, on the other
hand, consist in nothing else
than a discrepancy between the
concept of a thing and its
actual state. While, therefore,
on the one hand, the δυνάμει ὂν
cannot be itself evil, yet is it,
on the other hand, the ultimate cause and condition of it.
Accordingly Aristotle himself
speaks (*Phys.* i. 9, 192, a, 15) of
the κακοποιὸν of the ὕλη. He
admits that it is not evil in itself and in its essence, but only
in a secondary sense, and in
so far as, being without form, it
lacks also the quality of goodness
(cf. p. 324, n. 5, and p. 344, n. 1).
But it is precisely upon this want
and this indeterminateness that
the possibility of its turning out
bad as well as good depends.
Eternal reality excludes evil, since
it has either no matter at all, or
one which, as perfectly definite
and formed, is incapable of opposite de`erminations — while muta-
bility and change, on the other
hand, are sure indications of evil
and imperfection. (On this
subject cf also *Eth. N.* vii. 15,
1154, b, 28 : μεταβολὴ δὲ πάντων
γλυκύτατον, κατὰ τὸν ποιητὴν, διὰ
πονηρίαν τινά. ὥσπερ γὰρ ἄνθρωπος
εὐμετάβολος ὁ πονηρός, καὶ ἡ φύσις
ἡ δεομένη μεταβολῆς · οὐ γὰρ
ἀπλῆ οὐδ' ἐπιεικής.) And so we
shall find that Aristotle traces
all imperfect forms of natural
existence to the resistance which
the matter offers to the form : and
by a parity of reasoning he would
have been forced to refer the

fect and imperishable heavenly bodies are no less formed of a definite material.[1] In Matter alone we must seek for the cause of change and motion, which result from an innate striving of Matter after Form.[2] Matter, finally, is the source of individual existence, in all those things at least which are formed of the union of Matter and Form. Aristotle certainly did not treat of the principle of Individualisation with the universality and definiteness that we could have wished : and thereby he bequeathed to his followers in the Middle Ages a rich opportunity for scientific controversy. We shall find hereafter that, in addition to corporeal beings, he recognises in the Deity, the spheral spirits and the rational part of man, incorporeal beings free from any taint of Matter, which we must nevertheless regard as being also individual existences.[3] Yet when the Form becomes actual in any material, it is the latter alone which explains why the

source of moral evil to the body, which in his general scheme is alone passive and changeable, had he not, as we shall see hereafter, left this question wholly vague.

[1] Aristotle himself has not overlooked this objection. He meets it (*Metaph.* viii. 4, 1044, b, 6) with the remark : ἐπὶ δὲ τῶν φυσικῶν μὲν ἀϊδίων δὲ οὐσιῶν ἄλλος λόγος. ἴσως γὰρ ἔνια οὐκ ἔχει ὕλην, ἢ οὐ τοιαύτην (as the φυσικαὶ καὶ γεννηταὶ οὐσίαι) ἀλλὰ μόνον κατὰ τόπον κινητήν. Similarly xii. 2, 1069, b, 24. The ether, for instance, of which the heavens and the heavenly bodies consist, is said to have no ἐναντίωσις and therefore to be subject to no change in its substance. It has

none of the qualities on which rest the mutual opposition of the elements and their transformation into one another (cf. p. 358 sqq.). The question is, how it *can* be so, if it is really matter and if all matter is a δυνάμει ὂν and all δύναμις contains the possibility of opposite states.

[2] On this, more *infra*.

[3] The solution which the Schoolmen in their doctrine of angels devised, to the effect that each of these pure spirits, as specifically different from every other and itself the only member of the species, is therefore at once specifically and numerically single, is nowhere suggested by Aristotle.

Form is never present in it except under certain limiting conditions and with certain definite properties, which are not contained in the Form as such—that is, in the pure Concept of the thing. The Form or Concept is always a Universal,[1] denoting not a thing but a kind,[2] and capable of being thought, but not of existing, by itself apart from things.[3] Between the Individuals into which the *infimœ species* resolve themselves no difference of kind or Form any longer exists,[4] and consequently they must be distinguished from one another by their Matter.[5] Aristotle is unable to apply this principle unwaveringly[6] through-

---

[1] See p. 219, n. 4, and p. 221, *supra*; and upon εἶδος as the object of the conception see notes on pp. 216 and 341, &c., and cf. p. 173, n. 2.

[2] *Metaph.* viii. 8, 1033, b, 21 : the form is not something apart from definite material things, ἀλλὰ τὸ τοιόνδε σημαίνει, τόδε καὶ ὡρισμένον οὐκ ἔστιν, ἀλλὰ ποιεῖ καὶ γεννᾷ ἐκ τοῦδε τοιόνδε. But this is itself the distinctive mark of universality; see pp. 333, &c. *supra*.

[3] *Phys.* ii. 1, 193, b, 4 : ἡ μορφὴ καὶ τὸ εἶδος, οὐ χωριστὸν ὂν ἀλλ' ἢ κατὰ τὸν λόγον. *Metaph.* viii. 1, 1042, a, 26 sqq. ; *v. infra*, n. 6.

[4] See notes at pp. 216, 221,&c. *supra*.

[5] *Metaph.* vii. 8 *fin.* (cf. c. 10, 1035, b, 27 sqq.) : the form unites with the matter, τὸ δ' ἅπαν ἤδη τὸ τοιόνδε εἶδος ἐν ταῖσδε ταῖς σαρξὶ καὶ ὀττοῖς Καλλίας καὶ Σωκράτης · καὶ ἕτερον μὲν διὰ τὴν ὕλην, ἑτέρα γὰρ, ταὐτὸ δὲ τῷ εἴδει · ἄτομον γὰρ τὸ εἶδος ; x. 9, 1058, a, 37 : ἐπειδή ἐστι τὸ μὲν λόγος τὸ δ' ὕλη, ὅσαι μὲν ἐν τῷ λόγῳ εἰσὶν ἐναντιότητες εἴδει ποιοῦσι διαφοράν, ὅσαι δ' ἐν τῷ

συνειλημμένῳ τῇ ὕλῃ οὐ ποιοῦσιν. διὸ ἀνθρώπου λευκότης οὐ ποιεῖ οὐδὲ μελανία . . . ὡς ὕλη γὰρ ὁ ἄνθρωπος, οὐ ποιεῖ δὲ διαφορὰν [a specific difference] ἡ ὕλη · οὐκ ἀνθρώπου γὰρ εἴδη εἰσὶν οἱ ἄνθρωποι διὰ τοῦτο, καίτοι ἕτεραι αἱ σάρκες καὶ τὰ ὀστᾶ ἐξ ὧν ὅδε καὶ ὅδε · ἀλλὰ τὸ σύνολον ἕτερον μὲν, εἴδει δ' οὐχ ἕτερον, ὅτι ἐν τῷ λόγῳ οὐκ ἔστιν ἐναντίωσις.

[6] There are certainly passages in Aristotle in which that which constitutes the difference between individuals of the same species seems to be included in the conception of their εἶδος ; thus it cannot be overlooked that the conception, *e.g.*, of man, which according to the passage just quoted is an *infima species*, does not exclude certain individual differences which have a reference, not to the matter alone, but also to the form of the individual members of it (*e.g.* their bodily form). No clear distinction, however, is anywhere drawn between this individual form, and the universal form or class conception which expresses the common

out; but it is clear that his system leaves no room for

essence of several individual things; on the contrary, the former always resolves itself finally into the latter. *Metaph.* xii. 5, 1071, a, 27, it is said : καὶ τῶν ἐν ταὐτῷ εἴδει ἕτερα [sc. τὰ στοιχεῖά ἐστιν], οὐκ εἴδει, ἀλλ' ὅτι τῶν καθέκαστον ἄλλο, ἥ τε σὴ ὕλη καὶ τὸ κινῆσαν καὶ τὸ εἴδος καὶ ἡ ἐμὴ, τῷ καθόλου δὲ λόγῳ ταὐτά. While, however, accord-ing to this passage everyone has an εἶδος of his own different from that of everyone else, still the one does not differ from the other in kind. They will differ from one another, therefore, only in so far as they belong to different subjects : or in other words, in their actual embodiment, not in their cha-racter—ἀριθμῷ, not εἴδει. *Metaph.* vii. 3 (cf. p. 372, n. 3), 1029, a, 1, it is said : the name οὐσία seems to belong in the first place to the ὑποκείμενον πρῶτον· τοιοῦτον δὲ τρόπον μέν τινα ἡ ὕλη λέγεται, ἄλλον δὲ τρόπον ἡ μορφή, τρίτον δὲ τὸ ἐκ τούτων. Since, then, by ὑποκείμενον or substance the indi-vidual thing as the subject of all its predicates is elsewhere under-stood (cf. pp. 332 sqq., 300, &c.), we should naturally refer μορφή here to the form of the individual thing *qua* individual. But from the further explanation, c. 8, it appears that this μορφή ἐν τῷ αἰσθητῷ (1033, b, 5), this ὡς εἶδος ἢ οὐσία λεγόμενον, is only the un-realised form which first makes this definite thing into a thing which is defined in this or that way (τόδε into a τοιόνδε, l. 23) in the actual thing, *i.e.* in the matter, but which on the other hand itself stands related to individual things as man is to

Callias or Socrates. The only ground of individuality lies in the matter : ἐν παντὶ τῷ γενομένῳ ὕλη ἔνεστι, καὶ ἔστι [and there-fore is] τὸ μὲν τόδε τὸ δὲ τόδε (l. 18). Exactly the same is true of *Metaph.* viii. 1, 1042, a, 26 (ἔστι δ' οὐσία τὸ ὑποκείμενον, ἄλλως μὲν ἡ ὕλη . . . ἄλλως δ' ὁ λόγος καὶ ἡ μορφή, ὃ τόδε τι ὂν τῷ λόγῳ χωριστόν ἐστι. τρίτον δὲ τὸ ἐκ τούτων, οὗ γένεσις μόνου καὶ φθορά ἐστι καὶ χωριστὸν ἁπλῶς), and of the similar statement, *Metaph.* v. 8 (see p. 372, n. 2, *infra*). The form is a τόδε in so far as it expresses a definite kind of being (man, beast, &c.); but it becomes the form of a definite individual thing in being united with a definite material. Considered apart from this union it is a universal, and it is not true to conclude, as HERTLING does (*Form u. Mat.* 56), from the fact that *Phys.* iv. 3, 210, b, 29 sq., seems to reckon the εἶδος as well as the ὕλη a constituent element of the thing, that it is 'the con-stitutive principle of individual being.' This is true rather of the material in which the form is first individualised. Even *De An.* ii. 1, 412. a, 6 leads to no other conclusion. It is there said : λέγομεν δὴ γένος ἕν τι τῶν ὄντων τὴν οὐσίαν, ταύτης δὲ τὸ μὲν ὡς ὕλην, ὃ καθ' αὑτὸ μὲν οὐκ ἔστι τόδε τι, ἕτερον δὲ μορφὴν καὶ εἶδος, καθ' ἣν ἤδη λέγεται τόδε τι, καὶ τρίτον τὸ ἐκ τούτων. The thing is called this definite thing, *i.e.* a thing of this kind, because its material has received this form ; so the τόδε τι means here also, not the indivi-dual, but the specific peculiarity. —Still less in such passages as

individual Forms of sensible things.[1]   Every Individual

Metaph. xii. 5, 1071, a, 20 (ἀρχὴ
γὰρ τὸ καθ' ἕκαστον τῶν καθ' ἕκασ-
τον· ἄνθρωπος γὰρ ἀνθρώπου καθό-
λου· ἀλλ' ἔστιν οὐδεὶς, ἀλλὰ Πηλεὺς
'Αχιλλέως, &c.) it is (as HERTLING
says at p. 57), stated 'in plain
words that the form, like all first
principles, must be individual.'
Peleus, however, is not the mere
form of an individual but a real
individual; and he has become
so by the union of the form man
with this particular human body.
Moreover, ἴδιον εἶδος (*Metaph.* xii.
5, 1071, a, 14) refers, not to the
individual form of this or that
man, but to the form man in
general. So also the remark (*De
An.* i. 3, 407, b, 23) that any soul
may not enter any body, since all
have their ἴδιον εἶδος καὶ μορφὴν,
must be taken to refer to bodies
and souls of different kinds, and
to mean that the soul of a
man may not wander into the
body of a beast. And when *Gen.
An.* iv. 1, 766, a, 66 sqq. explains
the origin of the female sex on
the ground that the male principle cannot transform the
material into its ἴδιον εἶδος, it is
not dealing with the individual
type, but with the form of the male
sex. It does not alter the case
here that difference of sex according to *Metaph.* x. 9 (see p. 365, n. 2,
supra) resides not in the οὐσία
(= εἶδος) of the ζῷον but only in
the ὕλη and the σῶμα: for even
although it be true that to Aristotle this difference concerns, not
the essence of man or animal as
such, but only the form of the
body, yet it is not on that account
a mere question of individuality.
  [1] HERTLING (*Form u. Mat.* 48
sq.) believes that the form in
Aristotle must necessarily be an

individual thing, since it gives to
the individual its peculiar nature, and is thus distinguished
from the essence (τὸ τί ἦν εἶναι),
which is always, at least in sensible things, a universal. He admits, however, that these two
conceptions, which in certain
passages Aristotle undoubtedly
recognises as distinct, are as a rule
used interchangeably by him. It
seems more correct to say, on the
contrary, that it was Aristotle's
conscious intention to identify the
two, and to treat the form as well
as the essence as a universal.
If we find individual expressions
in him which do not wholly harmonise with this view, this is an
inconsistency which the actual
facts of the case forced upon
him. It is not the expression of
the view with which he started
and which was only afterwards
obscured. That the essence of
each thing lies in its form is to
Aristotle an incontrovertible position, and is stated by him with
the greatest definiteness. The
opposite he never stated in express words; it can only be
deduced from casual expressions
to which we cannot certainly
prove that Aristotle himself consciously attached this significance. As a matter of fact the
boundary line between the essential marks which constitute the
class conception, and the unessential which constitute mere
individual difference, is very im-
palpable. In every attempt to
define it and to explain certain
differences among things as class
differences, others as individual
varieties within the same class,
we shall come upon cases in
which a certain indefiniteness is

therefore implies a material element,[1] and everything that has a body is an Individual.[2] Aristotle uses the two terms 'object of sense' and 'individual' indifferently.[3] If Matter is the cause of all this, it is impossible to suppose that it is distinguished from Form only by privation and non-existence : rather must it contribute something of its own to Form.

Matter, viewed in this light, must be rated at even

inevitable. That Aristotle experienced this difficulty is undeniable : but it does not therefore follow that he did not make the attempt, and that he intended from those εἴδη which coincide with class conceptions to distinguish a second kind of εἴδη which represent, not what is common to the class, but what is peculiar to the individual. The truth is that there is no place in his scheme for such individual forms. For since according to the well-known view that the form has neither origin nor end (see p. 342 —and this must hold also of the form which as τόδε τι is in an individual existence—see preceding note) the individual forms of sensible things, if there are such, must be in actual fact separable from the things whose form they are; but this in Aristotle's view is wholly inadmissible.

[1] *Metaph.* vii. 11, 1037, a, 1 : καὶ παντὸς γὰρ ὕλη τίς ἐστιν ὃ μή ἐστι τί ἦν εἶναι καὶ εἶδος αὐτὸ καθ' αὑτὸ ἀλλὰ τόδε τι. *Ibid.* xii. 8, cited p. 339, n. *supra.* This only refers, however, as has there been already remarked, to the individual members of an *infima species.*

[2] See *e.g. Metaph.* i. 6, 988, a, 1 : Plato makes matter the source

of multiplicity, καίτοι συμβαίνει γ' ἐναντίως . . . οἱ μὲν γὰρ ἐκ τῆς ὕλης πολλὰ ποιοῦσιν . . . φαίνεται δ' ἐκ μιᾶς ὕλης μία τράπεζα : which, however, Plato did not deny, since it is just because the same material gives only one specimen, that material things constitute a plurality even when there is no distinction of kind between them —as Aristotle also holds.

[3] Cf. *Metaph.* iii. 4 (cited p. 342, n. *supra)* where he says : if there were nothing but individual things, there would be nothing but sensible existence ; xii. 3, 1070, a, 9 : οὐσίαι δὲ τρεῖς, ἡ μὲν ὕλη τόδε τι οὖσα τῷ φαίνεσθαι . . . ἡ δὲ φύσις (here = εἶδος) τόδε τι. εἰς ἦν, καί ἕξις τις · ἔτι τρίτη ἡ ἐκ τούτων, ἡ καθ' ἕκαστα. *De Cœlo,* i. 9, 227, b, 30 sq. (cf. p. 219, n.) : Form as such is something different from form in the material; and if, for instance, there existed only one single circle, *the* circle would still continue to be something different from *this* circle. The one would be the εἶδος, the other εἶδος ἐν τῇ ὕλῃ καὶ τῶν καθ' ἕκαστον. ἐπεὶ οὖν ἐστιν ὁ οὐρανός αἰσθητὸς τῶν καθ' ἕκαστον ἂν εἴη. τὸ γὰρ αἰσθητὸν ἅπαν ἐν τῇ ὕλῃ ὑπῆρχεν. 'Individual reality' and εἶδος ἐν τῇ ὕλῃ here signify the same thing.

a higher value, when we recollect that Aristotle allowed substantiality in its full sense *to the Individual* alone.[1] If the Individual alone is Substance, and if Form, as we have just seen, is always universal, and if therefore the true ground of individual existence is Matter—then we cannot escape the consequence that Matter supplies the ground also of substantial being, and that it is not pure Form, but the composite result of Form and Matter which alone is Substance. Indeed, since we have defined Substance as ' the substratum ' (ὑποκείμενον)[2] and have also recognised in Matter the substratum of all Being,[3] this would seem to give Matter the right to claim that it alone should be regarded as the primitive Substance of all things. Yet it is impossible for Aristotle to admit this. Full and original reality belongs to Form alone ; Matter, on the contrary, is no more than the bare Potentiality of that whereof the Actuality is Form. Not only, therefore, is it impossible that Matter can be substantial, but from its union with Form there can be produced nothing higher than pure Form. Moreover, there are innumerable passages in which Aristotle expressly identifies Form with Substance.[4] He declares that in all primitive and absolute existences, the intelligible essence is not different from the thing to which it belongs,[5] so that it constitutes the Substance

[1] See pp. 331 sqq.
[2] See pp. 300,'333, and notes.
[3] See pp. 344 sq.
[4] *E.g.*, *Metaph.* i. 3, 983, a, 27 ; iii. 4, 999, b, 12 sqq.; vii. 4, 1030, b, 5, c. 7, 1032, b, 1, 14 (εἶδος δὲ λέγω τὸ τί ἦν εἶναι ἑκάστου καὶ τὴν πρώτην οὐσίαν . . . λέγω δ' οὐσίαν ἄνευ ὕλης τὸ

τί ἦν εἶναι), c. 10, 1035, b, 32, c. 11, 1037, a, 29, c. 17, 1041, b, 8 ; viii. 1, 1042, a, 17, c. 3, 1043, b, 10 sqq.; ix. 8, 1050, a, 5; *Gen. et Corr.* ii. 9, 335, b, 6 ; *Meteor.* iv. 2, 379, b, 26, c. 12, 390, a, 5; *Part. An.* i. 1, 641, a, 25; *Gen. An.* i. 1, 714, a, 5. Cf. p. 214, n.
[5] *Metaph.* vii. 6 in answer to

of the thing. Further, he will not suffer anything else
to be considered absolutely real except absolutely immaterial Form, or pure spirit. It is not a sufficient solution to recall the different senses in which the term
Substance (οὐσία) is used,[1] since it is not here a question
merely of the use of language but of the claim to actuality
in the full and strict sense of the word. The question is
whether we are to assign it to individual things as such,
or only to their intelligible essence, *i.e.* to a Form which
is unaffected by change in the individual thing and
remains for ever self-identical. Here we detect a difficulty, or rather a contradiction, which threatens to
shake the very foundations of the system.

Aristotle did not succeed in evading it altogether.
In his Metaphysics he asks the question where we ought
to look for the substance of things—in the Form, or in
the Matter, or in the composite Whole produced by

the question (1031, a, 15) πότερον
ταὐτόν ἐστιν ἢ ἕτερον τὸ τί ἦν
εἶναι ἢ ἕκαστον; it is said that
they are different only in the
case in which a conception belongs to a thing κατὰ συμβεβηκὸς
(as mere predicate), whereas on
the other hand when the conception expresses the essence of the
thing itself they are one and
the same. *E.g.* the conception of
whiteness is different from the
λευκὸς ἄνθρωπος; on the other
hand the ἑνὶ εἶναι is not different
from the ἕν, the ἀγαθῷ εἶναι from
the ἀγαθὸν, nor again (c. 10, 1036,
a, 1, cf. viii. 3, 1043, b, 2) the
κύκλῳ εἶναι from the κύκλος,
the ψυχῇ εἶναι from the ψυχή.
Otherwise (not to mention other
reasons) conceptions would not

exist, things would not be known
(τῶν μὲν οὐκ ἔσται ἐπιστήμη, τὰ
δ' οὐκ ἔσται ὄντα 1031, b, 3).
This holds of all ὅσα μὴ κατ' ἄλλο
λέγεται, ἀλλὰ καθ' αὐτὰ καὶ πρῶτα.
1031, b, 13, cf. 1032, a, 5 : τῶν
πρώτων καὶ καθ' αὐτὰ λεγομένων τὸ
ἑκάστῳ εἶναι καὶ ἕκαστον τὸ αὐτὸ
καὶ ἕν ἐστι; c. 11, 1037, a, 33 sqq.
[1] Cf. the following notes and
Metaph. v. 8, 1017, b, 23 :
συμβαίνει δὴ κατὰ δύο τρόπους τὴν
οὐσίαν λέγεσθαι, τό θ' ὑποκείμενον
ἔσχατον, ὃ μηκέτι κατ' ἄλλου
λέγεται, καὶ ὃ ἂν τόδε τι ὂν καὶ
χωριστὸν ᾖ · [where, however, as
SCHWEGLER and BONITZ rightly
remark upon this passage, we
can only understand the λόγῳ
χωριστὸν to be meant; on which
cf. viii. 1 ; see p. 369, n. 6, *supra*]

the combination of both.[1] But his answer is far
from satisfactory. He admits that Matter cannot
properly be termed Substance,[2] yet, on the other hand,
he does not venture to deprive it altogether of this title,
since it is the substratum of all Being, the permanent
amid change.[3] Nor is it sufficient to maintain that
Matter is substantial in a different sense from Form,
the latter being actually, the former only potentially so;[4] for how can we conceive of a Substance

τοιοῦτον δὲ ἑκάστου ἡ μορφὴ καὶ
τὸ εἶδος.
  [1] VII. 3 init. (cf. at p. 370):
we may use ' substance ' in various ways: as equivalent to the
τί ἦν εἶναι, the καθόλου, the γένος,
the ὑποκείμενον. By the last,
again, we may understand either
the ὕλη or the μορφὴ or the composite product of both. Of
these, however, the καθόλου, and
with it the γένος (on the relation
of which to the κ2θόλου, see p.
213 sq.), are quietly set aside,
c. 13 (cf. p. 333, supra) and
since the μορφὴ coincides with
the τί ἦν εἶναι there only remain
the three above-mentioned significations of οὐσία. Cf. c. 13
init., viii. 1, 1042, a, 26 sqq.;
ibid. c. 2; De An. ii. 1 (see p.
369, n. 6, supra); Ind. Arist. 545,
a, 23 sq.
  [2] Metaph. vii. 3, 1029, a, 27,
after adducing several reasons
in support of the view that the
substance = the matter, he goes
on: ἀδύνατον δέ· καὶ γὰρ τὸ
χωριστὸν καὶ τὸ τόδε τι ὑπάρχειν
δοκεῖ μάλιστα τῇ οὐσίᾳ, διὸ τὸ
εἶδος καὶ τὸ ἐξ ἀμφοῖν οὐσία δόξειεν
ἂν εἶναι μᾶλλον τῆς ὕλης. Cf.
further, p. 345 sqq.
  [3] Metaph. viii. 1, 1042, a, 32:

ὅτι δ' ἐστὶν οὐσία καὶ ἡ ὕλη δῆλον.
ἐν πάσαις γὰρ ταῖς ἀντικειμέναις
μεταβολαῖς ἐστί τι τὸ ὑποκείμενον
ταῖς μεταβολαῖς. Cf. p. 344. Ibid. ix.
7, 1049, a, 34 : the substratum of
the τόδε τι is ὕλη καὶ οὐσία ὑλική;
vii. 10, 1035, a, 1 : εἰ οὖν ἐστὶ τὸ
μὲν ὕλη τὸ δ' εἶδος τὸ δ' ἐκ τούτων,
καὶ οὐσία ἥ τε ὕλη καὶ τὸ εἶδος καὶ
τὸ ἐκ τούταν. Phys. i. 9, 192,
a, 3 (cf. pp. 342 sqq. and notes) :
ἡμεῖς μὲν γὰρ ὕλην καὶ στέρησιν
ἕτερόν φαμεν εἶναι, καὶ τούτων τὸ
μὲν οὐκ ὂν εἶναι κατὰ συμβεβηκὸς,
τὴν ὕλην, τὴν δὲ στέρησιν καθ'
αὐτὴν, καὶ τὴν μὲν ἐγγὺς καὶ οὐσίαν
πως, τὴν ὕλην, τὴν δὲ στέρησιν
οὐδαμῶς. De An ii. 1 (see p. 669,
n. 6, supra).
  [4] Metaph. viii. 1, 1042, a, 26 :
ἔστι δ' οὐσία τὸ ὑποκείμενον, ἄλλως
μὲν ἡ ὕλη, . . . ἄλλως δ' ὁ λόγος
καὶ ἡ μορφὴ, . . . τρίτον δὲ τὸ ἐκ
τούτων; c. 2 init.: ἐπεὶ δ' ἡ μὲν
ὡς ὑποκειμένη καὶ ὡς ὕλη οὐσία
ὁμολογεῖται, αὕτη δ' ἐστὶν ἡ δυνάμει,
λοιπὸν τὴν ὡς ἐνέργειαν οὐσίαν τῶν
αἰσθητῶν εἰπεῖν τίς ἐστιν. Ibid.
fin. : φανερὸν δὴ ἐκ τῶν εἰρημένων
τίς ἡ αἰσθητὴ οὐσία ἐστὶ καὶ πῶς·
ἡ μὲν γὰρ ὡς ὕλη, ἡ δ' ὡς μορφὴ,
ὅτι ἐνέργεια· ἡ δὲ τρίτη ἡ ἐκ
τούτων; xiv. 1, 1088. b, 1 (against
the Platonic doctrine of an abso-

which is merely potential : that is, an absolute existence which does not yet actually exist? If we grant that Form is the proper Substance of things, actual existence in the highest sense, and that as such it is opposed not only to Matter but also to the composite product of Matter and Form,[1] yet Aristotle has done nothing at all to show how this is possible, considering that Form in itself is always a Universal, that the Individual is always burdened with Matter, and that Substance is originally individual Substance. In like manner he fails to tell us how mere Form can be the essence and substance of things which cannot be conceived apart from a definite material composition;[2] or again how Matter devoid of quality and determination can produce the individual determinateness of particular existences which are not related to each other as so many impressions of a die but are differentiated from one another qualitatively by definite properties. Finally, it is not easy to see why birth and extinction should pertain to things that are the joint product of Form and Matter, and yet not to Form

---

lutely great and small) : ἀνάγκη τε ἑκάστου ὕλην εἶναι τὸ δυνάμει τοιοῦτον, ὥστε καὶ οὐσίας · τὸ δὲ πρός τι οὔτε δυνάμει οὐσία οὔτε ἐνεργείᾳ.

[1] *Metaph.* viii. 3 *init.*: ἐνίοτε λανθάνει πότερον σημαίνει τὸ ὄνομα τὴν σύνθετον οὐσίαν ἢ τὴν ἐνέργειαν καὶ τὴν μορφήν, οἷον ἡ οἰκία πότερον σημεῖον τοῦ κοινοῦ ὅτι σκέπασμα ἐκ πλίνθων καὶ λίθων ὡδὶ κειμένων, ἢ τῆς ἐνεργείας καὶ τοῦ εἴδους ὅτι σκέπασμα ; vii. 3, 1029, a, 5 : εἰ τὸ εἶδος τῆς ὕλης πρότερον καὶ μᾶλλον ὄν, καὶ τοῦ ἐξ ἀμφοῖν ᾳρότερον ἔσται ; line 29 : τὸ εἶδος καὶ τὸ ἐξ ἀμφοῖν οὐσία δόξειεν ἂν

εἶναι μᾶλλον τῆς ὕλης. τὴν μὲν τοίνυν ἐξ ἀμφοῖν οὐσίαν, λέγω δὲ τὴν ἔκ τε τῆς ὕλης καὶ τῆς μορφῆς, ἀφετέον · ὑστέρα γὰρ καὶ δήλη.

[2] Aristotle frequently distinguishes between conceptions of pure form and of form inherent in a definite material ; the standing example of the latter is the σιμὸν as distinguished from the κοῖλον ; so also axe, saw, house, statue, and even soul. Cf. *Phys.* ii. 1, 194, a, 12, ii. 9 *fin.* *De An.* i. 1, 403, b, 2, ii. 1, 412, b, 11. *Metaph.* vii. 5, c. 10, 1035, a, 1 sqq. b, 74, c. 11, 1037, a, 29.

or Matter separately.[1] For even if we can suppose that Matter as such had no beginning, it is hard to imagine that the Forms of created things were uncreated, if they neither exist independently as Ideas nor are originally inherent in Matter. All these difficulties exhibit the same conclusion that we discerned in dealing with the notion of Substance. The fact is that Aristotle combines in his Metaphysics two different points of view, which he fails to harmonise. On the one side he adheres to the Socratico-Platonic principle that the true essence of things is to be found in their Concept, and this is always Universal. On the other side he acknowledges that this Universal has no existence apart from the Individual, which he therefore declares to be the Substance. He cannot explain how these two positions may coexist in one philosophy, and hence the above-mentioned contradictions arise. At one time the Form, at another the Individual which is the product of the union of Form and Matter, appears to be the Actual. Matter causes results incompatible with mere Potentiality. It is represented at the same time as indefinite Universality and as the ground of individual determinateness. So the un-

---

[1] *Metaph.* vii. 15 cited at p. 219, n. 4, *supra*, and the passage from c. 10 cited at p. 366, n. 1; *ibid.* viii. 1, 1042, a, 29 : τρίτον δὲ τὸ ἐκ τούτων [form and matter], οὗ γένεσις μόνου καὶ φθορά ἐστι ; c. 3, 1043, b, 10 : οὐδὲ δὴ ὁ ἄνθρωπός ἐστι τὸ ζῷον καὶ δίπουν, ἀλλά τι δεῖ εἶναι ὃ παρὰ ταῦτά ἐστιν, εἰ ταῦθ' ὕλη . . . ἡ οὐσία· ὃ ἐξαιροῦντες τὴν ὕλην λέγουσιν. εἰ οὖν τοῦτ' αἴτιον τοῦ εἶναι καὶ οὐσίας [so BONITZ], τοῦτο αὐτὴν ἂν τὴν

οὐσίαν λέγοιεν. ἀνάγκη δὴ ταύτην ἢ ἀΐδιον εἶναι ἢ φθαρτὴν ἄνευ τοῦ φθείρεσθαι καὶ γεγονέναι ἄνευ τοῦ γίγνεσθαι . . . τὸ εἶδος οὐδεὶς ποιεῖ οὐδὲ γεννᾷ, ἀλλὰ ποιεῖται τόδε γίγνεται δὲ τὸ ἐκ τούτων ; c. 5 *init.* : ἐπεὶ δ' ἔνια ἄνευ γενέσεως καὶ φθορᾶς ἔστι καὶ οὐκ ἔστιν, οἷον αἱ στιγμαί, εἴπερ εἰσὶν, καὶ ὅλως τὰ εἴδη καὶ αἱ μορφαί, οὐ γὰρ τὸ λευκὸν γίγνεται, ἀλλὰ τὸ ξύλον λευκόν. Cf. pp. 341 sqq., and notes there.

certainty goes on, until we cease to wonder that Aristotle's doctrine of Matter and Form, Particular and Universal, received the most various interpretations and supported the most contradictory assertions not only among the Greek Peripatetics but also and to a far greater extent among the logicians of the Middle Ages.

Yet the doctrine is of vital importance to the System. Aristotle finds the best solution of the difficulties which perplexed earlier philosophers in his distinction between Form and Matter, Potential and Actual. By means of this distinction he explains how Unity can also be Multiplicity; how the Genus and Differences form one Concept; how the many Individuals constitute one Species; how Soul and Body make one Being.[1] It is this alone which enables him to solve the problem of Becoming, over which Plato as well as all others had stumbled. Indeed, the distinction of which we are speaking serves especially, as has been seen, for the elucidation of this problem. Form and Matter being related to each other as Actual and Potential, they are in a position of essential correlation; the notion of the Potential implies the possibility of its becoming Actual; the notion of the Actual implies that it is the Actuality of the Potential. Everything that is to become actual must be potential; and conversely everything that is potential must at some time or other become actual, since what is never to be actual cannot be called potential.[2] Nor does Aristotle mean

---

[1] Cf. pp. 219, n. 2, 351, n. 1, and 369, n. 5. *De An.* ii. 1, 412, b, 6, c. 2, 414, a, 19 sqq.

[2] Aristotle, indeed (*Metaph.* ix. 3) controverts the Megarian assertion that a thing is potential only so long as it is actual; but he forbids us also to say (*ibid.* c. 4 *init.*) ὅτι δυνατὸν μὲν τοδὶ οὐκ ἔσται δὲ, since this could only

by Potentiality any mere logical or formal but also real Potentiality. Matter is in itself or in its capacity that whereof the Actuality is Form; and consequently Matter of itself implies Form, requires Form, owns a natural inclination or longing (as Aristotle expresses it) for it, is provoked by it to move and develop itself.[1] On the other hand Form is that which gives completeness to Matter by realising its potential capacities; it is the Energy or Entelechy of Matter.[2] But the

be said of that which by its very nature could not be; but this could not be potential, and he therefore denies (as was pointed out at p. 366, n. 1) that in things of eternal duration there can be any potentiality without actuality.

[1] Cf. the passage, *Phys.* 1, 9, quoted p. 314, n. 1. Matter is said by nature ἐφίεσθαι καὶ ὀρέγεσθαι τοῦ θείου καὶ ἀγαθοῦ καὶ ἐφετοῦ, and this is the principle upon which we must explain the movement of the world by God and of the body by the soul. Cf. such expressions as *Metaph.* xii. 7, 1072, b, 3 : κινεῖ ὡς ἐρώμενον; *ibid.* a, 26 : τὸ ὀρεκτὸν καὶ τὸ νοητὸν κινεῖ οὐ κινούμενον. The longing referred to is no conscious desire, but a mere natural impulse, and is frequently referred to by Aristotle as the cause of the natural movements of bodies. Thus (*Phys.* ii. 1, 192, b, 18) we are told : a work of art οὐδεμ'αν ὁρμὴν ἔχει μεταβολῆς ἔμφυτον, whereas the product of nature has. Cf. *Metaph.* v. 23, 1023, a, 8, where κατὰ τὴν αὐτοῦ φύσιν and κατὰ τὴν αὐτοῦ ὁρμὴν are parallel phrases; *Anal. Post.* ii. 11, 94, b, 37, where inner necessity, ἀνάγκη κατὰ τὴν

φύσιν καὶ ὁρμὴν, is distinguished from compulsion, ἀνάγκη παρὰ τὴν ὁρμὴν, and the falling of a stone quoted as an example of the former (similarly *Metaph.* v. 5, 1015, a 26, b, 1, c. 23, 1023, a, 17 sq., xii. 7, 1072, b, 12; cf. HERTLING, *Mat. u. Form*, 91). Nevertheless we cannot but recognise in the use of these expressions the psychological analogy from which the terminology is borrowed, reminding us as it does of the earlier hylozoism.

[2] Aristotle as a rule makes no distinction between these two terms (see TRENDELENBURG, *De An.* 296 sq.; SCHWEGLER, *Arist. Metaph.* iv. 221 sq., 173 sq.; BONITZ, *Ind. Arist.* 253, b, 35 sqq., also p. 348, n. *supra*), and if he seems to do so in individual passages, yet is the distinction of each from the other so loosely defined that in different passages the same is assigned to both. Thus motion is usually called the entelecheia of matter, the soul the entelecheia of the body (cf. *Phys.* iii. 1, 200, b, 26, 201, a, 10, 17, 28, 30, b, 4; viii. 1, 251, a, 9; *De An.* ii. i. 412, a, 10, 21, 27, b, 5, 9, 28, 413, a, 5 sqq., c. 4,

Entelechy of Matter or the actualisation of Potentiality is Motion.[1] The correlation therefore of Form and Matter leads us to consider Motion and its Causes.

(3) *Motion and the first Cause of Motion.*

Aristotle has himself explained what he meant by the definition we have quoted. Motion is the Entelechy of that which exists potentially—in other words, it is

415, b, 4 sqq.) ; yet *Metaph.* ix. 6, 8 (1048, b, 6 sqq., cf. l. 1, 1050, a, 30 sqq.) motion is defined as energetic, and yet again (*ibid.* c. 6, 1048, b, 18 sqq.) it is said to differ from energy as the incomplete from the complete, so that only such activity as contains its own end in itself, *e.g.* sight, thought, life, happiness, is called energeia, while on the other hand that which is subordinate to an end outside itself and ceases with its attainment, *e.g.* building, walking, &c., is called motion. (On these two kinds of activities, *v.* also c. 8, 1050, a, 23 sqq.) *Metaph.* ix. 3, 1047, a, 30 again seems to appropriate ἐντελέχεια to the state of completion, ἐνέργεια to the activity directed to its attainment, or to motion (δοκεῖ γὰρ ἐγέργεια μάλιστα ἡ κίνησις εἶναι), and so c. 8, 1050, a, 22. Also *De An.* ii. 5, 417, b, 4, 7, 10, 418, a, 4, ἐντελέχεια stands for the completed state (That *Metaph.* xi. 9, 1065, b, 16, 33, repeatedly uses ἐνέργεια where *Phys.* iii. 1 has ἐντελέχεια, is of no importance, on account of the spuriousness of the former passage.) Elsewhere motion is called ἐνέργεια ἀτελὴς, ἐν. τοῦ ἀτελοῦς, and as such is distinguished from the ἀπλῶς ἐνέρ-

γεια τοῦ τετελεσμένου (cf. n. 1 at p 383 *infra*). But ἐντελέχεια is used also in this sense, *e.g. De An.* ii. 5, 417, a, 28, and the same expression occurs *Metaph.* xii. 8, 1074, a, 35, c. 5, 1071, a, 36, as applied to the pure, immaterial form, viz. God. *Phys.* iii. 3 *init.* the action of the moving cause is called ἐνέργεια, the change effected in that which is moved ἐντελέχεια, a use which seems quite proper, as the latter and not the former is brought to completion by motion ; yet in the passage that follows ἐντελέχεια is used of both, and in *Metaph.* ix. 8, 1030, a, 30 sqq. it is said, with reference to the two kinds of activities distinguished above : in the case of those whose end is outside of themselves, the energeia is in that which is moved ; in the case of the others, in that which acts. It is therefore impossible to point to any fixity in the language used to express the distinction between these two terms.

[1] *Phys.* iii. 1, 201, a, 10, b, 4 : ἡ τοῦ δυνάμει ὄντος ἐντελέχεια ᾗ τοιοῦτον, κίνησίς ἐστιν . . . ἡ τοῦ δυνατοῦ, ᾗ δυνατὸν, ἐντελέχεια φανερὸν ὅτι κίνησίς ἐστιν ; c. 2, 202, b, 7 : ἡ κίνησις ἐντελέχεια τοῦ

the process by which that which existed previously only
in capacity is brought to reality, the determination of
Matter by Form, the transition from Potentiality to
Actuality.[1] The movement of building, for example,
consists in fashioning the materials of which a house
can be made, into an actual house. But motion is the
entelechy of potential existence only *qua* potential and
not in any other relation. The movement of the brass,
for instance, out of which a statue is cast, does not concern it in so far as it is brass—for *qua* brass it remains
unaltered and has always had a certain sort of actuality—
but only in so far as it contains the potentiality of being
made into a statue.[2] This distinction, however, can, it

κινητοῦ ᾗ κινητόν ; viii. 1, 251, a, 9 :
φαμὲν δὴ τὴν κίνησιν εἶναι ἐντελέχειαν τοῦ κινητοῦ ᾗ κινητόν. So
Metaph. xi. 9, 1065, b, 16, 33 ; see
preceding note.

[1] That only this transition and
not the condition attained by
means of it, only the process of
actualisation, not the actuality, is
meant by the expression entelecheia or energeia is obvious not
less from the nature of the case
itself than from the repeated
description of motion as an un-
completed energy or entelechy
(see pp. 383, n. 1, 379, n. 2). The
same distinction elsewhere occurs.
Pleasure, *e.g.*, is said not to be a
movement, because a movement
is at each moment incomplete,
whereas pleasure is complete. The
former is the pursuit, the latter
the attainment, of the end, a
result of the completed activity.
Eth. N. x. 3, 4, vii. 13, 1153, a, 12.

[2] In this way the previously
quoted definition is explained,

Phys. iii. 1, 201, a, 9, sqq. (and
therefore *Metaph.* xi. 9, 1065, b,
sqq.). BRENTANO'S explanation
(*Von der mannigf. Bedeutung des
Seienden nach Arist.* p. 58), according to which motion is the
actuality which transforms a
potential being into 'this potential being,' or 'which constitutes
or forms a potential as potential,'
is without support either in Aristotle's use of terms or in actual
fact. For, in the first place, the
entelechy of the δυνάμει ὂν is not
that by which the δυν. ὂν first
comes into being ; and, in the
second place, when, *e.g.*, the
bronze which is potentially a
statue is formed into the statue,
its κίνησις does not consist in its
becoming δυνάμει ἀνδριὰς, *i.e.*
bronze. Aristotle, however, has
stated the meaning of his definition unambiguously in the
passage immediately following,
and so has the author of
Metaph. xi. 9.

is clear, be only applied to the case of special or particular movement; for such movement is always carried on in material that has already an actuality of some sort of its own. If, on the other hand, we take the *general* notion of movement, it may be defined as the process by which Potentiality is actualised, the development of Matter by Form, since the material *qua* material is mere Potentiality which has not yet in any respect arrived at Actuality. This definition includes all Alteration of every kind, all coming into being and destruction. It does not, however, apply to absolute origination and annihilation, for this would necessitate the birth or destruction of matter, which is never assumed by Aristotle.[1] It follows from what we have said, that when he refuses to regard becoming and decaying as forms of motion, maintaining that though every motion is change, all change is not motion[2]—this distinction must be accepted as a relative one which does not hold of the general idea of motion; and so Aristotle himself on other occasions[3] employs motion and change as synonymous terms. The doctrine, however, of the different kinds of motion belongs to Physics.

We have seen that motion is intermediate between potential and actual being; it is Potentiality struggling into Actuality, and Actuality not yet freed from Potentiality—in other words, imperfect Actuality. It is distinguished from mere Potentiality by being an Entelechy, and from an Energy in its strictest sense by the fact that in Energy the activity which is directed

---

[1] See pp. 341 sqq. *supra.*
[2] *Phys.* v. 1, 225, a, 20, 34, and *passim*; see *infra.*
[3] *E.g. Phys.* iii. 1, 201, a, 9 sqq. c. 2 *init.* iv. 10 *fin.* viii. 7, 261, a, 9, and *passim.*

to an object has also attained its object—thought, for instance, is both a process of search and also a mental possession of the object of thought—whereas motion ceases in the attainment of the object, and is therefore only an unaccomplished effort.[1] Hence each particular motion is a transition from one state of being into an opposite—from that which a thing ceases to be into that which it has to become. Where there is no opposite, there is also no change.[2] Consequently all motion implies two principles—that which moves, and that which is moved, an actual and a potential being.

Mere Potentiality is unable to produce motion, for it lacks Energy : and so likewise is pure Actuality, since it contains nothing imperfect and undeveloped. Motion can only be conceived as the operation of the Actual or

---

[1] *Phys.* iii. 2, 201, b, 27 : τοῦ δὲ δοκεῖν ἀόριστον εἶναι τὴν κίντσιν αἴτιον ὅτι οὔτε εἰς δύναμιν τῶν ὄντων οὔτε εἰς ἐνέργειαν ἔστι θεῖναι αὐτὴν ἁπλῶς· οὔτε γὰρ τὸ δυνατὸν ποσὸν εἶναι κινεῖται ἐξ ἀνάγκης οὔτε τὸ ἐνεργε'α ποσὸν, ἥ τε κ'νησις ἐνέργεια μέν τις εἶναι δοκεῖ, ἀτελὴς δέ· αἴτιον δ' ὅτι ἀτελὲς τὸ δυνατὸν, οὗ ἐστὶν ἡ ἐνέργεια. It is therefore neither a στέρησις, nor a δύναμις. nor an ἐνέργεια ἁπλῆ (So *Metaph.* xi. 9, 1066, a, 17.) VIII 5, 257, b, 6 : κινεῖται τὸ κινητόν· τοῦτο δ' ἐστὶ δυνάμει κινούμενον οὐκ ἐντελεχείᾳ· τὸ δὲ δυνάμει εἰς ἐντελέχειαν βαδίζει. ἔστι δ' ἡ κίνησις ἐντελέχεια κινητοῦ ἀτελής· τὸ δὲ κινοῦν ἤδη ἐνεργείᾳ ἐστ'ν. *Metaph.* ix. 6, 1048, b, 17 : ἐπεὶ δὲ τῶν πράξεων ὧν ἐστὶ πέρας οὐδεμία τέλος ἀλλὰ τῶν περὶ τὸ τέλος, οἷον τοῦ ἰσχναίνειν ἡ ἰσχνασία, αὐτὰ δὲ ὅταν ἰσχναίνη οὕτως ἐστὶν ἐν κινήσει,μὴ ὑπάρχοντα

ὧν ἕνεκα ἡ κίνησις, οὐκ ἔστι ταῦτα πρᾶξις ἡ οὐ τελεία γε· οὐ γὰρ τέλος, ἀλλ' ἐκείνη ἐνυπάρχει τὸ τέλος καὶ ἡ πρᾶξις . . . οὐ γὰρ ἅμα βαδίζει καὶ βεβάδικεν, οὐδ' οἰκοδομεῖ καὶ ᾠκοδόμηκεν, &c. ἑώρακε δὲ καὶ ὁρᾷ ἅμα τὸ αὐτὸ καὶ νοεῖ καὶ νενόηκεν· τὴν μὲν οὖν τοιαύτην ἐνέργειαν λέγω, ἐκείνην δὲ κ'νησιν. Cf. c. 8, 1050, a, 23 sqq. and p. 379, n. 2, *supra* ; *De An.* ii. 5, 417, a, 16 : καὶ γὰρ ἔστιν ἡ κίνησις ἐνέργειά τις ἀτελὴς μέντοι ; iii. 7, 431, a, 6 : ἡ γὰρ κίνησις τοῦ ἀτελοῦς ἐνέργεια ἦν, ἡ δ' ἁπλῶς ἐνέργεια ἐτέρα ἡ τοῦ τετελεσμένου

[2] *Phys.* v. 1, 224, b. 26 sqq. 225, a, 10 ; *Metaph.* viii. 1, 1042, a, 32, xii. 2, 1069, a, 13: εἰς ἐναντιώσεις ἂν εἶεν τὰς καθέκαστον αἱ μεταβολαί· ἀνάγκη δὴ μεταβάλλειν τὴν ὕλην δυναμένην ἄμφω· ἐπεὶ δὲ διττὸν τὸ ὄν, μεταβάλλει πᾶν ἐκ τοῦ δυνάμει ὄντος εἰς τὸ ἐνεργείᾳ ὄν. Cf. p. 342 sqq.

Form upon the Potential or Matter:[1] even in that
which moves itself we always find the motive force
separate from what it moves, just as in living creatures
the soul is different from the body, and in the soul itself,
as we shall see below, the active part is different from
the passive.[2] While Becoming, therefore, is impossible
without matter or potential being, some Actuality is not
less indispensable as an antecedent and motive cause.
Even in cases where an individual has developed itself
from mere Potentiality to Actuality, and consequently
the former principle precedes the latter in *it*, yet another
individual must have come before it in actual existence.
The organic individual is produced from seed, but the

---

[1] *Phys.* iii. 2 (p. 383, n. 1), viii.
5, 257, b, 8; *Metaph.* ix. 8 esp. 1050,
b, 8 sqq. xii. 3; *Phys.* vii. 1 : ἅπαν
τὸ κινούμενον ὑπό τινος ἀνάγκη
κινεῖσθαι: even in the case of
that which apparently is self-
moved, the material which is
moved cannot be at the same
time the moving cause, since if
a part of it is at rest the whole
of it must also be at rest ; but
neither can rest and movement
in the self-moved be dependent
on anything else. The true explanation is to be found in the
above account, and *Phys.* iii. 2 ;
Gen et Corr. ii. 9 : neither form
in itself nor matter in itself explains becoming ; τῆς μὲν γὰρ
ὕλης τὸ πάσχειν ἐστὶ καὶ τὸ
κινεῖσθαι, τὸ δὲ ποιεῖν καὶ κινεῖν
ἑτέρας δυνάμεως.   See further,
p. 341 sqq.
[2] See preceding note and *Phys.*
iii. 4, 255, a, 12 : it is impossible
that a συνεχὲς καὶ συμφυὲς should
be self-moved ; ᾗ γὰρ ἓν καὶ
συνεχὲς μὴ ἁφῇ, ταύτῃ ἀπαθές [cf.

Metaph. ix. 1, 1046, a, 28] · ἀλλ᾽
ᾗ κεχώρισται, ταύτῃ τὸ μὲν πέφυκε
ποιεῖν τὸ δὲ πάσχειν.   Nothing
that is single, therefore, is self-
moved, ἀλλ᾽ ἀνάγκη διῃρῆσθαι τὸ
κινοῦν ἐν ἑκάστῳ πρὸς τὸ κινούμενον
οἷον ἐπὶ τῶν ἀψύχων ὁρῶμεν, ὅταν
κινῇ τι τῶν ἐμψύχων αὐτά · ἀλλὰ
συμβαίνει καὶ ταῦτα ὑπό τινος ἀεὶ
κινεῖσθαι. γένοιτο δ᾽ ἂν φανερὸν
διαιροῦσι τὰς αἰτίας : c. 3 257, b, 2 ;
ἀδύνατον δὴ τὸ αὐτὸ αὑτό κινοῦν
πάντῃ κινεῖν αὐτὸ αὑτό · φέροιτο
γὰρ ἂν ὅλον καὶ φέροι τὴν αὐτὴν
φορὰν, ἓν ὂν καὶ ἄτομον τῷ εἴδει,
&c., ἔτι διώρισται ὅτι κινεῖται τὸ
κινητόν, &c. (see p. 383, n. 1).
Therefore, we certainly hear nothing in Aristotle of any 'Identity
of   Mover and Moved' (BIESE,
Phil. d. Arist. i. 402, 7, 481)
nor does the existence of something which at the same time
moves and is moved (*Phys.* iii. 2,
202, a, 3 and above) in any way
prove it, if the above explanations are true.

seed is contributed by another individual—the egg is
not antecedent to the hen.[1] Conversely, where an actual
meets with a potential being, and no obstruction from
without intervenes, then the corresponding motion is
necessarily produced.[2] The object in which this process
takes place is the thing moved or Matter; that by which
it is effected is the motive power or Form. Motion,
therefore, is the common function of both, though it takes

[1] *Metaph.* ix. 8, 1049, b, 24 :
ἀεὶ ἐκ τοῦ δυνάμει ὄντος γίγνεται τὸ
ἐνεργείᾳ ὂν ὑπὸ ἐνεργείᾳ ὄντος, οἷον
ἄνθρωπος ἐξ ἀνθρώπου, μουσικὸς ὑπὸ
μουσικοῦ, ἀεὶ κινοῦντός τινος πρώτου.
1050, b, 3 : φανερὸν ὅτι πρότερον τῇ
οὐσίᾳ ἐνέργεια δυνάμεως · καὶ ὥσπερ
εἴπομεν, τοῦ χρόνου ἀεὶ προλαμβάνει
ἐνέργεια ἑτέρα πρὸ ἑτέρας ἕως τῆς
τοῦ ἀεὶ κινοῦντος πρώτως. xii. 3,
(cited in note to p. 356, *supra*) ;
xii. 5, 1071, b, 22 sqq. c. 6, 1072,
a, 9 : πρότερον ἐνέργεια δυνάμεως . . .
εἰ δὲ μέλλει γένεσις καὶ φθορὰ εἶναι,
ἄλλο δεὶ εἶναι ἀεὶ ἐνεργοῦν ἄλλως
καὶ ἄλλως. *Gen. An.* ii. 1, 734, b,
21 : ὅσα φύσει γίνεται ἢ τέχνῃ ὑπ᾽
ἐνεργείᾳ ὄντος γίνεται ἐκ τοῦ δυνάμει
τοιούτου. *Phys.* iii. 2 *fin.* : εἶδος
δὲ ἀεὶ οἴσεταί τι τὸ κινοῦν, . . . ὃ
ἔσται ἀρχὴ καὶ αἴτιον τῆς κινήσεως,
ὅταν κινῇ, οἷον ὁ ἐντελεχείᾳ ἄνθρωπος ποιεῖ ἐκ τοῦ δυνάμει ὄντος
ἀνθρώπου ἄνθρωπον. *Ibid.* c. 7 ;
viii. 9, 265, a, 22 ; *Metaph.* vii. 7,
c. 9 *fin.*, ix. 9 *fin.*, xii. 7, 1072, b,
30 sqq.; *De An.* ii. 4 *init.* iii. 7
init. ; cf. also p. 355-6, *supra*.

[2] *Phys.* viii. 4, 255, a, 34 sqq.
Only an apparent exception to
this is introduced by *Metaph.* ix.
5, where it is said (1047, b, 35):
we must distinguish between
irrational and rational forces ;

κἀκείνας . . . ἀνάγκη, ὅταν ὡς
δύνανται [under the conditions
which limit their activity and pas-
sivity] τὸ ποιητικὸν καὶ τὸ παθητικὸν
πλησιάζωσι, τὸ μὲν ποιεῖν τὸ δὲ πάσχειν, ἐκείνας δ᾽ οὐκ ἀνάγκη · αὐταὶ μὲν
γὰρ [the irrational] πᾶσαι μία ἑνὸς
ποιητική, ἐκείναι δὲ τῶν ἐναντίων,
ὥστε ἅμα ποιήσει τἀναντία (so that
if necessity forced this power of
choice to be exercised on both
alternatives, opposite effects must
be produced at one and the same
time). For even in the case of
the latter, so soon as the choice
has been made, the result necessarily follows : ὁπότερον γὰρ ἂν
ὀρέγηται κυρίως, τοῦτο ποιήσει,
ὅταν ὡς δύναται ὑπάρχῃ καὶ πλησιάζῃ
τῷ παθητικῷ (1048, a, 11); but
the will must decide on the one
side or the other, if the condition
of action is to be present : for to
produce opposite effects at the
same time is impossible, οὐ γὰρ
οὕτως ἔχει αὐτῶν τὴν δύναμιν οὐδ᾽
ἔστι τοῦ ἅμα ποιεῖν ἡ δύναμις (l. 22).
Finally, it follows also that the
effect is necessarily produced
when the active and passive principles are in the condition ὡς
δύνανται ποιεῖν καὶ πάσχειν ; and
the general reasons of this have
already been stated at p. 378-9.

opposite directions in each : [1] the motive power excites
the latent activity in the thing moved, while the thing
moved realises it for itself.[2] Aristotle conceives of the
operation of the motive principle upon the thing moved
as conditioned by continuous contact between them.[3]

[1] *Phys.* iii. 3, where this is
discussed at length. V. 1. 224, b,
4, *ibid.* l. 25 : ἡ κίνησις οὐκ ἐν
τῷ εἴδει ἀλλ᾽ ἐν τῷ κινουμένῳ καὶ
κινητῷ κατ᾽ ἐνέργειαν. vii. 3 : the
ἀλλοίωσις takes place only in the
material thing. *De An.* iii. 2,
426, a, 2 : εἰ δ᾽ ἔστιν ἡ κίνησις καὶ
ἡ ποίησις καὶ τὸ πάθος ἐν τῷ ποιου-
μένῳ . . . ἡ γὰρ τοῦ ποιητικοῦ καὶ
κινητικοῦ ἐνέργεια ἐν τῷ πάσχοντι
ἐγγίνεται. διὸ οὐκ ἀνάγκη τὸ κινοῦν
κινεῖσθαι . . . ἡ ποίησις καὶ ἡ πάθησις
ἐν τῷ πάσχοντι ἀλλ᾽ οὐκ ἐν τῷ
ποιοῦντι. See further p. 358–9.

[2] Cf. p. 378–9.

[3] *Phys.* iii. 2 *fin.* : ἡ κίνησις ἐντελέχεια τοῦ κινητοῦ ᾗ κινητόν· συμβαίνει δὲ τοῦτο θίξει τοῦ κινητικοῦ,
ὥσθ᾽ ἅμα καὶ πάσχει. vii. 1, 242,
b, 24, vii. 2, *init.* : τὸ δὲ πρῶτον
κινοῦν . . . ἅμα τῷ κινουμένῳ ἐστί·
λέγω δὲ τὸ ἅμα, ὅτι οὐδέν ἐστιν
αὐτῶν μεταξύ· τοῦτο γὰρ κοινὸν ἐπὶ
παντὸς κινουμένου καὶ κινοῦντός
ἐστιν—which is then shown to be
true of all kinds of motion. *Ibid.*
viii. 2, 255, a, 34, c. 1, 251, b, 1
sqq.; *Gen. et Corr.* i. 6, 322, b, 21,
c. 9, 327, a, 1; *Gen. An.* ii. 1, 734,
a, 3 : κινεῖν τε γὰρ μὴ ἁπτόμενον
ἀδύνατον ; *Metaph.* ix. 5. Cf. n. 1
supra, and p. 387, n. 3. That this
contact of the moving force with
that which is moved, is conceived
of by Aristotle as not merely a
momentary one giving the first
impulse only, but as lasting during the whole continuance of the
motion, is obvious especially
from his account of the motion

of throwing. Here the motion
of the thrown seems to continue
after contact with the thrower
has ceased. But this Aristotle
cannot admit to be the case. He
therefore assumes (*Phys.* viii.
10, 266 b, 27 sqq., 267, b, 11,
cf. iv. 8, 215, a, 14 ; *De Insomn.*
2, 459, a, 29 sqq.) that along
with the thing thrown the thrower
moves also the medium through
which it moves (*e.g.* the air or
water) and that the motion of
the thing which is moved is communicated to it from this, when
it has passed from the thrower.
But since this motion continues
after that of the thrower has
ceased, while (according to his
presupposition) the motion of the
medium must cease simultane-
ously with that of the thrower,
he adopts the curious solution
that the medium can still produce motion even when it has
itself ceased to be moved: οὐχ ἅμα
παύεται κινοῦν καὶ κινούμενον ἀλλὰ
κινούμενον μὲν ἅμα ὅταν ὁ κινῶν
παύσηται κινῶν, κινοῦν δὲ ἔτι ἐστίν
(267, a, 5). The law of inertia, according to which motion persists
until it is met by an opposing
force, was not, therefore, known
to him. How the natural motion
of the elements, which carries
each of these to its proper place,
can spring from contact with a
moving force, it would be hard
to say. By what is said of these,
however (*Phys.* viii. 4, 254, b, 33
sqq., *De Cœlo*, iv. 3 *fin.*), it is

Indeed, this appears to him so necessary that he asserts even of what is absolutely incorporeal that it acts only through contact: even thought apprehends its object by touching it [1]—the latter, however, is related to the thinking subject as Form to Matter [2]—and in like manner God, as the first cause of motion, is said, as we shall shortly see, to be in contact with the world.[3] But in what sense such expressions can be used of immaterial things, Aristotle has not further explained.

It follows from this that Motion is as eternal as Form and Matter, whose essential correlation it represents,[4] and that it has neither beginning nor end.[5] For if it had a beginning, the *movens* and the *motum* must either have existed before this beginning or not. If they did not exist, they must have come into being, and so a movement would have taken place before the first motion. If they did exist, we cannot suppose that they were at rest, since it was of their very nature to move. But if it be granted that they did move, some active force must have operated to endow them

---

not proved even that they are moved by anything else at all.

[1] Cf. p. 203, n. 3.

[2] *Metaph.* xii. 9, 1074, b, 19, 29; *De An.* iii. 4, 429, b, 22, 29 sqq.

[3] *Gen. et Corr.* i. 6, 322, b, 21: nothing can affect another without being in contact with it, and in the case of things which at the same time move and are moved, this contact must be mutual (323, a, 20 sqq.); ἔστι δ' ὡς ἐνίοτέ φαμεν τὸ κ.νοῦν ἅπτεσθαι μόνου τοῦ κινουμένου, τὸ δ' ἁπτόμε- νον μὴ ἅπτεσθαι ἁπτομένου [that

which touches is not touched by anything which touches it again] . . . ὥστε εἴ τι κινεῖ ἀκίνητον ὂν, ἐκεῖνο μὲν ἂν ἅπτοιτο τοῦ κινητοῦ, ἐκείνου δὲ οὐδέν · φαμὲν γὰρ ἐνίοτε τὸν λυποῦντα ἅπτεσθαι ἡμῶν, ἀλλ' οὐκ αὐτοὶ ἐκείνου. That this, however, is no more than a play upon words is obvious.

[4] See p. 341, n. 2, 345, n. 1.

[5] With what follows, cf. SIE- BECK, *Die Lehre d. Ar. v. d. Ewig- keit d. Welt (Untersuch z. Phil. d. Griechen* Halle, 1873, pp 137 189).

with the property of motion, and thus we should in this
case also arrive at a movement before motion. It is
equally impossible to conceive of motion as destructible.
The cessation of a movement is always conditioned by
another movement which puts an end to the first. As
in the former argument we were forced to admit a
process of change antecedent to the first, so here we
cannot escape one subsequent to the last.[1] Motion is
therefore without beginning or end; the world was
never created and it will never perish.[2]

Yet, although Motion from this point of view is infinite, there is another aspect in which it has its limitation. Since every motion presupposes a motive principle,
it follows that the idea of motion in general involves
the assumption of a first motive force which is not
moved by anything else. Without this assumption we
should be involved in an infinite series of moving causes,
which could never produce actual motion, because
they would never bring us to a first cause—and without

---

[1] The above account contains
the essence of the discussion in
Phys. viii. 1. That motion must
be eternal is also asserted in *Metaph.* xii. 6, 1071, b, 6: ἀλλ'
ἀδύνατον κίνησιν ἢ γενέσθαι ἢ
φθαρῆναι· ἀεὶ γὰρ ἦν. Further, if
Time is without beginning and
end (on this see *infra*, p. 406,
&c.) motion must be so also, since
Time, as we shall find, cannot be
conceived of apart from motion.
Cf. *Phys.* viii. 1, 251, b, 12: εἰ δή
ἐστιν ὁ χρόνος κινήσεως ἀριθμὸς ἢ
κίνησίς τις, εἴπερ ἀεὶ χρόνος ἐστίν,
ἀνάγκη καὶ κίνησιν ἀΐδιον εἶναι, and
after proving the infinity of time
in both directions he goes on at l.
26: ἀλλὰ μὴν εἴγε χρόνον, φανερὸν

ὅτι ἀνάγκη εἶναι καὶ κίνησιν, εἴπερ ὁ
χρόνος πάθος τι κινήσεως. With
reference apparently to this passage, *Metaph.* xii. 6 proceeds: οὐδὲ
χρόνον· οὐ γὰρ οἷόν τε τὸ πρότερον
καὶ ὕστερον εἶναι μὴ ὄντος χρόνου.
καὶ ἡ κίνησις ἄρα οὕτω συνεχὴς
ὥσπερ καὶ ὁ χρόνος· ἢ γὰρ τὸ αὐτὸ
ἢ κινήσεώς τι πάθος. The same
inference follows from the statement (*Phys.* vi. 6, 236, b, 32 sqq.;
Metaph. ix. 8, 1050, b, 3) that
every change and process presupposes a previous one.

[2] In this form, viz. the question as to the eternity of the
world, the present subject will
recur in Ch. IX. *infra.*

that, none of the succeeding causes could operate. This conclusion cannot be avoided by presuming that the object moved produces its own motion, since it is necessary for the motive force already to be what the object moved is to become : [1] and hence the same thing cannot at the same time and in the same relation be both moved and moving. We are forced, therefore, to admit a *primum mobile*. That principle, again, might be either something moved and therefore something self-moving, or something unmoved. The first of these cases, however, resolves itself into the second, for even in a self-impelling substance the motive force must of necessity be different from what it moves. Consequently there must be an Unmoved Substance, which is the cause of all motion.[2] Or—as this is elsewhere more briefly demonstrated—since all motion must start from a motive principle, a motion which has no beginning presupposes a motive principle which is as eternal as the motion itself, and which, as the presupposition of all motion, must be itself unmoved.[3] Thus, then, we obtain three elements : that which merely is moved and never causes motion, = Matter ; that which both causes motion and is itself moved, = Nature ; that which causes motion without itself being moved, = God.[4]

Our previous pages will have shown that this position

---

[1] Cf. p. 384, *supra*.

[2] *Phys.* viii. 5, cf. vii. 1 and ii. (a), 2, where it is agreed that neither efficient nor formal nor even final causes permit of a *regressus ad infinitum*.

[3] *Metaph.* xii. 6, 1071, b, 4 : ἀνάγκη εἶναί τινα ἀΐδιον οὐσίαν ἀκίνητον. αἵ τε γὰρ οὐσίαι πρῶται τῶν ὄντων, καὶ εἰ πᾶσαι φθαρταί,

πάντα φθαρτά. ἀλλ' ἀδύνατον κίνησιν ἢ γενέσθαι ἢ φθαρῆναι· ἀεὶ γὰρ ἦν. c. 7, 1072, a, 21 : ἔστι τι ἀεὶ κινούμενον κίνησιν ἄπαυστον . . . ἔστι τοίνυν τι καὶ ὃ κινεῖ.

[4] *Phys.* viii. 5, 256, b, 20; *Metaph.* xii. 7, 1072, a, 24 (as emended by BONITZ); *De An.* iii. 10, 433, b, 13.

is not an isolated one in Aristotle's philosophy. Actuality in the highest sense is synonymous with Pure Form devoid of Matter—the Absolute Subject which as perfect Form is at once the motive force and the end of the Universe.[1] The gradations of existence, ascending from the first formless Matter, reach their consummation in God. And this thesis actually formed the starting-point for a demonstration of the existence of God in Aristotle's treatise on Philosophy.[2] In the same work he deduced the belief in the gods from two principles—from reflection upon self-revealing traces of the divine nature in the presentiments of the soul and from the contemplation of the heavens.[3] A well-known fragment shows what stress he laid upon the witness of beauty and order in the universe to the existence of God.[4] Nor are these arguments without their justifi-

---

[1] Cf. pp. 355, &c., and the passages quoted, pp. 395 sqq., on God as highest form, pure energy and supreme end. *Metaph.* xii. 7, 1072, a, 35 : ἔστιν ἄριστον ἀεὶ [in every sphere of being] ἢ ἀνάλογον τὸ πρῶτον.

[2] SIMPL. *De Cœlo*, 130, *Schol. in Ar.* 487, a, 6 (*Ar. Fr.* 15): λέγει δὲ περὶ τούτου ἐν τοῖς περὶ Φιλοσοφίας (as to which see Ch. II. *supra*) " καθόλου γὰρ ἐν οἷς ἐστί τι βέλτιον, ἐν τούτοις ἐστί τι καὶ ἄριστον. ἐπεὶ οὖν ἐν τοῖς οὖσιν ἐστὶν ἄλλο ἄλλου βέλτιον, ἔστιν ἄρα τι καὶ ἄριστον, ὅπερ εἴη ἂν τὸ θεῖον."

[3] *Fr.* 13, b, SEXT. *Math.* ix. 20 : ᾿Αριστοτέλης δὲ ἀπὸ δυοῖν ἀρχῶν ἔννοιαν θεῶν ἔλεγε γεγονέναι ἐν τοῖς ἀνθρώποις, ἀπό τε τῶν περὶ τὴν ψυχὴν συμβαινόντων καὶ ἀπὸ τῶν μετεώρων. ἀλλ᾿ ἀπὸ μὲν τῶν περὶ τὴν ψυχὴν συμβαινόντων διὰ τοὺς ἐν

τοῖς ὕπνοις γινομένους ταύτης ἐνθουσιασμοὺς καὶ τὰς μαντείας. ὅταν γὰρ, φησὶν, ἐν τῷ ὑπνοῦν καθ᾿ ἑαυτὴν γένηται ἡ ψυχὴ, τότε τὴν ἴδιον ἀπολαβοῦσα φύσιν προμαντεύεταί τε καὶ προαγορεύει τὰ μέλλοντα. τοιαύτη δέ ἐστι καὶ ἐν τῷ κατὰ τὸν θάνατον χωρίζεσθαι τῶν σωμάτων. So Homer represents Patroclus and Hector as prophesying at death. ἐκ τούτων οὖν, φησὶν, ὑπενόησαν οἱ ἄνθρωποι εἶναί τι θεὸν τὸ καθ᾿ ἑαυτὸν [-ὸ] ἐοικὸς τῇ ψυχῇ καὶ πάντων ἐπιστημονικώτατον. ἀλλὰ δὴ καὶ ἀπὸ τῶν μετεώρων · θεασάμενοι γὰρ μεθ᾿ ἡμέραν μὲν ἥλιον περιπολοῦντα, νύκτωρ δὲ τὴν εὔτακτον τῶν ἄλλων ἀστέρων κίνησιν, ἐνόμισαν εἶναί τινα θεὸν τὸν τῆς τοιαύτης κινήσεως καὶ εὐταξίας αἴτιον.

[4] In the brilliant *Fr.* 14 (prob. also from the Π. φιλοσοφίας in

cation in his system, although there are, no doubt, certain points of them which must be interpreted in the light of a less rigid logic, or perhaps referred to an earlier form of his teaching more akin to Platonism. Presentiments which exhibit themselves in prophetic dreams and inspired states of feeling are only an obscure manifestation of the force which under the form of the Active Understanding unites the human and the divine intelligence.[1] The beauty of the world, the harmonious connection of its parts, the purpose observable in their arrangement, the splendour of the stars, and the inviolable order of their motions, point not only to astral spirits (in whom we shall have hereafter to recognise the guiding forces of the heavenly spheres), but also to a Being placed far above them, from whom alone the simple movement of the universe and the harmony between the whole and all the parts proceed.[2] Conse-

CIC. *N. D.* ii. 37, 95, which reminds us at the beginning, of Plato's picture of the dwellers in the cave (*Rep.* vii. *init.*): ' si essent, qui sub terra semper habitavissent . . . accepissent autem fama et auditione, esse quoddam numen et vim Deorum : deinde aliquo tempore, patefactis terræ faucibus, ex illis abditis sedibus evadere in hæc loca, quæ nos incolimus, atque exire potuissent : cum repente terram et maria cœlumque vidissent, nubium magnitudinem ventorumque vim cognovissent adspexissentque solem ejusque tum magnitudinem pulchritudinemque tum etiam efficientiam cognovissent, quod is diem efficeret toto cœlo luce diffusa :

cum autem terras nox opacasset, tum cœlum totum cernerent astris distinctum et ornatum lunæque luminum varietatem tum crescentis tum senescentis eorumque omnium ortus et occasus atque in omni æternitate ratos immutabilesque cursus : haec cum viderent profecto et esse Deos et haec tanta opera Deorum esse arbitrarentur.' According to CIC. *N. D.* ii. 49, 125, Aristotle seems to have pointed to the instinct of animals as a teleological argument for the being of God.

[1] For the fuller discussion of this see *infra.*

[2] Besides the passage from *De Cœlo,* i. 9 quoted *infra,* in n. 6 at p. 395, cf. *Metaph.* xii. 7, 1072, a,

quently the arguments which Aristotle puts forward,
in the passages indicated, to prove the existence of
God, though based, like those of Socrates and Plato,[1]
upon teleological principles—as well as the identification
which he elsewhere establishes between the force of
nature working to fixed ends and God[2]—are not a mere
adaptation of his views to unscientific notions, but are
in harmony with the spirit of his whole system. The

35 sqq., where God is described as
the ἄριστον or οὗ ἕνεκα, and as thus
the efficient cause of motion in
the world ; but especially c. 10,
where the question is discussed :
ποτέρως ἔχει ἡ τοῦ ὅλου φύσις τὸ
ἀγαθὸν καὶ τὸ ἄριστον, πότερον
κεχωρισμένον τι καὶ αὐτὸ καθ᾽ αὑτὸ,
ἢ τὴν τάξιν, ἢ ἀμφοτέρως, ὥσπερ
στράτευμα. In the case of an
army the good resides as well in
the general as in the order of the
whole : in the former, however, in
a still more primary sense than in
the latter. The universe is compared to an army : πάντα δὲ συν-
τέτακταί πως, ἀλλ᾽ οὐχ ὁμοίως, καὶ
πλωτὰ καὶ πτηνὰ καὶ φυτά· καὶ οὐχ
οὕτως ἔχει, ὥστε μὴ εἶναι θατέρῳ
πρὸς θάτερον μηθέν, ἀλλ᾽ ἐστί τι.
πρὸς μὲν γὰρ ἐν ἅπαντα συντέτακται,
except that each creature is more
fully subject to this order just in
proportion to the nobility of its
nature, even as in a household
the freeborn are subjected to
a stricter discipline than the
slaves. τοιαύτη γὰρ ἑκάστου ἀρχὴ
αὐτῶν ἡ φύσις ἐστίν. λέγω δ᾽ οἷον
εἴς γε τὸ διακριθῆναι ἀνάγκη ἅπασιν
ἐλθεῖν, καὶ ἄλλα οὕτως ἐστὶν ὧν
κοινωνεῖ ἅπαντα εἰς τὸ ὅλον. All
other systems are founded of
necessity upon the opposite principle : Aristotle's is the only exception, οὐ γάρ ἐστιν ἐναντίον τῷ

πρώτῳ οὐθέν (1075, b, 21, 24). If,
like Speusippus, we accept a
whole series of primary principles
we destroy the unity of all being
(see the passage, Div. I. p. 854,
1); τὰ δὲ ὄντα οὐ βούλεται πολι-
τεύεσθαι κακῶς. " οὐκ ἀγαθὸν πολυκοιρανίη · εἷς κοίρανος ἔστω."
Cf. xiv. 3, 1090, b, 19, where he is
again attacking Speusippus : οὐκ
ἔοικε δ᾽ ἡ φύσις ἐπεισοδιώδης οὖσα
ἐκ τῶν φαινομένων, ὥσπερ μοχθηρὰ
τραγῳδία. We have the same
point of view in Fr. 16, preserved
to us only by an unknown
scholiast, where Aristotle says :
given several ἀρχαί, they must be
either ordered or disordered. But
the latter is impossible, since
from disorder no natural order,
no κόσμος, could have arisen ; εἰ
δὲ τεταγμέναι. ἢ ἐξ ἑαυτῶν ἐτάχθη-
σαν ἢ ὑπὸ ἔξωθεν τινὸς αἰτίας ; but
even in the former case ἔχουσί τι
κοινὸν τὸ συνάπτον αὐτὰς κἀκεῖνο ἡ
ἀρχή. The comparison of the
order of the world with that of
an army is further developed in
SEXT. Math. ix. 26 sq., which
perhaps follows Aristotle Περὶ
φιλοσοφίας.
[1] See Div. i. p. 143 sq. 786
(ZELLER'S Plato, Eng. Tr. p. 281
sqq. 485).
[2] De Cœlo, i. 4 fin. : ὁ θεὸς καὶ
ἡ φύσις οὐδὲν μάτην ποιοῦσιν.

unity of the world and its adaptation to fixed ends can only be explained by the unity of the Supreme Cause. It is not without good reason, also, that Aristotle in his most important treatises· connected the proof of the reality of the Supreme Being with his theory of motion : for this is the point at which the Changeable is seen most directly to lean upon an Unchangeable, as itself the condition of all change.

The further characteristics of the Supreme Being may be determined from what has gone before. Motion being eternal, it must be continuous ($\sigma \upsilon \nu \varepsilon \chi \grave{\eta} s$), and so it must be one and the same throughout. But such a single motion is the product of a single *mobile* and a single *motum*. Hence the *primum mobile* is single and is as eternal as motion itself.[1] In the next place what has been said about the continuity and uniformity of motion implies that this motive principle is absolutely unmoved; since that which is moved, being itself subject to change, cannot impart an unbroken and uniform movement,[2] and consequently it is of the essence of the *primum mobile* to exclude the possibility of change.[3] It is unchangeable and absolutely necessary; and this unconditional necessity is the law by

---

[1] *Phys.* viii. 6, 259, a, 13 ; *Metaph.* xii. 8, 1073, a, 23 sqq., where in connection with the πρώτη ἀΐδιος καὶ μία κίνησις, that of the fixed stars, it is shown how single motion presupposes a single moving cause. Cf. p. 391, n. 2. On the constancy and unity of motion we shall have more to say in the next chapter.

[2] *Phys.* viii. 6, 259, b, 22, c. 10, 267, a, 24 sqq.

[3] In *Fr.* 15 (preserved to us by SIMPL. *De Cælo*, 130, 45, K., *Schol. in Ar.* 487, a, 6), from the treatise Π. φιλοσοφίας, the immutability of God is proved on the ground that the κράτιστον can neither suffer change from anything else nor feel in itself the need of any such change. (It must be granted to BERNAYS, *Dial. d. Arist.* 113, and HEITZ, *Ar. Fragm.* p. 37, that

which the universe is held together.[1] It is further involved in this that it is incorporeal. Only that is indestructible which cannot possibly cease to be ; on the other hand all that is merely potential is by nature destructible ;[2] only that can operate as *primum mobile* in which there is no element of unrealised possibility.[3] But the Potential is necessarily material. A Being that contains in itself nothing that is merely potential must

this amplification also belongs to the Aristotelian fragment. The passage in PLATO's *Republic*, ii. 380, D sqq., as Simpl. remarked, served as the original of it.) The same reason is assigned also in the *De Cœlo*, i. 9 (see p. 395, n. 6) for the immutability of God, and in *Metaph.* xii. 9, 1074, b, 26, for the doctrine that God must always think the same thing; cf. p. 397, n. 2.

[1] *Metaph.* xii. 7, 1072, b, 7 : ἐπεὶ δ' ἐστί τι κινοῦν αὐτὸ ἀκίνητον ὄν, ἐνεργείᾳ ὄν, τοῦτο οὐκ ἐνδέχεται ἄλλως ἔχειν οὐδαμῶς ... ἐξ ἀνάγκης ἄρα ἐστὶν ὄν · καὶ ᾗ ἀνάγκῃ καλῶς [*i.e.* in so far as it is necessary it is good, since, as is immediately explained, its necessity is neither external nor merely relative, but absolute—μὴ ἐνδεχόμενον ἄλλως, ἀλλ' ἁπλῶς ἀναγκαῖον] . . . ἐκ τοιαύτης ἄρα ἀρχῆς ἤρτηται ὁ οὐρανὸς καὶ ἡ φύσις.

[2] After showing that the ἐνέργεια precedes the δύναμις in all the three respects of λόγῳ, χρόνῳ and οὐσίᾳ Aristotle goes on, *Metaph.* ix. 8, 1050, b, 6 (following immediately on the passage quoted at p. 385, n. 1): ἀλλὰ μὴν καὶ κυριωτέρως [actuality has a higher reality than the δύναμις]. τὰ μὲν γὰρ ἀΐδια πρότερα τῇ οὐσίᾳ

τῶν φθαρτῶν, ἔστι δ' οὐθὲν δυνάμει ἀΐδιον. This he then goes on to prove. That which is merely potential can both be and not be. τὸ δ' ἐνδεχόμενον μὴ εἶναι φθαρτὸν, ἢ ἁπλῶς, ἢ τοῦτο αὐτὸ [relatively to that], ὃ λέγεται ἐνδέχεσθαι μὴ εἶναι [the former, if I say, ' it is possible for A not to be ; ' the latter, if I say, ' it is possible for A not to be in this place, or not to be so great, or not to have this quality '] ... ἁπλῶς δὲ τὸ κατ' οὐσίαν [but that is absolutely perishable whose substance can cease to be]. οὐθὲν ἄρα τῶν ἀφθάρτων ἁπλῶς δυνάμει ἐστὶν ὂν ἁπλῶς ... οὐδὲ τῶν ἐξ ἀνάγκης ὄντων.

[3] *Metaph.* xii. 6, 1071, b, 12 : if there were a κινητικὸν which did not realise itself in action there would be no eternal uninterrupted motion; ἐνδέχεται γὰρ τὸ δύναμιν ἔχον μὴ ἐνεργεῖν. But this would be equally true, εἰ ἐνεργήσει ἡ δ' οὐσία αὐτῆς δύναμις· οὐ γὰρ ἔσται κίνησις ἀΐδιος· ἐνδέχεται γὰρ τὸ δυνάμει ὂν μὴ εἶναι. δεῖ ἄρα εἶναι ἀρχὴν τοιαύτην ἧς ἡ οὐσία ἐνέργεια. The leading thought of this proof (ἐνδέχεσθαι ἢ εἶναι οὐδὲν διαφέρει ἐν τοῖς ἀϊδίοις) Aristotle states also *Phys.* iii. 4, 203, b, 30, and he shows in *Metaph.* ix. 4 that it is inadmissible to say,

be immaterial and therefore incorporeal.[1] Only the incorporeal can be unchangeable;[2] on the other hand, everything which has a material side is subject to motion and change,[3] and can alter its state.[4] Moreover all bodies have magnitude, and magnitude is always limited. But the limited cannot possibly produce an infinite activity like eternal motion, for its power is just as surely limited as that of the infinite is illimitable.[5] It follows that the *primum mobile* must be absolutely incorporeal, indivisible and unconditioned by space, motionless, passionless, changeless : in a word, it must be absolute Reality and pure Energy.[6]

ὅτι δυνατὸν μὲν τοδὶ, οὐκ ἔσται δέ, from which it immediately follows that we can never say of anything which by its very nature *can* cease to be, that it *will never* cease to be; and consequently it cannot be of the nature of that which never ceases to be (the ἀΐδιον).

[1] Cf. p. 347 sq. and *Metaph.* xii. 6, 1071, b, 20 : ἔτι τοίνυν ταύτας δεῖ τὰς οὐσίας εἶναι ἄνευ ὕλης. ἀϊδίους γὰρ δεῖ, εἴ πέρ γε καὶ ἄλλο τι ἀΐδιον. ἐνεργείᾳ ἄρα.

[2] After what has been said above, this does not require any further proof. All change is a transition from possibility to actuality, which is only precluded where there is no matter, and therefore no δυνάμει ὄν. Cf. (besides p. 359 sqq.) the proof in *Phys.* vi. 4, that everything which changes must be divisible. We shall thus find also that the soul is in essence unmoved.

[3] *Phys.* viii. 6, 259, b, 18. Cf. preceding n. and p. 366, n. 1.

[4] See p. 394, n. 3, and *Metaph.* vii. 7, 1032, a, 20, c. 10, 1035, a, 25.

[5] *Phys.* viii. 10, 266, a, 10 sqq. 267, b, 17. ; *Metaph.* xii. 7 *fin.*

[6] *Metaph.* xii. 7 (see p 394, n. 1, *supra*), c. 8, 1074, a, 35 ; cf. preceding and following n. *De Cælo*, i. 9, 279, a, 16 : ἔξω δὲ τοῦ οὐρανοῦ δέδεικται ὅτι οὔτ᾽ ἔστιν οὔτε ἐνδέχεται γενέσθαι σῶμα. φανερὸν ἄρα ὅτι οὔτε τόπος οὔτε κενὸν οὔτε χρόνος ἐστὶν ἔξωθεν· διόπερ οὔτ᾽ ἐν τόπῳ τἀκεῖ πέφυκεν, οὔτε χρόνος αὐτὰ ποιεῖ γηράσκειν. οὐδ᾽ ἐστὶν οὐδενὸς οὐδεμία μεταβολὴ τῶν ὑπὲρ τὴν ἐξωτάτω τεταγμένων φοράν, ἀλλ᾽ ἀναλλοίωτα καὶ ἀπαθῆ τὴν ἀρίστην ἔχοντα ζωὴν καὶ τὴν αὐταρκεστάτην διατελεῖ τὸν ἅπαντα αἰῶνα. After some remarks upon the expression αἰών, Aristotle proceeds : τὸ τοῦ παντὸς οὐρανοῦ τέλος καὶ τὸ τὸν πάντα χρόνον καὶ τὴν ἀπειρίαν περιέχον τέλος αἰών ἐστιν, ἀπὸ τοῦ ἀεὶ εἶναι εἰληφὼς τὴι ἐπωνυμίαν, ἀθάνατος καὶ θεῖος. ὅθεν καὶ τοῖς ἄλλοις ἐξήρτηται, τοῖς μὲν ἀκριβέστερον τοῖς δ᾽ ἀμαυρῶς, τὸ εἶναί τε καὶ ζῆν. It is thus seen that the highest Deity (τὸ θεῖον πᾶν τὸ πρῶτον καὶ ἀκρότατον) must be unchangeable.

By a converse process, it follows that, since all multiplicity partakes of matter, the *primum mobile* and that which it moves are single.[1] The cause of all motion, or God, is therefore Pure Being, absolute Form (τὸ τί ἦν εἶναι τὸ πρῶτον), incorporeal Substance—or, in other words, is Thought. Nothing but pure self-centred thought is free from materiality, for even the soul has an essential relation to the body, and in all corporeal substances form is involved with matter. Again, perfect activity exists in thought alone. Neither constructive (ποιητικὴ) nor practical (πρακτικὴ) activity is perfect, since the end of both is external to themselves, and therefore they require material to work with.[2] But the Supreme Being has no end beyond itself, because it is the ultimate end of everything.[3] It is

οὔτε γὰρ ἄλλο κρεῖττόν ἐστιν ὅ τι [nom.] κινήσει . . . , οὔτ᾽ ἔχει φαῦλον οὐθὲν, οὔτ᾽ ἐνδεὲς τῶν αὑτοῦ καλῶν οὐδενός ἐστιν. (Cf. p. 393, n. 3.) As to whether this account, indeed, was to be taken as referring to the primal mover or the primally moved (the outmost sphere) the old commentators held divided views: according to SIMPL. *in loc.*, Alexander as well as his Peripatetic predecessors, gave the preference to the second, the younger (Neoplatonic) expositors to the first explanation. Alexander's view seems to be supported by the words καὶ ἄπαυστον δὴ κίνησιν κινεῖται εὐλόγως, unless we alter κινεῖται with some of the MSS. used by Simpl. into κινεῖ; it is easy, however to supply ὁ οὐρανός as the subject, even although God is spoken of in what precedes,

and that we must do so is obvious from the fact that the subject of this explanation is expressly said to be that which is ἔξω τοῦ οὐρανοῦ, ὑπέρτην ἐξωτάτω φοράν—the incorporeal, immovable, all-embracing, the θεῖον πρῶτον καὶ ἀκρότατον, the cause of all being and life.

[1] *Metaph.* xii. 8, 1074, a, 31: ὅτι δὲ εἷς οὐρανὸς, φανερόν· εἰ γὰρ πλείους οὐρανοὶ ὥσπερ ἄνθρωποι, ἔσται εἴδει μία ἡ περὶ ἕκαστον ἀρχὴ, ἀριθμῷ δέ γε πολλαί· ἀλλ᾽ ὅσα ἀριθμῷ πολλὰ, ὕλην ἔχει· εἷς γὰρ λόγος καὶ ὁ αὐτὸς πολλῶν . . . τὸ δὲ τί ἦν εἶναι οὐκ ἔχει ὕλην τὸ πρῶτον· ἐντελέχεια γάρ.

[2] Cf. p. 400, n. 1.

[3] *De Cœlo*, ii. 12, 292, b, 4: τῷ δ᾽ ὡς ἄριστα ἔχοντι οὐθὲν δεῖ πράξεως· ἔστι γὰρ αὐτὸ τὸ οὗ ἕνεκα, ἡ δὲ πρᾶξις ἀεί ἐστιν ἐν δυσὶν, ὅταν καὶ οὗ ἕνεκα ᾖ καὶ τὸ τούτου ἕνεκα.

true that in analysing Thought we separate Potentiality from Actuality—the faculty of thinking from actual Thought (θεωρία). But this distinction does not apply to the Deity, for his substance contains no undeveloped potentiality; and even in the case of man, it is only his finite nature which renders him incapable of uninterrupted thought. The nature of the Deity consists of unceasing sleepless contemplation and absolutely perfect activity,[1] an activity that cannot alter, since to a perfect being alteration would involve a loss of perfection.[2] God, therefore, is the absolute activity of thought, and, as such, He constitutes absolute reality and vitality and is the source of all life.[3]

What, then, are the contents or subject-matter of this Thought? All thinking derives its value from the object of thought; but the Divine Thought cannot be dependent for its validity on anything beyond itself, nor can it relate to anything except the best. But the best is

---

[1] *Eth. N.* x. 8, 1078, b, 20 : τῷ δὴ ζῶντι τοῦ πράττειν ἀφαιρουμένου, ἔτι δὲ μᾶλλον τοῦ ποιεῖν, τί λείπεται πλὴν θεωρία ; ὥστε ἡ τοῦ θεοῦ ἐνέργεια, μακαριότητι διαφέρουσα, θεωρητικὴ ἂν εἴη. καὶ τῶν ἀνθρωπίνων δὴ ἡ ταύτῃ συγγενεστάτη εὐδαιμονικωτάτη. *Metaph.* xii. 7, cf. p. 398, n. 5 ; c. 9, 1074, b, 28 : we cannot think of the divine thought either as resting or as in a state of mere potentiality, for εἰ μὴ νόησίς [actual thought] ἐστιν, ἀλλὰ δύναμις, εὔλογον ἐπίπονον εἶναι τὸ συνεχὲς αὐτῷ τῆς νοήσεως. *Ibid.* 1075, b, 7 (following BONITZ's text) : pure reason is indivisible ; as is therefore the discursive thought of

man (ὁ ἀνθρώπινος νοῦς ὁ τῶν συνθέτων) at isolated moments when it contemplates perfection, not in broken fragments but in its entirety : οὕτως δ' ἔχει αὐτὴ αὑτῆς ἡ νόησις τὸν ἅπαντα αἰῶνα.

[2] *Metaph.* xii. 9, 1074, b, 25 : δῆλον τοίνυν ὅτι τὸ θειότατον καὶ τιμιώτατον νοεῖ καὶ οὐ μεταβάλλει · εἰς χεῖρον γὰρ ἡ μεταβολὴ καὶ κίνησίς τις ἤδη τὸ τοιοῦτον.

[3] *Metaph.* xii. 7, 1072, b, 28 : φαμὲν δὲ [δὴ] τὸν θεὸν εἶναι ζῷον ἀΐδιον ἄριστον, ὥστε ζωὴ καὶ αἰὼν συνεχὴς καὶ ἀΐδιος ὑπάρχει τῷ θεῷ · τοῦτο γὰρ ὁ θεός. *De Cælo*, ii. 3, 286, a, 9 : θεοῦ δ' ἐνέργεια ἀθανασία · τοῦτο δ' ἐστὶ ζωὴ ἀΐδιος.

nothing but itself.[1]   Consequently God contemplates
Himself, and his thought is the thought of thought.[2]   In
the thought of God, therefore, as must necessarily be the
case with Pure Spirit, thought and its object are identical.[3] This unalterable repose of thought upon itself—the
indivisible unity of the thinking subject and the object of
thought [4]—constitutes the absolute blessedness of God.[5]

---

[1] Still less, of course, can
God be affected by any emotion
from without. Hence the statement (*Eth. N.* viii. 9, 1158, b, 35,
1159, a, 4, or more definitely *Eud.*
vii. 3, 12, 1238, b, 27, 1244, b, 7,
1245, b, 14, and from this treatise
M. Mor. ii. 11, 1208, b, 27), that
God does not love but is only
loved, and that between Him
and man there is too wide a
separation to permit of mutual
φιλία.

[2] *Metaph.* xii. 9, 1074, b, 17:
εἴτε γὰρ μηθὲν νοεῖ, τί ἂν εἴη τὸ
σεμνὸν, ἀλλ᾿ ἔχει ὥσπερ ἂν εἰ ὁ
καθεύδων· εἴτε νοεῖ, τούτου δ᾿ ἄλλο
κύριον, . . . οὐκ ἂν ἡ ἀρίστη οὐσία
εἴη· διὰ γὰρ τοῦ νοεῖν τὸ τίμιον
αὐτῷ ὑπάρχει. ἔτι δὲ . . . τί νοεῖ;
ἢ γὰρ αὐτὸς αὑτὸν ἢ ἕτερόν τι. . . .
πότερον οὖν διαφέρει τι ἢ οὐθὲν τὸ
νοεῖν τὸ καλὸν ἢ τὸ τυχόν; ἢ καὶ
ἄτοπον τὸ διανοεῖσθαι περὶ ἐνίων;
δῆλον τοίνυν . . . (as at p. 397,
n. 2); further, at l. 29, if
νοῦς were the mere power of
thinking, δῆλον, ὅτι ἄλλο τι ἂν εἴη
τὸ τιμιώτερον ἢ ὁ νοῦς, τὸ νοούμενον·
καὶ γὰρ τὸ νοεῖν καὶ ἡ νόησις ὑπάρξει
καὶ τὸ χείριστον νοοῦντι· ὥστ᾿ εἰ
φευκτὸν τοῦτο, . . . οὐκ ἂν εἴη τὸ
ἄριστον ἡ νόησις· αὑτὸν ἄρα νοεῖ,
εἴπερ ἐστὶ τὸ κράτιστον, καὶ ἔστιν
ἡ νόησις νοήσεως νόησις. c. 7 (see
n. 4). *De An.* iii. 6, 430, b, 24 :
εἰ δέ τινι μή ἐστιν ἐναντίον τῶν

αἰτίων [?], αὐτὸ ἑαυτὸ γινώσκει
καὶ ἐνεργείᾳ ἐστὶ καὶ χωριστόν.

[3] See preceding note and *Metaph.* xii. 9 : φαίνεται δ᾿ ἀεὶ ἄλλου
ἡ ἐπιστήμη, . . . ἢ ἐπ᾿ ἐνίων ἡ
ἐπιστήμη τὸ πρᾶγμα ; ἐπὶ μὲν τῶν
ποιητικῶν ἄνευ ὕλης ἡ οὐσία καὶ τὸ
τί ἦν εἶναι, ἐπὶ δὲ τῶν θεωρητικῶν
ὁ λόγος τὸ πρᾶγμα καὶ ἡ νόησις.
οὐχ ἑτέρου οὖν ὄντος τοῦ νοουμένου
καὶ τοῦ νοῦ, ὅσα μὴ ὕλην ἔχει τὸ
αὐτὸ ἔσται, καὶ ἡ νόησις τοῦ
νοουμένου μία. *De An.* iii. 4 *fin.*
(cf. c. 5 and c. 7 *init.*): ἐπὶ μὲν
γὰρ τῶν ἄνευ ὕλης τὸ αὐτό ἐστι τὸ
νοοῦν καὶ τὸ νοούμενον.

[4] *Metaph.* xii. 9: 1075, b, 7:
ἀδιαίρετον πᾶν τὸ μὴ ἔχον ὕλην,
&c., see p. 397, n. 1, *supra*.

[5] This view is set forth in
the passage immediately following that quoted p. 394, n. 1: δια-
γωγὴ δ᾿ ἐστὶν [sc. τῷ πρώτῳ
κινοῦντι] οἷα ἡ ἀρίστη μικρὸν χρόνον
ἡμῖν. οὕτω γὰρ ἀεὶ ἐκεῖνό ἐστιν·
ἡμῖν μὲν γὰρ ἀδύνατον. ἐπεὶ καὶ
ἡδονὴ ἡ ἐνέργεια [so BONITZ,
rightly following Alexander,
instead of ἡ ἡδ. ἐνέργ.] τούτου· καὶ
διὰ τοῦτο [*i.e.* because not God's
activity alone, but activity in
general, is pleasant, for in this
passage, as often in this book,
lucidity is sacrificed to an exces-
sive brevity of style] ἐγρήγορσις
αἴσθησις νόησις ἥδιστον ἐλπίδες δὲ
καὶ μνῆμαι διὰ ταῦτα. ἡ δὲ νόησις ἡ

These propositions of Aristotle concerning the
Divine Spirit contain the first attempt to find a
scientific basis for Theism. Here first the idea of God
as self-conscious intelligence was logically deduced
from the principles of a philosophical system instead or
being borrowed from religious notions. And on the
very threshold we are confronted with the difficulty the
solution of which is the final problem of all systems of
theistic speculation : how are we to define the idea of
God so that while maintaining his essential difference
from all finite reality, we may yet preserve his personality, and *vice versa*? Aristotle represents God as
self-conscious Spirit ; on the other hand, he deprives
Him of body and senses, and, not content with this,
declares not only action and creation, but the direction
of the will itself towards an object, to be incompatible

καθ' αὐτὴν τοῦ καθ' αὐτὸ ἀρίστου
καὶ ἡ μάλιστα τοῦ μάλιστα [pure
thought has for its object that
which is absolutely best, and all
the more fitly the purer it is].
αὐτὸν δὲ νοεῖ ὁ νοῦς κατὰ μετάληψιν
τοῦ νοητοῦ· νοητὸς γὰρ γίγνεται
θιγγάνων καὶ νοῶν, ὥστε ταὐτὸν
νοῦς καὶ νοητόν. τὸ γὰρ δεκτικὸν
τοῦ νοητοῦ καὶ τῆς οὐσίας νοῦς,
ἐνεργεῖ δὲ ἔχων. ὥστ' ἐκεῖνο
[ἐνεργεῖν and ἔχειν] μᾶλλον τούτου
[*i.e.* more than the mere recep-
tivity] ὃ δοκεῖ ὁ νοῦς θεῖον ἔχειν,
καὶ ἡ θεωρία τὸ ἥδιστον καὶ ἄριστον
(and therefore actual knowledge,
and not the mere capacity of
knowing, is the best and most
blessed state. On this meaning
of θεωρία *vid.* BONITZ, *Ind. Ar.*
328, a, 50 sqq.) From l. 18
(ἡ δὲ νόησις ἡ καθ' αὐτὴν) this

passage is quite general, referring
neither to the divine nor to the
human reason exclusively ; l. 24,
however, continues : εἰ οὖν οὕτως
εὖ ἔχει, ὡς ἡμεῖς ποτὲ, ὁ θεὸς ἀεί,
θαυμαστόν· εἰ δὲ μᾶλλον ἔτι
θαυμασιώτερον. ἔχει δὲ ὡδί. καὶ
ζωὴ δέ γε ὑπάρχει. ἡ γὰρ νοῦ
ἐνέργεια ζωή, ἐκεῖνος δὲ ἡ ἐνέργεια·
ἐνέργεια δὲ ἡ καθ' αὐτὴν ἐκείνου ζωὴ
ἀρίστη καὶ ἀΐδιος. φαμὲν δή, . . ., as
at p. 397, n. 3, *supra.* Further cf.
Eth. x. 8, cited at p. 397, n. 1; *ibid.*
vii. 15, 1154, b, 25 : εἴ του ἡ φύσις
ἁπλῆ εἴη, ἀεὶ ἡ αὐτὴ πρᾶξις ἡδίστη
ἔσται· διὸ ὁ θεὸς ἀεὶ μίαν καὶ ἁπλῆν
χαίρει ἡδονήν ; and *Polit.* vii. 1,
1323, b, 23 : τῷ θεῷ . . . ὃς εὐδαίμων
μέν ἐστι καὶ μακάριος, δι' οὐδὲν δὲ
τῶν ἐξωτερικῶν ἀγαθῶν ἀλλὰ δι'
αὐτὸν αὐτὸς καὶ τῷ ποιός τις εἶναι
τὴν φύσιν.

with divine perfection,[1] and confines his thought within

[1] That neither ποίησις nor
πρᾶξις (on the difference between
them cf. p. 182 sq.) can be attributed to God is definitely stated
by Aristotle in many passages ;
e.g. Eth. x. 8, 1178, b, 7 sq The
position that perfect bliss consists
in thought alone, he there proves
by showing that everyone considers the gods blessed and that
the question then is : πράξεις
δὲ ποίας ἀπονεῖμαι χρεὼν αὐτοῖς ;
πότερα τὰς δικαίας ; . . . ἀλλὰ τὰς
ἀνδρείους . . . ἢ τὰς ἐλευθερίους ;
. . . αἱ δὲ σώφρονες τί ἂν εἶεν ; All
these being inconceivable (διεξ-
ιοῦσι δὲ πάντα φαίνοιτ᾽ ἂν τὰ περὶ
τὰς πράξεις μικρὰ καὶ ἀνάξια θεῶν),
he concludes : τῷ δὴ ζῶντι, &c.
(as at p. 397, n. 1). *De Cœlo* ii. 12,
292, a, 22 : ἔοικε γὰρ τῷ μὲν ἄριστα
ἔχοντι ὑπάρχειν τὸ εὖ ἄνευ πράξεως,
τῷ δ᾽ ἐγγύτατα [the heavenly
bodies of the outer sphere] διὰ
ὀλίγης καὶ μιᾶς. *Ibid.* b, 4, cited
p. 396, n. 3, *supra ; Gen. et Corr.* i.
6, 323, a, 12 : since every ποιεῖν
involves a corresponding πάσχειν,
we cannot ascribe a ποιεῖν to
every *movens,* but only to such as
must itself be moved in order
that it may in turn move ; κινεῖν,
therefore, is a more comprehensive conception than ποιεῖν.
These details are much too explicit to permit the assertion
(BRENTANO, *Psychol. d. Arist.*
247 sq.) that Aristotle desires to
deny to Deity only such actions
(πράττειν ; universal 'action'
must be ascribed to God on any
view) as result from a felt need,
and that therefore, while denying that πράττειν contributes anything to the blessedness of God,
he does not deny that it belongs
to Him generally. Aristotle does

not recognise any such limitation, which, moreover, would be
wholly inconsistent with his
other views (for since, according
to the passage quoted p. 394, n. 1,
all God's properties must be
absolutely necessary, none can
belong to Him which He does
not require for his perfection and
blessedness, and which therefore
He could not dispense with without prejudice to these). On the
contrary, he says without any
reservation (*Eth.* x. 8 ; see p. 397,
n. 1, *supra*), that neither ποιεῖν nor
πράττειν can be attributed to
God ; that perfection in action
(practical virtue) can only find a
place in human intercourse and
among beings who are subject to
human passions (*Eth.* x. 8, 1178,
a, 9, b, 5, vii. 1, 1145, a, 25) ; that
every action is a means to an end
different from itself, and therefore that it cannot be attributed
to God, for whom there is no end
not yet attained (*De Cœlo,* as
quoted above). Nor is it any
objection to this view that Aristotle elsewhere (*Eth.* vii. 15, see
p. 398, n. 5 *fin.* ; *Polit.* vii. 3, 1325,
b, 28) speaks of God's πρᾶξις, since
the word here used in the wider
sense in which it occurs in *Eth.* vi.
2, 5, 1139, b, 3, 1140, b, 6 (where
it is said that πρᾶξις differs from
ποίησις in having its end in itself,
εὐπραξία being the τέλος) and includes every form of activity,
even the pure activity of
thought. No other meaning will
suit the words, *Eth.* vii. 15, ἀεὶ ἡ
αὐτὴ πρᾶξις ; and in a similar
sense *Pol.*, as above, l. 16 sqq.,
distinguishes πράξεις πρὸς ἑτέρους,
τὰς τῶν ἀποβαινόντων χάριν γιγνο-
μένας ἐκ τοῦ πράττειν—in a word,

the limits of an isolated self-contemplation. But this

πράξεις ἐξωτερικαί, actions which elsewhere are called simply πρᾶξις in the narrower sense of the word—from τὰς αὐτοτελεῖς, καὶ τὰς αὐτῶν ἕνεκα θεωρίας καὶ διανοήσεις, and attributes only the latter to God, in opposing the view that the practical life is superior to the theoretic ; σχολῇ γὰρ ἂν ὁ θεὸς ἔχοι καλῶς καὶ πᾶς ὁ κόσμος, οἷς οὐκ εἰσὶν ἐξωτερικαὶ πράξεις παρὰ τὰς οἰκείας τὰς αὐτῶν. Still less is it a pertinent objection that in using popular language Aristotle ascribes ποιεῖν to God, as in *De Cœlo*, i. 4 *fin.* (ὁ θεὸς καὶ ἡ φύσις οὐδὲν μάτην ποιοῦσιν), *Gen. et Corr.* ii. 10, 336, b, 31 (συνεπλήρωσε τὸ ὅλον ὁ θεὸς, ἐντελεχῆ ποιήσας τὴν γένεσιν). Θεὸς here means the divine force which governs nature, whose relation to the first cause of motion is left, as we shall see, wholly undefined; nor can we draw any conclusion from this use as to Aristotle's view of God as the absolute supramundane reason, any more than from the frequent use of θεοὶ as in *Eth.* x. 8, quoted above, and *ibid.* viii. 14, 1162, a, 4, x. 9, 1179, a, 24, we may argue that Aristotle was a polytheist. Ποιεῖν also in these passages seems to be used quite generally and not to be limited any more than ποιητικὸν, *Metaph.* xii. 6, 1071, b, 12 (to which BRENTANO appeals, but which is nowhere directly applied to God by Aristotle) to the narrower sense discussed p. 182; it bears merely the general signification of creation or production, as in the phrase νοῦς ποιητικὸς, and merely indicates causality in general without further specification of its nature.—But if action does not belong to God, neither can will, for as will (προαίρεσις) is ἀρχὴ πράξεως and originates in turn in a desire on the one hand and the conception of an end on the other, it always presupposes an ἠθικὴ ἕξις (*Eth.* vi. 2, 1139, a, 31) : and these ideas it is impossible to reconcile with Aristotle's conception of God. Furthermore, βούλησις, *De An.* iii. 10, 433, a, 23, is defined as rational desire ; but desire cannot in any sense be ascribed by Aristotle to God; nor can we admit the assertion of BRENTANO, p. 246, that because he ascribes to Him ἡδονὴ, he must also have ascribed to Him something corresponding to desire in us. It is only of sensuous λύπη and ἡδονὴ that Aristotle says (*De An.* ii. 2, 413, b, 23) that it involves ἐπιθυμία ; he expressly adds that he is not here speaking of Nous ; and *ibid.* iii. 7, 431, a, 10 he declares ὀρεκτικὸν and φευκτικὸν to be identical with αἰσθητικὸν, and remarks iii. 9, 10, 432, b, 27, 433, a, 14, cf. *Eth.* vi. 2, 1139, a, 35, that the νοῦς θεωρητικὸς (therefore also the divine) does not deal with the φευκτὸν and διωκτὸν by which desire is always conditioned. It is evident that those passages in which Aristotle uses the common conceptions of God as generally admitted premisses from which conclusions may be drawn—*e.g.* *Top.* iv. 5, 126, a, 34 ; *Eth.* x. 9, 1179, a, 24, or, indeed, such quotations as *Eth.* vi. 2, 1139, b, 9, *Rhet.* ii. 23, 1398, a, 15—prove nothing. Such statements as that God ' in making Himself the

solution [1] is wholly unsatisfactory. On the one hand, personal existence implies activity of will no less than of thought. On the other hand, thought *qua* personal is always in transition from possibility to actuality—in other words, in a state of development—and is determined as much by the variety of its objects as by changes of intellectual states. Aristotle by destroying these conditions and confining the function of the Divine Reason to a monotonous self-contemplation, not quickened into life by any change or development, merges the notion of personality in a mere abstraction.

The difficulties which perplex us when we come to consider the operation of God upon the world are not

object of desire for his own sake desires the universe and the whole order of nature ' (BRENT. 247), receive no support whatsoever from Aristotle. Such a conception, on the contrary, is wholly irreconcilable with his idea of God, for all desire is an effort after something not yet attained, and in a φύσις τοῦ ἀρίστου τετυχηκυῖα (*Metaph.* xii. 8, 1074, a, 19) any such effort is inconceivable.

[1] On this point also Aristotle has expressed himself with a definiteness that leaves no room for doubt. Neither the view of BRENT. (*Psych. d. Arist.* 246 sq.), that in knowing Himself, God knows the whole creation as well, nor SCHNEIDER's modification of it (*De Causa finali Arist.* 79 sq.; cf. also KYM, *Metaphys. Unters.* 252, 256), to the effect that God knows the intelligible world as the totality of the forms that are contained in his thought, finds any justification in Aristotle's writings. The passage *Metaph.*

xii. 10 (see p. 391, n. 2, *supra*) offers no support to either. Aristotle is here inquiring in what way the world contains the good. The only answer which he gives, however, to this question is contained in the words καὶ γὰρ ἐν τῇ τάξει τὸ εὖ καὶ ὁ στρατηγός, καὶ μᾶλλον οὗτος· οὐ γὰρ οὗτος διὰ τὴν τάξιν ἀλλ' ἐκείνη διὰ τοῦτον ἐστιν. If we apply this to the idea of God and the world it certainly follows that the perfection of the universe resides in the first place in God as the first cause of motion, and secondly in the universal order that owes its origin to it. On the other hand, the comparison of the world to an army gives no clue to the method in which the order of the universe proceeds from God (for this was not the question under discussion). As we evidently cannot conclude from it that God sketches plans, issues commands to his subordinates, &c. (though this way of representing God's government of the

less weighty. Aristotle describes God, as we have seen, not only as the *primum mobile*, but also more generally as the highest principle [1] and the ground of the collective cosmos.[2] While we are not justified in attributing to him a belief in a Providence which extends its care to individuals,[3] we may yet see that he acknowledges the world to be the work of Reason,[4] that

universe is common enough), neither does it follow that God produces the order of the world by a process of thought which has for its object the world itself or its individual parts. That point can only be decided by a reference to declarations elsewhere made by Aristotle. Still further at variance with the spirit of the above comparison is the statement of KYM, p. 246 sq., that the good or God does not merely exist outside the world as an individual being, but is immanent in it as order and design. 'God' and 'the good' are not, however, to Aristotle convertible terms (cf. *e.g. Eth.* i. 4, 1096, a, 23, BONITZ, *Ind. Ar.* 3, b, 35 sqq.), and the general is quite different from the order of the army. Cf. further p. 413 sq.

[1] *Metaph.* xi. 2, 1060, a 27, cannot, indeed, be quoted in support of this statement; for the words εἴπερ ἔστι τις οὐσία καὶ ἀρχὴ τοιαύτη τὴν φύσιν οἵαν νῦν ζητοῦμεν, καὶ αὕτη μία πάντων καὶ ἡ αὐτὴ τῶν ἀϊδίων τε καὶ φθαρτῶν, not only, as may be seen from the context and from the parallel passage iii. 4, 1000, a, 5 sqq., leave it in doubt whether there be such an ἀρχή or not, but they do not speak of God as an individual being. The words in iii. 4, are:

πότερον αἱ αὐταὶ τῶν φθαρτῶν καὶ τῶν ἀφθάρτων ἀρχαί εἰσιν. On the other hand we read in *Metaph.* xi. 7, 1064, a, 34 sqq. : if there be an οὐσία χωριστὴ καὶ ἀκίνητος, ἐνταῦθ' ἂν εἴη που καὶ τὸ θεῖον, καὶ αὕτη ἂν εἴη πρώτη καὶ κυριωτάτη ἀρχή.

[2] *Metaph.* xii. 7, 10; see p. 394, n. 1, and p. 391, n. 2, *supra, De Cælo,* i. 9; see p. 395, n. 6.

[3] On this subject cf. p. 422, n. 1; see Ch. XVI. *infra.* How little the passages referred to are to be taken literally is obvious from the fact that the gods (θεοί) are always spoken of in them in the plural. But if we have thus first to translate them into language possible to the philosopher in order to discover his true meaning, it is a question whether we have not to make as great a deduction from their literal content as in the parallel cases which will be discussed *infra,* at the end of the section in Ch. IX. on the Universe.

[4] Anaxagoras is praised (*Metaph.* i. 3, 984, b, 15, cf. *Phys.* viii. 5, 256, b, 24) for having made νοῦς αἴτιος τοῦ κόσμου καὶ τῆς τάξεως πάσης, and it is remarked *Phys.* ii. 6, 198, a, 9, that αὐτόματον and τύχη always presuppose a νοῦς and a φύσις.

he recognises,[1] in the adaptations of nature, traces of the operation of God, and that he finds in human Reason an indwelling element of Divinity.[2] But if we attempt to bring these convictions into harmony with his theology as above discussed, we are met by many questions to which it is not easy to find an answer.

In the first place, it is obvious that if God exercises neither creative nor practical activity in relation to anything else, He cannot be the *primum mobile*. Here, however, we are met by the notion to which we have already alluded : that Form, without moving itself, exercises a power of attraction over Matter, causing it to move in its direction. ' God moves the world in this way : the object of desire and the object of thought cause motion without moving themselves. But these two motive forces are ultimately the same (the absolute object of thought is the absolutely desirable or pure good) ; for the object of desire is apparent beauty, while the original object of will is real beauty ; but desire is conditioned by our notion (of the value of the object) and not *vice versa*. Thought, therefore, is the starting-point or principle. Thought, however, is set in motion by the object of thought ; but only one of the two series is absolutely intelligible,[3] and in

---

[1] Cf. p. 421, and p. 460 sq.

[2] *Eth.* ix. 7, 9, 1177, a, 13, b, 30, 1179, a, 26 ; *Gen. An.* ii. 3, 736, b, 27, 737, a, 10 ; *De An.* i. 4, 408, b, 29 ; *Part. An.* ii. 10, 656, a, 7, iv. 10, 686, a, 28, 373.

[3] Νοητὴ δὲ ἡ ἑτέρα συστοιχία καθ᾽ αὑτήν. By this ἑτέρα συστοιχία we are to understand, as the more recent commentators right-ly point out, and as is obvious from l. 35, the series of being and good. The expression refers to the Pythagorean and Platonic doctrine of the universally preva-lent antithesis of being and not-being, perfection and imperfec-tion, &c., which Aristotle had discussed at length in the ᾽Εκλογὴ τῶν ᾽Εναντίων (see p. 61, n. 1,

this Being stands first, defined as simple and actual.'[1] 'The final cause operates like a loved object, and that which is moved by it communicates motion to the rest.'[2] God, therefore, is the *primum mobile* only in so far as He is the absolute end of the world,[3] the Governor, as it were, whose will all obey, but who never sets his own hand to the work.[4] And He fulfils this function by being absolute Form. As Form in general moves Matter by inviting it to pass from potentiality into actuality, the operation of God upon the world must be of the same sort.[5] Without doubt

supra) and often alludes to elsewhere ; cf. *Metaph.* iv. 2, 1004, a, 1, ix. 2, 1046, b, 2, xiv. 6, 1093, b, 12, i. 5, 986, a, 23 ; *Phys* iii. 2, 201, b, 25, i. 9, 192, a, 14 ; *Gen. et Corr.* i. 3, 319, a, 14.

[1] *Metaph.* xii. 7, 1072, a, 26 ; see BONITZ and SCHWEGLER.

[2] *Ibid.* 1072, b, 3 : κινεῖ δὲ ὡς ἐρώμενον, κινούμενον (better Cod. E T : κινουμένῳ) δὲ τἄλλα κινεῖ.

[3] As also do the movers of the celestial spheres (to be discussed *infra*, Ch. IX. in the section on the Spheres) ; these cause motion, according to *Metaph.* xii.8, 1074, a, 23, ὡς τέλος οὖσαι φοράς.

[4] Cf. *Metaph.* xii. 10 *init.* and *fin.*

[5] The subject, however, is here only treated generally : the question is not whether God moves the world but how He moves it, and it is therefore irrelevant when BRENTANO, *ibid.* 235 sqq., contests the assertion that God 'is not the first operative principle, but only the final cause, of being ' ; that according to Aristotle ' no operation at all belongs ' to Him. This assertion

would certainly be strange, for if God is the first mover He must be the first operator, since the κινητικὸν αἴτιον and the ποιητικὸν are the same (*De An.* iii. 5 *init.* ; *Gen. An.* i. 21, 729, b, 13 ; *Metaph.* xii. 6, 1071, b, 12 ; *Gen. et Corr.* i. 7, 324, b, 13 : ἔστι δὲ τὸ ποιητικὸν αἴτιον ὡς ὅθεν ἡ ἀρχὴ τῆς κινήσεως) and only a certain kind of ποίησις is denied of God (see p. 400, n. 1). But it is quite another thing to say that according to Aristotle God operates upon the world not directly but indirectly, not by Himself exercising activity upon it, but as perfect being by eliciting its activity by his mere existence ; He is efficient cause only in virtue of his being final cause. Nor is it sufficient to discredit this statement to adduce passages in which God is described in general as the moving or efficient principle of the world. No one doubts that this is so. To prove our view wrong, it would be necessary to produce passages in which direct action upon the world is attributed to Him ; it would be further neces-

this doctrine harmonises admirably with the whole system. It gives us, in fact, the proper coping-stone of the Metaphysics, by clearly exhibiting the ultimate unity of formal, efficient, and final causes, and their relation to the material cause. We find in it, moreover, the ultimate principle of union between the Metaphysics and the Physics—the point at which the investigations into the nature of the Unmoved and the Moved meet and find a common issue. It enables Aristotle to trace to absolutely immaterial and unmoved Being the ultimate source of all movement and change, and to make God the central, controlling principle of the universe without involving Him in its machinery on the one hand or disturbing the uniformity of natural law by personal interference with it on the other. It further furnishes him with the means of reconciling the eternity of the world with its dependence upon a divine supernatural Being. If the existence or the order or the motion of the universe be referred to definite acts of Deity, we are forced to assume that the world had a beginning, since every single act and that which is produced by it has a beginning in time.[1] On the other hand, a system which is gravitating towards a fixed and definite point, and which owes its motion to the attraction which is thus exercised upon it (and Aristotle's Cosmos is such a system), can be conceived of indifferently as with or without beginning. But the

sary to show how any such statement can be reconciled with those passages which explicitly deny any such action of Him; and finally to harmonise it with the Aristotelian conception of the nature of God as an absolutely unchangeable Being who is the only object of His own thought.

[1] Cf. p. 412, n. 1.

more important the above doctrine is for Aristotle, the
more obviously does it reveal the weak side of his
theory. The notion of the *motum* naturally desiring the
mobile, the Corporeal seeking the Divine, is so obscure [1]
as to be almost unintelligible to us.[2] Further, if, as

[1] As THEOPHRASTUS easily
discerned, *Fr.* 12 (*Metaph.*), 8:
εἰ δὴ ἔφεσις, ἄλλως τε καὶ τοῦ
ἀρίστου, μετὰ ψυχῆς, . . . ἔμψυχ᾽
ἂν εἴη τὰ κινούμενα. Similarly
PROCLUS, *in Tim.* 82, A (cf.
SCHRADER, *Arist. de Volunt.
Doctr.* Brandenb. 1847, p. 15, A,
42) asks : εἰ γὰρ ἐρᾷ ὁ κόσμος,
ὥς φησι καὶ ᾽Αριστοτέλης, τοῦ νοῦ
καὶ κινεῖται πρὸς αὐτὸν, πόθεν ἔχει
ταύτην τὴν ἔφεσιν ;
[2] We are not, of course, therefore justified. in denying that
Aristotle held this notion in the
face of his own plain and repeated statements and the interpretations of them in this sense
by the most faithful of his disci-
ples ; all the less as it is hard
indeed (as the discussion in
THEOPHRASTUS, *Fr.* 12, 5, clearly
proves) to say in what other way
motion can, on Aristotle's principles, be conceived of as proceeding from the absolutely unmoved.
BRENTANO (as above, 239 sq.)
thinks, indeed, that there is nothing so totally in contradiction to
the Aristotelian doctrine as the
view that ' matter is the efficient
principle because it moves of
itself to meet God, who is its
end.' As little, he says, can ' the
end produce anything of itself
without an efficient principle.'
But nobody has asserted either
the one or the other. When
it is said that God causes
motion by causing the desire

for his own perfection, it is
not meant that the matter in
which this desire is produced
causes the motion ; as little can
it mean that the end produces
it by itself alone, apart from any
efficient principle. The fact is that
the efficient cause is not here regarded as different from the
final. Though *we* should perhaps
in such a case conceive of two
independent causes at work,
the attractive force and the
thing that permits itself to be
attracted, Aristotle represents
the relationship otherwise. He
ascribes to the mover a δύναμις
ποιητική, to the motion merely a
δύναμις παθητική (*Metaph.* v. 15,
1021, a, 15, ix. 1, 1046, a, 16
sqq.). It is impossible, therefore,
for him to attribute to that which
owes its motion to something else,
any independent efficiency of its
own. On the contrary, the
efficient and the final cause, as
has been shown at p. 356 sq., he
conceives of as in essence one.
Their apparent severance under
certain circumstances is only a
phenomenon of the sensible
world, where form realises itself
in matter, and therefore (cf. pp.
368 sq.) in a plurality of individuals. In the intelligible world,
however, efficient and final cause
are always one and the same,
and accordingly it is impossible
to speak of an end producing
anything apart from a principle

Aristotle supposes, the *motum* must be in contact[1] with the *mobile*, it follows that the Universe must be in contact with the *primum mobile*, as, indeed, Aristotle explicitly states.[2] It is true that he endeavours to exclude the notion of contiguity in space from this idea; for he often employs the expression 'contact' when the context clearly proves that he does not allude to juxtaposition in space, but only to an immediate connection between two things.[3] Moreover, he asserts[4] that the *motum* is in contact with the *primum mobile*, but not *vice versa*. But even though we overlook the contradiction that is here involved, we find the notion

of efficiency.— Similar to the action of God Himself is that of the spheral spirits, which produce motion in their respective spheres as being themselves the end of the motion; cf. p. 405, n. 3.—It is still more strange that BRENTANO goes beyond the view which he combats, in saying. p. 240, that according to *Metaph.* xii. 7, 1072, a, 26: 'God moves as known;' for since matter, as he himself adds, cannot know God, it would follow from this that God does not move matter at all. The assertion, however, rests upon a misunderstanding. Aristotle says (cf. p. 404): τὸ ὀρεκτὸν καὶ τὸ νοητὸν κινεῖ οὐ κινούμενον . . . νοῦς δὲ ὑπὸ τοῦ νοητοῦ κινεῖται . . . . . κινεῖ δὲ ὡς ἐρώμενον. As νοητὸν God moves only Nous (to which, however, motion can be ascribed only in an improper sense; cf. Ch. XI. at the commencement and at the end.*infra*); the world, on the other hand, He moves as ἐρώμε-νον by means of the ὄρεξις which He causes. We, indeed, should

not think of ascribing any such quality to matter, and we should hesitate scarcely less to attribute to plants and animals a 'longing after the divine' as Aristotle does in *De An.* ii. 4, 415, a, 26 sqq. (see Ch. X. pt. 2, *infra*). Even the doctrine of a plant and animal soul would scarcely justify such a view in our eyes, as from such a soul the thought of God is necessarily excluded. But just as Aristotle here attributes to non-rational existence an unconscious yearning after τὸ θεῖον, so the conception of a world animate throughout, so natural to the Greek and yet resting ultimately on an untenable anthropological analogy, enables him to view the astral spheres, which he holds to be of a far higher nature than any earthly existence (see Ch. IX. on the Universe), in the same light.

[1] Cf. *supra*, p. 386.
[2] *Gen. et Corr.* i. 6, 323, a, 20.
[3] Cf. *supra*, p. 203, n. 3.
[4] *Gen. et Corr. ibid.*; see p. 387, n. 3, *supra*.

of existence in space forced upon us still more remark-
ably by the further assertion that God in setting the
world in motion starts from its circumference. For since
generally the primordial motion is taken to be motion
in space,[1] and of the original motions in space none is
absolutely continuous and uniform except circular
motion,[2] the operation of the first mover upon the
world must consist in the production of circular motion.[3]
According to Aristotle, this might be effected either
from the centre or the circumference of the world, for
both of these places are ἀρχαί, and command the whole
movement. He prefers the latter, however, because it
is clear that the circumference moves faster than the
centre, and that which is nearest to the cause of
motion ought to move at the quickest rate.[4] In defending
this position he might hope to evade the objection that
he places God in a particular locality by his peculiar
theory of space, which excluded from the notion everything that lay beyond the limits of the world.[5] It is
obvious, however, that we cannot accept this defence.
Again as the Deity, relatively to Himself, is confined to
the unvarying exercise of uniform self-contemplation,
so, in his relation to the world, He has no other function but that of monotonously causing circular motion.
To explain the rich variety of finite existence with the

---

[1] *Phys.* viii. 7, 9; see p. 421
sq.

[2] *Ibid.* c. 8 sq.; *De Cœlo,* i. 2;
Metaph. xii. 6, 1071, b, 10.

[3] *Phys.* viii. 6 *fin.,* c. 8 *fin.*;
Metaph. xii. 6 *fin.*; c. 8, 1073, a,
23 sqq.

[4] *Phys.* viii. 10, 267, b, 6; *De*

Cœlo, i. 9, 279, a, 16 sqq. (see p.
395, n. 6, *supra*). Hence the
assertion (SEXT. *Math.* x. 23;
Hypotyp. iii. 218) that God is
to Aristotle τὸ πέρας τοῦ οὐρανοῦ.

[5] Cf. *De Cœlo,* i. 9 (cited as
above, at p. 395, n. 6) and p. 432,
n. 5.

infinite diversities and subdivisions of its motion, by means of this simple and uniform activity, would be impossible. Aristotle himself admits as much with reference to the heavenly bodies; and accordingly he adds to the first mover a number of subordinate but equally eternal substances, whose business it is to cause the special motions of the planets.[1] The same provision must, however, be made to account for special motion of all kinds and for every separate property of things. As the First Cause of motion cannot have produced them, seeing that it exercises one general function in the world and nothing more, we are driven to assume some special cause for them.[2] Only it will not do to point merely to something which is equally general in its operation : for example, to the inclination of the orbit of the sun and planets, from which Aristotle deduces the phenomena of growth and destruction.[3] The special character of everything must be ascribed to its own particular nature and Form.[4] Here a new question rises : what position do these particular Forms, which operate as creative forces in finite things and constitute their peculiar essence, occupy with respect to the highest form, the primordial motive force, or God ? Or what are we to say of those beings which, belonging as they do to the supernatural world, are unaffected by

---

[1] *Metaph.* xii. 8, 1073, a, 26. For fuller explanation see Ch. IX. *infra.*

[2] *Metaph.* xii. 6, 1072, a, 9 : to secure the uniformity of the motion of the world (περιόδῳ l. 10 is prob. corrupt), δεῖ τι ἀεὶ μένειν ὡσαύτως ἐνεργοῦν. εἰ δὲ

μέλλει γένεσις καὶ φθορὰ εἶναι, ἄλλο δεῖ εἶναι ἐνεργοῦν ἄλλως καὶ ἄλλως.

[3] *Gen. et Corr.* ii. 10, 336, a, 23 ; see the section of Ch. IX. *infra*, which deals with the earthly world.

[4] Cf., besides p. 350 sq., the passages quoted *infra*, p. 432, n. 5.

the changes of birth and destruction—the heavenly spheres with the spirits that move and animate them, and the immortal part of the human soul?[1] What explanation does Aristotle offer us of the existence and peculiar nature of these beings? We cannot suppose them to be God's creatures;[2] for not only does such a notion obtain no support from his system and writings,[3]

[1] That these three classes of being are uncreated and indestructible not only follows from the eternity of the world and its motion, but is also expressly stated by Aristotle; cf. p. 474 sq. and Ch. IX. *infra.*

[2] As BRENTANO holds them to be, *Psych. d. Arist.* 198, 234 sqq. BULLINGER goes even further, *Des Arist. Erhabenheit über allen Dualismus* etc. (1878), p. 2 sq. According to his view, Aristotle supposed not only the whole world, but even the material of which it is made, to originate in a divine act of creation. Thus 'the material out of which God creates the world' would, according to Aristotle, be nothing else 'than the power and might eternally actual in God, whereby the world is actualised,' &c. (p. 15). It will be sufficiently evident from the account already given in the text that speculations are here attributed to Aristotle which are as foreign to the range of his thought as they are in conflict with his definite declarations.

[3] That God is called πρώτη ἀρχή (see p. 403, *supra*), proves nothing; for this may mean, not only that He has produced everything, but also that He is the condition of the eternal order and activity of the world: ἀρχή,

indeed (*Metaph.* v. 1, 1013, a, 16, 20 sq.), is used in as many senses as αἴτιον, and includes especially the conception of final cause. Since it is God who, as the most perfect being in the universe, gives unity of aim to the whole, and who causes the all-governing motion of the first sphere, He is also the πρώτη καὶ κυριωτάτη ἀρχή, on Him the whole order of the universe may be said to depend (p. 394, n. 1, and 395, n. 6), and to Him we are justified in applying " εἷς κοίρανος ἔστω " (p. 391, n. 2). The commander, however, is not therefore the creator of his subordinates. And as little does it follow from *Metaph.* ix. 8, 1050, b, 3 (see p. 385, n. 1, *supra*) that the creative activity of God precedes all being in time; for the ἀεὶ κινοῦν πρώτως does not (as Ps. ALEX. *in loc.* certainly thought) refer to God as the first cause of motion in the universe. On the contrary (as is obvious from the explanation upon p. 1049, b, 17 sqq. which the ὥσπερ εἴπομεν recalls), the reference is here to the fact that every individual thing presupposes as the condition of its production another similar already existing thing, and this likewise another, ἕως τοῦ ἀεὶ κινοῦντος πρώτως: *i.e.* until we come to the first member of the

but it would involve us in the contradiction of supposing the uncreated to be at the same time created, that which has been declared to be eternal to have had a beginning in time.[1] The same question arises with

series in question which has given the first impulse to the whole series, the *primum movens* in each case (not the πρῶτον κινοῦν); and this is the reason why the ἀεὶ κιν. πρ. is repeated from p. 1049, b, 26, where (as *Phys.* viii. 10, 267, a, 1, 3) this is undoubtedly its meaning. Aristotle was precluded from holding any theory of creation by his view of the eternity of the world. Such a theory, moreover, is incompatible, not only with the assertion that to God belongs neither πράττειν nor ποιεῖν (see p. 400, n. 1), but also with the principle *ex nihilo nihil fit* (*Phys.* i. 4, 187, a, 34, c. 7, 190, a, 14; *Gen. An.* ii. 1, 733, b, 24; *Metaph.* iii. 4, 999, b, 6, vii. 7, 1032, a, 13, 20, b, 30, c. 8 *init.*, ix. 8, 1049, b, 28, xi. 6, 1062, b, 24), from which we have not the smallest right to make an exception in favour of the Deity, as BRENTANO, 249, does.

[1] BRENTANO, p. 240, indeed, believes that the eternity in time of immaterial substances as little dispenses with the necessity of an efficient principle for them as the eternity of motion dispenses with the necessity of a mover; in other words, he endeavours to reconcile the eternity of the world with the theory of its creation by means of the conception of an eternal creative activity in God. But upon the principles of the Aristotelian as

of every subsequent theism this is impossible. One who conceives of God as the substance of the world, and of finite things as mere manifestations of the divine force immanent in them, may, and even must, in consequence, declare that the one is as eternal as the other. One, on the other hand, who treats God as a personal being outside the world, distinguishing other beings from Him as so many independent substances, would involve himself in a palpable contradiction were he to hold that the latter are eternally created by the former. Creation as an act proceeding from a personal will must necessarily be in time, and an individual being in order to produce other beings must necessarily exist before them. For only *causæ immanentes* have contemporaneous effects; *causæ transeuntes* always precede their effects: the father precedes the son, the artist the work of art, the creator the creature. Such a contradiction we should be justified in attributing to Aristotle, only if we could show that he held alike to the eternity of the world and to a creative activity of God. The opposite, however, is the case. Aristotle holds, indeed, quite definitely the doctrine of the eternity of the world, but of a creative activity in God we not only find no word in his writings, but he expressly de-

respect to the Forms of sensible things, and to the order
of nature which results from their union with Matter:
they also are uncreated.[1] It is equally impossible upon
Aristotle's showing to explain the adaptations of nature
as the result of any personal interference on the part of
God.[2] If, finally, the ancient Greek view of the
universe as interpenetrated by divine forces is in open
disagreement with Aristotle's dualistic theism,[3] this
does not, where the question is one of his scientific
views, justify us in setting aside or explaining away his
own definite and well-considered statements, on the
ground that he has neglected to bring them into harmony with views that were pressed upon him from
another side.

Brandis adopts another method of solving the above
difficulties. He believes that Aristotle regarded the
Forms as the eternal thoughts of God, whose self-
development produces alteration in individual things,
and the harmony of whose transmutations is guaranteed
by the fundamental unity which underlies them.[4] But,

clares that no ποιεῖν belongs to
Him at all. Cf. also *infra*, Ch.
XI. near the end.

[1] As is shown in reference to
the forms p. 341, n. 2; in reference
to the universe as a whole, p. 387.

[2] Such interference is expressly denied of God (see p.
368, n. 1), nor on the theory that
the world is eternal can we
understand when it could have
taken place ; cf. p. 412.

[3] Cf. *infra*, p. 420 sq.

[4] *Gr.-rom. Phil.* ii. b, 575,
where he says that in order to
fully understand Aristotle's meta-

physics, we must supply certain
important conceptions, and goes
on : ' Indeed, that all existences
must be traced back to, referred
ultimately to, living thoughts of
God, and that these must be
treated as the simple substrata
upon which concrete existences
and their mutations ultimately
rest, hardly requires to be expressly stated, and is indicated
by the question (*Metaph.* xii. 9,
see p. 298, n. 2, *supra*): If nothing
is attained by the thought of the
divine spirit, wherein consists its
worth ? We may, moreover, as-

in the first place, this statement can apply only to the Forms as such, and leaves the existence of the eternal substances (the spheral spirits, &c.) wholly unexplained. In the second place, it is untenable even with respect to the Forms. It finds no support in Aristotle's own utterances,[1] and in more than one point it contradicts what he indisputably taught. The object of Divine Thought, according to Aristotle's definite statement, cannot be other than God Himself: not only are finite existences, as these particular things, excluded, but even the specific concepts or forms, which constitute their internal essence, must remain remote from Him, since they are always something different from Himself, and stand far below that which alone can be matter of his thought—viz. divine and perfect

---

sume that Aristotle—anticipating Leibnitz's doctrine of monads— more or less consciously intended to refer the changes in the qualities or essence of individual existences to the self-development of the divine thought on which they rest, and the obstructions and disturbances in this self-development to its connection with matter or potentiality; and the harmonious variations in the developments of different individual existences, by an anticipation of the conception of a *harmonia præstabilita*, to the unity and perfection of the ultimate reality, the unconditioned spirit of God, which is their common substratum.' Cf. further his p. 578, where the central point of the Aristotelian theology is sought for in the doctrine 'that all determination in the world is referable to dynamic activities, and these again

to the eternal thought of God:' and p. 577 n.: 'That dynamic activities which have gone out from God, and therefore also finite being which is animated by these, should seek to return to Him, is quite comprehensible.' So also *ibid.* iii. a, 113 sq.

[1] Even *Metaph.* xii. 9 contains nothing to support BRANDIS's view (cf. also KYM, *Metaph. Unters.* 258). Aristotle there asks how we are to conceive of the thought of the divine spirit: if nothing is thought of by him (not: if 'nothing is attained by his thought') his power of thought must be as worthless as that exercised in sleep; if something other than Himself is thought of, then is the worth of his thought to be measured by the worthiness of its object? But this does not mean that the Divine thoughts constitute the essence of things.

being.[1] Conversely, the Forms of things cannot be thoughts of the Deity, since, according to Aristotle, the Form is the substance of the thing, and Substance can neither be predicated of nor belong to anything.[2] Thoughts cannot be substances, since they exist in the soul as their substratum.[3] Again, we find no analogy in Aristotle for the notion of a self-development of the divine thoughts : indeed, it is directly contradicted by the proposition [4] that there is no change in the thought of God, no transition from one thing to another. Finally, while Brandis maintains that all things strive towards Deity, because the active forces which emanate from Him struggle to return to Him again, Aristotle himself rather ascribes this striving, like all motion, to Matter, which desires to complement and complete itself by means of the forces.[5] Nor is it the least important objection to this view that it clashes with the whole character of Aristotle's system. For supposing the thoughts of Deity to be the supporters of concrete existences and of their mutations, the relation of finite reality to God would be one of immanence : the Deity would by virtue of his thoughts be inherent in things, and the latter would have in God the permanent ground of their shifting properties. Instead of Aristotle's dualistic theism, we should arrive at a system of dynamic pantheism.[6] But not only is it impossible to

---

[1] See p. 398, n. 1, and p. 397, n. 2, *supra.*

[2] See p. 330 sq., and p. 373 sq. *supra.*

[3] 'Επιστήμη is the very example which Aristotle mentions of that which is at once predicate and inherent attribute of a sub-stratum; see p. 214, n. 4 *fin. supra.*

[4] P. 397, n. 2, *supra.*

[5] Cf. p. 404 sq., p. 344, n. 1, and p. 379, n. 1, and on the doctrine that motion resides in the motum and therefore in the material, 386, n. 1.

[6] This is made still more

discover such a system in the works of the Philosopher,
but even his school were unacquainted with anything
of the sort, until the influence of Stoic opinions introduced that fusion of things diverse and fundamentally
distinct which meets us in the spurious book upon the
World and still more in Neoplatonism. Aristotle leaves
it quite uncertain how we are to define the relation of
the particular and individual Forms to the Deity.
From his utterances upon the subject we can only say
that he placed them side by side, without explaining
satisfactorily the existence and the special motions of
finite things by the operation of the Deity, or even
attempting such an explanation. They are given
factors, just as Matter is a given factor which he does
not attempt to deduce from Form or Deity. It is true
that the unity of his system, the οὐκ ἀγαθὸν πολυκοιρανίη, is thus rendered more than doubtful.[1]

This brings us to the conclusion of the Metaphysics.
God being defined as the First Cause of Motion, philosophy passes from the Unmoved to the Moved—or, in
other words, to Nature.

obvious by KYM; cf. *ibid.* p. 242
246 sq., 256, 258 sq., and p. 402, n. 1,
fin. supra. According to Kym,
God is said to be, not only the
creative conception, but also the
material cause of the world, the
indwelling purpose and the pro-
ductive force that is immanent
in it. This, however, is a mere
assertion, and is not proved to be
Aristotle's own opinion by any
detailed investigation into his
declarations on the subject.
　[1] Cf. THEOPHR. *Fr.* 12 (*Me-*

taph.), 7 : τὸ δὲ μετὰ ταῦτ' ἤδη
λόγου δεῖται πλείονος περὶ τῆς
ἐφέσεως, ποία καὶ τίνων, ἐπειδὴ
πλείω τὰ κυκλικὰ [the heavenly
spheres] καὶ αἱ φοραὶ τρόπον τινὰ
ὑπεναντίαι καὶ τὸ ἀνήνυτον [? we
should have expected ἀγαθὸν or
ἄριστον] καὶ οὗ χάριν ἀφανές. εἴτε
γὰρ ἓν τὸ κινοῦν, ἄτοπον τὸ μὴ
πάντα τὴν αὐτὴν [sc. φορὰν κινεῖ-
σθαι] · εἴτε καθ' ἕκαστον ἕτερον, αἵ
τ' ἀρχαὶ πλείους, ὥστε [?] τὸ
σύμφωνον αὐτῶν εἰς ὄρεξιν ἰόντων
τὴν ἀρίστην οὐδαμῶς φανερόν.

CHAPTER VIII

PHYSICS

A.—*The Idea of Nature and the most General Conditions of Natural Existence*

FIRST Philosophy, according to the view of Aristotle, has to deal, as we have seen, with unmoved and incorporeal reality : though, in treating of this its proper subject, we were in fact obliged to include some notice of the opposite principle. Natural Philosophy is occupied with the aggregate of corporeal existence which is subject to Motion.[1] All natural substances are bodies, or united to bodies ; and under the name of natural existence we include bodies and masses— everything, in fact, which possesses them or is related to them. Hence the whole domain of corporeal existence belongs to Natural Science.[2] But it regards form only in its connection with matter,[3] and the soul in its con-

---

[1] Cf. p. 183, n. 3.

[2] *De Cœlo*, i. 1 *init.*: ἡ περὶ φύσεως ἐπιστήμη σχεδὸν ἡ πλείστη φαίνεται περί τε σώματα καὶ μεγέθη καὶ τὰ τούτων εἶναι πάθη καὶ τὰς κινήσεις, ἔτι δὲ περὶ τὰς ἀρχὰς, ὅσαι τῆς τοιαύτης οὐσίας εἰσίν· τῶν γὰρ φύσει συνεστώτων τὰ μέν ἐστι σώματα καὶ μεγέθη [as the human body], τὰ δ' ἔχει σῶμα καὶ μέγεθος [as man], τὰ δ' ἀρχαὶ τῶν ἐχόντων εἰσίν [as the soul] ; iii.

1, 298, b, 27 : ἐπεὶ δὲ τῶν φύσει λεγομένων τὰ μέν ἐστιν οὐσίαι τὰ δ' ἔργα καὶ πάθη τούτων [by οὐσίαι, however, he here means both simple and composite bodies] . . . φανερὸν ὅτι τὴν πλείστην συμβαίνει τῆς περὶ φύσεως ἱστορίας περὶ σωμάτων εἶναι· πᾶσαι γὰρ αἱ φυσικαὶ οὐσίαι ἢ σώματα ἢ μετὰ σωμάτων γίγνονται καὶ μεγεθῶν.

[3] *Metaph.* vi. 1, 1025, b, 26 sq. (xi. 7) and elsewhere ; see *infra*.

nection with the body.[1]   It must, however, be remembered that material existence pertains to Nature and to Natural Philosophy only in so far as it is subject to motion and repose. Mathematical bodies are not natural bodies ; indeed, Mathematics may be distinguished from Physics by the fact that the former deals with immovable, the latter with movable, substances.[2] Furthermore, movable existence can only be regarded as 'natural' when it contains within itself the principle of motion ; and this is the point of difference between natural things and the productions of art.[3] The distinction, on the other hand, which is drawn between rational and irrational forces, on the ground that the former may act in either of two opposite directions, the latter only in one, and that the former, therefore, are free, the latter necessary—is only a subdivision within the realm of Nature.[4]   Yet since in all substance Form and Matter are distinguishable, we are met by this question : Does the essential reality of nature consist in the Form

---

[1] *Metaph.* vi. 1, 1026, a, 5: περὶ ψυχῆς ἐνίας θεωρῆσαι τοῦ φυσικοῦ, ὅση μὴ ἄνευ τῆς ὕλης ἐστίν. *De An.* i. 1, 403, b, 7. *Part. An.* i. 1, 641, a, 21, 32.

[2] *Phys.* ii. 2, 193, b, 31: the mathematician as well as the physicist is occupied with the form of bodies, ἀλλ' οὐχ ᾗ φυσικοῦ σώματος πέρας ἕκαστον· οὐδὲ τὰ συμβεβηκότα θεωρεῖ ᾗ τοιούτοις [sc. φυσικοῖς] οὖσι συμβέβηκεν. διὸ καὶ χωρίζει· χωριστὰ γὰρ τῇ νοήσει κινήσεώς ἐστι . . . . τὸ μὲν γὰρ περιττὸν ἔσται καὶ τὸ ἄρτιον, etc. ἄνευ κινήσεως, σὰρξ δὲ καὶ ὀστοῦν καὶ ἄνθρωπος οὐκέτι. Cf. what follows and 183, n. 3, *supra.*

[3] *Phys.* ii. 1, 192, b, 13 : τὰ μὲν γὰρ φύσει ὄντα πάντα φαίνεται ἔχοντα ἐν ἑαυτοῖς ἀρχὴν κινήσεως καὶ στάσεως, τὰ μὲν κατὰ τόπον, τὰ δὲ κατ' αὔξησιν καὶ φθίσιν, τὰ δὲ κατ' ἀλλοίωσιν· κλίνη δὲ καὶ ἱμάτιον, etc. . . . οὐδεμίαν ὁρμὴν ἔχει μεταβολῆς ἔμφυτον, as he proceeds in the rest of the chapter further to explain. *Metaph.* xii. 3, 1070, a, 7 : ἡ μὲν οὖν τέχνη ἀρχὴ ἐν ἄλλῳ [similarly ix. 2, 1046, b, 4] ἡ δὲ φύσις ἀρχὴ ἐν αὐτῷ.

[4] *Metaph.* ix. 2 *init.* c. 5, c. 8, 1050, a, 30 sqq.   *De Interpr.* c. 13, 22, b, 39.

or in the Matter ? In support of the second alternative
it might be asserted that everything requires some
material in order to be what it is.¹ Yet Aristotle is
forced to maintain the first alternative. The essence of
things invariably resides in the Form ; it is only by its
Form and purpose that a natural object becomes what it
is.² The true causes are the final causes ; the material
causes are only the indispensable conditions of natural
existence.³ If, therefore, we wish to determine the general definition of Nature, we must not consider what
in it is material so much as the moving and informing
force.⁴ Nature is the cause of motion and rest in everything which possesses these conditions of being originally
and not merely in some derivative fashion. A natural
thing is one that has such a motive force within itself.⁵

But Aristotle does not help us greatly in defining

---

¹ *Phys.* ii. 1, 193, a, 9–30.
Metaph. v. 4, 1014, b, 26.
² *Phys.* ii. 1, 193, a, 28 sqq. c.
2, 194, a, 12. *Metaph.* as above,
l. 35 sqq. *Part. An.* i. 1, 640, b,
28, 641, a, 29, b, 23 sqq.
³ For a fuller discussion of
this point see *infra* and p. 357–8.
⁴ *Part. An.* i. 640, b, 28 : ἡ
γὰρ κατὰ τὴν μορφὴν φύσις κυριωτέρα
τῆς ὑλικῆς φύσεως. 641, a, 30 : the
scientific investigator has to deal
with the soul still more than with
the body, ὅσῳ μᾶλλον ἡ ὕλη δι'
ἐκείνην φύσις ἐστὶν ἢ ἀνάπαλιν.
⁵ *Phys.* ii. 1, 192, b, 20 : ὡς
οὔσης τῆς φύσεως ἀρχῆς τινὸς καὶ
αἰτίας τοῦ κινεῖσθαι καὶ ἠρεμεῖν ἐν ᾧ
ὑπάρχει πρώτως καθ' αὑτὸ καὶ μὴ
κατὰ συμβεβηκός. l. 32 : φύσις μὲν
οὖν ἐστι τὸ ῥηθέν· φύσιν δὲ ἔχει
ὅσα τοιαύτην ἔχει ἀρχήν. *Metaph.*

v. 4 *fin.* : ἡ πρώτη φύσις καὶ κυρίως
λεγομένη ἐστὶν ἡ οὐσία ἡ τῶν
ἐχόντων ἀρχὴν κινήσεως ἐν αὑτοῖς ᾗ
αὑτά. vi. 1, 1025, b, 19 [xi. 7,
1064, a, 15, 30] : περὶ γὰρ τὴν
τοιαύτην ἐστὶν οὐσίαν [ἡ φυσικὴ]
ἐν ᾗ ἡ ἀρχὴ τῆς κινήσεως καὶ
στάσεως ἐν αὐτῇ (or l. 26 : περὶ
τοιοῦτον ὂν ὅ ἐστι δυνατὸν κινεῖσθαι). It is indifferent whether
nature is described as the substratum of motion merely, or of
rest as well, since, according to Aristotle, rest (ἠρεμία,
στάσις) belongs as an attribute
only to those things to which
motion belongs, or at least can
belong, and is merely στέρησις
κινήσεως. *Phys.* iii. 2, 202, a, 3,
v 2, 226, b, 12, c. 6 *init.*, vi. 3,
234, a, 32 c. 8 239, a, 13, viii.
1, 251, a, 26.

the character of this 'force' with accuracy. On the
one side he considers Nature as a Single Being,
attributing to her a life which permeates the world
throughout,[1] and a definite design which determines
and unifies all its parts. He talks of the aims which
she attempts to realise in her creations, although the
properties of matter often thwart her purpose. In a
word, he uses expressions that can scarcely be explained
except by the analogy of the human soul and the
Platonic *anima mundi*,[2] although he distinctly argues
against this idea as conceived by Plato. Though he
remarks that the designs of Nature are not determined
by deliberation like those of an artist,[3] and though in
general we cannot attribute to him any real and intentional personification of Nature, yet the analogy remains.[4] On the other side, however, he undoubtedly
regards living beings as individual substances. He
ascribes an individual principle of life to them, and he
never indicates, or sets himself to discover, how this
principle is related to the single force of Nature. Nor
does he teach us how Nature is related to the divine
causality.[5] When insisting upon the exact significance
of divinity, he denies it to any but rational beings ;[6]

[1] See the end of this chapter.
[2] Proofs of this are innumerable ; it will suffice to refer
to the discussion of design in
nature which follows in the text.
[3] As will be shown in its
proper place.
[4] By 'analogy' is meant, not
identity, but similarity.
[5] Cf. with what follows BRAN-
DIS, iii. a, 113 sqq.
[6] As in *Part. An.* ii. 10, 656,

a, 7 : ἡ γὰρ μόνον μετέχει [τὸ τῶν
ἀνθρώπων γένος] τοῦ θείου τῶν ἡμῖν
γνωρίμων ζῴων ἢ μάλιστα πάντων.
iv. 10, 686, a, 27 : man stands
upright διὰ τὸ τὴν φύσιν αὐτοῦ καὶ
τὴν οὐσίαν εἶναι θείαν · ἔργον δὲ τοῦ
θειοτάτου τὸ νοεῖν καὶ φρονεῖν.
Eth. N. x. 7, 1177, a, 13 sqq. (cf.
p. 165, n. 1) : νοῦς is the divine in
man, and therefore the highest
activity is the theoretic.

and from this point of view he will not allow that Nature as a whole is divine, but only demonic.[1] Yet there are other passages in which he seems to follow the popular theology of the Greeks, who recognised and revered an immediate exhibition of divine force in natural phenomena. Nature and God are so used synonymously,[2] and a share in divinity is conceded to all natural existences, however trivial.[3] Indeed, this vacillation of view is deeply rooted in Aristotle's philosophy. So far as God is the first cause of motion, all motions in the universe must proceed from Him; natural forces can only be an emanation of his force, and natural causes a manifestation of his causality. On the other hand, if we confine the functions of the *primum movens* to setting the outer sphere of heaven in motion, these conclusions are impossible. If even in the heavenly sphere we have to assume in addition to the Supreme Mover a series of subordinate and eternal beings, it is still more necessary in order to explain the much greater variety of movements in the realm of nature to assume a train of independent substances endowed with motive power of their own. How the harmony of these movements or their conjunction in an orderly system is effected, it is hard to say. It cannot be by the

[1] *Divin. p. S.* c. 2, 463, b, 12 : since beasts also dream, dreams cannot be divine ; they may, however, be demoniacal ; ἡ γὰρ φύσις δαιμονία, ἀλλ' οὐ θεία.

[2] *De Cœlo,* i. 4 *fin.*: ὁ θεὸς καὶ ἡ φύσις οὐδὲν μάτην ποιοῦσιν. *Gen. et Corr.* ii. 10, 336, b, 27 sqq. (see next chapter, *infra*). *Polit.* vii. 4, 1326, a, 32 : θείας γὰρ δὴ τοῦτο δυνάμεως ἔργον, ἥτις καὶ τόδε συν-

ἔχει τὸ πᾶν. *Eth. N.* x. 10, 1179, b, 21 : τὸ μὲν οὖν τῆς φύσεως [the moral disposition] . . . διά τινας θείας αἰτίας τοῖς ὡς ἀληθῶς εὐτυχέσιν ὑπάρχει. The θεῖαι αἰτίαι correspond here to the Platonic θεία μοῖρα, as to which see ZELLER's *Plato* and cf. p. 402 sqq. *supra.*

[3] *Eth. N.* vii. 14, 1153, b, 32 : πάντα γὰρ φύσει ἔχει τι θεῖον.

natural operation of the *primum movens* upon the world.
Aristotle's philosophy, moreover, excludes the conception
of God's immediate interference in the course of the
universe; and it would be illegitimate to attribute
to Aristotle the popular belief in Providence, on the
strength of a passing allusion to it in his writings.[1]
Consequently it remains in obscurity whether we are to
regard Nature as a single force or as an assemblage of
forces, as something independent or as an emanation
from the divine activity; or, on the other hand, whether
we ought to combine these two points of view, and, if
so, how we ought to do it. But meantime we may
permit Aristotle further to unfold his view of Nature.

The most important idea with which we have to
deal in the Philosophy of Nature is that of Motion. In
our earlier researches we had to examine this idea in its
general bearing; therefore what now remains is that we
should supplement our previous conclusions with an
analysis of physical motion in its stricter and more
special sense.

Motion was defined generally on p. 380 sq. as the
actualisation of what exists potentially. By analysing
the different sorts of Motion we arrive at the special
definition of its physical character. Aristotle distin-

---

[1] *Eth. N.* x. 9, 1179, a, 22 : ὁ
δὲ κατὰ νοῦν ἐνεργῶν καὶ τοῦτον
θεραπεύων καὶ διακείμενος ἄριστα καὶ
θεοφιλέστατος ἔοικεν εἶναι· εἰ γάρ
τις ἐπιμέλεια τῶν ἀνθρωπίνων ὑπὸ
θεῶν γίνεται, ὥσπερ δοκεῖ, καὶ εἴη ἂν
εὔλογον χαίρειν τε αὐτοὺς τῷ ἀρίστῳ
καὶ τῷ συγγενεστάτῳ (τοῦτο δ' ἂν
εἴη ὁ νοῦς) καὶ τοὺς ἀγαπῶντας
μάλιστα τοῦτο καὶ τιμῶντας ἀντευ-
ποιεῖν ὡς τῶν φίλων αὐτοῖς ἐπιμελου-
μένους καὶ ὀρθῶς τε καὶ καλῶς
πράττοντας. ὅτι δὲ πάντα ταῦτα τῷ
σοφῷ μάλισθ' ὑπάρχει, οὐκ ἄδηλον.
θεοφιλέστατος ἄρα. It is obvious
that Aristotle is here arguing
from popular conceptions; he
himself ascribes to God no external operation. Cf. pp. 389 sqq.
supra.

guishes three kinds: quantitative motion, or increase
and decrease; qualitative motion, or alteration; and
motion in space, or locomotion—to which may be added
as a fourth kind, birth and destruction.[1] Now all these
kinds of movement may be ultimately resolved into the
third kind—Motion in Space. For, if we examine
them more closely, we find that increase or growth, to
begin with, consists in the addition of fresh material to
matter which has already received a certain form: the
increment is potentially but not actually identical with
that which it augments, and assumes its form; in other

---

[1] *Phys.* v. 1, 225, a, c. 2, 226,
a, 23 (*Metaph.* xi. 11, 12), cf.
Metaph. viii. 1, 1042, a, 32, xii. 2
init., Phys. viii. 7, 260, a, 26, 261,
a, 32 sqq., vii. 2 *init.* *Gen. et
Corr.* i. 4, 319, b, 31; *De An* i.
3, 406, a, 12,; *Long.* v. 3, 465, b,
30; *De Cœlo,* iv. 3, 310, a. 25.
Cat. c. 14 *init.* Aristotle here
distinguishes generally three
kinds of change (μεταβολή):
transition from being to being,
from being to not-being, and from
not-being to being. The first is
motion in the stricter sense, the
second *destruction,* the third
origination. Motion he then
divides into the kinds mentioned
in the text (κίνησις κατὰ μέγεθος,
κατὰ πάθος and κατὰ τόπον, as he
calls them *Phys.* viii. 7, 260, b,
26), and, taking birth and destruction again together, thus enumerates four kinds of μεταβολή:
ἡ κατὰ τὸ τί (γένεσις καὶ φθορά), ἡ
κατὰ τὸ ποσόν (αὔξησις καὶ φθίσις),
ἡ κατὰ τὸ ποιόν (ἀλλοίωσις), ἡ κατὰ
τὸ ποῦ (φορά). That these are the
only categories under which motion can be thought, is shown
Phys. v. 2, where change of substance (birth and destruction) is
not admitted to be motion (similarly c. 5, 229, a, 30; cf. SIMPL.
Phys. 201, b, who extends the
statement to the Peripatetic
school in general, remarking, however, that Theophrastus, among
others, did not keep strictly to
this use of language); elsewhere
Aristotle treats this also as a form
of motion, and uses 'motion' as
synonymous with 'change.' See
p. 382, n. 3, *supra.* *Phys.* vii. 2, 243,
a, 21 (cf. *De An.* i. 3, 406, a, 4)
distinguishes two kinds of locomotion: that which is self-
originated and that which is
caused by something else. The
latter again is of four kinds:
ἕλξις, ὦσις, ὄχησις, δίνησις, the
third and fourth of which, however, may be resolved into the
first two. Cf. viii. 10, 267, b, 9
sqq.; *De An.* iii. 10, 433, b, 25;
Ingr. An. c. 2, 704, b, 22 (*Mot.
An.* c. 10, 703, a, 19); the
statement in *Rhet.* i. 5, 1361, b,
16, is less exact. Ὦσις is either
ὦσις in the stricter sense, or
πληγή; *Meteor.* iv. 9, 386, a, 33; *De
An.* ii. 8, 419, b, 13, and cf. *Probl.*

words, such increase is an augmentation of matter, the form remaining constant. Similarly decrease is the diminution of matter without change of form.[1] Quantitative alteration, therefore, implies both qualitative movement and locomotion.[2] But the second of these two is prior to the first; for every transformation results from the coincidence of something which produces it with something in which it is produced, of an active and a passive element[3] This coincidence, then, can only take place by local contact, for (although the converse is not necessarily true) the patient must always be touched by the agent, and contact cannot be effected without locomotion.[4]

Even the last species of change, birth and destruction, is eventually founded upon movement in space. If one were to assume an absolute beginning or end of existence, such a transmutation could not, indeed, be called a movement, since in such a case the substratum of the movement would itself begin or end. But birth and annihilation in this absolute sense are really impossible.[5] Everything starts from

xxiv. 9, 936, b, 38. IDELER, *Arist. Meteor.* ii. 509.

[1] *Vide* the full discussion in *Gen. et Corr.* i. 5.

[2] *Phys.* viii. 7, 260, a, 29, b. 13.

[3] Ποιεῖν in the physical sense is synonymous to Aristotle with ἀλλοιοῦν, πάσχειν with ἀλλοιοῦσθαι. Cf. *Phys.* iii. 3 *fin.*: ἀλλοίωσις μὲν γὰρ ἡ τοῦ ἀλλοιωτοῦ, ᾗ ἀλλοιωτὸν, ἐντελέχεια· ἔτι δὲ γνωριμώτερον ἡ τοῦ δυνάμει ποιητικοῦ καὶ παθητικοῦ ᾗ τοιοῦτον. *Gen. et Corr.* i. 6, 322, b, 9, 323, a, 17: οὐ γὰρ οἷόν τε πᾶν τὸ κινοῦν ποιεῖν, εἴπερ τὸ ποιοῦν ἀντιθήσομεν τῷ

πάσχοντι· τοῦτο δ' οἷς ἡ κίνησις πάθος· πάθος δὲ καθ' ὅσον ἀλλοιοῦται μόνον. On a further meaning of ποιεῖν see in n. 1 to p. 400.

[4] *Phys.* viii. 7, 260, b, 1 sqq., where it is further remarked that all qualitative changes are ultimately resolvable into rarefaction and condensation, which involve change of place. *Gen. et Corr.* i. 6, 322, b, 21 sqq. c. 9, 327, a, 1, cf. p. 386.

[5] *Gen. et Corr.* i. 3, among other arguments, shows that matter would in the end be all used up, if destruction were to

being of some sort, and is resolved into being again.[1]
It is only a particular object, as such, that begins and
ends its existence Its beginning is the end, and
its end the beginning, of something else.[2] Consequently, in so far as generation and destruction are
different from change, this difference only affects the
individual object. The individual changes when it sur-
vives as a whole, although its qualities alter, but it is
generated or destroyed when it, as a whole, begins or
ceases to exist.[3] If on the contrary we regard the
universe and not the individual, then generation and
destruction coincide partly with composition and division, partly with the transmutation of materials.[4] Now
both of these processes are occasioned by movement in
space.[5] Everything that comes into being has its
cause ; all ' becoming ' implies a ' being ' by which it is

mean actual annihilation (318, a,
13).

[1] *Phys.* viii. 7, 261, a, 3 :
δόξειέ γ' ἂν ἡ γένεσις εἶναι πρώτη
τῶν κινήσεων διὰ τοῦτο, ὅτι γενέσθαι
δεῖ τὸ πρᾶγμα πρῶτον. τὸ δ' ἐφ'
ἑνὸς μὲν ὁτουοῦν τῶν γινομένων
οὕτως ἔχει, ἀλλ' ἕτερον ἀναγκαῖον
πρότερόν τι κινεῖσθαι τῶν γινομένων
ὂν αὐτὸ καὶ μὴ γινόμενον, καὶ τούτου ἕτερον πρότερον. Cf. p. 384-7.

[2] *Gen. et Corr.* i. 3, 318, a,
23 : διὰ τὸ τὴν τοῦδε φθορὰν ἄλλου
εἶναι γένεσιν, καὶ τὴν τοῦδε γένεσιν
ἄλλου εἶναι φθορὰν ἄπαυστον ἀναγκαῖον εἶναι τὴν μεταβολήν. *Ibid.*
319, a, 20, ii. 10, 336, b, 24. Cf.
p. 387.

[3] *Gen. et Corr.* i. 2, 317, a, 20:
ἔστι γὰρ γένεσις ἁπλῆ καὶ φθορὰ οὐ
συγκρίσει καὶ διακρίσει, ἀλλ' ὅταν
μεταβάλλῃ ἐκ τοῦδε εἰς τόδε ὅλον.
'Αλλοίωσις is produced by change

in the πάθη, birth and destruction
by change in the ὑποκείμενον,
whether in respect of its form
(λόγος) or its matter ; c. 4, 319,
b, 10 : ἀλλοίωσις μέν ἐστιν, ὅταν
ὑπομένοντος τοῦ ὑποκειμένου, αἰσθητοῦ ὄντος, μεταβάλλῃ ἐν τοῖς αὐτοῦ
πάθεσιν . . . . ὅταν δ' ὅλον μεταβάλλῃ μὴ ὑπομένοντος αἰσθητοῦ
τινος ὡς ὑποκειμένου τοῦ αὐτοῦ . . .
γένεσις ἤδη τὸ τοιοῦτον, τοῦ δὲ
φθορά.

[4] Cf. *Meteor.* iv. 1, 378, b, 31
sqq., where he argues that generation is effected by definite
materials becoming transmuted
and determined in certain ways
by the agency of efficient forces ;
destruction, on the other hand,
by the conquest of the passive
matter over the determining
form.

[5] Cf. *Phys.* viii. 7, 260, b, 8 :

produced. Since this, as we saw in the case of alteration, cannot operate without movement in space, such
movement must precede all generation.[1] Again, if
movement in space precedes generation, it must of necessity precede growth, change, decrease, and destruction ; since these processes can only be carried on in that
which has previously been generated.[2] Therefore this
species of motion is the first in the order of causality, as
well as in the order of time and in the logical order also.[3]

Notwithstanding what has just been said, Aristotle
is far from explaining natural phenomena by the merely
mechanical principle of motion in space, as the Atomists
had done. Even purely physical occurrences cannot, in
his opinion, be satisfactorily accounted for by this
method, seeing that many of them are only to be
conceived as modes of qualitative alteration, or the
transmutation of materials.[4] Physics do not by any
means exhaust the conception of Nature. Final Causes

πάντων τῶν παθημάτων ἀρχὴ πύκνωσις καὶ μάνωσις . . . πύκνωσις δὲ
καὶ μάνωσις σύγκρισις καὶ διάκρισις,
καθ᾽ ἃς γένεσις καὶ φθορὰ λέγεται
τῶν οὐσιῶν. συγκρινόμενα δὲ καὶ
διακρινόμενα ἀνάγκη κατὰ τόπον
μεταβάλλειν.

[1] *Phys. ibid.* 261, a, 1 sqq.
Gen. et Corr. ii. 10 *init.*

[2] *Phys. ibid.* b, 7. It is here
further pointed out in proof of the
priority of ' movement in space,'
that, while it is presupposed by
the others, it does not presuppose them. Without the movement of the heavens, neither
generation nor destruction, neither growth nor material change,
could take place. Movement itself, on the other hand, is indepen-

dent of these conceptions, and
none of them are applicable to the
heavens (260, b, 19 sqq. *Gen. et
Corr.* ii. 10 *init.*). So also movement in space is the only one of
these conceptions which has to do
with the eternal, and is of infinite
duration (260, b, 29, 261, a, 27
sqq.). Aristotle also argues that
because it is the last in time in respect to individual existences, it
must be the first in nature (260,
b, 30, 261, a, 13) ; and he holds that
it causes the least change in the
nature of the thing moved, and is
the motion which the self-moving
produces in preference to every
other (261, a, 20).

[3] *Ibid.* 260, b, 15 sqq.

[4] See p. 304, n. 3, and p. 306, n. 5.

rise above the material causes which subserve them ; and these are not provided for in the philosophy of a Democritus.[1] Lastly, if it be true that 'becoming' is a transition from potentiality to actuality, or a process of development, and that the importance of Aristotle's natural philosophy consists, to a great extent, in having first made this notion of development possible and consciously given it the foremost place, it is clear that Aristotle could not favour opinions which started with an express denial of any 'becoming' or qualitative alteration, and left us nothing but a movement in space of unalterable materials. Therefore qualitative alteration must be added to locomotion, even in the domain of matter, as a second source of natural occurrences : but over against both, Aristotle sets the teleology of nature, which uses as means to its end all that is corporeal and determined by natural necessity.

Next to Motion in Space, and not without direct relation to it, come investigations by which Aristotle further illustrates the idea of motion in his Physics : and these include discussions upon the Infinite, Space, Time, the Unity and Continuity of Motion,[2] &c.

The Infinite [3] had played an important part in pre-

---

[1] See p. 307, n. 4, and cf. p. 359, sq. *supra*.

[2] He describes those conceptions, indeed, generally, iii. 1, 200, b, 15 sqq. c. 4 *init.*, as belonging to the discussion upon motion, and deals with the first three in bks. iii. and iv. before the section upon the kinds of motion ; but the way in which he treats them shows that he is thinking chiefly of locomotion.

[3] The discussion of this conception Aristotle introduces in *Phys.* iii. 1, 200, b, 15, with the words : δοκεῖ δ' ἡ κίνησις εἶναι τῶν συνεχῶν, τὸ δ' ἄπειρον ἐμφαίνεται πρῶτον ἐν τῷ συνεχεῖ ; c. 4 *init.* he remarks that natural science deals with masses, motion, and time, each of which is either finite or infinite. On what follows see ZELLER, *Ph. d. Gr.* pt. i. 186.

Aristotelian philosophy. Plato and the Pythagoreans went so far as to make it an element of all things, and therefore a substance. Aristotle begins by proving this to be impossible : ' infinity ' does not belong to the order of substances but of qualities.[1] Then he shows that an 'infinite magnitude' is inconceivable. For suppose it to be a body, body is that which is limited by superficies ; or if it be a number, numbers are capable of being counted, and that which can be counted is not infinite.[2] Lastly, and more especially, an infinite body could neither be composite nor simple. It could not be composite, since, the elements being limited in number, an infinite body could not be made up of them unless one of them were infinite in magnitude, and such an element would leave no room for the rest.[3] And to think of it as simple is equally impossible. In the first place, as far as this world is concerned, no bodies exist except the four elementary ones, nor can there be any out of which alone everything could come, since all becoming moves between two opposites ; and if there be several primitive bodies, it is quite impossible that one should be infinite.[4] Again, every body has its natural place, in which it abides, and to which it tends ; and this law determines the difference in weight between bodies ; every body without exception must exist in a definite space, in a locality ; but in the infinite there is no definite locality, no distinction of up and down, centre and circumference, before and after, right and left.[5] Moreover, whereas it is manifest that bodies

---

[1] *Phys.* iii. 5, 204, a ; see p. 312, n. 2, and p. 325, n. 2, *supra.*

[2] *Phys. ibid.* 204, b, 4.

[3] *Ibid.* 204, b, 11, cf. *De Cœlo,*

i. 7 *init.*

[4] *Phys. ibid.* 204, b, 22.

[5] *Ibid.* 205, a, 8 to end of chap., iv. 8, 215, a, 8. *De Cœlo,* i. 6

either move in a circle like the celestial spheres or in straight lines up and down like the elemental bodies, infinity admits of neither of these movements. The former is impossible, because circles are by their nature circumscribed, and circular movement is rotation round a centre, whereas in the infinite there is no centre;[1] the latter, because lineal motion has a starting point and end.[2] Indeed, ' infinity' could not move at all, since it would take infinite time to traverse the smallest conceivable space.[3] Finally, Aristotle uses an argument conclusive with Greeks, who could not imagine formless being : the infinite, as such, is incomplete and without shape—we call that infinite the magnitude of which is indeterminable, which is never finished and complete, which cannot be limited in such a way as not to leave some portion of it outside.[4] The infinite first becomes a whole and complete when it is enclosed by means of form. But the world cannot be conceived except as complete and a whole.[5] It is therefore impossible that

init. c. 7, 274, b, 8, 29, 276, b, 6 sqq. In c. 6, 273, a, 21 sqq., the same conclusion is reached by showing that infinite bodies must be infinitely heavy or light, but an infinitely heavy or an infinitely light body is an impossibility, since it must either exhibit infinite speed or be absolutely immovable.

[1] As is shown, at unnecessary length, *De Cœlo,* i. 5, 271, b, 26 sqq. 272, b, 17 sqq. c. 7, 275, b, 12.

[2] *De Cœlo,* i. 6 *init.* Also c. 7, 275, b, 15 sqq.

[3] *Ibid.* c. 6, 272, a, 21 sqq. *Phys.* vi. 7, 238, a, 36.

[4] Aristotle's words are : οὐ γὰρ οὗ μηδὲν ἔξω, ἀλλ' οὗ ἀεί τι ἔξω ἐστί, τοῦτ' ἄπειρόν ἐστιν, where, however, the antithesis is merely verbal, οὗ μηδὲν ἔξω meaning ' that beyond which nothing exists,' οὗ ἀεί τι ἔξω, on the other hand, 'that of which a part always remains beyond.'

[5] *Phys.* iii. 6 : see at p. 350, *sup.* *Gen. An.* i. 715, b, 14 : ἡ δὲ φύσις φεύγει τὸ ἄπειρον· τὸ μὲν γὰρ ἄπειρον ἀτελὲς, ἡ δὲ φύσις ἀεὶ ζητεῖ τέλος The objection (*Phys.* iii. 4, 203, b, 22 sqq.) that infinite space presupposes also an infinite body, he afterwards sets aside (iv. 5, 212, a, 31, b, 8, 16 sqq.;

the infinite, as such, should really exist as an interminable magnitude.[1]

Yet we cannot entirely do without it. Time, and
motion, which is measured by time, are without beginning or end. Magnitudes are capable of infinite
division, number of infinite increase.[2]   Hence we

cf. *De Cœlo*, i. 9, see p. 395, n. 6
supra) by his peculiar definition
of space as the 'boundary between
the enclosing and the enclosed.
The boundary of the world itself
is, therefore, according to his
view, not in space; beyond it
there is no space either void or
occupied.
    [1] *Phys.* iii. 5 *fin.*: ὅτι μὲν οὖν
ἐνεργείᾳ οὐκ ἔστι σῶμα ἄπειρον,
φανερὸν ἐκ τούτων. c. 6, 206, a, 16:
τὸ δὲ μέγεθος ὅτι κατ' ἐνέργειαν οὐκ
ἔστιν ἄπειρον, εἴρηται; *ibid.* b, 24.
    [2] *Phys.* iii. 6, *init.*: ὅτι δ' εἰ
μή ἐστιν ἄπειρον ἁπλῶς, πολλὰ
ἀδύνατα συμβαίνει, δῆλον. τοῦ τε
γὰρ χρόνου ἔσται τις ἀρχὴ καὶ
τελευτή, καὶ τὰ μεγέθη οὐ διαιρετὰ
εἰς μεγέθη, καὶ ἀριθμὸς οὐκ ἔσται
ἄπειρος. Aristotle proves in particular: (1) the eternity of time,
and with it the eternity of motion
which is measured by time. Besides the passages quoted p. 388,
n. 1, see *Phys.* viii. 1, 251, b; 10 sqq.
and cf. *Metaph.* xii. 6, 1071, b, 7.
He argues that as every present is the middle point between
the past and the future, and
every moment is a present, it is
wholly impossible to conceive of
any moment of time which has
not a before and after, and therefore of any which could be a
first or a last moment, a beginning or an end of time. (2) He
proves the infinite divisibility of
magnitudes, by showing that
nothing which is continuous, whe-

ther it be spatial size, or time, or
motion, can consist of what is
indivisible.   Continuous magnitude can only be constituted
(according to *Phys.* v. 3, 227, a,
10) by such elements as have a
common boundary, and, moreover, lie outside one another;
indivisible magnitudes, on the
other hand, must either lie wholly
outside one another, in which case
they would have no point of contact, or must wholly coincide
(*Phys.* vi. 1 *init.*, cf. *Gen. et Corr.*
i. 2, 317, a, 2 sqq., *De Cœlo*, iii.
8, 306, b, 22). The assumption of
indivisible bodily surfaces or
lines is not only incompatible
with the fundamental principles
of mathematics (*De Cœlo*, iii. 1,
298, b, 33 sqq. c. 5, 303, a, 20, c.
7, 306, a, 26: cf. the treatise Π.
ἀτόμων γραμμῶν), but it would
likewise make the most universal
of all physical phenomena, viz.
motion, impossible, for, magnitude and time being alike indivisible, it is impossible to traverse
one part before another. In respect, therefore, of each of the indivisible elements—and accordingly also of the whole which is
constituted by them—motion
could only be predicated as a thing
of the past, never as a thing of the
present (*Phys.* vi. 1, 231, b, 18
sqq.; cf. c. 2, 233, a, 10 sqq. c. 9,
239, b, 8, 31), and all difference of
velocity must also in like manner
vanish (*ibid.* c. 2, 233, b, 15 sqq.)

must conclude that the infinite exists in one sense and not in another: or in other words, that it has a potential but not an actual existence. The divisibility of magnitudes in space is indefinite; yet we may not therefore argue that there is an infinitely small particle. The multiplication of numbers has no limit; yet there is no infinitely great number.[1] In a word, the infinite can never be represented in actuality. It is always potential, and in its two manifestations takes opposite directions—extension being capable of infinite division, but not of infinite augmentation: number, on the other hand, of infinite augmentation, but not of infinite division, since the unit is the smallest number.[2] Real infinity is only possible in incorporeal substance—

Again, all change is excluded in things indivisible, for change involves division between an earlier and a later condition (*Phys.* vi. 4 *init.*). In particular, when we come to the indivisible elementary bodies and surfaces of Democritus and Plato, we shall find these beset by a whole series of new difficulties in addition to the above. (3) Lastly, as there is no highest number, number is capable of infinite multiplication. This, however, has never been disputed, and therefore requires no proof.

[1] *Phys.* iii. 6, 206, a, 12 sqq.: πῶς μὲν ἔστι [τὸ ἄπειρον], πῶς δ' οὔ. λέγεται δὴ τὸ εἶναι τὸ μὲν δυνάμει τὸ δὲ ἐντελεχείᾳ, καὶ τὸ ἄπειρον ἔστι μὲν προσθέσει ἔστι δὲ καὶ ἀφαιρέσει. τὸ δὲ μέγεθος ὅτι μὲν κατ' ἐνέργειαν οὐκ ἔστιν ἄπειρον, εἴρηται, διαιρέσει δ' ἐστίν· οὐ γὰρ χαλεπὸν ἀνελεῖν τὰς ἀτόμους γραμμάς· λείπεται οὖν δυνάμει εἶναι

τὸ ἄπειρον. Only we must not suppose that this potentiality can ever become actual, ὥστε τὸ ἄπειρον οὐ δεῖ λαμβάνειν ὡς τόδε τι . . . ἀλλ' ἀεὶ ἐν γενέσει ἢ φθορᾷ, &c.; c. 7, 207, b, 11 (on the infinity of number): ὥστε δυνάμει μέν ἐστιν, ἐνεργείᾳ δ' οὔ· ἀλλ' ἀεὶ ὑπερβάλλει τὸ λαμβανόμενον παντὸς ὡρισμένου πλήθους. ἀλλ' οὐ χωριστὸς ὁ ἀριθμὸς οὗτος τῆς διχοτομίας, οὐδὲ μένει ἡ ἀπειρία ἀλλὰ γίνεται, ὥσπερ καὶ ὁ χρόνος καὶ ὁ ἀριθμὸς τοῦ χρόνου. It is shown also, *Gen. et Corr.* i. 2, 316, a, 14 sqq., with respect to infinite divisibility, that it never can be actually realised in fact and therefore exists only potentially. It is just because it is merely ἐν δυνάμει that the Infinite is reckoned among material causes (see p. 350, n. 1, *supra*).

[2] *Phys.* iii. 7. Time, however, even Aristotle holds to be infinite in both directions.

as an infinity of force. This also, however, is manifested
only in a series which is never exhausted, and in the
endless motion of the world.[1]

In proceeding to the notion of Space, we may
remark, in the first place, that Aristotle did not regard
it as the boundary-line or shape of individual bodies;
for in this case bodies would not move *in* a space, but
with their space, and several bodies could not succes-
sively enter the same space. No more can it be identified with the matter of bodies, since this also is
inseparable from the body which is in space: nor is it
that which circumscribes, but that which is circumscribed. In the third place, we may not regard it as
the distance between the boundaries of bodies, since
this distance changes with the bodies, whereas space
remains always the same, whatever may exist and move
within it.[2] Space may more properly be defined as the
limit of the surrounding body in respect to that which
it surrounds.[3] The place of each particular body[4] is
therefore formed by the (internal) limits of that which
surrounds it, and space in general by the limits of the
world.[5]

---

[1] See notes to p. 395, *supra*.

[2] *Phys.* iv. 1–4, cf. esp. 211,
b, 5 sqq., 209, b, 21 sqq.

[3] Τὸ πέρας τοῦ περιέχοντος
σώματος, or, more accurately, τὸ
τοῦ περιέχοντος πέρας ἀκίνητον
πρῶτον. Cf. *De Cœlo*, iv. 3, 310,
b, 7.

[4] Ἴδιος τόπος, as it is called
Phys. iv. 2 *init.*, as opposed to
τόπος κοινός. It is also called ὁ
πρῶτος τόπος ἐν ᾧ ἐστὶν ἕκαστον;
ibid. c. 4, 211, a, 28.

[5] *Phys.* iv. 5, 212, a, 31, b, 18.

It is strange that space should
here be called as in c. 4, 212, a,
20 (cf. n. 3, *supra*) τοῦ οὐρανοῦ τι τὸ
ἔσχατον καὶ ἁπτόμενον τοῦ κινητοῦ
σώματος πέρας ἠρεμοῦν; for we are
told (*v.* below and p. 377) that
the vault of heaven moves continually in a circle. Aristotle
means, however (c. 4, 212, a, 18
sqq. c. 5, 212, a, 31 sqq., viii. 9,
265, b, 1 sqq.) that just as in the
case of a ball which spins round
its own axis without otherwise
moving the circumference is as

Aristotle obtains the notion of Time by a similar process.[1] Time cannot exist without motion, since it is only by the movement of thoughts that we perceive it. Yet it is not motion, since motion itself is inseparable from the object moved, and therefore is in one case faster, in another slower; whereas time is universally the same, and its movement is always equally fast. It follows that time stands in a special relation to motion, but is different from it. It is the measure or the number of motion in respect to what is earlier and later.[2] The unit of this number is the 'now.' Time is occasioned by the movement of the 'now.' It is this that makes time at once a continuous and a discrete magnitude: continuous, in so far as 'now' is the same in the present moment as it was in the past; discrete, in so far as its being is different in each moment.[3]

These notions of Time and Space involve the infinity of the former and the finitude of the latter; and we already know Aristotle's further reasons for this distinction between them.[4] In like manner his concep-

stationary as the centre, the circular motion affecting merely its parts, since only those change their position, so the highest heavens move only in a certain respect, and are in space only κατὰ συμβεβηκὸς, and in so far as their parts move and are in space (*De Cœlo*, v. 5, which passage BRAN-DIS, ii. b, 748, wrongly suspects). In a like sense it is said (212, a, 18) that the river is stationary, and that only the individual waves move.

[1] *Phys.* iv. 10, 11.
[2] Ἀριθμὸς κινήσεως κατὰ τὸ πρότερον καὶ ὕστερον, c. 11 *fin.*; *De Cœlo*, i. 9, 279, a, 14.

[3] *Phys.* iv. c. 11, cf. p. 220, a, 5: συνεχής τε δὴ ὁ χρόνος τῷ νῦν καὶ διῄρηται κατὰ τὸ νῦν; 219, b, 9: ὥσπερ ἡ κίνησις ἀεὶ ἄλλη καὶ ἄλλη, καὶ ὁ χρόνος · ὁ δ' ἅμα πᾶς χρόνος ὁ αὐτός · τὸ γὰρ νῦν τὸ αὐτὸ ὅ ποτ' ἦν · τὸ δ' εἶναι αὐτῷ ἕτερον. *Ibid.* c 13, *init.* : τὸ δὲ νῦν ἐστι συνέχεια χρόνου · ... συνέχει γὰρ τὸν χρόνον τὸν παρελθόντα καὶ ἐσόμενον, καὶ ὅλως πέρας χρόνου ἐστίν · ... διαιρεῖ δὲ δυνάμει· καὶ ᾗ μὲν τοιοῦτο, ἀεὶ ἕτερον τὸ νῦν, ᾗ δὲ συνδεῖ, ἀεὶ τὸ αὐτό ... ἔστι δὲ ταὐτὸ καὶ κατὰ ταὐτὸ ἡ διαίρεσις καὶ ἡ ἕνωσις, τὸ δ' εἶναι οὐ ταὐτό.
[4] Cf. p. 428 sqq., and 387, *supra.* Aristotle, however, here

tion of Space implies the impossibility of a vacuum. If Space is the limit of the enclosing body in relation to the enclosed, we cannot but conclude that there is no space where there is no body : empty space would be an enclosure that encloses nothing. Aristotle tries on this point, with minute and patient arguments, to confute the widely-received assumption of a vacuum, which, owing mainly to the teaching of the Atomists, had become part of the current Natural Philosophy.

The reasons with which they had supported it appear to him inconclusive. Movement does not need to be explained by such an hypothesis, since we can imagine that another body quits the space which the object in motion enters. Condensation may be referred to the exit of air or other matter from the bodies in question ; rarefaction to its entrance into them. The expansion which water, for example, experiences when passing into air (that is, into steam) may be explained by the alteration of materials, which necessitates another degree of rarity : or the phenomena of gravity by the tendency of the elements to reach their natural place.[1] The vacuum would rather put a stop to the possibility of motion. Since emptiness yields equally on all sides, one cannot imagine anything capable of determining a body to follow one direction rather than another. It would afford no distinction of natural localities. No special motion could take place in it. On the other hand, it

distinguishes, as Plato had done (*Tim.* 37, D, 38, B), between the endless time in which mutable existence moves, and eternity (αἰών) or the timeless being of the immutable. *Phys.* iv. 12, 221, b, 3. *De Cœlo,* i. 9, 279, b, 11–28 ; see p. 395, n. 6, *supra.*

[1] *Phys.* iv. 7, 214, a, 24 sqq., c. 8 *init.* c. 9.

would be equally impossible, on the hypothesis of infinite vacuity, to assign any reason for rest in Nature Again, if bodies fall or rise with a rapidity proportioned to the rarity of the medium through which they are moving, everything would have to fall or rise with infinite rapidity through the infinite rarity of the void. On the other hand, if, *ceteris paribus*, greater masses fall or rise quicker than smaller ones because they more easily overcome the withstanding medium, then in the void, where there is no resistance to overcome, the smallest would move as quickly as the greatest. Lastly, how are we to conceive that an empty space exists beyond the space occupied by bodies, since, if a body entered that space, there would then be two spaces, an empty and a full, the one within the other? And what is the use of such a void space, since every body has its own extension? [1] Besides, by maintaining that there is empty space or any space at all beyond the world, one would end in the contradiction of asserting that a body could be where no body can. [2]

If empty Space is impossible, empty Time, filled with no movement, is equally inconceivable, since Time is nothing but the number of motion. [3] Aristotle, in fact, maintains the eternity of motion as having neither be-

---

[1] *Phys.* iv. 8; cf. *De Cœlo*, iv. 2. In estimating the force of these arguments we must, of course, take account of the state of scientific knowledge at the time, and of the presuppositions which were shared by Aristotle and the Atomists alike. See p. 442, *infra*.

[2] *De Cœlo*, i. 9, 279, a, 11 : ἅμα δὲ δῆλον ὅτι οὐδὲ τόπος οὐδὲ κενὸν οὐδὲ χρόνος ἐστὶν ἔξω τοῦ οὐρανοῦ· ἐν ἅπαντι γὰρ τόπῳ δυνατόν ὑπάρξαι σῶμα· κενὸν δ' εἶναί φασιν ἐν ᾧ μὴ ἐνυπάρχει σῶμα, δυνατὸν δ' ἐστὶ γενέσθαι . . . ἔξω δὲ τοῦ οὐρανοῦ δέδεικται ὅτι οὔτ' ἔστιν οὔτ' ἐνδέχεται γενέσθαι σῶμα.

[3] *Phys.* viii. 1. 251, b, 10 : τὸ πρότερον καὶ ὕστερον πῶς ἔσται χρόνου μὴ ὄντος; ἢ ὁ χρόνος μὴ οὔσης κινήσεως; εἰ δή ἐστιν ὁ

ginning nor end.[1]　On this point he suggests the remarkable question : whether there could be Time without a soul?　And he answers it by saying that Time in its essence is implicit in motion, but that in reality it cannot be without the soul, because number does not exist without a calculator, and reason is the only calculator.[2]　But we should make a mistake if we sought to discover in this remark any inclination to the idealist theory of Time which has obtained so vast an importance in modern philosophy.　Its apparent bias towards Idealism proceeds from Aristotle's not conceiving the ideas of Time and Space in as pure and abstract a sense as is familiar to us.　Although he does not go so far as Plato, who identified Space with extended substance, and Time with the motion of the stars,[3] yet he never attempts to make an accurate distinction between Space and Time

χρόνος κινήσεως ἀριθμὸς ἢ κίνησίς τις, εἴπερ ἀεὶ χρόνος ἐστὶν, ἀνάγκη καὶ κίνησιν ἀΐδιον εἶναι.　*Ibid.* l. 26 : ἀνάγκη . . . εἶναι ἀεὶ χρόνον. ἀλλὰ μὴν εἴγε χρόνον, φανερὸν ὅτι ἀνάγκη εἶναι καὶ κίνησιν, εἴπερ ὁ χρόνος πάθος τι κινήσεως. *De Cœlo,* i. 9, 279, a, 14 : outside the world there is no time, for χρόνος ἀριθμὸς κινήσεως· κίνησις δ' ἄνευ φυσικοῦ σώματος οὐκ ἔστιν. Cf. p. 395, n. 6, *supra.*

[1] See p. 387, *supra.*

[2] *Phys.* iv. 14, 223, a, 16 sqq. esp. l. 25 : εἰ δὲ μηδὲν ἄλλο πέφυκεν ἀριθμεῖν ἢ ψυχὴ καὶ ψυχῆς νοῦς, ἀδύνατον εἶναι χρόνον ψυχῆς μὴ οὔσης, ἀλλ' ἢ τοῦτο ὅ ποτε ὄν ἐστιν ὁ χρόνος [apart from the soul time, as such, cannot exist, but only that which constitutes the essence of time, the reality that lies beneath it as the substratum

of its existence; *v.* TORSTRIK in *Rh. Mus.* xii. 1857, p. 161 sqq.], οἶον εἰ ἐνδέχεται κίνησιν εἶναι ἄνευ ψυχῆς.　Aristotle is not quite consistent in his answers to the question, what faculty of the soul it is that perceives time.　According to the above passage and *De An.* iii. 10, 433, b, 5 sqq., we must suppose that it is the reason, and that the sense of time is limited to rational beings.　In the *De Mem.* i. 450, a, 9–23, on the other hand, he assigns it to the πρῶτον αἰσθητικὸν, and attributes memory, which involves the perception of time (*ibid.* 449, b, 28), to many of the lower animals (*ibid.* and c. 2, 453, a, 7 sqq.　*Hist. An.* i. 1, 488, b, 25).

[3] See ZELL. *Ph. d. Gr.* Abth. i. pp. 613, 684, 2.

as universal forms of sense, and the existence in which they are manifested. We have seen [1] that he cannot conceive of space without physical locality, higher and lower, gravity and levity.[2] He limits existence in space, in its strictest sense, to that which is surrounded by another body different from itself, arguing from this position that there is no space beyond the world, and that the world as a whole is not in space, but only its single parts.[3] In the same way the homogeneous parts of a coherent body, as parts of the whole, are only potentially in space; they are not actually so until separated from the whole.[4] It is the same with Time. Time, being the number of motion, presupposes an object moved on the one hand, and on the other a counting subject. He remarks expressly, however, that when Time is called the number of motion, we must not understand by the word number that by which one counts, but what is counted.[5] Number, that is, must be taken not in its subjective but its objective sense. Far from considering Time as a mere form of our perception, he regards it rather as something pertaining to motion, and, indeed, to the body moved. Outside the world, where bodies cease, Time also ceases to exist.[6]

In the further discussion of Motion which is found in Aristotle's Physics, our attention is chiefly drawn to the points which bear more directly upon his doctrine of the *primum movens* and the structure of the universe. He

---

[1] P. 428, *supra*.

[2] He says, therefore, *Phys.* iv. 1, 208, b, 8: the movements of simple bodies (fire, earth, &c.) show οὐ μόνον ὅτι ἔστι τι ὁ τόπος, ἀλλ' ὅτι καὶ ἔχει τινὰ δύναμιν (a

real significance).

[3] See p. 429, n. 5, *supra*.

[4] *Phys.* iv. 5, 212, b, 4.

[5] *Phys.* iv. 11, 219, b, 5.

[6] *De Cælo*, i. 9; see p. 435, n. 3, *supra*, and p. 39⁵, n. 6.

defines the meaning of coexistence in space, of contact,
of intermediate space, of succession, of continuity, &c.[1]
He distinguishes the different relations in which the
unity of motion can be spoken of,[2] finding the absolute
unity of motion in continuous or unbroken movement—
that is, in such as belongs to one and the same object
in the same relation at one and the same time.[3] He
asks what constitutes uniformity of motion and its
opposite :[4] in what cases two movements, or movement
and repose, may be said to be opposed to each other ;
how far the natural or unnatural character of a movement has to be considered in either instance.[5] After
proving further that all continuous magnitudes are
divisible *ad infinitum*,[6] that time and space in this
respect correspond, and that in reality it is only with

---

[1] *Phys.* v. 3 : ἅμα μὲν οὖν
λέγεται ταῦτ᾽ εἶναι κατὰ τόπον, ὅσα
ἐν ἑνὶ τόπῳ ἐστὶ πρώτῳ, χωρὶς δὲ
ὅσα ἐν ἑτέρῳ, ἅπτεσθαι δὲ ὧν τὰ
ἄκρα ἅμα, μεταξὺ δὲ εἰς ὃ πέφυκε
πρῶτον ἀφικνεῖσθαι τὸ μεταβάλλον
. . . ἐφεξῆς δὲ οὗ μετὰ τὴν ἀρχὴν
μόνον ὄντος . . . μηδὲν μεταξύ ἐστι
τῶν ἐν ταὐτῷ γένει καὶ [join with
ταὐτῷ] οὗ ἐφεξῆς ἐστίν. . . .
ἐχόμενον δὲ [immediately suc-
cessive] ὃ ἂν ἐφεξῆς ὂν ἅπτηται
. . . . λέγω δ᾽ εἶναι συνεχὲς
[continuous], ὅταν ταὐτὸ γένηται
καὶ ἓν τὸ ἑκατέρου πέρας οἷς
ἅπτονται. In the συνεχὲς, therefore, there must be unity as well
as contact. On ἀφὴ cf. *Gen. et
Corr.* i. 6, 323, a, 3.

[2] *Phys.* v. 4 *init.* : motion is
either γένει or εἴδει or ἁπλῶς μία.
For other senses in which motion
is said to be 'one,' see *ibid.* 228, b,
11 sqq. Cf. vii. 1, 4, pp. 125, 139,

of Bekker's smaller edition.

[3] *Phys.* v. 4, 227, b, 21 : ἁπλῶς
δὲ μία κίνησις ἡ τῇ οὐσίᾳ μία καὶ τῷ
ἀριθμῷ, the latter is the case when
not only the thing moved and
the kind of its motion (ἀλλοίωσις,
φορὰ, &c., together with their
special varieties) but also the
time is the same, 228, a, 20 : τήν
τε ἁπλῶς μίαν [κίνησιν] ἀνάγκη καὶ
συνεχῆ εἶναι . . . καὶ εἰ συνεχῆς,
μία.

[4] *Ibid.* b, 15 sqq.
[5] *Phys.* v. 5, 6.
[6] *Ibid.* vi. 1 sq. ; see p. 430, n.
2, *supra*. The indivisible unit of
space and time (the point and the
moment) is therefore (as is shown
De An. iii. 6, 430, b. 17 sqq.)
never found existing actually and
independently as a χωριστὸν, but
only as contained potentially in
the divisible, and not ever known
except as a negation.

finite spaces traversed in a finite time that motion has to do—whereas infinite spaces are only said to be traversed in the same sense in which the time of motion is infinite [1]—he establishes the indivisibility of the present moment, and concludes that in this unit neither motion nor rest are possible.[2] He discusses the divisibility of motion and of the body moved,[3] remarking that every alteration attains completion in an indivisible moment, but that the moment of its beginning is never capable of being accurately determined.[4] He shows that it is equally impossible to measure a merely finite space in infinite time or an infinite space in finite time, and consequently that an infinite magnitude cannot move any distance at all in a finite time.[5] These conclusions supply him with the means of refuting Zeno's arguments against motion,[6] and enable him to prove that the indivisible can neither move nor change in any way.[7] Finally, he prepares the way for investigating the movement of the universe and its cause, by asking [8] whether there can be a single movement of infinite duration. After establishing the eternity of motion and

[1] *Phys.* vi. 2, 233, a, 13 sqq.
[2] *Ibid.* c. 3, and again c. 8, where he adds: in the transition from motion to rest, the motion lasts as long as the transition lasts ; while, therefore, a thing is coming to rest, it is moving still.
[3] *Ibid.* c. 4 (cf. also p. 430, n. 2). Motion according to this passage is divisible in a double sense : first in respect of the time occupied, and secondly in respect of the object moved.
[4] *Ibid.* c. 5, 6. We see from SIMPL. *Phys.* 230, a, m. 231, b,

m. and THEMIST. *Phys.* 55, a, m., that difficulties had already suggested themselves to Theophrastus and Eudemus in connection with this view.
[5] *Phys.* vi. 7 ; cf. p. 429, n. 3, *supra.* Aristotle shows, *Phys.* viii. 9, 265, b, 16, that his predecessors also treated motion in space as the most primary.
[6] *Phys.* vi. 9, cf. c. 2, 233, a, 21, viii. 8, 263, a, 4, and p. 311, *supra.*
[7] *Phys.* viii. 10.
[8] At the end of this chapter.

the necessity of a *primum movens*, he gives this answer : [1] if there is a continuous and single movement without beginning or end, it must be movement in space, for not only does this precede every other,[2] but every other is a transition between opposites ; [3] and where this is the case the first motion ceases at a certain point, at which a new movement may begin in another direction, but one and the same cannot continue without a break.[4] The same argument proves that only circular motion answers all the necessary requirements. If all movement in space must be either in a straight line, or circular, or mixed,[5] a mixed movement could only be of endless duration and continuous if both the others could. Movement in a straight line cannot have this character, since every finite rectilinear movement[6] has terminal points at which it ceases, and though between these terminal points it may be infinitely often repeated, yet these repeated movements do not constitute one continuous motion. Circular motion is, therefore, the only kind of movement which, continuing one and the same in unbroken sequence, can be without beginning and end.[7] It unites the repose of the universe with unceasing motion, since it enables it to move

---

[1] *Phys.* viii. 1–6; see p. 387 sq. *supra.*

[2] *Phys.* viii. 7 ; see p. 423 sq. *supra.*

[3] Generation from not-being to being ; destruction from being to not-being ; increase from less to greater ; decrease from greater to less ; alteration from one state to another, *e.g.* from water to steam.

[1] *Ibid.* 261, a, 31 sqq.

[5] Among mixed forms of motion we must in this division reckon all curves except the circle.

[6] An infinite one is impossible, not only in itself (see p. 430, n. 2, *supra*) but also because the world is not infinite.

[7] All this is explained at length, *Phys.* viii. 8, 261, a, 27–263, b, 3, 264, a, 7 sqq. c. 9 *init.*

without changing its place as a whole.[1] It is the measure for all other movement. It alone is entirely uniform, whereas in rectilinear [2] movement rapidity increases in proportion to the distance from the starting-point.[3] How this eternal rotation is brought about by the operation of the *primum movens* [4] we have already shown.

Important though movement in space is, as the most primitive kind of change on which all others are dependent, Aristotle cannot agree with the mechanical theory of physics in merging all forms of change in this one, and in assuming only the combination and separation, while rejecting the transmutation, of materials. Three questions arise upon this point. Is there a qualitative distinction between sorts of matter? Is there a qualitative alteration of materials? Is there such a combination of materials as to cause the change of their

---

[1] *Phys.* viii. 9, 265, b, 1 ; cf. p. 398, 4.

[2] Those, namely, which Aristotle treats as the natural motions of elementary bodies: in other words, the downward motion of heavy, and the upward motion of light bodies. With forcible movements the opposite is the case.

[3] *Phys.* viii. 9, 265, b, 8 sqq.

[4] The seventh book of the *Physics* is passed over in the above account, because it was not originally a part of the work (see p. 81, n. 2, *supra*). Its contents are as follows. After it has been explained in c. 1 that every movement must have its source in a *primum movens*, and in c. 2 (see p. 386, n. 3, and p. 423, n. 1, *ad fin.*) that the latter must move along with the motion, c. 3 goes on to show that ἀλλοίωσις concerns only the sensible qualities of things; c. 4 inquires in what case two movements are commensurable, and c. 5 finally proves that the same force moves half the mass in the same time twice as far, in half the time the same distance as the whole ; likewise that the same mass is moved, by the same force, in the same time, the same distance, in half the time half the distance, while half the mass is moved by half the force the same distance ; on the other hand, it does not follow that twice the mass is moved by the same force half as far as half the mass, or the same mass by half the force half as far as by the whole force ; for the force may not perhaps be able to move it at all. The same is true of the other kinds of change.

qualities? The Atomists answered all three of these questions, Anaxagoras and Empedocles at least the second and the third, in the negative. Aristotle feels himself obliged to answer all affirmatively, combating the mechanical theory of his predecessors, and seeking the solution of their difficulties in the peculiar tenets of his own system. That he wholly succeeded in this attempt the natural science of our day will certainly refuse to admit, and will even be frequently inclined, with Bacon,[1] to take the part of Democritus against him. Yet this is just a case in which we have to guard against a too hasty criticism of a man who occupies one of the first places among the scientific investigators as well as the philosophers of antiquity. In order to form an impartial judgment of Aristotle in his contest with the mechanical theory of physics, and to appreciate his own views, we must never forget that we have not here to do with the atomistic philosophy of our days, but with that of Democritus, which differed from it *toto cœlo*. Aristotle, like his opponents, possessed nothing but the scantiest rudiments of the methods and processes of observation which we have to so boundless an extent at our command. He had to define the elementary physical conceptions of an age whose observations did not extend beyond the reach of the naked eye, and whose experiments were confined to a few simple and for the most part very unreliable empirical processes. Of all[2] our mathematical, optical, and

---

[1] Cf. Kuno Fischer, *Franz Bacon*, 262 sqq. (Eng. tr.).

[2] Cf. also Brandis, ii. b, 1213 sq., 1220 sq., and Meyer's refer-ences (*Arist. Thierkunde*, 419 sq.) to Aristotle's method in testing heat.

physical instruments, he possessed only the rule and compasses, together with the most imperfect substitutes for some few others. Chemical analysis, correct measurements and weights, and a thorough application of mathematics to physics, were unknown. The attractive force of matter, the law of gravitation, electrical phenomena, the conditions of chemical combination, pressure of air and its effects, the nature of light, heat, combustion, &c.—in short, all the facts on which the physical theories of modern science are based, were wholly, or almost wholly, undiscovered. It would have been more than a miracle, if under such circumstances Aristotle had developed views in natural philosophy of which we could have availed ourselves without alteration at the present time. It is the business of a history to show how he explained phenomena consistently with the position of knowledge in his own day.[1]

None of the ancient systems presents so pure a form of mechanical physics as the atomic, to which the theory of the elements adopted by Plato from Philolaus is closely allied. Both deny qualitative variety in matter, and consider differences of shape and magnitude as the only original and real distinction. Aristotle opposes this view, not merely because it maintains the existence of infinitely small bodies or superficies, but also because it denies specific difference in matter. In both respects, according to his judgment, the weaknesses of the Platonic theory are most striking.[2] It contradicts mathematics, because it regards bodies as composed of superficies, which brings us logically to the assumption

---

[1] Cf. *supra*, p. 262 sq.   [2] Cf. ZELLER, *Platon. Stud.* . 270 sq.

of indivisible lines , [1] nay, further, to the resolution of magnitudes into points.[2] Again it destroys the divisibility of bodies.[3] Moreover, the figures of the elements assumed by Plato do not fill the space within the world, and yet he allows no vacuum.[4] Lastly, it is impossible to form any coherent bodies out of them.[5] Nor are the difficulties which beset this theory from the point of view of physics less important. For how can bodies which have weight consist of surfaces which have none?[6] And how, according to this hypothesis, could the specific gravity or levity of the single elements be produced? Fire would have to become heavier and ascend more slowly in proportion to its bulk; much air would be heavier than a little water.[7] Again, while experience shows that all the elements are mutually transmutable, Plato only admits this with respect to the three just mentioned;[8] even in their case difficulties arise from the circumstance that superfluous

---

[1] Plato, indeed, and Xenocrates actually adopted this assumption; cf. ZELL. *Ph. d. Gr.* pt. i. pp. 807, 2 *ad fin.* 868.

[2] *De Cœlo*, iii. 1, 299, a, 6, 300, a, 7, c. 7, 306, a, 23. Cf. *Gen. et Corr.* ii. 1, 329, a, 21 : since the πρώτη ὕλη of the *Timæus* is not a superficies, elementary matter cannot be resolved into superficies.

[3] *De Cœlo*, iii. 7, 305, b, 31, 306, a, 26 : primary atoms of the elements cannot be divisible (nor are they according to Plato and Democritus) seeing that when fire or water is divided, each part is again fire or water—whereas the parts of a ball or pyramid

are not balls or pyramids.

[4] *Ibid.* c. 8 *init.*; cf. ZELL. *Ph. d. Gr.* pt. i. 679, 3.

[5] *Ibid.* 306, b, 22 sqq.

[6] *De Cœlo*, iii. 1, 299, a, 25 sqq. b, 31 sqq. (where, however, we must read τὰ σώματα τῶν ἐπιπέδων, the gen. ἐπιπέδων being governed by πλήθει); cf. the corresponding objection to the Pythagoreans, p. 311, n. 5, 6 *supra*.

[7] *De Cœlo*, iv. 2, 308, b, 3 sqq. c. 5, 312, b, 20 sqq. It has already been shown how we are to interpret these objections in the mouth of Aristotle.

[8] *De Cœlo*, iii. 7, 306, a, 1 sqq. ZELL. *Ph. d. Gr.* pt. i. 676, 1, 2.

triangles are left over,[1] and that it is as easy to think of a superimposition of surfaces as of the composition assumed by Plato.[2] Furthermore, the theory of unchangeable type forms of the elements contradicts the fact that the shape of simple bodies—water and earth, for instance—is determined by the surrounding space.[3] In the last place, how are we to comprehend the qualities and movements of the elements by these hypotheses of Plato? Democritus supposed that fire was formed of globes, on account of its mobility and disruptive force ; Plato thought it was made of pyramids, but that the earth was made of cubes, on account of its comparative immobility. Yet both of these elements are hard to move in their own locality, and easy to move in a strange one, since they strive to escape from the latter and not from the former.[4] Aristotle is therefore forced to regard Plato's theory of the elements as in every respect mistaken.[5]

The Atomic theory of Democritus and Leucippus is treated by him with more respect ;[6] but he holds that

[1] *Ibid.* l. 20 ; cf. Plato, *Tim.* 56 D sq.

[2] *De Cœlo*, iii. 1, 299, b, 23.

[3] *Ibid.* c. 8, 306, b, 9.

[4] *Ibid.* 306, b, 29 sqq., where it is further objected that balls and pyramids are easily moved only in a circle, whereas fire has an upward movement. Again, if it is its corners that give to fire its heat-producing power, all elementary bodies must likewise produce heat as well as everything that has mathematical shape, for they all have corners. Fire changes things which it seizes into fire ; a pyramid or a ball does not change that with which it comes into contact into balls or pyramids. Fire separates only dissimilars, whereas it unites similars. Further, if heat be united to a particular shape, so also must cold.

[5] PROCLUS at a later date defended it in a separate treatise against his attacks ; SIMPL., *Schol. in Ar.* 515, a, 4.

[6] Cf. the discussion in *Gen. et Corr.* i. 2, 315, b, 30 sqq., the chief sentences of which are cited in ZELL. *Ph. d. Gr.* pt. i. 771, 4 ; also, on the Platonic theory, cf. *De Cœlo*, iii. 7, 306, a, 5 sqq.

it also is far from having proved that everything may be deduced from a primitive matter of absolutely homogeneous quality. In the first place, it is open to all the objections which beset the hypothesis of indivisible bodies.[1] Next, as in the case of Plato, it is clear that the materials could not adjust their shape to the space in which they find themselves, if we attribute a distinct elementary figure to them.[2] In the next place, we already[3] know the reasons why Aristotle is not inclined to admit an infinite variety of difference of shape among the atoms; and if the elementary atoms are to be distinguished only by their size, one element could not be developed from another.[4] If all the atoms are homogeneous, one does not see how they are separate, and why they do not join when brought into contact with one another. If they are composed of heterogeneous materials, we should have to seek the cause of phenomena in this circumstance, and not in the difference of shape, and then they would influence one another while in con-

---

[1] See, besides p. 306, the statements quoted p. 430, n. 2, all of which are more or less directly aimed at the atomists. Here also, we must continually remind ourselves of the state of science at the time, and of the peculiar character of the theory which Aristotle attacked. When, for instance, he shows that atoms could not cohere in a solid body, he is not speaking of the atoms of modern physics, which attract and repel one another, are held in equilibrium, &c., in many different ways, but of the atoms of Democritus, which act upon one another only mechanically by pressure or collision. It is certainly hard to see how a cohesive body could be constituted of such atoms. The means which Democritus adopted for securing this end by attributing corners and hooks to atoms, by which they may hang on to one another (ZELL. *Ph. d. Gr.* i. 796, 2, 798, 4), could not but appear to Aristotle, as they appeared (according to CIC. *Acad.* ii. 38, 121) to his follower Strato, fantastic and absurd.

[2] See p. 445, n. 3, *supra.*

[3] See p. 331 sq.

[4] *De Cælo,* iii. 4, 303, a 24 sqq. Cf. p. 306, n. 6.

tact, which is what the Atomists deny.[1] In the same way a reciprocal influence would exist between them if certain qualities—like warmth, for instance—were coupled with a certain shape ; it is, however, equally impossible to imagine the atoms without qualities and to suppose them endowed with definite properties.[2] Again, there is no reason why there should be only small and invisible atoms and not also large ones.[3] Lastly, if the atoms are moved by another power, they experience an influence, and their apathy is destroyed : if they move themselves, the motive force is either inside them and different from what is moved—in which case they are not indivisible—or opposite properties are united in one and the same object.[4]

Again, Aristotle believed that Democritus was quite as unable as Plato to explain the physical qualities of things. The one makes fire spherical, the other pyramidal in form, but both are equally wrong.[5] Aristotle, however, derives his most conclusive argument against the homogeneity of matter from the very phenomenon by which modern science is accustomed to support it—the phenomenon of gravity. Democritus, like Aristotle, was ignorant that all bodies mutually attract each other, that within the terrestrial atmosphere they all gravitate to the centre of the earth, that the inequality in the rate of their descent is caused by

---

[1] *Gen. et Corr.* i. 8, 326, a, 29 sqq., to which, however, it might be replied that they refuse to unite because they are not liquid but solid bodies.

[2] *Ibid.* 326, a, 1–24.

[3] *Ibid.* at line 24.

[4] *Ibid.* 326, b, 2.

[5] In the passage quoted p. 445, n. 4, *supra*, Aristotle attacks both views alike and on the same grounds. Cf. also *Gen. et Corr.* i. 8, 326, a, 3,

the resistance of the air, and that the pressure of the
atmosphere occasions the ascent of fire, vapour, &c.
Democritus believed that all the atoms fall downwards
in the void, but that the greater fall quicker than the
less, deducing from this hypothesis the concussion of the
atoms and the pressure by which the lesser are driven
upwards. For the same reason, he held that the weight
of composite bodies, supposing their circumference equal,
corresponds to their magnitude after subtraction of the
empty interstices.[1] Aristotle demonstrates[2] that this
hypothesis is false : there is no above or beneath in
infinite space, and consequently no natural tendency
downwards; all bodies must fall with equal rapidity in
the void,[3] nor can the void within bodies make them
lighter than they really are. But being equally unacquainted with the actual phenomena which have to be
explained, Aristotle repudiates the only true point in the
system of Democritus, in order to avoid the consequences
which he saw to be implied in the Atomic hypothesis,
but the truth of which Democritus was as far from recog-
nising as he was. On the strength of what he assumed
to be facts, he opposes a theory which, originally speculative, could only be supported by a verification of the facts
it had assumed, such as was wholly beyond the reach of
ancient science. It is true, as he says, that in a vacuum
everything must sink with equal rapidity ; but this

[1] Cf. Zell. *Ph. d. Gr.* i.
779 sq., 791 sq.
[2] *Phys.* iv. 8, 214, b, 28 sqq.
De Cœlo, iv. 2, 308, a 34–309, a,
18 ; see p. 428, n. 5, *supra.*
[3] Epicurus, indeed, had recognised this, not, however, as a

real advance upon the atomic
theory, but only as a means of
making his own arbitrary assumption of deviations in the atoms
comprehensible. See p. 307, n. 4,
supra.

appears to him so inconceivable that he considers it sufficient ground for rejecting the hypothesis of empty space.[1] He goes on to say that if all bodies be composed of the same matter, they must all be heavy, and there would be nothing that was in itself light and by virtue of its own nature disposed to rise, but only some things that remain behind in the downward movement or are driven upwards by something else. Although it may be that of two bodies of equal size, the denser might be the heavier, nevertheless a great mass of air or fire would necessarily be heavier than a small quantity of earth or water. This, however, he thinks impossible,[2] and he says it is manifest when we consider that certain bodies always tend upwards, rising quicker in proportion to the increase of bulk—a phenomenon which seems to Aristotle quite inexplicable on the hypothesis of absolute homogeneity in matter. If gravity be determined by bulk, then a greater mass of rarer material would be heavier than a small one of denser, and accordingly would move downwards. If, on the contrary, it is said that the more vacuum a body contains the lighter

---

[1] Cf. *Phys.* iv. 8, 216, a, 13 : ὁρῶμεν γὰρ τὰ μείζω ῥοπὴν ἔχοντα ἢ βάρους ἢ κουφότητος, ἐὰν τἄλλα ὁμοίως ἔχῃ τοῖς σχήμασι, θᾶττον φερόμενα τὸ ἴσον χωρίον, καὶ κατὰ λόγον ὃν ἔχουσι τὰ μεγέθη πρὸς ἄλληλα. ὥστε καὶ διὰ τοῦ κενοῦ. ἀλλ' ἀδύνατον. διὰ τίνα γὰρ αἰτίαν οἰσθήσεται θᾶττον; ἐν μὲν γὰρ τοῖς πλήρεσιν ἐξ ἀνάγκης· θᾶττον γὰρ διαιρεῖ τῇ ἰσχύϊ τὸ μεῖζον . . . ἰσοταχῆ ἄρα πάντ' ἔσται [in a vacuum]. ἀλλ' ἀδύνατον.

[2] *De Cœlo*, iv. 2, 310, a, 7 : τῷ [as PRANTL rightly reads, instead of τὸ] δὲ μίαν ποιεῖν φύσιν τῶν τῷ μεγέθει διαφερόντων ἀναγκαῖον

ταὐτόν συμβαίνειν τοῖς μίαν ποιοῦσιν ὕλην, καὶ μήθ' ἁπλῶς εἶναι μηθὲν κοῦφον μήτε φερόμενον ἄνω, ἀλλ' ἢ ὑστερίζον ἢ ἐκθλιβόμενον, καὶ πολλὰ μικρὰ [small atoms] ὀλίγων μεγάλων βαρύτερα εἶναι. εἰ δὲ τοῦτο ἔσται, συμβήσεται πολὺν ἀέρα καὶ πολὺ πῦρ ὕδατος εἶναι βαρύτερα καὶ γῆς ὀλίγης. τοῦτο δ' ἐστίν ἀδύνατον. Cf. previous n. *Ibid.* c. 5, 312, b, 20 sqq. (where, however, in l. 32 we must read ἐὰν δὲ δύο, τὰ μεταξὺ πῶς ἔσται ποιοῦντα, &c., as Prantl does in his translation, though not in his text).

it is, it may be answered that a great mass of denser and heavier substance includes more vacuum than a small one of the rarer sort. Finally, if the weight of every body corresponded to the proportion between its bulk and the empty interstices, ever so great a lump of gold or lead might sink no faster, and ever so great a bulk of fire rise no faster, than the smallest quantity of the same stuff. He concludes that we are driven to assume the existence of certain bodies heavy or light in themselves, which move respectively towards the centre or the circumference of the world ; [1] and this is possible only when we conceive of them as distinguished from each other by the qualities of the matter composing them and not merely by the figure or magnitude of the elementary ingredients. [2]

Not only are the materials of the world different in quality, but they are also subject to qualitative transformation. Unless we admit this, we must explain the apparent transmutation of matter either (with Empedocles, Anaxagoras and the Atomists) by a simple extrusion of existing materials, or (with Plato) by a change in the figures of the elements. [3] We have already seen [4] how far Aristotle is from agreeing with the latter solution as maintained by Plato. On the other hand, were we to imagine that one and the same corporeal substance, like wax, assumed first one and then another elementary form, and that this metamorphosis was in

---

[1] Aristotle here follows Plato's view; see ZELL. *Ph. d. Gr.* i. 678 sq. Strato, on the other hand, returned to that of Democritus; see *infra*, Ch. XX.

[2] *De Cœlo*, 308, a, 21 sqq. 309, b, 27 sqq. c. 5, 312, b, 20 sqq. Cf. the section concerning the Elements, *infra*.

[3] Cf. *De Cœlo*, iii. 7.

[4] P. 444 sqq.

fact the transmutation of materials, the indivisibility of these elementary substances would follow,[1] and this he finds to be at direct variance with the nature of corporeity.[2] As to the theory of Empedocles and the Atomists, it is clear that, according to them, those substances into which others seem to be transformed existed previously in a state of interminglement with the latter, and are merely extruded from them. Aristotle thinks that this conception is, in the first place, at variance with the testimony of our senses.[3] Experience shows us a metamorphosis of materials in which the elementary properties of substances alter. One substance passes into another, or a third is formed of several. When water freezes or ice melts, the phenomenon is not, he says, occasioned by a mere alteration in the position and order of the parts, nor has a mere separation or combination of materials taken place, but, while the substance remains the same, certain of its qualities have changed.[4] Again, when water is made from air, a body comes into existence heavier than air, yet not, he thinks, as a consequence of the separation and compression of certain portions of the air. Conversely, when air is produced

[1] *De Cœlo*, iii. 7, 305, b, 28 sqq., 306, a, 30. The meaning is that we may suppose the elements formed of atoms of a definite shape—earth of cubical, fire of quadrilateral, atoms—without adopting Plato's view of the constitution of these bodies, and that the conversion of one element into another may be explained, not as its resolution into its primal surfaces and the combination of these into a new form, but as a transformation of the material that underlies all the elements alike (as was actually done by Philolaus, cf. ZELL. *Ph. d. Gr.* i. 376 sq.). By thus conceiving of the atoms of the elements as divisible, however, we should involve ourselves in the difficulty already mentioned, p. 444, n. 3.

[2] See p. 430, n. 2, *supra.*

[3] *Gen. et Corr.* i. 1, 314, b, 10 sqq. *De Cœlo*, iii. 7, 305, b, 1. *Metaph.* i. 8, 989, a, 22 sqq.

[4] *Gen. et Corr.* i. 9, 327, a, 14 sqq.

by evaporation from water, the former occupies so large
a space in comparison with the latter that it even bursts
the vessel.   How is this to be explained on the hypothesis that it had previously existed in the water without change or difference ?[1]   If a body grows or dwindles,
it is not merely that new parts are added to it, but all
its parts increase or diminish in size—and this involves
a general change in the material.[2]   When bones and
flesh are formed from food, they are not taken ready
made from what we eat, like bricks from a wall or water
from a cask, but the food passes into a new material.[3]
Moreover, it is clear that the elements themselves come
into existence and perish : fire is kindled and goes out ;
water is precipitated from the air and passes into steam
again.   How are we to conceive of such formation
and dissolution ?   There must be definite points at
which they begin and end, as in the case of all Becoming, else we should be driven to suppose an infinite progression in two directions.   Yet these terminal points
cannot consist of indivisible bodies—whether absolutely
indivisible (or atoms) as we have already seen,[4] or such

---

[1] *De Cœlo*, as above, 305, b,
5 sqq. Aristotle's view of gravity
precludes the admission that the
greater weight of water as compared with steam is due merely
to its greater density. The atomists of that time could not possibly explain the expansion of
fluids into steam as the result of
increased repulsion in the atoms ;
at least the atoms of Democritus
are certainly incapable of internal
change.   Empedocles and Anaxagoras (with whom Aristotle, *ibid.*
l. 16 sqq., first deals) were obliged
to explain steam as a kind of air
which emanates from water ; nor
could atomists generally regard
it as other than a complex of
atoms emanating from water in
which they had previously been
imprisoned. As against such theories Aristotle's objections are valid.

[2] *Gen. et Corr.* i. 9, 327, a, 22.

[3] *Ibid.* ii. 7, 334, a, 18, 26 ; cf.
De Cœlo, iii. 7, 305, b, 1.   Cf. p.
457 sq.

[4] In the passage from *De Cœlo*,
iii. 4, cited at pp. 306, n. 6, and
446, n. 4.

as are divisible by nature but are never actually divided ; for why should the smaller resist division, when larger bodies of similar substance do not do so ? No more can the elements be produced from incorporeal substance,[1] or from a body different from themselves ; for if the latter were not one of the elements, it could have no gravity or natural locality, and hence would be a mathematical and not a physical body, and would not exist in space. Hence we are driven to suppose that the elements are developed from one another.[2] But this process can only be conceived as one of transformation. For if there were not a transformation of the elements, but only a putting forth of something which they already contained complete within themselves, one substance could not be *entirely* dissolved into another, but an insoluble remnant would be left : and so any complete transmutation of substances, such as is given in experience, would be impossible.[3] Coarse and fine materials could never be completely converted into each other.[4] Lastly, how are we to imagine the reciprocal influence of substances on one another, unless they are capable of qualitative change ? Empedocles and Democritus made bodies enter each other by means of ' pores.' But not only can this hypothesis be dis-

[1] As is proved at superfluous length, and with some obscurity, in the *De Cœlo*, iii. 7, 305, a, 16 sqq.

[2] *De Cœlo*, iii. 6.

[3] This objection is first brought against Anaxagoras in the *Phys.* i. 4, 187, b, 22 sqq. : in *De Cœlo*, iii. 7, 305, b, 20 sqq. it is used against all who explain material change as an extrusion—in the latter case with justice, since if steam, for example, consists of a different material or different atoms from water, steam might be extruded from water, but water could not be wholly resolved into steam.

[4] *De Cœlo*, iii. 4, 303, a 24. where the words ὑπολείψει γὰρ ἀεί, &c., must mean ' since the larger atoms would fail to obtain release,' so that in water, for example, a residuum would be left which could not be turned into air.

pensed with, since bodies only require to be divisible, and need not be actually divided in order to experience reciprocal influences; but it really serves no purpose, for, if two bodies cannot affect each other by contact, those parts of them which interpenetrate by means of pores will not do so either.[1] Therefore while the mechanical theory of nature confined itself to a movement of the elementary ingredients in space, Aristotle maintained their qualitative alteration. Where the former had explained apparent metamorphosis as a mere process of extension, Aristotle assumed the operation of real changes under certain conditions. His predecessors restricted the reciprocal operation of bodies to pressure and impulse: he extended it to the internal nature of bodies, whereby they transform their primitive qualities.

It is precisely this process which he understands by 'action and passion' in their stricter sense.[2] The conditions of such transformation, as of all movement, are contained in the correlation of potentiality and actuality. When two things meet, of which one is actually what the other is potentially, then, so far as this is the case, the latter is patient, the former agent:[3] and a change is produced in the one, which proceeds from

[1] *Gen. et Corr.* i. 8, 326, b, 6–28, c. 9, 327, a, 7 sqq.

[2] *Gen. et Corr.* i. 6, 323, a, 12: if the *movens* is likewise partly *motum*, partly *immobile*, this must be true also of the agent: καὶ γὰρ τὸ κινοῦν ποιεῖν τί φασι καὶ τὸ ποιοῦν κινεῖν. οὐ μὴν ἀλλὰ διαφέρει γε καὶ δεῖ διορίζειν· οὐ γὰρ οἷόν τε πᾶν τὸ κινοῦν ποιεῖν, εἴπερ τὸ ποιοῦν ἀντιθήσομεν τῷ πάσχοντι. τοῦτο δ' οἷς ἡ κίνησις πάθος. πάθος δὲ καθ' ὅσον ἀλλοιοῦ-ται μόνον, οἷον τὸ λευκὸν καὶ τὸ θερ-μόν· ἀλλὰ τὸ κινεῖν ἐπὶ πλέον τοῦ ποιεῖν ἐστίν.

[3] *Ibid.* c. 9 *init.*: τίνα δὲ τρόπον ὑπάρχει τοῖς οὖσι γεννᾶν καὶ ποιεῖν καὶ πίσχειν, λέγωμεν λαβόντες ἀρχὴν τὴν πολλάκις εἰρημένην. εἰ γάρ ἐστι τὸ μὲν δυνάμει τὸ δ' ἐντε-λεχείᾳ τοιοῦτον, πέφυκεν οὐ τῇ μὲν τῇ δ' οὐ πάσχειν, ἀλλὰ πάντῃ καθ' ὅσον ἐστὶ τοιοῦτον, ἧττον δὲ καὶ μᾶλλον ᾗ τοιοῦτον μᾶλλόν ἐστι καὶ ἧττον.

the other.[1]   Action and passion, like all movement,
presuppose on the one hand the distinction of a *movens*
and a *motum*, on the other their direct or indirect
contact.   Where one or other of these conditions fails,
no passion and no alteration is possible ; where both
are present, it is inevitable.[2]   Again, this consequence
depends upon the agent being partly similar and partly
opposed to the patient ; since of things which belong
to wholly different genera, as a figure and a colour, for
example, neither can produce any change in the other ;
and the same is true of such things as are completely
similar, since change is always a passage from one
condition into an opposite, and that which does not
stand in any opposition to another thing cannot produce
in it an opposite condition.   Hence the agent and the
patient must be generically similar, but specifically
different ; and so the old moot point as to whether likes
or unlikes influence each other is decided by the law
that neither the one nor the other do so absolutely, but
both in certain relations.[3]   The agent and patient are
opposed within the limits of the same genus ;[4] and
the change consists in the removal of this opposition,
in the agent's making the patient like itself.[5]   Hence

---

[1] It has been already shown,
p. 386, n. 1, that all motion has
its seat in the *motum*, not in the
movens.

[2] *Ibid.* 327, a, 1, c. 8, 326, b,
1. *Longit. Vit.* 3, 465, b, 15. Cf.
p. 378 sq. *supra.*

[3] *Gen. et Corr.* i. 7, 323, b, 15-
324, a, 14, with which cf. the
quotations on p. 340 sqq.

[4] Like all ἐναντία. See p. 224,

n. 3, *supra.*

[5] *Gen. et Corr. ibid.* 324, a, 9 :
διὸ καὶ εὔλογον ἤδη τό τε πῦρ
θερμαίνειν καὶ τὸ ψυχρὸν ψύχειν,
καὶ ὅλως τὸ ποιητικὸν ὁμοιοῦν ἑαυτῷ
τὸ πάσχον· τό τε γὰρ ποιοῦν καὶ τὸ
πάσχον ἐναντία ἐστὶ, καὶ ἡ γένεσις
εἰς τοὐναντίον. ὥστ' ἀνάγκη τὸ
πάσχον εἰς τὸ ποιοῦν μεταβάλλειν·
οὕτω γὰρ ἔσται εἰς τοὐναντίον ἡ
γένεσις.

the patient is in the position of the ' matter,' to which a determinate ' form ' is communicated by the agent.[1] In so far as it has not yet received this form or has another form, it is opposed to the agent ; inasmuch as it must be capable of receiving it, it is similar in kind. If the agent is also a patient, so that the two mutually act upon each other, both must be of the same material, and in this respect belong to the same genus.[2] But this condition does not universally apply to agents : for as the *primum movens* is unmoved, so the first active power is without passivity, and therefore without matter ; whereas, on the contrary, the lowest force that acts immediately upon another is material, and its operation is conditioned by a πάθος on its own part.[3] The reason why all parts of the patient are affected by this active influence and by the alteration it occasions, is to be found in the nature of corporeity. Body, as potential, is subject in its whole extent to the transition to actuality, *i e.* to change, and being divisible at all points, nowhere offers an absolute resistance to the active force.[4]

The question about the mixture of materials must be judged from the same points of view. A mixture[5] is a combination of two or more materials,[6] in which

[1] A relation obviously identical with that which he expresses in the passage quoted p. 454, n. 3, under the form of potentiality and actuality.

[2] *Ibid.* 324, b, 6 : τὴν μὲν γὰρ ὕλην λέγομεν ὁμοίως ὡς εἰπεῖν τὴν αὐτὴν εἶναι τῶν ἀντικειμένων ὁποτερουοῦν, ὥσπερ γένος ὄν. The γένος stands to the εἶδος generally in the relation of matter; see p. 219,

n. 2, *supra*.

[3] For the above, see *Gen. et Corr. ibid.* from 324, a, 15 to the end of the chapter; and cf. c. 10, 328, a, 17.

[4] *Gen. et Corr.* i. 9 *init.* (see p. 454, n. 3, *supra*). *Ibid.* 327, a, 6 sqq.

[5] According to *Gen. et Corr.* i. 10.

[6] Aristotle shows, *ibid.* 327, b,

neither the one is merged in the other,[1] nor both exist together unchanged, but a third is formed which is itself ὁμοιομερές.[2] In other words, it consists neither in the absorption of one sort of matter into another, nor in a merely mechanical junction or interminglement of both,[3] but in a chemical combination. When two materials are mixed, neither of them remains the same, preserving its original qualities. They are not merely blended in invisibly minute particles,[4] but both have wholly passed into a new material, wherein they remain only potentially, inasmuch as they can be again extracted from it.[5] Such a relation, however, only

13 sqq. 328, a, 19 sqq., that only the union of substances(χωριστὰ), not that of qualities or of the form with the matter or of the immaterial efficient cause with its passive object, can be called a mixture (μῖξις). To us this seems superfluous; but according to *Metaph.* i. 9, 991, a, 14 (cf. ZELL. *Ph. d. Gr.* i. 890, n. 4, and *ibid.* i. 881 sqq.) he had some occasion to make this reservation. That the substances, moreover, which are mixed can only be of a material nature is self-evident : for the incorporeal is ἀπαθές.

[1] As happens in the case of burning (*Gen. et Corr.* i. 9, 327, b, 10), where it is not a mixture that takes place, but the production of fire and the destruction of wood, or, in other words, the change of wood into fire. The same is true of nutrition, and generally of all cases in which one material is transformed into another (*ibid.* l. 13, 328, a, 23 sqq.). This is not a case of μῖξις but ἀλλοίωσις.

[2] *Ibid.* 328, a, 10: φαμὲν δ' εἴπερ δεῖ μεμῖχθαί τι, τὸ μιχθὲν ὁμοιομερὲς εἶναι [or as it is previously expressed : ἔχει τὸν αὐτὸν λόγον τῷ ὅλῳ τὸ μόριον] καὶ ὥσπερ τ΄ῦ ὕδατος τὸ μέρος ὕδωρ, οὕτω καὶ τοῦ κραθέντος. On the ὁμοιομερὲς see the end of Ch. IX. *infra*, and cf. ZELL. *Ph. d. Gr.* i. 879, n. 2.

[3] Σύνθεσις, as distinguished (*ibid.* 328, a, 5 sqq. cf. *Metaph.* xiv. 5, 1092, a, 24, 26) from μῖξις or κρᾶσις. In *Metaph.* vii. 2, 1042, b, 16 σύνθεσις is further distinguished as the class notion under which κρᾶσις comes.

[4] As Anaxagoras, the Atomists and, later, Epicurus supposed.

[5] *Ibid.* 327, b, 22 : ἐπεὶ δ' ἐστὶ τὰ μὲν δυνάμει τὰ δ' ἐνεργείᾳ τῶν ὄντων, ἐνδέχεται τὰ μιχθέντα εἶναί πως καὶ μὴ εἶναι, ἐνεργείᾳ μὲν ἑτέρου ὄντος τοῦ γεγονότος ἐξ αὐτῶν, δυνάμει δ' ἔτι ἑκατέρου ἅπερ ἦσαν πρὶν μιχθῆναι καὶ οὐκ ἀπολωλότα . . . . σώζεται γὰρ ἡ δύναμις αὐτῶν, just because they can be again separated ; and l. 31 sqq. In later usage com-

occurs when the materials brought together are mutually capable of acting and being acted on ; [1] and when, moreover, the forces of both stand in a certain equilibrium, so that one of them does not get merged in the other and its qualities absorbed like a drop of wine in a hundred gallons of water; and lastly when they are easily divisible, so as to act upon each other at as many points as possible, like fluids.[2] Where these conditions meet, materials affect each other in such a manner that both, while combining, change at the same moment. This combination, attended by the simultaneous transmutation of the materials combined, is mixture.[3]

Aristotle is not content with substituting the theory of qualitative differences and transformations in matter for that of the mechanical physicists. He goes further, and shows that he is far from being satisfied with that physical view of things which is confined to material causes and their laws. Material causes are only intermediate—merely the means and indispensable conditions of phenomena. Above them stand final causes ;

---

plete mixture of this kind (τὸ πάντῃ μεμῖχθαι, De Sensu, c. 3, 440, b, 11), as distinguished from a mere compound of smallest parts was called ἡ δι' ὅλου κρᾶσις.

[1] This is the case when their material is of the same kind but their qualities are of an opposite character; ibid. 328, a, 19 sqq. 31; cf. p. 454, supra.

[2] Ibid. 328, a, 18 towards the end of the c., where the above is thus expressed: mixture takes place ἐπείπερ ἐστὶν ἔνια τοιαῦτα οἷα

παθητικά τε ὑπ' ἀλλήλων καὶ εὐόριστα καὶ εὐδιαίρετα [according to what Aristotle says, ibid. 328, b, these two coincide with one another]. ταῦτα γὰρ οὔτ' ἐφθάρθαι ἀνάγκη μεμιγμένα οὔτ' ἔτι ταὐτὰ ἁπλῶς εἶναι, οὔτε σύνθεσιν εἶναι τὴν μῖξιν αὐτῶν, οὔτε πρὸς τὴν αἴσθησιν [the previously mentioned apparent mixture]· ἀλλ' ἔστι μικτὸν μὲν ὃ ἂν εὐόριστον ὂν παθητικὸν ᾖ καὶ ποιητικὸν καὶ τοιούτῳ μικτόν.

[3] Ibid. 328, b, 22: ἡ δὲ μῖξις τῶν μικτῶν ἀλλοιωθέντων ἕνωσις.

above material necessity, the design of the universe ; above the physical explanations of nature, the teleological.

Our researches up to this point have already led to the conclusion that everything in nature has its End. If Nature is the inner cause of motion, every motion has its goal by which its measure and direction are determined.[1] If the essence of things consists in their form, the form is not to be distinguished from their End.[2] If everything which moves must of necessity be moved by something else, it follows that the ultimate cause of movement resides in that which moves the universe as its Final Cause,[3] and movement in general can only be conceived as the action of form upon matter, in which the former is the ' object of desire,' and so the goal towards which the latter strives.[4] Aristotle cannot conceive of regulated and orderly events except under the analogy of human action directed towards an end. Hence while combating the theory of an *anima mundi* in the form in which it had been held by Plato, he adopts himself a similar view.[5] He

[1] See p. 341, n. 2, *supra*.

[2] See p. 356 sqq., p. 418, and p. 462, n. 2.

[3] See p. 404, and p. 396, n. 3.

[4] See p. 383, and p. 379, n. 1.

[5] *De An.* i. 3, 406, b, 25 sqq.; *De Cœlo*, ii. 1, 284, a, 27 sqq.; *Metaph.* xii. 6, 1071, b, 37. Aristotle rejects this theory in the first place because he cannot regard the soul as in any sense a *motum* and therefore not even as ἑαυτὸ κινοῦν (see the beginning of Ch. X. *infra*). He further objects that Plato conceives of the soul of the world as something extended in space. But it would be impossible to suppose that its thought consists of circular motion, or of any motion at all. It would be inconsistent with its perfect happiness that it should be inter-mixed with the body of the world and, burdened with the latter, should have unintermittently to produce, like an Ixion with his wheel, a motion which had no affinity with its nature and which therefore involved exertion. Nor, indeed, is it shown how it produces it. Lastly, the soul cannot be ἀρχὴ as asserted in the *Phœdrus*, if, according to the *Timœus*, it comes into existence only with the world.

refers not only the movement of the outermost sphere, which communicates itself to all others, but also that of the stars, like Plato, to the action of spirits, which are related to the spheres moved by them as the human soul is to the body.[1] He even treats the forces of nature in general, to a certain extent, from the same point of view : in the eternity of motion he recognises the immortal life of nature,[2] and he even ascribes a sort of animation to the elements.[3] Every vital activity is also, as we shall see,[4] an activity guided by a purpose, for everything in living beings is related to the soul as the incorporeal unity of the corporeal existence. Hence it follows that by regarding nature as a living whole,

[1] Cf. p. 373 sq. and see the section in the next chapter concerning the Spheres. Aristotle is so far justified from his own point of view in treating both the world as a whole, and its individual parts as animated with life, as he does also De Cœlo, ii. 12 followed by Eudemus (Fr. 76 b, SIMPL. Phys. 283 m. : cf. SIEBECK, D. Lehre d Ar. v. d. Leben d. Universum, in Fichte's Ztschr f. Phil. lx. 31). God is a part of the universe in the same sense in which reason is a part of the man ; and of the same nature is the relation of the spheral spirits to their spheres. Each of these spirits, however, animates only the sphere which it moves and the primum movens only the πρῶτος οὐρανός. While the movement of the latter, indeed, extends to all the other spheres, yet in their case it is something communicated from without like the motion of the driver on a carriage ; their own proper motion, on the other hand,

is due, not to the primum movens, but to particular motors. Although the whole world is thus animated, yet Aristotle refuses to call it with Plato ζῷον, because its life springs from no single principle of motion.

[2] Phys. viii. 1 init.: Πότερον δὲ γέγονέ ποτε κίνησις οὐκ οὖσα πρότερον, καὶ φθείρεται πάλιν οὕτως ὥστε κινεῖσθαι μηδὲν, ἢ οὔτ᾽ ἐγένετο οὔτε φθείρεται, ἀλλ᾽ ἀεὶ ἦν καὶ ἀεὶ ἔσται, καὶ τοῦτ᾽ ἀθάνατον καὶ ἄπαυστον ὑπάρχει τοῖς οὖσιν, οἷον ζωή τις οὖσα τοῖς φύσει συνεστῶσι πᾶσιν. In these words Aristotle seems to have in mind the passage from Heraclitus, quoted ZELL. Ph. d. Gr. i. 586, 2.

[3] Gen. An. iii. 11, 762, a, 18 : γίνεται δ᾽ ἐν γῇ καὶ ἐν ὑγρῷ τὰ ζῷα καὶ τὰ φυτὰ διὰ τὸ ἐν γῇ μὲν ὕδωρ ὑπάρχειν, ἐν δ᾽ ὕδατι πνεῦμα, ἐν δὲ τούτῳ παντὶ θερμότητα ψυχικὴν, ὥστε τρόπον τινὰ πάντα ψυχῆς εἶναι πλήρη.

[4] At the commencement of Chap. X. infra.

and deducing its movement from the incorporeal forms
which govern all material change and shape, Aristotle
is driven, as was Plato on similar grounds,[1] to adopt of
necessity a teleological theory of nature.[2] God and
nature, he says, do nothing without a purpose ; nature
always strives, as far as circumstances permit, to realise
perfection ; nothing is superfluous, profitless, or incomplete in her ; of her productions we may say with truth,
and far more truly than of those of art, that there is
nothing accidental in them, but that everything has its
own purpose ;[3] it is, indeed, this very prominence of
design in nature which constitutes the beauty of her
creations and the charm with which even the least of
them repay investigation.[4] The essence of Nature, as

---

[1] See ZELL. *Ph. d. Gr.* i. 642
sqq.

[2] With what follows, cf. RIT-
TER'S exhaustive treatment of
the whole subject, iii. 213 sqq.
265 sqq.

[3] *De Cœlo*, i. 4 *fin.* : ὁ θεὸς καὶ
ἡ φύσις οὐδὲν μάτην ποιοῦσιν. ii.
8, 289, b, 26, 290, a, 31 : οὐκ
ἔστιν ἐν τοῖς φύσει τὸ ὡς ἔτυχεν
. . . . οὐθὲν ὡς ἔτυχε ποιεῖ ἡ φύσις.
c. 11, 291, b, 13 : ἡ δὲ φύσις οὐθὲν
ἀλόγως οὐδὲ μάτην ποιεῖ. c. 5, 288,
a, 2 : ἡ φύσις ἀεὶ ποιεῖ τῶν ἐνδεχομένων τὸ βέλτιστον. *Polit.* i.
8, 1256, b, 20 : εἰ οὖν ἡ φύσις
μηθὲν μήτε ἀτελὲς ποιεῖ μήτε
μάτην. *Part. An.* i. 1, 639, b,
19 : μᾶλλον δ' ἐστὶ τὸ οὗ ἕνεκα καὶ
τὸ καλὸν ἐν τοῖς τῆς φύσεως ἔργοις
ἢ ἐν τοῖς τῆς τέχνης. iv. 10, 687,
a, 15 (cf. ii. 14) : ἡ φύσις ἐκ τῶν
ἐνδεχομένων ποιεῖ τὸ βέλτιστον,
c. 12, 694, a, 15 : οὐδὲν ἡ φύσις
ποιεῖ περίεργον. *De An.* iii. 9,
432, b, 21 : ἡ φύσις μήτε ποιεῖ

μάτην μηθὲν μήτ' ἀπολείπει τι τῶν
ἀναγκαίων πλὴν ἐν τοῖς πηρώμασι
καὶ τοῖς ἀτελέσιν. *Gen. et Corr.*
ii. 10, 336, b, 27 : ἐν ἅπασιν ἀεὶ
τοῦ βελτίονος ὀρέγεσθαί φαμεν τὴν
φύσιν. *De Vita et M.* c. 4, 469,
a, 28 : τὴν φύσιν ὁρῶμεν ἐν πᾶσιν
ἐκ τῶν δυνατῶν ποιοῦσαν τὸ κάλλι-
στον. *Gen. An.* ii. 6, 744, b, 36 :
οὐθὲν ποιεῖ περίεργον οὐδὲ μάτην ἡ
φύσις. Likewise c. 4, 739, b, 19.
Ingr. An. c. 2, 704, b, 15 : ἡ φύσις
οὐθὲν ποιεῖ μάτην ἀλλ' ἀεὶ ἐκ τῶν
ἐνδεχομένων τῇ οὐσίᾳ περὶ ἕκαστον
γένος ζῴου τὸ ἄριστον · διόπερ εἰ
βέλτιον ὡδὶ, οὕτως καὶ ἔχει κατὰ
φύσιν. Even in the most insignificant products of nature we may
perceive the effort after perfection ; cf. foll. n. and *Eth. N.* x.
2, 1173, a, 4 : ἴσως δὲ καὶ ἐν τοῖς
φαύλοις ἐστί τι φυσικὸν ἀγαθὸν
κρεῖττον ἢ καθ' αὑτά, ὃ ἐφίεται τοῦ
οἰκείου ἀγαθοῦ. vii. 14, 1153, b, 38 :
πάντα γὰρ φύσει ἔχει τι θεῖον.

[4] *Part. An.* i. 5, 645, a, 15 :

he shows, is Form, but the form of everything is determined by the function for which it is designed.[1] All
Becoming has its goal, and the terminal point of all
motion is also its end or object.[2] This pursuit of fixed
designs in nature is demonstrated to our experience by
the order and coherence of the universe and the regularity with which certain effects are produced by certain
means. It is impossible to ascribe to chance what
happens always or even usually.[3] He lays especial
stress upon the motions of the heavenly bodies, the
birth of living creatures from seed, the instinct of
animals, the evidences of design in the structure of
animals and plants, and also upon human action, inas-

διὸ δεῖ μὴ δυσχεραίνειν παιδικῶς τὴν
περὶ τῶν ἀτιμωτέρων ζῴων ἐπί-
σκεψιν. ἐν πᾶσι γὰρ τοῖς φυσικοῖς
ἔνεστί τι θαυμαστόν. As Heraclitus bade the strangers welcome
to the bakery where they found
him, saying that God was there
also, περὶ ἑκάστου τῶν ζῴων προσιέναι
δεῖ μὴ δυσωπούμενον ὡς ἐν ἅπασιν
ὄντος τινὸς φυσικοῦ καὶ καλοῦ. τὸ
γὰρ μὴ τυχόντως ἀλλ᾽ ἕνεκά τινος
ἐν τοῖς τῆς φύσεως ἔργοις ἐστὶ καὶ
μάλιστα · οὗ δ᾽ ἕνεκα συνέστηκεν
ἢ γέγονε τέλους τὴν τοῦ καλοῦ
χώραν εἴληφεν. (Cf. c. 1, cited
in previous n.)

[1] Cf. also Meteor. iv. 12, 390,
a, 10 : ἅπαντα δ᾽ ἐστὶν ὡρισμένα
τῷ ἔργῳ · τὰ μὲν γὰρ δυνάμενα
ποιεῖν τὸ αὐτῶν ἔργον ἀληθῶς ἐστὶν
ἕκαστα, οἷον ὁ ὀφθαλμὸς [sc. ἀληθῶς
ὀφθαλμὸς ἐστιν] εἰ ὁρᾷ, τὸ δὲ μὴ
δυνάμενον ὁμωνύμως, οἷον ὁ τεθνεὼς
ἢ ὁ λίθινος.

[2] Phys. ii. 2, 194, a, 28 : ἡ δὲ
φύσις τέλος καὶ οὗ ἕνεκα · ὧν γὰρ

συνεχοῦς τῆς κινήσεως οὔσης ἔστι
τι τέλος τῆς κινήσεως, τοῦτο ἔσχατον καὶ τὸ οὗ ἕνεκα. c. 8, 199, a, 8 :
ἐν ὅσοις τέλος ἐστί τι, τούτου ἕνεκα
πράττεται τὸ πρότερον καὶ τὸ
ἐφεξῆς, &c. I bid. l. 30, see p. 356,
supra. Part. An. i. 1, 641, b, 23 :
πανταχοῦ δὲ λέγομεν τόδε τοῦδε
ἕνεκα, ὅπου ἂν φαίνηται τέλος τι
πρὸς ὃ ἡ κίνησις περαίνει μηδενὸς
ἐμποδίζοντος, ὥστε εἶναι φανερὸν
ὅτι ἔστι τι τοιοῦτον, ὃ δὴ καὶ
καλοῦμεν φύσιν. Phys. ii. 1, 193,
b, 12 : ἡ φύσις ἡ λεγομένη ὡς
γένεσις [see Metaph. v. 4 init.]
ὁδός ἐστιν εἰς φύσιν . . . ἡ ἄρα
μορφὴ φύσις. De An. ii. 4, 415,
b, 16 : ὥσπερ γὰρ ὁ νοῦς ἕνεκά του
ποιεῖ, τὸν αὐτὸν τρόπον καὶ ἡ φύσις.

[3] Phys. ii. 8, 198, b, 34, 199,
b, 15, 23 ; Part. An. iii. 2, 663, b,
28 ; Gen. An. i. 19, 727, b, 29, cf.
p. 362, n. 5 ; De Cælo, ii. 8, 289, b,
26 : οὐκ ἔστιν ἐν τοῖς φύσει τὸ ὡς
ἔτυχεν, οὐδὲ τὸ πανταχοῦ καὶ πᾶσιν
ὑπάρχον τὸ ἀπὸ τύχης.

much, that is to say, as all art is an imitation or completion of nature, and the design of the one therefore implies that of the other.[1] If we cannot deny the evidences of design throughout the world of mortal things, he argues that we must admit the same in a far greater measure with regard to the universe at large, where the order is more strict, and the regularity more unbroken. Whence, indeed, could the laws which govern the former have sprung except from the latter?[2] Consequently the discovery of final causes forms the first and most important problem of natural science. It must direct its attention, not to the individual, but to the whole which the individual subserves—not to the matter but to the form.[3] But if it is suggested that, in

---

[1] *Phys.* ii. 8, 198, b, 32–199, b, 26, cf. viii. 1, 252, a, 11 : ἀλλὰ μὴν οὐδέν γε ἄτακτον τῶν φύσει καὶ κατὰ φύσιν· ἡ γὰρ φύσις αἰτία πᾶσι τάξεως. *Part. An.* i. 1, 641, b, 12–30 ; *De Cœlo,* ii. 8, 289, b, 25 ; *Gen. An.* iii. 10, 760, a, 31 ; *Metaph.* xii. 10, xiv. 3 ; see p. 391, n. 2, *supra.*

[2] *Part. An.* i. 1, 641, b, 12 : ἡ φύσις ἕνεκά του ποιεῖ πάντα. φαίνεται γὰρ, ὥσπερ ἐν τοῖς τεχναστοῖς ἐστὶν ἡ τέχνη, οὕτως ἐν αὐτοῖς τοῖς πράγμασιν ἄλλη τις ἀρχὴ καὶ αἰτία τοιαύτη, ἣν ἔχομεν καθάπερ [as well as] τὸ θερμὸν καὶ ψυχρὸν ἐκ τοῦ παντός. διὸ μᾶλλον εἰκὸς τὸν οὐρανὸν γεγενῆσθαι ὑπὸ τοιαύτης αἰτίας, εἰ γέγονε, καὶ εἶναι διὰ τοιαύτην αἰτίαν μᾶλλον ἢ τὰ ζῷα τὰ θνητά· τὸ γοῦν τεταγμένον καὶ τὸ ὡρισμένον πολὺ μᾶλλον φαίνεται ἐν τοῖς οὐρανίοις ἢ περὶ ἡμᾶς, τὸ δ' ἄλλοτ' ἄλλως καὶ ὡς ἔτυχε περὶ τὰ θνητὰ μᾶλλον. οἱ δὲ τῶν μὲν ζῴων ἕκαστον φύσει φασὶν εἶναι καὶ γενέσθαι, τὸν δ' οὐρανὸν

ἀπὸ τύχης καὶ τοῦ αὐτομάτου τοιοῦτον συστῆναι, ἐν ᾧ ἀπὸ τύχης καὶ ἀταξίας οὐδ' ὁτιοῦν φαίνεται. Cf. also ZELL. *Ph. d. Gr.* i. 650, 579, 1.

[3] *Phys.* ii. 9, 200, a, 32 (after the passage quoted p. 360, n. 1) : καὶ ἄμφω μὲν τῷ φυσικῷ λεκτέαι αἱ αἰτίαι, μᾶλλον δὲ ἡ τίνος ἕνεκα· αἴτιον γὰρ τοῦτο τῆς ὕλης [inasmuch as Nature chooses her materials with a view to the thing that is to be produced] ἀλλ' οὐχ αὕτη τοῦ τέλους. *Gen. et Corr.* ii. 9, 335, b, 29 : it is not sufficient to give the material causes of a thing. Matter is merely the *motum,* the *movens* in the province both of nature and art is something quite different ; the κυριωτέρα αἰτία is the form. Materialistic physics, instead of giving us the real causes, can tell us only of implements of production : as if one in answer to the question ' Who saws the wood ?' were to reply,

order to pursue definite ends, Nature must be capable
of conscious deliberation, Aristotle considers this unreasonable Even Art, he remarks, does not reflect,
but works in the artist unconsciously.[1] Moreover, it is
just this which, as we already know, forms to Aristotle's
mind the distinction between Art and Nature, that the
productions of the former have their motive principle
outside themselves, and those of the latter within.[2] We
thus arrive for the first time at the important conception of immanent design, a point so essential to
Aristotle's system that we might define Nature, according to his view, as the realm of internal activity toward
a fixed end.

' The saw.' Cf. p. 360, n. 1, and
the passages quoted p. 303, n. 3,
and p. 307, n. 4, and ZELL. *Ph.
d. Gr.* pt. i. 788, 1, 3, 893,
2, on the neglect of final causes
in ancient physics. *Part. An.* i.
1, 639, b, 14 : φαίνεται δὲ πρώτη
[sc. αἰτία] ἣν λέγομεν ἐνεκά τινος ·
λόγος γὰρ οὗτος,, ἀρχὴ δ' ὁ λόγος
ὁμοίως ἔν τε τοῖς κατὰ τέχνην
καὶ ἐν τοῖς φύσει συνεστηκόσιν.
Ibid. c. 5, 645, a, 30 : in the
investigation of the animal or-
ganism the question is, not of the
individual parts or the matter,
but of the ὅλη μορφή, of the
σύνθεσις and the ὅλη οὐσία.

[1] *Phys.* ii. 8, 199, b, 26 : ἄτοπον δὲ τὸ μὴ οἴεσθαι ἕνεκά του
γίνεσθαι, ἐὰν μὴ ἴδωσι τὸ κινοῦν
βουλευσάμενον [= ἐὰν μὴ βουλεύη-
ται τὸ κινοῦν, for the poirt is
missed by Döring, who, in his
Kunstl. d. Arist. 68, puts a false
emphasis on ἴδωσι], καίτοι καὶ ἡ
τέχνη οὐ βουλεύεται · καὶ γὰρ εἰ ἐνῆν
ἐν τῷ ξύλῳ ἡ ναυπηγική, ὁμοίως ἂν
φύσει ἐποίει · ὥστ' εἰ ἐν τῇ τέχνῃ

ἔνεστι τὸ ἕνεκά του, καὶ ἐν φύσει.
Aristotle has here in view the
art that has become a fixed habit
and second nature in the artist.
Such art he conceives of, however, not as belonging to the
artist, but as inherent in ' Art '
itself, seeing that the creative
principle resides, not in the artist,
but in the artistic conception
which operates in him, and which
Aristotle therefore identifies with
the τέχνη itself ; cf. the passages
quoted from *Metaph.* vii. 7, *Gen.
An.* ii. 4, *Part. An.* i. 1, in n. 1,
p. 356, and *Gen. et Corr.* i. 7, 324,
a, 34 : ὅσα γὰρ μὴ ἔχει τὴν αὐτὴν
ὕλην, ποιεῖ ἀπαθῆ ὄντα, οἷον ἡ
ἰατρική · αὐτὴ γὰρ ποιοῦσα ὑγίειαν
οὐδὲν πάσχει ὑπὸ τοῦ ὑγιαζομένου.

[2] See p. 418, n. 3, *supra.* In
this sense Nature, as the internal
operative principle *in* living
things, is also expressly opposed
to the human understanding,
which operates upon them *from
without* (θύραθεν νοῦς) ; cf. *Gen.
An.* ii. 6, 744, b, 21.

But this action in obedience to purpose cannot obtain a complete mastery in nature : for, along with the free operation of form, we have the necessary element of matter which cannot be entirely overcome by form. We have already shown (p. 359 sqq.) that Aristotle finds in matter the groundwork of chance and blind natural necessity. Both, in fact, ultimately coincide, since chance is precisely that which does not happen as the fulfiment of some design, but is produced by the way, in consequence of the operation of intervening causes which are indispensable to the attainment of a further end. This characteristic of natural existence renders it impossible to assign a purpose for everything in the world. Nature, indeed, works towards definite ends, but, in the realisation of her plans, she produces many things parenthetically, by the way, from mere necessity ; [1] yet she still endeavours as far as possible to make use of such chance products, employing her superfluities for purposes of her own, and, like a good housewife, taking care that nothing be lost.[2] It follows that natural science, in like manner, cannot always proceed with the same rigour, but must take into account the disturbances introduced into the designs of nature by necessity and chance, admitting exceptions to rules, and feeling satisfied when her generalisations hold in the majority of instances.[3]

[1] See p. 361, n. 1, *supra*.

[2] *Gen. An.* ii. 6, 744, b, 16 : ὥσπερ οἰκονόμος ἀγαθὸς, καὶ ἡ φύσις οὐθὲν ἀποβάλλειν εἴωθεν ἐξ ὧν ἔστι ποιῆσαί τι χρηστόν. He points especially to uses to which superfluous materials (περιττώματα, on which see *Gen. An.* i. 18, 724, b, 23 sqq.) are put in the formation and nutrition of animal organisms; *Gen. An.* ii. 4, 738, a, 3/ sqq., iii. 2, 663, b, 31. Cf. also p. 361, n. 1, and *Part. An.* iv. 5, 679, a, 29, where he says of the juice of the cuttle-fish : ἡ δὲ φύσις ἅμα τῷ τοιούτῳ περιττώματι καταχρῆται πρὸς βοήθειαν καὶ σωτηρίαν αὐτῶν.

[3] *Part. An.* iii. 2, 663, b, 27,

It is from this resistance offered by matter to form
that Aristotle derives all irregular natural phenomena
(τέρατα), such as abortions and the like. He regards
them as the stoppage of nature in the midst of an
unfulfilled design, as a mutilation [1] and failure of the
result which she originally intended.[2] Such phenomena arise from form not being completely master over
matter.[3] Moreover, we may note that he even considers it a kind of abortion or failure of the ends of
nature when children do not resemble their parents,
and especially their father,[4] when a good man begets
a bad son and *vice versa*,[5] when the nature of the body

cf. *Metaph.* ii. 3 *fin.* and p. 168,
n. 1, 2, *supra.* Ritter's statement
(see his p. 212) that the doctrine
of Nature rests according to Aristotle rather on opinion than on
science, seems to be due to a
mistranslation of *Anal. Post.* i.
33, 89, a, 5, where ἡ φύσις ἡ
τοιαύτη (i.e. τὸ ἐνδεχόμενον καὶ
ἄλλως ἔχειν, as is clear from the
context) is taken as = ἡ φύσις
τοιαύτη—and Nature is so also
(i.e. ἀβέβαιος).

[1] *Gen. An.* iv. 3, 759, b,10 sqq.
Aristotle is here speaking of abortions which want essential parts
of the human body as well as
those which have more than the
proper number, and applies the
above explanation to both : τέλος
γὰρ τῶν μὲν κινήσεων (form-giving
motion) λυομένων, τῆς δ' ὕλης οὐ
κρατουμένης, μένει τὸ καθόλου
μάλιστα · τοῦτο δ' ἐστὶ ζῷον . . .
τὸ τέρας ἀναπηρία τίς ἐστιν. Cf.
also 767, b, 13 : τὸ δὲ τέρας οὐκ
ἀναγκαῖον πρὸς τὴν ἔνεκά του καὶ
τὴν τοῦ τέλους αἰτίαν, ἀλλὰ κατὰ
συμβεβηκὸς ἀναγκαῖον.

[2] *Phys.* ii. 8, 199, b, 1 : εἰ δὴ

ἔστιν ἔνια κατὰ τέχνην ἐν οἷς τὸ
ὀρθῶς ἕνεκά του, ἐν δὲ τοῖς ἁμαρ-
τανομένοις ἕνεκα μέν τινος ἐπιχει-
ρεῖται ἀλλ' ἀποτυγχάνεται, ὁμοίως
ἂν ἔχοι καὶ ἐν τοῖς φυσικοῖς καὶ τὰ
τέρατα ἁμαρτήματα ἐκείνου τοῦ
ἕνεκά του.

[3] *Gen. An.* iv. 4, 770, b, 9 :
ἔστι γὰρ τὸ τέρας τῶν παρὰ φύσιν
τι, παρὰ φύσιν δ' οὐ πᾶσαν ἀλλὰ
τὴν ὡς ἐπὶ τὸ πολύ · περὶ γὰρ τὴν
ἀεὶ καὶ τὴν ἐξ ἀνάγκης οὐθὲν γίνεται
παρὰ φύσιν (a proposition which
was afterwards applied by theo-
logians to the miracles, and in
this application has become
famous, although it is not generally known that it comes from
Aristotle). Even a τέρας, therefore, is in a certain sense κατὰ
φύσιν, ὅταν μὴ κρατήσῃ τὴν κατὰ
τὴν ὕλην ἡ κατὰ τὸ εἶδος φύσις.
Cf. previous n.

[4] *Gen. An.* ii. 3, 767, b, 5 : ὁ
μὴ ἐοικὼς τοῖς γονεῦσιν ἤδη τρόπον
τινὰ τέρας ἐστίν.

[5] *Polit.* i. 6, 1255, b, 1 :
ἀξιοῦσι γὰρ, ὥσπερ ἐξ ἀνθρώπου
ἄνθρωπον καὶ ἐκ θηρίων γίνεσθαι
θηρίον, οὕτω καὶ ἐξ ἀγαθῶν ἀγαθόν ·

does not correspond to that of the soul.[1] Indeed, he looks on all the female sex as imperfect and mutilated in comparison with the male, because the informing force of the man was insufficient to overcome the matter taken from the woman in the act of procreation.[2] Again the brutes are dwarfish as compared with human beings, because the upper members of their body are not properly proportioned to the lower ;[3] they are the imperfect attempts of nature to make men—a form of development analogous to that of children.[4] Moreover, among the animals we may discern a further malformation in the case of single tribes—the mole, for instance[5] —or, to speak more accurately, we may distinguish between more perfect and less perfect animals : such as have blood are more perfect than such as have none ;[6] the tame than the wild ;[7] those which possess but one centre of organic life than those which are provided with several.[8] In like manner, vegetables, as compared

η δε φύσις βούλεται μεν τοῦτο ποιεῖν πολλάκις, οὐ μέντοι δύναται.

[1] Polit. i. 5, 1254, b, 27 : βούλεται μεν οὖν ἡ φύσις καὶ τὰ σώματα διαφέροντα ποιεῖν τὰ τῶν ἐλευθέρων καὶ τῶν δούλων, . . . συμβαίνει δὲ πολλάκις τοὐναντίον.

[2] Cf. infra, the section in Ch. X. on Sex in Animals.

[3] Part. An. iv. 10, 686, b, 2, 20 : πάντα γάρ ἐστι τὰ ζῷα νανώδη τἄλλα παρὰ τὸν ἄνθρωπον. Cf. c. 12, 695, a, 8. Children also, for the same reason, are νανώδη; Part. An. iv. 10, 686, b, 10 ; Ingr. An. 11, 710, b, 12 ; De Mem. c. 2 fin. and passim.

[4] Hist. An. viii. 1, 588, a, 31 : the soul of children hardly differs from that of a beast.

[5] Hist. An. iv. 8, 533, a, 2.

[6] Gen. An. ii. 1, 732, a, 16.

[7] Polit. i. 5, 1254, b, 10 : τὸ μεν ἥμερα [ζῷα] τῶν ἀγρίων βελτίω τὴν φύσιν. Aristotle admits, however, himself, Part. An. i. 3, 643, b, 3, that the division of animals into tame and wild is a false one, as all tame animals are found also in a wild condition. The greater perfection of tame animals is therefore something that is acquired ; so far as it is φύσει, it consists in a mere capacity.

[8] Part. An. iv. 5, 682, a, 6, where also it is added : nature, indeed, desires to give to such creatures only one central organ, but, being unable to do this, she is forced to give them several. In the Problems (x. 45) the writer goes so far as to say that

with animals, are incomplete.[1] They display design but in a less developed form;[2] and they too, as we shall see, have an animate existence, although only in the lowest stage of its development and in its most rudimentary outline. Aristotle even goes further and recognises a degree of life, though the least possible, in what appears to be inorganic.[3] Thus Nature as a whole is the gradual conquest of Form over Matter—a continual progression towards more perfect development of life. That which is absolutely first, or Form, in its temporal origin is last, since all Becoming is a movement out of Matter into Form, and the beginning (that which comes first in the order of thought) is also in every case the end.[4] It follows that complex existences must be posterior to simple ones—the organic to the inorganic.[5] Aristotle, however, does not carry this thought beyond the sphere of earthly existence. He applies it chiefly to organic nature, in which he first had the insight to discover a continuous progress from inanimate to animate, from imperfect to perfect forms of existence.

nature produces wild plants and animals in greater quantity than tame ones, because it is easier to make what is imperfect than what is perfect, and because nature, like art, is only able to create the better after long practice. This, however, is an exaggeration of the Aristotelian doctrine of nature's weakness.

[1] Cf. *Gen. An.* iii. 7, 757, b, 19, 24.

[2] *Phys.* ii. 8, 199, b, 9: καὶ ἐν τοῖς φυτοῖς ἔνεστι τὸ ἕνεκά του, ἧττον δὲ διήρθρωται.

[3] See p. 460, n. 3, *supra*; and

Ch. X. *infra*, at the end of pt. i.

[4] *Part. An.* ii. 1, 646, a, 25: τὰ ὕστερα τῇ γενέσει πρότερα τὴν φύσιν ἐστὶ, καὶ πρῶτον τὸ τῇ γενέσει τελευταῖον . . . τῷ μὲν οὖν χρόνῳ προτέραν τὴν ὕλην ἀναγκαῖον εἶναι καὶ τὴν γένεσιν, τῷ λόγῳ δὲ τὴν ἑκάστου μορφήν. *Metaph.* ix. 8, 1050, a, 7: ἅπαν ἐπ᾽ ἀρχὴν βαδίζει τὸ γιγνόμενον καὶ τέλος· ἀρχὴ γὰρ τὸ οὗ ἕνεκα, τοῦ τέλους δ᾽ ἕνεκα ἡ γένεσις. See also p. 205, n. 2, *supra*.

[5] *Part. An.* 646, b, 4. *Meteor.* iv. 12, 389, b, 29: ἀεὶ δὲ, μᾶλλον δῆλον [τί ἕκαστον] ἐπὶ τῶν ὑστέρων καὶ ὅλως ὅσα οἷον ὄργανα καὶ ἕνεκά

CHAPTER IX

CONTINUATION

B.—*The Universe and the Elements*

TURNING now from these more general inquiries into nature to the consideration of the actual constitution of the world, Aristotle comes upon a question which had occupied a leading place in previous metaphysical discussions—the question, namely, of creation. His predecessors had without exception assigned to the world in which we live a definite beginning in time—some, such as Anaxagoras, Plato, and the Pythagoreans,[1] holding that this world is the only one; others that the world we see is only one among an infinite series of other worlds both past and present.[2] Aristotle was the first to declare that our world is eternal and unbegotten.[3] This conviction seems to have early forced itself upon him.[4] Although in his system it is not

---

του. We have a clearer idea of the true nature of man than of flesh, bones, &c., and a better idea of the nature of the latter than of the elements. Τὸ γὰρ οὗ ἕνεκα ἥκιστα ἐνταῦθα δῆλον ὅπου πλεῖστον τῆς ὕλης· ὥσπερ γὰρ εἰ τὰ ἔσχατα ληφθείη, ἡ μὲν ὕλη οὐθὲν ἄλλο παρ' αὐτήν, ἡ δ' οὐσία οὐθὲν ἄλλο ἢ ὁ λόγος, τὰ δὲ μεταξὺ ἀνάλογον τῷ ἐγγὺς εἶναι ἕκαστον, ἐπεὶ καὶ τούτων ὁτιοῦν ἐστιν ἕνεκά του.

[1] On the latter cf. ZELL. *Ph.*

d. Gr. pt. i. 378 sqq. 410 sq.

[2] The atomic school held the existence of both; Anaximander, Anaximenes, Diogenes, and Empedocles placed the series in the past. On Heraclitus cf. ZELL. *Ph. d. Gr.* pt. i. 586, 2 *ad fin.* 629, 1 *ad fin.*, and on Xenophanes, *ibid.* 498, 3 *fin.*

[3] As he says himself in the *De Cælo*, i. 10, 279, b, 12.

[4] CIC. *Acad.* ii. 38, 119 (*Ar. Fr.* 18), quotes probably from

placed in direct connection with the doctrine of the eternity of motion,[1] yet it follows, equally with it, from the consideration that the operation of creative force in the world must be as eternal and unchangeable as that force itself, and that therefore the universe which is produced by it, however the individual parts may change,[2] cannot as a whole have had a beginning in time. Aristotle, indeed, nowhere expressly states this result in the works that have come down to us, although he approaches very near to it.[3] He contents himself, in

the treatise Π. φιλοσοφίας (see p. 56 sq. *supra*), at any rate from one of the dialogues, as Aristotle's view: ' Neque enim ortum esse unquam mundum, quod nulla fuerit novo consilio inito tam praeclari operis inceptio, et ita esse eum undique aptum ut nulla vis tantos queat motus mutationemque moliri, nulla senectus diuturnitate temporum existere ut hic ornatus unquam dilapsus occidat.' (Cf. PLATO, *Tim.* 34, B, 68, E, and elsewhere.) So PS. PHILO, *Ætern. M.* ii. 489 (*Ar. Fr.* 17), where it is declared to be δεινὴ ἀθεότης to regard the ὁρατὸς θεὸς as no better than any human product.

[1] See p. 387, *supra.* The latter is even quite compatible with the doctrine of the birth and destruction of the world.

[2] On this, cf. p. 468, n. 3.

[3] *Phys.* viii. 1, 251, a, 20 sqq. where, in opposing the view that motion had ever a beginning, he says : had the *movens* and the *mobile* existed without producing any motion, the transition from rest to motion could only have been effected by a previous change

either in one or both of them, and we should have to suppose a προτέρα μεταβολὴ τῆς πρώτης. Similarly we should have to conclude that as a preliminary to the transition from creation to destruction of the world or *vice versa* a change must take place in the creative force or in the material upon which it works. If both remain unchanged their mutual relation must also remain unchanged, and therefore also the resultant effect. But according to Aristotle, God is eternal, and unchangeable ; matter, on the other hand (setting aside the doctrine of the immutability of the material of which the heavens are made), we know can only suffer change through the operation of the moving cause. If, therefore, the latter is unchangeable, its relation to the matter and the universe which is its product must be unchangeable. This is the argument indicated by Cicero in the passage quoted above, where Aristotle declares it to be inconceivable that so perfect a product as the world could

his investigations into the origin of the world, with
proving that motion is eternal, and refuting the doctrine
that the world has a beginning but no end.[1] The doctrine, however, is clearly involved in his metaphysics.
For if the *primum movens* is unchangeable, the effect
which it produces upon the world must always be the
same. It cannot at one time act as a creative, at another
as a destructive, force. The same conclusion follows also
from Aristotle's scientific doctrine of the immutability
of the material of which the heavenly spheres and the
stars are made. Not only, therefore, does the doctrine
of a beginning and end of the world in the sense of an
absolute birth and destruction find no place in Ari-

have had a beginning *novo
consilio inito*; whence it may
be concluded that the creative
force must have produced the
best from all eternity in virtue
of its own unchangeable perfection.

[1] Aristotle devotes *De Cœlo*,
i. 10–12, to the proof that the
heavens are without beginning
and end, confining himself, however, almost exclusively to the attack on the Platonic view, that,
while they will endure for ever,
they yet had a beginning in time.
His chief argument against it is
that beginning and endlessness,
end and beginninglessness, are
mutually exclusive. That which
exists for an endless period can
neither begin nor cease to be ;
in either case there must be a
time in which it is not (see c. 12,
281, b, 18 sqq. where, however,
it is proved in too formal a way).
Why, moreover, should that
which has not existed for all
eternity begin to be at this particular moment ? or why should
that which has been from all
eternity cease at this particular
moment to exist ? (283, a, 11)
It is its own nature which constitutes a thing without beginning
or end, and this in such a case
excludes the possibility of not-
being ; the nature of that which
has had a beginning and is liable
to perish must, on the other hand,
include it. The latter, therefore,
cannot last for ever any more
than the former can begin or
end (l. 29 sqq.; cf. p. 366, n. 1, *fin.*
and the passage quoted, *ibid.
init.* from *Metaph.* ix. 8). The
views, on the other hand, of those
who hold that the world has
both beginning and end are
here only lightly touched upon.
The atomic view Aristotle considered that he had disposed of
by his doctrine of the unity of
the world, while in reference to
the view of Heraclitus and Empedocles he contents himself
with remarking (c. 10, 280, a,

stotle's system, but even such a fundamental change in the constitution of the world as is presupposed by Heraclitus and Empedocles is wholly inconsistent both with his cosmology and his metaphysics. The question for Aristotle is not of any origin of the world in time, but only of its actual character and constitution.

The universe is divided, according to Aristotle, into two halves of opposite character—the one terrestrial, and the other celestial. This opposition is at once revealed by the testimony of our senses : and Aristotle can hardly have come to it in any other way. The unalterable nature of the stars and the changeless regularity of their movements form, in his opinion, so strong a contrast [1] to terrestrial corruptibility and change, that we are forced to recognise two essentially different realms, subject to different laws. The more important this opposition seems to him to be, the more he strives to demonstrate its necessity. All natural bodies, he argues, are capable of movement in space. But movement in space is either rectilineal or circular or a compound of both. The third of these being derived from the first two, it follows that the latter alone are simple and original—rectilineal motion proceeding from the centre to the circumference, or *vice versa*, and circular motion revolving round the centre. If these are the first natural motions, there must be certain bodies which by reason of their nature are the subjects of such movement, and which are consequently the

1 l sqq. ; cf. ZELL. *Ph. d. Gr.* pt. i. 629, 1 *ad fin.*) that it attributes to the world a mere change of form and not a veritable birth and destruction.

[1] That it was the observation of this which led Aristotle in the first instance to make his

most primitive and ancient bodies. Those, on the contrary, which exhibit a composite movement, must be formed by combination from them, and receive their particular bias from the constituent which preponderates in their composition. That which is natural is always earlier than that which is opposed to nature and violent. It follows that circular, and also rectilineal, movement must be naturally fitted for some body or other, the more so that rotation is the only unbroken and interminable movement, and nothing that is contrary to nature fulfils these conditions. Accordingly there must exist two sorts of simple bodies—the one originally destined for rectilineal, the other for circular, movement.[1] Rectilineal movement has opposite directions : it is either upwards or downwards, passing from centre to circumference, or *vice versa*. Consequently, the bodies which exhibit it must be of opposite natures, destined for the one or the other kind of motion : that is, they must be either light or heavy. Circular motion, on the other hand, exhibits no such contraries. It starts from any point towards any point in the circumference. So the body which is naturally qualified for it must likewise be without contrariety. It can neither be heavy nor light, since it does not rise or fall, and in fact it cannot exhibit any kind of rectilineal motion. It is even impossible to communicate either upward or downward motion to it by force, since if the one were unnatural to it the other must[2] be

distinction between two realms of being is obvious from his whole treatment of the subject. Cf. also p. 366, n. 1.

[1] *De Cælo*, i. 2, 268, b, 14 sqq.

[2] According to the principle already laid down (c. 2, 269, a, 10, 14) as the basis of the discussion (see p. 224, n. 3), ἐν ἑνὶ ἐναντίον, which, when thus universally expressed, is certainly open to dispute.

its natural motion.[1] The body that is destined for circular motion is also without beginning or ending, subject to neither increase nor diminution, neither impression nor change.[2] His argument for this is that everything that comes into being springs from its opposite, and everything that perishes is resolved into the same;[3] all increase and decrease depend upon addition or subtraction of the matter out of which a thing has grown, and therefore that which, being without beginning, possesses no such matter, cannot increase or decrease; all bodies, finally, which alter, either increase or decrease, and where there is no such process neither is there any alteration.[4]

---

[1] *Ibid.* c. 3, 269, b, 18–270, a, 12; nor can the position βίᾳ μὲν γὰρ ἐνδέχεται τὴν ἄλλου καὶ ἑτέρου [sc. κίνησιν κινεῖσθαι] (c. 2, 269, a, 7) be accepted except provisionally as of universal validity. As is shown in the sequel, it is inapplicable to the æther. The position upon which the latter conclusion rests, (viz. that movement in a circle has no opposite). Aristotle, indeed, endeavours (c. 4) further to establish by special proofs. But he cannot prove that the motion may not be crooked or oblique ; for if we have two opposite motions on the same or on parallel lines which deviate in opposite directions, it does not make the slightest difference whether the lines are straight or circular. Moreover, the courses of the fixed stars and of the planets are actually in opposite directions ; why may these bodies not, then, consist of different ætherial substance ? We are not warranted, however, with MEYER

(*Aristot. Thierkunde*, 393) in casting a doubt upon Aristotle's clearly expressed meaning, merely on the ground of the actual difficulties that beset the theory.
[2] He says, *De Cœlo*, i. 3, 270, a, 13, b, 1 : ἀγένητον καὶ ἄφθαρτον καὶ ἀναυξὲς καὶ ἀναλλοίωτον, ἀΐδιον καὶ οὔτ' αὔξησιν ἔχον οὔτε φθίσιν, ἀλλ' ἀγήρατον καὶ ἀναλλοίωτον καὶ ἀπαθές. Cf. *Metaph.* viii. 4, 1044, b, 7, xii. 1, 2, 1069, a, 30, b, 25.
[3] On this point, cf. also p. 341 sq.
[4] *De Cœlo*, i. 3, 270, a, 13–35. The immutability of the body which has no opposite might have been proved more simply and conclusively from the proposition (p. 341, and p. 353 sq. above) that all change means transition from one state into its opposite, and that a thing can only be operated upon by its opposite. Aristotle, however, does not here adopt this method, as his investigation into the conception of change and affection was not published until later—in his

This position draws further support from experience. For he contends that if the spaces of the heavens, as well as the intermediate space between heaven and earth, were full of air or fire, then the bulk of these elements, considering the magnitude of the stars and their distance from each other, would be so hugely disproportioned to that of the remaining elements that the latter could not preserve their equilibrium, but would be swallowed up by them. A proper proportion between the elements [1] can therefore only be maintained on the hypothesis that the celestial space is filled with a body different from the matter of the elements.[2] We are also led to believe that this body is superior to all change, by the fact that antiquity, so far as tradition reaches, furnishes us with no evidence of the least alteration in the fabric of the heaven or its parts.[3] Finally, the unthinking belief of humanity harmonises with this conviction, and such a belief deserves respect as the inheritance of unnumbered generations.[4] All nations have placed the residence of the gods in heaven, because they were convinced of its immortal and divine nature. The name ' æther ' may be traced to the same source, for Aristotle, like Plato,[5] derives it from ἀεὶ θεῖν, from the restless rotation of

---

treatise on birth and destruction.

[1] Such a proportion involves that there is as much air and as much fire as will be produced by the transformation of all water into air and all air into fire on the basis of the existing quantitative extent of these bodies.

[2] *Meteor.* i. 3, 339, b, 13–340, a, 18.

[3] *De Cœlo,* i. 3, 270, b, 11.

[4] οὐ γὰρ ἅπαξ οὐδὲ δὶς ἀλλ' ἀπειράκις δεῖ νομίζειν τὰς αὐτὰς ἀφικνεῖσθαι δόξας εἰς ἡμᾶς. *De Cœlo,* 270, b, 19. See *Meteor.* 339, b, 27, where the same reason is given in almost the same words, and *Metaph.* xii. 8 *ad fin.* See *infra,* the section of Ch. IX. on the Heavens, and Ch. XII. pt. 2.

[5] PLATO, *Crat.* 410, B.

the celestial globes, and not from $ai\theta\epsilon\iota\nu$.[1] The conclusion is that the æther must be distinguished from all elementary matter.[2] Without opposition and without

[1] *De Cœlo*, i. 3, 270, b, 4–25; *Meteor.* i. 3, 339, b, 19 sqq.; and following these passages *De Mundo*, c. 2, 392, a, 5. On the name 'æther,' cf. ZELL. *Ph. d. Gr.* i. 897, 4 *ad fin.*

[2] Although it is called πρῶτον στοιχεῖον, *De Cœlo*, iii. 1, 298, b, 6; *Meteor.* i. 1, 338, b, 21; c. 3, 339, b, 16, 340, b, 11, τὸ τῶν ἄστρων στοιχεῖον; *Gen. An.* iii. 3, 737, a, 1, it is yet expressly distinguished in these passages from the four στοιχεῖα. *Gen. An.* ii. 3, 736, b, 29, it is called ἕτερον σῶμα καὶ θειότερον τῶν καλουμένων στοιχείων; *Meteor.* i. 3, 340, b, 7 (cf. p. 488, n. 3, *infra*), ἕτερον σῶμα πυρός τε καὶ ἀέρος; and *De Cœlo*, i. 2, 269, a, 30: οὐσία σώματος ἄλλη παρὰ τὰς ἐνταῦθα συστάσεις θειοτέρα καὶ προτέρα τούτων ἁπάντων; cf. *ibid.* c. 3 (following n.). If, therefore, we understand by στοιχεῖα only such simple bodies as stand to one another in the relation of opposites, and pass into one another, we cannot reckon the æther among these. Only when we extend the meaning of the word to embrace *all* simple bodies can we call it a στοιχεῖον. On the other hand, it is, to say the least of it, inaccurate and misleading to say that according to Aristotle the celestial spheres have 'no material substratum' (BRENTANO, *Psychol. d. Arist.* 198; HERTLING, *Mat. und Form*, 22), that 'the æther consists of a material which is no material, of an immaterial material' (KAMPE, *Erkennt-*

nissth. d. Arist. 30 sq.) that all that is meant by the ὕλη of the stars is the potentiality they possess of motion and change in space, and that in this sense we might even attribute ὕλη to νοῦς (HERTLING, *ibid.* 23). Aristotle certainly says, *Metaph.* viii. 4, 1044, b, 7: in the · case of γεννηταὶ οὐσίαι, we have to deal both with their matter and form; it is otherwise with φυσικαὶ μὲν ἀΐδιοι δὲ οὐσίαι. 'ἴσως γὰρ ἔνια οὐκ ἔχει ὕλην, ἢ οὐ τοιαύτην ἀλλὰ μόνον κατὰ τόπον κινητήν.' Matter, however, is denied of the heavenly bodies only in the sense in which it belongs to temporal things. Aristotle means that if we understand by ὕλη that of which a thing is made, the ὑποκείμενον γενέσεως καὶ φθορᾶς δεκτικὸν (as it is defined, *Gen. et Corr.* i. 4, 320, a, 2), the uncreated and eternal has no ὕλη in this sense; but if we take it in the more general sense of the substratum of change, the δυνάμει ὄν, it has ὕλη, inasmuch as it is capable of movement in space. That this is all that Aristotle means is obvious from the parallel passages, xii. 2, 1069, b, 24: πάντα δ' ὕλην ἔχει ὅσα μεταβάλλει . . . καὶ τῶν ἀϊδίων ὅσα μὴ γεννητὰ κινητὰ δὲ φορᾷ, ἀλλ' οὐ γεννητήν, ἀλλὰ πόθεν ποι; viii. 1, 1042, b. 5: οὐ γὰρ ἀνάγκη, εἴ τι ὕλην ἔχει τοπικήν. τοῦτο καὶ γεννητὴν καὶ φθάρτην ἔχειν; c. 8, 1050, b, 20: οὐδ' εἴ τι κινούμενον ἀΐδιον, οὐκ ἔστι κατὰ δύναμιν κινούμενον ἀλλ' ἢ πόθεν ποι· [only in respect of

mutation, it stands above the strife of the elements: these belong to the terrestrial, it to the celestial, world : of it are formed the heavenly spheres and stars ; it is the god-like in the realm of matter.[1]

The four elements are different in all respects. If circular movement is peculiar to the æther, their movement is rectilineal. But, as we have remarked, rectilineal motion follows two opposite directions, up and down, toward the circumference and toward the centre. That which tends naturally downwards is heavy ; that which rises is light. Accordingly the elements exhibit the opposites of heavy and light.[2] This opposition cannot, he holds, be reduced to quantitative differences of magnitude, of mathematical figure, or density ; it is original and qualitative. The peculiarities of the elementary materials we cannot explain either, with Plato and Democritus, by the mathematical qualities of atoms, or, with the elder physicists, by the rarefaction and condensation

---

locality can it be said to move merely δυνάμει and not ἐνεργείᾳ, inasmuch as it is not yet in the place to which it is moving] τούτου δ' [ι.ᵉ. τοῦ πόθεν ποι κινεῖσθαι] ὕλην οὐθὲν κωλύει ὑπάρχειν. *De Cœlo*, i. 9, 278, a, 10 sqq. Aristotle expressly says : ὁ οὐρανὸς as a universal conception is different from ὅδε ὁ οὐρανός ; the former is εἶδος καὶ μορφή, the latter τῇ ὕλῃ μεμιγμένον. Still less can we infer from *Metaph.* viii 4, that the celestial globes are incorporeal beings (like the æther, they are frequently called θεῖα σώματα, &c. : see *Ind. Ar.* 742, a, 43–60) ; we cannot, therefore, suppose for a moment that

ὕλη is denied of them in the same sense as it is denied of the immaterial Nous, or that it can be attributed to the latter in the same sense as to the former.

[1] It is called θεῖος, *Meteor.* i. 3, 339, b, 25 ; also, similarly, *De Cœlo*, i. 3, 270, b, 11, 20 : ἡ πρώτη οὐσία τῶν σωμάτων, τὸ πρῶτον σῶμα, ἕτερόν τι ὂν παρὰ γῆν καὶ πῦρ καὶ ἀέρα καὶ ὕδωρ. *Ibid.* ii. 1, 284, a, 4 Later philosophers, such as Cicero's Epicurean (*N. De.* i. 13, 33, cf. KRISCHE, *Forsch.*, 306 sqq.) and the pseudo-Justin Cohort. c. 5, 36, identify on this ground God and the æther.

[2] See p. 473 sq.

of one and the same primitive material. We have already proved this point with regard to the first hypothesis.[1] But those who deduce the differences of matter from a condensation and rarefaction of some one original element are, besides other arguments, met by the objection that they do not explain the distinction between light and heavy substance. They confine the difference between the elements to a mere relation of magnitudes, and accordingly represent it as something merely relative.[2] To Aristotle's mind, the opposition of rectilineal movements and natural localities at once demands a qualitative difference between the elements. Rectilineal motion being just as primitive as circular motion, there must be certain bodies which are especially designed for it.[3] Again, since it includes two tendencies, upward and downward, we must in the first place assume two bodies, of which one naturally sinks, the other rises, the one tending to the centre, the other to the circumference of the world. In the second place, we must imagine an intermediate element, or rather a pair of elements, the one approximating to the former, and the other to the latter. Of these four bodies, the first two are earth and fire, the other two water and air. Earth is absolutely heavy and entirely devoid of lightness; fire is absolutely light and entirely devoid of heaviness. The one moves straight to the centre, and therefore sinks below all other bodies; the other moves straight to the circumference, and therefore

---

[1] See p. 443 sqq.

[2] Aristotle discusses this view *De Cœlo*, iii. 5, cf. iv. 5, 312, b,

20; *Metaph.* i. 8, 988, b, 29 sqq.

[3] See p. 473.

rises above all other bodies. Water and air, on the other hand, are only relatively heavy, and therefore also relatively light. Water is heavier than air and fire, but lighter than earth ; air heavier than fire, but lighter than water and earth. Under no possible circumstances, unless compelled by forcible movement, does fire sink of itself into the place of air ; nor, again, does earth rise into that of water. Air and water, on the contrary, sink into the lower regions when the matter which fills them is withdrawn.[1] Earth is everywhere heavy; water, everywhere except in earth ; air, everywhere except in earth and water ; [2] fire, nowhere.[3] Therefore of two bodies the one which holds the more air may be heavier in air but lighter in water than the other—a hundred-weight of wood, for instance, than a pound of lead.[4]

We may arrive at these four elements even more definitely by another process of reasoning.[5] All

[1] Properly, indeed, they ought to rise into the higher ; Aristotle admits himself, *De Cœlo*, iv. 5, 312, b, sqq., that this does happen unless external force be applied, —without, however, explaining a circumstance which has so important a bearing upon his theory.

[2] That even air has weight is obvious from the fact that a bladder full of air is heavier than an empty one ; *ibid.* c. 4, 311, b, 9.

[3] Aristotle, in the passage just referred to, finds in this theory an explanation of the difference between absolute and specific gravity.

[4] *De Cœlo*, iv. 3–5. The same ideas occur, in a somewhat different application, ii. 3, 286, a, 12 sqq. It is there said that the

world cannot consist of æther alone, for it must have an immovable centre. There must therefore be a body whose nature it is to rest at the centre and move towards it, and therefore also one of an opposite nature. We thus have earth and fire, which in turn require water and air as intermediate elements.

[5] For what follows, see *Gen. et Corr.* ii. 2, 3. The true author of this theory of the elements is said to be Hippocrates (according to IDELER, *Arist. Meteor.* ii. 389, who appeals to GALEN, *De Elem. sec. Hippocr.* i. 9, *Opp.* ed. Kühn, i. 481 sq.). This, however, is uncertain for several reasons. In the first place, neither of the works here referred to, Π. φύσιος ἀνθρώπου and Π. σαρκῶν, can be

bodies capable of being perceived by the senses are prehensible; but all qualities perceptible by the sense of touch, with the exception of gravity and levity,[1] are reducible to four—warmth, cold, dryness, moisture.[2] Aristotle regards the first two of these properties as active, the others as passive.[3] Now, by joining these

attributed to Hippócrates. The former is without doubt the work, or an extract from a work, of Polybus, his son-in-law : the latter is of post-Aristotelian origin, cf. KÜHN, *Hippocr. Opp.* I. cxlvii., clv. ; LITTRÉ, *Œuvres d' Hippocrate*, i. 345 sqq. 384. Again, while the treatise Π. φύσιος ἀνθρώπου recognises (c. 1 *init.*) Empedocles's four elements and even makes heat and cold, dryness and moisture the constituent elements of every living thing (c. 3), it yet does not bring these two positions together as Aristotle does, or deduce each of the four elements from the various combinations of those four properties into pairs ; nor, indeed, does GALEN (see *supra*) claim this for it. The treatise Π. σαρκῶν, on the other hand, refers (at i. 425, K) to the Aristotelian account of the elements, but this merely proves that it is later than Aristotle. That heat and cold, dryness and moisture, were regarded as the elements of things in the medical schools of his time, is corroborated by PLATO, *Sym.* 186, D. 187, D. The early physicists regarded the conflict of heat and cold as the primary principle of evolution and frequently united with it that of dryness and moisture, without, however, as yet expressly combining these four as the primary properties of things.

Cf. ZELL. *Ph. d. Gr.* i. 205, 241, 519 sq. 897.

[1] We have not here to do with these, as they do not indicate a particular kind of action and passion; the elements, on the other hand, stand to one another in that particular relation of action and passion (*ibid.* 329, b, 20), which the treatise on birth and destruction chiefly discusses.

[2] *Ibid.* 329, b, 24 : θερμὸν δὲ καὶ ψυχρὸν καὶ ὑγρὸν καὶ ξηρὸν τὰ μὲν τῷ ποιητικὰ εἶναι τὰ δὲ τῷ παθητικὰ λέγεται · θερμὸν γάρ ἐστι τὸ συγκρῖνον τὰ ὁμογενῆ [from which it follows that fire sepaiates heterogeneous elements], ψυχρὸν δὲ τὸ συνάγον καὶ συγκρῖνον ὁμοίως τά τε συγγενῆ καὶ τὰ μὴ ὁμόφυλα, ὑγρὸν δὲ τὸ ἀόριστον ᾿οἰκείῳ ὅρῳ εὐόριστον ὄν, ξηρὸν δὲ τὸ ἀόριστον μὲν οἰκείῳ ὅρῳ, δυσόριστον δέ. (Cf. *Meteor.* iv. 4, 381, b, b, 29.) The qualities λεπτὸν, παχὺ, γλίσχρον, κραῦρον, μαλακὸν, σκληρὸν are reduced to these primary qualities ; διερὸν and βεβρεγμένον form two kinds of moisture, ξηρὸν in its narrower sense and πεπηγὸς of dryness.

[3] *Meteor.* iv. 1 *init.*: ἐπεὶ δὲ τέτταρα διώρισται αἴτια τῶν στοιχείων, . . . ὧν τὰ μὲν δύο ποιητικὰ, τὸ θερμὸν καὶ τὸ ψυχρὸν, τὰ δὲ δύο παθητικὰ, τὸ ξηρὸν καὶ τὸ ὑγρόν · ἡ δὲ πίστις τούτων ἐκ τῆς ἐπαγωγῆς. φαίνεται γὰρ ἐν πᾶσιν ἡ μὲν

four properties in pairs, we obtain, after eliminating
two impossible combinations, four that are possible, in
which one active and one passive property are always
united, and thus four simple bodies or elements are
exhibited [1]—warm and dry, or fire; warm and moist,
or air; [2] cold and moist, or water; cold and dry, or
earth. [3] These are the four sorts of matter of which all
composite bodies consist, which are excreted from all,

θερμότης καὶ ψυχρότης ὁρίζουσαι
καὶ συμφύουσαι καὶ μεταβάλλουσαι
τὰ ὁμογενῆ καὶ τὰ μὴ ὁμογενῆ, καὶ
ὑγραίνουσαι καὶ ξηραίνουσαι καὶ
σκληρύνουσαι καὶ μαλάττουσαι, τὰ
δὲ ξηρὰ καὶ ὑγρὰ ὁριζόμενα καὶ
τἆλλα τὰ εἰρημένα πάθη πάσχοντα.
Cf. c. 4 *init.* c. 5, 382, a, 27 sqq.
c. 10, 388, a, 21, c. 11, 389, a, 29.
[1] In his description of these
four primary substances and their
fundamental attributes Aristotle
is not quite consistent. Thus
Gen. et Corr. ii. 2, 329, b, 7, 13,
c. 3, 330, a, 30, 33, and *Meteor.* i.
2, 339, a, 13, he calls the latter
(heat, cold, &c.) both στοιχεῖα and
ἀρχαί, the bodies of which they
are attributes, ἁπλᾶ σώματα, *Ind.*
Arist. 76, b, 15 sqq. Again, they
are frequently called στοιχεῖα
with the addition τὰ καλούμενα
[*Phys.* i. 4, 187, a, 26, iii. 5, 304,
b, 33. *Gen. et Corr.* ii. 1, 328, b,
31, 329, a, 26. *Meteor.* i. 3, 339,
b, 5. *Gen. An.* ii. 3, 736, b, 29.
Metaph. i. 4, 985, a, 34 : τὰ ὡς ἐν
ὕλης εἴδει λεγόμενα στοιχεῖα],
Part. An. ii. 1, 646, a, 13 even
τὰ καλούμενα ὑπό τινων στοιχεῖα,
so that we clearly see that he is
merely following in this the
usage of others. On the other
hand, στοιχεῖον—which in its
most general sense indicates constituent parts of any kind (ἐνυπάρχοντα), and thus even the component parts of a conception or a
demonstration, as well as the
form as constituent part of the
thing, but in a more special
sense the ἐνυπάρχον ὡς ὕλην
(BONITZ, *Ind. Arist.* 702, a, 18
sqq.)—stands for the ultimate
material constituents of bodies
themselves, that εἰς ὃ διαιρεῖται τὰ
σώματα ἔσχατα, ἐκεῖνα δὲ μηκέτ᾽ εἰς
ἄλλα εἴδει διαφέροντα [*Metaph.* v.
3, 1014, a, 32 ; cf. i. 3, 983, b, 8],
εἰς ὃ τἆλλα σώματα διαιρεῖται, ἐνυπάρχον δυνάμει ἢ ἐνεργείᾳ, αὐτὸ δ᾽
ἔστιν ἀδιαίρετον εἰς ἕτερα τῷ εἴδει
(*De Cœlo*, iii. 3, 303, a, 15). So
Gen. et Corr. ii. 7 *init.* ; *Meteor.*
i. 1 *init.* (τῶν στοιχείων τῶν σωμα-
τικῶν) ; ii. 2, 355, b, 1, iv. 1 *init.* ;
De Cœlo, iii. 3 *init.* c. 5 *init.*, and
innumerable other places. The
original oppositions, moreover,
which succeed primary substance
as the second principle of existence (as the elements are the
third, *Gen. et Corr.* ii. 1, 329, a,
32),are called αἴτια τῶν στοιχείων,
Meteor. iv. 1 *init.*
[2] 'Οἶον ἀτμὶς γὰρ ὁ ἀήρ,' *Gen.*
et Corr. ii. 3, 330, b, 4.
[3] *Gen. et Corr.* ii. 3. *Meteor.*
iv. 1 *init.*

and into which all are resolved.[1] Their own primitive and indecomposable nature is proved by the fact that though they can, by transmutation, pass into each other, they never excrete any other body from themselves.[2] Every composite body in the terrestrial kingdom contains all of them.[3] Yet they are never revealed to our experience in perfect purity.[4] For example, elemental fire must not be confounded with a flame, which is produced by an intensification of its warmth, as ice is by an intensification of the cold natural to water. Elemental fire is caloric, or warm and dry evaporation;[5] flame, on the contrary, is no constant

[1] *De Cœlo*, iii. 3. *Metaph*. v. 3, see p. 481, n. 1, and elsewhere.

[2] *De Cœlo*, iii. 3, 302, a, 19 sqq.

[3] As is more fully proved, *Gen. et Corr*. ii. 8.

[4] *Gen. et Corr*. ii. 3, 330, b, 21: οὐκ ἔστι δὲ τὸ πῦρ καὶ ὁ ἀὴρ καὶ ἕκαστον τῶν εἰρημένων ἁπλοῦν, ἀλλὰ μικτόν· τὰ δ᾽ ἁπλᾶ τοιαῦτα μέν ἐστιν, οὐ μέντοι ταὐτὰ [ταῦτα], οἷον εἴ τι τῷ πυρὶ ὅμοιον, πυροειδές, οὐ πῦρ, καὶ τὸ τῷ ἀέρι ἀεροειδές· ὁμοίως δὲ κἀπὶ τῶν ἄλλων. Cf. *Meteor*. ii. 4, 359, b, 32, where, referring to the distinction between wet and dry vapour, which is discussed below, he says: ἔστι δ᾽ οὔτε τὸ ὑγρὸν ἄνευ τοῦ ξηροῦ οὔτε τὸ ξηρὸν ἄνευ τοῦ ὑγροῦ, ἀλλὰ πάντα ταῦτα λέγεται κατὰ τὴν ὑπεροχήν. *Ibid*. ii. 5, 362, a, 9 : dry vapours are only produced where moisture is present. *Ibid*. iv. 8. According to *Phys*. iv. 7, 214, a, 32, air is intermingled with water; whereas, in *De Sensu*, c. 5, 443, a, 4, this is controverted; cf. MEYER, *Arist. Thierkunde*, 404 sq.

[5] *Gen. et Corr*. ii. 3, 330, b, 25 ; τὸ δὲ πῦρ ἐστιν ὑπερβολὴ

θερμότητος, ὥσπερ καὶ κρύσταλλος ψυχρότητος· ἡ γὰρ πῆξις καὶ ἡ ζέσις ὑπερβολαί τινές εἰσιν, ἡ μὲν ψυχρότητος ἡ δὲ θερμότητος. εἰ οὖν ὁ κρύσταλλός ἐστι πῆξις ὑγροῦ ψυχροῦ, καὶ τὸ πῦρ ἔσται ζέσις ξηροῦ θερμοῦ. διὸ καὶ οὐδὲν οὔτ᾽ ἐκ κρυπτάλλου γίγνεται οὔτ᾽ ἐκ πυρός. The same remark is made about fire, *Meteor*. i. 3, 340, b, 21, c. 4, 341, b, 22 ; cf. l. 13 : πρῶτον μὲν γὰρ ὑπὸ τὴν ἐγκύκλιον φοράν ἐστι τὸ θερμὸν καὶ ξηρὸν, ὃ λέγομεν πῦρ· ἀνώνυμον γὰρ τὸ κοινόν, &c. What is called ' fire ' is a kind of inflammable material (ὑπέκκαυμα)which, like smoke, can be kindled by a little motion. Heraclitus had identified fire with heat in general (see ZELL. *Ph. d. Gr*. i. 588 sq.); the distinction between fire and the heat of fire appears in his school (PLATO, *Crat*. 413, C). Aristotle had a special reason for emphasising this distinction, as is indicated by the above passage from the *Meteorology*. For it was impossible that between the aërial and the celestial sphere there should

material, but a phenomenon occasioned by the transmutation of moist and dry substance (air and earth).[1] Again, while each of the elements exhibits two essential properties, one of which in each case is its proper and distinctive characteristic—the dryness of earth, the cold of water, the 'moisture' or fluidity of air, the warmth of fire.[2] Since, finally, each element includes a passive and an active quality,[3] it follows that all act upon and are acted on by one another, that they mingle and are transformed into one another—a process, indeed, which would not otherwise be conceivable.[4] Each element may pass into all the rest, for everything goes from

be a region of fire, as he was forced to hold there was, if 'fire' included only visible flame.

[1] *Meteor.* ii. 2, 355, a, 9 : ἡ μὲν γὰρ φλὸξ διὰ συνεχοῦς ὑγροῦ καὶ ξηροῦ μεταβαλλόντων γίγνεται καὶ οὐ τρέφεται [with which that which is improperly called τροφή, *Long. Vit.* 3, 465, b, 24, *Vita et M.* c. 5, 470, a, 2, does not conflict]· οὐ γὰρ ἡ αὐτὴ οὖσα διαμένει οὐθένα χρόνον ὡς εἰπεῖν. *Ibid.* c. 3, 357, b, 31 : καθάπερ τὸ τῶν ῥεόντων ὑδάτων καὶ τὸ τῆς φλογὸς ῥεῦμα. *Vita et M.* c. 5, 470, a, 2.

[2] *Gen. et Corr.* ii. 3, 331, a, 3 : οὐ μὴν ἀλλ' ἁπλῶς γε τέτταρα ὄντα [τὰ στοιχεῖα] ἑνὸς ἕκαστόν ἐστι, γῆ μὲν ξηροῦ μᾶλλον ἢ ψυχροῦ, ὕδωρ δὲ ψυχροῦ μᾶλλον ἢ ὑγροῦ, ἀὴρ δ' ὑγροῦ μᾶλλον ἢ θερμοῦ, πῦρ δὲ θερμοῦ μᾶλλον ἢ ξηροῦ. *Meteor.* iv. 4, 382, a, 3. In the latter passage Aristotle says, among other things, that earth and water alone are inhabited by living beings (on which *vide* below), because they alone are ὕλη τῶν σωμάτων. For although cold is held by Aristotle

to be the primary quality of water, moisture of air, he yet tells us here : λέγεται δὲ τῶν στοιχείων ἰδιαίτατα ξηροῦ μὲν γῆ, ὑγροῦ δὲ ὕδωρ . . . τιθέμεθα δὲ ὑγροῦ σῶμα ὕδωρ, ξηροῦ δὲ γῆν (iv. 4, 5, 382, a, 3, b, 3); and since dryness and moisture are regarded as the passive or material qualities (see p. 480, *supra*), earth and water are held to be the matter of all bodies. Fire, on the other hand, represents in a special sense the element of form (*Gen. et Corr.* i. 8, 335, a, 9 sqq.), for here, as elsewhere, the containing element stands to the contained in the relation of form to matter (*De Cœlo*, iv. 4, 312, a, 11) Similarly, more reality is attributed to heat than to cold, inasmuch as the former is a positive, the latter a negative, attribute ; the one is classed as being, the other as not-being (*Gen. et Corr.* i. 3, 318, b, 14).

[3] See pp. 479 sq. *supra*.

[4] *Gen. et Corr.* ii. 2, 329, b, 22, c. 7, and elsewhere; see pp. 450 sq. *supra*.

opposite to opposite; but the elements are all opposed
to each other just in the same way as their distinctive
properties (warmth, cold, dryness, and moisture) are
opposed. The more complete this opposition is, the
more difficult and the slower is the process of transition
from one to the other; the less complete, the easier.
Therefore, when two elements exhibit respectively a
conflict of both their essential properties, the process is
slower and more difficult than when they have one
property in common and conflict only in respect of the
other. In the latter case the alteration of one property
in one of them occasions a complete transmutation into
the other; while in the former case we only gain one
step by such a change—for only the element intermediate between the two that are opposed is produced, and
it requires a second transmutation before the metamorphosis is complete. For instance, by removing the
cold of water, we obtain air; but it is only when the
humidity common to water and air has been removed
that we obtain fire. If the humidity of water dis-
appears, earth is produced; but in order to generate
fire, the coldness common to earth and water must be
withdrawn. Hence it follows that the elements which
are wholly opposed to one another are metamorphosed
by an indirect process; those which are but partially
opposed are transformed directly. Fire passes directly
into air or earth, indirectly into water; air directly into
fire or water, indirectly into earth; water directly
into air or earth, indirectly into fire; earth directly
into water or fire, indirectly into air.[1] Thus all the

---

[1] *Gen. et Corr.* ii. 4.

elements, as Heraclitus and Plato had already demonstrated,[1] form together one complete whole, a self-
contained circle of generation and destruction,[2] the parts
of which are incessantly undergoing transformation, but
steadfastly maintaining the law of their metamorphosis,
preserving the same forms and proportions in the midst
of the ceaseless transmutation of their matter.[3]

These propositions concerning the nature of the
elementary bodies are enough to prove that there is
only one world. For if each body has its natural place,
and if its very essence consists in its having it, then all
bodies, unless hindered by force, must move to these
their natural localities—earth to the centre, æther to
circumference, and the other elements to the intermediate spaces. Hence it is impossible that there
should be more than one region of earth, water, air,
fire, and æther, and consequently that there should be
another world besides the one in which we live. We
cannot suppose that a body is forcibly retained in a
locality beyond the world, since such a locality must be

[1] Cf. ZELL. *Ph. d. Gr.* i.
619, and *ibid.* ii. 680.

[2] *Gen. et Corr. ibid.* 331, b, 2:
ὥστε φανερὸν ὅτι κύκλῳ τε ἔσται ἡ
γένεσις τοῖς ἁπλοῖς σώμασι, &c.

[3] *Meteor.* ii. 3, 357, b, 27 : it
is asked, πότερον καὶ ἡ θάλαττα
ἀεὶ διαμένει τῶν αὐτῶν οὖσα μορίων
ἀριθμῷ, ἢ τῷ εἴδει καὶ τῷ ποσῷ
μεταβαλλόντων ἀεὶ τῶν μερῶν,
καθάπερ ἀὴρ καὶ τὸ πότιμον ὕδωρ
καὶ τὸ πῦρ. ἀεὶ γὰρ ἄλλο καὶ ἄλλο
γίνεται τούτων ἕκαστον, τὸ δ' εἶδος
τοῦ πλήθους ἑκάστου τούτων μένει,
καθάπερ τὸ τῶν ῥεόντων ὑδάτων καὶ
τὸ τῆς φλογὸς ῥεῦμα. φανερὸν δὴ

τοῦτο καὶ πιθανόν, ὡς ἀδύνατον μὴ
τὸν αὐτὸν εἶναι περὶ πάντων τούτων
λόγον, καὶ διαφέρειν ταχυτῆτι καὶ
βραδυτῆτι τῆς μεταβολῆς ἐπὶ πάντων τε καὶ φθορὰν εἶναι καὶ γένεσιν,
ταύτην μέντοι τεταγμένως συμβα΄-
νειν πᾶσιν αὐτοῖς. 358, b, 29:
οὔτε ἀεὶ˙τὰ αὐτὰ μέρη διαμένει, οὔτε
γῆς οὔτε θαλάττης, ἀλλὰ μόνον ὁ
πᾶς ὄγκος. καὶ γὰρ καὶ περὶ γῆς
ὁμοίως δεῖ ὑπολαβεῖν · τὸ μὲν γὰρ
ἀνέρχεται τὸ δὲ πάλιν συγκατα-
βαίνει καὶ τοὺς τόπους συμμετα-
βάλλει τά τ' ἐπιπολάζοντα καὶ τὰ
κατιόντα πάλιν. Cf. also ZELL.
Ph. d. Gr. i. 2, 576, 620.

the natural place of some other body ; and if all bodies
in this one world have their place, there can be no body
outside it, and consequently no space, since space is
only that in which a body is or can be.[1] The same
conclusion is arrived at also from another side. Several
worlds would presuppose several first causes of motion,
which would be specifically similar, and consequently
only different in their matter. But the *primum movens*
has no matter : it is single and complete in itself. It
follows that the world which derives its continuous and
eternal motion from the first cause must be so too.[2]
If, however, we are told that the concept of the world,
like all concepts, must manifest itself in several individuals, Aristotle bids us answer that this argument
would be only conclusive if there were an extra-mundane
matter in which this concept could incorporate itself,
but since our world embraces the whole of matter, it is
of necessity single in its kind, although we ought
always to distinguish between its concept and the
phenomenal manifestation of the same which is present
to our senses.[3] If there are not several worlds now in
existence, no more can there be such in the future, or
have been at any past period. This world of ours is
one, and single, and complete.[4]

[1] *De Cælo*, i. 8, c. 9, 278, b,
21 sqq. 279, a, 11.
[2] This metaphysical proof,
held in prospect *De Cælo*, i. 8,
277, b, 9, is given *Metaph.* xii. 8,
1074, a, 31 sqq.; cf. also p. 388
sq., and on matter as the source
of multiplicity, p. 368 sq.
[3] *De Cælo*, i. 9 ; cf. p. 222.
[4] *Ibid.* 279, a, 9 : ὥστ' οὔτε νῦν

εἰσὶ πλείους οὐρανοὶ οὔτ' ἐγένοντο
οὔτ' ἐνδέχεται γενέσθαι πλείους ·
ἀλλ' εἷς καὶ μόνος καὶ τέλειος οὗτος
οὐρανός ἐστιν. *Ibid.* i. 1 *fin.*:
particular bodies are infinite in
number ; τὸ δὲ πᾶν οὗ ταῦτα μόρια
τέλειον ἀναγκαῖον εἶναι καὶ καθάπερ
τοὔνομα σημαίνει, πάντῃ, καὶ μὴ τῇ
μὲν τῇ δ' οὔ.

Furthermore, the shape of the universe is determined by the nature of the five simple bodies. Since circular motion is proper to one of them, and rectilinear motion to the rest, we obtain in the first place the distinction, touched upon above, between the two chief regions of the world—that in which circular motion rules, and that in which the opposite movements up and down hold sway : *i.e.* that which is full of æther, and that which contains the four elements. In both of them the materials lie in spherical layers one above the other. For since similar materials uniformly strive to reach their natural localities, which in turn are determined by their distance from the centre of the world, it follows that the materials of each sort are conglobated in spheres which are at all points equidistant from the centre. In the middle of the whole lies the earth—a solid sphere,[1] but in extent a relatively small portion of the world.[2] Its fixture in this locality proceeds partly

---

[1] Besides the argument quoted in the text, Aristotle proves the rotundity of the earth (*De Cœlo*, ii. 14, 297, a, 6 sqq.) from the form of its shadow on the moon during an eclipse, from the different stars visible in the north and the south, and the fact (already touched on 296, b, 18) that falling bodies do not move in parallel lines but only at similar angles towards the earth. With regard to the last, there is room for doubt whether it had been ascertained by accurate observation and experiment, or whether it was not an inference from the theory that all bodies which have weight gravitate towards the centre.

[2] In proof of this statement Aristotle, *Meteor*. i. 3, 339, b, 6, 340, a, 6, refers generally to the ἀστρολογικὰ θεωρήματα, *De Cœlo*; as above. 297, b, 30 sqq., he adduces the fact that when we move even a short distance north or south, some of the stars visible over the horizon seem to change their positions. He remarks here that mathematicians reckon the circumference of the earth at 400,000 stadia (50,000 miles : about double, therefore, the true measurement), and that as compared with the size of the celestial bodies this is a comparatively small figure. The hypothesis (so important in later times for Columbus's discovery)

from the nature of its material,[1] and partly from its position in the universe :[2] observation, moreover, assures us of the fact.[3] The hollows on the surface of the earth are filled with water, the upper surface of which is spherical.[4] Around the water and the earth are hollow spheres—first of air, then of fire. Aristotle, however, not unfrequently identifies the two last, remarking that what we call air is composed partly of moist and partly of dry vapour, the latter produced from earth, the former from water and the moisture of the earth : the drier kinds mount upwards, the more humid, from their

that the Indian and Atlantic Oceans are all one sea, he further thinks worthy of respect. *De An.* iii. 3, 428, b, 3, *Meteor.* i. 8, 345, b, 2, he tells us that the sun is larger than the earth.

[1] *De Cœlo,* ii. 14, where Aristotle opposes the view that the earth moves, both in the form in which it was held by Philolaus (ZELL. *Ph. d. Gr.* i. 388), and in the form given to it by Hicetas, Ecphantus, Heraclides (*ibid.* i. 459, ii. 1, 8×7 sq.), and attributed also to Plato (*ibid.* ii. 1, 682, 2). His chief reason is (296, a, 27, b, 6, 25) that circular motion is contrary to the elemental nature of the earth, in virtue of which its proper motion is rectilinear and toward the centre. For the same reason all other motions must be denied of it. For since its natural motion is toward the centre, and all bodies rest when they arrive at the place toward which they naturally gravitate, motion away from the centre cannot belong to any part of it and the whole must be at rest.

[2] The rotation of the world presupposes a fixed centre, which Aristotle conceives of as corporeal ; see p. 480, *supra.*

[3] Thus, heavy bodies when thrown upwards in a straight line return to their starting-point (*ibid.* 296, b, 25 sqq.). Moreover, astronomical phenomena find a satisfactory explanation on the hypothesis that the earth rests (297, a, 2), while on the opposite hypothesis irregularities must result ; for instance, the stars could not always rise and set at the same points (296, a, 34 sqq.). The ' motion ' referred to in *Anal. Post.* ii. 1, 89, b, 30, is the earthquake.

[4] The proof of this, *De Cœlo,* ii. 4, 287, b, 1 sqq., is as follows : as water always accumulates in the deepest parts, and the nearer the centre the deeper any part is, water must continue to flow towards the centre until all the deep places are filled up, *i.e.* until its surface is at all points equidistant from the centre. The proper place for water is the space occupied by the sea, *Meteor.* ii. 2, 355, a, 35, b, 15, 356, a, 33.

greater gravity, sink downward; so the former fill the upper, the latter the lower, region of the atmosphere.[1]

The spherical form of the lower world involves that of the celestial region which surrounds the former and touches it at all points.[2] But considered in themselves, the heavens could scarcely be supposed to have another shape,[3] since the sphere is the first and most perfect figure, and therefore the one appropriate to the first body. Moreover, it is only this figure which can revolve within the space which it encloses,[4] and external to the heavens there is no space. Lastly, the motion of the heavens, being the measure of all movement, must be the most rapid; but the most rapid is that which has the shortest journey, and a circle is the shortest road from the same point to the same point.[5]

---

[1] *Meteor.* i. 3, 340, b, 19 sqq. 341, a, 2, c. 4, 341, b, 6–22; cf. i. 7, 344, b, 8, c. 8, 345, b, 32; ii. 2, 354, b, 4 sqq.; *De Cœlo*, ii. 4, 287, a, 30; on the difference between dry and moist vapours (ἀναθυμίασις, or καπνὸς and ἀτμίς), *v.* also *Meteor.* ii. 4, 359, b, 28, 360, a, 31, iii. 6. 378, a, 18.

[2] *De Cœlo*, ii. 4, 287, a, 30 sqq. As there can be no space which is void (see pp. 432 sq.), it follows that the celestial and the fiery spheres are at all points in contact with one another.

[3] For what follows see *De Cœlo*, ii. 4.

[4] *Ibid.* 287, a, 11. This statement is certainly strange, for as ALEX. *apud* SIMPL. *in loco*, *Schol.* 493, b, 22, observed at an early date, a whole series of figures share this attribute with the sphere, viz. all those which are described by the spinning of a smooth body, and of which, therefore, each section which cuts the axis at right angles forms a circle whose centre is on the line of the axis. Simplicius gets out of the difficulty by remarking that, while in the case of other shapes there is only one axis that will serve the purpose, in a sphere you may take any you please; an explanation with which we may rest content on so trifling a point.

[5] Or as SIMPLICIUS, *in loco*, explains it: of all lines which return to the point from which they started, and thus inclose a space, the circle is the shortest; just as of all surfaces of equal extent that which is circular, of all bodies of equal bulk that which is globular, has the smallest circumference. Even with this

The finer and more uniform its matter is, the more
perfectly spherical will be the shape of the celestial
world : [1] as, indeed, in the most perfect body matter
must be perfectly adapted to its form, and as the arguments by which the spherical shape of heaven is proved [2]
require. Still we cannot regard the matter of the
heavens as uniformly homogeneous. Nature, in Aristotle's opinion, reconciles all opposites by a gradual
process, and the purity of the æther, which composes
heaven, diminishes as it approaches the terrestrial
atmosphere.[3]

In proceeding to investigate the disposition of the
heavens, Aristotle is guided by observation.[4] All the

explanation the argument is a
lame one. It is obvious that
Aristotle accepts the globular
form of the earth on the direct
evidence of the senses, and
merely adds these other proofs
as supplementary evidence.

[1] *Ibid.* 287, b, 14 : ὅτι μὲν οὖν
σφαιροειδής ἐστιν ὁ κόσμος δῆλον
ἐκ τούτων, καὶ ὅτι κατ᾽ ἀκρίβειαν
ἔντορνος οὕτως ὥστε μηθὲν μήτε
χειρόκμητον ἔχειν παραπλησίως
μήτ᾽ ἄλλο μηθὲν τῶν παρ᾽ ἡμῖν ἐν
ὀφθαλμοῖς φαινομένων, no terrestrial body being so completely
adapted for an exactly symmetri-
cal form.

[2] According to the above
argument, the smallest elevation
or depression in the outer surface of the celestial globe would
presuppose a void space outside
of it.

[3] *Meteor.* i. 3, 340, b, 6 : τὸ
μὲν γὰρ ἄνω καὶ μέχρι σελήνης
ἕτερον εἶναι σῶμά φαμεν πυρός τε
καὶ ἀέρος, οὐ μὴν ἀλλ᾽ ἐν αὐτῷ γε τὸ
μὲν καθαρώτερον εἶναι τὸ δ᾽ ἧττον

εἰλικρινές, &c. KAMPE is wrong
in supposing that it is the
air as the matter of the fiery
region and not the æther that is
here spoken of. The ἄνω μέχρι
σελήνης does not mean the region
below the moon, but the upper
regions reaching down as far as
the moon, and lying between it
and the starry heavens. Moreover, σῶμα ἕτερον ἀέρος cannot
possibly mean the air, but, as
l. 10 immediately says, the
πρῶτον στοιχεῖον κύκλῳ φερόμενον
or the æther. We must not,
however, conceive of a mixture
of elementary substances which
cannot extend to the region
of circular motion, but merely of
differences in the degree of
density.

[4] According to Eudemus (in
SIMPL. *De Cœlo, Schol. in Arist.*
498, a, 45) Plato had thus stated
the problem of astronomy : τίνων
ὑποτεθεισῶν ὁμαλῶν καὶ τεταγμένων κινήσεων διασωθῇ τὰ περὶ τὰς
κινήσεις τῶν πλανωμένων φαινόμενα,

heavenly bodies seem daily to move from east to west,
but seven of them [1] move besides in longer periods of

and from this time forth Greek
astronomy held to the view that
its function consisted in dis-
covering hypotheses which would
explain the phenomena as satisfactorily as (on their somewhat
hardy assumption) the motion
of the stars is explained by
the theory of uniform motions.
The highest criterion of the truth
of a theory is τὸ σώζεσθαι τὰ
φαινόμενα. To take only a few instances : cf. the quotations from
and about Heraclides, in ZELL.
Ph. d. Gr. i. 881, 1, and in
BÖCKH, D. kosm. Syst. d. Platon,
134 sqq. ; Aristotle's statements
about Callippus, Metaph. xii.
8, 1073, b, 35 : τῷ δ᾽ ἡλίου καὶ
τῷ σελήνης δύο ᾤετο ἔτι προσθέ-
τεας εἶναι σφαίρας, τὰ φαινόμενα
εἰ μέλλει τις ἀποδώσειν ; the statements and quotations from
Geminus, in SIMPL. Phys. 64, b,
and what the latter says of
the old astronomers partly
following Eudemus and Sosigenes, De Cœlo, Schol. in Arist.
472, a, 42, 498, a, 43, 499, a, 7,
500, a, 25, 501, b, 28, 502, b, 5
sqq. 503, a, 23, 504, b, 32 sqq.
Aristotle adopts the same criterion. He asserts only those
positions which are warranted
by the facts ; where the latter are
inadequately known, or do not
speak with sufficient plainness,
he makes no pretence of absolute certainty, but is content
with probability. Thus Metaph.
xii. 8, 1073, b, 38, 1074, a, 14,
after declaring (1073, a, 11) that
the investigation is not yet concluded, he says : ἀναγκαῖον δὲ εἰ
μέλλουσι συντεθεῖσαι πᾶσαι τὰ

φαινόμενα ἀποδώσειν, καθ᾽ ἕκαστον
τῶν πλανωμένων ἑτέρας σφαίρας
μιᾷ ἐλάττονας εἶναι, &c. . . . τὸ
μὲν οὖν πλῆθος τῶν σφαιρῶν ἔστω
τοσοῦτον . . . τὸ γὰρ ἀναγκαῖον
ἀφείσθω τοῖς ἰσχυροτέροις λέγειν.
De Cœlo, ii. 12, 292, a, 14 : περὶ
δὴ τούτων ζητεῖν μὲν καλῶς ἔχει
καὶ τὴν ἐπὶ πλεῖον σύνεσιν, καίπερ
μικρὰς ἔχοντας ἀφορμάς, &c.; c. 5,
287, b, 28 : the desire to explain
everything is a mark either of
great zeal or great folly. The
extent, however, to which
the attempt is open to blame
depends upon the motive which
inspires it, and the strength of a
man's conviction of the truth of
his views : πότερον ἀνθρωπίνως ἢ
καρτεριχώτερον, ταῖς μὲν οὖν ἀκρι-
βεστέραις ἀνάγκαις ὅταν τις ἐπι-
τύχῃ, τότε χάριν ἔχειν δεῖ τοῖς εὑρ-
ίσκουσι, νῦν δὲ τὸ φαινόμενον ῥητέον.
Cf. also Part. An. i. 5, 644, b, 31,
where it is said that the study of
the heavens possesses an infinite
charm, εἰ καὶ κατὰ μικρὸν ἐφαπτόμεθα : and on the necessity of
observation, cf. ibid. c. 1, 639, b, 7:
πότερον, καθάπερ οἱ μαθηματικοὶ τὰ
περὶ τὴν ἀστρολογίαν δεικνύουσιν,
οὕτω δεῖ καὶ τὸν φυσικὸν τὰ
φαινόμενα πρῶτον τὰ περὶ τὰ ζῷα
θεωρήσαντα καὶ τὰ μέρη τὰ περὶ
ἕκαστον, ἔπειθ᾽ οὕτω λέγειν τὸ διὰ
τί καὶ τὰς αἰτίας, ἢ ἄλλως πως.
(That Aristotle would decide for
the former method is obvious.)
Aristotle himself was a most
careful observer of known facts ;
see p. 46, n. 1, supra.
    [1] Aristotle speaks, of course,
only of the stars known to the ancients, and visible to the naked
eye.

very unequal lengths in the opposite direction, *i.e.* from west to east, around the earth. That these bodies could move freely in space was a thought beyond the reach of ancient astronomers. They fancied each star fixed in its sphere, and therefore were obliged to imagine at least as many celestial spheres as they saw stars differing in their movements and periods.[1] Aristotle does not get beyond this view. The stars, he says,[2] as well as the whole heaven, appear to move; and since the earth is fixed, this phenomenon must be explained by a real movement of the heaven or the stars, or of both. It is not conceivable that both should

[1] Many of the older philosophers held that the stars were carried round by the air or the rotation of the world. Besides Xenophanes and Heraclitus, who held that the stars were nebulous masses, this view was shared by Anaxagoras, Democritus, and perhaps even Anaximenes; Empedocles held that it was true of the planets but not of the fixed stars, which were set immovably in the arch of heaven (see ZELL. *Ph. d. Gr.* i. 226 sq. 500, 622, 715, 799, 898, 3). Anaximander seems to have been the first to start the theory of spheres (*ibid.* 206 sq.) which was subsequently adopted by the Pythagoreans(*ibid.* 384, 1, 449) and by Parmenides (*ibid.* 528). Plato adopted it from the Pythagoreans (*ibid.* i. 685), and was followed by Eudoxus and Callippus, the leading astronomers of Aristotle's time (see p. 497 sq., *infra*). It seemed forced upon them by the difficulty they had in conceiving of a free motion of the stars, the idea of universal gravitation not yet having dawned upon them. It seemed, moreover, to be demanded by the nature of the stellar motions themselves, which, if they were one and the same every day round the earth, were more naturally explained by a single motion of the whole sphere of the fixed stars than by a number of separate motions. A like hypothesis seemed to afford the best explanation of the movements of the planets, including the sun and moon; their proper motion being the result of the rotation of their spheres, which takes place, however; in a direction opposite to that of the fixed stars, while their daily course was to be explained on the ground that the rotation of the stellar regions included them also.

[2] *De Cœlo*, ii. 8. This argument is stated with some fullness, because it shows the important fact that Aristotle already presupposes the existence of *different* stellar spheres.

move independently, for in this case how could we explain the exact correspondence between the rate at which the stars move and that of their spheres? We cannot refer an invariably regular phenomenon to an accidental coincidence. The same may be said about the hypothesis that the stars move while their spheres are fixed. In this case also the rate of the astral movement would have to correspond to the size of their circle, although there is no real connection between the two. Hence we are driven to suppose that the spheres move, but the stars are fixed and carried round by them.[1] This hypothesis satisfactorily explains why, among concentric circles, the larger move at a more rapid rate. It is further seen to be necessary because the stars, from their spherical shape,[2] in order to get into motion, must either roll or spin. Mere rolling, however, would not carry them on their way;[3] and the fact that the moon always shows us the same side proves that they do not spin. Moreover, their shape is the least adapted to progressive movement, since they are devoid of locomotive organs,[4] obviously because nature has not intended them for any such movement.[5]

[1] Τοὺς μὲν κύκλους κινεῖσθαι τὰ δὲ ἄστρα ἠμερεῖν [*i.e.* they have no motion of their own within their own spheres, but move with them] καὶ ἐνδεδεμένα τοῖς κύκλοις φέρεσθαι, 289, b, 32.

[2] That this is their form is demonstrated, *ibid.* c. 11, both by the shape of the moon in its different phases, and by the teleological argument that since nature does nothing in vain she must have given the stars, which require no organs of locomotion, the corresponding shape, viz. rotundity.

[3] Moreover, Aristotle adds, it is only the sun which appears to roll at its rising and setting: and this, like the twinkling light of the fixed stars, is merely an optical delusion.

[4] Cf. also ZELL. *Ph. d. Gr* i. 681, 1.

[5] In his refutation of the doctrine of the harmony of the spheres (c. 9 *fin.*), which we

Now in order to explain the motion of the heavenly bodies upon this hypothesis, it was assumed that every sphere revolved on its own axis at a perfectly uniform rate. Accordingly, so far as the movements of the separate stars varied from a perfect circle, or progressed at unequal rates, they were regarded as composite movements capable of being analysed into pure and uniform rotations. Therefore, each star required as many spheres as were found necessary for the resolution of its apparent movement into pure circular revolutions. Aristotle was bound to accept these various hypotheses, since even he never doubted that the heavenly spheres and the matter which composed them performed such revolutions only as our eyesight seems to witness to; moreover, he was obliged to suppose that the spheres contained within the universal globe, in which there was no vacuum whatever, had no room for any other kind of movement.[1] He went further, and connected

may omit, Aristotle gives another reason, viz. that infinite confusion would result if the movements of the stars were free.

[1] Cf. what has already been said upon the movement of the heavens, p. 489, and on the circular movement of the primeval body, p. 473. It was a universal presupposition among ancient astronomers, traceable to Plato (see p. 490, n, *supra*, and the references to Eudoxus and Callippus, p. 500 sq. *infra*), that the movement of the spheres must be perfectly uniform. Aristotle endeavours to establish its truth in the first instance in connection with the πρῶτος οὐρανὸς, the sphere of the fixed stars. In-

crease and decrease of velocity is possible only, he asserts, in a movement which has beginning, middle, and end; it is impossible in circular motion, which is alike without beginning and end. Unequal motion presupposes change either in *motum* or *movens*, or both, but this is impossible with regard to the heavens. For it is obvious to the senses that the parts of the (highest) heavens are uniform in their movements, while with regard to the heavens as a whole the same conclusion is forced upon us when we consider that unequal motion is only possible where force is either added or withdrawn, and that every with-

his peculiar theory of motion with these views. All motion depends upon the contact of a mobile with a motive body, and this law must apply to the motion of the spheres, since one *movens* in the same matter can only produce one kind of motion,[1] and since every motion ultimately proceeds from an unmoved cause, and every motion which has no beginning from an eternal cause of movement,[2] we must imagine as many eternal and unmoved substances for the production of the movement of the spheres as there are spheres required for the phenomena to be accounted for.[3] The heavenly bodies are no dead masses, but living beings ;[4] there

drawal of force (ἀδυναμία) is an unnatural condition inapplicable to the heavens, &c. All these reasons hold equally of the spheres of the planets considered individually and apart from the influence of their spheres upon one another as of the first heaven. Aristotle, at 288, a, 14 of the passage quoted above, confines himself to the latter only. The movements of the lower spheres are compounded of those of the higher. The true account of the motions of the planets (attributing to them acceleration and retardation of velocity) is declared to be παντελῶς ἄλογον καὶ πλάσματι ὅμοιον, 289, a, 4.

[1] *Phys.* viii. 6, 259, a, 18 (*v.* above p. 293, n. 1): μία δ' [ἡ κίνησις] εἰ ὑφ' ἑνός τε τοῦ κινοῦντος καὶ ἑνὸς τοῦ κινουμένου.

[2] Cf. p. 388 sq., and on the way in which motion is produced by the unmoved mover, p. 404.

[3] After showing the necessity of an eternal incorporeal cause of motion, *Metaph.* xii. 7, Aristotle asks, c. 8 : πότερον μίαν θετέον τὴν τοιαύτην οὐσίαν ἢ πλείους, καὶ πόσας ; and answers, 1073, a, 26 : ἐπεὶ δὲ τὸ κινούμενον ἀνάγκη ὑπό τινος κινεῖσθαι, καὶ τὸ πρῶτον κινοῦν ἀκίνητον εἶναι καθ' αὑτό, καὶ τὴν ἀΐδιον κίνησιν ὑπὸ ἀϊδίου κινεῖσθαι καὶ τὴν μίαν ὑφ' ἑνός, ὁρῶμεν δὲ παρὰ τὴν τοῦ παντὸς τὴν ἁπλῆν φορὰν ἣν κινεῖν φαμὲν τὴν πρώτην οὐσίαν καὶ ἀκίνητον, ἄλλας φορὰς οὔσας τὰς τῶν πλανήτων ἀϊδίους . . . ἀνάγκη καὶ τούτων ἑκάστην τῶν φορῶν ὑπ' ἀκινήτου τε κινεῖσθαι καθ' αὑτὸ καὶ ἀϊδίου οὐσίας. ἢ τε γὰρ τῶν ἄστρων φύσις ἀΐδιος οὐσία τις οὖσα, καὶ τὸ κινοῦν ἀΐδιον καὶ πρότερον τοῦ κινουμένου, καὶ τὸ πρότερον οὐσίας οὐσίαν ἀναγκαῖον εἶναι. φανερὸν τοίνυν ὅτι τοσαύτας τε οὐσίας ἀναγκαῖον εἶναι τήν τε φύσιν ἀϊδίους καὶ ἀκινήτους καθ' αὑτὰς καὶ ἄνευ μεγέθους. BRENTANO'S view that these eternal beings were created by God has already been discussed at p. 412, *supra*.

[4] *De Cœlo*, ii. 12, 292, a, 18 (cf. b, 1): ἀλλ' ἡμεῖς ὡς περὶ σωμάτων αὐτῶν μόνον καὶ μονάδων τάξιν

must be as many ' souls,' to preside over their motions, as there are spheres. The fabric of the heavens consists, therefore, of a system of concentric hollow balls or spheres, so placed within each other as to leave no empty interspace.[1] The centre of this system is called the bottom, the circumference the top; and so the outer spheres are uppermost, the inner are nethermost, and each locality in space is higher, or lower according as it has a greater or less distance from the centre.[2] It is only indirectly, and relatively to the motion of the

μὲν ἐχόντων ἀψύχων δὲ πάμπαν διανοούμεθα· δεῖ δ' ὡς μετεχόντων ὑπολαμβάνειν πράξεως καὶ ζωῆς. It is true that αὐτῶν seems to refer to the stars, not to their spheres, and that we are at liberty to picture with KAMPE (*Erkenntnissth. d. Arist.* 39 sq.) each individual star as animated by a spirit; but the passage does not compel us to do so, for if the spheres are animate the stars which are part of them must share their life and action. Elsewhere, however, *Metaph.* xii. 8 (see p. 501 sq. *infra*, and cf. previous note), he expressly says that there cannot be more eternal unmoved beings than there are spheres, and this is only what we should have expected from him, since it is only from the movement of the stars that he infers, in the way indicated in the preceding note, the existence of such beings. Moreover, it is only the spheres, and not the stars, which are said by him to be moved. It is only these, then, that have ' souls' of their own, or, to speak more strictly, it is only these which

are united severally to spiritual beings which stand in the same relation to them as the human soul does to the body which it moves without being itself moved (see *infra*, vol. ii., *init.*). *De Cælo,* ii. 2, 285, a, 29: ὁ δ' οὐρανὸς ἔμψυχος καὶ ἔχει κινήσεως ἀρχήν. So 284, b, 32; cf. *Part. An.* i. 1, 641, b, 15 sqq. As, however, the mover of the highest sphere lies outside the world and is unmoved, Plato's conception of the ' world-soul ' (which, indeed, Aristotle expressly rejects, see p.459, n. 5) is as inapplicable to it in its relation to its sphere as it is to the other spheral spirits in their relation to theirs.

[1] Aristotle denies that there is any ' void ' (see p 433, sq. *supra*), and accordingly conceives not only of the astral spheres but of all the others, even the lowest, as in immediate contact with one another. *Meteor.* i. 3, 340, b, 10 sqq. 341, a, 2 sqq.; *De Cælo,* ii. 4, 287, a, 5 sqq.

[2] Cf. pp. 473 and 478, *supra*; *Phys.* iii. 5, 205, b, 30 sqq.; *De Cælo,* i. 6 *init.* ii. 4, 287, a, 8, and elsewhere.

spheres, that the terms above and beneath are applied to opposite points in the circumference, and consequently that we come to speak of right and left, front and back, in the world. In this case, reckoning from the sphere of the fixed stars, we call the southern half of the globe the upper, reckoning from the planetary sphere, the northern.[1] Each sphere has its own peculiar

[1] See *De Cœlo*, ii. 2 (cf. *Phys.* passage just referred to) and the lucid explanation in BÖCKH, *D. kosm. Syst. d. Platon*, p. 112 sqq. The differences here spoken of apply only to motion, and therefore properly only to that which is living and self-moved; to such the upper is (285, a, 23) τὸ ὅθεν ἡ κίνησις, the right hand τὸ ἀφ' οὗ, the front τὸ ἐφ' ὃ ἡ κίνησις. (Cf. *Ingr. An.* c. 4, 705, b, 13 sqq.) If we apply this to the world, that is the right side of the πρῶτος οὐρανὸς from which its motion proceeds—in other words, the east. This motion is conceived of (285, b, 19), as it was by Plato (see ZELL. *Ph. d. Gr.* i. 684, 1), as proceeding in a circle towards the right, as when in a circle of men anything (as, for instance, the cup or the talk at table, PLATO, *Symp.* 177, D, 214, B, C, 222, E, 223, C) is passed along by each to his neighbour on the right. The πρῶτος οὐρανὸς is therefore represented (285, a, 31 sqq.) as standing inside the circle of the heavens in the line of its axis, touching one of the poles with its head, the other with its feet, and as giving the ball at some point upon its equator the push with its right hand which sets it spinning. The natural direction of such

motion will be that which carries the point in the periphery which has received the push past one who stands in the line of the axis in front of him: in other words, that which proceeds from the right in a forward direction and thence to the left. This, however, will be the case with the motion of the sphere of the fixed stars only if the head of one standing inside of it be upon the south pole; with that of the spheres of the planets which move from west to east, on the other hand, only on the opposite supposition. According to Aristotle, therefore, our antipodes are in the upper hemisphere, which he also calls (obviously from a different point of view than that just indicated) the right side of the world; we in the lower hemisphere and on the left side. On the other hand, reckoning from the courses of the planets, ours is the upper and right-hand, theirs the lower and left-hand, side. He points out, indeed, that we cannot properly speak of a right and a left at all in connection with the world as a whole (284, b, 6-18: ἐπειδὴ δέ τινές εἰσιν οἵ φασιν εἶναί τι δεξιὸν καὶ ἀριστερὸν τοῦ οὐρανοῦ . . . εἴπερ δεῖ προσάπτειν τῷ τοῦ παντὸς σώματι ταύτας τὰς ἀρχάς

motion, communicated by the presiding incorporeal being : but in all cases the motion is uniform, without beginning or ending, round an axis ; but the direction and the rapidity of this rotation vary in the several spheres. At the same time the spheres are connected with each other in such a way that the inner, or lower, are carried round by the outer, just as if the axis of each sphere were inserted at its poles into the next above.[1] Consequently, the problem arises how we are, under the

. . εἰ δὲ δεῖ καὶ τῷ οὐρανῷ προσάπτειν τι τῶν τοιούτων). Nevertheless, *Phys.* iii. 5, 205, b, 33, he says that the distinctions above and below, before and behind, right and left, exist οὐ μόνον πρὸς ἡμᾶς καὶ θέσει, ἀλλὰ καὶ ἐν αὐτῷ τῷ ὅλῳ ; *Ingr. An.* 5, 706, b, 11, he finds it natural that motion should proceed from the upper front and right side, ἡ μὲν γὰρ ἀρχὴ τίμιον, τὸ δ' ἄνω τοῦ κάτω καὶ τὸ πρόσθεν τοῦ ὄπισθεν καὶ τὸ δεξιὸν τοῦ ἀριστεροῦ τιμιώτερον (though it might be said with equal truth, ὡς διὰ τὸ τὰς ἀρχὰς ἐν τούτοις εἶναι ταῦτα τιμιώτερα τῶν ἀντικειμένων μορίων ἐστίν). So in *De Cælo,* iii. 5, to the question why the heavens move from east to west and not in the contrary direction, he gives the answer that since nature orders everything in the most perfect possible way, and forward motion is superior to backward, the heavens have received that motion which, according to the description of right and left in c. 2, is to be regarded as a forward one. The allusion, *Meteor.* ii. 5, 362, a, 32 sqq., to the north pole as the upper, the south pole as the lower, is an unimportant use of ordinary language.

[1] A similar connection of the inner with the surrounding spheres Plato had conceived of as existing between the spheres of the planets and of the fixed stars, when in *Tim.* 36, C, 39, A (cf. *Ph. d. Gr.* i. 683), he represents the axis of the former as inserted in the latter, and accordingly attributes to the planets a spiral motion compounded of the motions of both circles. One would suppose from ARIST. *Metaph.* xii. 8, 1073, b, 18, 25, SIMPL. *De Cælo, Schol. in Arist.* 498, b, 36, that Eudoxus and Callippus also conceived of the stars collectively as carried round by the sphere of the fixed stars, and the planets collectively by a sphere moving in the line of the ecliptic. It is clear, however, from the further explanations of Simplicius and from Aristotle's enumeration of the spheres(which differed from that of Callippus only in the addition of the σφαῖραι ἀνελίττουσαι) that this was not the case. Plato's proof that the spheres of the planets are carried round by the sphere of the fixed stars appeared to them fantastic. Only those spheres they conceived of as connected with one another which belonged

specified circumstances, to determine both the number
of the spheres and also the direction and rapidity of
their rotation, so as to explain the motions of the stars
revealed to us by observation.[1]

For this purpose Eudoxus, the famous astronomer
of Cnidos, who may be regarded as the first founder of
a complete theory of the spheres based upon accurate
observation,[2] sketched out a system of twenty-seven
spheres, twenty-six of which belong to the planets.
Considering the simple nature of its motion, he thought
one sphere enough for the heaven of the fixed stars, and
in this sphere the whole assemblage of the stars was
fastened. On the other hand, he assigned four spheres
to each of the five upper planets, and three apiece to
the sun and moon, which, in agreement with Plato, he
placed lowest in the planetary scale. The first sphere
of each planet was intended to explain its daily revolution in concert with the heaven of the fixed stars,
since it accomplished every day a rotation from east to

to the same planet. Aristotle, on
the contrary, extended Plato's
doctrine to the relation of all the
upper spheres to those that are
contained within them, as is
clear from his hypothesis of
retrogressive spheres (see *infra*).
(Cf. also *De Cœlo*, ii. 12, 293, a,
5 : πολλὰ σώματα κινοῦσιν αἱ πρὸ
τῆς τελευτα'ας καὶ τῆς ἐν ἄστρον
ἐχούσης· ἐν πολλαῖς γὰρ σφαίραις
ἡ τελευταῖα σφαῖρα ἐνδεδεμένη
φέρεται. *Ibid.* c. 10.) He justi-
fies this view on the ground that
the upper spheres stand to the
lower as the form to the matter,
De Cœl, iv. 3, 4, 310, b, 14, 312,
a, 12 ; *v. supra*, p. 325, n. 2); and
that, as all spheres are in close and
immediate contact with one another (see p. 496, n. 1, *supra*), each
can communicate its motion to the
one next below it. This relation
need not apply with equal strictness to the elementary spheres as
to the heavenly, seeing that they
do not, like the latter, consist of
a body whose nature it is to
move in a circle. Aristotle,
however, supposes in *Meteor.* i.
3, 341, a, 1, ii. 4, 361, a, 30 sqq.
that the winds circle round the
earth, being carried round by the
rotation of the world.

[1] Cf. p. 490, n. 4, *supra*.

[2] Eudemus and Sosigenes in
SIMPL. *De Cœlo, Schol. in Ar.* 498,
a, 45, b, 47, cf. *supra*, p. 451, n. 2,

west. The second, which was fastened into it, revolved in the opposite direction, completing its course in the space of time required by each planet (in the sun's case 365¼ days) to traverse the zodiac in the plane of the ecliptic. The others, likewise carried round by the surrounding spheres, but differing from them in direction and the period of rotation, were meant to explain the variations which are observable between the apparent motion of the stars and that produced by the two first spheres. The lowest sphere of each planet supports the star itself.[1] Callippus [2] added seven other spheres— two apiece for the sun and moon, and one apiece for Mercury, Venus, and Mars.[3] Aristotle approves of this, as being the more probable theory,[4] without remarking

---

and IDELER on Eudoxus, *Philosoph. Abh. d. Berl. Akad.* 1830, p. 67 sq.

[1] For a fuller account of the theories of Eudoxus and Callippus, see besides the scanty allusion in Aristotle (*Metaph.* xii. 8, 1073, b, 17) SIMPL. *ibid.* 498, b, 5–500, a, 15, who depends partly upon the work of EUDOXUS Π. Ταχῶν, partly upon the account of Sosigenes, but has not altogether avoided falling into mistakes, and THEO. *Astronom.* p. 276 sqq. ed. Martin, in whom, however, his editor (p. 55 sq.) points out serious errors. In explanation, cf. IDELER, *ibid.* 73 sqq. KRISCHE, *Forschungen,* p. 288 sq., who are followed by BONITZ, *Arist. Metaph.* ii. 507 sq., and SCHWEGLER, *Arist. Metaph.* iv. 274 sq.; PRANTL, 'Αριστ. π. οὐρ. 303 sqq.

[2] According to SIMPL. *ibid.* 498, b, 28, 500, a, 23, this astronomer was a pupil of Eudoxus (or perhaps only of his pupil Polemarchus) who on the death of the latter betook himself to Aristotle at Athens. Simplicius knows of no work by him, but gives some account, taken from Eudemus's *History of Astronomy,* of the reasons which led him to dissent from Eudoxus.

[3] ARIST. *ibid.* 1073, b, 32; SIMPL. *ibid.* 500, a, 15 sqq.; THEO, *ibid.* 278 sq. ; IDELER, 81 sq.; KRISCHE, 294 sq.

[4] It is obvious from the passage quoted p.490, n. 4,*supra,* that he did not attribute complete certainty to it. According to SIMPL. 503, a, 3, he even brought forward several objections to it in the *Problems.* The passage, however, does not occur in this treatise as we have it, which makes it all the more difficult to decide upon its genuineness.

that his own doctrine of the connection of the spheres
in one coherent whole renders the first sphere assigned
by Eudoxus and Callippus to each planet superfluous.[1]
At the same time he judges an important rectification
of the theory to be needful, on account of this very
coherence of the heavenly system. For if each sphere
carries round in its course all those which are contained
in it, the motions of the lower planets must be greatly
disturbed by those of their superiors, and the whole
result of the assumed spheral system would be altered
unless precautions be taken to neutralise the communication of movement from the spheres of one planet to
those of another. To meet this difficulty Aristotle,
accordingly, inserts some other spheres between the
lowest of each planet and the highest of that which
comes next beneath, meaning them to obviate the
action of the first upon the second. But the premises
of the whole theory require that these fresh spheres
should move at the same rate as those which they are
destined to neutralise, but in an exactly opposite
direction;[2] and again that there should be as many

---

[1] For, as Simplicius also remarks, 503, a, 38 sqq. (where,
however, l. 41, we must read συν-
αποκαθιστῶσαν), a special sphere
is not required to explain the
daily rotation of the planets from
east to west, since, in consequence of this connection the
motion of the spheres of the fixed
stars communicates itself to all
that are contained in it.

[2] For if two concentric
spheres, whose axes lie in the
same line, and of which the inner

one is fixed to the outer by the poles
of its axis, spin round the common
axis with relatively equal veloci-
ties in the opposite directions,
each point of the inner sphere is
at each moment precisely in the
position in which it would be if
both spheres were at rest. The
two motions have completely
neutralised one another in their
effect upon the inner sphere and
all that depends upon it, as Sosigenes, in SIMPL. *ibid.* 500, b, 39,
truly explains.

retrogressive or retarding spheres [1] as the movements
they are used to obviate. In other words, the collective
motions peculiar to each planet have to be considered :
none of these may be communicated to another planet,
whereas the daily revolution from east to west excited
in each planet by its first sphere does not require to be
neutralised.[2] It is only the moon which requires no
retrogressive sphere beneath the one which carries her,
since there is no planet below the moon that she could
interrupt. Aristotle, consequently, adds twenty-two
retrogressive spheres to the thirty-three of Callippus,
three apiece for Saturn and Jupiter, four apiece for

---

[1] Σφαῖραι ἀνελίττουσαι (supply τὰς τῶν ὑποκάτω φερομένων ἄστρων σφαίρας, not as Sosigenes
does, SIMPL. *ib.* 502, a, 43, τὰς τῶν
ὑπεοάνω κινήσεις, 1074, a, 2–12),
i.e. 'spheres which serve to turn
those beneath them backwards,'
to communicate to them a motion
opposite to that of the next
above them, and in this way to
keep them in the same position
relatively to the fixed stars as
they would have held had the
planetary spheres above them
produced no effect upon them at
all ("τὰς ἀνελιττούσας καὶ εἰς τὸ
αὐτὸ ἀποκαθιστάσας τῇ θέσει τὴν
πρώτην σφαῖραν ἀεὶ τοῦ ὑποκάτω
τεταγμένου ἄστρου"); *Metaph.*
ibid. 1074, a, 1 sqq Theophrastus
called these spheres ἀνταναφέρου-
σαι, because they carry those
that are beneath them back,
and ἄναστροι, because not only
some, but all of them are starless (SIMPL *ibid.* 498, b, 41,
where, however, the retrogressive spheres appear to be confounded with the starless spheres

of individual constellations); cf.
ibid. 502, a, 40.

[2] This supposition is as
erroneous as the view, discussed
p. 501, *supra*, that the theory of a
special sphere for each of the
planets with daily rotation from
east to west is compatible with
Aristotle's system of the spheres.
For since, according to his view,
the sphere of the fixed stars in
its revolution carries round with
it all that is contained in it, each
further sphere which revolved in
the same direction and at the
same velocity would only add one
more to the number of the daily
rotations of the spheres contained
in it, unless this result were ob-
viated by a special arrangement
of retrogressive spheres. Aristotle has obviously overlooked
this. If he had remarked it, he
would not have neutralised the
action of the primeval spheres
of each planet which run parallel
with the heaven of fixed stars,
but would have abolished them
altogether.

Mars, Venus, Mercury, and the sun; giving in all
fifty-five or, if we add in the sphere of fixed stars,
fifty-six spheres, together with as many eternal incorporeal unmoved entities from whom the motions of the
spheres proceed.[1] The progress of observation could
not fail to show that the theory of spheres, even as thus
conceived, was inadequate to explain the phenomena:
accordingly, as early as the middle of the third century
before Christ, Apollonius of Perga advanced his theory of
' epicycles' triumphantly against it.[2] Yet even the ant-
agonists of Aristotle's system admitted that his theory
of retrogressive spheres was an ingenious attempt to
rectify and supplement the hypothesis of Eudoxus.[3]

---

[1] *Metaph. ibid.* cf. SIMPL.
ibid. 500, a, 34 sqq.; KRISCHE,
ibid. 206 sqq.; IDELER, *ibid.* 82;
BONITZ and SCHWEGLER on the
passage in the *Metaphysics.*
There Aristotle expressly says,
l. 17 sqq., that more spheres are
not required, for, since every
motion exists for the sake of
that which is moved, there can
be no motion and therefore no
sphere in the heavens which is
not there for the sake of a star.
εἰ δὲ μηδεμίαν οἷόν τ' εἶναι φορὰν μὴ
συντείνουσαν πρὸς ἄστρου φορὰν,
ἔτι δὲ πᾶσαν φύσιν καὶ πᾶσαν
οὐσίαν ἀπαθῆ καὶ καθ' αὑτὴν τοῦ
ἀρίστου τετυχηκυῖαν τέλους εἶναι
δεῖ νομίζειν, οὐδεμία ἂν εἴη παρὰ
ταύτας ἑτέρα φύσις [sc. ἀπαθὴς
&c.], ἀλλὰ τοῦτον ἀνάγκη τὸν
ἀριθμὸν εἶναι τῶν οὐσιῶν. εἴτε γάρ
εἰσιν ἕτεραι κινοῖεν ἂν ὡς τέλος
οὖσαι φορᾶς. (Instead of τέλους,
however, in l. 20, we must clearly
read with Bonitz τέλος; BREN-
TANO'S objection to this emenda-
tion, *Psychol. d. Ar.* 344 sq., is

groundless; the traditional reading is obviously meaningless.)
Here also we can see that his
theory is founded upon observation. In l. 12 he remarks that if
we were to leave the sun and the
moon out of our reckoning, the
number of the (planetary)
spheres would be 47; but the
difficulty is so obvious that Sosigenes conjectured this to be a
slip for 49 (SIMPL. *ibid.* 502, a,
11 sqq.). Krische, with whom
Bonitz and seemingly also
Schwegler agree, refers the remark to the eight retrogressive
spheres under Mercury and the
sun; but it is not easy to see
how the σφαῖραι ἀνελίττουσαι belonging to the sun and the moon
could have been left out.

[2] Upon which cf. esp. IDELER,
ibid. 83 sq., LÜBBERT, ' On the
Greek Theory of the Moon's Orbit,'
Rhein. Mus. xii. (1857), 120 sq.

[3] Of the Peripatetic Sosigenes
(as to whom, see ZELL. *Ph.
d. Gr.* i. 696, 701) SIMPL. says,

One circle of fixed stars, or the ' first heaven,' as Aristotle called it, is the most perfect portion of this celestial world. Stationed next to Deity, the best and most perfect object, it accomplishes its purpose by a single motion. In its single sphere it carries an innumerable multitude of heavenly bodies.[1] Its motion is pure, unalterable, uniform rotation,[2] starting from the better side and following the better direction, from right to right.[3] Moving without trouble, it requires no Atlas to support it nor any sail to carry it round by

ibid. 500, a, 40 : ταῦτα τοίνυν τοῦ Ἀριστοτέλους συντόμως οὕτως καὶ σαφῶς εἰρηκότος, ὁ Σωσιγένης ἐγκωμιάσας τὴν ἀγχίνοιαν αὐτοῦ &c. SIMPL. proceeds, 502, b, 5 sqq., to give the arguments which he brought against Aristotle's theory.

[1] *De Cœlo*, ii. 12, Aristotle asks how it is that the number of motions belonging to each planet does not increase with their distance from the *primum movens*, but the three middle planets have one motion more than the two above and below them ; and, further, why the first sphere contains so many stars while the converse is the case with the others, several spheres being assigned to each star. In reply to the former question (292, a, 22) he says that whereas the Most Perfect needs no action (see p. 396, n. 2, 3, and p. 397, n. 1), of all that is beneath Him one thing attains its end by a few actions, another requires many, others still make no effort to attain their end at all, but content themselves with a distant approach to perfection. The earth does not move at all, that which lies nearest to it has

few motions, the next above that and the next again reach higher attainments, the former by the aid of many, the latter by the aid of few, motions. Finally the highest heavens attain the highest with one single motion. In answer to the second question, Aristotle remarks that the first sphere far excels the others in vital and original energy (νοῆσαι γὰρ δεῖ τῆς ζωῆς καὶ τῆς ἀρχῆς ἑκάστης πολλὴν ὑπεροχὴν εἶναι τῆς πρώτης πρὸς τὰς ἄλλας, 292, a, 28); but that the nearer each is to first the more are the bodies which it carries, seeing that the lower spheres are carried round by the upper. Aristotle himself seems, from the way in which he introduces them, 291, b, 24, 292, a, 14 (cf. p. 169, n. 3, and p. 490, n. 4) to place no great reliance upon these explanations. The problem, however, appears to him too important to be altogether passed over. There are questions which he approaches with a species of religious awe, but which nevertheless lie very near his heart.

[2] See p. 494, n. 1, *supra*.

[3] See p. 497, n. 1, *supra*.

force.[1]   Its motion embraces all and generates all motion. Unbegotten and indestructible, affected by no earthly distress, comprehending in itself all time and space, it rejoices in the most complete existence that has been allowed to any bodily thing.[2]   Less perfect is the region of the planetary spheres. Instead of one sphere bearing countless heavenly bodies, we here perceive a multiplicity of spheres, several of which are required to bear one star on its course. Their motion proceeds from the left side of the world, and though, considering each sphere by itself, it is a pure and uniform rotation, yet the general result is not so, since the lower spheres are carried round by the upper, and as a consequence motions composite and deviating

[1] See p. 459, n. 5.

[2] *De Cœlo*, ii. 1 *init.*: ἔστιν εἶς καὶ ἀΐδιος [ὁ πᾶς οὐρανὸς : Aristotle, however, has principally in view the πρῶτος οὐρανὸς, which, in i. 9, 278, b, 11, is called by preference simply οὐρανός] ἀρχὴν μὲν καὶ τελευτὴν οὐκ ἔχων τοῦ παντὸς αἰῶνος, ἔχων δὲ καὶ περίεχων ἐν αὐτῷ τὸν ἄπειρον χρόνον . . . διόπερ καλῶς ἔχει συμπείθειν ἑαυτὸν τοὺς ἀρχαίους καὶ μάλιστα πατρίους ἡμῶν ἀληθεῖς εἶναι λόγους, ὡς ἔστιν ἀθάνατόν τι καὶ θεῖον τῶν ἐχόντων μὲν κίνησιν ἐχόντων δὲ τοιαύτην ὥστε μηθὲν εἶναί πέρας αὐτῆς, ἀλλὰ μᾶλλον ταύτην τῶν ἄλλων πέρας. τό τε γὰρ πέρας τῶν περιεχόντων ἐστί, καὶ αὕτη ἡ κυκλοφορία τέλειος οὖσα περιέχει τὰς ἀτελεῖς καὶ τὰς ἐχούσας πέρας καὶ παῦλαν, αὐτὴ μὲν οὐδεμίαν οὔτ᾽ ἀρχὴν ἔχουσα οὔτε τελευτήν, ἀλλ᾽ ἄπαυστος οὖσα τὸν ἄπειρον χρόνον, τῶν μὲν αἰτία τῆς ἀρχῆς τῶν δὲ δεχομένη τὴν παῦλαν. The

ancients were right when they assigned the heavens, as alone indestructible, to the gods, for it is ἄφθαρτος καὶ ἀγένητος, ἔτι δ᾽ ἀπαθὴς πάσης θνητῆς δυσχερείας ἐστίν, πρὸς δὲ τούτοις ἄπονος διὰ τὸ μηδεμιᾶς προσδεῖσθαι βιαίας ἀνάγκης, ἢ κατέχει κωλύουσα φέρεσθαι πεφυκότα αὐτὸν ἄλλως · πᾶν γὰρ τὸ τοιοῦτον ἐπίπονον, ὅσωπερ ἂν ἀϊδιώτερον ᾖ, καὶ διαθέσεως τῆς ἀρίστης ἄμοιρον. I. 9, 279, a, 10: εἶς καὶ μόνος καὶ τέλειος οὗτος οὐρανός ἐστιν. The passage which follows (quoted p. 395, n. 6), refers partly to the same subject, even although the description contained in it refers primarily to God and not to the heavens. All that was said of the æther, p. 473 sq., is equally applicable to the πρῶτος οὐρανὸς, which, according to the account p. 490, n. 3, is formed of the purest æther.

from the circle are produced.[1] Moreover the rate of these motions is affected by the relation of the lower to the upper spheres,[2] which in itself is a further proof of their less complete self-sufficingness. Nevertheless, these spheres belong to the most divine part of the visible universe, to that which is removed from mutability and impression from without, and which partakes of perfection.[3] As the æther is superior to the four elements, so the stars without exception occupy a position of superiority to the earth. They form the celestial world, in comparison with which the terrestrial seems but an unimportant and transient portion of the whole.[4]

[1] Cf. p. 494 sqq. *supra*.

[2] *De Cælo*, ii. 10: the velocity of the planets (by which, however, Aristotle, as PLATO, *Tim.* 39, A sq., *Rep.* x. 617, A, *Laws*, vii. 822, A sq., here means, not their absolute velocity, but merely the time of their revolutions, and accordingly calls those swifter which take a shorter time; on the other hand, see c. 7, 289, b, 15 sqq., *Meteor.* i. 3, 341, a, 21 sqq.) is in inverse ratio to their distance from the earth. The further each is the longer it takes to complete a revolution, inasmuch as the motion of the stellar heavens from east to west has a stronger counteractive influence upon that of the planets from west to east the nearer it is to it. As Aristotle expressly appeals to mathematical proofs for the truth of the latter proposition, we must understand it to mean that of concentric circles or spheres which revolve round their axes in the same time, the outer ones move swifter than the inner,

and that therefore the velocity of their motion (in the present case that of the daily motion round the earth) constantly decreases towards the centre.

[3] Cf. pp. 474 and 505, n. 2, *supra*, and *Phys.* ii. 4, 196, a, 33 : τὸν οὐρανὸν καὶ τὰ θειότατα τῶν φαινομένων. *Metaph.* xii. 8, 1074, a, 17 (see p. 503, n. 1, *supra*). The stars are therefore called θεῖα σώματα, *Metaph. ibid.* l. 30, *De Cælo*, ii. 12, 292, b, 32 ; likewise the heavens, *ibid.* 3, 286, a, 11.

[4] *Part. An.* i. 1, 641, b, 18 : τὸ γοῦν τεταγμένον καὶ τὸ ὡρισμένον πολὺ μᾶλλον φα′νεται ἐν τοῖς οὐρανίοις ἢ περὶ ἡμᾶς τὸ δ′ ἄλλοτ′ ἄλλως καὶ ὡς ἔτυχε περὶ τὰ θνητὰ μᾶλλον. *Metaph.* iv. 5, 1010, a, 28 : ὁ γὰρ περὶ ἡμᾶς τοῦ αἰσθητοῦ τόπος ἐν φθορᾷ καὶ γενέσει διατελεῖ μόνος ὤν · ἀλλ′ οὗτος οὐθὲν ὡς εἰπεῖν μόριον τοῦ παντός ἐστιν. By thus dividing the universe into a terrestrial and a celestial part, Aristotle intends to distinguish between the sublunary world, the materials of which are

Aristotle, like Plato, thought the stars were bodies animated by rational spirits, and ascribed to these beings a nature far more godlike than man's.[1] Therefore he attributes a priceless value to the smallest iota of knowledge which we can boast to have acquired about them.[2] In this view we can trace the consequences of a metaphysic which deduced all motion ultimately from incorporeal essences; but it is also possible to recognise in it a reflection of those modes of

supplied by the four elements, and in which birth, death, and qualitative change take place, and the world of the heavenly spheres,which consists of ætherial matter and which, while exhibiting motion in space, admits neither growth nor transformation of any kind. Similarly, *De Cœlo*, i. 2, 269, a, 30, b, 14: πέφυκέ τις οὐσία σώματος ἄλλη παρὰ τὰς ἐνταῦθα συστάσεις, θειοτέρα καὶ προτέρα τούτων ἁπάντων .... ἔστι τι παρὰ τὰ σώματα τὰ δεῦρο καὶ περὶ ἡμᾶς ἕτερον κεχωρισμένον τοσούτῳ τιμιωτέραν ἔχον τὴν φύσιν ὅσῳπερ ἀφέστηκε τῶν ἐνταῦθα πλεῖον ; c. 8, 276, a, 28 sqq. b, 3, ii. 12, 292, b, 1, where τῶν ἄστρων and ἐνταῦθα are opposed ; *Meteor.* ii. 3, 358, a, 25 : τοῦτ' ἀεὶ ·γίνεσθαι κατά τινα τάξιν, ὡς ἐνδέχεται μετέχειν τὰ ἐνταῦθα τάξεως. In ordinary language ἐνταῦθα and ἐκεῖ indicate respectively the upper and the under world (*e.g.* SOPH. *Ajax*, 1372 ; PLATO, *Rep.* i. 330, D, v. 451, B; *Apol.* 40, E, 41, B sq., and elsewhere), in Plato also the sensible and ideal world (*Theæt.* 176, A, *Phædr.* 250, A), as also in Aristotle, where he is describing the Platonic

doctrine, *Metaph.* i. 9, 990, b, 34, 991, b, 13, iii. 6, 1002, b, 15, 17, 22, 467.

[1] *Eth. N.* vi. 7, 1141, a, 34 : ἀνθρώπου πολὺ θειότερα τὴν φύσιν, οἷον φανερώτατά γε ἐξ ὧν ὁ κόσμος συνέστηκεν. *De Cœlo*, i. 2 ; see preceding note.

[2] *Part. An.* i. 5 *init.*: the beings in the world are either unbegotten and imperishable, or begotten and perishable : συμβέβηκε δὲ περὶ μὲν ἐκείνας τιμίας οὔσας καὶ θείας ἐλάττους ἡμῖν ὑπάρχειν θεωρίας ... περὶ δὲ τῶν φθαρτῶν φυτῶν τε καὶ ζῴων εὐποροῦμεν μᾶλλον πρὸς τὴν γνῶσιν διὰ τὸ σύντροφον. ἔχει δ' ἑκάτερα χάριν. τῶν μὲν γὰρ εἰ καὶ κατὰ μικρὸν ἐφαπτόμεθα, ὅμως διὰ τὴν τιμιότητα τοῦ γνωρίζειν ἥδιον ἢ τὰ παρ' ἡμῖν ἅπαντα, ὥσπερ καὶ τῶν ἐρωμένων τὸ τυχὸν καὶ μικρὸν μόριον κατιδεῖν ἥδιόν ἐστιν ἢ πολλὰ ἕτερα καὶ μεγάλα δι' ἀκριβείας ἰδεῖν· τὰ δὲ διὰ τὸ μᾶλλον καὶ πλείω γνωρίζειν αὐτῶν λαμβάνει τὴν τῆς ἐπιστήμης ὑπεροχὴν, ἔτι δὲ διὰ τὸ πλησιαίτερα ἡμῶν εἶναι καὶ τῆς φύσεως οἰκειότερα ἀντικαταλλάττεταί τι πρὸς τὴν περὶ τὰ θεῖα φιλοσοφίαν. Cf. also *De Cœlo*, ii. 12 (*supra*, p. 169, n. 3).

thought which lay at the root of the natural religion of
the Greeks, and which stamped themselves in similar
notions upon the philosophy of Plato.[1] Aristotle himself, indeed, is perfectly conscious of this connection
between his theories and the ancient faith of his nation.[2]

The relation between the terrestrial world and the
celestial spheres gives rise to the motions and change of
earthly things. The laws that govern the earth are
necessarily different from those of heaven,[3] because of
the difference of materials, if for no other reason.

The nature of the elements forces them to move in
opposite directions and to exhibit opposite qualities, to
act and be acted upon, to pass into and to inter-
mingle with one another.[4] But since everything that
is moved must be moved by something else, it follows
that the reciprocal interaction of the elements receives

[1] ZELL. *Ph. d. Gr.* i. p. 686 sq.

[2] See p. 505, n. 2, *supra*,
and p. 475, *supra.   Metaph.*
xii. 8, 1074, a, 38 : παραδέδοται δὲ παρὰ τῶν ἀρχαίων καὶ παμ-
παλαίων ἐν μύθου σχήματι κατα-
λελειμμένα τοῖς ὕστερον ὅτι θεοί τέ
εἰσιν οὗτοι [the starry heavens]
καὶ περιέχει τὸ θεῖον τὴν ὅλην
φύσιν. τὰ δὲ λοιπὰ μυθικῶς ἤδη
προσῆκται πρὸς τὴν πειθὼ τῶν
πολλῶν καὶ πρὸς τὴν εἰς τοὺς νόμους
καὶ τὸ συμφέρον χρῆσιν · ἀνθρωποειδεῖς τε γὰρ τούτους καὶ τῶν
ἄλλων ζῴων ὁμοίους τισὶ λέγουσι,
καὶ τούτοις ἕτερα ἀκόλουθα καὶ
παραπλήσια τοῖς εἰρημένοις · ὧν
εἴ τις χωρίσας αὐτὸ λάβοι μόνον τὸ
πρῶτον ὅτι θεοὺς ᾤοντο τὰς πρώτας
οὐσίας εἶναι θείως ἂν εἰρῆσθαι νομί-
σειεν καὶ κατὰ τὸ εἰκὸς πολλάκις
εὑρημένης εἰς τὸ δυνατὸν ἑκάστης
καὶ τέχνης καὶ φιλοσοφίας καὶ πάλιν

φθειρομένων καὶ ταύτας τὰς δόξας
ἐκείνων οἷον λείψανα περισεσῶσθαι
μέχρι τοῦ νῦν. ἡ μὲν οὖν πάτριος
δόξα καὶ ἡ παρὰ τῶν πρώτων ἐπὶ
τοσοῦτον ἡμῖν φανερὰ μόνον.

[3] Both Christian and heathen
opponents (*e.g.* the Platonist
ATTICUS, see EUSEB. *Præp. Ev.*
xv. 5, 6 ; ATHENAG. *Supplic.* c.
22, S, 88 P ; CLEMENS, *Strom.* v.
591, D ; EUSEB. *ibid.* 5, 1 ;
CHALCID. *in Tim.* c. 248 and
elsewhere ; cf. KRISCHE, *Forsch.*
347, 1) have distorted this to
mean that the Divine Providence
reaches only as far as the moon
and does not extend to the earth.
How far this representation
agrees with the true Aristotelian
doctrine may be gathered from
what has been already said,
at pp. 403, 410, and 421.

[4] See pp. 453 sq. 477 sq. *sup.*

an impulse from without. The immediate sources of these motions are the heavenly bodies.[1] Their movement occasions the changes of warmth and cold, which, in the opinion of Aristotle, are the most generally active forces in the elementary bodies.[2] Although the stars and their spheres are neither warm nor cold,[3] yet, by their movement, they generate light and heat in the stratum of air that lies nearest to them; as, indeed, all swiftly moving bodies warm and even set fire to surrounding substances by friction. This is particularly true of the place in which the sun is fastened, since it is neither so far off as the fixed stars,[4] nor yet

---

[1] *Meteor.* i. 2, 339, a, 21 : ἔστι δ' ἐξ ἀνάγκης συνεχής πως οὗτος [ὁ περὶ τὴν γῆν κόσμος] ταῖς ἄνω φοραῖς, ὥστε πᾶσαν αὐτοῦ τὴν δύναμιν κυβερνᾶσθαι ἐκεῖθεν. . . . . ὥστε τῶν συμβαινόντων περὶ αὐτὸν πῦρ μὲν καὶ γῆν καὶ τὰ συγγενῆ τούτοις ὡς ἐν ὕλης εἴδει τῶν γιγνομένων αἴτια χρὴ νομίζειν, . . . τὸ δ' οὕτως αἴτιον ὡς ὅθεν ἡ τῆς κινήσεως ἀρχὴ τὴν τῶν ἀεὶ κινουμένων αἰτιατέον δύναμιν ; c. 3, 340, a, 14.

[2] See p. 480, n. 3, *supra*.

[3] It is impossible that they should be, seeing that the æther, of which they consist, admits none of the opposites which constitute the qualities of the elements. Some further reasons against the view that they are of a fiery nature are given, *Meteor.* i. 3 *fin.*

[4] *DeCælo*, ii. 7, 289, a, 19 : the stars do not consist of fire. ἡ δὲ θερμότης ἀπ' αὐτῶν καὶ τὸ φῶς γίνεται παρεκτριβομένου τοῦ ἀέρος ὑπὸ τῆς ἐκείνων φορᾶς. Motion causes wood, stone, and iron to

burn, and the lead of arrows and bullets to melt (on this widely spread error of the ancients, cf. IDELER, *Arist. Meteor.* i. 359 sq.); it must therefore heat the air that surrounds them. ταῦτα μὲν οὖν αὐτὰ ἐκθερμαίνεται διὰ τὸ ἐν ἀέρι φέρεσθαι, ὃς διὰ τὴν πληγὴν τῇ κινήσει γίγνεται πῦρ· τῶν δὲ ἄνω ἕκαστον ἐν τῇ σφαίρᾳ φέρεται, ὥστ' αὐτὰ μὲν μὴ ἐκπυροῦσθαι, τοῦ δ' ἀέρος ὑπὸ τὴν τοῦ κυκλικοῦ σώματος σφαῖραν ὄντος ἀνάγκη φερομένης ἐκείνης ἐκθερμαίνεσθαι, καὶ ταύτῃ μάλιστα ᾗ ὁ ἥλιος τετύχηκεν ἐνδεδεμένος. διὸ δὴ πλησιάζοντός τε αὐτοῦ καὶ ἀνίσχοντος καὶ ὑπὲρ ἡμᾶς ὄντος γίγνεται ἡ θερμότης. That the sun has this effect is explained, *Meteor.* i. 3, 341, a, 19, in the course of an exposition which agrees with the passage just quoted, in terms similar to the above. See further *Meteor.* i. 3, 340, b, 10, i. 7, 344, a, 8. The whole account, however, would suggest many difficulties even to an Aristotelian. For how can light and heat proceed from a

so slow of motion as the moon. Again the solar movement frequently causes the fire which has raised the
air, to burst and rush violently downward.¹ If the
motion of the sun were uniformly the same in relation
to the earth it would produce a simple and unvarying
effect either of generation or of destruction. But the
inclination of the sun's path makes it unequal. The
sun is sometimes nearer and sometimes further from the
different parts of the earth, and the alternation of birth
and death is a result of this circumstance.² Whether
one connects the former with the proximity and the
latter with the remoteness of the sun, the one with the
approach of warmer and the other with that of colder
seasons of the year,³ or whether one regards generation
as the consequence of a proportionate mixture of heat
and cold, and destruction as produced by a prepon-

single celestial body like this,
when it is the motion of the
whole sphere that produces them?
We should require in that case to
suppose that the sun stands out
of its sphere like a promontory.
Or how does it agree with the
account here given that the fire
and air region is separated from
the solar sphere by the lunar ?
    ¹ *Meteor.* i. 3, 341 a, 28.
    ² *Gen. et Corr.* ii. 10 : ἐπεὶ ἡ
κατὰ τὴν φορὰν κίνησις δέδεικται
ὅτι ἀίδιος, ἀνάγκη τούτων ὄντων καὶ
γένεσιν εἶναι συνεχῶς· ἡ γὰρ φορὰ
ποιήσει τὴν γένεσιν ἐνδελεχῶς διὰ
τὸ προσάγειν καὶ ἀπάγειν τὸ γεννητι-
κόν. . . . But as both birth and
death are eternal, φανερὸν ὅτι
μιᾶς μὲν οὔσης τῆς φορᾶς οὐκ ἐνδέχεται γίνεσθαι ἄμφω διὰ τὸ ἐναντία
εἶναι· τὸ γὰρ αὐτὸ καὶ ὡσαύτως
ἔχον ἀεὶ τὸ αὐτὸ πέφυκε ποιεῖν.
ὥστε ἤτοι γένεσις ἀεὶ ἔσται ἢ φθορά.

δεῖ δὲ πλείους εἶναι τὰς κινήσεις καὶ
ἐναντίας, ἢ τῇ φορᾷ ἢ τῇ ἀνωμαλίᾳ·
τῶν γὰρ ἐναντίων τἀναντία αἴτια.
διὸ καὶ οὐχ ἡ πρώτη φορὰ αἰτία ἐστὶ
γενέσεως καὶ φθορᾶς, ἀλλ' ἡ κατὰ
τὸν λοξὸν κύκλον· ἐν ταύτῃ γὰρ
καὶ τὸ συνεχές ἐστι καὶ τὸ κινεῖσθαι
δύο κινήσεις . . . τῆς μὲν οὖν συνε-
χείας ἡ τοῦ ὅλου φορὰ αἰτία, τοῦ δὲ
προσιέναι καὶ ἀπιέναι ἡ ἔγκλισις·
συμβαίνει γὰρ ὁτὲ μὲν πόρρω γίνεσθαι ὁτὲ δ' ἐγγύς. ἀνίσου δὲ τοῦ
διαστήματος ὄντος ἀνώμαλος ἔσται
ἡ κίνησις· ὥστ' εἰ τῷ προσιέναι καὶ
ἐγγὺς εἶναι γεννᾷ, τῷ ἀπιέναι ταὐτὸν
τοῦτο καὶ πόρρω γίνεσθαι φθείρει.
καὶ εἰ τῷ πολλάκις προσιέναι γεννᾷ,
καὶ τῷ πολλάκις ἀπελθεῖν φθείρει·
τῶν γὰρ ἐναντίων τἀναντία αἴτια.
Cf. *Meteor.* i. 9, 346, b, 20, ii. 2,
354, b, 26.
    ³ As is done in the preceding
note and in the passages quoted,
p. 512, n. 1, *infra.*

derance of one over the other,[1] still the facts are the
same. The double movement of the heavens occasions
the interaction of the elements upon one another, and,
by causing their mutual metamorphosis, prevents their
flying to the different localities which, if prevented by
no controlling influence, they would severally occupy.
The materials of the world are thus continually con-
ducted in a never-ceasing stream of reciprocal transmutation downwards from above and upwards from
below.[2] The endlessness of this process communicates
a sort of infinity to perishable things. The substances
which are further removed from the highest cause having
no right to indestructible existence, the Deity has endowed them with perpetual ' becoming ' instead, and has
thus left no gap or discontinuity in the universe.[3]

[1] *Gen. An.* iv. 10, 777, b, 16 :
the generation, evolution, and
the life of animals have their
natural periods, which are determined by the revolution of the
sun and the moon, as we might
expect: καὶ γὰρ θερμότητες καὶ
ψύξεις μέχρι συμμετρίας τινὸς
ποιοῦσι τὰς γενέσεις, μετὰ δὲ ταῦτα
τὰς φθοράς. τούτων δ' ἔχουσι τὸ
πέρας καὶ τῆς ἀρχῆς καὶ τῆς τελευ-
τῆς αἱ τούτων κινήσεις τῶν ἄστρων.
The changes in the temperature
of the air depend upon the sun
and moon ; those in the water
upon air and wind. Whatever is
or comes into being in them must
adjust itself to their state. (Then
follows the passage quoted p.
363, n. 4.)

[2] *Gen. et Corr.* ii. 10, 337, a,
7 : ἅμα δὲ δῆλον ἐκ τούτων ὅ τινες
ἀποροῦσιν, διὰ τί ἑκάστου τῶν σωμάτων εἰς τὴν οἰκείαν φερομένου χώραν
ἐν τῷ ἀπείρῳ χρόνῳ οὐ διεστᾶσι τὰ

σώματα. αἴτιον γὰρ τούτου ἐστὶν ἡ
εἰς ἄλληλα μετάβασις· εἰ γὰρ
ἕκαστον ἔμενεν ἐν τῇ αὑτοῦ χώρᾳ
καὶ μὴ μετέβαλλεν ὑπὸ τοῦ πλησίον,
ἤδη ἂν διεστήκεσαν. μεταβάλλει
οὖν διὰ τὴν φορὰν διπλῆν οὖσαν·
διὰ δὲ τὸ μεταβάλλειν οὐκ ἐνδέχεται
μένειν οὐδὲν αὐτῶν ἐν οὐδεμιᾷ χώρᾳ
τεταγμένη. Here also it is only
by variations of temperature that
the sun effects the constant
transmutation of the elements, as
is placed beyond a doubt by the
arguments in the *Meteorology*
which are discussed below.

[3] *Gen. et Corr.* ii. 10, 336, b,
26 : τοῦτο δ' εὐλόγως συμβέβηκεν·
ἐπεὶ γὰρ ἐν ἅπασιν ἀεὶ τοῦ βελτίονος
ὀρέγεσθαί φαμεν τὴν φύσιν, βέλτιον
δὲ τὸ εἶναι ἢ τὸ μὴ εἶναι, . . . τοῦτο
δ' ἀδύνατον ἐν ἅπασιν ὑπάρχειν διὰ
τὸ πόρρω τῆς ἀρχῆς ἀφίστασθαι, τῷ
λειπομένῳ τρόπῳ συνεπλήρωσε τὸ
ὅλον ὁ θεὸς ἐντελεχῆ (better :
ἐνδελ.) ποιήσας τὴν γένεσιν· οὕτω

Accordingly a higher order is mirrored in the law of this mutation : for as the heavenly bodies approach the earth and move away from it at fixed and equal intervals, nature has ordained that birth and death should occur coincidently with these periods ; [1] and as the movement of the heavens is circular, the opposite motions of the elements in the terrestrial world also accomplish their kind of circle, inasmuch as each of them passes into all the others, and finally returns upon itself.[2]

Aristotle's *Meteorology* is occupied with the phenomena produced by the motion, reciprocal action and mixture of the elements.[3] He first [4] describes those which belong to the fiery circle ; next [5] those of the lower portion of the atmosphere ; [6] and finally [7] those

γὰρ ἂν μάλιστα συνείροιτο τὸ εἶναι [in this way no gap will be left in nature] διὰ τὸ ἐγγύτατα εἶναι τῆς οὐσίας τὸ γίνεσθαι ἀεὶ καὶ τὴν γένεσιν. *Ibid.* c. 11 *fin.* : perishable things complete the circle of their being ἀριθμῷ not εἴδει. Cf. also ZELL. *Ph. d. Gr.* i. p. 512.

[1] *Ibid.* at 336, b, 9 : ἐν ἴσῳ χρόνῳ καὶ ἡ φθορὰ καὶ ἡ γένεσις ἡ κατὰ φύσιν. διὸ καὶ οἱ χρόνοι καὶ οἱ βίοι ἑκάστων ἀριθμὸν ἔχουσι καὶ τούτῳ διορίζονται · πάντων γάρ ἐστι τάξις καὶ πᾶς βίος καὶ χρόνος μετρεῖται περιόδῳ,πλὴν οὐ τῷ αὐτῷ πάντες. Experience, moreover, is in harmony with this theory : ὁρῶμεν γὰρ ὅτι προσιόντος μὲν τοῦ ἡλίου γένεσίς ἐστιν, ἀπιόντος δὲ φθίσις, καὶ ἐν ἴσῳ χρόνῳ ἐκάτερον. It is true that in many cases death takes place quicker. The reason of this, however, is to be found in the disproportionateness of the materials.

[2] *Ibid.* 337, a, 1, c, 11, 338, b, 3, 11 sqq. ; cf. c. 4 (see p. 484,

supra), and on the circle of generation, *Phys.* iv. 14, 223, b, 23 sqq.

[3] The object of the treatise is set forth thus, in c. 1 : ὅσα συμβαίνει κατὰ φύσιν μὲν, ἀτακτοτέραν μέντοι τῆς τοῦ πρώτου στοιχείου τῶν σωμάτων, περὶ τὸν γειτνιῶντα μάλιστα τόπον τῇ φορᾷ τῶν ἄστρων, . . . ὅσα τε θείημεν ἂν ἀέρος εἶναι κοινὰ πάθη καὶ ὕδατος, ἔτι δὲ γῆς ὅσα εἴδη καὶ μέρη καὶ πάθη τῶν μερῶν. With these investigations ought to be connected the discussion of organic being (*ibid.* and iv. 12 *fin.*).

[4] *Meteor.* i. 3–8.

[5] *Ibid.* i. 9—iii. 6.

[6] τόπος τῇ θέσει μὲν δεύτερος μετὰ τοῦτον [*i.e.* after the fiery circle], πρῶτος δὲ περὶ τὴν γῆν ; and again : τόπος κοινὸς ὕδατός τε καὶ ἀέρος, i. 9 *init.*

[7] *Ibid.* iii. 6, 378, a, 15 sqq. according to BELCHER'S reckoning, or iii. 7 according to that of IDELER.

which are exhibited within the sphere of the earth. The latter part of his treatise does not seem to have been finished. Aristotle appears, instead of continuing the work, to have composed the separate essay which now forms the fourth book of the *Meteorology* and which offers a proper point of transition to the science of animate existence in its discussion of topics which we should refer to the province of inorganic and organic chemistry.[1] In the first of these sections various phenomena, such as meteors and aerolites,[2] together with the Comets and the Galaxy, are explained to be collected masses of dry and inflammable vapours set on fire by the motion of the stars.[3] Comets are bodies of this vapour in a state of slow combustion, moving freely or in the train of a star.[4] Similar in kind is the Milky Way, its vaporous material being excreted and inflamed by the movement of the whole heaven.[5] In the lower portion of the atmosphere are observable all circumstances connected with the formation of the clouds. Under the influence of solar warmth the moisture on the surface of the earth evaporates. The rising mists cool themselves in the higher regions of the air, imparting a portion of their heat to the fiery

[1] See p. 83, n. 2, *supra*.
[2] *Meteor.* i. 4, 5.
[3] Cf. pp. 482, n. 4, 479, n. 4, 490, n. 3, and 509, n. 4.
[4] *Ibid.* c. 6–7, especially 344, a, 16 sqq. and c. 8, 345, b, 32 sqq. In harmony with the account of the nature of comets which he here gives, Aristotle endeavours (344, b, 18 sqq.) to explain those meteorological phenomena (*e.g.* storm and drought) which they

were thought to forecast. On *Meteor.* i. 396 IDELER points out that Aristotle's account of comets held its ground among the most distinguished astronomers until the time of Newton.
[5] *Ibid.* c. 8, esp. 346, b, 6 sqq. where the attempt is made to explain in detail, on the basis of this supposition, the form and appearance of the Milky Way.

sphere, and losing the rest in contact with the chillness of the upper atmosphere.[1] Then they condense, change from air to water,[2] and fall again to earth. In this manner there is formed a stream of air and water, moving up and down in a circle : when the sun is near, the column of air, or warm exhalation, rises ; when it retreats, the stream of water flows downwards.[3] Aristotle makes use of this phenomenon to explain the clouds and mists,[4] dew, rime, rain, snow and hail,[5] and goes on to connect with it the nature and origin of rivers[6] and of the sea.[7] The former are produced in part by the products of the atmosphere and in part by a transmutation of vapour into water within the earth. The sea, though no less eternal than the world, is always yielding a portion of its waters in the form of vapour, which returns to it through the rivers after having been again transformed into water in the atmosphere and discharged in this form. Its salt and bitter taste is occasioned by earthy particles which obtain their bitterness in combustion : for when dry vapours are generated in the earth, a change ensues from earth to fire—in other words, combustion. These vapours, then, carry the result of this combustion aloft with them, which mingles with the water of the rain and the streams, and being by reason of its weight unaffected by evaporation, it remains

---

[1] The reason of this is given, *ibid.* i. c. 3, 340, a, 26.

[2] Air, which is a compound of moisture and heat, when it cools down, is transformed into moisture and cold, *i.e.* water : see p. 484, *supra*.

[3] *Ibid.* i. c. 9.

[4] *Ibid.* at 346, b, 32.

[5] *Ibid.* c. 10–12.

[6] *Ibid.* c. 13, 349, b, 2–c. 14 *fin.*, where he gives a survey of the most noted rivers and their sources. The matter of c. 14 will be further touched upon *infra*.

[7] *Ibid.* ii. c. 1–3.

behind in the sea. Dry evaporation causes wind, as moist evaporation rain. Both are mingled in the lower atmosphere, but the dry exhalations rise aloft and are carried round by the rotation of the upper regions. This excretion of the warmer matter causes the remaining moisture to cool and be condensed into rain ; and this refrigeration being communicated to the warm vapours of the upper strata, causes them to rush towards the earth in the shape of wind.[1] Consequently, the alternations of wind and rain depend upon the fluctuations of moist and dry vapours continually changing place with one another.[2] Masses of vapour penetrating the interior of the earth as winds produce earthquakes.[3] Similar in their origin are thunder and lightning, whirlwinds and simooms,[4] while halos round the sun and moon, rainbows, parhelia, and light-streaks in the clouds [5] may be explained by the reflection of light in moist exhalations and water. In the earth itself stones are produced from dry exhalations, together with all other minerals which are incapable of fusion ; damp vapours, on the other hand, by hardening, before passing into water, become metals.[6]

At the end of the third book of the *Meteorology*

---

[1] *Ibid.* i. ç. 13, 349, a, 12 sqq., ii. 4–6, especially c. 4, where the subject is further developed. Cf. also IDELER, i. 541 sqq. ; *Meteor.* i. 3, 341, a, 1 ; *Probl.* xxvi. 26.

[2] Upon this ἀντιπερίστασις, a conception which plays a great part in Aristotle's philosophy of nature, as it did in Plato's before, and in the Stoics' after, him, see also *Meteor.* i. 12, 348, b, 2 ; *De*

Somno, 3, 457, b, 2.

[3] *Meteor.* ii. 7, 8. An enumeration of the various hypotheses advanced by the ancients to explain earthquakes is given by IDELER, *in loco*, 582 sqq.

[4] *Ibid.* ii. 9, and iii. 1.

[5] These phenomena are dealt with in *Meteor.* iii., chapters 2–6.

[6] *Meteor.* iii. 6, 7, 378, a, 15 sqq.

Aristotle promises to give a fuller description of these bodies. But the fourth book, which is not properly connected with the others,[1] makes a new start. Taking the four elementary characteristics, and regarding warmth and cold as active, dryness and moisture as passive, principles,[2] Aristotle first considers the former and then the latter, in their several manifestations.

From warmth and cold he derives generation on the one hand and corruption on the other[3]: generation, when these principles, being combined in due proportion and acting on the material substratum of a being, obtain complete ascendency over its substance[4]; corruption, when the warmth peculiar to the moist elements of a being is withdrawn by some external heat, and consequently form and distinctness are destroyed.[5]

Among phenomena of a similar description, but not involving generation or destruction, may be reckoned digestion, ripening, boiling, roasting, &c.[6] Of the two

---

[1] Cf. p. 513, *supra*.

[2] See p. 480, n. 3, *supra*.

[3] *Meteor.* iv. 1, 378, b, 28: πρῶτον μὲν οὖν καθόλου ἡ ἀπλῆ γένεσις καὶ ἡ φυσικὴ μεταβολὴ τούτων τῶν δυνάμεών ἐστιν ἔργον καὶ ἡ ἀντικειμένη φθορὰ κατὰ φύσιν.

[4] *Ibid.* l. 31: ἔστι δ' ἡ ἀπλῆ καὶ φυσικὴ γένεσις μεταβολὴ ὑπὸ τούτων τῶν δυνάμεων, ὅταν ἔχωσι λόγον, ἐκ τῆς ὑποκειμένης ὕλης ἑκάστῃ φύσει· αὗται δ' [ὕλη] εἰσὶν αἱ εἰρημέναι δυνάμεις παθητικαί. γεννῶσι δὲ τὸ θερμὸν καὶ ψυχρὸν κρατοῦντα τῆς ὕλης.

[5] *Ibid.* 379, a, 2: ὅταν δὲ μὴ κρατῇ, κατὰ μέρος μὲν μώλυσις καὶ ἀπεψία γίνεται, τῇ δ' ἀπλῇ γενέσει ἐναντίον μάλιστα κοινὸν σῆψις.

πᾶσα γὰρ ἡ κατὰ φύσιν φθορὰ εἰς τοῦθ' ὁδός ἐστιν. L. 16: σῆψις δ' ἐστὶ φθορὰ τῆς ἐν ἑκάστῳ ὑγρῷ οἰκείας καὶ κατὰ φύσιν θερμότητος ὑπ' ἀλλοτρίας θερμότητος· αὕτη δ' ἐστὶν ἡ τοῦ περιέχοντος. Corruption may also be described as the joint effect of ψυχρότης οἰκεία, and θερμότης ἀλλοτρία. Moisture, however, is (acc. to l. 8 sqq.) a necessary means, all generation being the result of the action of moisture (which is εὐόριστον; see p. 480, n. 2, *supra*) upon dryness in obedience to the efficient force of nature; destruction begins ὅταν κρατῇ τοῦ ὁρίζοντος τὸ ὁριζόμενον διὰ τὸ περιέχον.

[6] πέψις, πέπανσις, ἕψις, ὄπτησις

passive principles moisture and dryness, the former is
in its nature the more easily determinable; moisture,
therefore, must needs determine the characteristics of
dryness and not *vice versa*; neither of the two, however,
can exist without the other, but both (and therefore
also the two elements, whose fundamental qualities they
are) must subsist together in all bodies.[1] This combination produces the opposition of hard and soft.[2]
Every body, again, which has its own definite form[3]
must be stiff, and all stiffness is a form of dryness.[4]
Consequently, we are next led to treat of the nature and
kinds of drying, melting, and stiffening, together with
the materials subject to these processes.[5] Homogeneous bodies are formed of earth and water by the influence of warmth and cold.[6] Aristotle proceeds at once

as effects of heat, ἀπεψία, ὠμότης,
μώλυσις, στάτευσις as effects of
cold. Cf. *Meteor.* iv. 2 sq.

[1] *Ibid.* c. 4 : εἰσὶ δ' αἱ μὲν
ἀρχαὶ τῶν σωμάτων αἱ παθητικαὶ
ὑγρὸν καὶ ξηρόν . . . ἐπεὶ δ' ἐστὶ τὸ
μὲν ὑγρὸν εὐόριστον, τὸ δὲ ξηρὸν
δυσόριστον [see p. 480, n. 2, *supra*],
ὅμοιόν τι τῷ ὄψῳ καὶ τοῖς ἡδύσμασι
πρὸς ἄλληλα πάσχουσιν· τὸ γὰρ
ὑγρὸν τῷ ξηρῷ αἴτιον τοῦ ὁρίζεσθαι
. . . καὶ διὰ τοῦτο ἐξ ἀμφοῖν ἐστὶ τὸ
ὡρισμένον σῶμα. λέγεται δὲ τῶν
στοιχείων ἰδιαίτατα ξηροῦ μὲν γῆ,
ὑγροῦ δὲ ὕδωρ [see p. 483, n. 2, *sup.*].
διὰ ταῦτα ἅπαντα τὰ ὡρισμένα
σώματα ἐνταῦθα [added because
the statement does not apply to
ætherial regions] οὐκ ἄνευ γῆς καὶ
ὕδατος.

[2] *Ibid.* 382, a, 8 sqq. c. 5 *init.*

[3] τὸ ὡρισμένον σῶμα οἰκείῳ ὅρῳ
(cf. p. 480, n. 2), as distinguished
from that which has its form
imposed on it from without, as

water in a vessel.

[4] *Ibid.* c. 5 *init.*

[5] *Ibid.* c. 5–7.

[6] *Ibid.* c. 8 *init.* c. 10, 388, a,
20 sqq. On the nature of homogeneity, cf. Part I, 879, 2. Homogeneous bodies (ὁμοιομερῆ) are
defined in general as those composed of one kind of material,
whether that material be simple
and elementary or compound, in
the narrower sense as those composed of the latter. Opposed to
the homogeneous is the heterogeneous (ἀνομοιομερὲς), or that
which is composed of different
materials mechanically held
together, as is the case especially
with organic bodies. See, besides
the passages referred to above,
Meteor. iv. 10, 388, a, 13. c. 12
init.; *De An.* i. 5, 411, a, 16–21,
cf. b, 24 sqq , where besides
ὁμοιομερὴς we have ὁμοιειδὴς,
which is further expanded into τὸ

to describe their qualities and composition,[1] passing to
the detailed discussion of living beings with the remark
that homogeneous bodies serve as the matter of heterogeneous ones, and that the designs of nature are more
clearly exhibited in the latter than in the former.[2] In
fact, however, everything which we find scattered over
the later writings about the objects of sense-perception,
light, colour, sound, smell, &c., belongs to that portion of
physics which is treated of in the *Meteorology*. We cannot
therefore here do more than refer to these suggestions,[3]

ὅλον τοῖς μορίοις ὁμοειδές, *Part. An.*
ii. 9, 655, b, 21, where ὁμοιομερῆ
is explained by συνώνυμα τοῖς ὅλοις
τὰ μέρη ; cf. the *Ind. Arist.* under
the word. According to PHILOP.
Aristotle distinguished in his
Eudemus between elementary
homogeneous and organic bodies.
In a quotation from this dialogue
occur the words (*Ar. Fr.* 1482,
a, 10, cf. p. 482, *supra*): ἀσυμ-
μετρία ἐστὶ τῶν στοιχείων ἡ νόσος
. . . τῶν ὁμοιομερῶν ἡ ἀσθένεια . . .
τῶν ὀργανικῶν τὸ αἶσχος ; they are
perhaps, however, only inserted
by the reporter by way of explanation.

   [1] *Ibid.* c. 8–11. Caps. 8 and 9
treat especially of stiffening by
heat and cold ; of melting by
heat and moisture ; of softening,
bending, extending ; of breaking,
bruising, splitting, &c. ; caps. 10
and 11 treat of the constituent
elements of homogeneous bodies
and the properties by which they
may be known. For a fuller
account of Aristotle's treatment
of the latter subject see MEYER,
Arist. Thierkunde, 416 sqq. 477.

   [2] *Ibid.* c. 12.

   [3] Aristotle gives the following
account of Light, *De An.* ii. 7,

418, b, 3 sqq. ; *De Sensu*, c. 3,
439, a, 18 sqq. : transparency is a
common property (κοινὴ φύσις καὶ
δύναμις) of many bodies with
whose other properties it is in-
separably united (οὐ χωριστή).
That which gives actuality to
this property (ἡ τούτου ἐνέργεια
τοῦ διαφανοῦς ᾗ διαφανές—ἡ ἐντελέχεια τοῦ διαφανοῦς, 418, b, 9,
419, a, 10) and as it were colour
to the transparent object is light,
which again is caused by fire or
æther (ὑπὸ πυρὸς ἢ τοιούτου οἷον τὸ
ἄνω σῶμα), and may therefore be
defined as πυρὸς ἢ τοιούτου τινὸς
παρουσία ἐν τῷ διαφανεῖ. At the
same time he controverts (*De
An.* 418, b, 20 ; *De Sensu*, c. 6,
446, a, 25 sqq) the view of Empedocles that light is motion
passing from heaven to earth, on
the ground of the immense distance at which we see it. Light,
to Aristotle, is the effect of motion
(see 468 sq. *supra*), but is not *per
se* a motion, but rather a definite
state which is produced in a body
as a whole in consequence of a
qualitative change (ἀλλοίωσις)
such as freezing (*De Sensu*, c. 6,
446, b, 27 sqq.) It is asserted at
the same time that vision is the

as it will be now necessary to pass at once, in the next volume, to Aristotle's observations and conclusions as to Organic Nature.

result of a motion which passes from an object to the eye through the transparent medium (*De An.* ii. 7, 419, a, 9, 13, iii. 1, 424, b, 29. c. 12, 435, a, 5; *De Sensu*, 2, 438, b, 3).—That, he says, which by its presence causes light, by its absence darkness, is also that which on the border of transparent things produces Colour. For colour resides only on the surface of bodies, and belongs, therefore, only to those which have definite limits: as light is said to be ἐν ἀορίστῳ τῷ διαφανεῖ (*De Sensu*, c. 3, 439, a, 26), so colour is defined (*ibid.* 439, b, 11) as τὸ τοῦ διαφανοῦς ἐν σώματι ὡρισμένῳ πέρας. White and black correspond on the surface of bodies to light and darkness (439, b, 16), and from these two primary colours come all the others, not merely by the mechanical confusion of their atomic elements, nor by the shining of one through the other, but also by a real process of mixture, such as is described at p. 420. If they are mixed in simple numerical proportion, we have pure colours; if otherwise, impure. Inclusive of black and white, Aristotle enumerates in all seven primary colours (*ibid.* 439, b, 18 to the end of the chapter, and also c. 6, 445, b, 20 sqq., and c. 4, 442, a, 19 sqq. Cf. *De An.* ii. 7 *init.*; *ibid.* 419, a, 1 sqq.; *Meteor.* iii. 4, 373, b, 32 sqq., i. 5, 342, b, 4). The treatise upon colour starts from somewhat different premisses; *vide* PRANTL, who treats Aristotle's doctrine of colour from different

points of view in the most exhaustive manner, pp. 86-159, as also BÄUMKER, *Arist. Lehre v. d. Sinnesvermögen* (1877), p. 21 sqq.—Sound is said to be motion caused by the concussion of hard bodies and transmitting itself through the medium of the air. It was to describe this idea of the sound-medium that Theophrastus and other Peripatetics invented the word διηχὲς, formed upon the analogy of διαφανὴς, just as in like manner they invented δίοσμος to describe the medium by which smell is transmitted, PHILOP. *De An.* L, 4; cf. *ibid.* M, 8, o. 10, o. Those notes are high which make a forcible impression on the ear in a brief time, *i.e.* quick notes; those on the other hand are deep which take a longer time to produce a weak impression, *i.e.* slow ones (*De An.* ii. 8, 419, b, 4-420, b, 5). Bodies which are fastened into others and carried round by them as the stars are, produce no sound by their motion (*De Cælo*, ii. 9, 291, a, 9 sqq.)—Smell is held to be caused by dry materials which are dissolved in moisture, *i.e.* in water or air (ἔγχυμος ξηρότης, 443, a, 1, b, 4; note that the earlier and provisional description of ὀσμὴ as καπνώδης ἀναθυμίασις, *De Sensu*, 2, 438, b, 24, is rejected, *ibid.* c. 5, 443, a, 21). This is how they become objects to the sense (*De Sensu*, c. 5, 442, b, 27-443, b, 16; *De An.* ii. 9, 421, a, 26 sqq., 422, a, 6; cf. BÄUMKER, 28 sq.)—In the same way Taste is the effect of the union of dry or earthy material with moisture, which, however, in this case is not that of water and air, as in the case of smell, but of water alone. The object of the sense of taste is χυμοί : χυμὸς again is defined as τὸ γιγνόμενον ὑπὸ τοῦ εἰρημένου ξηροῦ [viz. τοῦ τροφίμου ξηροῦ] πάθος ἐν τῷ ὑγρῷ, τῆς γεύσεως τῆς κατὰ δύναμιν ἀλλοιωτικὸν εἰς ἐνέργειαν [i.e. which causes our sense or faculty of taste actually to feel a sensation, 441, b, 19], τοῦ τροφίμου ξηροῦ πάθος ἢ στέρησις (ibid. l. 24). As all colours are a mixture of white and black, so all tastes (λιπαρὸν and ἁλμυρὸν, δριμὺ and αὐστηρὸν, στρυφνὸν and ὀξὺ) are a mixture of sweet and bitter; if these elements are mingled in a certain proportion we have pleasant tastes; otherwise, unpleasant ones (De Sensu, c. 4 ; De An. ii. 10, BÄUMK. 32 sq.). In this way

the law discovered by the Pythagoreans which declared that the harmony and discord of sounds depended upon certain numerical relations is considered also to apply, not only to colours, but to tastes (χυμοί). De Sensu, 4, 442, a, 19 sqq. c. 7, 448, a, 15. Aristotle compares seven principal tastes to the seven primary colours. Further investigations into the nature of χυμοὶ he reserves (De Sensu, c. 4 fin.) for the φυσιολογία περὶ τῶν φυτῶν. Upon the treatise attributed to him π. χυμῶν, see p. 84, n. 1.—The sense of Touch has for its object all those general qualities of bodies (De An. ii. 11, 422, b, 25, 423, b, 26), which are ultimately resolvable into terms of the elementary oppositions referred to on p. 479, supra, and do not, therefore, call for further special notice here.

END OF THE FIRST VOLUME.